D1554734

A HISTORY OF MERTON COLLEGE, OXFORD

Frontispiece: The Library and the Tower from the Meadows, with Grove Building to the left and Fellows' Quad to the right

Oxford University Press, Great Clarendon Street, Oxford OX2 6DP

Oxford New York
Athens Auckland Bangkok Bogota Bombay
Buenos Aires Calcutta Cape Town Dar es Salaam
Delhi Florence Hong Kong Istanbul Karachi
Kuala Lumpur Madras Madrid Melbourne
Mexico City Nairobi Paris Singapore
Taipei Tokyo Toronto Warsaw

and associated companies in
Berlin Ibadan

Oxford is a trade mark of Oxford University Press

Published in the United States
by Oxford University Press Inc., New York

British Library Cataloguing in Publication Data
Data available

Library of Congress Cataloging-in-Publication Data
Martin, G. H. (Geoffrey Haward), 1928–
A history of Merton College, Oxford / G.H. Martin and J.R.L.
Highfield.
Includes bibliographical references and index.
1. Merton College——History. I. Highfield, J. R. L. (John Roger
Loxdale) II. Title.
LF645.M37 1997 378.42'57——dc21 97-34
ISBN 0-19-920183-8

1 3 5 7 9 10 8 6 4 2

Typeset by Selwood Systems, Midsomer Norton
Printed in Great Britain
on acid-free paper by
Butler & Tanner Ltd,
Frome and London

A History of
Merton College,
Oxford

G. H. MARTIN

AND

J. R. L. HIGHFIELD

OXFORD UNIVERSITY PRESS

1997

Preface

OVER the centuries, the House of the Scholars of Merton has accumulated more history than histories. The last comprehensive survey was B. W. Henderson's *Merton College*, which appeared in 1899 in the series of College Histories published by Robinson, though there have been many specialized studies, by H. W. Garrod and others, since then. The contrast between the College Histories, admirable in their day, and the scale of the current *History of the University of Oxford* marks the attention which the evolution of the academic community has attracted in that time. The end of the twentieth century therefore seems an appropriate season for the present study, which seeks to relate the history of Merton to the larger issues of national life, with a particular emphasis upon the last three hundred years. The work has been generously supported by the warden and fellows of the House from inception to publication.

The authors first met in a post-war Oxford which in some respects now seems as remote as the Renaissance. Since then they have communed on many topics, and much on the history of Merton, but in the completed text chapters 1–7 and 10 are substantially the work of GHM, and chapters 8, 9, and 11–13 of JRLH.

The illustrations have been chosen to enhance the text, but naturally their scope could be greatly extended. In particular the riches of the library are only lightly represented, and there are no examples of the college silver of a date earlier than 1938, as there is a complete and handsomely illustrated inventory in the *Catalogue of the Plate of Merton College, Oxford* by E. A. Jones, published in that year by Oxford University Press.

Merton College   G.H.M.
August 1996   J.R.L.H.

Acknowledgements

AMONGST many obligations to friends and colleagues we are particularly grateful to Professor J. D. North of the University of Groningen for his helpful comments on Chapter 3. Dr S. J. Gunn, Mr Philip Waller, and Dr J. M. Roberts kindly read and commented on Chapters 8, 12, and 13 respectively. Mr C. H. Martin provided editorial and other advice, and Miss Judith Kirby, Fellows' Secretary, and Mrs Joan Barton, formerly Warden's Secretary, typed and retyped many forbidding drafts with patient goodwill.

Of the illustrations, our warm thanks are due to Miss Elizabeth Lipsett, executrix of the late Wim Swaan, for permission to reproduce the frontispiece and nos. 2, 6, 7, and 16; to Mr J. S. G. Gloag, the College land-agent, for no. 5; to the Trustees of the Dyson Perrins Museum at Worcester for their courtesy in making no. 23 available; to the John Gibbons Studio for Fig. 2 and Plates nos. 1, 8, 9, 11, 13, 14, 20, 29, 32, 42, and II–III; to Thomas-Photos of Headington for Nos. 3, 4, 12, 15, 17–19, 21–2, 24, 26–8, 30–1, 35–6, 38, 40–1, 43–5, and V–VIII; to Messrs Gilman and Soame for nos. 39(a) and 46; to Jim Chambers for 39(b); to the Trustees of the British Museum for permission to publish nos. 25 and 47; to the Trustees of the Imperial War Museum for no. 37; and to the Trustees of the National Portrait Gallery for nos. 33 and 34. Mr A. J. Bott kindly made his plan of the college buildings available to us for Fig. 1.

We are also grateful to Mrs D. Blunt of Panty-y-Cae, Clyro, for permission to quote the extracts from Warden Mure's autobiography, 'The Impact of a War', on pp. 326–9; to Random House UK Ltd., for the quotation about H. W. Garrod from George Mallaby's *From My Level* (1965) on pp. 331–2 and to Curtis Brown, Ltd for the extracts from Angus Wilson's essay 'My Oxford' in *Encounter* (April, 1977), quoted on pp. 335–6. We thank David Higham Associates for permission to quote from A. J. P. Taylor's *A Personal History* (Hamish Hamilton, 1983) on p. 333, and Messrs Faber and Faber similarly for the extract on

Acknowledgements

pp. 334–5 from Louis MacNeice, *The Strings are False* (1965). We are able to quote from Ernest Barker, *Age and Youth* (1953) (see pp. 302–3) by permission of Oxford University Press.

The executors of the estate of the late J. R. R. Tolkien gave us permission to reproduce the Runic inscription on the fly-leaf of the copy of *The Hobbit*, presented to Professor Norman Davis (see Plate 42). We are particularly grateful to Dr Nicholas Tyacke and to the Oxford University Press for making available proofs of vol. IV of the *History of the University of Oxford* before its publication.

G.H.M.
J.R.L.H.

Contents

List of Illustrations

Abbreviations

(Place of publication is London unless stated otherwise)

Ackermann, *Oxford*	Ackermann, R., *History of the University of Oxford*, i (1814)
Aubineau	Aubineau, M., *Codices Chrysostomi Graeci*, i. *Britanniae et Hiberniae* (Paris, 1968)
Aubrey, *Brief Lives*	Aubrey, John, *'Brief Lives', chiefly of contemporaries set down by John Aubrey between the years 1669 and 1696*, ed. A. Clark, 2 vols. (Oxford, 1898)
Baigent and Millard, *Basingstoke*	Baigent, F. J., and Millard, J. E., *History of the Ancient Town and Manor of Basingstoke* (Basingstoke, 1889)
Balliol Deeds	*Balliol Oxford Deeds*, ed. H. E. Salter, OHS lxiv (1913)
Bibl. Bod. Cat.	*Bibliothecae Bodleianae Catalogus*, 7 vols. (Oxford, 1843–51)
Binns, *Intellectual Culture*	Binns, J. W., *Intellectual Culture in Elizabethan and Jacobean England* (Leeds, 1980)
Birley	Birley, R., 'The history of Eton College Library', *London Bibliographical Society* (1956), 231–61
BL	British Library
BLR	*Bodleian Library Record*
Bott, *Monuments*	Bott, Alan, *The Monuments in Merton College Chapel* (Oxford, 1964)
Bott, *Short History of the Buildings*	Bott, Alan, *Short History of the Buildings of Merton College, Oxford* (Oxford, 1993)
BQR	*Bodleian Quarterly Review*
Brodrick, *Memorials*	Brodrick, G. C., *Memorials of Merton College, Oxford*, OHS iv (1885)

BRUO	*Biographical Register of the Members of the University of Oxford to 1500*, ed. A. B. Emden, 3 vols. (Oxford, 1957–9)
Buxton and Williams, *New College*	Buxton, John and Williams, Penry (eds.), *New College, Oxford, 1379–1979* (Oxford, 1979)
Camden Soc.	Camden Society
CChR	*Calendar of Charter Rolls*
CCR	*Calendar of Close Rolls*
Chamberlain, *Letters*	Chamberlain, John, *Letters (1597–1626): A Selection*, ed E. McC. Thomason (1963)
CHLMP	*Cambridge History of Late Medieval Philosophy*, ed. Norman Kretzmann, Anthony Kenny, and Jon Piborg (Cambridge, 1982)
Clarendon, *Life*	Clarendon, earl of, *The Life of Edward, Lord Clarendon, written by himself* (Oxford, 1759)
Close Rolls	*Close Rolls, Henry III* (1902–75)
Colvin, *Dictionary*	Colvin, H. M., *Dictionary of British Architects, 1600–1840* (1978)
Cooke, 'Harvey'	Cooke, A. M., 'William Harvey at Oxford', *Journal of the Royal College of Physicians of London*, ix/2 (1975), 185–6
Costin, *History of St John's*	Costin, W. C., *The Early History of St John's College, Oxford, 1598–1860*, OHS n.s. xii (1958)
Cox, *Recollections*	Cox, G. V., *Recollections of Oxford* (1863)
Coxe	Coxe, H. O., *Catalogus Codicum MSS qui in collegiis aulisque Oxoniensibus hodie adservantur*, i (Oxford, 1852)
CP	*Complete Peerage*, ed. V. Gibbs, G. E. C., and G. H. White, 13 vols. (1910–40)
CPL	*Calendar of Papal Letters 1198–1492*, ed. W. H. Bliss *et al.*, 14 vols. (1894–1961)
CPR	*Calendar of Patent Rolls*
Creighton, *Life and Letters*	Creighton, L., *Life and Letters of Mandell Creighton, D.D.*, 2 vols. (1904–6)
CSP. Domestic	*Calendar of State Papers Domestic*
CSP. Foreign	*Calendar of State Papers Foreign*
DNB	*Dictionary of National Biography*
EHR	*English Historical Review*
EPNS	English Place-Name Society

Elizabethan Oxford	*Elizabethan Oxford*, ed. C. Plummer, OHS viii (1886)
ERMC	*The Early Rolls of Merton College*, ed. J. R. L. Highfield, OHS n.s. xviii (1964)
FH	*Flores Historiarum*, ed. H. R. Luard, RS, 3 vols. (1890)
Feingold	Feingold, Mordechai, *The Mathematicians' Apprenticeship. Science, Universities and Society in England 1560–1640* (Cambridge, 1984)
Foster, *Alumni Oxonienses*	Foster, Joseph, *Alumni Oxonienses 1500–1714*, 4 vols. (Oxford, 1891–2); *1715–1886*, 4 vols. (Oxford, 1888)
Garrod, *Study of Good Letters*	Garrod, H. W., *The Study of Good Letters*, ed. J. Jones (Oxford, 1963)
Green, *Commonwealth of Lincoln College*	Green, V. H. H., *The Commonwealth of Lincoln College, Oxford, 1427–1977* (Oxford, 1979)
Handbook of British Chronology	*Handbook of British Chronology*, ed. E. B. Fryde, D. E. Greenway, G. Porter, and I. Roy, 3rd edn., Royal Historical Society (1986)
Harvey, *Cuxham*	Harvey, P. D. A., *A Medieval Oxfordshire Village: Cuxham, 1240–1400* (Oxford, 1965)
Hearne, *Collections*	*Hearne's Collections*, ed. C. E. Doble, OHS ii, vii, xiii, xxxiv, xlii, xliii, xlviii, l, lxv, lxvii, lxxii (1884–1918)
Henderson	Henderson, B., *Merton College* (1899)
Highfield, 'An autograph commonplace book ...'	Highfield, J. R. L., 'An autograph manuscript commonplace book of Sir Henry Savile', *BLR* vii. 2 (1963)
Historical Monuments Commission (City of Oxford)	*An Inventory of the Historical Monuments in the City of Oxford*, Royal Commission on Historical Monuments (England) (1939)
History of Northumberland	*History of Northumberland*, ed. E. Bateson, M. H. Dodds, and others, 12 vols. (Newcastle-upon-Tyne, 1895–1920)
Holdsworth, *History of English Law*	Holdsworth, Sir William S., *History of English Law*, 17 vols. (1903–72)
Hudson, *Memorials*	Hudson, Robert, *Memorials of a Warwickshire Parish* (1904)

HUO	*The History of the University of Oxford* i. *The Early Oxford Schools*, ed. J. I. Catto (1984) ii. *Late Medieval Oxford*, ed. J. I. Catto and T. A. R. Evans (1992) iii. *The Collegiate University*, ed. J. McConica (1986) iv. *The Seventeenth Century*, ed. N. Tyacke (1997) v. *The Eighteenth Century*, ed. L. S. Sutherland and L. G. Mitchell (1980) viii. *The Twentieth Century*, ed. B. Harrison (1994)
Injunctions	*Merton College: Injunctions of Archbishop Kilwardby, 1276*, ed. H. W. Garrod (Oxford, 1929)
JEH	*Journal of Ecclesiastical History*
Jones, *Catalogue of the Plate*	Jones, E. A., *Catalogue of the Plate of Merton College, Oxford* (Oxford, 1928)
Kenny	Kenny, Anthony (ed.), *Wyclif and his Times* (Oxford, 1986)
Ker, 'Oxford Libraries'	Ker, N. R., 'Oxford college libraries in the sixteenth century', *BLR* vi. 3 (1959), 459–515
Knighton's Chronicle	*Knighton's Chronicle, 1337–96*, ed. G. H. Martin (Oxford, 1995)
Knox, *Reminiscences*	Knox, E. A., *Reminiscences of an Octogenarian* (1934)
LTAW	*The Life and Times of Anthony Wood*, ed. Andrew Clark, OHS, 5 vols. (1890–1900)
Maude, *Memories*	Maude, John, *Memories of Eton and Oxford, the Mountains and the Sea* (1936)
Maxwell-Lyte, *History of Eton College*	Maxwell-Lyte, H. C., *History of Eton College 1440–1884* (1889)
MBMC	F. M. Powicke, *Medieval Books of Merton College, Oxford* (Oxford, 1931)
MCR	Merton College Record
Mert. Coll. Reg.	*Merton College Register, 1900–1964* (Oxford, 1964); 2nd edn. *1891–1989* (Oxford, 1990)
MM	*Merton Muniments*, ed. H. W. Garrod and P. S. Allen, OHS lxxxvi (1928)

MMC	*Memorials of Merton College*. ed. G. C. Brodrick, OHS ix (1885)
Morrish, *Bibliotheca Higgsiana*	Morrish, P., *Bibliotheca Higgsiana: A Catalogue of the Books of Griffin Higgs (1589–1659)* (Oxford Bibliographical Soc. occasional publication no. 22, 1990)
MR	Merton Roll
MS	*Medieval Studies*
Munimenta Academica	*Munimenta Academica, or Documents illustrative of Academical Life and Studies at Oxford*, ed. H. Ansty, 2 vols., RS 1 (1868)
Nias, *Dr John Radcliffe*	Nias, J. B., *Dr John Radcliffe: A Sketch of his Life with an Account of his Fellows and Foundations* (Oxford, 1915)
Nichols, *Literary History*	Nichols, John, *Illustrations of the Literary History of the Eighteenth Century*, 8 vols (1817–58)
Ornsby, *Memoirs*	Ornsby, John, *Memoirs of James Robert Hope-Scott*, 2 vols. (2nd edn. 1884)
Oxford City Documents	*Oxford City Documents*, ed. J. E. Thorold Rogers, OHS xviii (1891)
Oxford Council Acts	*Oxford Council Acts 1666–1701*, ed. M. G. Hobson, OHS n.s. ii (1938)
OHS	Oxford Historical Society
Pattison, *Casaubon*	Pattison, M., *Isaac Casaubon, 1557–1614* (1875)
Philip, *The Bodleian Library*	Philip, I., *The Bodleian Library in the Seventeenth and Eighteenth Centuries* (Oxford, 1983)
PL	*Patrologia Latina*
Pollard, *Records*	Pollard, A. W., *Records of the English Bible* (1911)
Poole, *Catalogue of Oxford Portraits*	Poole, Mrs R. Lane, *Catalogue of Oxford Portraits*, OHS lvii, lxxxi, lxxxii (1911–24)
RACM 1483–1521	*Registrum Annalium Collegii Mertonensis 1483–1521*, ed. H. E. Salter, OHS lxvi (1921)
RACM 1521–67	*Registrum Annalium Collegii Mertonensis 1521–67*, ed. J. M. Fletcher, OHS n.s. xxii (1972)
RACM 1567–1603	*Registrum Annalium Collegii Mertonensis 1567–1603*, ed. J. M. Fletcher, OHS n.s. xxiv (1976)
'Repertorium Mertonense'	Weisheipl, J. A., 'Repertorium Mertonense', *MS* xi (1969), 174–224
Rev. Eng. Stud.	*Review of English Studies*

Riewald	Riewald, J. G., *Sir Max Beerbohm: Man and Artist* (1953)
Ross, *Malden*	Ross, K. N., *A History of Malden* (New Malden, 1947)
Roth, *Jews of Medieval Oxford*	Roth, C., *The Jews of Medieval Oxford*, OHS n.s. ix (1951)
Rot. Parl.	*Rotuli Parliamentorum*, Record Commission, 6 vols. (1783–1832)
Rowse, *Court and Country*	Rowse, A. L., *Court and Country: Studies in Tudor Social History* (Brighton, 1987)
RS	Rolls Series
Sandys, *History of Classical Scholarship*	Sandys, J. E., *History of Classical Scholarship*, 3 vols. (Cambridge, 1903–8)
SCH	*Studies in Church History*
Sinclair and Robb-Smith	Sinclair, H. M., and Robb-Smith, A. H. M., *History of Anatomy at Oxford* (Oxford, 1958)
Sophismata	*The Sophismata of Richard of Kilvington: Introduction, Translation and Commentary*, ed. N. and B. E. Kretzmann 2 vols., (Cambridge, 1990)
SS	Salter, H. E., *Survey of Oxford*, OHS n.s. xiv (1960), xx (1969)
Statutes and Ordinances	*Statutes of the Colleges of Oxford: Merton College* (1853)
Stone, *The University in Society*	Stone, Lawrence, *The University in Society: Oxford and Cambridge from the 14th to the early 19th Century*, 2 vols. (Princeton, 1975)
Trans. Jew. Hist. Soc.	*Transactions of the Jewish Historical Society*
Trecentale	*Trecentale Bodleianum* (Oxford, 1913)
Trevor-Roper, *Laud*	Trevor-Roper, H. R., *Archbishop Laud* (2nd edn. 1962)
TRHS	*Transactions of the Royal Historical Society*
Tyacke, 'Science and Religion'	Tyacke, N., 'Science and Religion at Oxford University before the Civil War' in *Puritans and Revolutionaries*, ed. D. Pennington and G. Aylmer (Oxford, 1981)
Ungerer, *Spaniard in Elizabethan England*	Ungerer, G., *A Spaniard in Elizabethan England*, 2 vols. (1974)
VCH	*Victoria County History*

Abbreviations

Venn, *Alumni Cantabrigienses*	*Alumni Cantabrigienses*, ed. I. and J. A. Venn, 2 prints (to 1751; 1752–1900), 4 and 6 vols. (Cambridge, 1922–54)
Ward, *Georgian Oxford*	Ward, W. R., *Georgian Oxford* (Oxford, 1968)
Wood, *Athenae Oxonienses*	Wood, Anthony, *Athenae Oxonienses to which are added Fasti Oxonienses*, 3rd edn., ed. P. Bliss, 3 vols. (1813–17)
Wood, *Historia et Antiquitates*	Wood, Antonius, *Historia et Antiquitates Universitatis Oxoniensis*, 2 vols. (Oxford, 1674)
Wood, *History and Antiquities*	Wood, Anthony, *History and Antiquities of the University of Oxford*, ed. T. Gutch, 2 vols. (1786–90), Appendix (1790)
YAJ	*Yorkshire Archaeological Journal*

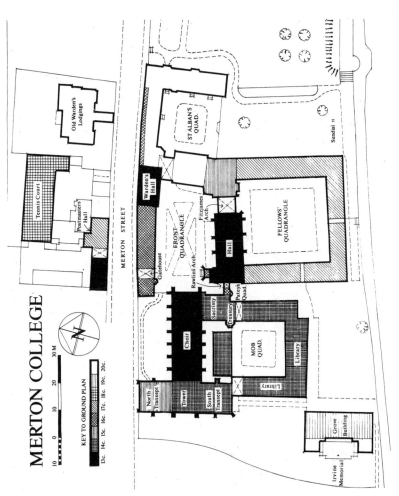

MERTON COLLEGE

KEY TO GROUND PLAN

13c. 14c. 15c. 16c. 17c. 18c. 19c. 20c.

Old Warden's Lodgings

Tennis Court

Postmaster's Hall

MERTON STREET

Warden's Hall

ST ALBAN'S QUAD.

Gatehouse

FRONT QUADRANGLE

Fitzjames Arch

Rawlins' Arch

Hall

Patey's Quad.

Sacristy

Treasury

FELLOWS' QUADRANGLE

Choir

MOB QUAD.

Library

North Transept

Tower

South Transept

Library

Sandial

Irvine Memorial

Grove Building

Fig. 1 Merton College: the buildings

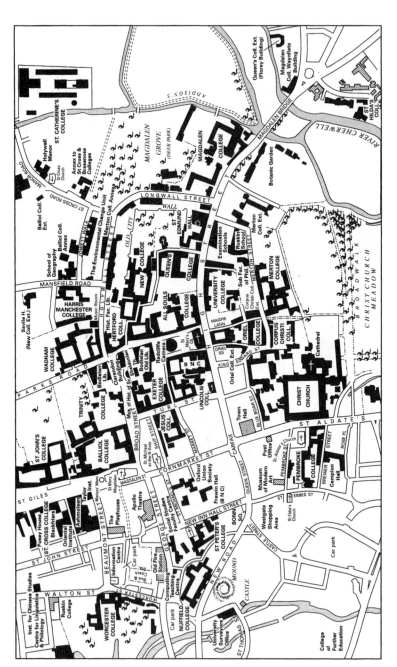

Fig. 2 The College in its university setting

I

The Founder and his Foundation

MERTON COLLEGE was founded in 1264. Its founder, Walter de Merton, king's clerk and lately chancellor to Henry III, had sketched it in a different form two years earlier, and he elaborated it in 1270, and then again in 1274, in the light of a decade's experience. During those years he had served again as chancellor, while Edward I was abroad, and had then retired from royal service to become bishop of Rochester. In its earliest years the college had two locations, but it maintained students in Oxford from the first, and the founder's statutes of 1274 recognized that it could function best if it were unified there, upon its present site. By that time most of its members had been settled in the city for some years, in the earliest of the buildings which house the college today. It could therefore properly be called Merton College, Oxford, the name by which the House of Scholars of Merton is now generally known.

By that time also Merton had established a character which not only distinguished it then, but has since become the mark of almost all the other colleges of Oxford and its sister university Cambridge. That decisive feature is an endowment of property appointed to support an academic community, and vested in the members of the community themselves. It has influenced not only the development of those universities, but the ordinary meaning of the word college in the English-speaking world.

A college is essentially and simply an association, a group of people joined together for a particular purpose. The word university originally had similar connotations, and it is not beyond imagination that either should have taken on the other's meaning. As it happens, and following the example set by Walter de Merton more than seven hundred years ago, colleges have come to be seen as constituents of universities, rather than the other way about. Largely for that reason they are also commonly seen as embodied in the buildings which they occupy. In guide books, picture-postcards, and daily conversation,

Merton College is taken to be an entity mainly on the south side of Merton Street, just as King's College, Cambridge, might be described, when speaking informally, as standing on the west side of King's Parade. There is something to be said for such notions, incomplete as they are. Even its street front reveals a good deal of Merton's history, from the college church, standing in its own churchyard, to the lugubrious Edwardian bulk of the former Warden's Lodgings on the other side of the road. The turreted gatehouse and the adjoining range of buildings have much of the Gothick prettiness of an Ackermann print, and might seem at first glance to be of no greater antiquity.[1] Closer inspection, however, will reveal that the gatehouse has kept its fifteenth-century gates and vaulted entrance-hall, and a variety of sculptures (Pl. 2), whilst the range to the east preserves the identity of one of the original houses bought to accommodate Walter de Merton's students in the 1260s.

Beyond that building again, there are details in the stonework and fenestration of what is now the Merton Street front of St Alban's quadrangle which mark the former presence there of two academic halls, which were functioning before there were any colleges in Oxford. They were merged before the sixteenth century, and rebuilt as St Alban Hall in 1599, but their separate origins are still declared in the stone, and remind us that this was once a populous and busy part of the early medieval town.[2] The passer-by, advised in 1997 that the college is not open to visitors until the afternoon, does not need to enter its gates to read something of its past, and even of its prehistory.

The visitor sees colleges as groups of buildings, venerable in appearance or reputation, open or closed to inspection, perhaps welcoming or inhospitable in aspect, and in distinguishing their faces thus may come to recognize them as so many building-blocks of the university. The members of colleges see them in a different way, though the buildings still bulk large in their perceptions, peopled either by their present inhabitants, or by those who were there perhaps thirty or forty years ago. Such intuitions are readily understandable, but are obviously only part of the story.

Academic colleges are complex bodies, and although their primary purpose, which is to maintain and promote learning, can readily be

---

[1] The street-front of the range was refaced in 1836–8 under the direction of Edward Blore, the architect of Abbotsford. For Blore, see below, pp. 283–4.

[2] On the two halls, Nun Hall and St Alban Hall, see below, pp. 8, 125, 129.

stated, it is apt to attract less attention than the means which they deploy to that end, and the places in which the work is done. Few members of colleges, even their bursars, can hold every aspect of the corporate life in view, though it may be that bursars come closest to the truth. What we understand today by a college is, just as it was in the Middle Ages, a device for getting things done in a domestic setting. A college is, first and last, a household.

The continuity both of Merton's academic and domestic life and of its physical setting, over more than seven centuries, is a tribute not only to the founder's benevolence, but also to his vision. His foundation not only played a decisive part in developing the medieval and later university, but has since weathered two great social revolutions. The first, still known as the Reformation, was both expressed in and accomplished by radical changes in religious practice in England in the sixteenth and seventeenth centuries. It bore heavily and decisively upon the university because the university was, and remained for some centuries, an ecclesiastical institution. The second, the Industrial Revolution, was effected when mechanical power was exploited and assimilated in industry and transport in the nineteenth and twentieth centuries, and all society was transformed. The second has led on to a third great alteration in human affairs, the management of knowledge by automatic means, which is still in train. It is impossible at present to assess its continuing effects, but it is a change that might, in its apocalyptic character, appeal more to Walter de Merton than would either of its predecessors.

Seen in those terms, the life of the college would bear some fuller consideration. Walter de Merton was explicit enough about his intentions, but they have in the first place to be read, and elucidated, in the context of his own times and experience. The development of the college, and of the university in which it has functioned for more than 730 years, has to be assessed against social and other movements in which both institutions have had an influence of their own. To describe the most ordinary of historical events incurs a great risk of over-simplifying them, and even the busiest periods of history are foreshortened when we define them. Their reality, of which college life itself is only one manifestation, has always been a continuum.

We shall probably never know what experience of the life and work of the university Walter de Merton had had before he resolved to endow a college to encourage learning there. He may have had a brief opportunity to study at Oxford in the 1230s, when he was certainly

3

known to two of the most talented scholars of his day,[3] but he spent the greater part of his life in the king's service, as a lawyer and administrator. As a royal official and counsellor he had evidently had an opportunity to consider the university's functions, and its potential as a store of talent. Though he was almost certainly not himself a graduate, he worked for most of his life with graduates, and he came to think well of them.

There were other and more readily discerned influences in Walter de Merton's life. His father was a man of modest substance, apparently a tradesman, once referred to as a cook, in Basingstoke, a royal manor, who was connected with a ministerial family, the Heriets, or Herriards, one of whom was a judge in the reigns of Richard I (1189–99) and John (1199–1216). Walter's mother, Christina Fitzace, inherited property in Basingstoke, and bequeathed a small freehold estate to him.[4]

Walter received some other modest gifts or bequests of land, from kinsmen on either side of his family. He might therefore have spent his life as a minor landlord in Hampshire, a freeholder and juror of a royal manor, though for security and reassured contentment in thirteenth-century England he would have needed a patron of some greater means. In the event, he would probably have found one.

His abilities, ambitions, and some unknown chance worked to take him further. His first support must have come from his family, and throughout his life he remembered his obligations to his kinsmen. He was grateful to his parents, whose memory he honoured by his first charitable foundation, the hospital of St John in Basingstoke.[5] He was also strongly mindful of his duty towards his seven sisters and their children. He was able to express his gratitude in a striking way because he found a rewarding employment for his own talents, and a career that took him into the innermost circle of government, as a member of the clergy.

Walter owed his professional career, and most probably the first

---

[3] He was commended as a candidate for holy orders in a letter written *c.* 1236 by Adam Marsh, OFM, to a brother Franciscan named Bechesoveres, who was probably then a member of Robert Grosseteste's episcopal household at Lincoln. There is an implication that Walter de Merton was in Oxford at the time, and therefore in Grosseteste's diocese: see further *ERMC*, pp. 9–10.

[4] For Walter's parentage, and his local property, see *ERMC*, pp. 5–6. Some of his other lands in Basingstoke came from Christina Basing and Walter son of Alexander, who may have been kin either on his father's or his mother's side (loc. cit.).

[5] The hospital, an almshouse endowed between 1240 and 1245, eventually came under the college's control: see below, p. 324 and n.; and *VCH Hants.*, ii. 208–11.

stages of his education, to the Augustinian priory of Merton, in Surrey.[6] We know him only as a cleric, and first find him, about the year 1230, acting as an agent of the priory.[7] He was evidently not professed as a canon, but in 1233 he was appointed to one of the priory's local benefices, at Cuddington. He had plainly proved himself a useful man, and the connection with the priory was in turn deeply important to him. He seems to have taken on the name of Merton in compliment to the house, and the canons were much in his mind a quarter of a century later, when he came to plan and found his college. Well before the end of the decade, however, he moved from Merton and Surrey into the king's service, and devoted the rest of his life, at least until he was made bishop of Rochester in 1274, to the business of government.

A notable servant of the crown, Walter de Merton was also active in the administration of the church in his earlier years, and between 1242 and 1247 he was an official of Bishop Nicholas Farnham in the diocese of Durham. Both as a cleric and a scholar, Farnham seems to have had a particular personal influence upon his more talented clerks, Walter amongst them. As bishop, Farnham exercised a delegated royal authority in the palatinate of Durham, and he was well placed to recruit and encourage able men. His distinguished household there must in many ways have resembled the royal chancery itself, to which Walter returned, richer from the proceeds of several benefices, in 1247.[8]

The administrative life was evidently congenial to him, and his years in Durham enlarged his experience and his skills. His career thereafter was beset with the hazards of high politics, but it exposed him to many of the great issues of his times. It also served to make the fortune which he subsequently bestowed upon the church, the world of learning, and those members of his kin who proved apt for study.[9]

---

[6] On Merton Priory, a rich and influential house, see A. Heales, *The Records of Merton Priory in the County of Surrey, chiefly from early and unpublished Documents* (London, 1898); and *VCH Surrey*, ii. 94–102. It was the scene of a royal council in 1235 which produced the enactments known as the Statute of Merton (20 Henry III), and has its place in the prehistory of parliament.

[7] He acted on occasions as an attorney, and probably as a conveyancer: *ERMC*, pp. 8–9.

[8] See *ERMC*, pp. 15–18, and on some connections between the diocese of Durham and the earliest colleges in Oxford, p. 68. Walter de Merton's benefices there were Sedgefield and Staindrop in Co. Durham, and Haltwhistle in Northumberland.

[9] For some examples of Walter de Merton's transactions in land, which combined patience, watchful assiduity, and a keen eye for a bargain, see *ERMC*, pp. 12–15.

Walter was a royal clerk of some standing in the writs office by 1238, four years before he moved to Durham, and when he resumed work in the chancery a decade later he first became prothonotary,[10] and eventually chancellor and keeper of the great seal in 1261. He remained close to Henry III in the great crisis of the reign, when a substantial number of barons turned against the king under the leadership of Simon de Montfort. He was then displaced as chancellor by Nicholas of Ely, a baronial nominee,[11] but made his peace well enough with de Montfort to be able to endow and establish Merton College in 1264. After de Montfort's defeat and death at Evesham in 1265 Walter remained in the king's service, and held a number of judicial commissions, sitting on occasion with the justices for the Jews. Upon Henry III's death in 1272 he became chancellor again, and directed the government of England in Edward I's absence on crusade and in Gascony from 1272 to 1274. On Edward's return, however, he readily resigned his office, and turned to other concerns.

Walter de Merton's appointment as bishop of Rochester in 1274 was a reward for which he might have looked earlier in other and more settled times. In the remaining years of his life, down to his death in 1277, he busied himself with his college, and with a residuum of public affairs, at least as much as with the concerns of his small diocese.[12] He would undoubtedly have said, had he been challenged, that he was using his talents in the best interests of the church.

If Walter de Merton did study in Oxford, his studies can only have been brief, and of a general and basic kind.[13] His talents were plainly those of an administrator and negotiator, and they were sustained by his knowledge of the common law, which, like his expert touch as a conveyancer, was not among the objects of academic study at the

---

[10] The king referred to him as *clericus noster*, our clerk, in 1249 when he granted him the right of free warren over his lands at Malden. Free warren gave the lord the right to keep and take small game on his own lands. Walter was evidently building up an estate in Surrey, and it would be interesting to know whether his final purpose was already maturing at that time.

[11] See below, pp. 19–20.

[12] The monks of the cathedral priory of Rochester evidently regretted the time and the means which Walter expended on his college, and felt that he might have done more for them than he did: *Flores Historiarum*, ed. H. R. Luard, RS xcv (London, 1890), iii. 44

[13] The evidence of Adam Marsh's letter, mentioned above, n. 3, raises a chronological problem. If, as seems probable, Walter de Merton was born *c.* 1200–5, the most likely time for him to have attended the Oxford schools would have been *c.* 1220. It may be that he took a later opportunity for a short period of study on the threshold of his public career, under the sponsorship of Merton Priory.

time.[14] The university schools did, however, teach critical analysis by the deployment of logic, and by the time that Walter became chancellor he would have been able to assess some of its results in his younger colleagues.[15]

In the 1260s the university in Oxford, as a centre of systematic higher studies, was probably not much more than a century old, though the prehistory of its schools stretched back to the end of the eleventh century.[16] It was a self-governing association of masters, in its origins most probably a gild.[17] It was recognized as a corporate body by the pope in 1254,[18] when it had well-established courses of study, but even at that time it had no buildings of its own, and little in the way of common resources. The academics of medieval Europe were notably foot-loose, and as a general rule had little beyond personal loyalties and enthusiasms to tie them to a particular place.[19]

University students in general began their studies in their early teens, and needed seven years to complete the course in the liberal arts which led to a master's degree.[20] They were for the most part housed in licensed hostels known as halls. The halls might or might not be owned by their principals, the masters of arts who instructed and disciplined their lodgers, but they characteristically lacked the endowments which enabled the colleges to prevail over them in later centuries.[21] The only Oxford hall to survive until the twentieth century

[14] See e.g. *ERMC*, p. 12.

[15] For some contemporary examples of the sponsored training and employment of graduates, see F. Pegues, 'Royal support of students in the thirteenth century', *Speculum*, xxxi (1956), 454–62.

[16] See R. W. Southern, 'From schools to university', in *The Early Oxford Schools*, ed. J. I. Catto, *HUO* i. 1–36.

[17] Of the forms of voluntary association available at the time, the gild, a self-sustaining surrogate family, was by far the most flexible and, for all ordinary purposes, secure. See further G. H. Martin, 'The early history of the London saddlers' gild', *Bulletin of the John Rylands University Library of Manchester*, lxxii (1992), 145–54. As late as the middle of the 15th cent. 'it is very clear ... that the university received a much more substantial income from being a gild than it did from being a landlord': T. A. R. Evans and R. J. Faith, 'College estates and university finances', *HUO* ii. 703.

[18] As *universitas magistrorum et scholarium Oxonie*: see M. B. Hackett, 'The university as a corporate body', in *HUO* i. 50 and n.

[19] Hence the periodic migrations in time of trouble, and even in a more settled age, the alarms which a threat of migration aroused: see below, p. 98.

[20] On the liberal arts, see below, p. 52.

[21] The variety of lodgings in Oxford and Cambridge was no doubt very great: many students will have slept where they could, whilst those with substantial means maintained their own households: see below, p. 29 and n. The halls were undoubtedly a valuable amenity both to the students and to the masters who ran them. See further n. 22.

was St Edmund Hall, which eventually became a college in 1957,[22] but there were at least 120 halls in the university by the early fourteenth century, and even in their decline they greatly outnumbered the colleges until after the Reformation. A substantial group of them were standing in St John's Lane, later Merton Street, when Walter de Merton began to buy his properties there. Of his two immediate neighbours then, Nun Hall succumbed almost at once, but St Alban Hall, reinforced later by the buildings of Nun Hall and an even narrower tenement to the east, called Hart Hall, withstood the looming presence of Merton College until it was gathered up and swallowed in 1881–4.[23]

The abundant halls of the thirteenth century, like the university itself, were eloquent of a great change in the church during the preceding 150 years. The clerics of western Christendom were historically divided into the religious, who were members of the monastic and religious orders, and the seculars, who worked in the world either as parochial or diocesan clergy, or, whilst subject to ordinary clerical discipline, as expert agents of the king or other lay patrons and employers. For the first seven centuries of western European Christianity almost the entire learning and professional skills of the clergy were commanded by the monasteries, whose members also controlled in their endowed lands much of the church's wealth. The conversion of the barbarian kingdoms of western Europe had been largely accomplished, and was certainly consolidated, by monks, and though by the early twelfth century the religious played a smaller part in secular administration than they had in earlier times, the management of their own large estates gave them a formidable record of expert practice.

The oldest monasteries were those of the Benedictines. From the tenth century onwards they were joined first by the Cluniacs, and then by the Cistercians, whose austerities, practised like their service of prayer in the interests of society as a whole, attracted huge benefactions from a grateful laity. The emergence of the order of Augustinian canons, to which Merton Priory belonged, can be seen as an attempt to strengthen the secular clergy, and perhaps even to super-

---

[22] St Edmund Hall is the subject of an illluminating study by A. B. Emden, *An Oxford Hall in Medieval Times, being the Early History of St Edmund Hall* (2nd edn., Oxford, 1948). Individually the halls are poorly documented, and their rapid erosion in early modern times has obscured their importance in the medieval university.

[23] It took a little longer to digest, though the process was complete by the time that Champneys rebuilt it in 1904–10. See further below, pp. 308–9.

sede them. The canons regular seemed able to provide a force which could undertake pastoral work amid the tumult of lay society, while sustained by a monastic discipline and, equally valuable, a monastic endowment. Like the Cistercians, however, the Augustinians often found themselves overwhelmed by their endowments, and especially by the gifts of parish churches which were heaped upon them, and which they could not hope themselves to serve.[24]

In the course of the twelfth century, however, although the wealth of the monastic houses remained imposing, their pre-eminence and authority were challenged by a remarkable enhancement of the power and authority of the secular clergy. The change was produced partly by the growing strength of the church as a whole, and its direction by the papal monarchy through the elaboration of the canon law, but principally by the parallel enrichment of lay society, the labours of which provided and sustained the church's wealth. The augmented resources of an expanding population and economy were applied in increasing measure to develop lay institutions. In particular they went to enhance the power of kings and princes, who borrowed their skilled administrators in ever greater numbers from the church. The rise of the universities, which came into being in western Europe to meet the demands for trained men from ecclesiastical and lay authorities alike, was a notable sign of the times.

Late in the same period there was a further movement of reform and development in the church, with the appearance at the beginning of the thirteenth century of the mendicant friars. The followers of St Dominic and of St Francis of Assisi might have riven the church with their enthusiasm, but their orthodoxy was acknowledged, or secured, by Innocent III at the fourth Lateran Council in 1215. The friars were quick to recognize the importance and potential of the universities as a training ground. Unlike the older religious orders they were committed from the beginning to pastoral work in the lay world, and they took care to establish their houses where they could best advance their cause. Work in the universities simultaneously widened their audience and refined their skills. There was a Dominican house in

---

[24] See further J. C. Dickinson, *The Origins of the Austin Canons and their Introduction into England* (London, 1950), pp. 58, 131–53; and A. H. Thompson, *The Abbey of St Mary of the Meadows, Leicester* (Leicester, 1949), pp. 4–8. Dickinson emphasizes, in a European context, the contemplative element in the Augustinian movement, but the nature and endowment of the English houses, and their patronage by courtiers and administrators, suggest that their pastoral role was predominant here.

Oxford by 1221, and a Franciscan by 1224. The university had gained an access of disciplined and well-directed energy, and in the longer run a threatening rival.[25]

The friars' houses in Oxford grew in number during the century. The two older orders were joined by the Carmelites in 1256, and by the Augustinian or Austin friars, who settled on the north side of the city, outside Smith Gate, in 1266–7. Between them they established a pattern which the other religious orders came to copy, and by their presence they strengthened a movement which eventually produced the secular colleges, and thence an even greater change in the university.

In that as in almost every other respect Oxford in the middle of the thirteenth century was a smaller and less imposing version of the university of Paris, where there were eleven colleges by the 1260s. They were very various in their nature and purposes, but without exception they depended upon funds which were held and administered by other institutions or authorities. The most celebrated, and in the event the longest-lived of them, was the establishment known as the Sorbonne, founded as recently as 1257 by a royal chaplain, Robert de Sorbon. The Sorbonne provided quarters and support for a chosen company of graduates who were permitted to read both for the degree of master of arts and, when they were qualified to do so, for advanced degrees in theology. A privileged communal life of that kind was an amenity which had previously been available only to members of those religious orders, notably the friars, which had established houses in the university.

What had been done in Oxford by that time was, though significant, on a much smaller scale. The foundation now known as University College had its origins around 1250 in a benefaction made by William, archdeacon of Durham, one of a number of Parisian masters who came to England in the 1220s at the invitation of Henry III's ministers. William's bequest established a fund administered by the university, which was used to buy some houses, none of them on the site of the present college, and to make loans to students from the rents. Balliol College began in fulfilment of a penance placed upon John de Balliol for assaulting the bishop of Durham, Walter Kirkham, in 1255. In the 1260s Balliol's agents paid a weekly allowance to a number of poor

---

[25] On the mendicant houses, and others, see M. Sheehan, 'The religious orders, 1220–1370', *HUO* i. 193–224.

scholars, and by 1266 he had leased a hostel in what is now Broad Street to accommodate sixteen of them. The dole was continued precariously after John's death in 1269, until in 1284 his widow, the Lady Devorguilla, vested an endowed fund in the hands of trustees, one of whom was to be a Franciscan friar.

Such were the examples, at home and abroad, available to Walter de Merton when in 1262, in a moment of some political danger, he began to realize his plans to provide for his kin, and to honour his friends and patrons, in a manner beneficial to both church and state. The earliest record of his intentions appears in the text of a charter uttered by Gilbert de Clare (1222–62), seventh earl of Gloucester.[26] The earl, as the chief lord of the fee, licensed and confirmed Walter's grant of the Surrey manors of Farleigh and Malden, with part of Chessington, to Merton Priory. The priory was to hold the property in trust to maintain clerks studying in the university of Oxford, according to regulations which Walter would frame. It appears, however, that the priory was not then formally enfeoffed with the manors, but that their rents were paid over privately.[27] In September 1264, immediately after uttering the college's first statutes, Walter named eight of his nephews as beneficiaries of the foundation, whilst reserving the right on the one hand to name a number of additional scholars, and on the other to lodge in the manors himself, with his travelling household, as and when he chose. The deed probably gave formal effect to an arrangement which had obtained at least since the grant of 1262.[28]

The charitable trust of 1262, whatsoever its details, was entirely superseded in 1264. It was rational and effective, and it fittingly expressed Walter's regard for Merton Priory, but its chief and immediate object had no doubt been to preserve the intended endowment from the hands of his political enemies.[29] In the event the manors did suffer some damage,[30] and in the uncertainty of the time there was

---

[26] On 7 May 1262. The original charter has been lost, but it was transcribed by Joseph Kilner, as printed in his *Account of Pythagoras's School*, p. 51, and reprinted in *MM*, p. 8.

[27] See *ERMC*, p. 22 and n.

[28] See *ERMC*, p. 26 and n. 4. For the text of the deed, see *MM*, p. 9, where it is provisionally dated to 1262.

[29] He had also arranged during the summer of 1262 for the king to take on the patronage of St John's hospital, Basingstoke, to the same end: *CChR 1257–1300*, p. 44.

[30] Malden, Chessington, and Cuddington were sacked in 1263 by agents of Peter de Montfort, and Malden and Farleigh occupied by Gilbert de Clare, who was at that time an ally of Simon de Montfort, from March to September 1264. Londoners sympathetic to

nothing better to be done. As soon as he was able to act, however, at a moment when it appeared that the baronial party had established an effective regime, Walter felt able to entrust his project to a foundation of his own. He thereupon established an independent college at Malden to be known, in honour of the priory of St Mary of Merton, as the house of the scholars of Merton, and endowed it with the manors of Malden and Farleigh, as before.[31]

The college consisted of a warden[32] and a chapter of two or three priests, who were to reside at Malden with a small household staff and administer its lands. Its object was to support twenty students in Oxford, or in any other place where learning might flourish, by an annual allowance which they were to receive at the warden's hands. The income was derived from the rents and dues of the endowed lands, and the warden's management of the estate was subject to the students' scrutiny. The beneficiaries were to be drawn in the first instance from the founder's own kin, after whom preference would be given to clerks who were natives of the diocese of Winchester. The first warden, who held office until 1286, was Master Peter Abingdon (Pl. 1b). An Oxford graduate, Abingdon was a trusted colleague who had previously been master and a benefactor of the hospital at Basingstoke, and whom Walter subsequently named as the principal auditor of his will.[33]

In his new venture Walter de Merton was on uncharted ground. His original appointment of Merton Priory to oversee his benefaction may have been only a temporary expedient, but it had carried the assurance that his endowment would be protected and administered by a great religious house, with more than a century of experience in such matters. The new college would be conveniently close to Merton, to which its officers could turn for advice if they chose, but it was unmistakably intended to be independent,[34] and the price of independence was the risk of incompetence, maladministration, and

---

de Montfort also attacked Walter de Merton's prebendal estates. See futher *ERMC*, pp. 22–3; and J. A. R. Maddicott, *Simon de Montfort* (Cambridge, 1994), pp. 266, 305.

[31] See *ERMC*, pp. 25–7; *MM*, pp. 15–17; and above, n. 30. Beyond the circumstances of its foundation, practically nothing is known of the college at Malden, which functioned for only a decade. There is a valiantly uninformative note of it in *VCH Surrey*, ii. 128–9. Its records, whatsoever they were, were presumably brought to Oxford in 1272, but do not appear amongst the present college muniments. See further below, n. 60.

[32] On the connotations of the term *custos*, and some other monastic influences detectable in the organization of the college, see *ERMC*, pp. 68–9.

[33] See *ERMC*, pp. 1–2; *BRUO*, p. 4. See further below, pp. 69–70.

[34] See below, pp. 19–20.

failure. Its regulation called for careful consideration, and the statutes show an interesting mixture of confidence and cautious prescription.

The first statutes,[35] which cover some twenty topics, begin with the endowment and constitution of the college, and then prescribe the students' numbers and allowances, and their appointment. They provide for the appropriate education of any orphans amongst the founder's kin, within the available resources of the house.[36] They go on to require an annual examination of the warden's work by the senior scholars, an arrangement which at once ties the college closely to the university schools, and they also bind the house to an increase in the number of scholars as often as its resources will allow: a recurrent theme. There follow rules for the household at Malden, provision for the sick and superannuated, including members of the founder's own household, a provision for appointing the warden, and injunctions that the beneficiaries remember the house in the days of their prosperity, as well as praying regularly for the good estate of their patrons.

The statutes are of a fairly simple kind, but they have one significant and striking feature. They bear a faint impress of the *Regula ad servos Dei* of the Augustinian order,[37] which Walter de Merton might naturally have had in mind, but the obedience which is enjoined upon the students, unlike the members of a religious house, is rather to the house and its statutes than to its head. On the other hand there is a system of checks and scrutinies, which was progressively developed, by which the college's entire resources were to be conserved and the more effectively applied by the beneficiaries themselves.

Except for the superannuated household staff, who were to be

---

[35] See *MM*, pp. 15–17, and Plate II; and *ERMC*, pp. 377–8. The document is undated, but probably followed immediately upon the vesting of the endowment on 14 Sept. 1264. See also below, n. 42.

[36] The nature of the special provision for orphans in 1264 and 1270 (see below, p. 14) shows that the foundation was from the beginning intended for established students, and indeed for those able to proceed to advanced studies. The founder would not have subjected the warden's conduct in office to the scrutiny of boys in the earliest stages of the arts course. From 1270, however, the presence of the grammar master would provide for the regular education of younger children, the *parvuli*, who remained a feature of the house for some decades. They do not seem all to have been of the founder's kin, though it was equally not intended that the seniors should all, or even predominantly, be recruited from their number. See also below, p. 21.

[37] Cf. *PL* xxxii, 1377–84. The reference is, however, far removed from Dr H. Mayr-Harting's demonstration of the derivation of the statutes of Peterhouse, Cambridge, from the rule of St Benedict: 'The foundation of Peterhouse, Cambridge (1284), and the rule of St Benedict', *EHR* ciii (1988), 318–38.

employed about the college as their capacities allowed, and the indispensable chaplains, all the beneficiaries of the foundation were to be apt for advanced study. They were then to be diligent in their work and, though it has proved a forlorn hope, they were to dress in a uniform style in token of their common life. They would forfeit their places if they entered a religious order, a choice which some of them did make from time to time,[38] or if their conduct were seriously unsatisfactory. The ordinances distinguished the generations of the founder's kin, the orphans being described as *parvuli*, little boys, who remained at Malden under the warden's care and instruction until 1270, and the older men as *scolares*, scholars, or students in the schools at Oxford, who must have been at least bachelors of arts, and who subsequently came to constitute the fellowship of the college. As we have seen, the scholars were not simple beneficiaries, but had a duty to inquire annually into the warden's management of the estate. In the same way, the twelve most advanced[39] were to be responsible, in consultation with the rest, for proposing the name of a warden, upon any vacancy, to the bishop of Winchester as protector, father, and defender of the house. Those are provisions which reveal the emergent autonomous college against the generally prescriptive background of the regulations.

Whilst the warden was to see to the instruction of any orphans of the founder's kin, the college was to take responsibility for scholars who fell incurably sick, and for those of the founder's servants who had no other resource. None but male servants were to be employed, at least upon the main site. Those scholars who prospered were again enjoined to remember their debt of gratitude to the college itself, to the founder's hospital of St John at Basingstoke,[40] and to Merton Priory. They were to pray together, at least on one or two formal occasions every year, not only for the founder himself, but for all their other benefactors, both living and dead.[41]

The bishop of Winchester, as diocesan, stood as patron of the

---

[38] See below, pp. 139–40.

[39] The term is *provectiores*, who would most probably, but not necessarily, be senior in years as well as accomplishment.

[40] The inclusion of the hospital, which subsequently became an asylum for all those who retired from the house, is a further and interesting reflection of Walter's concern to serve family piety and public duty together. See further below, p. 324 and n.

[41] This obligation, which would also have been discharged in daily services, was subsequently associated directly with the formal scrutinies. See above, n. 35, and below, p. 21.

college, and the deed of foundation was sealed with the great seal of England, the bishop's seal, the seal of his cathedral chapter, and Walter de Merton's own seal (Pl. 1*a*). The charter is dated only by the year, but the officers of the college were formally seised of the manor of Malden on 14 September 1264, the feast of the Exaltation of Holy Cross, an anniversary which the house still celebrates.[42]

The college was now established, and operating in two places to a common end, like many charitable trusts today. Its principal offices, in both the medieval and the modern sense, were in Surrey, where the warden and chaplains supervised the estate, and maintained the constant service of prayer which was the first business of any college of clerics, and to which the supplications of the students themselves were ancillary. To its contemporaries the prayers were the chief and essential function of the house, and their performance a guarantee that its contingent business would be duly and effectively performed. The students' perception would be much the same, though they would judge the practical work of the college by their own experience. Even in its first few years the college was a force in Oxford,[43] yet it also had its being elsewhere: the community of students was merely one local manifestation of its life, as the daily prayers at Malden and its agents in the manors were others.

Those few years, however, worked a great and rapid change. In the first place, within two years, and probably within an even shorter time, Walter de Merton began to buy property in Oxford, and on a substantial scale. The campaign was apparently a brief one, though it probably took longer, if not to plan, then to execute, than the dates of the title deeds might suggest.[44] Between January 1266 and the autumn of 1268 Walter acquired and consolidated more than an acre of ground in St John's Lane, just inside the south wall of the town, and secured the king's permission to enclose it. He also received the advowson of St Peter's-in-the-East, Oxford, from the king, and the

[42] The significance of the occasion is that it is the date upon which the founder at last recovered possession of the property which had been taken from him by members of the baronial party the previous year: *ERMC*, pp. 25–6. See also above, p. 11 and n.

[43] See below, p. 19. The warden was evidently a familiar figure in Oxford by 1268: see below, p. 34.

[44] The acquisition of property in the 13th cent., and particularly the business of establishing an unencumbered title, was at least no speedier than it is today. Walter de Merton was well versed in the procedures, and he is unlikely ever to have moved precipitately. The conveyance of St John's church in Jan. 1266 (see below, p. 26) marks the end of, or a significant stage in, a process that must have taken some months to negotiate. See also below, p. 29 and n.

manor of Holywell with it, and acquired other properties. In the second place, his community of scholars had plainly grown both in numbers and potential. The daily life of Mertonians in and about the schools had become not so much a function as a constituent of the college.

The middle stage of the foundation was therefore reached in 1270, when Walter issued new statutes for the house.[45] They are more than twice the length of those of 1264, which they begin by confirming, but which they then elaborate extensively. They are in all respects much closer to the final statutes of 1274 than to those of 1264, though the college chapter is still at Malden, the scholars are still to be supported at Oxford 'or elsewhere', and the priests, still at the heart of the college, are now to number three or four rather than two or three. That addition marks the increasing responsibilities of the warden and his colleagues as administrators. Like the scholars' place of study, the college itself could be removed elsewhere: to Farleigh, or to one of its other manors, as circumstances might require. The provision clearly prepares the way for the removal to Oxford which was completed by 1274, though it has also to be read in the context of the many disturbances and migrations that marked the early history of Oxford. It was less than a decade since the university had seemed threatened by a rival establishment in Northampton during the civil wars.[46]

At the same time the academic work and organization of the foundation were carefully considered, presumably in response to several years' experience in Oxford. The scholars' studies were prescribed in more detail, and in terms that looked forward to advanced work rather than to the routines of the schools, for they extended through the arts to philosophy, and on to theology, with some marginal provision for the study of canon and civil law. There were now to be two sub-wardens, one to concern himself with the college household, the other to look to the 'congregation of scholars'. There had probably been a sense of some untidiness in the arrangements at Oxford in recent years, and again the provision testifies to the increasing import-

---

[45] Printed in *Statutes of the Colleges of Oxford (Merton College)* (Oxford, 1853), pp. 10–20; and *ERMC*, pp. 378–91.

[46] See c. 45; and below, p. 19. For Northampton, see *HUO* i. 128–9. F. W. Maitland said delicately that Walter de Merton acquired land in Cambridge 'for reasons that I dare not guess': *Township and Borough* (Cambridge, 1898), p. 6. In the event the next serious migration, which was also the last, was to Stamford in 1333. See below, p. 98.

ance of the operations there.[47] The bishop of Winchester was no longer named as patron, but the chancellor and a proctor of the university, in place of the 'chancellor or rector' invoked in 1264, were to resolve any disagreements over the admission of new fellows. It was a further sign of the growth of the community, and also of its position in the university.[48]

Beyond the evident success of the establishment in Oxford, the most substantial reason for the changes worked in 1270 was that the endowment had been greatly increased. The original provisions of 1262, and the emergent college of 1264, with the issues and resources of two-and-a-half manors at its disposal, were on the scale of a well-endowed private chantry, to which the acquisitions in Oxford had added several houses and another manor, and the patronage of four churches, two in Oxford and two in Surrey.[49] The founder now bestowed seven more manors upon the college, one of them an important urban property in Cambridge, and the rights of presentation to six parish churches, together with an income from another estate, at Kibworth Harcourt in Leicestershire.

The seven new manors, which represented in some measure the spoils taken from the rebels after the battle of Evesham and the siege of Kenilworth, in 1265–6, were Cheddington in Buckinghamshire, Cuxham in Oxfordshire, Gamlingay and Dunnings in Cambridgeshire, Ibstone in Buckinghamshire, Thorncroft in Leatherhead, Surrey, and Stillington in County Durham. The churches were Diddington in Huntingdonshire, Horspath in Oxfordshire, Lapworth in Warwickshire, Ponteland in Northumberland, Stratton St Margaret in Wiltshire, and Wolford in Warwickshire.[50] It was a resource unmatched in either university until William of Wykeham, with Merton before his eyes, founded New College in 1379.[51]

The allowance from Kibworth is a particularly interesting item in

---

[47] See below, pp. 27–32.

[48] See c. 6. *Proctor* might be read in this context as a proxy or deputy, especially in view of the vagueness of the phrase 'chancellor or rector' used in 1264. However, the university's government was effectively established by this time, and the founder was evidently prepared to leave the matter to an academic authority. See further *HUO* i. 52–8; and below, p. 20 and n.

[49] The college was given the patronage of Farleigh and Malden in 1264: *ERMC*, p. 41.

[50] Statutes, c. 33. On the income available from churches, see D. Postles, 'The acquisition and administration of spiritualities by Oseney Abbey', *Oxoniensia*, li (1986), 69–77, and on seisin and titles, ibid. 70–1. Not all the churches could be secured at once, and the college never obtained Horspath. See further below, n. 52; and p. 18.

[51] See A. B Cobban, 'Colleges and halls, 1380–1500', *HUO* ii. 581–2; and below, p. 111.

an imposing tale of benefactions. One of the new churches, St Giles's, Horspath, was a gift to Merton from Henry III's brother Richard, earl of Cornwall and titular king of the Romans. In the event the college never secured the patronage of the living, although it went to law to establish its title, but in the mean time the addition of a prince to the roll of benefactors was an accomplishment in itself.[52] Walter de Merton underlined the prize by providing a stipend from Kibworth for three chaplains and twelve poor scholars to pray for Richard and, ironically, for his son Henry, who was murdered a year later at Viterbo by two of Simon de Montfort's sons. The arrangement, which in effect established a chantry within the college, was eloquent of Walter's own standing and connections, of the pieties of patronage, and perhaps of some unspoken anxiety about Horspath. It was also a reminder that there can be many a slip between a title conferred and an income enjoyed.[53]

The lordship of Kibworth itself was not subsequently bequeathed to the college, but had to be acquired from Walter's heirs, a process which took several years.[54] Both Ponteland, and the rectory of Embleton, Northumberland, which Edmund of Lancaster granted to the college in 1275, had to be fought for, against a rich variety of opponents. The founder did not live to see the Statute of Mortmain (1279), which controlled gifts of estates to such corporations as abbeys and colleges by forbidding them entirely, and so allowed the king to circumvent the statute by licensing exceptions. The college discovered subsequently that in accepting Embleton it had erred in not taking note of the statute before it was enacted, but that was the least of its troubles, and as the founder himself knew, public offences are a universe of themselves.[55]

The much-enlarged endowment brought wider responsibilities to

---

[52] Walter probably had hopes of other members of the royal family: see below, pp. 33–4. Horspath eventually came into the hands of Magdalen College.

[53] Advowsons, which commonly entangled lay and ecclesiastical titles, were a fruitful source of trouble to many who acquired them. Dower was another, and the college's interest in Ponteland involved both: see below, p. 65. See also the negotiations involved, with the founder's direct participation, in securing possession of the church of Elham, Kent, given to the college by the Lord Edward (later Edward I), in 1267: *ERMC*, p. 44. On Richard of Cornwall's poor scholars, see further below, pp. 48–9.

[54] For the heirs' seisin of the property in the summer of 1278, and the release of their individual titles to the college later in the year, see *CCR 1272–9*, pp. 465, 510, and 512.

[55] The statute *De viris religiosis* is Stat. 7 Edw I, 1279. On its workings, see S. Raban, *Mortmain Legislation and the English Church, 1279–1500* (Cambridge, 1982); for Embleton, see below, pp. 66–8.

the foundation, which the statutes sought to accommodate in part by providing for manorial officers who would share in the common life of the college.[56] In the mean time suitably qualified members of the house were to be appointed as supervisors of studies, and those of the company who were best fitted to do so were to look to the pastoral needs of the churches of which the college was now the patron, a provision again reminiscent of the founder's association with the Augustinian order, and one which, as in Augustinian houses, was likely to prove increasingly difficult to observe as the fortunes of the house prospered. The hospital at Basingstoke was now confirmed as a refuge for superannuated scholars, and an income assigned to it from the estates at Cheddington and Ibstone. The institution as a whole had manifestly come a long way since 1262.

It had, however, still further to go. The statutes of 1270 do not refer explicitly to the property in Oxford, which the house already enjoyed and which was emerging as the most significant part of the endowment. In 1274 the founder therefore issued new statutes,[57] under which, with some amendments over the centuries, the college has effectively been governed ever since. The first clause decreed that the House of Scholars of Merton was to be entirely domiciled in Oxford, and to become a self-governing corporation there, duly reinvested with the Surrey manors. The role and qualifications of the warden, as the supervisor of every aspect of the college's work, were prescribed in detail for the first time, on the experience of a decade's practice and probably with an eye to Peter Abingdon's eventual successor.[58] In future the warden was to be chosen by the visitor from a short list of three names, drawn up by a committee of the seven senior members of the house after detailed consultation with all their fellows.

The visitor is not named in the new statutes, but he emerges two years later not as the bishop of Winchester, as in 1264, but as the

---

[56] See cc. 16–18. The *yconomi* have overtones of the contemporary Cistercian lay-brothers, or *conversi*, who by the thirteenth century were managers of the abbeys' granges rather than manual workers: see C. Platt, *The Monastic Grange in England: A Re-assessment*, (London, 1969), pp. 76–7. The intention at Merton is clearly to asssociate, if not to equate, the two functions of the college as the manager of an estate and as a place of learning. On the estates, see also below, pp. 68–9.

[57] In August, immediately upon Walter de Merton's retirement from the chancellorship and his election to the bishopric of Rochester at the end of July. Their drafting must have preoccupied him at least over his busy last months in office, if he had not had them in hand since 1270. They are printed and reproduced in facsimile in *MM*, pp. 21–6, and translated in *MMC*, pp. 317–40.

[58] See cc. 5–6, 27–9, 31–3, 41. See also below, pp. 69–70.

archbishop of Canterbury. The change is rich in nuances. Between Malden and Oxford the administration of the college had moved from the diocese of Winchester into the diocese of Lincoln. The bishop of Winchester from 1268 to 1280 was Nicholas of Ely, the old political rival who had probably driven Walter de Merton from the chancery in 1260, and who, as the Montfortian nominee, certainly ousted him as chancellor in July 1263.

Those events may have rankled, even in the very different circumstances of 1274. On the other hand, the bishop in 1264 had been John Gervais, who appeared for the Montfortians before Louis IX of France at Amiens when Walter was the principal spokesman for Henry III. The change of diocese may well have been of more consequence than the change of diocesan. There is no record of the authority upon which Archbishop Kilwardby first acted as visitor in 1276: he was deeply interested in the work of the university, and may simply have taken the responsibility upon himself. On balance, however, it seems likely that Walter took the opportunity tactfully to divest the college of its association with the bishop, though not with the diocese, of Winchester, and welcomed the access of dignity which came with Kilwardby's benevolent interest in the foundation.[59]

Whatsoever its origins, the provision said as much about the nature and new status of the foundation as did the fact that the warden and eight or ten seniors now had the power to add to the statutes. Not only was the college formally housed in Oxford, but the entire management of its affairs, under the warden, was put into the hands of its academic community, which might now reasonably be termed the fellowship. With the house unified there was to be a single sub-warden, but the financial affairs of the college, the whole business of collecting and spending the revenues, were committed to three bursars. The bursars were to be chosen from amongst the fellows, and with the sub-warden and five other colleagues they were to supervise the local officers of the college manors. The warden was formally charged with the annual duty of riding to visit the estates, to review them and estimate the value of their produce, so that the college should know its resources and potential from harvest to harvest. In greatly changed circumstances, the visitation is still a feature of the college year.

---

[59] See further below, pp. 46–50. On the nuances of the visitorship, and Walter's relationship with Nicholas of Ely, see *ERMC*, pp. 75–6 and n.

The internal affairs of the house were also closely regulated by the statutes, which again prescribed a systematic augmentation of the fellowship. The founder was anxious both that the individual stipend of the fellows should be maintained at fifty shillings a year, and that their number should be kept at the fullest extent that the revenues could reasonably bear. The warden, who was already installed in one of the houses in St John's Lane,[60] had his own household there, in which the sub-warden and the chaplains, now to number at least three, and up to five servants, dined with him. There were to be three annual chapters or scrutinies, held after the end of each teaching term, to examine in detail the conduct of the whole company,[61] to maintain discipline and sound economy, and to approve candidates for admission, who were to serve a probationary period of one year.

Preference in elections was to be given as before to the founder's kin, then to candidates from the diocese of Winchester, and then to those from the other dioceses, now quite numerous, in which the college held land. The fellows' studies were prescribed in the same broad terms as in 1270, with provision for up to five suitably qualified graduates to study canon and civil law, and the grammar master was to continue his work, with an allowance for books and other needs. Up to thirteen of the founder's younger kin were to be taught Latin, and encouraged to progress to degrees as they were able. There were to be public readings at meals, and where conversation was permitted it was to be in respectable Latin.

Almost all the provisions of the earlier statutes were repeated and elaborated, though the college was no longer expected to serve its own churches.[62] There was now explicit provision for the warden's superannuation, and for the care of the college's own servants in retirement. As before, all members of the college were to remember their benefactors in prayer, and those who prospered were enjoined as before to assist the foundation, and the hospital of St John at Basingstoke.

The drafting of the statutes displays some oddities, particularly in the light of Walter de Merton's experience as a conveyancer. Although

[60] He may already have taken up lodgings in the city by 1268. At that time the college was formally embodied in Malden, but it was recognized that the warden would ordinarily be available in Oxford to conduct business there: see below, p. 34.

[61] By what Jeremy Bentham later described as Universal Delation, or the Non-Connivance-Tolerating Principle.

[62] Presumably because of the demands which they would have made upon the time of any fellows who happened to be in priestly orders. See also above, p. 19.

there are broad groupings of subjects, and some continuity of phrasing, both the major series are loosely constructed, and leave an impression that certain clauses have been inserted as they came to mind. One matter upon which Walter evidently felt strongly was that the substance of the house should not be consumed by litigation, and that it should be a condition of every appointment that members could be expelled from the house on due process without any right of appeal.[63] The clauses relating to the warden's status in 1274 are separated, not altogether illogically, but at a considerable remove, from those which concern his further duties, allowances, and election. He is then debarred from appealing against dismissal only in the penultimate clause, after various other matters, and before the attestation of the document. If a dramatic emphasis was intended, it miscarried in the drafting.

It is difficult to suppose that Walter de Merton did not scrutinize the texts closely, and very reasonable to think that he did. It seems that his experience of life reinforced a temperament given to prescription, and that sometimes his anxieties overcame his other promptings, as they might well do. He had made handsome provision for the welfare of the house and the furtherance of its work, and he was now anxious that its achievement should not be impaired by private interests and inclinations.

The statutes lay down careful procedures for the punishment of delicts and the ultimate removal of offenders, though seeking to maintain discipline with an appropriate leniency. All the regulations were to be closely observed, and in particular neither the warden nor the existing fellowship were to resist the admission of additional fellows in order to enhance their own allowances. New members were to take an oath upon their admission not only to obey the statutes but, as we have seen, to renounce any right of appeal against their decrees. The house, a beacon to the world, was also to be an island.

The most pragmatical note in the new statutes is perhaps in the rules for providing and regulating the college's horses, a matter as important as any in the conduct of affairs. The warden had an allowance for two horses, but he could be accompanied by a servant on a third, and could send a rider with messages, which might well justify keeping four. The provision of stabling was probably one of the immediate benefits which Peter Abingdon sought when he bought

---

[63] See 1270, c. 7, and 1274, c. 16.

tenements on the other side of St John's Lane: he certainly established his horses there, to be nourished with hay from Holywell.[64] The stables were in effect the warden's second household; besides their stalls the horses needed fodder, clothing, and harness, which all had to be stored, and regular shoeing as well as tending, and they also needed, or at any rate received, constant cosseting with potions and unguents. Stables have a shifting and largely inscrutable clientèle, and except in the most rigorously-conducted establishments it is often difficult to account for the whole number of those attendant on the livestock at any particular moment. If the warden sensed that there might be difficulties in keeping his horses on the main site he was prescient.[65]

Officers of the manors also could have horses at the college's expense if they needed them, a provision no doubt subject to a good deal of interpretation. Mertonian horses were sold as well as bought, and there may have been some systematic breeding on the manors.[66] Under the statutes the horses that the college provided for its officers, other than the warden, were to be competent but not of the most expensive kind, another fertile matter for debate.[67]

However, other members of the college had their own horses, which had also to be accommodated on or conveniently near the site.[68] There may have been space for a paddock to the south, towards the city wall, but such stabling as the original houses afforded cannot have lasted long amongst the new buildings. It is clear that the founder would not have wished even his kinsmen's horses to share the common manger, though they may well have done so on occasions. He did, however, order that the college's cavalry was not to eat its way through the estates on private journeys. Mertonians hacking home to the Leicestershire wolds, or to the mild valley of the Test, were not to call at the manors to feed their horses at the common

---

[64] What was known later as Postmasters' Hall was for some time called the warden's *curia*. See, for example, the entries for the stables, farrier's work, and harness in the earliest surviving sub-warden's accounts, between 1298 and 1301: *ERMC*, pp. 179–97, particularly pp. 193–4.

[65] See the tribulations of Warden Wyntle, below, pp. 248–55. The warden came to believe that the fellows' horses not only stole his hay, but were trained to steal it.

[66] See the horses sold at Reading in 1300, including the chestnut called Shyrf, who may merely have been a well-known character: *ERMC*, p. 359.

[67] See further below, p. 72.

[68] Horses were hired by fellows for some particular journeys, but many fellows would have kept their own, whether or not they always used them: *ERMC*, p. 218.

expense.[69] If they resolutely withstood those and other mundane temptations, fellows could ultimately be buried in the college church. It cannot be said that the founder had left anything unnecessarily to chance.

[69] 'Take him round and rub him down, there's a good chap. Oh, and just give him a handful of oats'. At least there were some occasions when the founder's ingrained optimism outweighed his anxieties.

2

The College Established

WE do not know at what point Walter de Merton made the momentous decision to allow his scholars to manage their own affairs in a single community, but he was almost certainly planning to acquire a substantial property for them in Oxford when he drew up the statutes of 1264. The site on which he developed his college there was apparently determined by the availability of something over an acre of land in the south-eastern quarter of the town, in St John's parish. The whole block, which included the parish church and churchyard, lay between St John's Street, also called St John's Lane, and now called Merton Street, to the north, and the city wall, or the roadway running inside it, to the south (*Frontispiece*). The properties there were in various hands, however, and could not be acquired without some negotiation. By the time that he bought the first plot, at the beginning of 1266,[1] it seems that he had already found some regular accommodation for his students in Bull Hall, St Aldate's, on the north side of what is now Pembroke Street. It is therefore possible that when he turned to the land at St John's his first intention was only to provide some additional, or more convenient, quarters for them.[2] The way in which he went to work, however, and the inclusion of the church, suggests that he had already conceived a more ambitious plan, and was preparing a fitting site for his transformed college.

The block of property which he eventually secured was bounded on the north by the street, and to the east by a small tenement called Nun Hall, which belonged to the Benedictine priory of Littlemore, and which is now covered by the western part of St Alban's quad-

---

[1] In the Middle Ages the year was commonly reckoned to begin on 25 Mar., and the deed (MCR 1, on which see pp. 26–7, below) is therefore dated 18 Jan. 1265, which is sometimes rendered as 1265/6, and is regarded now as 1266. The modern convention has been adopted here throughout.

[2] Bull Hall was later granted to the college by Jacob, son of Moses, in 1270–1, and was used to house the poor scholars of Richard of Cornwall's chantry, and some of the *parvuli*. See *MM*, p. 20; *ERMC*, p. 73 n. 2; and below, p. 113.

rangle.[3] On the west it extended as far as the western side of the strip of land now known as the Grove, which follows the line of a stream. The hollow of the stream is still marked by a long, shallow dip in the surface of Merton Street between Logic Lane and Oriel Square. By the early fourteenth century it was known as the Gutter, giving its name to Gutter Hall, which stood on its east bank.[4] To the south the boundaries of the constituent tenements stopped some way short of the city wall, which was supported by an inner rampart, of which the bank in the present college garden is in part a remnant. There seems to have been a track or pathway at the foot of the rampart to give continuous access to the wall-walk, but there were also several water-courses there, one or more of which passed under the wall.[5]

The main plot comprised the parish church of St John the Baptist,[6] its churchyard, and some vacant ground to the north and west. The site of the church is now occupied by the north wing of Mob Quad, which may incorporate some of its masonry. There were various other buildings on the site, but the principal house, which seems to have stood to the west or north-west of the church, had disappeared by 1266. To the east of that plot there were three other houses, facing on to Merton Street with courtyards behind them. The fact that the church stood so far to the south of the present street strongly suggests that there was another lane or path which served it, either running

[3] A patch of rough masonry visible in the passage between Front Quad and St Alban's may be the last original relic of Nun Hall. However, the irregular line of the string-courses on the street-front of the building still marks the original division of the two properties. See further above, p. 2, and below, pp. 125, 129.

[4] The stream was subsequently buried in a conduit (and perhaps in more than one), but the sinuous line of the path and boundary, which is the only curved line on the main site, suggests that it was originally a natural watercourse. It evidently overflowed into one of its old channels after a cloudburst in Aug. 1672, when Anthony Wood recalls that the water ran through the church, presumably north to south through the transepts. It then flooded the ground-floor chambers and the lower treasury in Mob Quad, and the sexton carried a fellow and two bachelors to dinner in hall on piggy-back: *LTAW* ii. 249.

[5] Wood says that 'most part of the wall on this side the city was formerly built on arches', and speaks of three visible in his own day: *MMC*, p. 302. His story there of a regular landing under the wall may be exaggerated, but there was a good deal of water to drain off the college site, and no doubt more than one channel in what are now the Meadows.

[6] St John's was sometimes known as St John's-within-the-Walls, to distinguish it from the extra-mural hospital of St John, of which Magdalen College now occupies the site. Merton's association with the saint goes back to the Basingstoke hospital (above, p. 4), and the dedication of the parish church must have seemed a happy augury to the founder. The present church, which today serves only as the college chapel, is dedicated to St Mary and St John. See also below, p. 39 and n.

parallel with Merton Street along the present north walk of Mob Quad, or north and south along either the east or the west side of the present quadrangle.

Whatsoever the pattern of the plots, the titles were quite complicated. Churches trail many rights, and St John's had an incumbent in occupation.[7] Then the first of the houses to the east belonged to St Frideswide's Priory, and the next was owned by a leading member of Oxford's congregation of Jews, Jacob, whose father, Master Moses of London, also held property in St Aldate's, close by Walter's tenement of Bull Hall.[8]

That association may perhaps explain Walter's original interest in the main site, but whether or not he found his own way to the place, he had long since shown himself to be a patient and practised negotiator, and he acquired what he wanted in the course of a few years. The principal component, the substantial plot on the west side, belonged to Reading Abbey, which had acquired it in 1235.[9] Although there was no identifiable house on the site in 1266, the capital messuage there was once a property of some consequence. The holding had comprised one of the *mansiones murales* of eleventh-century Oxford, a category of properties which is mentioned in Domesday Book, and was charged with maintaining the adjoining stretch of the city wall.[10]

The riverside settlement which became known as Oxford was probably first fortified under Alfred (849–901), or early in the tenth century, when its east wall seems to have cut across the present High Street by St Mary's church.[11] There was presumably a gateway there, but if there

[7] William of Chetyndone (?Cheddington), who died in 1292: *MM*, p. 18; and below, p. 39.

[8] See *MM*, p. 20; and below, n. 34. The tenement known as Moyses Hall stood on the south side of the street: H. Hurst, *Oxford Topography: An Essay* (OHS xxxix, 1899), pp. 48–9. Jacob may have specialized in building and/or leasing halls: see Roth, *Jews of Medieval Oxford*, pp. 145–8; and above, n. 2.

[9] *Close Rolls 1234–7*, p. 204. The tenement, which had been granted to Reading by Peter FitzHerbert, had been impounded for murage unpaid, and was formally restored to the abbey in that year.

[10] See H. Turner, 'The mural mansions of Oxford: attempted identifications', *Oxoniensia*, lv (1991), 73–9; and H. E. Salter, 'An Oxford mural mansion', in *Historical Essays in Honour of James Tait*, ed. J. G. Edwards, V. H. Galbraith, and E. F. Jacob (Manchester, 1933), pp. 299–303. Reading acquired the site of the *mansio*, which was probably a member of the manor of Watlington, from Peter FitzHerbert: ibid., pp. 300–1.

[11] See *VCH Oxon.* iv. 300; and B. Durham, 'The Thames crossing at Oxford', *Oxoniensia*, xlix (1985), 57–100. The low-lying ground to the south and east, on which Merton College now stands, was gathered in by the expansion of the late Anglo-Saxon town.

was, it gave on to an expanding suburb. The town's defences were therefore subsequently extended towards the Cherwell, enclosing the eastern curve of High Street, and the cluster of tenements along St John's Lane to the south, and so bringing new properties under the charge of maintaining the ditches and banks.

The presence of St John's church, and the fact that its advowson, the right to present the incumbent to its rectory, went with the title to the land, suggests that the church was originally founded for the tenants of the *mansio* and its subsidiary and neighbouring properties. The parish bounds of St John's subsequently included tenements to the north beyond the present line of Kybald Street, and others to the east as far as the new city wall. The territory of early parishes was defined by the land which tithed to their churches. If St John's was not a pre-Conquest foundation, it was certainly founded and endowed before the development of canon law in the twelfth century, and the consequent hardening of existing rights, made the assignment of tithe to new churches an operation of forbidding difficulty.

St Alban's Quad today occupies the site of no fewer than three such tenements. There were then at least seven other plots between St Alban Hall and the south-east angle of the town walls. They were Hart or Hertheved Hall, which belonged to Balliol, St Stephen's Hall, which the college acquired in 1329 and demolished in 1360, Elm Hall, which belonged to Godstow, then four tenements of St Frideswide's: Little and Great Bileby, Marshall's tenement, and at the east end Runceval, which was functioning as an academic hall when Merton took the whole block on a long and renewable lease from the priory in 1328.[12] The history of the site, and the extensive subdivision of the neighbouring plots, especially to the east, therefore looks back to a period of quite intense commercial activity, and at least a moderately dense settlement of the area in the twelfth century. The putative presence of a brothel or brothels in what is now, and irreproachably, known as Magpie Lane may represent an earlier turning point in the fortunes of the area.[13]

At all events, the subsequent decay of the principal tenement by St John's seems to reflect a general decline in the southern part of the town. For some centuries thereafter commercial development in

[12] See further *VCH Oxon.* iii. 98; and below, p. 135 and n.

[13] Magpie Lane was known as Grope Lane, an occupational title, by the mid-13th cent. at the latest. See M. Gelling (ed.), *Place-Names of Oxfordshire* (EPNS xxiii, Cambridge, 1953–4), pp. 40–1.

Oxford, as distinct from the business of housing academics, was largely confined to the area of the central markets round Carfax, and an area outside the north wall. On the other hand, the neighbouring properties in St John's Lane were all tenanted in the later thirteenth century, and whilst St John's, known to the college as the old church, *vetus ecclesia*, may have seen better days, or at the least a larger congregation,[14] the advent of a courtier and former royal chancellor of extensive means seems to have stimulated the local market in property. If his influence had not been as imposing as his other resources, the founder might have had to pay out even more than he did.

Within the main plot, and probably within the bounds of the churchyard, there was a building known as *domus reclusa*, which was unusual amongst anchorites' cells in having its own stable.[15] Outside, to the east of the churchyard, there were the three further houses where the north range of Front Quadrangle now stands, which were apparently in good condition, and immediately more useful to the college than the ground on which the church stood. One of them, in the middle of the row, formerly John Halegod's house,[16] had recently come into the hands of Jacob the Jew,[17] and was occupied by two aristocratic students: Antony Bek, later bishop of Durham (1283–1311), and his brother Thomas, who became bishop of St David's.[18] The Beks' tenancy was protected for three years from Walter's acquisition of the property in February 1267, during which time they presumably lived beside his scholars, if not amongst them. There are now no certain signs of divisions in the range of Front Quadrangle, which was rebuilt by Warden Savile in 1589,[19] but the Beks' lodgings are represented by

[14] See also above, pp. 8 and 28.
[15] *ERMC*, pp. 63 and n. 9, 293. The stabling may rather have belonged to the decayed capital messuage.
[16] Halegod's is usually spoken of as one house, though Jacob's charter (MCR 188) refers to it as 'our houses'. It does not seem likely that the Beks would deliberately have set up two households under one narrow roof, but the property may have housed more than one tenant for some time past.
[17] Jews could not, technically speaking, hold property in medieval England, though Christian society could not have functioned and developed as it did if the Jews had not been willing to lend money on such security. Walter de Merton had long experience in that precarious and irritable market: *ERMC*, pp. 29, 36. See also below, p. 33.
[18] Antony Bek was appointed to Durham from the king's service in 1284. On his tastes, and perhaps some echo of his early studies, see A. Bennett, 'Anthony Bek's copy of *Statuta Angliæ*', *England in the Fourteenth Century*, ed. W. M. Ormrod (Woodbridge, 1986), pp. 1–27.
[19] See *MMC*, p. 61; and below, p. 176–7.

Staircases 2 and 3 there. They may well have seen the beginnings of the college hall in their backyards.

The house to the west, which covered the site of the present gate-house, was known as Herprut's, and belonged in 1266 to St Frides-wide's, to which it had been granted by Henry, son of Elfred Herprut, about 1250.[20] Walter de Merton acquired it at some time between Michaelmas 1267 and Michaelmas 1268, when it was described as lying on the east side of St John's church, between the church and the house formerly of Jacob the Jew.[21] The prior and chapter granted the property 'at the instance' of King Henry III. The deed does not refer to any consideration beyond an annual payment of one halfpenny to St Frideswide's shrine by way of service, although the canons had received annual rents of 9s. o½d. from the premises in the recent past. The plot was evidently a valuable component of the college site, and its acquisition through royal patronage was another mark of the founder's watchful care, as well as of his good fortune. Henry also gave oaks from Bernwood and Wychwood to further the building works.[22]

The front gate of Herprut's tenement probably served from the beginning as the principal entrance to the college grounds.[23] It was certainly the site of the gate-keeper's house which was being built in 1286,[24] and although the other houses are likely to have had a cart-entrance from the street, Herprut's could also be made to serve the church and churchyard, and had no settled tenants to consult on the finer points of access. The curtilages behind the two houses, Herprut's and Jacob's, were probably soon thrown into one: Walter had licence from the king to enclose the site of St John's as early as the summer of 1266,[25] but that was to secure and unify the ground, not to divide it.

[20] See MCR 189, *MM*, p. 20; and *Cartulary of the Monastery of St Frideswide*, ed. S. R. Wigram (OHS xxviii), i (1894), 400, 410.

[21] The abutments given in the deed suggest that Herprut's lay at the east end of the church, though it evidently had a street frontage, and may also have abutted onto the church's north wall. Either way it appears that the small lodging to the west of the gatehouse, which was built in the 17th cent., stands inside the original bounds of the tenement.

[22] An original grant of eight oaks was renewed in 1268 as four from Bernwood and four from Wychwood: *Close Rolls 1268–72*, p. 11. It is interesting that the original grant referred to work not on the house of scholars but on the scholars' houses (*domorum scholarium*).

[23] It is remarkable that the warden's house was also serviced through what is now Front Quad (or conceivably through Nun Hall, when that property was acquired). It had, probably as a result of its remodelling in 1268–70, no doorway on to the street until 1836.

[24] MR 3616; *ERMC*, p. 219.

[25] MCR 195: *MM*, p. 18.

The most important provision in that grant was that the consolidated enclosure could now be extended southwards to the line of the city wall, to which the king reserved only ready access in time of war.

The easternmost house, called Flixthorpe's, or Herlwyn's, was bought from Robert Flixthorpe, in 1268, for the substantial sum of thirty-two marks, £21. 6s 8d. sterling. The transaction has many interesting features. They include a title which extended back in a series of deeds to the 1240s,[26] but the most important are that the property thus acquired served as the warden's house from the last years of Henry III's reign to the middle of Edward VII's, and that a considerable part of it still stands at the north-east corner of Front Quadrangle, constituting Staircase 4. What has survived is the original hall, now divided into two floors, but with its fine roof intact (Pl. 4), and the shell of the screens passage at its east end. The present first floor, lit only by the traceried heads of the windows, serves as the Middle Common Room.

The hall of Flixthorpe's was long known as the Little Hall, as distinct from the Great Hall of the college, and was the heart of the warden's house throughout the Middle Ages. As the hall and screens passage fill the whole street front of the narrow plot, the kitchen must always have been to the south, but it moved as the house expanded, and only its later positions are known. The hall and its south wing were apparently remodelled immediately after the property was acquired, to make it ready for the warden and his household from Malden.[27] Even so, the *parvuli* had to be accommodated elsewhere, at first on the other side of the road, and then next door to the warden, in Nun Hall.[28]

The addition of Flixthorpe's house marks the end of a buying campaign, short but intense, which in its last stages was clearly directed to the further development of the site. If the statutes of 1270 are considered in that context, their provision for moving the college from Malden takes on an extra significance. It might indeed happen that the scholars would be forced in some unforeseen crisis to seek other schools than Oxford, but in the immediate future they evidently had some prospects there. The lands at Malden and Chessington were no longer the college's principal resource, though in 1270 there was no precedent in Oxford or anywhere else for managing an estate from

---

[26] See *MM*, p. 20; and *ERMC*, pp. 395–409.

[27] On the layout of the warden's house, see *ERMC*, pp. 61–2.

[28] See below, p. 35.

an academic hostel. There were no doubt many reasons for supposing that such a venture might not succeed, but in the event it did, and there was then no need for other expedients.

An episode in 1268 throws an interesting light both on the status of the emergent college and on its founder's intentions. Oxford had an important congregation of Jews, and its numbers had been increased for a time by the excitements and dangers of the civil war, when refugees from other places had gathered in the city for safety.[29] There was a consequent threat of disorder, and some of the Jews' records seem to have been destroyed by Christians whose natural zeal for their faith had been further inflamed by the irksome obligations of their debts. The Jewish congregation in England was still quite numerous, and held a good deal of property under royal protection, but it was also very vulnerable. In 1268 the Oxford Jews were accused of sheltering some one or more of their number who had rabbled a religious procession staged by the parochial clergy of Oxford on Ascension Day (17 May) and had cast down and broken a crucifix.

The details of the event are obscure and, as they stand, not wholly convincing, but as the procession, making for St Frideswide's, would have passed by the principal Jewish houses in the town there probably was some local excitement, and a zealous expectation of trouble.[30] Trouble followed, and in the event all the Jews of Oxford were ordered to pay compensation for it. The money was to cover the substantial cost of making a marble cross with images and a suitable inscription, to be raised as a permanent memorial to the outrage, and a processional cross of silver, *crux portabilis*, as large as that customarily carried before an archbishop, which could be paraded from time to time to the same pious end.

A royal letter of December 1268 explains that it was originally intended to build the stone cross upon the site of the battle in the street, but that that could not be done without inconvenience and loss to the burgesses. By way of balancing the claims of God and Mammon it was therefore proposed that the cross should be raised immediately outside the synagogue in St Aldate's.[31] Further reflection

---

[29] See *Close Rolls 1261–4*, pp. 363–4 and Roth, *Jews of Medieval Oxford*, pp. 28–9.

[30] See Roth, *Jews of Medieval Oxford*, pp. 151–4.

[31] The synagogue stood at the north-west corner of what is now Tom Quad, Christ Church: see the map in Roth, *Jews of Medieval Oxford*. The citizens were apparently reluctant to have the cross in the street, and the king thought it unwise and improper to put it on what was effectively Jewish ground.

had prompted some objections to that course, as well it might. It had then been suggested, apparently by the Lord Edward, the king's son, that Walter de Merton's house of scholars could provide both a fitting site for the stone cross, on their *placea* by St John's church, and safe keeping for the processional cross, which originally was to have been lodged with the proctors of the university.[32]

The king approved and endorsed the proposal, and issued instructions to his officials in February 1269 to distrain the Jewish congregation for funds.[33] It is interesting to note that, notwithstanding the original intention that all the Jews should be made to pay, Jacob, son of Master Moses, and two of his sons had been exempted from the levy in 1268, as they were known to have been in London when the brawl took place. They were also, and probably more to the point, known to be associates of Walter de Merton, and may already have contributed some incremental value to the college.[34]

There were delays in building the marble cross: the money was misappropriated, and the work was still in train in 1276. The *placea* by St John's church may have proved no more accommodating than the roadway of St Aldate's. There is a tradition that the cross was eventually raised well to the south of the church, by the site of the later college brewhouse, but that sounds like malicious folklore. The most obvious place for such a memorial would have been the churchyard to the north, or the comparatively narrow space to the west of the church, for the base of the cross need not have been very large.[35] Its position remains uncertain. Nor is there any evidence that the college ever numbered the processional cross amongst its plate: the piece is said to have been lodged later in St Frideswide's, but there is no more precise record even of that.[36]

[32] The university had as yet no secure premises of its own.

[33] See *Close Rolls 1264–8*, pp. 14–15, for an account of the offence and the king's instructions to levy compensation, and pp. 22–3 for the revised proposals.

[34] See *Close Rolls 1264–8*, pp. 553–4. Jacob's sons were another Moses, and Benedict. Moses, son of Jacob, more usually known as Moses of Northampton, was one of the most learned and distinguished survivors of the English congregation: see Roth, *Jews of Medieval Oxford*, pp. 113–16, 125, 166 and n. 5.

[35] See Roth, op. cit., pp. 153–4, and *Munimenta Academica*, i. 36–7, where a note added in the 17th cent. says that the cross was at St Frideswide's. That may confuse the stone cross and the portable cross. John Rous of Warwick may well have seen a cross in the grounds of Merton in the 15th cent., just as he said he did, but the subsequent discovery of fragments of building stone near the brewhouse does not prove that it stood there. See further below, n. 36.

[36] There was, however, somewhere an outdoor preaching cross known as St Frideswide's cross, for the restoration of which Bishop Marshall of Llandaff (1478–96), paid in 1492:

Nevertheless the original proposal says much not only of Walter's own standing at court, but of the early repute of his foundation both there and in the university. Howsoever the idea came to Prince Edward, it clearly carried with it no suggestion that the establishment in St John's Street was temporary or experimental. It assumed, indeed, that the house of scholars itself was in Oxford, not in Malden, and by that time to most appearances it was. The bond for a debt which fell due to the founder in 1269 stipulated that it should be paid either to him personally, or in Oxford to the warden of his house of scholars.[37]

The scale of the undertaking in St John's Street was evidently now quite imposing, and from the founder's point of view it warranted some reorganization. It may be, indeed, that the innovative device of allowing or requiring the fellows to take a part in managing the estates was a deliberate alternative to enlarging the number of priests who were attendant upon the warden, which would have produced an institution of a very different kind. The growth of the college probably set its own agenda. The compact block of ground around St John's church was only one of the acquisitions which had transformed the endowment by 1270. The founder had not only added properties in St Aldate's, but also the advowson of the church of St Peter's-in-the-East, and its dependent chapels of St Cross and Wolvercote, which he acquired from the king in 1266, and with it the whole extra-mural manor of Holywell.[38]

Its title to Holywell, the lands of which stretched over the site of the present Parks to the junction of Parks Road and the Banbury Road, made the college one of the most substantial landlords in Oxford.[39] The new estate was, however, only an adjunct to the land inside the

RACM 1483–1521 157. Marshall was a former fellow and notable benefactor of Merton. It is not clear that he had any particular interest in St Frideswide's priory, and it may be that what he paid to restore was after all, or was reputed to be, the Jews' cross. See further below, p. 138. The issue is complicated by a later fanciful tradition of a 'Jew's cross' in St Frideswide's church, for which see B. J. Marples, 'The medieval crosses of Oxfordshire', *Oxoniensia*, xxxviii (1974), 299–311, at pp. 304–5 and 308.

[37] See *Close Rolls 1264–8*, p. 552.

[38] The grant was made on 7 Sept. 1266, even before the purchase of Herlwin's and Halegod's: *MM*, p. 19. St Peter's and St John's were then both appropriated to the college by the bishop of Lincoln on 13 Sept., securing the rectories and the great tithe of both churches to the house, and instituting two vicarages to serve the parishes: *ERMC*, pp. 405–6.

[39] See below, pp. 322–3, 342 for the piecemeal disposal of that large site in the course of the nineteenth and twentieth centuries to the university, the city, and other colleges.

walls, and the fact that over the following year the founder negotiated permission to construct a watercourse from the Cherwell to the site in St John's Street suggests that he was already intent upon a major development there.[40]

Twenty or more fellows with servants and other staff made up a substantial household, which was almost doubled when the warden, chaplains, *parvuli*, and the rest moved to Oxford from Malden. On his arrival in Oxford the warden bought the property on the opposite side of St John's Street now represented by Postmasters' Hall and its neighbouring buildings, which he seems first to have used to accommodate the *parvuli* and their master, and also to provide stabling.[41] The college subsequently took a lease of Nun Hall, in 1300, and refitted the property for the boys and the other members of their household. A private water-supply was not an extravagance.[42]

Over the following two centuries the college gradually acquired a further seven tenements in the south-eastern angle of the city walls, outflanking St Alban Hall, and extending the grounds over the site of the present garden (Pl. VII). The transactions were long-drawn-out and intricate, and the stone wall on the south side of Merton Street preserves some interesting reminders of them.[43]

The college also bought most of the land to the west of the Grove as far as the precinct of St Frideswide's priory, where the Canterbury gate of Christ Church now stands. It was on that side of the main site, until the ground was presented to Corpus Christi College in the early sixteenth century, that the gardens and orchards were laid out. There seem to have been no gardens within the main enclosure, though it may have been possible so to use some of the ground

[40] See the grant, dated 3 Sept. 1267, in *ERMC*, pp. 406–7, and n.; and below, pp. 36, 38. A stretch of the conduit was uncovered when the city's defences were strengthened by the king's army in April 1643: see *LTAW* i. 96–7.

[41] See *ERMC*, pp. 413–14, 419–21, and pp. 22–3, above. The small stable-block which still screens the yard to the west of Postmasters' Hall is probably the last remnant of the original property, and therefore the oldest entire building on the college site.

[42] The new conduit was a considerable undertaking, and the work was probably made an occasion to improve the general drainage of the site. The springing of the old west door of the kitchen shows that the ground level of the site has risen by several feet (rather less in Front Quad than elsewhere), and the subterranean watercourses represent some serious engineering. See the notes made by Twyne: *LTAW* i. 96–7; and below, p. 38.

[43] The wall, which is of various dates, runs from the east side of St Alban's Quad to the new Warden's Lodgings where Merton Street turns north. It is built in sections, the alignment of which can be seen still to reflect the street fronts of the principal tenements. There is also one blocked doorway surviving, of *c.* 1500. See further below, p. 236 n. 3.

towards the city wall.[44] The brewhouse stood by the Grove in later centuries, and was probably there from the beginning.[45] There would also have been workshops, and there was a masons' lodge which seems to have been kept in repair after the hall and the church were built,[46] besides open and closed stores, and simple dumps. For several decades the central part of the site must have looked like a builder's yard.

St John's church served the college adequately well for some twenty years; it has suffered something in esteem because the records subsequently refer to it as the old church, but that was a simple statement of fact. The college spent money on its fabric and furnishings for several years, and seems to have maintained there without difficulty the various daily and commemorative services enjoined by the statutes. The church would also have enjoyed some accession of plate and vestments when the warden and chaplains arrived from Malden. For their part, though they may not have rejoiced to exchange the sweet air of Surrey for the dank vapours of the Cherwell and Isis meadows, the priests probably found their altars better housed in St John's than they had been at Malden.

The most urgent need on the new site was for domestic accommodation. The warden was evidently at pains not to encroach upon what was available, but though sleeping quarters might be improvised for a time, the common life undeniably demanded meals in common. The answer was to build a great hall, and the work was almost certainly in hand before 1270. The present hall, though unyieldingly Victorian in its outward appearance, occupies not merely the site but the precise volume of its original being, for the undisturbed masonry of the east and west walls shows that the pitch of Scott's handsome roof is itself an ancient feature (Pl. I). The pattern and size of the paired and transomed side windows, now filled with sombre heraldic glass, seem also to have preserved an original feature.

Measuring eighty by thirty feet, the hall was planted immediately east of, and roughly in line with, St John's church. Its eastern wall is in turn aligned with the west end of the Little Hall, which strongly

---

[44] There was a hall garden by 1511, when its walls were repaired: E. A. Gee, 'Oxford masons 1370–1530', *Archaeological Journal*, cix (1952), 84. It presumably stood within the site of Fellows' Quad, and may have been there since the earliest times. It may also, conceivably, have been the kitchen garden.

[45] See above, n. 34; and below, p. 317.

[46] See *ERMC*, p. 332, and below, pp. 39–43.

suggests that there was a north-to-south fence or wall at that point, and that what is now the site of the FitzJames archway always stood within the warden's curtilage.[47] The masonry of the end walls also shows that the hall always had an undercroft, and the fact that in Loggan's view of the college there are narrow windows in what is now the wine cellar and cold store suggests that the lower floor may originally have been intended for other uses than storage. Such an arrangement would have been logical, but highly unusual, and the windows may have been no more than a draughtsman's flight of fancy. First-floor halls themselves are a comparative rarity in England, but we do not know what influences may have played upon the founder, or upon the college, at the time.[48]

There must therefore always have been a stairway to the main entrance to the hall, and although the present porch was built in 1579 it replaced an earlier one. It is also clear that the main door of the hall, with its scrolled iron strap-work, is an original fitting, and has never been exposed to the weather (Pl. 3). The high quality of the iron-work, the only decorative feature to have survived from the original building, suggests that the hall's necessary furnishings were not stinted.[49]

Inside the hall there was at first almost certainly no dais, but a common table, or tables, originally warmed by a central hearth over the site of which Loggan's view shows a louvre or lantern in the roof.[50]

---

[47] Loggan's view of the college, taken when the FitzJames arch had become the entrance to the Great Quadrangle, shows a similar wall much closer to the lodgings, built flush with the front of the porch in Front Quad which leads into the present estates bursary and the stairs to the Queen's Room. See also below, pp. 134–5.

[48] The hall at Acton Burnell stands over an undercroft, but that at Stokesay, which is quite close in time to Merton, and the great hall of the bishop's palace at Wells, built in 1283, are both at ground level. See further M. Thompson, *The Medieval Hall: The Basis of Secular Domestic Life, 600–1600 A.D.* (Woodbridge, 1995).

[49] The finest ironwork of the period surviving is the grille on Queen Eleanor's tomb at Westminster: Royal Commission on Historical Monuments, *An Inventory of the Historical Monuments of London: 1, Westminster Abbey* (London, 1921), p. 29. Much other good work has been lost, and there is now little available for comparison. Walter de Merton would, however, have known of the leading craftsmen at work both in iron and in other materials.

[50] The original smoke-vent was probably a hole in the roof, and the louvre a refinement introduced when the central hearth was abandoned. Wood speaks of the hall being warmed by charcoal braziers brought in on winter feast days, and of a declaiming desk which had an empty space before it in the middle of the floor: *LTAW* i. 133–4. The date of the present chimney in the south wall is uncertain, but a mason repaired the hall fireplace in 1517: E. A. Gee, 'Oxford masons', p. 84. In 1509 William Neele left money to floor the upper part of the hall and provide hangings about the dais, which sounds as though there were a high table by that time: *BRUO*, p. 1342.

The hall was evidently in use by the time that the bursars' accounts begin, in 1277, when it was refreshed from time to time, and especially for festivals, with new straw and rushes on the floor. There is a reference to a great table in 1299, and earlier references to table-cloths, at least for special occasions.[51] Some monks from Durham were entertained in 1289; they stand out from other visitors only because the 5s. laid out on their meat and drink would have sufficed for wine on any three ordinary feast days.[52] The hall, with its great door, has been in continuous use since the earliest days of the college's presence in Oxford, serving for many centuries as a place for teaching and for meetings, occasionally for services, and at least once for a lying-in-state,[53] as well as a refectory, chapter-house, and common-room.

The unbroken masonry of the west wall of the hall suggests that the kitchen has always occupied its present site to the south of the screens passage, extending over approximately one half of the ground floor of what is now the west side of Fellows' Quadrangle. It had wells and dipping-hatches to its own water-supply under the floor, and must from the first have been serviced, as it still is, from the pathway which leads out of Front Quad under the west wall of the hall.

The arch and first-floor passage-way which now connects the hall screens to the sacristy is of sixteenth-century date, and seems to be of a piece, though the sacristy stair turret has a plain pointed arch over its door on the ground floor, which looks earlier than the bridge to which it leads. There are, however, some plain corbels projecting from the hall which suggest that there may have been an earlier timber structure there. It is not easy to see its purpose, but the corbels are set high in the wall, and it is conceivable that they supported a penthouse of some kind which straddled rather than obstructed the pathway below.

Any such structure would have stood between the hall and St John's church. The present bridge was spoken of as affording the warden a covered walk from his lodging to the chapel, but that amenity also depended upon the existence of the FitzJames archway, and necessarily led into the college church through the sacristy.[54] An earlier

---

[51] See e.g. *ERMC*, pp. 221, 241.

[52] *ERMC*, p. 225, where there is also a note that the warden paid 1s. 8d. for wine for the fellows at St Mary's Assumption (15 Aug.).

[53] For Edward Wood, who died 22 May 1655, in the fourth week of his proctorship: *LTAW*, i. 197–8; and below, p. 226.

[54] The sacristy is unlikely to have been used regularly as a thoroughfare, even by the head of the house, until after the Reformation.

gallery, which gave the company in hall direct access to the chancel of the church, and was then abandoned when the church was moved and the present sacristy built, would have had something to recommend it.[55] However, the sixteenth-century doorway to the present bridge is quite narrow, and any earlier arch there would have been minute. There is no trace of another opening in the wall at any level, though there are some remains of a heavy string-course older than, but level with, the floor of the present bridge.

The hall, with its high roof-ridge, is still a striking building, and would have been even more impressive when it first rose over the motley structures which surrounded the site.[56] When it was first raised it was the largest secular building in Oxford outside the castle, and it was certainly large enough for the early collegiate household, which even with all its staff probably still fell short of a hundred. It was, nevertheless, only an earnest of good intentions, and though it had necessarily taken first place in the college's programme there were more imposing plans in hand.

Work on the new church of St Mary and St John, which is now generally known as Merton College chapel,[57] started late in the 1280s, and the building seems to have been ready to be furnished and equipped by 1291, after some intensive work by masons, sculptors, and others in the course of that year.[58] Some material was removed then from the old church, but the vicar who was in possession of St John's in 1266 survived until 1292, and seems to have ministered to his parishioners there for as long as he lived. After his death parochial services were first provided in the new church by one of the fellows, Master William Streetly. The college's delicate connections with the order of Augustinian canons were therefore complemented by the

---

[55] There seems to have been an analogous arrangement, at a later date, at Peterhouse, Cambridge, where Little St Mary's served as the college chapel: see R. Willis and J. W. Clark, *Architectural History of the University of Cambridge,* i. 22, 53, 56.

[56] It is now lost in most distant views, being masked by the high roofs of Fellows' Quad, but when it was new it would have stood out strongly from the meadows, and also from the north-west until the new church was built.

[57] The church was, and in some particular senses still is, both parochial and collegiate, though St John's parish was amalgamated with St Peter's-in-the-East in 1891. In the early chapters of the present work the church as a building is distinguished from the college chapel, which down to the Reformation can best be regarded as an institution housed in the church. In the later chapters chapel is used in its current sense, for the building as well as the institution.

[58] See *ERMC*, pp. 304–15.

fact that part of its church, as in almost every Augustinian house in England, served the parish in which it stood.

The new building was only the chancel of the present college church, and we do not know how it was finished at its western end. It seems likely, however, that the great arch there, which is now the eastern arch of the tower, was included in the first building campaign. However, after 1292 the college had also to provide some accommodation for the parishioners of St John's, which could hardly have been elsewhere than on the site of the present crossing. There may have been a timber structure there, but there is a reference in 1297 to masons working on a doorway in the outer vestibule of the church, which suggests a large porch or antechamber which could most usefully have opened to the west or the north.[59]

The first phase of building therefore produced a chancel of seven bays, 110 feet long and 40 feet wide, enclosing substantially more space than the college hall, and more even than the hall and the warden's hall combined. The chancel's most imposing feature, beyond its scale, is the assured quality of its design and execution, most evidently in the seven pairs of windows in the side walls. Twelve of the windows retain their original glass, set in Decorated tracery which is varied throughout by a lively but competently restrained hand.[60] The members of any of the religious houses then in the town might have looked enviously at the setting of the fellows' stalls.

The figured and grisaille glass in the side windows was given between 1289 and 1296 by Henry Mansfield, fellow and benefactor of the college, later chancellor of the university, and dean of Lincoln, whose pious munificence is commemorated twenty-four times in the inscriptions and figures.[61] Those windows are complete, but they are now all that survives of the earliest furnishings, except for some heraldic glass and an Annunciation in the east window, the carved

[59] See *ERMC*, p. 332; and below, p. 41. There was a good deal of other building work going on at the time, in particular repairs to the roofs of the hall and the church, which had been damaged by a high wind.

[60] The broad expanse of the east window seems to represent a second stage of design, perhaps simply to frame more glass. It is now filled partly with glass gathered up from the transept windows, and from the warden's house, but would originally have had its own iconographic themes. On some stylistic affiliations of the architecture, see further J. Bony, *The English Decorated Style: Gothic Architecture Transformed, 1250–1350* (Oxford, 1979), pp. 12, 17, 74–5.

[61] For Mansfield, also known as Mamesfield, see *BRUO*, pp. 1211–12; and *MBMC*, p. 106. His figure in the windows is by a few years the earliest Mertonian icon. He also gave or bequeathed at least seven MSS to the college library.

corbels under the vaulting shafts, and some other fragments of sculpture. The original fittings included a free-standing set of stalls for the warden and fellows, draught-proofed after a fashion and canopied, and probably returned, or screened off, at their western end in the sixth bay from the high altar.[62] The backs or outer face of the stalls were decorated with paintings, either from the beginning or added at some later date.[63]

There were some secondary altars, though as only the warden and chaplains were necessarily in priestly orders there would not at first have been need for any large number. There must also have been at least one lectern, or reading desk, and probably two.[64] The parishioners of St John's, meanwhile, had needs of their own.

It is not clear whether the parochial space at the west end lay partly within or wholly outside the chancel. Although the sedilia and sacristy doorway seem to have been remodelled by Butterfield in 1849–50, it is very unlikely that he enlarged them, or that the original sanctuary occupied less space than the two easternmost bays of the chancel. It is just possible that the original stalls were confined to the next three bays, but even that would have left only two bays for the parish, which could hardly have been accommodated in a smaller space. The homogeneity of the design, however, makes it likely that the college chapel, strictly so called, was meant to enjoy the whole of the chancel, and the parish church was always to the west of the great arch, unless its principal altar was set against the chancel screen.[65] Its accommodation, whether or not it extended into the chancel, required, besides an altar, at least a pulpit and a font, which could all have been brought in from the old church. There would also have been stoups, a cupboard of some kind, because it is unlikely that the parish had ready access to the sacristy, books, and images. The college paid 8s. for six paintings in the church in 1296–7, but we do not know where or precisely what they were.[66]

---

[62] The great classical screen erected in the chapel in 1671 (see below, p. 217), and of which three arches are now set under the tower arch, was originally placed between the sixth and seventh bays of the chancel, and would certainly have been west of the medieval stalls. See also below, n. 63.

[63] The stalls were replaced in 1491, when the church was expensively refurnished and redecorated: *RACM 1483–1521*, pp. 101, 103. See also below, n. 64; and p. 138.

[64] The present fine brass lectern was installed in 1504: see below, p. 138.

[65] All other considerations apart, the inconvenience of carrying the Host through the chancel makes it most probable that the parish always had an altar of its own.

[66] See *ERMC*, p. 332. The entry says six painted images, which suggests murals or painted

There was at that time literally no model for the chapel of an academic college, just as there was none before 1270 for a college hall, though halls, chapels, and colleges of other kinds were ubiquitous. The most useful experience was likely to be found amongst the friars, although their domestic planning was closer to monastic than to secular practice, whilst their churches were designed to house substantial lay congregations, at least for sermons, as well as to provide for the friars' common and individual devotions. It is therefore not wholly surprising, but certainly interesting, to find an Augustinian friar, Brother Thomas, regularly consulted by the college during 1291. He was evidently closely concerned with the building of the chapel, and may have brought in colleagues, though the nature of his expertise cannot be deduced from the laconic entries in the accounts.[67]

The Augustinian friary in Oxford, of which Brother Thomas was presumably a member,[68] stood on the site occupied since 1610 by Wadham College. It has not been fully excavated, but both the Dominicans and the Franciscans, whose houses were on the south-western side of the city, had churches with chancels of a size comparable with Merton's.[69] Those chancels were, however, structurally closed off from the public parts of the church, whereas the plan at Merton, at least by the early fourteenth century, envisaged a conventional cruciform space with a large open crossing and wooden screens. If that plan had been followed through the college would have had to acquire the land immediately to the west of the Grove, which belonged to St Frideswide's.[70] The plots were in fact bought in piecemeal over the next century, but eventually the T-shaped space provided by the chancel and the broad transepts proved adequate for the needs both

---

panels rather than statues. They were too few for the backs of the stalls, unless they were part of a series there.

[67] See e.g. *ERMC*, pp. 304–5, 310–11. The building account rolls do not begin until 1287, and there is relatively little information on work on the church until 1291. As H. W. Garrod remarked, it is a characteristic of medieval building accounts to record almost everything except what is actually being built. See also below, p. 122.

[68] If he was not from Oxford, he was most probably a member of the Augustinian friary in Broad Street, London, a major house which was under the patronage of the Bohuns.

[69] See M. W. Sheehan, 'The religious orders 1220–1370', *HUO* i. 222–3. The chancels of the friars' churches served much larger congregations than Merton's, with a larger proportion of priests amongst them.

[70] That is to say, the properties known as Gutter Hall (acquired 1331), and Christopher Hall and Urban Hall, which were not secured until 1338: see below, pp. 69, 114. The land to the south-west, which became the bachelors' garden, was acquired in 1321 (*MMC*, pp. 308–9). If the western limb of the church had ever been built it would have straddled the Gutter, though the stream was probably enclosed in a conduit by the 15th cent., if no earlier.

of the college and the parish.[71] There remains a slight but interesting possibility that what was first contemplated was an asymmetrical plan with a western limb aligned north and south like the so-called north nave of the Oxford Dominicans' church. On balance, however, it is most likely that the common interest with the friars was in the scale of the church, rather than the nature of the accommodation which it provided. For the rest, the college was intent upon work of high quality, which it duly achieved.

The completion of the new church left the old one available for other uses, the simplest of which was to dismantle it for its materials. The removal of timbers from St John's in 1291, and the presence of pieces of reused carved stone in the new church show that there was some reworking, but there is also some evidence that the main fabric of the old church was absorbed early in the fourteenth century into a new set of chambers, which is now the north wing of Mob Quadrangle (Pl. 6). That development marks a new stage in the life of the college, in which its resources were used to cultivate scholarship in a fashion which the founder had envisaged, but probably upon a larger scale, and even sooner, than he could have expected.

Mob, known earlier as the Bachelors' Quadrangle,[72] is often referred to as the first quadrangle in Oxford, though the building of the new church had already served to define Front Quad by closing off its western side. Mob may have been planned as early as 1290, when the prospect of using the site and fabric of St John's church allowed the college to contemplate a second stage of development. The northern and eastern ranges of the new quadrangle, with their lavish provision of chambers opening off staircases, were the first specialized accommodation in the college, and once again they proved models of their kind.

The scale of the work reflects both the early success and the comfortable resources of the foundation: we know the names of more than 100 Mertonians before the end of the century.[73] The rooms in the

---

[71] New College, which had no parochial congregation to accommodate, subsequently made shift with a nave or ante-chapel of two bays. The resemblance between the two plans seems to have been a coincidence, but one or the other, or both, had an enduring effect on the design of college chapels for several centuries. See further H. M. Colvin, *Unbuilt Oxford* (New Haven, 1983), pp. 2–3.

[72] On the name of Mob, see Bott, *Short History of the Buildings*, p. 16.

[73] The biographical material assembled by A. B. Emden in *BRUO* was analysed, with some supplementary data, for use in *HUO*. It has produced the names of 57 members of Merton College before 1281, and a cumulative total of 136 by 1299. Those so listed

north wing of Mob were, however, preceded by the building, between 1288 and 1291, of a fire-proof treasury just to the south-west of the hall, with a vaulted passage running beneath,[74] and then of the adjoining sacristy, *c.* 1310, on the axis of the old church and the new chambers (Pl. 7). In the mean time work seems to have begun on the east wing of the quadrangle in 1299–1300.[75]

The sequence of those buildings is interesting. In the first place, there was evidently no thought of providing a cloister: the college was a religious house, but its daily life and work were focused on the hall and the chapel, and then on the schools outside. Cloisters are found at a later stage of collegiate development, when founders and their beneficiaries were thinking in terms of monumentality rather than of utility.[76] Merton's specialized buildings were all of a pragmatic kind.

The treasury probably took precedence over the sacristy because St John's church had a sacristy or vestry of its own, where the chapel plate could remain while the new church was building. The new strong room could then accommodate the plate, and probably the common seal, of which we first hear in 1276,[77] but it was chiefly intended to be the repository, as it still is, of the muniments of the college. The archives began with the earliest deeds of title, the founder's statutes, and the accounts deposited by Walter de Merton's executors when they completed probate in 1282.[78] They were soon supplemented by material relating to the college's long disputes over its rights in Embleton and Ponteland.[79] The title deeds were systematically arranged as well as being carefully stored, and were treated

throughout the Middle Ages are, by definition, the more prominent members of the house, but they provide minima of great interest. On the original exercise, see T. H. Aston, 'Oxford's medieval alumni', *Past and Present*, lxxiv (1977), 3–35.

[74] Locks were made for the windows of the treasury in 1288, and the floor was paved in 1291: *ERMC*, pp. 221, 237. The paving is still in place. The passage-way beneath opens on to the north walk of Mob Quad, which probably gave access to the old church, and now leads on to the south transept of the new (Pl. 6).

[75] See *ERMC*, p. 356 and n.

[76] See below, p. 111–12.

[77] See below, p. 49 and n.

[78] The archives were calendared in 1888 by W. H. Stevenson, whom the college employed on the recommendation of E. A. Freeman (see below, p. 320 and n.), and Stevenson's MS calendar was published in facsimile by the National Register of Archives in 1961. The executors' accounts, the earliest of the college officers' accounts, running from 1277 to 1301, and the title deeds down to 1300 are printed, calendared, or listed in *ERMC*, pp. 90–452. See further below, pp. 68, 318.

[79] See below, pp. 64–8.

with some formality. The replacement of documents in the common chest following its repair in 1288 was marked by the consumption of three-and-one-half-pennyworth of wine, though that was evidently a special occasion.[80]

The exchequer chamber on the ground floor, the furniture of which included a literal chequer-board table for reckoning accounts,[81] served as a counting-house and estates office, informed by the records above. The college's first books, or the more valuable of them, were probably also kept in the treasury, though there were others in circulation from an early date.[82]

The sacristy and the treasury completed the managerial accommodation of the college: since 1310 all Merton's new buildings, except perhaps for the boathouse in 1939, and the sports pavilion in 1967, can be said to have been raised for domestic and academic purposes.[83] In the opening years of the fourteenth century the business of establishing the college was therefore complete. It was united on one site, where its common table was handsomely, and its chapel sumptuously, housed. Its members were responsible for the administration of the widespread estates which supported them, as well as for the work of inquiry, reflection, and instruction which was the end to which they had been assembled, and which daily prayer and the seasonal issues of the manors were to sustain and advance. By delivering the endowment to be managed by the warden and fellows, its principal beneficiaries, the founder had given his creation an untrammeled potential. It now remained to be seen what impression the house of Merton's scholars would make upon the wider world.

---

[80] See *ERMC*, p. 221.

[81] The royal exchequer itself takes its name from a checked table-cloth, which was used with coins or counters as an abacus for those arithmetical operations, notably long multiplication and division, which cannot gracefully be performed using Roman numerals: see further *Dialogus de Scaccario*, ed. C. Johnson, Nelson's Medieval Classics (London, 1950), pp. xxxv–xxxvii. Merton's *mensa conputatoria* was made in 1291: *ERMC*, p. 313.

[82] See below, p. 77.

[83] They have, nevertheless, and unsurprisingly, quite often been turned eventually to administrative uses, like the east side of Fellows' Quad, which by the 1990s was largely occupied by the offices of the bursary. Much older than the boathouse and pavilion, the tennis court behind Postmasters' Hall is another reminder of the variety of domestic building. See further below, pp. 322–3, 354–6.

3

Metaphysicians, Mathematicians, and Others

THE earliest commentary upon the life of the college in Oxford is in the injunctions issued by Robert Kilwardby, OP, archbishop of Canterbury, at Easter 1276, a year before the founder's death.[1] Like the college the archbishop himself was something of a novelty, for he was a Dominican friar, an eloquently learned member of a learned order, and the first friar to hold the primacy. As a secular clerk he had studied and taught in Paris, and he was prior provincial of the Dominicans in England for more than a decade before he was moved to Canterbury, in 1272, by papal provision. He was therefore well acquainted with the academic life of his day, and he had a reputation of his own as a theologian.[2]

Kilwardby seems to have descended upon Merton College while he was holding a visitation of the university, and to have taken its affairs in hand. Visiting the university was itself an operation of some delicacy, and the more so because at the time the archbishop was also engaged in a general visitation of the diocese of Lincoln, of which the university was an often unbiddable member. He may therefore have welcomed, and perhaps even have devised, the opportunity to regulate the college, both to review an experiment worthy of his attention and care, and as a fitting diversion from the more exacting affairs of the university at large.

Whether or not Walter de Merton had invited Kilwardby's attentions he duly counter-sealed the injunctions which the archbishop then made. Kilwardby's successor at Canterbury, John Peckham, OFM, when warning the college in 1280 to brace itself for another inquisition, said that the founder himself had entrusted the visitorship to the primate because the archbishopric was eminent in authority, judgement, wise counsel, and zeal. There is no other record

[1] See *Injunctions*. Walter de Merton died 27 Oct. 1277.
[2] The college's MSS subsequently included ten of his works, of which eight still survive: *MBMC*, nos. 207 (bis), 513, 515, 567, 970, 983 (bis).

46

of such a resolution on Walter de Merton's part, but it seems likely enough, and Kilwardby's injunctions are a fact.[3]

Whether he acted on his own initiative or at his suffragan's invitation, Kilwardby would certainly have been aware of the novelty and the significance of the occasion. Merton College, Oxford, was barely a decade old. The time was one of much academic excitement in the aftermath of the reign of Aquinas in the university of Paris, and Kilwardby was keenly interested in the state of the university's schools. As a conservative theologian he moved in the following year to condemn some Thomist opinions current in the faculty of arts which he believed would over-heat theological debate and corrupt the faith. The positions condemned seem to have been manifestations of modistic thought, so called from expositions beginning *De modis significandi*, 'the ways of signifying meaning'. Modism sought to relate the classical rules of grammar to Aristotelian philosophy, which Aquinas had striven to accommodate in Christian doctrine. The movement helped to establish the intensive study of grammar as a discipline of its own, rather than as a mere preliminary to the effective uses of language.[4]

After several decades of theological debate in Paris, the chief issue in the university of Oxford, and in such a focus of talent as Merton now became, was still how Aristotelian thought, as a manner of understanding and discussing both the natural world and its supernatural order, was to be assimilated to the advanced study of the Bible. The study of Aristotle's works had been transformed in the course of the century by the reception of new and superior texts from the Islamic world, in particular the Physics and the Posterior Analytics. St Thomas Aquinas's great synthesis had apparently reconciled faith and reason to the limits of human ingenuity, but strong rearguard actions were fought on two sides, by traditionally-minded Aristotelians on the one hand and by conservative theologians such as Peckham on the other. What was usually discussed was the significance of parts of speech and the logic of grammar: such questions as whether a verb had meaning without the qualification of person and tense. What was at issue behind the stylized but impassioned exchanges, beyond the manoeuvres attendant upon all institutional life, was the validity of human experience as a measure of the divine.

---

[3] See also pp. 19–20, above. The injunctions survive only in a later transcript, having disappeared from the muniment room at some time after 1598, perhaps even a century later: *Injunctions*, p. 5.

[4] See further *HUO* i. 116–17, and 419–20. See also below, pp. 52–3.

Those who took part in academic debates were usually allowed to express themselves freely, and even extravagantly, and they were jealous of those and other privileges. However, the universities' success in attracting and cultivating intellectual talent had made them a powerful force, and the church, like the lay power, had come in a very short time to depend on the skills which graduates deployed. Popes and bishops were correspondingly anxious to maintain control over the places from which the clergy's most influential recruits were drawn, and to curb the unpredictable excesses of academic speculation.

In a university which was already conscious of a novel strength, Merton's house of scholars was a phenomenon, and the archbishop was not likely to waste the opportunity which it presented. His provisions were entirely practical, though they raise some unanswerable questions about the nature of his powers. He began by appointing a sub-warden and bursars, matters which should have fallen to the fellows themselves, and we cannot tell whether in doing so he was displacing officers already in post, or filling gaps which he found in the administration. He also nominated three deans as disciplinary officers.[5]

There may have been some officiousness in the archbishop's actions, though the record of later visitations shows that for the most part the matters with which he was concerned needed regular attention.[6] He enjoined a careful watch over the accounts, which were to be independently audited each year. The bursars were responsible between them for three equal periods of the financial year, and were to see to the proper application of the funds allocated to the fellows' weekly commons.[7] If any part of the fifty marks (£33. 6s. 8d.) allowed to the warden should remain unspent at the end of the year it was to be returned to the general fund. On the other hand the bursars and deans were each to receive an additional 3s. 4d. a year for their cares.

A special scale of allowances was assigned to 'scholares in villa degentes': students living in the town, that is to say, away from the main site. In origin the pensioners may have been the poor scholars

[5] One of his appointees, Thomas Barnby, who was probably a foundation fellow, entered the Franciscan order *c.* 1290, and taught at the Oxford house: *BRUO*, p. 111.

[6] See below, pp. 50–1, 248–54.

[7] As Garrod points out (*Injunctions*, pp. 6–7), the sums allocated to the support of the warden and fellows were budgetary allowances, not monetary stipends. Members of the medieval college were assured of their keep, not of an income, though they might and often did have incomes of their own.

whom Walter de Merton had appointed to pray first for the good estate and then for the soul of Earl Richard of Cornwall and his son.[8] They were grouped according to their allowances, which were fixed at 8*d.*, 6*d.*, or 4*d.* a week, but those who could contribute something of their own might move to a house of a superior grade.[9] The provision seems to imply the existence of three distinct houses, though of them only Bull Hall can be identified, and the others may have been bursarial concepts rather than actual dwellings.[10] Payments were made to the remittance men over some decades, and Adam Petersfield received the bounty for fifty years, though in that time he seems to have been, or also to have been, the grammar master to the *parvuli*.[11] An additional payment equal to a bursar's fee was also to be made to what Kilwardby called the fellows of the founder's kin, a category of which there is no other record, but which presumably comprised those of the kin who had qualified for fellowships on normal terms.

The common seal of the college was to be kept under five locks, and used only in the presence of the five officers: the warden, sub-warden, and bursars. It authenticated the most solemn acts of the college, most notably the assignment of proprietorial rights.[12] It was soon supplemented by a vesica-shaped seal, known as the seal *ad causas*, that is to say for particular occasions, which in a later form is still in occasional use. The bursars were also to be responsible for the safe-keeping of the archives, which have survived in some numbers, and of the books belonging to the college.

There is some irony apparent in the archbishop's concern for the muniments, for when in 1278 he retired from Canterbury to a cardinalate he took many of the records of the see with him to Italy, and they were never recovered by his successors. Nevertheless Merton benefited from his injunction, as it did also from his order that if a fellow died, or vacated his fellowship by entering a religious order, his books, in so far as they were not assigned to discharge his debts,

---

[8] See above, p. 18; and below, p. 113.

[9] *Injunctions*, pp. 7–8, 14–15. See also below, n. 10.

[10] The expression *domicilium* for the residences does not preclude the possibility of their lodgings being adjacent, or on a single site.

[11] See *VCH Oxon.* iii. 103; and for Petersfield, *Injunctions*, pp. 7–8; and *BRUO*, p. 1470.

[12] The seal, or its early successor, was remodelled in some fashion in the 18th cent., probably by having its borders trimmed. It is inscribed SIGILLVM SCHOLARIVM DE MERTON, and shows Christ receiving five of the company into his bosom, with the legend 'Dominus est assumptio nostra', which invokes Psalm 26 (27): 10: 'Quoniam pater meus et mater mea dereliquerunt me, Dominus autem assumpsit me'.

should pass to the college.[13] The chapel would always have had service books, and there were most probably other common texts on the premises from the beginning. The new decree may well reflect a difference between the concerns of the founder, as a man of administrative experience, and those of the archbishop, as an author and academic. It was probably the most important service which Kilwardby rendered the college.

Eight years later, and five years after the founder's death, disagreements between the warden and the fellows excited another visitation, this time by commissioners of Archbishop John Peckham, Kilwardby's successor, and like Kilwardby a learned friar.[14] Once again the injunctions are all concerned with practical matters, and although their effects were uneven they were of great importance to the college. They are also eloquent of the dissensions which provoked them.

The archbishop sought first to arrest the growth of professional studies in the college by forbidding the admission of students of medicine, and permitting the study of canon law only under particular conditions and with special leave.[15] The physicians were apt to claim that their science was a manifestation of natural philosophy, which the archbishop perceived it not to be. It was certainly, on the other hand, the door to rewarding professional work at a time when lay society offered few such amenities to the merely talented. Something of the same kind lay behind the proscription of legal studies, though the church itself needed canon and civil lawyers. Neither injunction had any lasting effect: physicians came and went, and lawyers were hardly stinted. Nevertheless Peckham had his own view of the founder's intentions, and he did his best to further them.

The archbishop's first provisions may or may not have been a reproof to the warden's supervision of the college. Those which followed were probably closest to the recent dissensions. The warden was not to be excluded from the weekly accounting, the fellows were not to receive dividends from the surplus of the common fund, and vacancies were to be promptly filled and not left open to enlarge the surplus. There seems to have been some bias in recruitment: the

---

[13] Profession as a monk or friar was equated to civil death, and a postulant's goods could accordingly then be devised. If a fellow withdrew from college to a living, however, he could take his own books with him, but was expected to make some appropriate amends in his will. There are many examples of such bequests. See further below, pp. 152–4.

[14] See *Registrum Epistolarum Iohannis Peckham*, ed. C. T. Martin, RS lxxvii, 3 vols. (1882–3), iii. 811–18.

[15] See also below, pp. 257–8, 292.

indigent and worthy were not be be disparaged, and candidates were to be sought, as the founder had wished, in the dioceses in which the college had estates.[16] On the other hand candidates who were merely deficient in learning were not to be rejected as a nuisance, but instructed. It is not clear how their merits and potential were to be assessed.

A teacher of grammar was to be appointed, in accordance with the statutes. Private tastes were not to be indulged by the fellows, and the emoluments of the cook and the brewer were to be reduced, no doubt to that same end. If so, it might have been better to pay them more, and so strengthen their resistance to blandishment. There was also to be a more rigorous decorum at table: henceforward there were to be readings from St Gregory's *Moralia on Job*, and other edifying works of a readily assimilable kind, and all public conversation was to be, as the founder intended, in Latin.[17]

For the general good, and by no means for the grammar-master and his junior pupils alone, the college was to acquire three works of reference, Papias's *Vocabularium Latinum*, Hugutio de Vercelli's *Liber derivationum*, also known as the *Vocabularium* or *Etymologicum*, and the *Vocabularium Biblie* of the Franciscan Guillaume Brito Armoricus. They were to be made available in the library, chained to a suitable reading-desk, for all who wished to consult them.[18]

It was clearly Peckham's intention that the house should be rigorously managed, that it should maintain its character as a place of advanced learning, and that it should specialize first in the liberal arts, as the key to all learning, and then in theology in obedience to the founder's precepts. The injunctions did not achieve all their purposes, for many cooks flourished in the college kitchen over the centuries, and some Mertonian physicians even prospered in the warden's lodgings, but their general consequences were decisive and powerful.

---

[16] See further below, pp. 149, 255.

[17] There were at least four MSS of the *Moralia on Job* amongst the college's medieval books, but all came in the fourteenth cent. or later as gifts or bequests. One of them survives as Merton MS G.2.1. The fellows would almost certainly have lapsed into French when they were at their ease: English was probably not used in hall for another century.

[18] *super mensam honestam alligati*. The Brito seems to have survived into the 15th cent. (*MBMC*, no. 581). For Hugo, see Merton MS L.2.7 (op. cit., no. 319); and on his standing, R. W. Hunt, 'Hugutio and Petrus Helias', in *Collected Papers on the History of Grammar in the Later Middle Ages*, ed. G. L. Bursill-Hall (Amsterdam, 1980), pp. 145–9. See also below, p. 88.

Yet what happened during the next half-century was probably far from what Kilwardby and Peckham envisaged, familiar as they were with the academic world and its processes. The liberal arts were duly cultivated in Merton, and theology encouraged, but excellence in those works led on to a remarkable efflorescence of mathematics and science. The disposing factors were first the availability of the college's resources, and then the intoxicating power of logical argument.

The liberal arts comprised grammar, dialectic, commonly called logic, and rhetoric, which were together known as the trivium, and arithmetic, astronomy, geometry, and music, the four subjects which made up the quadrivium. In theory, and originally in practice, the skills which the trivium imparted – a sense of the significance of language, a capacity for analytical argument, and some knowledge of the arts of persuasion – were applied to the themes of the quadrivium to produce an educated mind. The ideal had taken shape in the world of pagan antiquity, but both the means and the end could be freely adapted to the needs of the Christian church.[19] Whilst the proper concern of the educated Christian was to apprehend and glorify God, grammar was an indispensable key to the Vulgate, rhetoric could promote pious eloquence in the clergy, and dialectic could inform the techniques of administration, as it still does in the guise of critical-path analysis.

Beyond those considerations, learning could be pursued to higher levels: prosaically to improve the means of instruction, and ultimately to comprehend the nature and purposes of God. In the process, it could be pursued at all levels for its own sake. St Thomas Aquinas had reordered Aristotelian philosophy, which afforded an approach to the observed world of nature, through physics, and beyond the physical world, through metaphysics, to the divine. Lively minds could and did engage both the means and the ends of speculation to any purpose, and at the end of the thirteenth century dialectic was the most potent instrument to hand. The nature of disciplined speculative thought, securing each proposition before proceeding to the next, naturally carried investigation to extremes: to the nature of God, to the definition of divine power, to the nature of the infinite.

Merton emerged into prominence in a period during which the general metaphysical debate was dominated by two Franciscans, John Duns Scotus and William Ockham, a much younger man who may

---

[19] On the tensions implicit throughout the Middle Ages in the use of pagan literature and learning to further Christian ends, see E. H. Harbison, *The Christian Scholar in the Age of the Reformation* (New York, 1956).

have been a pupil of Duns Scotus and was of comparable and perhaps even greater talents. Their eminence marks the beginnings of Oxford's maturity as a centre of scholarship.

Duns Scotus, *doctor subtilis*, reacted against Aquinas's efforts to match Aristotle's terms to the divine order, and argued that God could be discerned only as being. He asserted the unity of reality, and the supremacy of the will over the intellect, in conclusions that ranged over almost the entire ground of fourteenth-century debate.[20] It is a curious measure both of his influence and of the changing face of the university in his time, that he has long been taken, perversely but insistently, to have been a fellow of Merton College.[21]

As a Franciscan, Duns Scotus had no need of Merton, but the college was busy in recruiting talent.[22] Its commanding role seems to have begun with the arrival of Thomas Wilton, who was a fellow in 1288–9, and a nominee for the wardenship in 1299.[23] Wilton, whose name suggests the college's connections with the diocese of Salisbury, is the most distinguished figure amongst the early generations of fellows, though we cannot tell now what repute his contemporaries may have had, or how his name first came to the electors.[24] His career was exemplary in several senses, for like Duns Scotus he migrated from Oxford to Paris, and taught theology there, and he later returned to a canonry at St Paul's, where he probably died in 1327 as chancellor of the cathedral. His time in Paris is especially notable, however, for the fact that in 1310 he was followed there from Merton by Walter

[20] On Duns Scotus and his influence in Oxford, see J. I. Catto, 'Theology and theologians 1220–1320', *HUO* i. 471–517, at pp. 505–12.

[21] It appears that Duns Scotus was educated entirely within the Franciscan order, and that he would therefore have been ineligible for membership of Merton (*BRUO*, pp. 607–10). The tradition of his association appears only in the 15th cent. (see *MBMC*, no. 984), though during his most active years in Oxford (1300–4) he would have had both associates and opponents in the college. On the factitious portrait of Duns in the college hall, see below, pp. 262–3. All things considered, it is wholly appropriate that his ghost is reputed to walk the Old Library, which was built 60 years after his death.

[22] The cumulative total of known members of the college rises to 190 by 1320. See above, p. 43 n. 73.

[23] See *BRUO*, pp. 2054–5. For the leading Merton masters of the period and their works, see J. A. Weisheipl, 'Repertorium Mertonense', *MS* xxxi (1969), 174–224; and *CHLMP*, pp. 866 (Dumbleton), 880 (Billingham), 882 (Kilvington), 885 (Swineshead), 887 (Bradwardine), 888–9 (Burley), and 897 (Heytesbury).

[24] We can reasonably assume that there was academic gossip at the time, but can only rarely and fortuitously discover the topics. The building of the hall may well have caused some stir in the schools, the work on the chapel in 1290 assuredly did. Peckham (above, p. 51) was clearly anxious that it should not be supposed that only such stylish characters as the Beks need apply for places at Merton.

Burley, who later referred to him as his master, though Burley seems to have completed his doctorate in Paris before Wilton.[25]

Burley was a fellow by 1305, when his immediate contemporaries included the physician, John Gaddesden,[26] and he spent at least five years in college. He was the most celebrated and apparently the most prolific of the early Mertonians, a logician and metaphysician who was known to scholastic philosophers as *doctor planus* or *perspicuus*, the clear-headed. His transparency is less readily perceived by those who are not professional philosophers, but he had a powerful influence upon his own generation and his pupils, and in historical perspective he is still recognized as a formidable opponent to William Ockham. Like Duns Scotus, Ockham had a name which has outlived the world in which he was originally famous,[27] and like Scotus he was appropriated to Merton by later generations. He was the principal exponent of Nominalism, the system of thought which maintains that only phenomena that can be perceived and tested are real, and that other concepts are products of the mind, and the mental process of apprehension.

The opposing view, that beyond such phenomena there are absolutes, and forms of reality such as categories that transcend their individual constituents, is known as Realism or Universalism. The fundamental issues became lethally important later in the century, in the time of Wyclif and the Lollard movement, though within the university the extreme positions on either side were always qualified by the fluidity and freedom of academic debate. Indeed, Ockham's own thought was given an artificial rigidity when it was officially condemned by the papacy in 1326, and by the conscientious refutation thereafter of particular theses which their author might himself have chosen to modify.[28] In the context of Merton College and the Mertonians of the early fourteenth century, however, the most significant philosophical contentions were those concerned with the principles

---

[25] On Burley, see *BRUO*, pp. 312–14; and J. A. Weisheipl, 'Ockham and some Mertonians', *MS* xxx (1968), 163–213, at pp. 174–88.

[26] For Gaddesden, who was the author of an immensely successful medical treatise, and became a member of Prince Edward's household, see H. P. Cholmeley, *John of Gaddesden and the Rosa Medicine* (Oxford, 1912); and *BRUO*, p. 739.

[27] The principle attributed to Ockham, *quod entia non sunt predicanda preter necessitatem*, that the simplest solution to a problem is, other things being equal, to be preferred, still has some currency on its own account. The proverbial razor with which he removed superfluities has become detached from the arguments which it served.

[28] See *BRUO*, pp. 1384–7; and 'Repertorium Mertonense', pp. 173–4.

of motion, in the various Aristotelian senses of the word.

The preoccupations and devices of medieval philosophers were only lightly related to everyday life at the time, and they seem even further removed from the later courses of scientific thought, though the distances involved are not always as great as they appear to be.[29] It is also commonly believed that scholastic discussion of both the natural and the divine order was expressed in fanciful terms, and the image of angels frisking upon pin-points has been widely and dismissively invoked. It is clear that their attitudes towards authority, together with an enduring taste for allegory, often led disputants and others to repeat statements about causes and effects which simple observation of daily life might have served to contradict. The medieval relish for allegory was part of a wider taste for symbolism which powerfully influenced the graphic art of the time, and which is now only recoverable in part.

If, however, we were tempted to suppose that medieval visual and intellectual perceptions differed radically and wholly from our own, there are other works surviving which show that they did not. That same period in which Merton attracted and flourished its scientific talent is also marked off in England by two great monuments of art and architecture, the vestibule of the chapter house of Southwell Minster, completed in the 1290s, and the octagon of Ely cathedral, raised between 1322 and 1342. Each shows in its own way that theory and practice could run very smoothly together. The plant-sculptures at Southwell combine an exacting observation of the natural world with an astonishing mastery of technique. The octagon displays a boldly imaginative design with an equally remarkable command of materials. There is no mistaking the artistic skill of either or the engineering competence displayed at Ely. In the same fashion the scientists of the day advanced knowledge by devising and refining conceptual systems. In doing so they carried their speculations about the natural order of things much further than contemporary technology could allow the eye to see.

Walter Burley tested received knowledge by the use of suppositions, statements of which the ascertained truth or unsoundness, under logical examination, either advanced or consolidated what could be generally agreed. Some of Burley's investigations were pressed further by the *sophismata*, intrinsically puzzling or paradoxical statements,

---

[29] See further below, p. 58.

propounded and elucidated by a younger scholar called Richard Kilvington.[30] Like the great Franciscans, Kilvington has been credited to Merton, more rationally, for he was a secular, and an Oxford man, and his work is close to Burley's, but probably as mistakenly. There is no documented connection between Kilvington and the college, though it is clear that Kilvington was closely acquainted with Burley's work, and may have been in some sense his pupil. He also stands close to Bradwardine, and other mathematicians of the Merton school, though he himself uses no mathematical techniques.[31]

There were many strands of inquiry in the recent past which led scholars in the early fourteenth century to consider the nature of motion and time. Contemplating the power of God entailed definitions of eternity and infinity, the perennial discussions of God's foreknowledge of events raised questions about time, as did Aristotle's notion of *continua*: that everything that is continuous is divisible into divisibles that are infinitely divisible. Aquinas had considered whether angels, as immaterial beings, could move from one place to another without passing through intervening space. Those were matters discussed in various guises by Scotus and Ockham,[32] and they were carried to new refinements in conceptual terms by the work of Burley and others, especially Kilvington. The most striking change in contemporary thought, which points forward to Galilean concepts and techniques, and which seems to have come about at Merton in the third and fourth decades of the century, lay in the introduction of mathematics to the debate.

The most celebrated and certainly one of the most innovative of the Mertonian mathematicians was Thomas Bradwardine. He appears at Balliol in 1321, but moved to Merton by 1323, perhaps attracted by the reputation of John Maudith, the astronomer. He retained his fellowship there until 1335, when he became one of Richard de Bury's chaplains at Durham, in company, at various times, with Burley and Kilvington. His subsequent career saw him chaplain of the royal household and confessor to Edward III, canon and chancellor of St Paul's from 1337, and then successively nominated archdeacon of

---

[30] See *The Sophismata of Richard Kilvington*, ed. N. and B. E. Kretzmann (Auctores Britannici Medii Aevi, xii, 2 vols., Oxford, 1990), for the text, and the commentary in N. and B. E. Kretzmann, *The Sophismata of Richard Kilvington: Introduction, Translation and Commentary* (Cambridge, 1990).

[31] See *Sophismata: Introduction*, pp. xix–xx.

[32] See e.g. J. D. North, *HUO* ii. 78–9.

Norwich and dean of Lincoln. In the last year of his life he became archbishop of Canterbury. He died of the plague in the summer of 1349, within a few days of his return from his consecration at the papal court at Avignon.

Bradwardine's writings, though less extensive than those of Burley, had a notably wider range.[33] In his own age he was principally admired as a theologian, but his fame as a logician and mathematician endured, first through the work of the younger Mertonians, and then through the diffusion of his treatises on the Continent, into the age of the printed book. His most celebrated work, the *Summa de causa Dei contra Pelagios*, expounds an uncompromising Augustinian doctrine of grace, and of God's foreknowledge of events, against notions of the efficacy of the unaided human will. Amid his other preoccupations in the 1340s Bradwardine urged its principles upon his younger colleagues in Merton, when his correspondence has a nostalgic reference, rare in its age, to his former companions and life in the college. Of the *Summa*, he explains, perhaps with some innocent exaggeration, that he had undertaken to write it 'at the repeated requests of his beloved brethren, the warden and fellows of Merton Hall'.[34]

In his mathematical works Bradwardine had displayed a more creative power of reasoning, and revelled particularly in the scope which the axiomatic method of geometry gave to his gift of logical argument. The mathematics of classical arithmetic and computation in medieval Europe were greatly enriched from the twelfth century onwards by the Greek learning which the Arabs transmitted to the west. Euclid's works and the spherical trigonometry of Menelaus of Alexandria were amongst the texts which came through Spain, and the Arabic masters' own development of algebra and the techniques of sexagesimal computation stimulated both pure mathematics and astronomical calculations.

About the time at which he moved to Merton Bradwardine displayed his dialectical powers in a work known as *De insolubilibus*, or the *Insolubilia*, in which he applied logic to the resolution of para-

---

[33] See 'Repertorium Mertonense', pp. 177–84. Some of Bradwardine's associates can be identified through the MSS of his works: see *MBMC*, pp. 120, 134. A minor work attributed to him, either as a by-product of his own work or a guide for other students, is a tract *De arte memorativa*, in BL MS Sloane 3744, which propounds a scheme of mental filing by the systematic association of topics.

[34] The college was known indifferently through the Middle Ages as Merton or Marton Hall, and Mertonhall, as well as Merton College. Formally speaking it was, as it still is, the House of Scholars of Merton.

doxes. His best-known mathematical work is the *Tractatus de proportionibus*, which followed in 1328. In it he brought a number of current ideas to bear on the relationship between changes in the velocity of a moving object, itself a concept not very rigorously defined in Aristotelian physics, and the forces of impulsion and resistance which work upon it. His argument brought him to the conclusion that velocity depended upon the ratio of the motive power to the power of resistance, but that the proportions involved were not simple but geometric proportions.

In so far as there are convergences between Bradwardine's thought and later physics they tend to obscure rather than to enhance his achievements. His object was not to determine the laws of nature for their own sake, and certainly not to do so in order to meddle with the structure of the physical world. It was rather to test and refine the philosophical system within and through which the Christian world sought to understand both God's purpose and its own part in the system. That said, intuition took the informed mind to the limits of techniques available to it. There was evidently much zest in the inquiries themselves, in the gratification of making discoveries, in occasionally convincing contemporaries, and in enthusing younger scholars. What emerges from beneath the stylized forms of debate can seem as familiar as the sharply observed naturalism of the foliage at Southwell. It is also remarkable that whilst both the quests and the techniques of medieval science appeared to be perverse and ridiculous when set against the billiard-ball certainties of nineteenth-century physics and chemistry, they can seem less remote from some of the perceptions of quantum mechanics and the universe of particles.

Bradwardine's most productive years were probably in the 1320s, although he was a proctor in 1325–7, and seems to have taken his theological doctorate at some time between 1337 and 1348, when he was deeply immersed in public affairs. He almost certainly lectured in divinity at that same time, as chancellor of St Paul's, an appointment which he did not relinquish until he was elected to the archbishopric. The text of *De proportionibus velocitatum* was in circulation during those years; the *Summa de causa* was completed by 1344. He was evidently in close touch with many other academics throughout his career, and Richard de Bury's household was an academy in itself,[35]

---

[35] See *BRUO*, pp. 323–6; and N. Denholm-Young, 'Richard de Bury, 1287–1345', *TRHS* 4th ser. XX (1937), 135–68.

but the time of his decisive influence seems to have been the decade which he spent in the college.

The intermittent nature of the college records down to the later fifteenth century makes it difficult to determine the body of fellows resident at any particular time.[36] The college was content to know itself: the self-regulating community seems to have had no thought of keeping a register, and there are no records of elections, and only incidental references to office holders and some others in the accounts.[37] The notes on the statutory college meetings, or scrutinies, which survive from 1338–9, are isolated fragments, and though full of interest they suggest that the company's livelier minds were not always engaged on those occasions.[38] There were, however, three periods in the earlier part of the century during which Merton attracted outstanding talent, that is to say around 1305, in the first half of the 1320s, and around 1330.[39]

By 1305, when Walter Burley, Richard Campsale, William Eastry, and John Gaddesden first appear as fellows, Thomas Wilton and William Hennor had been in the college for five years or more. Wilton may already have left for Paris by that time, though his connections with Burley make it likely that they met at Merton.[40] Eastry and Hennor both took livings, Eastry in Kent, which was most probably his native county, in 1315, and Hennor in Derbyshire, where he died in 1340. They are oddly associated by the presence of copies of their only known works, on Aristotle's Physics and Metaphysics respectively, amongst the books of St Augustine's abbey, Canterbury.[41] Both were therefore effectively active in the schools, though nothing more is known of their careers within either the college or the university.[42]

[36] The cumulative total of Mertonians reaches 238 by 1320, but the number falls over the next two decades to 170. On the fellowship in the time of the plague, see below, pp. 93–4.

[37] On the compilation of the first lists of fellows, see below, pp. 116–17.

[38] But see also below, p. 73.

[39] See the list of Merton masters and their writings in 'Repertorium Mertonense'.

[40] See above, pp. 53–4.

[41] The MSS may have come to the abbey library, though they are not so ascribed, from Abbot Thomas Poucyn, or Poucy (1334–43), who was a DD by 1334, and gave the house a number of his working texts, including some of Burley's writings: see *BRUO*, p. 1508; and A. B. Emden, *Donors of Books to St Augustine's Abbey, Canterbury*, Oxford Bibliographical Society, Occasional Publications, iv (Oxford, 1968), p. 4. St Augustine's had another, less gratifying connection with Merton in the person of Peter Dene: below, pp. 66–7.

[42] Except that Eastry also gave or bequeathed a MS of Aquinas to the college library: *MBMC*, no. 55; and below, p. 84. Eastry was presented to the rectory of Stowting, Kent, and Hennor to the rectory of Longley, Derbysh.: *BRUO*, pp. 651, 909.

Walter Burley's career brought him canonries at Chichester, Wells, and Durham. Like Bradwardine he was a member of Richard de Bury's household, and held an appointment at court, where he was almoner to Queen Philippa. His active life extended into the 1340s, and encompassed the writing of many books. Campsale, who, like Bradwardine some fifteen years later, came to Merton from Balliol at the outset of his professional life, was an active theologian who served three times as bursar. He was also a proctor in 1308, and acted for the university on several other occasions.[43] He was present in Balliol when the statutes of the college were determined in 1325, and he acted for Merton in negotiations with Worcester cathedral priory to attract recruits from that diocese.[44]

The next significant appointment was made in or before 1309, when the mathematician John Maudith is named as a fellow. He served as a bursar in 1311. He vacated his fellowship in 1319, but then secured permission from his diocesan, the bishop of Worcester, for a further period of study. He subsequently became one of Richard de Bury's learned clerks, and later served John, seventh earl of Warenne.[45] He wrote at least one theological tractate, but he is particularly remembered for his astronomical tables, upon which he was working between 1310 and 1316.[46] The substance of the tables, which were widely circulated, was derived ultimately from Arab sources through Toledo, but they demanded extensive calculation to relate the material to the latitude of Oxford. Their particular interest here is that in the first place they take Mertonian mathematics and astronomy back to the first decade of the century, and in the second that their accompanying text is much concerned with the technicalities of making astronomical instruments, another characteristic interest of the college in later generations.[47]

The admissions of the 1320s put a more distinctive stamp on the house. Walter Segrave, a logician who was made chancellor of Durham by Richard de Bury, was a fellow at least from 1321 to 1337. John

[43] See E. A. Synan, 'Richard of Campsale: an English theologian of the fourteenth century', *MS* xiv (1952), 1–8; and *BRUO*, pp. 344–5. Campsale took his doctorate in or before 1322.

[44] See *BRUO*, pp. 344–5.

[45] On Warenne, a powerful figure whose energies and resources were almost entirely consumed by his efforts to legitimize his mistress's children, see F. R. Fairbank, 'The last earl of Warenne and Surrey', *YAJ* xix (1907), 193–264.

[46] See further *HUO* ii. 143–4.

[47] See below, pp. 91, 110.

Ashenden, the astronomer and author of an apocalyptic *Summa judicialis de accidentibus mundi*, was a fellow by 1322, and survived until the mid-1350s.[48] He was followed by Bradwardine in 1323, and by Thomas Buckingham in 1324. Buckingham was third bursar in 1338, and vacated his fellowship in 1340 when he was made rector of Deene, Northamptonshire. Shortly afterwards he went to the university of Paris, where he is said to have disputed with Bradwardine. It seems an unlikely conjunction at that time, although Buckingham did differ from Bradwardine over the doctrine of free will, and must often have debated with him on other occasions.

Six years after Buckingham's appearance there came Simon Bredon, a mathematician and astronomer who was a notable benefactor of the college library.[49] Bredon, besides practising medicine, was a logician whose work provides a link between the advanced dialectical techniques of Kilvington and the Mertonian mathematicians. William Sutton, who appears in Merton in the same year as Bredon, was a logician and opponent of Ockham whose works were long admired on the Continent. Sutton spent his entire career in Oxford, holding office as bursar three times between 1338 and 1343, and as sub-warden in 1344–5. He took the college living of St Peter's-in-the-East in 1346 and died in 1349, perhaps of the plague. William Collingham, a commentator on Aristotle's *Physics*, was a fellow by 1331, and seems to have stayed at Merton without holding office until 1341, when like William Heytesbury, the logician and natural philosopher, he was nominated by Robert de Eglesfield as one of the original fellows of Queen's College.

A more celebrated figure, the logician and mathematician John Dumbleton, follows in 1338. Dumbleton was the author of an incomplete but imposing *Summa logice et philosophie naturalis*, and like Heytesbury provides connections between some earlier logicians, including Ockham, with whom he sympathized more openly than did Heytesbury, and the mathematical philosophers who followed upon Bradwardine.[50] He too was nominated to a fellowship of Queen's,

[48] See *BRUO*, pp. lviii and 56. See also K. V. Snedegar, 'John Ashenden and the *Scientia astrorum Mertonensis*, with an edition of Ashenden's *Prognosticaciones*', Oxford D.Phil. thesis (1988).

[49] See *BRUO*, pp. 257–8; *MBMC*, pp. 138–42; and below, pp. 87–8.

[50] For an authoritative sketch of Dumbleton's *Summa*, see Weisheipl (above, n. 25), 199–207.

but seems never to have left Merton, and as he disappears after 1349 he may well have been another victim of the Black Death.

After Dumbleton came a final group elected in the years before the plague, beginning with a logical analyst called [?John] Tewkesbury, by 1340, and continuing with Richard Billingham, William Rede, later bishop of Chichester and a notable benefactor of Merton and of other colleges, and Richard Swineshead, known as the Calculator, who were all fellows by 1344. They were among the dominant figures in the learned world of the second half of the century.

At any time before the plague there were up to fifty fellows in the college besides the warden and the other members of the house. The authors named here, of whom there are fewer than a score, can be identified only because some part of their work has survived in manuscript or in notices by other commentators. They had their own friends and colleagues, of whom some would have been Mertonians whom we can no longer distinguish, others disputants in the schools, some others even correspondents and coadjutors at a distance. The nexus of English scholarship beyond Oxford most notably embraced Richard de Bury, but again his is a name and influence of which we are aware, and there were assuredly other patrons and benefactors whose identity has been lost.

The setting in which Merton developed and flourished was anything but propitious. The half-century before the onset of the Black Death was a time of almost continuous political crisis and economic stress, from the strains of Edward I's last futile campaigns in Scotland, through the mayhem of Edward II's reign, to the first stages of the Hundred Years' War with France. The political crises had little direct effect upon the university, though one of its chief benefactors, Walter Stapledon, bishop of Exeter and founder of Exeter College, was murdered by a London mob at the doors of St Paul's when Edward II fell. The university nevertheless had its own problems, of which the most anguishing, though it was eventually resolved against all the perceptible odds, arose from its determination not to allow the friars academic autonomy within the system.[51]

---

[51] See further M. W. Sheehan, 'The religious orders 1220–1370', *HUO* i. 205–13; and *Formularies which bear on the History of Oxford, c. 1204–1420*, ed. H. E. Salter, W. A. Pantin, and H. G. Richardson (OHS n.s. iv–v, 1942), i. 1–79. The university's pertinacity, in a struggle which over several decades ranged it in opposition to the friars (themselves resourceful and articulate, a formidable crew), the king, and the pope, was truly remarkable.

That same troubled period, however, saw the foundation of three new colleges or collegiate halls: Exeter Hall by Walter Stapledon and his brother Sir Richard in 1312, the House of Scholars of St Mary, subsequently known as Oriel College, by Adam Brome, royal almoner and chancery clerk, in 1324–6, and the most ambitious, the Hall of the Queen's Scholars, or the Queen's College, by Robert Eglesfield, another royal clerk, in 1341. Stapledon sought the closest possible connections with the diocese of Exeter, stipulating that eight of the twelve scholars on the foundation should be drawn from Devon and four from Cornwall. He also, although he allowed the scholars to elect their own rector each year, entrusted the endowment of the hall to the dean and chapter of Exeter. Brome, who wished his house to specialize in theology and canon law, with an eye to the royal service, drew upon Merton's statutes for its constitution. Queen's, like Exeter, was marked by a strong regional affiliation, giving preference first to the founder's kin, as at Merton, and then to natives of Cumberland and Westmorland. Eglesfield nevertheless drew on Merton in the first instance for his foundation fellows. He specified theology as the principal discipline of the house, and wished the fellows to take orders as soon as they were eligible.

The general crisis of the early fourteenth century was continuous, cumulative, and affected the whole of Europe, though at the time it was not well understood, and probably not well perceived. It came at the end of several centuries of economic growth, when the expanding population of the continent could no longer be sustained by the resources that were available to it, and in particular when the cultivation of marginal lands ceased to offer an effective return. In an over-extended and unresilient economy bad weather, poor harvests, diseases of cattle, and interruptions of trade, which seemed endemic in the first decades of the century, became a cumulative burden. When the bubonic plague came, in the 1340s, it was rather as the climax than as the harbinger of demographic catastrophe.

As a landlord, and indeed the most substantial landlord within the ambit of the university, Merton was exposed to those problems, and they make the college's accomplishments the more impressive.[52] The endowment was substantially complete when the founder died, though it was then supplemented by a bequest of 1,000 marks (£666.

---

[52] On the management of the estates, see T. H. Aston, 'The external administration and resources of Merton College, to *c.* 1348', *HUO* i. 311–68.

13*s*. 4*d*.), and the residual value of Walter de Merton's estate.[53] It took a little time to buy out the family and other interests in Kibworth and elsewhere, and there were much greater difficulties over the rectories of Embleton and Ponteland. Embleton was not effectively secured to a Merton incumbent until 1341, after long frustration and many journeys undertaken by the warden and fellows.[54]

Although the immediate grounds of contention in Embleton and Ponteland were different, the two episodes, which were exemplary, had some significant features in common, of which the most important was the simple factor of distance. The college had no local support in the pursuit of its rights, and faced a good deal of hostility as an interloper. As it happened, both properties came to Merton through the sieve of bargaining and manoeuvring that followed the confiscations of rebel lands after 1266. Simon de Montfort had acquired the lordship of Embleton in 1255, and Edmund of Lancaster, to whom Henry III granted Simon's confiscated estates, granted the advowson to the college in 1275. Ponteland came direct from Peter de Montfort, who had sacked the Surrey manors in 1263, but it was not the Montfortian dispossessed who proved most obdurate in the contests that followed.

The advowson of the parish church of St Mary, Ponteland, was given to the college by Peter de Montfort in 1268. The grant refers to the college as founded by de Montfort's friend, Walter de Merton, and there is not so much as a whiff of burnt farmsteads about the transaction.[55] The mischief was that the rectory, which in this context might better be called the manor of the rectory, had been divided some time before into three parts, which were in turn unhelpfully called prebends.[56] The college believed that what it had acquired

---

[53] See *ERMC*, pp. 82, 84. The thousand marks was a very large sum, several times larger than the whole cost of the college's site in Oxford.

[54] See T. H. Aston and R. Faith, 'The endowments of the university and colleges to *c*. 1348', *HUO* i. 298–9; and G. H. Martin, 'Road travel in the Middle Ages: some journeys by the warden and fellows of Merton College, Oxford, 1315–1470', *Journal of Transport History*, iii (1976), 159–78, at pp. 164–70.

[55] On Ponteland, see *A History of Northumberland*, xii, ed. M. H. Dodds (Newcastle upon Tyne, 1926), pp. 407–45. There is a detailed recital of the imbroglio, drawn up in or shortly before 1302, in MCR 578.

[56] A prebend is simply an allowance, or the title to an allowance. In historical usage, however, it has come to be associated exclusively with the estate appointed to support a canon of a cathedral or other capitular church. The three portions of the rectory of Ponteland were therefore rightly called prebends, but they might equally well have been called estates, manors, or allotments. They may have reflected some familial division of the rectory, or even some earlier division of the lordship of Eland, but their creation made

was what might be termed the rectorial prebend and with it an unencumbered title to the advowson, or right to present to the living. It had not. All that de Montfort had bought, in 1261, and bestowed upon the college in 1268, was the advowson itself, sold over the head of the incumbent, Robert Driffield, and sketchily reinforced with a tenement of two bovates.

The weakness of the college's position was revealed in 1275, when Roger Bertram III, the lord of Mitford, died. Robert Driffield still enjoyed the beatitude of glebe and tithe, and he claimed the associated right to present to both the other prebends. Beyond that issue, Merton's impatient desire to appropriate the living and institute a vicarage was deeply repugnant to him.[57] He scouted the college's title, but before the warden and fellows could gather their forces for the fight, they found themselves under attack from another direction. Driffield had been presented, together with the incumbents of both the other prebends, in or soon after 1243, by Agnes Bertram, widow of Roger II, when she held the advowson as her dower. Now Agnes's daughter-in-law, Ida, the widow of Roger Bertram III, claimed dower in the rectory in her turn.

Dower was a notoriously potent right. It was possible, though expensive and cumbrous, to debar a woman's claim to dower in property of which her husband had disposed, even with her professed consent, during his lifetime, but any attempt to short-circuit the process could lead straight to catastrophe. What is more, under the tontine rules of the common law, if a widow remarried and then predeceased her husband, her dower remained with him for life. Ida showed no sign of fragility,[58] but she was now married to Robert Neville of Raby, a man of ominously wide interests and influence. Together they took the Scholars of Merton into King's Bench, and emerged with one-third of the advowson. In 1276 the college was awarded an unwelcome and probably unenforceable compensation from Peter de Montfort's lands in Warwickshire.

In the mean time what remained of the lordship of Mitford had passed to another Bertram, Agnes, who bestowed it on Eleanor, the

no difference to the parochial or juridical status of the church itself: see further *History of Northumberland*, xii. 407–8.

[57] By impropriation the college became the corporate rector of the living, reserving to itself the great tithe, the tithe of grain, and instituted a vicarage which was supported by the lesser tithes. See further below, n. 61.

[58] On the contrary, she survived Robert Neville and married a third husband, John Fitzmarmaduke, whom she outlived in turn. She was still alive in 1315: *CP* ix. 496.

wife of Robert de Stuteville. The Stutevilles duly regarded themselves as the patrons of the next vacant prebend, and appointed Master Hugh Woodhall to it. It was evidently time for the college, with or without the formalities of action at law, to buy out everyone in sight.

In 1286, however, on the death of Robert Driffield, Merton carelessly over-played its hand. Its proctor exacerbated local feeling by entering the church and rectory so promptly that he interrupted Driffield's funeral, and the parish and the shire united in opposition to the interlopers. The college then tried to present Richard Worplesden, its new warden,[59] to the living, but the bishop, who was now none other than Anthony Bek, once the college's tenant, denounced both the title and the proposed vicarage, and instituted a new rector under the Bertram title, together with two new prebendaries for good measure.

The new incumbent, Adam Driffield, proved himself a resourceful opponent. When in 1302 the college procured papal letters in support of its claims the rector struck back in two ways. His congregation rallied with sickles and billhooks to expel the college's proctor and his coadjutors, who had to retire to read their act of sequestration in the safety of St Nicholas's, Newcastle, some twelve miles from the front line. At the same time Driffield himself appealed to the pope, referring to Merton as a haunt of scholars studying physic and law, a barbed invocation of Peckham's injunctions which probably came to him out of the bishop of Durham's household rather than by direct revelation.[60] However, his appeal was rejected by Boniface VIII, who had irredentist problems of his own, and Bishop Bek was constrained to institute a vicarage at Ponteland in August 1303.[61] The college, remembering that it was the corporate heir not only to its founder's pertinacity, but also to his circumspection, bought out Ida Neville, now Ida Fitzmarmaduke, in the same year.

At Embleton, the scene of an even more protracted campaign, the trouble was caused directly by the donor and his heirs.[62] Edmund of Lancaster gave Holy Trinity church (Pl. 5) to the college in 1275, but then absent-mindedly presented his own candidate to the living in 1279. The college succeeded in displacing the intruder and in installing two rectors in succession, but in 1307 Edmund's son, Earl Thomas of

[59] See below, p. 70.

[60] See above, p. 50.

[61] For a detailed valuation of the tithes and dues of the vicarage, which was worth £29. 2s. per annum in 1302, see *History of Northumberland*, xii (1926), 415–16 and n.

[62] For the passion of Embleton, see *A History of Northumberland*, ii (1895), pp. 49–63.

Lancaster, emerged from his minority and presented Dr Peter Dene. Thomas was not renowned for mildness and self-abnegation, and a local jury convened to testify to the facts was unable to remember that the college had ever presented an incumbent.[63]

Peter Dene was a doctor of canon and civil law, and from 1308 chancellor of York.[64] He was a busy and acquisitive man who was so closely identified with Earl Thomas that after the battle of Boroughbridge, in the spring of 1322, when a royal army defeated Thomas's allies and the earl was beheaded outside his own castle of Pontefract, he had to flee from the North. He found sanctuary in the abbey of St Augustine, Canterbury, of which he had been an agent in the past, where he took vows as a monk and began a further remarkable career.[65] However, he had resigned Embleton before 1321, and Earl Thomas presented another rector to the living in that year.

After Thomas's fall and execution Merton began an action in Common Pleas to recover the advowson. It won the day, but the king's lawyers observed that the college had no licence to hold the advowson in mortmain, having acquired it before the statute of 1279 was enacted.[66] The licence was duly bought, but in the mean time the king presented Thomas Bamburgh to the living. The college eventually succeeded in instituting a vicarage in 1332, though at the price of allowing Bamburgh to enjoy the great tithe for the rest of his life. When Bamburgh died, however, the earl, who was now Henry of Lancaster, Thomas's brother, maintained family traditions by again presenting one of his own clerks to the living. Again there was brawling in the churchyard, and the earl's bailiff personally ejected the college's proctor, John Hotham.[67] A new appeal again established Merton's right, but the college had to buy off the earl at a substantial

---

[63] The college's proctor, Peter de Lisle, reported that there was still strong feeling against the college locally over its actions at Ponteland in 1286: *History of Northumberland*, xii. 417 and n.

[64] See the notice of his career in *BRUO*, pp. 2168–9.

[65] See *History of Northumberland*, ii. 54–7. St Augustine's took him in because he had been a valuable agent and benefactor of the house, but he absconded once in a melodramatic fashion, in the hope of pursuing a secular career again, and after his return, under restraint, misappropriated a substantial quantity of bullion and silver plate. He seems to have made amends posthumously: see Emden, *Donors of Books*, pp. 18, 64.

[66] Edmund of Lancaster's grant predated the statute (see above, pp. 18, 64), and the college undeniably had no licence for a transaction which did not require a licence when it was undertaken. However, time does not run against the crown in either direction.

[67] Fellow and bursar of Merton, and provost of Queen's 1350–61. He has a memorial brass at Chinnor: *BRUO*, pp. 969–70.

price before Hotham took formal possession of the church in the presence of the warden, Robert Tring, in November 1341, and William Humberston was installed in the vicarage.[68]

Those adventures apart, the college had moved swiftly and successfully to establish its titles and gather its income. The archives show that deeds of title were kept with great care from the earliest times.[69] The *Liber ruber*, a register of properties and deeds compiled before 1290, arranges the properties by counties, and shows that the documents relating to each manor were kept in a series of lettered receptacles.[70] There is no trace now of the original furniture of the muniment room, but its management was certainly up to the best practice of the day.[71] On the other hand the administrative records of the estates were evidently preserved more informally. They have survived in substantial numbers,[72] but they were used at once more intensively and more casually than the deeds. There is evidence that the college had assembled surveys of all but its northern lands by the 1290s, and abundant evidence that the administration and supervision of the estates engaged the energies of the warden and a substantial proportion of the fellows at all times.[73] Almost all the property was managed directly by the college.

Except for Embleton, which became freely available at a time when attitudes were changing, even the more distant estates were not leased, though except at Cuxham, and to a lesser extent in Holywell, the proceeds of the harvest, stock, and customary and other dues were taken in cash rather than kind. The resulting income amounted to some £340 a year. Careful leasing would almost certainly have produced more: close and continuous supervision of the individual properties was impossible, although everyone knew that it was necessary. There must have been many unauthorized local levies upon both the harvested and the threshed grain, and in bad years, of which there were too many between 1314 and 1330, the landlord who lacked the comfort of a lease was as exposed in his own way as were his

---

[68] For Tring, see below, p. 70; and for Humberstone, *BRUO*, p. 982.

[69] See above, p. 44. The proceedings over Ponteland are exceptionally well documented, even by Merton's generous standards.

[70] See *MM*, p. 29; and *ERMC*, pp. 366–7.

[71] See further G. H. Martin, *The Early Court Rolls of the Borough of Ipswich* (Occasional Papers in English Local History, Leicester, 1954), pp. 30–1 and nn.

[72] See e.g. P. D. A. Harvey, *Cuxham 1240–1400*, (Oxford, 1965); and R. Evans, 'Thorncroft', in *Medieval Society and the Manor Court* ed. Z. Razi (Oxford, 1996). pp. 199–259.

[73] See further T. H. Aston (above, n. 52), pp. 313–21, 333–41.

unfortunate tenants in theirs. Yet the income was quite evenly maintained, and it can be seen to have served the needs of the house.[74]

The practice of direct management probably derives from the first endowment of the college. Cuxham had been farmed directly by its previous lords, but for the warden and his colleagues personal supervision of their comparatively compact estate was a positive act of trusteeship. Once the practice was established it was likely to be changed only by some convulsion, which duly came after half a century.

In the mean time the prime purpose of the foundation was handsomely met, and further properties were acquired on either side of the main site, including Gutter Hall at the head of the Grove.[75] Money was spent consistently on maintenance, and there was also some new building. The south wing of the warden's house was probably remodelled around 1315, or a little earlier.[76] In the early 1330s work was resumed on the church. The crossing was completed, and two transepts added. The north transept was reconstructed early in the fifteenth century, though it seems that in the south transept only the windows were then renewed. It is clear from the details of the west wall of the church that there was to be an aisled nave to the west, as well as a central tower, and it is difficult not to think that that was the end to which the neighbouring ground was acquired. In the mean time the churchyard on the street front to the north of the church seems to have been enclosed with a wall running from the porter's lodge to the north transept.

There is no suggestion that those or any other operations were hindered by want of means, though as T. H. Aston observed, the college seems to have kept its spending close to the limit of its income, and there may have been occasions when officers had to wait for cash to come in.[77] Almost all the money came directly to the bursars, and was laid out by them, and on the whole there seems, despite some skirmishing, to have been little friction. Peter Abingdon, the first warden, resigned in 1285–6. Archbishop Peckham had sent com-

---

[74] See further D. Postles, 'Some differences between seignorial demesnes in medieval Oxfordshire', *Oxoniensia*, lviii (1994), 219–32.

[75] See *MMC*, p. 310, and above, p. 42.

[76] See *ERMC*, p. 61. The windows shown in J. Skelton, *Oxonia Antiqua Illustrata* (Oxford, 1823), p. 154, suggest that the work was undertaken at the same time and by the same hands as the building of the sacristy.

[77] There was at least one occasion in the early years when the warden's dinner depended upon an infusion of cash from the bailiff of Cuxham: *ERMC*, p. 62 and n.

missioners to investigate complaints against Abingdon in the spring of 1284, but on leaving the college Abingdon retired only to Nuneham Courtenay, and remained on amiable terms with his successor, Richard Worplesdon, and the fellows. Worplesdon had been closely associated with Abingdon, and some ambiguity about the date of his wardenship may reflect an agreed transfer of responsibilities.[78] It seems that Abingdon was the administrator who launched the college, with the founder's full and justified confidence, and Worplesdon the first scholar to direct the house.[79]

Worplesdon's successor, John de la More, who was a fellow by 1284 and a proctor in the 1280s, served for only four years, from 1295 to 1299, after which he withdrew to the living of St Peter's-in-the-East, where he died in 1310. The college bought a sword for him in 1296, for a modest sum. John Wanting, who followed him, held the office from 1299 to 1328. He was an executor of the will of Ela, Countess of Warwick, a benefactor who spent her last years in the nunnery at Godstow. The college helped to build her quarters there, and she took a close interest in its affairs, corresponding with the warden, and providing amongst other things a dole for wine on St Matthew's day.[80]

Wanting may have been growing old by the mid-1320s, though in 1326 the fellows spoke warmly of his administrative ability when someone complained of him to Archbishop Reynolds.[81] When Wanting died, by the summer of 1329 at the latest, Robert Tring, a fellow since 1313, was elected to succeed him, and served until 1351. Tring was responsible for the later phases of the negotiations over Embleton, which consumed much time and money, and added anxieties about tenure in mortmain to his other preoccupations.[82] The early years of his wardenship also saw the celebrated secession of

---

[78] Worplesdon, together with Henry Temple, a canon of Merton Priory, and Richard St John, an agent of Walter de Merton's whom the college continued to employ for some years, was a proctor to whom Abingdon granted power to appoint attorneys during his absence abroad in 1274: *CCR 1272-9*, p. 117.

[79] See further their respective bequests to the library (*MBMC*, p. 95), though the point may be distorted by the fact that Abingdon had borne the demanding affairs first of the college and then of the founder's estate during twenty years which Worplesdon had spent in Oxford.

[80] See *ERMC*, pp. 27, 262, and 446-9.

[81] See *MMC*, p. 156. Wanting died in 1328 or early in 1329 and was buried in the choir of the church before the high altar. His grave, which was noted by Anthony Wood, is now unmarked, but some fragments of its slab may remain. See Bott, *Monuments*, p. 107 and n.

[82] See the transactions in *CPR 1327-30*, pp. 259, 260; and *CPR 1330-34*, pp. 23, 102; and above, pp. 66-8.

northern masters from Oxford to Stamford in 1333. The migration was apparently led by a fellow of Merton, William Barnby, but it does not seem to have caused serious divisions in the college, which was in fact the last place in the university likely to be so disturbed. Barnby had, ironically enough, been one of the university's proctors at Avignon when its dispute with the Oxford Dominicans was argued in the papal curia in 1317.[83]

The college withstood two incidental attacks upon its property during Tring's office. The first was a clumsy but pertinacious attempt by the Augustinian friars to appropriate some of the Holywell lands outside Smith Gate, in 1336–7. The other was a simple fraudulent intrusion into the mastership of St John's Hospital, Basingstoke, in 1344. Both were effected by misrepresentation to royal officers, and both were countered by orders under the great seal.[84] The warden's appointment in 1339, together with the chancellor and the mayor of the city, to a commission to improve the sanitary condition of Oxford probably owed as much to the college's lordship of Holywell manor and its watercourses as to its weight in university affairs. The king's action in authorizing the commission almost certainly came from the university, and the intention was to clean the streets, forbid the slaughter of cattle within the walls, and if necessary to find another site for the meat market. Later in the year the mayor appeared before the royal justices to say that the city was unable to move the shambles from their accustomed place, and the vice-chancellor and the sheriff of Oxfordshire were left to do what they could in the king's name, which proved to be not very much. However the university achieved control of the city markets in the aftermath of the St Scholastica's day riots in 1355, and acquired some new points of view with that felicity.[85]

Warden Tring was also appointed with other commissioners to adjudicate upon the first statutes of Oriel College in 1348, and to negotiate with the bishop of Lincoln over the chancellorship of the university, a matter of frequent contention, in 1350.[86] He died in 1351, and was buried at the foot of the steps before the high altar, beside his predecessor, John Wanting. Tring's memorial slab is now reset in the north transept of the church. It had a brass inlay, with an effigy showing the warden, tonsured and wearing a tunic, standing within

[83] See *BRUO*, p. 112. Barnby gave several Aristotelian texts to Merton: *MBMC*, pp. 100–1.

[84] See *CPR 1334–8*, pp. 300–1, 396; and *CPR 1343–5*, pp. 258, 308.

[85] See *CPR 1338–40*, pp. 186, 306. For St Scholastica's day, see below, pp. 95–6.

[86] See *BRUO*, p. 1908; *HUO* i. 44–50: *CPR 1338–40*, pp. 186, 306.

a floriated cross, and an inscription round the border of the slab: 'Here lies buried Master Robert Tring, once warden of this house. May his soul find favour with God'. The inscription has long been lost, and the cross is broken, but most of the figure remains, and is the earliest depiction of a warden of the house.[87]

As it happens, the only early record of the college scrutinies, which were held three times each year, dates from Tring's time. It records meetings held in July and December 1338, and one in March 1339, and refers to thirty-five fellows, who cannot all be identified in other sources.[88] The document, which is in poor condition, was quite casually compiled, and it is interesting that there were several complaints at the time about the way in which the scrutinies were recorded.

The contents are much what might be expected in a self-intent and privileged community: that the warden does not listen to complaints, and that he is frequently absent, and indeed the records show him, like the bursars, travelling far and frequently on the college's business. Some fellows kept dogs, which were a distraction from study. It was also observed that some of the fellows, and on occasions William the chaplain, wore unsuitable and unseemly boots, which may well have been so. It was said further that the younger members of the college were lacking in respect for their seniors, and that they went out into the town too frequently. They then brought strong drink with them when they returned, and they were apt to spend their time gossiping in the hall doorway, all which is also quite likely.

There were fellows present at the meetings, with some distinguished names amongst them, who made no observations at all. The most vocal of the company was John Wanting, of whom no more is known than that he was a fellow at the time. His complaints ranged from the cost of the warden's apparel and housekeeping to the fact that there were too many horses on the premises, and those of an expensive kind, that accounts and collegiate duties were neglected, and that, perhaps not surprisingly, his own remonstrances were apt to go unheeded. He was recognizably a busy man, though others urged against him that he had detained money paid to him by the bailiff at

[87] See Bott, *Monuments*, pp. 56–7 and Pl. 3. The inscription was recorded by Captain Symonds, a young officer of the Royalist garrison of Oxford in 1643, but had been destroyed by 1659, when Anthony Wood noted that it was missing. The slab may have survived thereafter less from piety than because it was reused for Robert Wood (d. 1686), Anthony's elder brother.

[88] MCR 4249, reproduced in *MM*, pp. 33–6, and printed in *MMC*, pp. 341–7.

Elham, and that he had sold horses there and kept the money. He was also said to have absented himself from meetings, and from attendance at the common table on a feast day when he was sulking.

Amid those exchanges, however, and some pained reflections upon a want of charity between members of the company, there are some more substantial themes, of which the most important was that more fellows should be appointed. It may be that the warden and some of the fellows were deliberately enhancing the common fund, but it may also be that at that time it genuinely seemed wise to do so. A larger number of fellows might have spread communal duties more effectively, but the cost of appointing them might equally have been too high. As the record stands, the matter now seems, like the offending accidents of the chaplain's boots, beyond resolution.

Some other fellows made representations about the library: that it should be more accessible, that some funds had improperly been withheld from it, that its fabric should be repaired. There were also requests, from Ashenden and Dumbleton amongst others, for formal distributions of books, and for the provision of texts of canon law in the library. It is interesting that on the whole those who spoke about the library expressed no opinion on other matters, and that those who inveighed at greater length never mentioned the library. As with some of the other topics canvassed, we cannot be sure that what was said was incontrovertible, but at least the discussions reveal that the college still had a library, that it was not always open when fellows wished it to be, and that it might usefully have had more books in it. Those at least were words which proved to have fallen on fertile ground.

4

The Library in the Fourteenth Century

Iᴛ is natural to think of the library of Merton College as embodied in the western and southern ranges of Mob Quad, where the greater part of the college's books have been housed since the late fourteenth century. At all times, however, there have been library books in other places: the sacristy long accommodated manuscript books as well as some archival material, and a collection of texts and journals known as the Law Library, first assembled in the 1950s on Staircase 4 of Front Quad, in Flixthorpe's house, was subsequently rehoused in a room in the Old Warden's Lodgings. Then there are library books in use or at rest in the rooms of individual Mertonians, on or off the main site, besides others which are simply elsewhere.

The books themselves, whether at home or at large, are only part of the tale. Libraries, ancient and modern, have something organic about them. They are as difficult to define as the people who use them, and the more so, because a book can be both in and out of the library at the same time. A library is at once an accumulation of books, maintained and managed to some end, and the place or places where they are or ought to be found. Since the later Middle Ages any unqualified reference to the library in Merton has invoked Mob Quad, but the old library there was once, indeed twice, the new library, and its contents have a rich and complex history.

In its various manifestations the library is an institution almost as old, if it is not literally as old, as the college itself. The college at Malden needed service books, including psalters and Bibles, from the first moment of its existence, and there may also have been some books in common ownership amongst the scholars housed in Bull Hall, in Pennyfarthing Street. As soon as college services began in St John's church, which is to say from the day on which the officers took possession of the site, the chapel had two locations, and much of its equipment, including its books, would necessarily have been duplicated. Books for teaching were also needed in two or more places, for the *parvuli* were taught under the warden's eye, and the more advanced students gave and received instruction both on and off the premises in Pennyfarthing Street and in St John's Street from their first occupation of either. The warden certainly had books of his own, and Peter Abingdon subsequently gave or bequeathed at least three to the college, the first of many such benefactions from wardens and others. They were one-half of the Psalter with a gloss, or commentary, written in the margins of the text, that is to say, a copy for study rather than a service book; Job and twelve minor prophets, with other texts; and a volume containing the Song of Songs, Lamentations, and the canonical epistles. All the texts were glossed, like the psalms, and were presumably intended for study or teaching. None of them has survived, and the third was noted as lost by the middle of the fourteenth century.[1]

Undergraduate students did not need books of their own because they were taught by lectures, that is to say, by public readings, which were conducted by bachelors and masters from the texts prescribed for their courses. The readings were expositions which incorporated a critical commentary (commonly enshrined in a marginal gloss) upon the substance of the work, and in a community with a capacity for retaining the spoken word prodigiously more powerful than our own, lecture notes were the equipment of the reader rather than of the audience. Nevertheless undergraduates could well have taken notes which at their most elaborate would be indistinguishable from their instructors' glossed texts.[2] They may also occasionally have acquired other books: it would be a matter of taste and means.[3] The instructors, on the other hand, those bachelors who had begun to dispute and read in public, and the regent masters and others who taught, needed texts from which to lecture, together with what other works they could obtain for their own studies. The library, with its expensive works of reference and an expanding stock of texts which could be borrowed, was not the least of Merton's amenities.

It was open to the literate to copy a text at any time, and that was

---

[1] See *MBMC*, p. 95. Abingdon's successor, Richard Worplesdon, gave the college five books, one of which survives as Merton Coll. MS L.3.3.: *BRUO*, p. 2017; and below, p. 84 n. 37.

[2] See further e.g. B. Smalley, *The Study of the Bible in the Middle Ages* (2nd edn., Oxford, 1952), pp. 200–1.

[3] Anthony Bek, who though not a commonplace passman was also not a unique figure in his time, seems to have collected books for their own sake, a weakness which is sometimes manifested in youth: see above, p. 29.

the way in which many, perhaps even most, over the whole spectrum of university studies, were handed down.[4] At the same time, however, there were plenty of books for scholars to buy: university and cathedral towns abounded in scribes, illuminators, and binders. There were also publishers and booksellers, in the sense of those who variously commissioned, supervised, co-ordinated, assembled, and delivered the works of such craftsmen to those who did not choose, for whatsoever reason, to make their own arrangements directly with their suppliers.[5] The work was well organized, and books evidently commanded a ready sale. The more elaborate of them were also quite expensive, and could be expected to keep their value.[6] They seem often to have been bought, or at any rate were owned, by consortia of scholars. Where they had a single owner, they might be the most valuable things that he possessed.[7]

There would therefore have been at least a handful of working texts in the buildings in St John's Street as soon as there were beds and meals to be had there. We cannot say positively that any of them were the college's own books until Archbishop Kilwardby's visitation in 1276, after which they might all have been deemed to be vested in the house.[8] On the other hand, it is most likely that a college as bounteous as Merton provided some working texts for the common use of its members from the beginning. Some such consideration may lie behind Kilwardby's sweeping order that the house was entitled to keep a member's books on the demise of his fellowship.[9]

---

[4] See below, pp. 79 and 152. As the history of Merton's manuscripts shows, the medieval texts which we have today, whether surviving in their original institutions or in other libraries, are only a small selection of the many which were available at the universities and elsewhere. They are also most often the more formal and stately examples of their kind, eventually preserved because they were valuable and beautiful, as well as useful and interesting. There were, as Merton's early catalogues show, many more working texts which were subsequently discarded (see below, pp. 79–86).

[5] See further M. B. Parkes, 'The provision of books', *HUO* ii. 462–6. Some of Merton's circulating texts are described as *pecie*, that is to say professional booksellers' copies: see below, p. 81.

[6] They were frequently pledged to raise loans, in the various chests appointed for the purpose in colleges and the university, and no doubt in other places as well. For Rede's chest at Merton, see below, p. 91. For the university loan chests, see the account by Graham Pollard in *The Register of Convocation, 1448–63*, ed. W. A. Pantin and W. T. Mitchell (OHS n.s. xxii, 1972), pp. 418–20. What seems surprising now is that college texts in the hands of individual fellows were legitimately and quite frequently pawned in that way: *MBMC*, pp. 16–18.

[7] See below, p. 80 n. 24.

[8] See above, pp. 49–50.

[9] See also above, p. 50 n. 13.

It is also possible, however, and even likely, that the archbishop, himself a friar, saw Merton as in that sense a religious house, in which the individual's rights were fittingly subsumed by the common good. His provision that the books so acquired should be used in the first instance to pay the fellow's debts raises several interesting considerations. Merton had no power of probate, and the settlement of debts, which was prescribed for the good of the deceased's soul as well as for the comfort of creditors, was the business of his executors, and a matter in which the college had at the time no standing whatsoever.[10] It seems likely therefore that the books were deemed not to be part of a fellow's estate, and that the house had a vested interest in them, either because it had provided them, or because it might have provided them. It may also be that the debts are to be understood as debts to the college, though even so they should have fallen to the executors to settle.

Kilwardby's further order that the bursars should keep the college's books in a strongbox may therefore have covered some scholarly texts as well as service books, which were often richly ornamented. The oldest of the chests now in the library may well be the box, or one of the boxes, in question, for it seems to date from the earliest years of the foundation.[11] The order implies no very substantial collection, though it recognizes the value of the books, and only a century or so earlier a mere assemblage of nine titles was held to be enough to equip a new Cistercian monastery.[12] The next direct reference to books, however, which comes in 1284, in Archbishop Peckham's injunctions, shows that they already had a place of their own in the college.[13] The three works on grammar which the archbishop prescribed were to be kept chained in the library, and although the suitable table (*mensa honesta*) on which they were to be displayed may have been no more than adequately rugged, it is very likely that it had a lectern top. A chained book needs, or its readers need, a book-rest, and on a desk the chains are most conveniently secured below the reading surface.

If the college heeded the archbishop's precept, we could take the

---

[10] Warden Sever (1456–71) received a commission from Archbishop Bourchier in 1459 to prove wills of persons dying within the college: *BRUO*, p. 1672.

[11] See P. Eames, 'Furniture in England, France, and the Netherlands from the twelfth to the fifteeenth century', *Furniture History*, xiii (1977), 139 and 155.

[12] See J. W. Clark, *The Care of Books* (Cambridge, 1902), p. 72 n. 4. The early Cistercians were not a strenuously intellectual order, but the comparison is interesting.

[13] See above, p. 51.

works of Brito, Papias, and Hugutio to have been the first known titles in the college library. None of the three appears amongst the college manuscripts today, though the names of two of them occur in the medieval records.[14] We need not assume that they were the first of their kind, for the archbishop had the intensive study of grammar particularly in mind, and was prescribing works in which he had confidence. However, they provide a starting-place.

Although college libraries were an absolute novelty in the thirteenth century,[15] there were many established monastic libraries which could provide rules and examples for their management. The western church had grown in authority by cultivating literary skills in an unlettered world, and as Walter de Merton realized, the more elaborately and successfully it was organized the more important the written word became. Literacy was nurtured first to instruct the clergy, and then to enable them to apply their learning to the needs and in the service of lay society. By the time the universities emerged, in the course of the twelfth century, the monasteries were past their heroic age of learning, but large and small they had their libraries, and they maintained the principle that their members should study to the best of their ability. An annual distribution of books to that end was an established feature of monastic life, though the common provision that a monk might keep a text for a year suggests that the religious were not all voracious or demanding readers. Academic colleges came to follow a broadly similar pattern, but more intensively. Some of their consequent problems are still familiar.

Kilwardby's and Peckham's injunctions give us small but welcome clues to the early existence and nature of the books which the college possessed, but after that time we have for several centuries no explicit account of the library as an institution, and relatively little, by the generous standards of the rest of the college's muniments, on the ownership, availability, and use of books. We have, however, some incidental documents and references, which are sparse at first, but later become more numerous; and there are also, happily, a respectable

---

[14] See *MBMC*, p. 125 and n. (Brito and Hugutio); p. 188 and n. (Brito).

[15] And, *a fortiori*, university libraries too. The university of Oxford had no premises of its own until 1320, when the convocation house was built in the north-eastern angle of St Mary's church. The chamber above it was subsequently used to house such books as the university acquired before the building of Duke Humfrey's library in the middle of the 15th cent. The hall below, in its time the scene of some elevating and much peevish debate, has been an exemplary tea-room since 1987.

number of the books themselves.[16] The resulting archive, extending from the late thirteenth century to the eve of the Reformation, is unsurpassed in either university, and of prime importance for the intellectual history of that period in England.

Today some 320 codices, bound manuscripts, survive from the very much larger collection which the college accumulated in the Middle Ages. Of those, seven remain from the hundred or more which were acquired during the first half-century of the college's existence, and twenty-five others survive from the 235 manuscripts which we know to have been added to the holdings by the middle of the fourteenth century.[17] The rest were accumulated between the later fourteenth century and the early years of the sixteenth.

In all we can name more than 1,200 manuscripts which belonged to the medieval college, and there were undoubtedly others which have left no distinct trace. The bald number of volumes also hides a very much longer list of texts, or as we might say titles, because it was a common practice, for various reasons, to bind separate and often quite disparate works between the same covers.[18] Although the survivors include some handsomely written and decorated texts, they represent for the most part a working collection of books which were used for teaching and research, some of them copied by the fellows themselves.

It emerges that Merton followed the practice established in monastic libraries, and also found at the Sorbonne and elsewhere, of keeping some books chained in the library, where they could be consulted by anyone qualified to use them, whilst a substantially larger collection of texts circulated amongst the fellows. The college called the annual distribution of the circulating books an *electio*, an election or choosing, and in the fourteenth century we have two records of such elections from the 1370s, as well as some incidental references to the practice. The earliest document relating to the library is, however, a catalogue or inventory.[19]

---

[16] The best account of the medieval college library is in *MBMC* which, as Powicke scrupulously says, is not a history of the library. It is none the less a learned and discriminating survey of such books as we know were available to members of the college before the age of print.

[17] See the account in *MBMC*, pp. 8–9.

[18] See e.g. the eight texts assembled within the boards of Merton MS E.1.3, some of which were written in the 13th and the rest in the 14th cent., and all bound or rebound in the 17th cent. (*MBMC*, p. 150; and Coxe 267. All citations from Coxe are of numbered items, unless distinguished as page references).

[19] See Merton MS F.1.1., partly reproduced in *MM*, p. 44, and printed in full in *MBMC*, pp. 47–51.

The list headed *Libri philosophie de aula de Merton*, 'The philosophy books of Merton Hall',[20] contains eighty-five titles arranged in three categories: Philosophy, Mathematics, and Grammar. Though full of interest it is not, at first sight, an elegant document, for the college was not given to wasting expensive parchment and calligraphic flourishes on administrative memoranda.[21] Its heading is truthful but not perfectly informative. It seems to be an inventory rather than a finding-list, in the sense that the books are not arranged in any obvious order within the various categories, though it may be that whether or not they were kept in the library they are to some extent listed as they were stored, in chests or boxes.[22] The list was originally written out in the 1320s, and has some additional notes on gifts and legacies of books which were made in the following decade.[23]

Each entry gives a summary title of a work, or of the principal contents of a codex, and its price. The prices vary between £1. 4s. and a few pence.[24] There is also a note of the opening words of the text on the second folio of each volume, a reliable and widely used means of identifying a manuscript, as the vagaries of copying by hand meant that the arrangement of a particular text was almost invariably unique.[25] The provenance of the book is frequently noted, giving us in all the names of eight donors, and that many clues to the growth of the collection. It is an interesting feature of the list that the thirty benefactions, whether gifts or legacies, are priced like the other entries, which suggests that some at least of the prices are valuations.

[20] See above, p. 57 n. 34.

[21] See e.g. the other library list, below, p. 82, and more particularly the records of the scrutinies, above, p. 72. Even the *Liber ruber*, above, p. 68, which uses coloured initials to differentiate the entries, is business-like rather than ornate. On the other hand, the bursar did provide extra parchment after the warden had expressed dissatisfaction with the condition or appearance of some document in 1288, and patiently noted the fact in his accounts: *ERMC*, p. 220.

[22] See the notes on order, below, p. 82.

[23] The additions are probably to be dated to 1338 or 1339 by the inclusion of Stephen Gravesend, bishop of London (1318–38), the last of the donors named, who died in April 1338 and left eleven books to the college: *BRUO*, pp. 805–6; *MBMC*, p. 51.

[24] The most expensive book in the main list is a commentary on the Physics, written on vellum, and priced at £1. 4s. It was bequeathed to the college by Mr William Burnell, the incumbent of many canonries and a substantial benefactor of Balliol College, who has no other known connection with Merton. The later bequests include a Physics and other texts from Mr William Wood (or Boys), a former fellow, and chancellor of the university in 1308–9, which cost £1. 6s. 8d., the value of five weeks' commons (*MBMC*, pp. 48, 50).

[25] As in the two copies of the chronicle of Martinus Polonus noted in the theological catalogue, below, p. 82, which are distinguished one from the other only by the opening words of the second folio. The phrase in question was also known as the *dictio probatoria*.

The list is therefore the work of someone concerned with the nature and the value of the books, and probably also with their condition, for there is a note that one quire was missing from a copy of Aristotle's *De anima* (price 20*d*.), and another that it had been found. A text of Priscian's *De constructionibus*, among the grammatical books, is also said to be defective, the last part being missing or damaged. Eighteen of the works listed are said to comprise single volumes: for example, 'The Old Logic with the New, in one volume, of the gift of Master John Martyn'.[26] However, the references to the second folio are given for every title, but never to the second folio of a second or subsequent volume. It seems too that many of the other works are quite small, so the purpose of the distinction is not clear. In a similar fashion the bindings of some volumes are described summarily ('in bare boards', or 'covered in red'), whilst a few others are noted as being in quires, that is to say, apparently, sewn but not bound, and two of the mathematical books are described as 'in pieces', which were not fragments but the standard unbound parts of works supplied by professional booksellers.[27]

The list therefore appears to be the work of an officer responsible for the college's books. It might be too much to speak of a librarian, for the care of the books was spread between the sub-warden and the bursars, but as the catalogue is a record of numbers, value, and condition, and to that extent an administrative document, it is most probably the sub-warden's work.[28] It is, however, also thematic, and so academic. The titles which it contains are those of works required for the arts course, namely the writings of Aristotle and his commentators, beginning under Philosophy with a commentary by Averroes on the Physics and *Parva naturalia*, and ending with the books of the Politics.

The mathematical books include Euclid and Archimedes, and texts by Arabic mathematicians and astronomers. Amongst them is the Arithmetic (known as *Algorismus*) of al-Khwarizmi, through whose work, together with the Islamic astronomical tables, the Hindu-Arabic numerals were disseminated in the west. There are also several planetary tables and, besides various treatises on the use of the astrolabe,

---

[26] John Martyn was a fellow in 1295, and became rector of Broad Hinton, Wilts., in 1299: *BRUO*, p. 1235.

[27] See above, p. 76 n. 4.

[28] See further H. W. Garrod, 'The library regulations of a medieval college', *Trans. Bibliographical Soc.* n.s. viii (1927–8), 312–35, at p. 329. Later indentures for books show that at least from the time of Henry Abingdon (1421–37) there were some books permanently in the warden's keeping.

two astrolabes in leather cases. The grammatical works amount only to some six titles, three of them Priscian, in four volumes. One of those, Priscian's *De constructionibus*, and a collection of *Questiones* on logic and metaphysics bequeathed by John Sandwich, whose legacy is recorded at the end of the list, and who probably died *c.* 1330, are the only survivors today from among the eighty.[29]

The whole constitutes a useful, conservative but still reasonably up-to-date armoury for those teaching and studying the liberal arts. It is not, however, a large collection, given a company of up to fifty fellows. The fact that many of the items are quite modestly priced, and some unbound, makes it seem likely that it represents part of the college's circulating library rather than its static collection. If so, then it may imply the existence of some other record of the actual distribution of texts, such as we have from the end of the century. It also suggests, as we might suppose, that the losses of the early arts texts were even more extensive than those which we can trace. It is interesting that amongst the complaints about books which were registered at the college scrutinies was one that philosophical works were taken and kept out of circulation by those who were not engaged in teaching Aristotle's physics.[30] It may only have been a mark of inconsiderate behaviour, which can break out at any time, but it might also be a sign of some pressure on the collection.

The uncertainty about the status of the books in the philosophy list does not attach to the books named in the second surviving inventory, which is known as the theological catalogue.[31] The document has no general heading, but its 250 entries are arranged in an order common in systematic lists of theological texts, though in the larger categories it does not consistently separate the books of the Old and the New Testament, or present the Evangelists in their conventional scriptural order.

The list begins with biblical and ecclesiastical histories, including the *Historia scholastica* of Peter Comestor. It then proceeds through *postille*, which are intensive commentaries upon books and parts of

[29] They are Merton MSS H.3.9 and K.1.6 (Coxe 309 and 296). The *Questiones* were said in the 14th cent. to be in 17 quires sewn without boards, but they are now in a 17th-cent. binding. For Sandwich, a fellow in the early 1320s, see *BRUO* iii. 1639.

[30] See above, p. 73.

[31] Merton MS F.1.2. It was for some time in the Bodleian library, as MS Oxford Roll 25, and was restored to the college in 1927. The text is printed in *MBMC*, pp. 52–60.

the Bible,[32] and through standard glosses on the Bible, to the Sentences of Peter Lombard, the mainstay of all theological courses, and to other commentaries and patristic texts. Like the philosophical catalogue it gives the prices of books, and notes the *dictiones probatorie*. It also pursues the provenance of books more consistently than the earlier list, including notes that some had been bought rather than given or bequeathed: eleven in all, against 184 donations. It takes no particular account of the physical condition of the books, or the manner of their binding, beyond noting that one text was imperfect,[33] and that two of the *postille* were in quires and another unbound.[34] It does, however, record that thirty-one of the 250 manuscripts listed were kept in the library.

The theology catalogue therefore offers us a conspectus of the books available in the college for what would probably now be called research: they are the texts which sustained the higher studies which the founder most wished his beneficiaries to undertake. It also distinguishes those books, the minority, which remained in the library, from the collection of more than two hundred which, not being so confined, could be circulated amongst the fellows. That other assemblage of texts was, as most members of the college at that time understood the matter, Merton's working library. At any moment some of the fellows would have books of their own, some of which would come in due course to the common chests, or more rarely, to be chained to the library desks, but most depended for teaching and probably for some part of their own studies on the texts which the *electiones* made available year by year.

The study of theology was normally open only to those who had already qualified as masters of arts. It began with an intensive study of the Bible in the Vulgate text, the words of which were long familiar from daily usage, but which had now to be examined as a whole in the context of universal history and the history of the church in particular. The historical section of Merton's library included a small holding of chronicles, one of which was the widely admired and much copied Polychronicon of Ranulf Higden of Chester, present

---

[32] The word seems to derive from the tag *post illa verba*: 'after those words', originally signalling the presence of a gloss in the text. See further Smalley (above, n. 2), pp. 270–1; and also below, p. 84 n.

[33] A copy of Bartholomeus Anglicus, *De proprietatibus rerum*, MBMC, p. 60, no. 247.

[34] *non ligate*. If that were to be read as not chained, it would raise difficult questions about the disposition of many of the other titles. It can, however, be taken as meaning that the quires were stitched together without boards.

there because it began with the Creation and worked towards a history of England through the ages of mankind.[35] Particular books of the Bible were studied with the aid of the intensive commentaries in the *postille*, of which the catalogue contains eighteen on the Old Testament and nine, with another noted as missing, on the New. The same apparatus could be used in conjunction with the universal chronicle for the broadest studies of God's purpose.[36]

The unifying themes of the discipline came mainly from the study and exposition of the *Sentencie* of Peter the Lombard, a pupil of Abelard, who became bishop of Paris and died there in 1160. The Sentences, which nourished theological studies until the Reformation and beyond, were a monument of the dialectical theology which characterized the nascent university of Paris in the twelfth century. The catalogue contains fifteen copies of the work, all apparently in circulation, though it seems unlikely that there would not have been some other or others in the library. Peter's text set out to resolve scriptural conflicts and the *cruces* of the faith by assembling Biblical and patristic texts on contentious points, and arguing out the issues that arose from them. Every aspirant theologian had first to assimilate the Sentences, and subsequently to expound them. They became themselves the subject of many expert commentaries, which extended from those of St Thomas Aquinas, of which there are fourteen in the list, to more recent works by John Duns Scotus and William Ockham.[37] The catalogue includes five copies of Duns Scotus's commentaries on

[35] On the Polychronicon, see J. Taylor, *The Universal Chronicle of Ranulf Higden* (Oxford, 1966). The copy in the theology catalogue, which was subsequently lost, had belonged to Thomas Buckingham, the logician and theologian (see above, p. 61). The college's present copy of the Polychronicon (Merton MS L.3.2 (Coxe 121)) is an early 15th-cent. version, brought up to date by continuations in other hands, which came to the college from John Wood, fellow, and archdeacon of Middlesex, who died in 1475: see further *MBMC*, p. 209 and n.

[36] Dr J. G. Clark has suggested to me that there was probably some connection between the popularity of the Polychronicon amongst theologians in the 14th cent. and the concurrent spread of the compendious Postille of Nicholas de Lyra, and that together they lent themselves notably well to the literal and historical study of scripture. On the MSS of Nicholas de Lyra, see N. R. Ker, *Fragments of Medieval Manuscripts used as Pastedowns in Oxford Bindings, with a Survey of Oxford Binding, c. 1515–1620*, Oxford Bibliographical Society Publications, n.s. v (Oxford, 1954).

[37] Two volumes of St Bonaventure's commentaries, one on the second, and one on the third and fourth books of the Sentences, were amongst the books left to the college by the second warden, Richard of Worplesdon. Bonaventure (1221–74), who was known as the Seraphic teacher, held the Franciscan chair of theology in Paris when Aquinas held the Dominican. Both of his titles are marked in the catalogue as 'in the library', and both are in the college today (Merton MSS L.2.8 and L.3.3 (Coxe 115–16)).

the Sentences, but none of Ockham's. If Ockham's works were current in Merton, and no doubt they were, they would seem to have been then in the hands of individuals. The college's own copies apparently came in at a later date.

The preponderant authority invoked by the Sentences themselves was St Augustine, and for a different reason he also dominates the college's theological collection. There are forty-nine copies of Augustine's works in the list, including nine of *De civitate Dei*, and seven of his commentary upon the book of Genesis. His imposing presence most probably reflects the influence of Bradwardine's theological studies, and especially the discussions of predestination and of the nature of God's foreknowledge of events which exercised both Bradwardine and his followers, and those who, like Buckingham, challenged their views. At the heart of its wide interests Merton was, in one sense at least, an Augustinian college.

Though Merton was still resonating to the theological debates of the 1320s and 30s, however, there are few echoes in the surviving lists of the advanced mathematical work which had distinguished the college in that same period. The mathematical titles in the philosophical list presumably served for ordinary curricular purposes, but more serious work could hardly have been supported on the meagre fare of the *libri mathematicales* listed there. If there were more substantial holdings in the library or elsewhere in the college at that time no record of them has survived. Yet despite the comparative scarcity of such texts Merton would have been a likely place in which to find them. The entire disappearance of Bradwardine's books is a regrettable loss, but William Rede's bequests and gifts show what a single-minded scholar could assemble only a little later. There were, however, lesser men, and probably some other high fliers, who would have had to look to the library itself if they could not depend upon the elections to sustain their work.

The lists could therefore well be misleading if they were taken at their face value. They cover two important categories of books, but they may not be complete in themselves, and they reflect other categories only incidentally. Medicine and canon law flourished in Merton despite Archbishop Peckham's admonitions, and they did not flourish without texts. Classical literary works are also underrepresented, and were probably to be sought amongst the volumes secured in the library or those which individual fellows owned. In either instance we have only accidental references to them, though they show William Rede collecting Cicero's works,[38] and in the fifteenth century Thomas Bloxham's books included Pierre Bersuire's *Ovidius moralizatus* and extracts from Boccaccio's *De Genealogia Deorum libri X V.*[39] The library benefited greatly over the centuries from both large and small bequests, but several shelffuls of books probably went astray between probate and the library door.

The conclusions to be drawn from the catalogues are plainly conditioned by the nature of the documents themselves. On the face of things the two lists are complementary, and might be taken as successive instalments of a systematic catalogue. On that view the differences between them could be explained as marking the effects of experience in their compilation, even though they are separated one from another by a quarter of a century. The theological is certainly tidier and more effectively systematic than the philosophical list, and it might be supposed that the notes on bindings came to be seen as matters of less consequence than the questions of value and provenance. On the other hand it is remarkable that the earlier list makes no distinction between the circulating and the static collections, and difficult to suppose that it is other than a list of the circulating books. That in turn raises the question of what there may have been in the way of any such works chained in the library. There are also the other categories of books, such as literary texts, which may not have been in general demand, but were none the less significant. It is worth noting, in passing, that there is no reference in either list to particular titles being in the hands of individuals at the time of compilation.

As things stand therefore we cannot be sure even that all the philosophical books were in circulation in the 1320s and 30s, though we know from the records of scrutinies that there were elections of books, and that not everyone was satisfied with the results. Equally we cannot tell whether the same rules and practices applied in the 1350s as in earlier decades, though we can draw a line at that time between the static and the circulating library. The first election of which we have any precise knowledge is that held in 1372, when eighteen fellows, who cannot all be positively identified, received 133 books between them. On that occasion Master Walter Stanton, whose allocation of twenty-four books was already the largest on the list,

---

[38] See *MBMC*, nos. 550, 565.
[39] See *MBMC*, pp. 210–12.

received an additional three books, valuable works on medicine, from the recent bequest of Simon Bredon.[40] That new resource was also a mark of impending change.

Simon Bredon, a Gloucestershire man, and William Rede, who came from the diocese of Exeter, were together in Merton during the 1340s, and remained friends throughout their careers. There was probably a difference of a decade or more in their ages: the first reference to Rede occurs only in 1344, and Bredon had been a fellow since 1330. There is no evidence that either was a gremial Mertonian, but equally it does not appear that either was connected with any other college before they came to their fellowships. However, as a Devonian Rede most probably started his career at Stapledon Hall, to which he subsequently gave £20 for work on the library, and twenty-five books.[41]

Bredon, who wrote on the Ethics and on mathematical problems, studied medicine in the 1350s and took an MD before 1355. He was engaged in a public career by 1356, when he enjoyed the patronage of Simon Islip, Bradwardine's successor as archbishop of Canterbury, and held several livings in Kent. He died a prebendary of Chichester in 1372. Rede, who proceeded to a DD in or before 1362, was archdeacon of Rochester from 1359, and became bishop of Chichester by papal provision in 1368. Both men were active in astronomical studies and other branches of mathematics, as well as being busy administrators, and both were collectors and benefactors.

Bredon left books to Balliol, Oriel, Queen's, and to University College, but his principal bequest was of twenty-four manuscripts to Merton, besides an astrolabe, and a large mazer cup to cheer the company. The manuscripts include a fine copy of Avicenna's Canon of Medicine, and three other major medical texts, which are still in the college.[42] At least one other of Bredon's books came into the

---

[40] On the election, see N. R Ker, 'Books of philosophy distributed at Merton' in *Books, Collectors, and Libraries*, ed. A. G. Watson, pp. 331–78. Bredon, who died in 1372, was one of the fellows who pressed for an election of books in 1338: *MMC*, p. 343; on his career and bequests, see *BRUO*, pp. 257–8, and below, n. 41. Stanton retired to St John's Hospital, Basingstoke, in 1386 with an incurable illness. He bequeathed to the college a number of medical works which are now in the British Library: *BRUO*, p. 1770.

[41] See *BRUO*, p. 1559.

[42] The Avicenna is now Merton MSS N.3.9 (Coxe 224). The others are the Pantegni of Ali ben al-Abbas, translated by Constantinus Africanus, H.3.5 (Coxe 231); the Passionarium of Gariopontus of Salerno, C.2.1 (1) (Coxe 250 (1)); and the Compendium Medicinae of Gilbert, or Gilbertus Anglicus, MS N.3.9 (Coxe 226). See further *MBMC*, pp. 84 and 138–41.

library subsequently,[43] and he may well have made other gifts during his lifetime.

It seems that by the time Bredon died the college had resolved to build a new library, and from the support which Bishop Rede immediately gave to the project it is very likely that the matter had been under discussion, between the warden and fellows and the two friends, for some time. We do not know where the library had previously been housed. It was a locked room, and it had leaded, and therefore glazed windows, though we do not know how many there were. Its walls were plastered in 1346–7, perhaps in belated response to some of the complaints raised in the scrutinies nine years before,[44] and in 1350 it was equipped or refurnished with reading desks, probably with lectern tops, and benches. A further and interesting gesture to amenity was made by the provision of rush matting in 1353–4.[45]

When the bursars were first charged with the safe-keeping of the college books there was no treasury, and valuables were probably kept either in the warden's house or in the undercroft of the hall. There was still no treasury in Peckham's time, when a library was first mentioned, but the chained books could have been moved from one place to another over the years. The library of the 1350s may have been quite small, but it was evidently something more than a store room. It is difficult to see where it could have stood unless it was already on the south side of what is now Mob Quad, the north and east wings of which, except for the treasury, seem always to have been intended for domestic accommodation.[46]

Whether or not the ground was partially occupied, Mob was an obvious site for a new building, and by 1370 the college had formally engaged a master mason, William Humberville, who was already supplying stone from his own quarries in Taynton for the project.[47] The clerk of the works was John Bloxham, then fellow and bursar, who became warden in 1375 (Pl. 8). Bloxham took Humberville to

---

[43] Peter Quesnel, *Directorium juris*, Merton MS N.3.6 (Coxe 223).

[44] The lead time for urgent work in academic libraries may be a constant.

[45] See further J. R. L. Highfield, 'The early colleges', *HUO* i. 257.

[46] There are differences in the stonework of the upper and lower storeys of the library wings, which raise the possibility that there was something on the site before the library was built. However, the vaulted passage through the west wing which gives access to the church is of a piece with the structure of the library above, and if there was anything substantial on the site before the 1370s it was more probably on the south side of the quadrangle.

[47] See E. A. Gee, 'Oxford masons, 1370–1530', *Archaeological Journal*, cix (1952), 54–131, at p. 61.

consult with Bishop Rede, and they also rode together to examine the library of the Dominicans' house in London, probably then the best-equipped centre of theological studies outside the universities.[48] Bloxham subsequently travelled to Salisbury, Sherborne, and Winchester, almost certainly to inspect libraries, though no such work of the late fourteenth century survives in those places today. It is likely that though both the patron and the clerk of the works had opinions to express, the design of the building was Humberville's responsibility.[49] It seems from the contract for stone that the broad outline of the plan, and the location of the library on the first floor, had been determined early, though the internal arrangements of the building, and therefore probably the details of its fenestration, were reviewed while the work was in hand.

The present shell of the western and southern wings of the quad is substantially as the builders left it in the 1380s. The principal changes are that the dormer windows were added early in the seventeenth century, when the south wing was extended to take in some small chambers which stood at the south-eastern corner of the quad. The bay window there was added at the same time.[50] Almost all the external cut stone has been restored, but enough detail remains to demonstrate the original design. The library occupied the first floor of the two wings, and was lit, as it still is, by single lancet windows in both wings, in both the interior and exterior walls of each of seven bays, and by two two-light windows in the square vestibule where the wings meet at the south-western corner. In their present form those windows seem to be of fifteenth-century date, and to have replaced the 'great window' in the south wall and the 'two great windows' to which the accounts refer in 1378 and 1390.

The relatively small size and the disposition of the side windows suggest that each wing of the library had a central aisle, and that when the work was complete each was equipped with either twelve or fourteen desks. The under-framing of the present shelving, and the heavy oak planks which serve as benches between the presses, or at least those in the west wing, are probably part of the original fittings.[51]

---

[48] In 1382 Bloxham attended the council convened at Blackfriars by Archbishop Courtenay to condemn the teachings of John Wyclif: see below, p. 109.

[49] See E. A. Gee's comment on the design of the window in the southern gable, in 'Oxford masons', p. 61.

[50] See further below, p. 199.

[51] See the observations in B. H. Streeter, *The Chained Library: A Survey of Four Centuries in the Evolution of the English Library* (London, 1931), pp. 127–49, esp. p. 136.

It seems likely too that the wood of the original lectern tops was reused for the present desks when the sixteenth-century presses were installed.

The first phase of the building-work lasted through the 1370s, with a master carpenter, Robert Bath, engaged from the outset, and a number of other craftsmen and labourers coming and going under his charge.[52] The carpenters supplied the masons with tables for drawing templates to cut freestone or ashlar, the dressed stone which was used for detailed work and for some of the facing. They also made a windlass, in 1377–8, and the centring for a vault in the following year,[53] as well as roofing and furnishing the building. Bath supplied a considerable quantity of timber in 1379, when he was installing the first desks. The fifty-five planks bought then were presumably used for the desk-tops and shelves, and perhaps for the seats, and if so some of them have been reused, and survive. Other timber was supplied for ground-sills, which were the footings into which the desks and benches were framed.

It seems that the west wing was furnished first, with a lectern-topped reading desk in each bay, and the oak benches, which later and more effete generations have found hard sitting, framed in between them in much the same way as they are at present. The lecterns would have had rods or hasps for the chains which secured the books, and the survival of horn-covered labels on the boards of some of the books shows that they were normally kept flat on the desk tops, though others may have stood on shelves underneath. Forty-eight chains were bought and fitted to the desks in 1387.

Like the present presses which replaced them, the original lecterns were comparatively narrow, and any shelves provided underneath them would have been quite small. Even with the full complement of desks in either wing it would seem that only the most frequently used books in the collection could have been kept on the shelves. Chains not only ensured the safety of the books in the library, but meant that they could only be consulted where they were housed. Nevertheless the provision of some fifty places in the library was a generous allowance for a fellowship of that number, for those wishing or needing to read there were unlikely ever to attend in droves.

---

[52] See E. A. Gee, 'Oxford carpenters, 1370–1630', *Oxoniensia*, xvii–xviii (1953), 120–1.

[53] See Gee, 'Oxford masons', pp. 55 and 57. The centring was probably to build the vaulted passage leading through to the south door of the church from the north-west corner of the quad. See above, p. 88 n. 46.

Access to the library was probably always from the doorway which stands in the south wing by the angle of Mob Quad. The door which opens into the lobby there came to the library from the house of Carmelite friars at Beaumont, a friendly gesture at a time when relations between the secular masters and the mendicant orders were often uneasy. The first staircase was probably a temporary one, reset or replaced in 1390. There is an unconformity about the present wooden stairs and the stone steps on which they rest that suggests that there may have been more than one change there since the building was opened.

Work on the library was powerfully assisted by a donation of £100 which William Rede made to the college, together with a gift of one hundred books, in 1374. The money was received by John Bloxham in London in October of that year,[54] when the bishop also made gifts to Exeter and Queen's. The books were accompanied by a number of mathematical instruments and a map, as well as a silver-gilt chalice. Rede's last service to the college was the bequest of a further £100 to fund a loan chest, in which fellows could pledge their own, and on some occasions the library's books.[55]

Rede died in 1385, having seen the new building in commission. Its furnishing was continued or resumed in the 1390s. Walter Ramsbury, DD, a fellow and former bursar of Merton and canon of Hereford, then gave £10 for desks in the library and ten marks for stalls in the choir of the church. He also gave the library two substantial volumes of homilies, and a commentary on the Sentences by Robert Cowton, OFM. A carpenter called John was employed on the library staircase and a screen in 1390–1, having previously worked on some of the windows.[56] Either then or shortly afterwards the windows were filled with painted glass, the remnants of which are now reset in the west wing.

The planning and building of the library ran parallel, and perhaps not wholly coincidentally, with the planning and establishment of William of Wykeham's New College. The effect of William Rede's munificence, following upon Bredon's generosity, was to give Merton a library which could stand comparison, both in its fittings and its

---

[54] See H. W. Garrod and J. R. L. Highfield, 'An indenture between William Rede, bishop of Chichester, and John Bloxham and H. Stapilton, fellows of Merton College, Oxford, London, 22 October 1374', *BLR* x (1978–82), 9–19.

[55] See e.g. the transactions of Mr Thomas Gauge in 1450: *MBMC*, p. 17.

[56] Gee, 'Oxford carpenters', p. 160.

contents, with Wykeham's provisions. New College was the first college in which a library was a feature of the original plan, though in that as in other respects it had the example of Merton before it. For its own part, Merton had gained a well-contrived building, and had added the larger part of the working libraries of two distinguished scholars to the holdings which it had accumulated over the past century. It had no immediate need, at least as a home of learning, to look apprehensively at any of its new congeners in the university.

5

Wyclif, Rede, and Wyliot

BRADWARDINE was probably the most distinguished victim of the first outbreak of the plague in England, but in the history of the college and the university his death might be seen rather as a symbolic than as a climactic event. He had been involved in diplomacy and other public affairs for some ten years. Though his academic voice remained influential, his austerely prescriptive theology showed in the 1340s little of the boldness and subtle vigour that characterized his thought during his earlier years in Merton. It may be that his striking mathematical talent had simply burned itself out after 1330, but wheresoever his theological work might have led him, his appointment as archbishop obviously committed him deeply to the administrative affairs of the church, as well as to the duties of one of the king's principal counsellors. As primate he would no doubt have concerned himself with the university, just as he had maintained his affection for and his connections with Merton, but his influence there both in practical matters and in scholarship might not have been very different from that of his successor Simon Islip.

Of Bradwardine's closest contemporaries Segrave also died in the summer of 1349, but Buckingham remained chancellor of Exeter Cathedral, and Ashenden was still working in Merton in 1355. There were also others, from the successive generations of younger scholars, Billingham and Rede amongst them, who were developing new themes in logic, mathematics, astronomy, and theology. Scholarship of the kind that the founder had envisaged, as well as of other kinds which he had not, continued to distinguish the college. Nevertheless Bradwardine's remained a commanding figure, and a measure disadvantageous to the general run of men.

It is difficult to determine the direct effect of the plague upon either the university or particular colleges. The average of the number of fellows known to have been at Merton, which may have reached a peak above fifty in the 1330s, and seems to have fallen to between

forty and fifty in the decade before the plague, then declined by
almost one half. It did not reach the level of the 1340s again until the
last years of the century.[1] The details cannot be pressed into certainties,
for the documents are not continuous and all their references to
individuals are incidental, but it is reasonable to assume that overall
numbers were reduced quite sharply.

Over that time, until the establishment of New College in 1379,
Merton was still the largest and best found of the colleges in Oxford,
but its condition seems in a measure to reflect the condition of the
university as a whole. We know even less about the total numbers of
masters and students in residence than we do about the individual
colleges, for much the same reasons. It does, however, appear that
there was strong pressure on accommodation in the first decades of
the century, and that it was relaxed even before the plague and was
not felt again. In the later fourteenth and the fifteenth century the
university was probably smaller than it had been in Edward II's reign,
and if it did not absolutely decline in numbers it had at least ceased
to grow.[2] Yet it was better provided than it had been: the university
itself had acquired accommodation and institutions of its own, and
there were more places in colleges for the talented and fortunate.
There seem to have been fewer halls, but that was partly a result of
amalgamations. The halls which remained after the shocks of the
plague were generally larger, better provided, and perhaps better
administered.[3] One of them was St Alban Hall, which maintained a
precarious independence under Merton's increasingly close scrutiny.[4]

The university was a privileged community, and that not only in a
juridical sense.[5] The plague inflicted heavy casualties on the clergy as
a whole,[6] but various factors, including the mechanism of infection

---

[1] See T. Evans and R. Faith, 'The number, origins, and careers of scholars', *HUO* ii. 492–
4 and nn. The vigesimal totals for 1340, 1360, and 1380 are 170, 136, and 174 respectively,
falling to 150 by 1400.

[2] Something similar could be said of the city as a whole: J. I. Catto, 'Citizens, scholars,
and masters', *HUO* i. 159 and nn.

[3] See further ibid. 178–80.

[4] The early history of St Alban Hall (and some of the later) is, however, largely a matter
of inference. See below, p. 194.

[5] See further C. H. Lawrence, 'The university in state and church', *HUO* i. 132–3 and nn.

[6] The common assertion that one-third or more of the population died of the plague
itself is a simple exaggeration, though the cumulative effects of plague, other epidemics,
and social dislocation may have tended to such a proportion. The parish clergy were
exposed to infection, and probably suffered more than other groups: see e.g. A. H.
Thompson, 'The registers of John Gynewell, bishop of Lincoln, for the years 1347–50',
Archaeological Journal, lxviii (1911), 301–60.

and perhaps levels of nutrition, worked to lighten its incidence amongst the upper classes, including the higher clergy.[7] Despite Bradwardine's death, which came immediately upon his return from Avignon and has, so to speak, every appearance of an accident, casualties were light amongst the bishops and prebendaries, who had, like fellows of Merton, country estates to which they could withdraw. Students at large in the universities might have only modest means, but they were free to move, and dispersal was the first and most natural defence against infection. The university was not as vulnerable as it might seem, and it was neither paralysed by the plague, nor stagnant in the years that followed. There were deaths in colleges and halls, but no perceptible break in academic or other administration. There was a contest over the chancellorship which was followed by a riot at St Mary's in the spring of 1349, when the plague was spreading out of London and even dedicated committee-men might have been expected to have other things on their minds.[8]

Destructive and horrifying as the epidemic was, one of its effects was, paradoxically, to widen professional responsibilities, and to intensify demand for the skills which the clergy deployed. It may have been difficult to discern and recruit new talent, but the university was committed to the business of training, and there were more rather than fewer opportunities of employment for graduates, both in church and state. At the same time there was also much vocal disappointment over their rewards. Faced with a shortage of labour the royal administration not unnaturally chose to restrict wages by the sanguine expedient of fixing them at the levels believed to have obtained before the plague. There were penalties for both employers and employees who broke the law, but at the cost of much discontent and some misery the law was proved unenforceable. In the mean time similar efforts were made to control the stipends of the lower clergy, with no greater success.[9]

Those large social movements had their effects on academic life, but the processes were indirect and slow. The university's relations with the city of Oxford were neither worse nor better than they had been. In the rioting that began on St Scholastica's day, 10 February

---

[7] The disease was spread by rat fleas transferring to human hosts. On the process of infection see J. F. D. Shrewsbury, *A History of Bubonic Plague in the British Isles* (Cambridge, 1971), pp. 17–36.

[8] See below, p. 97.

[9] See further *Knighton's Chronicle*, pp. 102, 103 n.; and below, p. 105.

1355, when sixty members of the university were reckoned killed, Mertonians were safe behind their walls, unless any of them went out to look for a fight. Trouble of a less dramatic kind was endemic, but there was generally more harmony than strife between the parties. St Scholastica was something of a surprise to both sides. Several students were killed, and probably some halls were sacked. Either side graphically described the origin and progress of the mayhem as the exclusive and wilful act of the other. The university, supported by the king, took an extensive revenge upon the town, but the occasion was more remarkable for the long-lived penance which was imposed upon the city than for the damage suffered on either side.[10] In the absence of other developments the city had really no choice but to live on the university, and therefore to do so upon the university's own terms.[11]

The university had its own copious springs of dissension, in addition to the differences of opinion which sometimes arose on academic issues. One deeply rooted was the tribal strife between northerners and southerners, which in Oxford took the place of the hostilities between the groups designated nations at Paris and elsewhere.[12] Merton is commonly though erroneously regarded as a southern college. The division of the kingdom thus expressed was a matter of subtle administrative and ecclesiastical geography rather than simple regional affiliations, but it is permanently commemorated in the office of the university's two proctors, who until the later sixteenth century were rigorously appointed to represent one the rugged and virtuous pastoralists of the North (including Lincolnshire), and the other the effete cereal-growers, pluralists, and usurers of the South.[13] The groups concerned manifestly adjusted

---

[10] The university exacted a formal annual penance from the citizens until 1825, by which time it had long since ceased to pray for the souls of the slain, and indeed for any other souls, though it had no difficulty in taking the money. See *HUO* i. 166–7; and R. Fasnacht, *A History of the City of Oxford* (Oxford, 1954), pp. 65–70. In recent years there has been an interesting decline in the significance attached to the episode and its aftermath, which in the late 20th cent. has come to seem embarrassing to both city and university.

[11] C. H. Lawrence, 'The university in state and church', *HUO* i. 133–40. The importance of St Scholastica to the university was that it enabled it to close its grip upon the city's markets and retail trade.

[12] As it still does, in a much attenuated form, and when there is nothing better to do: see below, pp. 364–5. For the medieval 'nations', see P. Kibre, *The Nations in the Medieval Universities* (Cambridge, Mass., 1948).

[13] See further A. B. Emden, 'Northerners and Southerners in the organisation of the University to 1509', in *Oxford Studies presented to Daniel Callus* (OHS n.s. xvi, 1964), pp. 1–30.

their working shibboleths from time to time, and there were shifting associations both with and against the Welsh and the Irish,[14] but the broad arrangement and its various amenities endured.

As it happened, Merton's oldest rivals, each with strong connections with Durham, developed mainly as communities of northern scholars. University College had a general obligation to give preference to applicants from the diocese of Durham. Balliol seems to have developed a similar policy, which probably derived from the foundation's close association with the bishopric and then came to sustain itself naturally.[15] Merton, however, despite a preponderance of estates in the south, seems consistently to have taken talent from either end of the country. If there were anxieties about recruitment such a policy would have much to recommend it, especially if it were backed by other thrifty precautions, such as the provision for recruiting from the diocese of Worcester.[16] The most obvious risk, that the community would be disrupted by quarrels imported from outside, seems to have been avoided, and on the whole Mertonians, though given to captiousness at scrutinies, and some bickering in between, managed to project most of their animosities outwards.[17]

One episode which implies such a union of parties in Merton is the dispute over the election of the chancellor in 1349. John Wyliot, a fellow of Merton by 1338, and bursar and sub-warden in the 1340s,[18] opposed William Hawkesworth, then provost of Oriel College. When Hawkesworth was elected to the post some of Wyliot's party rabbled him at mass in St Mary's. Hawkesworth died a month or so later, more probably of the plague than of any harm done to him by his opponents, but either way life must go on, and Wyliot was then elected in his place.

Hawkesworth was an unimpeachable northerner from the diocese of York. He was a fellow of Balliol by 1341, active in college affairs, and a nominated foundation fellow of Queen's College in 1341, who took

---

[14] See e.g. *HUO* i. 186.

[15] See A. B. Emden, 'Northerners and Southerners', p. 9; and *ERMC*, pp. 67–8.

[16] See above, pp. 17 and 60. Wolford was in the diocese of Worcester.

[17] Which is, as F. M. Cornford observed, one of the qualities which distinguish a college from a boarding-house: *Microcosmographia Academica* (5th edn., Cambridge, 1953), p. 20. A relatively late but undated recension of the college statutes requires fellows to refrain from opprobrious epithets or deeds invoking the division between north and south, and the like: *ERMC*, pp. 418–19. It could have found application in the twentieth cent.: below, p. 364.

[18] On Wyliot see also below, pp. 112–14.

up his fellowship there before 1348, in which year he was appointed provost of Oriel. Wyliot, who was later a significant benefactor of Merton, was from South Mimms, and spent the later years of his life as a canon and prebendary of Exeter. He is not known as an author, but the college owns a manuscript of commentaries on Aristotle by Albertus Magnus of which part is copied in Wyliot's own hand.[19] His active supporters included two of his most distinguished colleagues in Merton: Richard Billingham,[20] a theologian and logician, and Richard Swineshead, the Calculator.

Billingham sounds like a Durham man, and Swineshead was from Lincolnshire, and so a titular northerner. Wyliot's connections with them must have derived from Merton, and flourished upon some affinities other than those which might be presumed from the geographical accidents of birth. His party was, however, supposed to have favoured secession from the university if Hawkesworth's cause had prevailed. The most recent and alarming secession had been to Stamford, in Lincolnshire, and such migration was on that account regarded as a northern proclivity. However, people may while brawling in church make declarations which are not considered statements of policy, and even in universities they may have opinions attributed to them which they have neither entertained nor expressed.

Having secured the chancellorship, however, Wyliot vacated it and left the university in the next year when he took up his prebend at Exeter. He there became chancellor of the cathedral, a post which carried responsibility for education in the diocese, and which he held until he died in 1383, though in the last decade of his life he was also a canon of St Paul's. We do not know how active he was at Exeter, but he probably lectured in theology there, like other chancellors of the time. At any event, he continued to think about Merton and its needs. In the mean time he was succeeded as chancellor of the university in the early 1350s by his colleague William Heytesbury, a busy scholar who was able to find time for administration.[21]

Another Mertonian of Wyliot's party, Robert Wickford, who was of

---

[19] Merton MS O.2.1. (Coxe 285): Albert the Great and al-Gazâli. Wyliot most probably copied the commentaries for his own studies; we do not know of any other MSS belonging to him. See also below, pp. 113–14.

[20] Billingham gave the college a work now lost, described in the *Catalogus vetus* as 'a table of philosophy and logic' of his own compilation (*BRUO*, p. 189). The word *tabula* suggests a scheme of cross-referencing or indexing, and presumably an aid to research, though of a different kind from Bradwardine's tract on memorizing (above, p. 57 n. 33).

[21] See below, pp. 113–14.

the founder's kin and was elected to a fellowship in 1344, survived the hazards of both riot and plague, and of something more. After a period of study abroad, during which he probably acquired his doctorate of canon and civil law, he entered and rose in the royal service. He became archbishop of Dublin by papal provision in 1375, in which year he was also constable of Bordeaux, and was chancellor of Ireland from 1377 to 1384.[22] Having skated gracefully over wafer-thin ice in the political crisis of 1387–8, he died in 1390, and bequeathed money and some ornamental hangings to the college.[23]

The principal academic issue in Merton as in the university in the later fourteenth century became international in its scope, and deeply perturbing to the English church. In the manner of such controversies it drew in and realigned other causes, embroiling every faculty and interest in the university, and spilling into the world of secular politics. Its begetter was John Wyclif, a formidable master of logical disputation, whose doctrines threatened both to divide and destroy the church and to work radical change in secular society.

Wyclif was an archetypal academic, both in the sense of his commanding authority in the intellectual life of his day, and also, prosaically, because all that we know of his origins and early life has to be deduced from the imperfect record of his academic career.[24] We do not know his parentage, or even from which county he came, though it seems a reasonable guess that he was a Yorkshireman. He appears in Oxford in 1356 as a bachelor fellow of Merton, his name preserved there only because it fell to him, during one of the periods when Richard Billingham was bursar, to account for the sums expended on the common table. He therefore laid out some £4 to entertain the college's guests on Ascension Day (2 June 1356), who numbered eighteen.

Wyclif's routine tenure of the stewardship of hall, which was an arrangement made to spare the bursar's time and energies, gave some

---

[22] *BRUO*, p. 2046.

[23] Richard II assembled a panel of judges at Nottingham in August 1387 and secured an opinion from them that the opposition lately raised against him in parliament was treasonable. Wickford and Bishop Gilbert of Hereford were the only witnesses to the judges' declaration who subsequently avoided proscription by the lords appellant. See further *Westminster Chronicle, 1381–94*, ed. L. C. Hector and B. F. Harvey, Oxford Medieval Texts (Oxford, 1982), pp. 200–2; 226–30.

[24] See *BRUO*, pp. 2103–6; and J. A. Robson, *Wyclif and the Oxford Schools: The Relation of the 'Summa de ente' to Scholastic Debates at Oxford in the Later Fourteenth Century* (Cambridge, 1961), pp. 9–18.

trouble to his earlier biographers, who saw him variously as a sizar, making his way through college on broken meats, a diet-master who stinted the clamant fellows, and a reckless entertainer of private guests.[25] The record shows him rather as officer of the week, in an unassumingly domestic role.

There is no further contemporary reference to Wyclif's time in Merton, which was apparently short. It is noteworthy, however, that his early writings on logic, which have some innovative features, continued work on the proofs of propositions begun by Richard Billingham. Wyclif could only have entered the college as a bachelor, and within four years of his appearance at Merton he was at Balliol, and master of that house. He was also by that time a master of arts, which is consistent with his having entered the university about 1350. Within the next two years he was presented to the Balliol living of Fillingham, in Lincolnshire, from which he was granted leave of absence in 1363 to resume his studies, this time in theology. He then returned neither to Merton nor Balliol, but to Queen's College.

Those restless movements, baffling and misleading if we try to relate them to the prescribed routines and loyalties of the later collegiate university, were highly characteristic of the medieval schools and their shifting population.[26] The only respect in which Wyclif was exceptional was his ability, of which his early appearance at Merton is an incidental measure. On balance it seems almost certain that he was a northerner: there was another Wyclif amongst the fellows of Balliol in 1360, William, who later became rector of Wycliffe in the North Riding, and they may well have been connected. On the other hand, John Wyclif's means seem to have been modest, and certainly not to have extended to a family living. Queen's College was an economical place in which to live in the 1360s, and probably congenial and convenient to a man who, though powerfully ambitious, was not minded for the moment to try for competitive college appointments.

From his new base in Queen's Wyclif began to apply himself with formidable energy to lecturing and disputing in the schools. By the early 1370s he was the acknowledged master of academic debate in a community which prized that talent above all others, and which had

[25] See further H. B. Workman, *John Wyclif: A Study of the English Medieval Church* (Oxford, 1926), i. 66–7.

[26] A point first made by K. B. McFarlane, in *John Wycliffe and the Beginnings of English Nonconformity* (1952), pp. 12–25, but which subsequent work on the history of the medieval university has rendered a commonplace.

an international reputation of its own. During the same years he had secured what seemed a valuable preferment, being appointed master of Canterbury College by Archbishop Simon Islip, Bradwardine's successor, though he was soon to be disappointed in it.

Wyclif was a prolific writer by any reckoning: the standard edition of his known works in Latin runs to more than twenty volumes, and the extent of his writings in English, though substantially smaller, is still a matter of research.[27] The subject and the style of his arguments in metaphysics, on the nature of being, are highly technical, and represent the climax of the intense debates which had occupied the philosophers and theologians of Oxford and Paris since the middle of the previous century. The difficulty of establishing the sequence and development of Wyclif's ideas is increased by the fact that after his posthumous condemnation his works were proscribed and destroyed, and many survive only in late copies. Nevertheless it seems that by the early 1370s he had completed the metaphysical treatises which go under the name of the *Summa de ente*, a compendious work with the concept of being as its theme, and that his thought had matured in the processes which he had found in the university twenty years before. At the end of the first and triumphant stage of his career he could be said to stand as a conservative theologian, a realist and an Augustinian in the tradition of Bradwardine. The junior fellow of 1356 had become a luminary, and his light carried far beyond Oxford.

When Wyclif entered Merton there were distinguished philosophers in the college, but its reputation in the second half of the century derived rather from its mathematicians and astronomers, such as Swineshead and Rede, than from its metaphysicians. We do not know what pride Merton may initially have taken in its association with John Wyclif the metaphysician, though it would be strange if no one had reflected that the unanimously acclaimed master of the schools in his prime was the very model of the man for whom the founder had intended his bounty. Any such reflection, however, would have been short-lived. By the beginning of the fifteenth century the connection had become painful to the house: there could be no open enthusiasm for Wyclif the theologian and heresiarch.

Wyclif's advance to the pre-eminence which he enjoyed around 1370 was inevitably marked by disputes with colleagues which carried

---

[27] See The Wyclif Society, *Wyclif's Latin Works* (London, 1883–1922); *Select English Works of Wyclif*, ed. T. Arnold (3 vols., 1869–71); and A. Hudson, 'Wyclif and the English language', in *Wyclif in his Times*, ed. A. Kenny (Oxford, 1986), pp. 85–103.

accusations of unorthodoxy, of a kind that might be regarded as a risk inherent in his occupation. In the following decade he was particularly embroiled with the Benedictines, and it was supposed by some, and by more after the event, that he was embittered against them by the circumstances in which he was deprived of the mastership of Canterbury College. Archbishop Islip had first intended a college which, a century after Walter de Merton's innovatory experiment, would admit both secular clerks and also monks released from Christ Church, Canterbury, to study in the university's schools. He then, perhaps because the cathedral convent was luke-warm in its support, turned about, established in 1365 a college exclusively for seculars, with a constitution like Merton's, and installed Wyclif as the master. William Durrant, warden of Merton (1351–75), donated his interest in part of the site, and Richard Benger, a fellow of Merton, became a fellow of the new foundation.

The convent's apathy or mistrust may have contributed to Islip's change of policy, but the monks at once saw the move as a betrayal which justified their deepest misgivings. They were passionately jealous of the archbishop's patronage. They had a long communal memory, and nurtured the tradition of a bitterly fought victory over Archbishop Hubert Walter, who had tried and failed to found an endowed college of priests at Lambeth in Richard I's reign.[28] Archbishop Islip's plans were undone by a petition to the pope, Wyclif and his colleagues were expelled, and Canterbury College reverted to the rule of St Benedict. Wyclif entrusted Benger, with whom he remained on friendly terms, with an appeal to the pope, which was formally disallowed in 1370.[29] Islip's successor was able to delay the process, but not to save the seculars' expectations.[30]

Wyclif was only an incidental casualty of the dispute, and there is nothing in the rest of his career to suggest that the episode played any part in the formulation of his thought. In the course of the 1370s

[28] See C. R. Cheney, *Hubert Walter* (Oxford, 1967), pp. 137–55. Hubert Walter's intention, horrifying to the monks, was to provide prebends for his chaplains and clerical aides: a century later he would have turned to the university as a nursery of expertise.

[29] Benger subsequently became rector of Donnington, Berks, by papal provision: *BRUO*, p. 167.

[30] Canterbury was eventually recast as an independent college linked to Christ Church, Canterbury, by Archbishop Courtenay in 1384, and dissolved in 1540 as a religious house: *Canterbury College: Documents and History*, ed. W. A. Pantin (OHS n.s. vi–viii, 1947–50). Its site was then absorbed by Christ Church, Oxford, where the Canterbury Gate is its continuing memorial.

he turned to apply his metaphysical reasoning to the nature of the eucharist, and his views on the doctrine of grace to the nature of lordship. There was no distinction between the two courses of speculation, which were closely interrelated, and open together to all the other influences that played upon his thought, but they threatened the profoundest consequences to church and state.

The doctrine of Christ's bodily presence in the consecrated host required in conservative scholastic thought a process of transubstantiation, through which the act of consecration entirely changed the substance of the bread and wine into the body and blood of Christ, leaving only the appearance, or accidents, of the original elements. It was a doctrine refined over several centuries of theological debate, and most recently consolidated in the aftermath of St Thomas Aquinas's efforts to assimilate Aristotelian philosophy to Christian dogma. The developed belief was central not only to the faith, but to the power of the clergy, for the priest alone was the agent of the miracle. Over the past half-century it had been strongly reinforced amongst the laity by the devotional cult of Corpus Christi, of which a striking recent manifestation was the foundation of a college in Cambridge by a gild of Corpus Christi in the town.[31]

Wyclif's conclusion that accidents could not be separated from substance, and that what continued to look like bread and wine must in some sense continue to be bread and wine, dismissed the priest's power to effect the miracle of transubstantiation, and with it the whole structure of clerical privilege. From the international authority of the papal monarchy to the incumbent's right to the tithes of the parish, including such corporate incumbents as Merton College, there was no manifestation of the clergy's privileges that was not vulnerable to such a challenge.

Even the priest's prescriptive right to expound the Scriptures was threatened. Wyclif's reflections on divine grace and the nature of holy writ led him to the conclusion that in the church defined as the body of the elect there could be no distinction before God between clergy and laity. The clergy had their sacramental and pastoral duties to perform, but it was the duty and privilege of every Christian to discover the truth directly from the Bible, a perception which would come assuredly and only to those in a state of grace. It followed that

---

[31] See further M. Rubin, *Corpus Christi: The Eucharist in Late Medieval Culture* (Cambridge, 1991); and for some notable complications, M. Aston, '*Corpus Christi* and *corpus regni*: Heresy and the Peasants' Revolt', *Past and Present*, cxliii (1994), 1–47.

the Bible should be made available in English to those who spoke English, and in all the other tongues of Christendom as there was need. The Latin text which St Jerome had prepared, the Vulgate, which the Western Church had come to regard as the authentic word of God, and which the clergy in the West had come to treat as a treasure exclusive to themselves,[32] was now to be only one of the ways in which God's word might be expressed to Christendom.

Wyclif is most generally remembered today for those aspects of his doctrine which prefigured Protestant beliefs, that is to say for his denunciations of clerical privilege, and as the instigator and champion of the English Bible. The translation and transmission of a complete text of the Bible in the vernacular is the most formidable achievement of his disciples. It is not clear that Wyclif took any direct part in the work himself, but we know that he preached in English upon occasions, and his extensive works, which have survived, and his utterances, of which we have a less certain record, provided examples and justification for the most enthusiastic of his disciples when they undertook to publish and popularize his message. He was, however, an academic, whose power was concentrated in the university schools. He undertook diplomatic and political commissions for the government,[33] but he was most sure of himself in teaching, and above all in debate. The question for those most alarmed by his proclivities was whether the ensuing mischief could be confined to and controlled within the lecture hall.

The period of Wyclif's greatest influence in the university, and also of his direct participation in public affairs, was one of disillusionment and acerbity in English politics and of crisis in international relations. When the war in France was resumed in 1369 the English found themselves at a disadvantage. They were unable on the one hand to hold their own in sieges, in the face of superior French artillery, and on the other to force battles in the open field of the kind that had brought them such stunning success in the 1340s and 50s. The south coast was exposed to destructive raids from the sea, and the taxes which were levied for the war brought neither security at home nor military success abroad. The shortage of labour in a society ravaged and dislocated by the plague also made for popular discontents, which were not all related to economic distress.

---

[32] See *Knighton's Chronicle, 1337–96*, pp. 242–4.

[33] Summarized conveniently in McFarlane, *John Wycliffe*, pp. 58–88, though McFarlane's disdain for Wyclif weakens much of what he says about him.

The mixture of dissatisfaction and disillusionment was dangerous in itself, and was not confined to the laity. The clergy, who were regularly constrained to render their goods to Caesar, were also vexed by papal taxes, which rose sharply when the popes added war in Italy to the high costs of administering their court and the international agencies which functioned there in Avignon. The endowed clergy saw themselves paying twice for what they were allowed to keep, and the unbeneficed fretted under policies which tried to depress stipends in the same way as the secular authorities strove to control wages and prices.[34] The efforts were equally unsuccessful, and served only to promote unrest: Merton College, like other employers with work to be done, regularly paid what its contractors and workmen asked, rather than what the government prescribed.[35]

Wyclif's developed thought posed in fact two dangers. The first was that as the acknowledged master of academic debate he wielded exceptional power and influence within the university, and that the university's graduates, charged with his ideas, were destined for high office in church and state. The second was that the most enthusiastic of his followers fastened swiftly upon his conviction that the laity deserved instruction in their own tongue. They busied themselves with translating the Bible and a number of exegetical works, and they also took their master's message into the countryside. One of them was Philip Repingdon, an able young Augustinian canon from Leicester Abbey, who later became an orthodox but open-minded bishop of Lincoln. Repingdon preached Wyclif's opinions at Brackley, in Northamptonshire, and took friends back with him to Leicester to spread the word in the Midlands. His closest associates included a fellow of Merton, John Aston, whom a critical observer described as an indefatigable traveller in the Lollard cause.[36]

The origin of the term Lollard for a Wycliffite is obscure, but its most likely derivation is from *lolium*, a tare or darnel-grass: to the orthodox, the Lollards showed themselves adept sowers of tares.[37] By the time that the university authorities moved to suppress the movement it was too late, and its dangerous notions were current far

---

[34] See above, p. 95.
[35] As with Nicholas Carpenter of Oxford, who worked for Merton on the roof of the chancel in 1391–2, and was fined three times for taking stipends beyond the rates prescribed under the Statute of Labourers (25 Edw. 3, Stat. 7; 12 Ric. 2, cc. 3–9).
[36] See *Knighton's Chronicle*, pp. 284, 285 n.
[37] Matt. 13: 25. See further *Knighton's Chronicle*, p. 286 and n.

beyond the settings of academic discussion. The heresy spread so quickly that it must have found opinions and beliefs already sympathetic to it. At the same time the homogeneity of much Lollard thought, and within it the vocabulary which was one of the most striking characteristics of early Lollard preaching and exhortation, make it exceptionally difficult to distinguish its academic and its popular elements. The recondite language of the schools evidently evoked a startling public response.

We have no clear record of opinion in Merton or any other college on the matter of Wyclif's teaching, but the fact that dissent is perceptible at all suggests that the Wycliffite element was quite strong at the time. Wyclif's association with the house was quite brief, and after his condemnation there was a disposition to deny that he had even been a member.[38] Orthodoxy was well and reassuringly represented, for it was William Barton, who had been a fellow with Wyclif in 1356, and was elected chancellor of the university in 1379, who took occasion late in 1380 to assemble a panel of theologians to examine and condemn Wyclif's eucharistic teaching. Barton seems to have chosen a conservative-minded group, there being only four secular doctors amongst the twelve members. In the early stages of his critical assault on the endowed clergy Wyclif had found allies amongst the friars, but by the winter of 1380–1 his radical theology had frightened them almost all away. Nevertheless the voting on the panel seems to have been only seven to five against him, which is a measure both of the high technicality of the subject and of his own formidable reputation and skills.[39]

The commission's verdict, delivered in Hilary term 1381, is reported to have taken Wyclif by surprise, and later that year he retired from the university to his rectory at Lutterworth, a crown living to which he had been appointed in 1374 as a reward for his diplomatic work. He had been silenced in the university, but he devoted his time to writing and to correspondence with his followers, until his death from a stroke at the end of 1384. He was attended at Lutterworth by a secretary and close companion called John Purvey, who was himself an active preacher, but it is no longer believed that Wyclif took any substantial part during those years, with or without Purvey's assistance, in the great work of making and disseminating the English

---

[38] See below, p. 117.
[39] See further J. I. Catto, 'Wyclif and Wycliffism at Oxford, 1356–1430', *HUO* ii. 175–261, at pp. 213–14.

texts with which the Lollard movement was nourished.[40] He had
given the enterprise its first impetus, but it was continued by other
hands.

The extent of Merton's involvement with Lollardy is a matter of
particular consequence because the Lollard Bible and its attendant
texts were a product not of untutored enthusiasm, but of a scholarly
venture which required extensive resources.[41] The assembly and comparison of texts, and the refinement of drafts, needed space, time,
and ready access to libraries. If those requirements were concentrated
in Oxford, and it is difficult to suppose that in the crucial early years
of the movement they were to be found elsewhere, a college would
be their most likely setting. Its resources evidently make Merton a
strong possibility, though on balance the effort was more probably
focused upon The Queen's College.

Nevertheless Merton's Lollard connections were more positive and
extensive than the immediately following generations were willing
to admit. Chaucer's friend Ralph Strode was a contemporary who
opposed Wyclif's views but remained on friendly terms wih him. John
Aston was a pertinacious preacher who defied Archbishop Courtenay,
and spent some years in proselytizing outside the university, but
seems at the last to have retained or resumed his fellowship at Merton
without renouncing his beliefs. Thomas Brightwell, who was later
recruited on the poacher-gamekeeper principle as a local commissioner against Lollardy in Leicestershire, was cited by Courtenay
in 1382 as an abettor of Wyclif's supporters. He submitted to the
archbishop on that occasion with no great alacrity, and his behaviour
was matched by that of Thomas Hulman, a fellow since 1366 and a
candidate for the wardenship in 1387.[42] A younger man, John Corringham, was presented to the college living of Diddington, in
Huntingdonshire, and taught Lollard precepts there until he was
discovered by Bishop Buckingham.[43] It would have been difficult both

---

[40] See, A. Hudson, *The Premature Reformation*, p. 242.

[41] Ibid.

[42] See *BRUO*, pp. 266–7, 981. Brightwell became dean of the college and hospital of the
Newarke, Leicester, a Lancastrian living, in or before 1388: A. H. Thompson, *The Hospital
and the New College of the Annunciation of St Mary in the Newarke, Leicester* (Leicester, 1937),
p. 139. There was some piquancy in his being commissioned to search for Lollard books,
but at least he would have known what they looked like. Thomas Hulman subsequently
became rector of Kibworth Beauchamp, where he found, if he did not himself import,
dissent: see below, p. 118.

[43] See further A. K. McHardy, 'Bishop Buckingham and the Lollards of Lincoln diocese',
Studies in Church History, ix (1972), 131–3, 143.

for Aston to have maintained his connections with the college and for Corringham to have secured a living without some degree of toleration and support from the fellowship. The likelihood is rather that Lollardy was viewed sympathetically for more than a decade by a majority of members of the house who had either never professed it or, like Brightwell, had made their peace by some formal recantation.

Such attitudes were readily compatible with feeling in the university, despite William Barton's stand. Indeed Barton's immediate successor, Robert Rigg, another Mertonian and a member of Barton's commission in 1380, actively supported Nicholas Hereford, a leading Wycliffite, in 1382, and consorted openly with him after the Ascension Day sermon that year (15 May) which marked the high point of dissent in the university after Wyclif's withdrawal. Another close associate of Rigg's, the Mertonian William James, was imprisoned for Lollardy in 1395 and deprived of his fellowship for a time on that account, though on his release he was ostentatiously welcomed back to the college and reinstated.[44]

Besides the state of opinion in Merton and other colleges, there were several other factors at work in the ambiguous politics of the university during the rest of the century. Despite the large issues and the passionate beliefs involved in the controversy, the university's principal desire in those years was to maintain its independence of direct episcopal supervision, and its freedom to regulate, as far as possible, every aspect of its own conduct. Freedom of debate, if it had been so defined, would have been seen rather as a consequence of administrative independence than as its purpose. It was, nevertheless, an important and delicate issue.

In the immediate aftermath of Barton's action it seemed that he had taken a successful stand against a threat of disruption and scandal, and although he had not made, and perhaps did not seriously intend, a clean sweep of Wyclif's followers he had attained his principal objective. As it happened, Simon Sudbury, the archbishop of Canterbury who was murdered by the rebels in London in June 1381, was not greatly disposed to interfere with the affairs of the university. He had begun an inquiry into Wyclif's views in 1376, from which he was deflected by political influence, and he seems generally to have been

---

[44] James subsequently held a number of college offices, but continued in his beliefs: see further below, p. 118 and n.

tentative rather than asssiduous in the management of his province.[45] It is not surprising that Wyclif's followers took heart, and that they received some countenance from colleagues who were not necessarily of their party.

The new archbishop, William Courtenay, was of a very different kind. A former chancellor of the university, and active there as an arbitrator, he had as bishop of London supported and perhaps instigated Sudbury's first proceedings against Wyclif.[46] However, Courtenay did not receive the temporalities of the see of Canterbury until the autumn of 1381, or the pallium until the following May, and in the mean time was also appointed lord chancellor. He was unable to give serious attention to Lollardy until the spring of 1382, when he began a series of energetic actions. The first was to call a council at Blackfriars in London, to examine Wyclif's teaching in greater detail than the commission at Oxford had pursued. When the council had distinguished and condemned ten heretical and twelve erroneous propositions, Courtenay issued general letters to his suffragans for the suppression of heresy, and referred the matter to a small committee of bishops for further consideration. Meanwhile he summoned the principal dissidents from Oxford, together with Rigg, the chancellor, to secure their recantation. Repingdon and Rigg conformed, after some initial defiance. Aston and Hereford proved more intractable, but the university was brought to heel after a fashion, and for the moment. It took another thirty years to impose a reassuring conformity, but the archbishop had restored the decencies, and he kept as close an eye on events as his other concerns allowed.[47]

In those circumstances it was possible for Merton to survive its involvement with Lollardy without any notable ructions, and later to

---

[45] Sudbury was reputed to have a critical view of the abuse of papal indulgences and of some of the extravagant aspects of pilgrimages, but in 1381 he was fiercely unpopular wih the rebels as a minister and royal counsellor: *DNB*. He had, as it happened, worked with Wyclif on the diplomatic mission of 1373–4.

[46] Courtenay also disliked Wyclif as an agent of John of Gaunt's. There was a rich interplay of patronage, political and theocratic sensitivities, and personal feeling in Gaunt's subsequent protection of Wyclif against the ecclesiastical authorities. See A. Goodman, *John of Gaunt: The Exercise of Princely Power in Fourteenth-Century Europe* (Harlow, 1992), pp. 241–71.

[47] Courtenay was not able to make a visitation of the diocese of Lincoln until 1389, when Lollardy was quite strongly established in Leicester, despite Bishop Buckingham's early proceedings against it. See further J. H. Dahmus, *The Metropolitan Visitations of William Coutenay, Archbishop of Canterbury, 1381–96* (Urbana, Ill., 1950), pp. 48–50, 163–70; and *Knighton's Chronicle*, pp. 532–4.

play down the connection when it became embarrassing and more dangerous. If there were disputes within the house, they were not more sharply focused by the issues of Wyclif's teaching than by any others, and they left no obvious marks. At the time, the college may well have given more attention to its other preoccupations.

By the measures which we have, Merton's chief academic interests and distinction in the second half of the century were in mathematics and its associated disciplines of astronomy and astrology. Rede's benefactions came to a college which was respectably well equipped with books, amongst which there were several scientific treatises by members of the house. The presence of astronomical instruments in the library reinforces the impression that scientific studies were still an active concern. We cannot be certain that the books were read or that the astrolabes were levelled at the sky, but their currency together is suggestive.

The two principal benefactors of the library, Rede and Bredon, were in a manner survivors of an earlier generation.[48] Simon Bredon was a fellow by 1330, and continued in Oxford for at least a decade, holding office as junior proctor in the later 1330s. He was an MD by 1355, when he was in the service of Richard earl of Arundel, and in which year he also became a canon of Chichester under Arundel's patronage.[49] William Rede was a fellow by 1344, and sub-warden in 1353–4. He was archdeacon of Rochester by 1359, and was provided to the see of Chichester by Urban V in 1368. Like his friend Bredon, Rede was close to the Arundels, and may have been instrumental in bringing the young Thomas Arundel, later archbishop of Canterbury, to study at Oriel College.[50] Bredon died in 1372, but Rede survived until 1385. His principal gifts to Merton library were made in 1374, though he made others on other occasions, and augmented them in his will.[51]

It would be difficult to find a modern equivalent to Rede's benefaction, ranging as it did over the whole field of scholarly and much practical knowledge, and including scientific instruments of high intrinsic value. Its immediate significance was two-fold. It acknow-

[48] See above, p. 87.

[49] On Bredon's relations with the Arundels, see further M. Aston, *Thomas Arundel: A Study of Church Life in the Reign of Richard II* (Oxford, 1967), pp. 10–12.

[50] Arundel was already bishop of Ely when he came to Oriel, where he endowed and built the college chapel. Rede, who was on friendly terms with Thomas's brother Richard, the ninth earl, subsequently included Oriel amongst the recipients of his books: M. Aston, *Thomas Arundel*, p. 12.

[51] See above, p. 91.

ledged the established importance of Merton as a centre of studies, and it also served to attract new talent to the college. The gesture was a timely one, for William of Wykeham's New College of St Mary, formally established in November 1379, was about to displace Merton from its position as the best-found house of learning in either university.

Wykeham looked to Merton not only as an example, but also as a source of expertise. He modelled the statutes of his college on those of Walter de Merton, and on Robert Eglesfield's plans for Queen's College, and he drew on Merton for agents, for the master of his scholars in Oxford while the new foundation was being planned and built, and for its first warden. What was most strikingly new about the New College, apart from its explicit association with a school which would supply it with students, was its scale.[52] From the beginning it assembled and accommodated a collegiate body of one hundred, including ten chaplains and sixteen choristers, and deployed an endowment calculated to protect them adequately from want. The provision of horses for the warden was eloquent: he was allowed a string of six, twice as many as the warden of Merton. Seven academic halls were submerged in the main site of the college, for the titles to which Wykeham negotiated with a dozen landlords. The warden and fellows of Merton were numbered amongst them.[53]

Wykeham's buildings had some particular features besides their monumental quality, which was unmatched until Wolsey planned Cardinal College in the early sixteenth century.[54] Whilst Merton had grown by domestic accumulation, Wykeham laid out his Great Quadrangle on a long east-west axis. The chapel and hall stand protectively on the north side, with a gate-tower, apparently the first in Oxford, on the west, and a corresponding gateway leading into open ground on the east. The upper storey of the gate-tower housed the warden, who also had an oratory to the north looking into the antechapel. The library was accommodated in the eastern range of the quadrangle.

The work is grandly conceived, but its effect as a model college is moderated by the inclusion of a cloister to the west of the chapel. The cloister seems to have been intended, as it has long been used, as

---

[52] On Wykeham's intentions, and the models available to him, see further A. B. Cobban, 'Colleges and halls, 1380–1500', *HUO* ii. 593–4.

[53] See further *HUO* ii. 581–2, 642–8.

[54] The casual elements in the plan of Magdalen, which was conceived as sumptuously as either, reflect the assimilation of older buildings on the site.

a burial ground rather than, as in a monastic house, a place for study, which would in turn have been superfluous where study was mainly corporate, disputatious, and public. It is a feature of the college that has been admired and widely imitated, but which might be described as regressive in character.

If New College was seen in Merton as a challenge, it was also clearly an asset to the university at large, though in the nature of things it was likely that the newcomers would recruit from Merton, at least in the first place, and that there would be little return. For the time being Merton had the advantage of an established position, and its resources were still substantial, though they were shortly to come under some pressure from the inflation of prices. For the moment, however, if the college felt any anxiety about recruitment it was probably related to questions of quality rather than to numbers. The foundation established by John Wyliot should probably be seen in that light.

Wyliot remained in Oxford for only a short time after the excitements of his election as chancellor.[55] Having held the office for a normal term he spent the rest of his career outside the university, for the most part as a canon of Exeter, though he also held a prebend at St Paul's and maintained other connections around London. He died in the early 1380s, and over the last decade of his life planned an endowment which for the first time provided systematic support for undergraduate students at Merton.[56]

Aware, by his own account, that he had not the means to endow a college, Wyliot chose instead to assist meritorious students, and the terms of the grant show that he had undergraduates in mind. The beneficiaries were to be chosen first from Wyliot's own kin, and then from a group of counties, Bedfordshire, Buckinghamshire, Hertfordshire, Huntingdonshire, and Oxfordshire, and from the diocese of London, because those were places in which he had held estates. Middlesex was his native county. The chancellor of Exeter cathedral was also given the nomination of two scholars, to commemorate Wyliot's long membership of that chapter. The properties conveyed in trust to the college included a number in the city of Oxford,

---

[55] See above, pp. 97–8.

[56] The chronology of Wyliot's benefaction is uncertain, not least because the date of his death is unknown, but also because the document reciting the intention and terms of his gift (MCR Deed 3028; *RACM*, pp. 514–17) is a late and undated copy, which appears to conflate a deed uttered by Wyliot with the text of a subsequent college order.

amongst them the Fleur de Lys inn. The Fleur de Lys stood on the south-west side of Carfax, at the top of St Aldate's. It was one of the principal inns in the city, with long civic connections, and later was a profitable source of income to Anthony Wood's family.[57]

Those appointed to the scholarships were to be competent in Latin, and able to proceed in the liberal arts course. If they were apt, they could be supported for up to five years, which would have taken them well towards, and the more experienced of them up to, the master's degree. They were to have a bachelor fellow to oversee their studies, who was to receive an annual fee of a mark (13s. 4d.) The fund allowed a weekly allowance, a *portio*, for each scholar, which was normally to be 6d. but could be adjusted to the current price of grain up to a maximum of 9d. The beneficiaries duly became known as *portioniste*, which was later corrupted to postmasters, a term first found in the name of Postmasters' Hall, the tenement on the north side of Merton Street in which they were lodged in the sixteenth century.[58]

There are several echoes of the college's own endowment in Wyliot's foundation, most obviously in the provision for founder's kin, and in the territorial associations of the grants, but also in the donor's desire to make some return, by furthering learning, for the blessings of his own career. Another consideration is that in his last years in residence in Merton, when he was successively bursar and sub-warden, between 1345 and 1347, Wyliot had seen the demise of the band of poor scholars 'living in the town', whose duties included daily prayers for Richard of Cornwall.[59] In the course of the fourteenth century special provision for undergraduates and their teaching had become an issue in the university, and one in which the colleges had a particular interest. Robert Eglesfield had proposed to maintain up to seventy-two poor boys at Queen's, though the reality proved to be much more modest.

---

[57] See further J. Munby, 'Zacharias's: a fourteenth-century Oxford new inn, and the origins of the medieval urban inn', *Oxoniensia*, lvii (1993), 245–309, at pp. 304–5. The Fleur de Lys, or Floure de Luce, originally known as Batte's Inn, was conveyed to the college in 1374. See also below, p. 224.

[58] Another form of the name, which may or may not have have been intermediate, was *postministri*, which later was fancifully rationalized as servitors who stood behind their seniors' chairs, though nothing is less likely. The expression postmaster has been used in more recent times, like scholar in other colleges, or demy in Magdalen, to designate the holder of a major award on the foundation. Originally neutral and local, it has been a source of some confusion outside the college. Since 1986 postmasterships have been awarded only as college prizes: see below, pp. 343–4.

[59] See further J. R. L. Highfield, 'The early colleges', *HUO* i. 249; and above, p. 18.

Wyliot's thinking was presumably influenced by his own experience, and by observation and consultation in the university.

The scheme which Wyliot devised both preserved tradition and made provision for a future in which a lien on talent would be an increasingly valuable asset. That is not to say that Wyliot, or Wykeham, or anyone else foresaw a time when colleges would maintain the whole business of recruiting and instructing students. They were responding to the needs of the church, the university, and the colleges as they perceived them. The purpose and first result of their actions was to secure the colleges in their peculiar role, yet in the process they changed the university .

The 1370s therefore saw Merton's resources considerably enhanced, in accordance with the founder's precepts. Wyliot's foundation served piety and learning to the advantage of the house in one fashion, as did Rede's munificence in another. There is nothing to suggest that the college felt a need for more domestic accommodation, though there may have been a small net gain from the works undertaken in Mob Quad. What is clear is that the new library was designed and furnished, as well as being equipped, to a high standard. At the same time there seems to have been further thought of extending the church. The south transept was built in 1367–8, and a consortium of fellows secured Christopher Hall and Neville's Inn, which subsequently constituted a major part of the site of Corpus Christi College, and conveyed them to the college in 1388.

A larger church would have added much to the dignity of the foundation. The age admired imposing and richly decorated buildings, and the works at New College no doubt roused the spirit of emulation. There were also many practical reasons for building a nave and aisles: both college and parish would benefit from the additional space for liturgical elaboration, including provision for chantries, which were also a source of income, and for sermons, which were greatly in fashion. Wyliot wished those of his foundationers who could sing to take part in all college services as choristers, and as the parish had established rights in the church there may also have been plans to preach to larger congregations. Above all, the completion of the church would restore the balance of intercessory prayer and scholarship which the college had achieved in its earliest days, and which had been the most striking mark of its success. If a new age set new standards, Merton wished to be seen to meet them.

6

The Age of Orthodoxy

THE fifteenth century begins in Merton with heterodoxy, archi-episcopal visitations, building works, and some archival research, and ends with orthodoxy apprehensions of change, more building, an episcopal translation, and what would later be called records management. In 1401 the warden was Edmund Beckenham, a mathematician and theologian, elected in 1398, who acted as chancellor of the university in 1411, and died in office in 1416.[1] In 1501 the warden was Richard Fitzjames, a royal chaplain and almoner, who had been bishop of Rochester since 1497. At that time he was still technically resident in Oxford. He became bishop of Chichester in 1503, and he resigned the wardenship only in 1507, when he had been bishop of London for two years.

When the century began Merton was still an active, though perhaps no longer an outstanding focus of Wycliffite opinions, and Arch-bishops Arundel and Chichele at their visitations, like Kilwardby and Peckham before them, found themselves as much concerned with the day-to-day observance of the statutes by the warden and fellows as with fine points of doctrine. The endowment, which had sustained the college handsomely over its first century, came under strain in a new age, and sometimes there were uncomfortable choices to be made. Chichele in particular denounced in plangent terms the college's failure to elect additional fellows. Yet Merton continued to attract talent and to find preferment for its members, Cardinal Kemp amongst them. By the time that Fitzjames moved to London the college had a striking range of new buildings to set against the others that had lately risen in Oxford, and its general tone was evidently unimpaired. Fitzjames himself then seemed to be in the middle of a successful university and public career, though the onset of blindness

---

[1] There is a record in Merton MS 261 of Beckenham having lectured in arithmetic and geometry: see *MBMC*, p. 34 and n., where the lectures are attributed to Thomas Buckingham; and *BRUO*, p. 155.

later prevented him from applying his full energies to the large responsibilities of his new see.

He had nevertheless left a lasting mark on Merton. His true memorial there is not the vaulted archway and chamber which he added to the warden's lodgings, though it is for them that he is most readily remembered today. His most distinctive contribution to the life of the college was in the register of acts which he inaugurated, and which he kept in his own hand for the greater part of his wardenship. It was an innovation significant in the history of the university, as well as of the college.[2] The events which it records run smoothly in the tradition of the house as it had functioned since its first foundation, but there is both in the undertaking itself, and in Fitzjames's explicit reflections upon it, much sense of impending change.[3]

The early fifteenth century also had its alarms, and may even have seemed a more troubled time to those who lived in it than did its closing years to Fitzjames and his contemporaries. It too witnessed a distinctive addition to the college archives, for the first systematic record of the fellowship, the list celebrated since Anthony Wood's time as the *Catalogus Vetus*, was compiled during Henry IV's reign (1399–1413).[4] The work was undertaken, apparently on his own initiative, by Thomas Robert, a fellow since 1395, and third bursar in 1411–12.[5] He seems to have been moved by an historical curiosity which would be commonplace enough in later ages, but was novel in its day.[6] He extracted the names of fellows from the bursars' accounts over the previous century, and as he made his first rough lists on the dorse of old wardens' and sub-wardens' rolls, it seems most likely that he began them while he held that office and had daily access to records in the treasury. The fact that the fellows are not listed in chronological order of their election until the reign of Henry V (1413–22) strengthens the probability that his researches were completed by 1422, when he took up his benefice at Kibworth Beauchamp.

[2] See below, p. 134 and n.

[3] See *RACM 1483–1521*, 1; and below, p. 134.

[4] See *MM*, p. 37; and *MMC*, pp. vii–ix. The catalogue is dated *c.* 1422 in *MM*, but its structure suggests that Thomas Robert began to compile it in the first decade of the century, probably about 1410.

[5] See *BRUO*, p. 1579. Robert was appointed incumbent of the free chapel of Kibworth by the college in 1422, and seems then to have left the university. He died in 1446.

[6] There are contemporary examples enough from religious houses, as in the chronicle of Meaulx Abbey or the work of Thomas Walsingham at St Albans, but the abbeys had an established historiographical tradition and a domestic *pietas* which lent itself readily to such work. Robert deserves at least a footnote in the history of college histories.

The *Catalogus* has several points of interest. In the first place it is both an historical list and a continuing register. It seems that the college had previously kept no dedicated record of its members; Robert evidently found nothing earlier that he could turn to account. His enterprise may have owed something to the formal register of admissions kept in New College from its foundation, but he made no gesture to formality himself beyond instituting the record. He did nevertheless leave it in a shape in which it could readily be kept up to date, as it has been ever since. He simply extracted all the names that he could find in the bursars' rolls, and then put them into an overall order by grouping them under reigns. On the other hand he did then organize them further by ranging them alphabetically under their initial letters. The device is far short of a true alphabetical index, but once again it matches the best current practice.[7]

John Wyclif duly appears amongst the entries for Edward III's reign, between Thomas Underdown, who was a fellow in the 1340s and later held livings in Kent and Surrey, and John Wendover, who was warden from 1387 to 1398. However, officious hands subsequently annotated the list, and Wyclif was then smugly noted as never having been a fellow of Merton, because he did not complete his probationary year. That is eminently the kind of explanation that makes things worse, but it has some interest as an early, and perhaps even the earliest, essay in the pious obfuscation of Wyclif's career.[8] Those who had known him, and the generations of scholars immediately following them, were in no more doubt about his identity than about his abilities and his influence. It clearly did not occur to Robert himself to disown the connection, and it probably took more than a half-century for anyone else to think it worth while.

There were, nevertheless, some grounds for anxiety at the time, though they were not peculiar to the college. Issues as fundamental as those raised by Wyclif's teachings were both disruptive in themselves, and certain to exacerbate other controversies. Just as the university's zeal for its academic freedom had protected Lollards against a variety of archiepiscopal strictures, so within the colleges and halls there were opinions, parties, and unresolved issues that might be of

---

[7] On some contemporary uses of alphabetical order, see G. H. Martin, *The Husting Rolls of Deeds and Wills, 1252–1485: Guide to the Microfilm Edition* (Cambridge, 1990), pp. 15–16.

[8] See further the arguments reviewed by Henderson, pp. 290–1. The great army of Wyclifs was eventually mustered and shown to be one by K. B. McFarlane in *John Wycliffe*: see above, p. 100, n. 26.

more consequence at particular moments than the largest questions of ecclesiastical authority or human understanding. There is some evidence of such feeling in Merton: Wycliffites and anti-Wycliffites evidently had other and additional means of classifying, assessing, and working with or against particular colleagues.

There were Mertonian Lollards in and out of the college from the earliest days of the movement, and they seem to have acted with fair impunity into the 1390s. Then Warden Wendover was at odds with some of them, most notably with William James, who was both outspoken and long-lived at a time when those qualities were not often found together.[9] In 1395 James was arrested on royal authority and imprisoned in Beaumaris Castle, adequately remote from the chief scenes of dissent, with three other fellows of Merton: John Gamlingay, Thomas Lucas, and Richard Whelpington. The warden then went to law to recover money from them. While he was trying to escape arrest, James seems to have misappropriated funds from Kibworth, a parish in which Lollardy was flourishing more than a decade later, but it is not clear that the warden himself was resolutely orthodox, or that anything more than accountancy and domestic propriety were at stake. However, Wendover resigned the wardenship in 1398, in an instrument drawn up in the garden adjoining his lodgings,[10] and it may be that he had lost some of his authority when Archbishop Arundel was driven into exile by Richard II. Whatsoever the cause, his successor, Edmund Beckenham, welcomed James back to the college with some warmth.

Yet Beckenham, a theologian as well as a mathematician, evinced no obvious sympathy with Lollardy. In 1411 he replaced a chancellor who had been obstructive to Archbishop Arundel's purge of the university, and he was again acceptable as the chancellor's vice-gerent in 1414. What he did show, like Wendover before him, was a persistent concern for the recovery of debts, which kept him busy in the courts, and fuelled if it did not always occasion a series of disputes with the fellows. One of them, fought out with Thomas Rodbourne, a future warden, probably lies behind a royal mandate of 1411, protecting the

---

[9] See further *BRUO*, pp. 1012–13; and A. Hudson, *The Premature Reformation*, pp. 88–90. James eventually abjured before Archbishop Chichele, in 1420, and was allowed to practise medicine in the archbishop's college at Maidstone, a provision that may account for his immunity from greater trouble

[10] Described by Anthony Wood: *MMC*, p. 158 and n. The garden was presumably at the lower end of the plot to the south of St Albans Quadrangle, where Lady Clayton subsequently had her summer house, and the old mulberry tree now (1997) grows.

college from violent intrusion.[11] Rodbourne was intent at that time on recovering his fellowship after having vacated it for what had proved to be an unsatisfactory benefice. He had a party amongst the fellows, and eventually carried his point with the visitor's aid. Whilst other passions may have been involved, however, the warden was probably chiefly unwilling to part with a stipend which he might have saved. He had some claim to be an economist as well as a mathematician.

That Lollardy faded in Merton in Beckenham's time is rather a coincidence than a matter of policy. If the Wycliffites could not command the university they would have to make their way outside it, though they could and did still draw nourishment from it. Although popular Lollardy survived more than a century of persecution, the energy which Wyclif's followers had applied to theological radicalism was often diverted by their successors to contemplative devotions, private prayer, and a new and intense regard for the setting of worship. Those are substantially the characteristics of the collegiate body in the fifteenth century.[12]

Though there were unrepentant Lollards in Merton in 1400, there was also much conservative feeling. Merton had lent countenance to Aston and James, but it also provided three members of the commission appointed on Archbishop Arundel's orders to examine and condemn Wycliffite teachings and literature. The commission condemned 267 propositions as heretical or erroneous, and one by-product of its labours was a formal bonfire of condemned books which is illustrated in an historiated initial letter in the college's copy of the *Doctrinale fidei* by Thomas Netter of Walden, OC (Pl. 9).[13] It is also remarkable that Robert Stoneham, who took two of Wyclif's works with him to the Council of Pisa, where he died in 1409, left £20 to the college to buy a silver cross and candlesticks for the chapel.[14]

The archbishop's Mertonian commissioners were Robert Gilbert,

---

[11] See further M. Jurkowski, 'Heresy and factionalism at Merton College in the early fifteenth century', *Journal of Ecclesiastical History* xlviii (1997). The writ is dated 15 May 1411, and is published in *MM*, pl. XVIa and p. 36.

[12] See further *MBMC*, p. 35 and n.

[13] Coxe 319, fo. 41ʳ. Netter, a tireless inquisitor, was probably the most learned and certainly the most persistent opponent of Lollardy in the generation after Wyclif. The illuminated initial is a worthy memorial to him.

[14] Stoneham, who was a canon of Lincoln and rector of Oakham, was an author and a collector. He left three books of practical worth, including a copy of the Decretals, to Oakham church. His bequests to Merton included a Polychronicon and a copy of the *Rosa medicine*: *BRUO*, pp. 1789–90.

John Luke, and Thomas Rodbourne. Gilbert, like Rodbourne, was later appointed warden. Both served, with John Kemp and other Mertonians, as royal chaplains to Henry V in France, Gilbert being dean of the chapel royal from 1418 to 1432, and both subsequently became bishops. Rodbourne, who was a busy man, apparently resigned the wardenship in 1417 to accompany Henry V to Normandy, and he enjoyed a number of prebends and deaneries before he became bishop of St David's in 1433. He undertook diplomatic missions in 1435 at Arras, in company with William Lyndwood, the canonist,[15] and 1439 at Calais. In 1436 he was nominated to the see of Ely by the king, but the chapter declined to elect him, and though the pope moved to provide him to Worcester in 1437 he remained at St David's until he died in 1442. He appears to have written a chronicle, somewhere in the interstices of his professional life.[16]

Robert Gilbert was an even busier man, and assembled a remarkable tale of preferments, including the deanery of York, before he became bishop of London in 1436. The second Mertonian to hold that see, to which he followed John Kemp, he may be first amongst his fellows in the number and quality of the benefices that he enjoyed, though a precise calculation of that kind would be as difficult as it would be invidious.[17] He had vacated his fellowship in 1402, on receiving his first rectory, but returned immediately to the university to teach, and took a doctorate of theology in 1406. Besides sitting on Arundel's commission, he conducted a visitation of the university as a commissary of the bishop of Lincoln in 1413, by which time he was precentor of Lincoln. He preached at the opening of the Canterbury convocation in 1416, and the next year spoke eloquently and, as he was then already warden of Merton, generously of the need to reward with benefices and academic posts those who had spent their vital energies in the service of the university. He attended general councils of the church at Constance in 1417 and Pavia in 1423, and was provided to the see of London in 1436.

Gilbert and Rodbourne, like Kemp, an older man who outlived

[15] *BRUO*, pp. 1191–2. Lyndwood was one of Chichele's commissioners for the visitation of 1425, above, p. 115.

[16] The chronicle is referred to by John Rudbourne, OSB, who wrote a chronicle of his own, and who has to be distinguished from Thomas Rodbourne: *DNB*.

[17] Gilbert is depicted in painted glass in the north aisle of St Etheldreda's, Horley, of which he held the rectory as prebendary of Sutton-cum-Buckingham, Lincs, from 1420 to 1436. That the figure is the oldest surviving portrait of a warden is yet another of the bishop's accomplishments.

them both, notably fulfilled Walter de Merton's hopes that the college would equip men to serve the church and the state, and on the face of things the fortunes of the house were prosperous in their time. Like Warden Beckenham, however, they had their anxieties. Merton's endowment was still substantial, and the college maintained a building programme throughout the century. It continued to attract both gifts and new recruits, and its library remained the best of its kind down to the eve of the Elizabethan settlement.[18] Yet the resources which had made the college rich in the thirteenth and even for much of the fourteenth century proved only competent in changed times. There was some truth, though also much exaggeration, in Archbishop Chichele's pronouncement in 1425 that Merton, which had once been as a blazing light to the church, was in danger of extinction if it did not enlarge its fellowship. Chichele commanded the college to maintain a full complement of forty-four fellows, oblivious of the fact that its sustainable income had been diminished by the inflation that followed upon the economic crises of the previous century.[19]

What the college needed was not so much exhortation as new founts of patronage. Its influence upon the life of the university had been profound, and its success enabled those who followed to improve upon its example. Both Wykeham, at New College, and Waynefleet, at Magdalen, made provision for the effects of inflation in their endowments. There were also new resources to be won from the confiscated endowments of alien religious houses, made available for pious and educational uses by an act of Henry V's first parliament.[20] The act was a positive disappointment to the Lollards, who had been urging a general disendowment since the 1380s, a signal opportunity to influential churchmen, and a dormant menace, eventually set loose by Cardinal Wolsey, to the English religious orders at large. Merton, first in those as in other affairs, had enjoyed a modest but comforting refreshment from that source long ago, in 1269,[21] but there was no further benison for the college under the Lancastrians.

That is the context in which Warden Beckenham's lawsuits should

---

[18] See [N. Ker], *Oxford College Libraries in 1556* (Oxford, 1956), p. 6; and below, pp. 152–3.

[19] The cumulative totals fall from 150 in 1400 through 132 by 1420, to 102 in 1440 and 97 in 1460. They then rise to 112 by 1480.

[20] Stat. 1 Henry 5, c. 7, 1413.

[21] The church of Stratton St Margaret, Wilts, acquired from the abbey of Ste Trinité, Tiron, in a rather different climate. In the 1450s, however, it became a useful focus for an enlargement of the estate after the contention with the crown over the endowments seized for King's College, Cambridge: below, p. 126.

be viewed, whatsoever other influences may have played upon them. Beckenham seems to have met his match in William Lucas. Lucas had chosen the common law for his career, a choice which might have surprised and might well not have pleased Walter de Merton, but which carried him through competence into gentility within a decade.[22] The warden too was probably irritated to see such an avenue of advancement opened to his contentious colleagues, but he did rather better when he turned from the formidable Lucas to his other suits. He had some need to do so.

Although Beckenham undertook no major building the college always had work in hand in Oxford and on its other properties. A mason, Roger Meriot, was working on St Cross church in 1406, probably on the north aisle, which was rebuilt in the nineteenth century. After some commissions for other colleges Meriot also built a stone wall for a new house in the developing suburb of Holywell. The next college building was the gate-tower, an amenity which had been an integral part of the design of New College, and one which Archbishop Chichele duly provided for All Souls' in 1437. There is a certain piquancy in the fact that the tower, which was designed to provide security as well as adornment, was begun under a licence obtained from the crown by Warden Rodbourne, for his predecessor Beckenham had apparently taken to the law to exclude Rodbourne from the college when he threatened a violent entry only five years earlier.[23]

The licence to build and crenellate a stone tower over the north gate came in 1418,[24] but it seems that what was built then was only the shell of the present gatehouse, probably with a timber upper-storey, the vault, sculptures, and battlements being added some decades later.[25] With the gate-tower in hand, however, work began on the church again. The north transept was built or rebuilt between 1416 and 1425, and the south transept, then some fifty years old, was apparently provided with its matching windows during that time. The whole was on as handsome a scale as the chancel, and arches were provided in both transepts to open westwards into the aisles of the still unbuilt nave. The end wall of the north transept was finished with an ornamented doorway on the street with large niches flanking the window above, as befitted the public entrance to the parish church

[22] See further Jurkowski (above, n. 11).
[23] See above, n. 11.
[24] 4 April 1418, dated at Bayeux during the campaign in Normandy: *MM*, p. 36, pl. XVIb.
[25] See below, pp. 127–9.

(Pl. 10). A variety of donors, John Kemp amongst them, paid for painted glass in the new windows, only fragments of which now remain.[26] The work was ready for a rededication of the church in 1425, which was also the year and perhaps the occasion of Chichele's unwelcome visitation.

There was then a pause in major building work for twenty years, during which two new colleges were founded in Oxford: Lincoln in 1427, and All Souls' in 1437. The warden in that time was Henry Abingdon, who succeeded Gilbert in 1421 and died in 1437. His previous college offices had included the mastership of Wyliot's foundation. He was a theologian, and as a senior representative of the university at the Council of Constance he had secured precedence for the English delegation over those of Castile, though he was unsucccessful in arguing the seniority of Oxford over the university of Salamanca, an issue which might raise irresoluble contention today. Abingdon had a working library of his own, from which he lent fifteen volumes to John Hanham, fellow and bursar.[27] One of them seems to have been a copy of what is now an extremely rare work of John Wyclif's, *De dominio civili*, which had escaped the holocaust in 1411.[28] Another short text by Wyclif, on the papal schism, was copied about the same time by John Mainsforth, who was admitted in 1425 or 1426, elected a fellow by 1429, and later became sub-dean of Chichester.[29] Only one book given by Warden Abingdon is recorded in the library,[30] but his other benefactions to the college included a great tenor bell to complete a peal for the church, which must have hung in a temporary frame until the central tower was built.[31]

[26] See H. W. Garrod, *The Ancient Painted Glass of Merton College, Oxford* (Oxford, 1937), pp. 10–11, 26–30. Some glass from the transept windows has been remounted in the windows of the south range of the library. The early-15th-cent. glass in the west range, sometimes said to have come from the church, is more probably the library's own, perhaps installed when the transept windows were being glazed.

[27] See *MM*, pl. xxv and p. 46. Richard Fitzjames received 68 books by indenture when he became warden in 1482: ibid. See also below, pp. 139.

[28] See *MBMC*, p. 76 and n.

[29] *De scismate*, one of more than twenty short texts copied by Mainsforth into the volume which is now Bodleian MS 52 (S.C. 1969), which was removed from Merton at some time in the 16th cent., and presented to the Bodleian by Bishop Cotton of Exeter in 1605: *BRUO*, p. 1250; *MBMC*, pp. 208–9.

[30] Merton MS M. 3. 4 (Coxe 154): Hugh of St Cher on Ecclesiasticus, bound with a dissertation on confession. In 1484 John Hanham bequeathed three books of his own to the library, two of which survive (MSS M. 1. 8 and H. 1. 8, Coxe 141 and 201).

[31] A frame could have been raised over the crossing, and probably was. New College had a free-standing bell tower, but the note on a subwarden's roll of 1422 which speaks of the

Henry Abingdon's successor was Elias Holcote, who as a Wiltshire man might have been a gremial Mertonian, but who had migrated from Exeter Hall in 1414. He resigned in 1455, when he was a canon and prebendary of York, but his earlier benefices, besides canonries at Beverley, Hereford, and Southwell, had included the rectory of Higham Ferrers, Archbishop Chichele's birthplace, and in 1430 the wardenship of the college which Chichele re-endowed there.

In 1437 Chichele began work on All Souls' College, where the master mason and designer, Richard Chevington, had a deputy and probable former pupil called Robert Janyns, who had worked with him at Abingdon Abbey. Janyns came to Merton in 1448 as master mason, that is to say, the architect and builder, of the church tower.

The tower has been the principal feature of the college ever since its completion. Its ground plan was determined by the preliminary work on the crossing, of which the eastern arch seems to be part of the original design of the chancel, and which was completed by the building of the north transept. Above the level of the ridge tiles, however, Janyns's work is original and distinctive, and was widely influential in its time. Its chief characteristics are the relatively broad proportions of the belfry stage, with its wide windows framed by carefully clustered buttresses, and the contrasting but subtly balanced height of the pierced parapets and the array of tall pinnacles above. The effect is distinctive and impressive from every angle of view, combining a stately mass with delicate texture (Pl. 6).

The tower was built in two campaigns, the first extending up to the window openings, and ending in or before the summer of 1450. The second continued in 1451, but the accounts do not show when the work was completed. Seventeen masons are known to have been at work during the first four years, and there would have been many other workmen of various kinds at the quarries and on the site. One of the masons, Nicholas Baseley, came from the college's estate at Gamlingay in Cambridgeshire.[32] A substantial part of the cost was raised by private donations. The total recorded expenditure was £185, a considerable sum in itself, and certainly exceeded over the whole

expediency of raising such a building (*edificium*) presumably refers to a crossing-tower. The note points out that donors are available, and apparently engaged to contribute to the work, which could be sustained with timber from the estates in Surrey. If the lower stages of the tower were built then, they cannot now be distinguished. See further Henderson, pp. 206–7.

[32] E. A. Gee, 'Oxford masons, 1370–1530', *Archaeological Journal*, cix (1952), 112.

work. Janyns is described in 1450 as master of the works, and he was still giving advice in 1455, though by that time his regular visits had ceased and it is likely that only details remained to be settled.

Janyns was a talented sculptor as well as a designer. His origins are uncertain, beyond his association with Richard Chevington at Abingdon. The college had a tenant family of his name in Northumberland, though his employment might as well be a result of his work at All Souls' and Warden Holcot's connections with Chichele. The influences which originally played upon Janyns are therefore only a matter for conjecture, though his response to them is striking enough. Merton's tower apparently owed nothing to anything else then in sight, but it clearly influenced the design of Magdalen's campanile, and its high pierced parapets are a feature of many later towers in the south-west and elsewhere. It was a distinguished addition to the repertory of fifteenth-century architecture, as well as to the skyline and townscape of Oxford.

Elias Holcot played no large part in university affairs, though he was a trustee for money bequeathed by Cardinal Beaufort towards building the Divinity School, and appeared with John Gygour, principal of St Alban Hall and later warden of Merton, as a surety for John Godson or Godsoud, an Oxford stationer, in the chancellor's court.[33] The records of the library reveal no books written or donated by him. He nevertheless laid out his funds to advantage, and took the opportunity to negotiate a lease of the garden of St Alban Hall from Littlemore Priory at a time when the priory had lost interest in the hall. The tower, raised and probably completed during his term of office, is not an extravagant memorial to him.

Holcot was succeeded in 1456 by a more celebrated warden, Henry Sever, who is commemorated on his brass as an outstanding benefactor, and 'in a manner of speaking a founder', of the college (Pl. 12). He was a candidate for the wardenship in 1438, in which year he took his DD, and he served as a proctor in 1427–8, and chancellor in 1442–4. Like Holcot he was a notable builder, but there is some irony as well as much of interest in his career. Sever entered Merton in 1419 as of founder's kin, a category relatively rare by the fifteenth century,

---

[33] *Registrum Cancellarii Oxonieusis 1434–69*, ed. H. E. Salter (OHS xciii–xciv, 1932), i. 319; ii. 250–3. He also held a schedule of William Lyndwood's books and other effects for Lyndwood's executors: op. cit., ii. 164–5.

and of diminishing importance.[34] He became a bachelor fellow a year later, and a full fellow in 1423, the year after he took his bachelor's degree. He was a DD by 1438, having rented and presumably conducted a school belonging to Exeter Hall in 1425. His preferments began in 1435, with a prebend in the royal chapel at Bridgnorth; by 1437 he was an acknowledged chaplain to the king, and almoner by 1448. He was therefore close to Henry VI at a time when the king was intent upon his pious foundations, and Sever duly became the first provost of Eton College in 1440. His later benefices included the deanery of Bridgnorth, and the chancellorship of St Paul's, of which he had been a canon since 1445.

Sever's provostship began a long and close association of Merton with Eton, but with Wykeham's example in mind Henry fashioned his collegiate school to supply his foundation at Cambridge, King's College. The famous chapel of King's, almost the only part of the king's careful designs to be accomplished, was explicitly shaped to exceed the dimensions and, in the most rigorous taste, the splendour of Wykeham's work.[35]

Henry evidently admired New College, and was associated with Chichele in the foundation of All Souls', which had the character of a Lancastrian memorial, but for his great benefaction he chose not Oxford but Cambridge, where he swept the hinterland of the town quays bare to accommodate the complex of buildings which he planned. Not content, however, with bestowing his favours there, he proceeded to endow King's College in part by challenging Merton's title to its Cambridge lands. The college was involved in prolonged and expensive litigation, and although it received some compensation from lands in Wiltshire, which enlarged its estate at Stratton St Margaret, and kept other property in Cambridge, it evidently suffered losses.

In the face of that harassment neither a royal grant of 1443, con-

---

[34] They still had a distinct household in 1448, which was in the care of Simon Philip, manciple of St John the Baptist Hall on Magpie Lane: MCR 4116; and J. M. Fletcher and C. A. Upton, 'The cost of undergraduate study in Oxford in the fifteenth century: the evidence of the Merton College Founder's Kin', *History of Education*, xiv (1985), 1–20. Nine members of the kin became fellows between 1404 and 1487. They were Walter Lugardyn and John Odiham (1404), Richard Peddington (1405), Henry Sever (*c.* 1423), Nicholas Yardley (*c.* 1443), Nicholas Wright (1457), Thomas Lee (1462), Edward Bernarde (1483), and William Sheffield (1488). For Lee and Sever, see below, pp. 129, 138–9.

[35] R. Willis and J. W. Clark, *Architectural History of the University of Cambridge*, 4 vols. (Cambridge, 1886), i. 368–80.

ferring exemption from taxation,[36] nor admonition from Archbishop Bourchier in 1455 to appoint more fellows, offered much relief or assistance. The contention lasted well into Sever's wardenship, and was aggravated by a dispute with Richard Scarborough, sub-warden in 1461–2, over the money which Scarborough had laid out in pursuit of the college's rights. Scarborough, described moderately by F. M. Powicke as 'an energetic, lavish, troublesome man', must often have seemed more trouble than he was worth to his long-suffering colleagues.[37] He was, nevertheless, a connoisseur of manuscripts who undertook valuable work in ordering and maintaining the library, and his virtuously detailed accounts of his ridings to and from Cambridge and London afford a vivid picture not only of his travels, but of much parliamentary lobbying, and treats for counsel.[38]

Like Holcot, Sever did what he could and sometimes, it may be, more than he had hoped. He extended the warden's lodgings towards the south with two cross-wings, the first containing a private chapel, of which the east window survived into the twentieth century, until the building of St Albans Quadrangle. The wing to the south provided a kitchen, which served, with some nineteenth-century adaptation and extensions, until the lodgings were abandoned in 1907. Sever probably also built the vaulted entrance turret in the south-east corner of Front Quad which now leads into the estates bursary. Its plinth and string courses do not run with those of the Fitzjames arch to the south, and the style of the vault is much plainer and looks earlier than what we have of Fitzjames's acknowledged work.[39]

Besides those domestic works, which the development of the college and the usage of the times fully justified, Sever completed the gate-tower, including the vaulted gate-hall, and the richly-symbolic sculptured panel which is now set above the entrance arch, but was previously above the first-floor window (Pl. 2).[40] It is a *chef-d'œuvre* of Robert Janyns and his son, but no doubt represents much careful discussion of its imagery within the college. The Janynses personally

[36] *MM*, pl. xviii and pp. 38–9.

[37] See e.g. *MBMC*, p. 235.

[38] Merton MS Sacristy E.2.21. See further G. H. Martin, 'Road travel in the Middle Ages: some journeys by the warden and fellows of Merton College, Oxford, 1315–1470', *Journal of Transport History*, iii (1976), pp. 159–78, at pp. 171–2.

[39] The porch also does not lead directly into Fitzjames's rooms, though it does give access to Warden Brent's fine staircase: see below, p. 200.

[40] See further A. J. Bott and J. R. L. Highfield, 'The sculpture over the gatehouse of Merton College, Oxford 1464–5', *Oxoniensia*, lviii (1994), 233–40.

chose the stone at Taynton, and fitted the finished panel above the gate in the façade of the gate-tower in 1464, together with a representation of the Holy Trinity, which was set in the top stage of the tower, and finally proved too much for protestant susceptibilities or some other improving spirit in the seventeenth century.[41] Other adornments included the arms of Warden Sever, and of his friend and contemporary John Chedworth.[42] Since his time in Merton Chedworth had been a fellow and then provost of King's College, and was bishop of Lincoln from 1451 to 1471.

The gate-hall is roofed with two bays of tierceron-star vaulting with richly carved bosses, a provision quite beyond any structural needs in so modest a space, but delicately managed. The bosses make a subtle display of patronage, with symbols not only of the Yorkists who had displaced the house of Lancaster in 1461, but also of Edward IV's marriage to Elizabeth Woodville which, with her Lancastrian connections, later brought the dynasty to ruin. In the 1460s, however, there seemed to be some prospect of peace and stability in the kingdom. The vault also contains the monogram of Thomas Beckington, a royal counsellor and bishop of Bath and Wells, as a benefactor of the college.

Like any noble house, Merton was displaying both its origins and its accomplishments over the two centuries of its existence. The statues on the north face of the transept were probably added in the same building campaign as the final ornamentation of the gate-tower. The Virgin Mary and St John the Baptist as patron saints of the parish welcomed the world to the church, whilst the façade and gate-hall of the entrance tower proclaimed to those who sought the college, or merely regarded it in passing by, its aspirations, auspices, and achievements (Pl. 10). Until that time the outside world had only the scale of the buildings to admire: the furnishings of the chancel and

---

[41] Anthony Wood notes the restoration and colouring of the panel and the statues in 1682, adding 'It had been defaced in Oliver's raign. The picture of an old man sitting in a chair over that with a glove in his right hand, cut downe in Oliver's raigne': *LTAW* iii. 27. It is most interesting that the image of the Trinity should have survived so long, and the explanation is perhaps to be found in the fact that puritan animosity against sculpture *per se* was less strong in Oxford than elsewhere, and also that even Wood, as a careful student of antiquities, did not recognize the theme. See further below, p. 228.

[42] The arms were carved on the corbels on either side of the gate arch, and survived in a mutilated state until Blore's restoration of the front in 1836–8. They were 'Azure a chevron between three wolves or foxes heads erased, or' (Chedworth, to the right) and 'A fesse nebule between three annulets' (Sever, to the left). Sever's arms appear under the flanking canopies of his brass in the church (Pl. 12). See further Bott, *Monuments*, pp. 62–3, 113.

above all the fittings of the library were for the few. Now the house displayed its purpose for all to see.

Sever died in 1471; his fine memorial brass, which has been reset in the north transept, shows him in an ornate cope and amice over his surplice and cassock, and the inscription proclaims his services to the house. During the last years of his office he gave twenty-one manuscripts to the library, some of which contain the press marks of his personal collection, and at least one of which he had bought for himself in Paternoster Row.[43] He had earlier pledged a valuable missal to raise funds from one of the university chests to pay for his building work.[44] His other benefactions to the college included gifts of property in London and Essex. He also negotiated a ninety-nine-year lease of St Alban Hall and Nun Hall from Littlemore priory, the second of three long steps to the college's outright acquisition of St Alban Hall in 1548.

It is no disparagement of Sever's generosity to say that it was in a measure enhanced by the flatness of the surrounding landscape. The college had more competitors to match, and more needs on which to spend its funds, whilst would-be benefactors had more demands to meet, and might find themselves beset by conflicting loyalties. The most eminent Mertonian of his time was John Kemp, fellow 1395–1407, DCL in 1414, later a cardinal, archbishop successively of York (1425–52) and of Canterbury (1452–4), and in the course of his public career chancellor of Normandy and of England. Kemp supported the work on the church, paying for the glass in the west window of the south transept. He also enlarged the patronage of the college when he founded a college of priests and a school at Wye in Kent, his birthplace, and stipulated that the provostship should be reserved in the first instance for Mertonians.[45]

As his purpose in establishing Wye college was to benefit the secular priesthood Kemp no doubt had Walter de Merton's example in mind. A lawyer and diplomat of great experience, he was probably not a reading man, and his one bequest of a book was to Durham College, the Benedictine house in Oxford. He was, however, a notable bene-

---

[43] *MBMC*, pp. 201–4. The volume from the bookshop, Merton MS N. I. 6 (Coxe 212), contained an admonition from a former owner, provost of Oriel, that it was to pass only by bequest to priests from the priest to whom he gave it. His intentions were presumably realized after a fashion.

[44] And may have lost it thereby: *Munimenta Academica*, i, pp. xlii–xliii.

[45] C. S. Orwin and S. Williams, *History of Wye Church and College* (Ashford, 1913), pp. 1–20.

factor of the university, augmenting Cardinal Beaufort's bequest of 500 marks for the Divinity School and the library with 1,000 marks of his own. Kemp's nephew Thomas, who succeeded Robert Gilbert as bishop of London, gave Merton a gilt cross and rich cloth for vestments, but he also gave 1,000 marks and ninety volumes to the university library. There Mertonians shared in a general benison, but Thomas Kemp did give the college a notable £400 to provide an annual allowance for the fellows' clothing, and so relieved the pressure of inflation upon the stipendiary funds. The money was eventually invested in land at Gamlingay.[46]

Sever's successor was John Gygour, whose career touches some of the same themes. He was a foundation fellow of All Souls', then a fellow, bursar, and sub-warden of Merton, and principal of St Alban Hall, which in the 1440s was well on its way to becoming an adjunct of the college.[47] He was a fellow of Eton College from 1453 to 1457, but in the following year became warden of Lord Cromwell's college of the Holy Trinity at Tattershall, a benefice which he held throughout his wardenship at Merton, from 1471 to 1483, and to which he then retired, dying there in 1504. He gave some plate to Merton, probably on his retirement, and twenty books, mainly theological and philosophical, of which only three now survive. He subsequently gave some other books, including Peter Lombard's Sentences and a grammatical text, to Tattershall.

Gygour's library seems to have been a theologian's collection. He took a BD in 1460, and was incorporated at Cambridge in 1480, probably with his removal to Tattershall in mind. The library at Tattershall was mindlessly dispersed like very many others when the college was dissolved in 1545, whilst Gygour's books at Merton were probably amongst the host that fell foul of the Edwardian commissioners when they strove to purify the university in 1549.[48] One of the most interesting of Gygour's benefactions was the alabaster altarpiece of English workmanship which he presented to Santiago

[46] See *BRUO* ii. 133. Pope Innocent VI had recognized even in 1355 that the fellows' statutory allowance of 50s. each *per annum* was 'barely enough for their food, without any clothing at all': *CPL* iii. 561.

[47] Mertonians were as likely as anyone to become principals of halls, but their prevalence in the halls in and around Merton Street suggests something of a campaign. Gygour was only one of seventeen Mertonian principals of St Alban Hall: Appendix A (ii), pp. 371–2.

[48] See below, pp. 150–1.

de Compostela, an act which reinforces the general impression of his pietism, and a Mertonian regard for the shrine.[49]

Theology remained the principal study of the college throughout the century and beyond. It was supplemented as in the past by medicine: two notable recruits in the middle decades were Thomas Bloxham in 1446, who took his MD in 1459, and Henry Sutton in 1458. Sutton was also celebrated as an astronomer. Bloxham, who was master of Wyliot's foundation in 1460–1, died in 1483, leaving several pieces of plate to the college and all his books other than medical works, and excepting also a handsome Bible which he bequeathed to All Souls'. Twelve of his books survive in Merton, reflecting 'the interests of a scholarly and conservative theologian', and including some interesting classical texts.[50] Bloxham asked to be buried in St Frideswide's church, where he had been ordained an acolyte, and bequeathed two copes to the fine church of St Mary's, Bloxham, which was presumably his native or his family's parish.

Sutton, who besides taking the MD became a notary public, put up caution money for several halls in the 1460s, and was a keeper of the Chichester chest in the university. His preferments included canonries at Lincoln and St Paul's, the wardenship of De Vaux college at Salisbury, and the treasurership of Salisbury cathedral. He was denounced for, but survived, some part in Sir William Stanley's conspiracy with Perkin Warbeck in 1495. On his death in 1501 he bequeathed 20*d.* to every fellow of Merton in priest's orders. He had earlier contributed generously to the furnishing of the church, giving 26*s.* 8*d.* to the cost of the organ, and presenting a set of black damask vestments for celebrants.[51]

Medicine and the law were profitable interests, just as Archbishop Peckham had feared they would be. Mathematics was also cultivated, though not with the flair and intensity of the early fourteenth century, and with it astronomy, which was its principal academic application. Astronomy at all times shaded into astrology, which in turn had its applications in medicine. The best known of the astronomers was John Killingworth, a Northumbrian who appears first as a secular scholar of Durham College, and was admitted to Merton in 1432. He

---

[49] See the letter from W. H. Grattan Flood in *The Times Literary Supplement*, 26 Aug. 1926, and M. V. Rodriguez, *La Tumba del Apostol Santiago* (Santiago, 1924). For other Mertonian pilgrimages to Compostela, see below, p. 139.

[50] *MBMC*, p. 210, and above, p. 86.

[51] *RACM*, pp. 110, 178.

held college and university offices, and was successively principal of Corner Hall, one of the tenements later absorbed by Corpus Christi College, and of Olifant Hall, on the north side of the High Street. He seems to have remained an active member of the university and not to have sought a career or secured preferments outside. He was an exceptionally able mathematician, who compiled astronomical tables and wrote a substantial mathematical treatise as well as works on the phenomena of twilight and clouds. There is no trace of any of them now in the college library, but several of his books were at King's College in the early sixteenth century.[52] He died in 1445, and part of his figured memorial brass remains in the south transept of the church.[53]

Killingworth had some younger colleagues whose work and interests he probably influenced even if they were not technically his pupils. The first of them was Walter Hart, from the diocese of Worcester, admitted in 1438 and a full fellow from the early 1440s. He is named with John Gygour in a small group of fellows admitted together to confraternity by the English Hospital of the Holy Trinity and St Thomas the Martyr in Rome.[54] He resided in Lincoln College in 1455–6, the year in which he received his first benefices, and later became a canon and prebendary of St Paul's and dean of the collegiate church of St Cuthberga at Wimborne, Dorset. The *Catalogus Vetus* describes him as a distinguished astronomer, and Bishop Tanner noted some material on eclipses and other themes from a book attributed to him. He owned a copy of Simon Bredon's *Trifolium de re medica* which he promised to the college and which, after his death early in 1484, his brother delivered to the warden for the library.[55]

A less fortunate student of astronomy and the associated arts of astrology was John Stacey, elected as a bachelor in 1462 and a fellow a few years later. Stacey rented the school of metaphysics in Schools Street, presumably to use as a hall, in 1461–2. He was ordained acolyte in 1467, but he followed a lay career, apparently in London, and became, if he had indeed not always been, a gentleman. He studied astronomy with Thomas Blake, who was a chaplain at Merton, and

[52] *BRUO*, pp. 1049–50.
[53] Bott, *Monuments*, p. 19.
[54] *BRUO*, pp. 841, 882. Others were John Marshall, for whom see below, pp. 152–4, John Wymark, who later gave the college a copy of the Polychronicon (*MBMC*, p. 223), and John Warkworth, later master of Peterhouse, Cambridge, and a notable benefactor of that college (ibid., p. 224; and *BRUO*, pp. 1992–3).
[55] His brother and executor, John Hart, was a citizen of London: *MBMC*, p. 218.

whom the *Catalogus Vetus* describes as notably more learned in the science.

Astrology, whether taken as indicating probabilities or as absolutely predicting events, was esteemed as a practical application of astronomy, and it was a short step for an astrologer's clients to proceed from examining the future to seeking to influence it.[56] Blake and Stacey were suspected of abetting a lady of title in her attempts to rid herself of her husband, though the leaden images which she employed, with or without scientific sanction, proved ineffective.[57] The astrologers were then accused of plotting, in treasonable collusion with a member of the duke of Clarence's household, the death of Edward IV and Edward prince of Wales by 'art, magic, necromancy, and astronomy'. They protested that they had calculated the king's and prince's nativities in all innocence, but that was never a wise thing to do without the sovereign's consent, and their confederate Thomas Burdett was said to have spread rumours of the king's impending demise on the strength of their investigations. All were convicted of treason. Blake's life was spared on the petition of Bishop Goldwell of Norwich, a trusted counsellor of Edward IV, but Stacey was executed at Tyburn in May 1477, the first though not the last Mertonian to die there.[58]

The tradition of predictive astronomy was continued more respectably but no more happily by Thomas Kent, elected as bachelor in 1480, who served as dean, bursar, and chaplain of Merton, and was a chaplain of the university. The *Catalogus* refers to him as a good astronomer, and he is said to have predicted the severe winter and dearth of 1490, but before they came he succumbed untimely to plague, in 1489.

On John Gygour's resignation in 1482 the fellows, in accordance with custom, submitted the names of three candidates for the wardenship. The more senior, by a considerable margin, were Thomas Pash, a canon and prebendary of St George's, Windsor, and a royal almoner, and Richard Newbridge, vicar of Farnham, Surrey, who had both been elected to Merton in 1436. The successful candidate was markedly younger: Richard Fitzjames, DD, a Somerset man, admitted

---

[56] On astrology and popular superstitions, see further J. D. North, 'Astronomy and mathematics', *HUO* ii. 103–74, at pp. 104–9.

[57] See *BRUO*, p. 1749. The reference there to Lady Beauchamp cannot be substantiated.

[58] Stacey's wife, Marion, was granted all his goods shortly after his execution: *CPR 1476–85*, p. 43. The swift restitution of his estate suggests that his execution was seen as something of a technicality, a nuance which probably escaped him.

as a bachelor in 1465, and a fellow since 1468 (Pl. II). He was a veteran of the usual college offices, served as senior proctor in 1473–4, and was the chancellor's commissary, or vice-chancellor of the university, in 1481. He had been principal of St Alban Hall from 1477 to 1481. His external preferments began in 1476, and at the time of his appointment he was a canon of Wells, but his public career largely followed upon his wardenship, though the college obviously knew him already as a purposeful administrator.

Fitzjames's first act was to institute a register and act book, the need of which, as he observed, the college had felt for many years. Immediately upon his introductory statement he recorded Gygour's resignation and his own appointment, and he then kept the register in his own hand for some fifteen years, with only minor intermissions, until his bishoprics and a growing tale of public commitments took him out of Oxford. In the mean time he set a pattern which transformed the records of the house, noting not only the admission and departure of fellows, but their academic progress, college acts and resolutions, and the domestic and other ceremonial of the common life. It was a notable and bold innovation on the part of a deeply conservative man.[59]

Fitzjames's name is now most usually associated with the vaulted archway and chamber which he added to the warden's lodgings. The connection is not unjust, for he was an enthusiastic builder, and what is generally referred to as the Fitzjames arch is an eloquent structure. The whole work added a further cross-wing to the lodgings, and its scale speaks of its purpose: the warden had many public duties, and on occasions he needed accommodation of a princely sort. The chambers above and to the east of the arch, later known as the Queen's Room and the Breakfast Room, are generously proportioned, and with hangings and other appropriate furnishing could offer the kind of elegant comfort that the rest of the lodgings probably lacked.[60]

All the internal details have since been swept away, but the purpose of the work is plain. Outside, the lierne vault of the archway is sumptuously executed, and shows at once that the warden did not

---

[59] A. B. Emden desribed it as the 'most enviable of all college records covering the Tudor period': *BRUO 1501–40*, p. xix. See also below, pp. 142–3.

[60] Richard Nash, mason, built a fireplace and did some work in the lodgings in 1483: Gee, 'Oxford masons', p. 114. The early 16th-cent. inventories do not refer to panelling in the lodgings, though it was by then a fashionable refinement: see below, p. 144. The Queen's Room housed Tsar Alexander I in June 1814: Henderson, p. 165.

spare expense. The imagery is also expressive. The arms displayed towards Front Quad celebrate the warden's appointment to the see of Rochester in 1497. The royal arms at the centre of the vault attest his loyalty, and the zodiacal theme of the surrounding bosses proclaims his learned interest in astronomy. We know from a later reference that the building's horoscope was cast when the first stones were laid, and recorded in a window which Warden Lydall removed from the lodgings in 1693, in pursuit of modernity.[61]

The archway now leads into the Great Quadrangle, known as Fellows' Quad, but Fellows' was raised by Warden Savile more than a century later, and in 1497 its site was only a paddock, with a garden or two by the hall. It may be that Fitzjames had some more elaborate plan in mind, and would have raised a quadrangle of his own there if he had stayed in Merton. If so, he had the eventual satisfaction of adding a handsome new courtyard to Fulham Palace, which still stands to be admired. His energies were by no means consumed in enlarging the lodgings, however, and in his own day, and for some time later, his work in the college church probably won more attention than the archway.

The college gave up the idea of building a nave and aisles to the west of the crossing only at a late date; the moulded arches built to open into the western limb were not finally walled up until the end of the fifteenth century, and the blocking of the tower arch for the west window conceals the springing of a nave arcade. That resolution, or resignation, was compensated by a sustained campaign to refurnish the church.[62] Fitzjames's principal contribution to the work was the roodloft, commissioned in 1486 from John Fisher, citizen and joiner of London.[63]

A roodloft was a screen and gallery which took its name from the rood or crucifix which it supported. It was a feature of monastic and other large churches from an early date, but became widely used in parish churches only from the fourteenth century. The loft, which

---

[61] *LTAW* iii. 436. Wood attributed Lydall's zeal for redecoration, like his acquisition of a carriage, for the first time in the history of the college, to the fact that he had a wife and five daughters to keep in countenance. See also below, p. 228 and n.

[62] It may be that the implied resignation of interest in the land beyond the Grove, of which Warden Rawlins improvidently disposed in 1513 (see below, p. 146–7), coincided with the consolidation of the plots to the east which the college had acquired over the century, and which became the fellows' garden. Henry Milton and a mason called Blake were employed in making a wall 'for the great garden' in 1500: Gee, 'Oxford masons', p. 82. The work may mark the consolidation of the front walls of the properties on Merton Street: see above, p. 35.

[63] See the contract, 11 Aug. 1496, in *RACM 1483–1521*, pp. 520–2.

supported an array of lights and statues, and sometimes housed an altar, was used particularly to read the Gospel during the mass.[64] The college church would certainly have had a screen to close off the choir as soon as it had a western limb,[65] but the explicit commission of 1486 seems to have been prompted partly by a desire piously to excel Magdalen College, and partly from Fitzjames's clear determination to elaborate college services and their setting.[66]

Fisher was to provide all the material except English timber, which the college would supply from its own resources. The work below the loft was to match, but improve upon, the roodloft at Magdalen, whilst the loft itself and its parapets were to be modelled on the loft in St Mildred's-in-the-Poultry, London, but 'of better [effect] than it is there'. The doors of the screen were flanked with tabernacle work for two altars, one dedicated to St Andrew, to the north, and one to St Jerome to the south,[67] for which Fisher supplied effigies of those saints, as well as a number of other figures for the parapet of the loft.[68] The loft was to have an ornamented coving, and the whole work was to be finished in a year, at a cost of £27 together with food and drink for Fisher and up to three workmen.[69] In 1488 Fitzjames contributed £5 towards the cost of an organ, and announced on the same occasion that the provost of Wye, Nicholas Wright, had subscribed £2 to the cost of the roodloft.[70] The contract for the organ was drawn up at

---

[64] Upon the precept of Isaiah: 40: 9.

[65] See above, p. 41.

[66] It was decided in 1488 to postpone some elections to the fellowship in order to maintain funds for work on the church: *RACM 1483–1521*, pp. 108–9.

[67] The altars were dedicated by the bishop of Lincoln in March 1488, when the warden and the bishop's chaplain celebrated the first masses, the warden choosing St Jerome's altar to mark his reverence for the saint. He had personally met part of the cost of furnishing the altar: *RACM*, p. 110.

[68] The rood customarily included the figures of St Mary and St John the Evangelist, at the foot of the cross, but the contract specifies a display of figures two feet high over a distance of 32 feet, perhaps in the panels of the parapet. The college was to specify the subjects: loc. cit. It would be interesting to know what they were, and whether they included benefactors as well as saints.

[69] In the event the work continued until Michaelmas 1488, probably because the college dispersed during an outbreak of plague in the summer of 1487: *RACM*, p. 92.

[70] Wright was of the founder's kin, a fellow from 1457 to 1462, who rented several halls in 1458–61 and became provost of Wye in 1461. He died in 1499: *BRUO*, p. 2097. There are many such gifts recorded in the Register, especially towards the roodloft and the organ, and they are most likely to have been the product of a campaign by the warden. See e.g. *RACM*, pp. 77, 98, for Dr Thomas Balsall, a notable benefactor. Fitzjames subsequently installed organs in the parish churches of Fulham, London, Much Hadham, Herts., and Wickham Bishops, Essex, when he became bishop of London: *BRUO*, p. 692.

once with William Wotton of Oxford, and the instrument completed in 1489. The organist was provided with a lectern or desk called an *ambo*, which probably served as a music rest.[71] The whole structure of the roodloft was decorated by Henry the painter, at the high cost of £16. 13s. 4d., in 1491.

With the organ installed, John Davers, a chaplain and bible clerk, was appointed precentor, and John Lawrence, one of the warden's scholars, was paid 20s. to play the organ. He was succeeded by a scholar named Bulger, and then by John Frampton, who in 1503, when he had taken orders, gave the college a breviary.[72] The organist's stipend was later raised to 26s. 8d. By 1507 all portionists and commoners were expected to sing plain song, with some of the portionists providing 'cantus fractus'. There were four choirmasters available for services on the major festivals, who were instructed to sit in pairs, and not all four on one bench, lest they should crush their expensive copes.

Music had evidently come to hold the kind of place which Wyliot had envisaged for it a century earlier, though we have little information about what was performed. Only a few fragments of the college's musical manuscripts have survived, as pastedowns in the bindings of books. However, Thomas Danet, a fellow in 1455 and subsequently principal of St Alban Hall, composed a *Gloria in excelsis*, a *Credo*, and probably a *Gloria, qui tollis*. They survive, with other settings from St George's chapel, in the volume known as the Old Hall Manuscript which Danet himself began to compile when he was at Windsor as a canon of St George's and a royal almoner.[73] Danet had a younger colleague, John Atkins, who was elected in 1467 and died in 1471 only a short time after he became a full fellow. Atkins is noted in the *Catalogus Vetus* as an outstanding musician, but there is no other trace of his work.

There were several more subsidiary altars in the church: at least four besides those already named, and probably others. Two, dedicated to the Virgin Mary and St Catherine, were in the south transept, which was principally appropriated to college use. The recess which contained St Catherine's altar is still marked by the wheel in the remains

[71] MCR 4012.

[72] *RACM*, pp. 177, 276.

[73] See *The Old Hall Manuscript*, ed. A. Ramsbotham, H. B. Collins, and A. Hughes, 3 vols. (London, 1933–8), i, pp. x–xi, xv–xvi. Danet was a member of the family which held Danets Hall, Leicester.

of its carved canopy. Elsewhere more windows were filled with painted glass, and new vestments and ornaments were either bought or presented by Mertonians and other benefactors. Robert Gosbourn, a bachelor fellow in 1471, later senior proctor, and chaplain to Richard duke of York, one of the princes in the Tower, gave 20*s*. towards the new organ. John Martock, elected in 1458 and subsequently a celebrated physician, gave plate and ornaments to St Andrew's altar and the high altar, and on his death in 1503 bequeathed the enormous sum of £100 for vestments, besides books and more plate. The college marked its gratitude by appointing a perpetual obit for him, and his executors rounded off his good works by presenting the fine brass lectern which still adorns the chancel.

A new set of choir stalls was built in 1491, and was decorated at the expense of John Marshall, bishop of Llandaff. Marshall was admitted as a bachelor in 1446, and was a fellow from 1449 to 1457. He rented several halls, and was a proctor, and keeper of one of the university chests. His benefices included canonries of York, Lincoln, and St George's, Windsor, before he was provided to Llandaff in 1478. He died and was buried there in 1496. He had previously paid for the restoration of a preaching cross in Oxford called St Frideswide's cross, which may originally have been the celebrated Jews' cross of 1268. On his death he bequeathed £20 and his books to Merton, with a silver-gilt cup for the warden's use.[74] The monetary legacy was used to ceil the chancel. The paintings on the backs of the choir stalls depicted apostles, saints, and prophets, each with a scroll bearing verses from the creed and paternoster. There was a kneeling figure of Bishop Marshall somewhere in the sequence, which gained sanctuary in the library until the middle of the seventeenth century, when it was removed by idle hands.

Fitzjames's care for the chapel continued into the years of his absence on other duties. He spent more than £200 on twenty-four copes in 1505, and bought fine cloth for the Easter sepulchre in 1506, the year before his resignation. He was also busy with the library throughout his wardenship. He used a timely donation from Thomas Lee with some other gifts to re-roof the library,[75] and to furnish it with

---

[74] For the Jews' cross, see above, pp. 32–3. For the books, including two given in 1491, see *MBMC*, pp. 219, 222. The books, mostly theological texts, but including one medical work, were all subsequently lost.

[75] Lee was of the founder's kin, deriving his claim through Walter de Merton's mother (MCR 3088), and a former fellow (1462–74), who had kept a number of halls and served

1 a) Seal of the founder,
Walter de Merton, bishop of
Rochester (8 Jan. 1277)
MCR 2817

1 b) First seal of Peter Abingdon
(first warden, 1264–86)

2 Merton College, the gateway (15th cent.) with the Janyns sculpture above (1464–5)

3 The door of the Hall (*c.*1275)

4 The roof of the Warden's Hall (*c.1270*), now the Middle Common Room

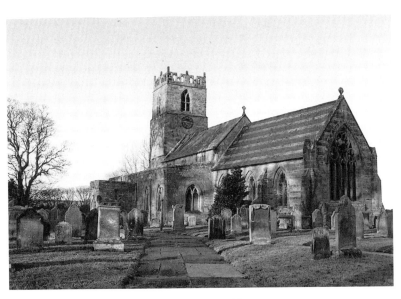

5 Holy Trinity, Embleton

6 Mob Quad and the Tower

7 Mob Quad, from the north-east, with the solid stone roof of the Treasury
in the foreground

Ricardus dei gra [...] er Angl [...] francie [...]
dominus scolarium de Merton in Oxon [...]
manerdur Thomas Gryne Baldus [...]
tii [...] cona cum [...] shopis [...] solarium [...]
[...] regentii [...] in [...] misericordia comon [...] mes [...]
in auxilium sustentacois paupium scolarium in scolis regencii [...]
colore cum scia magnificis p Estriecwarden [...] E [...] imp Regis Ang [...]
Thomas Baldus Johannes [...] [...] dau mesuagu sine hospic [...]
[...] maxim Oxon sibi [...] successorib; suis ad opus de dominis sin [...]
din adquisierunt pdam hospicium cum ptin caput sint in manu [...]
in Cuna nostra allegauimus [...] ipi dau hospicium cum ptin in [...]
[...] collusionem statim pdca adquisierunt ptin pdcam magnificen [...]
Merton Johem Thomam Baldum Johem [...] Fran capitam [...] pd [...]

8 King Richard II,
   Warden Bloxham, and
   five fellows of Merton
   (licence to acquire
   property in Mortmain,
   5 Oct. 1380) MCR 370

lut hetic [...]
restituam[...]
tellus. mon [...]
or libano p [...]
circumaso [...]
fiartharui [...]
poribus se [...]
multitou [...]
nelmt. Ju [...]
vi[...] proter [...]

9 Thomas Netter,
   Doctrinale Fidei (Coxe
   319 fo. 41r, 15th cent.):
   the burning of heretical
   books

10 Statue of the Virgin Mary on the north transept (after 1450)

11 'Maniculum' of John Tiptoft in the oldest book in the Library, Eusebius's *Chronicon* (Mert. MS Coxe 315, fo. 132ᵛ, 9th cent.), which was in Germany in the 14th cent. Tiptoft's marginalia suggest that it was in Padua in the mid-15th cent.

cena nihil se in illo die cuiquam prestitisse d

Mons uesouius ruptus in uertice tant ut regiones uicinas & urbes cum ho

Titus musonium rufum philosophu Titus amphitheatrum romae aedifi quinque milia ferarum occidit

Romanae aecclesiae secundus conse Romae plurimae aedes incendio co

CCXV OLYMPIAS Titus morbo periit in ea uilla qua p

ROMANORVM · VIIII · REGNAVIT · XV · MENS · V ·

Domitianus titi frater iunior ·

Domitiani uxor augusta appellatur Decreto senatus titus inter deos ref

12 Brass of Warden Sever (d. 1471) in the north transept

13 Geoffrey Chaucer, *The Canterbury Tales* (Caxton, Westminster, c.1478), p.1 with the arms of the Haberdasher's Company

14 Aristotle, *Opera Omnia* (Aldus, Venice, 1495), colophon to vol. i. Presented by Sir Basil Blackwell (postmaster and hon. fellow; d. 1984)

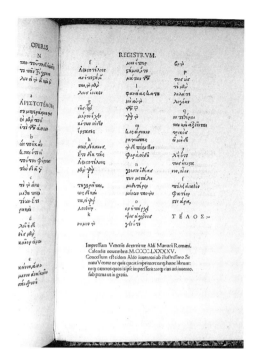

15 Monument of Sir Thomas Bodley (fellow; d. 1613) in the north transept

16 The Library, west wing, showing the the presses of *c.* 1589
and the arch of 1623

17 The Tower of the Four Orders, Fellows' Quad (1610)

18 Monument of Sir Henry Savile
(warden; d. 1621) in the south transept

19 Queen Henrietta Maria, after
Van Dyck, in the Old Common Room.
Given by Edward Lucie-Smith
(postmaster)

20 The title-page of William Harvey
(warden; d. 1657), *De Generatione
Animalium* (London, 1651)

21 Monument of Anthony Wood
(postmaster and bible clerk; d. 1695)
in the north transept

22 The Summer House (1709), now the Music Room

23 John Wall (fellow; d. 1776),
by an unknown artist

24 David Hartley (fellow; d. 1813),
by Lewis Vaslet

25 Thomas Tyrwhitt (fellow; d. 1786),
from a mezzotint by J. Jones after a
portrait by Benjamin Wilson

26 James Hope-Scott (fellow; d. 1873),
by George Richmond

27 Mandell Creighton (fellow; d. 1903), by Herbert Herkomer

28 Interior of the rooms of R. Helmes (commoner, 1870–3)

29 The annexation of St Alban Hall (1881). L to R: E. Knox (sub-warden),
the Hon. G. C. Brodrick (warden), Dr H. Robinson (St Alban Hall),
the Revd G. N. Freeling (chaplain of Merton)

30 Joseph Chamberlain
(bursary clerk)

31 Max Beerbohm (commoner and hon.
fellow; d. 1956), self-portrait

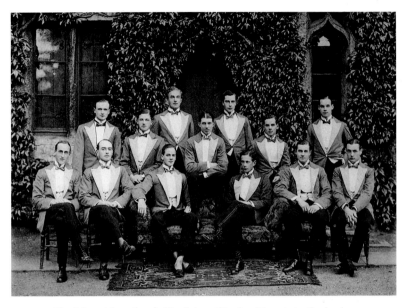

32 The Myrmidons (1913). The future Warden Mure is in the back row,
3rd from L.

W. Bullivant   A. Newall   G. R. G . Mure   E. A. Collymore

E. G. Thompson   M. R. Thompson (Prest)   W. H. E. Nield

C. L. Domville   T. H. Peach   H. A. Pelly   E. K. Stephenson   D'A. J. J. Hartley   R. W. Beeson

33 Lennox Berkeley, (commoner
and hon. fellow; d. 1989), by
Caroline Hill (1972)

34 Louis MacNeice (postmaster;
d. 1963)

35 Edmund Blunden (fellow; d. 1974)

36 Sir John Miles (warden, 1936–47; d. 1963), by Rivière

37 Group Captain G. L. Cheshire, vc, om, (hon. fellow; d. 1992)

38 G. R. G. Mure (warden, 1947–63; d. 1979), self-portrait

39 a) Merton College 1st VIII (1951), when Merton went Head of the River

P. D. Leuch (4)   K. R. Spencer (2)   N. W. Sanders (Bow)   C. D. Milling (3)   R. L. Arundel (5)
A. J. Smith (6)   D. R. Tristram (Str.)   H. M. C. Quick (7)
(Cox) D. W. Bannister

39 b) Merton College Women's VIII in Torpids (1991), on their way to winning their blades.

Stroke, Rachel Willmot; 7, Emma Haynes; 6, Julee Greenough; 5, Susanne Erb; 4,
Nicola Audhlam-Gardiner; 3, Hannah Tooze; 2, Harriet Drybrough; Bow, Lucy Wyles;
Cox, Lindsay Dow

40 Head of the River Bowl (1951)

41 A. R. W. Harrison (warden,
    1963–69; d. 1969), by G. W. Shield
    (schoolmaster student)

42 Professor J. R. R. Tolkien (fellow;
    d. 1973), *The Hobbit*, Runic
    inscription on flyleaf of copy
    presented to Professor Norman
    Davis (fellow; d. 1989)

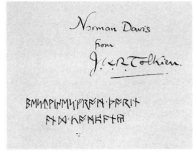

43 Sir Rex Richards (warden, 1972–84) as Vice-Chancellor, by Brian Organ (1977)

44 Sir Richard Southwood (Linacre Professor of Zoology) as Vice-Chancellor, by Mark Wickham (1990)

45 J. M. Roberts (warden, 1984–94), by Tai-Shan Schierenberg (1994)

46 The sub-warden, the warden-elect, and fellows (1994)

Dr Sunetra Gupta Mr R. Mighall Mr S. Jarvis Mr R. C. Loader Dr F. Oditah Dr Ulrike Tillmann Dr Z. Molnár Dr C-H. L. Ong Dr Fiona Robb
Dr P. B. Kronheimer Ms Mindy Chen-Wishart Professor G. K. Radda Dr Eleanor Dickey Dr J. J. Coulton Dr Sarah Bendall Dr Mary E. Phillips Dr M. G. Bowler
Dr P. Harvey Mr I. G. Thompson Dr S. J. Gunn Dr R. A. McCabe Dr E. A. Newsholme Mr D. C. Witt Dr R. N. Gildea Dr S. J. R. Vessey Dr D. J. Paterson
Dr C. J. H. Watson Dr L. M. Harwood Dr C. J. G. Morgan Dr T. P. Softley Mr J. L. Barton Mr D. Bostock Mr D. J. Markwell Dr D. E. Olleson Dr N. J. Richardson
Dr J. M. Baker Mr P. J. Waller Dr Jessica M. Rawson (Warden, from 26. 10. 94) Mr V. R. Joshi (Sub-Warden) Mr T. F. R. G. Braun Mr C. R. Webb
The Revd M. Everitt Professor M. G. Gelder

Absent: Professor R. Alexander, Dr J. J. Binney, Professor J. Carey, Dr P. Chamberlain, Dr M. S. Dunnill, Dr J. A. Jones, J. R. Lucas, Professor A. J. Macintyre,
Dr G. Major, Professor Sir Richard Southwood, Dr J. A. D. Welsh

47   J. M. Rawson (warden, 1994–)

wainscoting, which was subsequently replaced when the library was remodelled, and a new wooden ceiling, ornamented with bosses, which still serves.[76] He also gave the library more than twenty books, most of them after he moved to London.[77] He had at least one of his own sermons printed, so he was aware of printers and no doubt of what they portended, but in college he seems to have dealt only in manuscripts. A fourteenth-century missal which belonged to him and which he took with him to London is preserved in Minehead parish church.[78]

The conservative piety evinced by Fitzjames was not unrepresentative of Merton, which had certainly nurtured a tradition of personal devotion at least since the middle of the century. The appeal of confraternal prayer has been noted, and John Gygour's interest in St James of Compostela was continued, with John Trowell and another master planning a pilgrimage there in 1490, and John Beverston, principal of St Alban Hall, drowned on his way home from Spain in 1507. John Blackman, bachelor fellow and fellow in the 1430s, and later a fellow of Eton and warden of King's Hall, Cambridge, entered the Charterhouse at Witham, in Somerset. He was followed there in 1498 by Henry Corslegh, who resolved to leave Merton and take vows during his probationary year. John Trowell subsequently became a monk in the Brigittine house at Syon, Middlesex, and confessor general there. He gave three books to Merton when he resigned his fellowship in 1491, and ten others to Syon, of which seven were printed works, on his death in 1523.[79] By that time Thomas Person,

---

as a university officer. His gifts in 1487 included plate, £30 in cash, and a further £20 to establish a loan chest subsequently known as Mr Lee's hutch: *BRUO*, p. 1124. He died in 1502 and was buried before St Mary's altar, in the north transept of the church, where his grave-slab has survived with the impression of a brass. He was also commemorated by a portrait (*effigies*) in hall, most probably a figure in a window: Bott, *Monuments*, p. 15; *RACM*, pp. 262, 263.

[76] See J. M. Fletcher and C. A. Upton, 'The renewal and embellishment of the Merton College library roof, 1502–3', *Library History*, viii/4 (1989). The bosses judiciously associate the devices of the Tudors with the arms of the college and of Fitzjames.

[77] See *MBMC*, pp. 221–2, 225–30.

[78] Fitzjames was vicar of St Michael's, Minehead, Somerset, from 1485 until his election to Rochester. The missal contains a supplication in Fitzjames's hand, and a note attesting his ownership of the MS which was added by Cuthbert Tunstall, his successor in the see of London: C. H. Bullivant, *The Missal of Richard Fitzjames* (2nd edn., Minehead, 1984), p. 3.

[79] See *Catalogue of the Library of Syon Monastery, Isleworth*, ed. M. Bateson (Cambridge, 1898), p. xxvii and n.

elected to a fellowship in 1520, had also left the college to join the Observant Friars.

Fitzjames's time in London was embittered by disputes with John Colet, then dean of St Paul's, and by what he saw in Colet's circle and elsewhere as threats to the unity of the church. It is not unknown for bishops and deans to be at odds, but the friction does not often extend to formal denunciations of heresy such as Fitzjames laid before Archbishop Warham.[80] Colet's commitment to the new learning and his radical approach to the Bible seemed deeply dangerous to Fitzjames, whom Erasmus denounced as an embattled Scotist. So he was, not because his mind was locked into the disputes of the fourteenth century, but because established routines and tradition seemed to him to be the only means of securing the church against disruption.[81] He had sought to strengthen Merton against change on the eve of a cataclysmic upheaval. His forebodings were not unjustified, but his precautions were ineffectual. Yet some of his works have endured, long beyond the controversies and misgivings of his time.

[80] *DNB* (Colet).

[81] He would have been much of the mind of John Sheprey, reader in Greek at Corpus Christi, whom his colleagues denounced in 1538 for saying that 'the studiying off the scriptures was subversion of goode order': *BRUO*, p. 513. See also *MBMC*, p. 35 and n. The re-emergence of Scotist thought in the late 15th cent. probably accounts for the violence of the reformers' denunciations of John Duns as the archetype of scholastic philosophers.

7

The Onset of the Reformation

FITZJAMES was succeeded as warden by Thomas Harper, who by the time of his appointment in 1507 had held most of the established college offices and also the seasonal appointment known as the king of the beans. The king was a master of revels who ruled in hall over Christmas, and who first comes to notice in the later fifteenth century. He was either the most senior of the fellows who had never before held the post, or the most recent recipient of an adequately rewarding benefice who happened still to be in residence. His seniority was at odds with one common feature of the Saturnalian tradition, which is that rank should be overturned during the festival, but he was evidently expected to regale the company, and had therefore to be a man of some means. The first king named in the register was John Bird, appointed in 1486 out of turn, but recently collated to the rectory of Acton, Middlesex. His successor in 1487, William Neale, had a vicarage in hand and a canonry of St David's in prospect.[1]

There are some apparent relics of the kingship dating from the middle years of the fifteenth century, but it is likely to go back in some form to the earliest years of life in hall.[2] New Year was also regularly marked by a visit by the Oxford city waits, who sang, and then, unlike some later carol singers, were rewarded only if they did not uncivilly insist upon the reward as a right.[3] It fell to the second

---

[1] *Rex Fabarum*, the king of the beans, was also sometimes called king of the college, and sometimes simply king. For John Bird, see *RACM 1483–1521*, p. 94. For Neale, see ibid., p. 104. Neale, a fellow since 1477, had just been appointed vicar of Old Sodbury, Glos., and was a canon of St David's by the end of the year. He was a nominee for the wardenship in 1508: *BRUO*, p. 1342; *RACM*, p. 368.

[2] See the extravagantly allusive letters of *c.* 1450 from BL Royal MS 10 which order the nomination of a king, quoted by H. E. Salter in *RACM*, pp. xviii–xx. See further E. K. Chambers, *The Medieval Stage* (Oxford, 1903), i. 260–1, 407–13.

[3] The waits are described as *satrapes* (*RACM*, p. 312), and H. E. Salter identifies them as the mayor's serjeants from a Magdalen reference (ibid., pp. xx–xxi). *Satrapis* for serjeant (*serviens*) is a learned flourish, characteristic of the period, but apart from their other functions as officials of the city courts, the fact that they sang suggests strongly that they embodied the musical component of the city's watch, and were in effect the town band.

bursar, for some other reason now (perhaps happily) lost, to lead the Christmas hymn in hall after the annual assembly on New Year's Eve. Such domestic details are the small change of the register, and a welcome addition to the rather meagre picture of college life which the earlier records afford.

Thomas Harper, as well as having taken his turn as a lord of Yule, was a theologian who had been a university preacher, and had served as vice-chancellor in 1498. Like Fitzjames he was a Somerset man, from Axbridge. His benefices included a prebend at Chichester, and from 1503 the priorate of the house of Kalendars, a famous priestly gild in Bristol, where he was also vicar of St Nicholas's church. He was warden of Merton for little more than a year, dying at Bristol on 11 November 1508. He had not then been long in that city, for he had conducted a visitation of some of the Surrey and Buckinghamshire manors over Michaelmas, and when he died had cash still in hand, 16s. 8d., arising from a sale of timber at Ibstone.

The fellows recovered the cash, and found that the warden had bequeathed some plate to the college, including a large silver-gilt cup with a cover, and another standing cup. He also left a broad and sumptuous coverlet for the warden's use, and a legacy of £20 to secure his obit from the fellowship for a nicely calculated twenty years.[4] The plate, and some books intended to be distributed amongst the fellows, were duly delivered to the college by the Bristol carrier in the spring of 1509. Similar references at large in the register reveal a network of carriers in the late fifteenth century, which was probably long established.[5]

Harper was an active scholar,[6] and his benefice with the Kalendars suggests that he may have been given to personal pieties. In his short tenure of office he made no particular mark on the house,[7] but he was commemorated in the church by the unusual device of a memorial shared with his contemporary and friend Ralph Hamsterley. As Hamsterley, who was something of a connoisseur of funeral monuments,[8]

---

[4] See *RACM*, pp. 366–7, 369.

[5] See *RACM*, p. 387. In 1489 Fitzjames sent up a silver-gilt cross of Bishop Kemp's bequest, weighing 120 oz., by a London carrier named Barker: ibid., p. 119. See further G. H. Martin, 'Road travel in the Middle Ages', pp. 161–3.

[6] He received 73 books by indenture when he became warden, and he seems to have replaced or renewed a number of titles before his death: *MBMC*, pp. 224–5.

[7] See *BRUO*, pp. 878–9; and above, n. 6.

[8] He is commemorated in St Andrew's, Oddington, which is probably where he is buried, by a cadaver brass, a comparative rarity. Pevsner describes it clinically as 'A 27½-inch worm-

did not die until 1518 the two had presumably come to some agreement in Harper's lifetime. Only the indents of their twin brass effigies now remain, on a slab in the south transept.

Hamsterley was, with Harper himself, Richard Rawlins, and William Neale a member of the panel of senior fellows who put forward names for the wardenship in 1507, and he acted thus again in 1508, when Rawlins became warden. In 1509 he was made master of University College. His election was strongly resented by some of the fellows there as he was the first master appointed from outside the house. There was some uncomfortable strife, and it may be that he accepted a consolatory offer of accommodation from Merton in the last years of his life,[9] though he then enjoyed other resources, including a canonry of Durham, several rectories, and the mastership of St John's hospital at Banbury. Bishop Fitzjames tried to compose the discord between Hamsterley and his opponents, but apparently without success; viewed from University College he perhaps seemed more Mertonian than episcopal. One of the alien Hamsterley's innovations was a register like the Merton register, which his watchful colleagues spurned, not wishing to be written down.[10]

It was presumably not Hamsterley's remoter origins which had made him unacceptable at University College, for he was from the diocese of Durham, and his benefices were mostly in the north. When he died in 1518 he secured a memorial brass in University College chapel and an obit at Queen's, as well as other brasses in Durham College chapel and at Oddington, but he shared his pious fame only at Merton, where he had also provided £20 and other funds for the college to maintain an obit.[11]

Thomas Harper was succeeded by Richard Rawlins, another highly regarded theologian, whose name had been put forward with Harper's in 1507.[12] He was elected as a bachelor in 1481, was a fellow from 1484, and had since been a college officer under various titles, a canon of

eaten effigy in a shroud'. It is illustrated in M. Norris, *Monumental Brasses: The Craft* (London, 1977), p. 61; the inscription leaves blank the date of Hamsterley's death, which suggests that he had commissioned the brass himself. For Hamsterley's negotiations with the college over commemorative prayers, see *RACM*, pp. 449, 459; and below, n. 9.

[9] See *BRUO*, p. 424.

[10] No doubt on Lord Eldon's principle that any change, at any time, for any reason whatsoever, is to be deplored. See *BRUO*, p. 864; and Bodleian Library MS Bodl. 282.

[11] On Hamsterley's numerous memorials, see further Bott, *Monuments*, pp. 21–2 and n.

[12] *RACM*, pp. 334, 370. The third candidate on both occasions was Dr Hugh Saunders, later a canon of St Paul's and vicar of St Mary Matfelon, Stepney, the original White Chapel, who was one of Fitzjames's executors: *BRUO*, pp. 1643–4.

St George's, Windsor, and a royal chaplain. He wrote his letter accepting the wardenship from Windsor, and in 1511 he was called to Westminster to preach at the funeral of the infant Prince Henry, the first of Queen Catherine's sad children.[13] As well as being a royal official and a courtier, Rawlins seems to have favoured the new learning. Where Fitzjames could see only the contagion of literary criticism spreading destructively to holy writ, many other scholars saw new means to understanding. At all events Rawlins extended a cautious hand to innovation, and in reply to his official welcome in the college gate-hall he sounded a muffled warning against the toils of Scotic speculation. His words signalled at least an impending departure from the Fitzjames tradition.

Rawlins entered upon his office, on 17 February 1509, in high style. The fellows gathered in the gate-hall, in gowns and hoods, to receive him in traditional form with speeches, greetings, and embraces, and the company then progressed through Mob Quad and the south door of the church to a service in the choir, after which the fellows took the warden to his lodgings, and drank with him there. Then on the following evening, after a play performed in hall, Rawlins entertained the whole fellowship in the lodgings, together with a number of guests from neighbouring halls. There was an elegant buffet, and the evening ended with part-songs from the bachelors.

Thereafter, sooner or later, the warden began an extension or adaptation of the lodgings that lasted throughout his period of office, though it is not easy to see from the surviving inventories whether he added any rooms or merely reordered the interior. He also built the bridge leading from the screens passage of the hall to the sacristy stair turret, signing his work with a punning device on a shield over the archway there. In 1512 he proposed that the college should set up a refuge to which the company could retire in times of plague, by restoring a ruined tenement at Hampton Poyle.[14] He gave another notable party for all the masters in college in January 1513, and on that occasion there was 'a splendid play' in the hall.[15] The plays, of which we have no further details, were probably, though not certainly,

---

[13] B. Harvey, *Westminster Abbey and its Estates in the Middle Ages* (Oxford, 1977), p. 384 and n.

[14] See *RACM*, pp. 429–30. There had been occasional deaths in the preceding years, and in August 1507 some of the fellows and bachelors had withdrawn to Cuxham when plague broke out in St John's parish: *RACM*, p. 348.

[15] *ludus optimus*: *RACM*, p. 434.

derived from the liturgical drama associated with Easter and the festival of Corpus Christi. As the warden appears to have ordered them, and evidently enjoyed them, it is possible that they also included some early manifestations of the Latin comedies, masques, and interludes which proliferated at court and in the universities later in the century.[16] The warden's hospitality on those and other occasions was not stinted, and by 1516 the resources of his household were large enough for him to lend a quantity of plate, including twelve bowls and two censers, to Bishop Fitzjames for the term of the bishop's life.[17]

In June 1513 Rawlins accompanied Henry VIII to France, on his expedition to Thérouanne, and duly made account with the college before leaving. On that occasion he paid in £10 of unspecified receipts, which were put by in the jewel chest, to be reserved for the repair of the Fleur de Luce inn. There may nevertheless have been some breeziness about the warden's proceedings which bred suspicions and resentment, though his record of events in the register naturally does not dwell on trifles. He accompanied the king to France again in 1520, when Henry met the emperor, Charles V, at Gravelines. The summit of his public and social career came in 1518 when Catherine of Aragon visited the shrine of St Frideswide, in the hope of enjoying a healthy pregnancy. Resisting the blandishments of other colleges she came to Merton to honour the royal almoner, a gesture to which Dr Rawlins responded rapturously, comparing her majesty, in its discriminating condescension, to the glory of Juno and, for good measure, Minerva.[18]

Close behind Minerva, however, came Nemesis. In the winter of 1520–1 a majority of the fellows denounced the warden for a wide category of offences against the statutes and the interest of the house, and in September 1521 he was formally removed from office by the visitor, Archbishop Warham.[19] In the context of the register the thunderbolt comes from an empty if not from a blue sky, for there are no entries between the end of October 1520 and the letters of dismissal. In the mean time, however, the warden had been indignant, obdurate,

---

[16] Two such plays are named in the register in 1567: *Wylie beguylie*, in English, and the *Eunuchus* of Terence, both then performed in the warden's house by the *scolares*, in the presence of the rest of the college: *RACM 1521–67*, pp. 273, 276. Cf. *HUO* iv. 655.

[17] 26 Feb. 1516: *RACM 1483–1521*, p. 459. The plate was mostly if not entirely of Fitzjames's own gift to the lodgings.

[18] See further J. R. L. Highfield, ' Catherine of Aragon's visit to the shrine of St Frideswide', *Oxoniensia*, liii (1988), 274–5. Minerva was commonly identified with Athena and wisdom, but she was also a patron of playwrights and actors.

[19] *RACM*, pp. 502–8.

evasive, and ultimately unbiddable. He was summoned at least once to Lambeth, and there promised a reformation of his ways, but the archbishop finally took the fellows' part. There is nothing in the previous record of chapters, elections, and decrees to suggest a systematic dereliction by Rawlins, though some of his proceedings against delinquent fellows may have laid up ill will against him.[20] He was said nevertheless to have absented himself from the college and his duties, and he failed to co-operate with the archbishop's commissary, Dr John Cox, who was sent to investigate and compose the differences that had arisen in the house. The number of fellows had fallen to seventeen, in part no doubt because the administration of the college had recently been paralysed. The circulation of books by elections also seems to have come to a stop in Rawlins's time, but that may be a further symptom of academic change rather than a simple neglect. The last distributions of works of philosophy and theology took place at the end of 1519, and Merton evidently then had more books at its disposal than had other colleges.[21] Beyond all that, however, the warden had not only misappropriated revenues, alienated the college's lands, and victimized those fellows who challenged his policies, but had introduced three unauthorized horses into his stables.

It was almost certainly the alienation of land which brought the warden down, though the illicit horses are better documented than the transfer of title. Builders had been at work on the land to the west of the Grove since 1512, though it was only in 1513 that Bishop Foxe of Winchester formally published his intention to raise a college there.[22] Since then Corpus Christi College had appointed its first fellows, in 1517, and housed them on a site largely composed of the Merton properties of Nevill's Inn, Corner Hall, and Urban Hall. The bishop evidently had an agreement with the warden, no doubt discussed between them at court, and probably believed that he had an

---

[20] Rawlins's dealings with John Tutt, who in the summer of 1520 was accused of sexual misbehaviour with boys, and who fell sick and died before the truth of the matter could be established, seem rather to have been informed by humanity and common sense: *RACM*, pp. 496–7.

[21] See further *RACM*, pp. xxx–xxxi, 496–7. The system had been in decay for some time, and a substantial number of books had been lost: see e.g. ibid., p. 360. On that occasion, in April 1508, under Harper, the theological election was held in the warden's lodgings and the philosophical books were distributed in hall. See further H. W. Garrod, 'The library regulations of a medieval college', above, p. 81, n. 28, and below, pp. 324–6.

[22] See further *HUO* iii. 18–29.

agreement with the college. The outcome was that Corpus has ever since enjoyed the usufruct of the lands for an annual rent of £4. Mertonians who pass by, or upon occasion enter its gates, rejoice that scholarship has been so signally and economically maintained there over the centuries. Though his zeal for humane learning was misinterpreted by his colleagues Warden Rawlins was not entirely bereft, for in 1523 he was provided to the see of St David's, where he died in 1536. Nor did he show himself ungrateful to the king. Notwithstanding the eminent merits which he had once seen in Queen Catherine he was one of the small number of bishops who urged Henry VIII to divorce her.

The foundation of Corpus Christi was a portent, quite apart from its disruptive effect on Merton. Foxe was as orthodox as the dedication of his college suggests, but he was concerned to promote the new learning, and he sought to provide readers in Greek, Latin, and theology at Corpus whose lectures would be open to the whole university. At the same time Cardinal Wolsey, a thoughtful reformer of all shortcomings but his own, was intent on establishing university lecturers in theology and the humanities. He also appointed Thomas Musgrave, a Mertonian physician who had also lectured in astronomy, as reader in medicine at Corpus.[23] A series of other distinguished speakers appeared in Oxford under Wolsey's auspices between 1519 and 1524. In that year, however, that general enterprise was superseded by his imposing plans for Cardinal College, which grew magnificently upon a diet of confiscated monastic endowments until it foundered in the wreck of the cardinal's own career in 1530.[24]

Amid those manifestations of change Merton's conservatism did not make it a negligible force. In all outward appearance it was still a wealthy foundation, and it did not lack instincts of self-preservation. Over the previous century the college had benefited, whether by conscious policy or as a simple function of its position in the university, by the numbers of its members who kept academic halls, mainly though not exclusively in the immediate neighbourhood.[25] The college's reputation drew in recruits, but there was also a force of Mertonian observers at large, watching for talent. With the halls declining in numbers and new colleges arising which took in under-

---

[23] Musgrave, sometimes referred to as Mosgroff, had been dean, bursar, and sub-warden of Merton in previous years. He died in 1527: *BRUO*, pp. 406–7.

[24] See further *HUO* iii. 349–41.

[25] See above, pp. 131, 137–8.

graduates as a matter of course, Merton decided in 1519 to concentrate the portionists in their own hall, and to regard them positively as potential recruits for the fellowship.[26] Whether by those or other means, of which personal influence is now the most elusive, men of ability were drawn in to the elections.

Wolsey did not wish his new establishment to supersede the existing colleges but merely to excel them, and the warden of Merton was appointed with other heads of houses to appoint the professors at Cardinal College. When the first royal visitors descended upon Oxford under Thomas Cromwell's stimulus in 1535 they were looking not for the amendment of doctrine but for more efficient instruction, and Merton was one of the colleges charged then with the support of a university lecturer in Latin.

The college had either maintained or recovered its balance since Rawlins's departure. His successor was Roland Philipps, an Oriel man, and like the unfortunate Hamsterley at University College the first head of the house to be appointed from outside. Philipps was a celebrated preacher, and as the incumbent of two city parishes, St Margaret Pattens and St Michael, Cornhill, and a canon of St Paul's he appeared frequently in the famous pulpit at St Paul's Cross.[27] Like many of his predecessors he was a royal chaplain, and also in his time chaplain to Wolsey, though he resisted Wolsey's efforts to raise a subsidy from the clergy in 1523. He did not stay long in Merton, resigning in 1525. He appears to have offered to resign in the previous year if Dr Musgrave's name were put forward to succeed him, but the college declined the proposal.[28] He lived until 1538, and was then reputed to be 'of the popish sort' though he had accepted the royal supremacy.

Philipps was followed by John Chambers, a bachelor fellow in 1493 who studied at Padua from 1503 to 1506, and returned to become physician to Henry VII, and then to Henry VIII. He was a canon of St George's, Windsor, of Wells, and of St Stephen's, Westminster, where he was dean from 1522. Chambers was a renowned and humane physician as well as a courtier, but his public duties left him the less

[26] *RACM 1483–1521*, p. 491. The college nevertheless matriculated only 7 per cent of all the undergraduates recorded in those years: *HUO* iii. 71.

[27] See *BRUO*, p. 1478. He evidently preached too long at Bishop Ruthall's funeral in Westminster Abbey in 1523, where his aristocratic congregation were impatiently intent upon the baked meats which were to follow: S. Gunn, 'The structure of politics in early Tudor England', *TRHS* 6th ser., v (1955), 59–90, at p. 83.

[28] See *MMC*, p. 163; and *DNB*, (Philipps).

time for the affairs of the college. College business continued under the sub-warden, with regulations for lectures on Latin and Greek texts in hall in 1539, but the scrutinies ran down in that time. On the other hand the college accepted the estate of Thomas Linacre, the great humanist physician, in 1549, and it seems that both Warden Chambers and Merton's established reputation in medicine influenced that outcome.[29] The high standing of Mertonian physicians for the rest of the century was a continuing mark of Chambers's influence. The warden himself was the first president of the college of barber-surgeons in London when the company was incorporated in 1540.

Chambers's presence at court was no doubt a reassurance and perhaps a service to the college in a troubled time, but he resigned from the house in 1544. His preferred successor, Henry Tyndall, a former vicar of Embleton and senior proctor, survived for only eighteen months before dying while on progress in Cambridgeshire.[30] One of the few acts made during his office was a resolution that the college would ignore the creation of the Henrician dioceses, Bristol, Chester, Gloucester, Oxford, and Peterborough, and would continue to admit candidates from the historic territories of the older dioceses.[31] There were, however, changes of a quite different order impending, and the management of the college in the next stages of the protestant reformation fell to Thomas Raynolds, a theologian who after his election to a fellowship in 1524 had been a fellow of Cardinal College. Raynolds, then a canon of St Peter's, Westminster, took up office by proxy on 30 December 1545.

It seems now that the only tangible sign in Merton of the coming storms was the acquisition of the great English Bible which had to be displayed for use in every church from the autumn of 1538. For the

[29] On Linacre and his wide-ranging scholarship, see *Linacre Studies: Essays on the Life and Work of Thomas Linacre, c. 1460–1524*, ed. F. Maddison, Margaret Pelling, and C. Webster (Oxford, 1977), and on the complex story of his estate and the eventual endowment of the lectureships which bore his name, J. M. Fletcher, 'Linacre's lands and lectureships', ibid., pp. 107–97.

[30] It is a measure of Chambers's standing that he was allowed to take the unusual step of himself proposing the names of the candidates from whom the warden was chosen. His other nominees were Walter Morwent, rector of St Matthew's, Friday Street, and John Poxwell, rector of Cossington and some other Somerset livings. Tyndall was admitted 23 June 1544. He died at Gamlingay on 12 December 1545, and is buried there: *RACM 1521–67*, p. 114.

[31] *RACM 1521–67*, p. 110. The purpose of the act is not clear, but it was presumably intended to retain candidates who might have been lost by a literal reading of the rules. On the other hand there was no professed intention to recruit from the new dioceses at large, which would have increased the supply of recruits.

rest the services and furnishings of the church appear to have been maintained in their customary style. We know, for example, that lists of benefactors were still displayed in the chancel to inform intercessory prayers.[32] There were some prominent conservatives among the fellows, and if there were any radical sympathies in the college they found no public encouragement, for despite his other innovations Henry VIII consistently frowned upon liturgical change. In the first year of Edward VI's reign, however, the royal injunctions and a book of homilies were acquired, and shortly afterwards a single copy of the new order of the service of communion. At the beginning of 1549 parliament ordered the use of the new prayer book from Whitsunday, and the sub-warden, to whom the maintenance of the chapel fell, bought copies not only for use in college services, though learned congregations could continue with a Latin liturgy if they chose, but also for the dependent churches. The old service books were probably not discarded at once,[33] and the vestments were retained for a decade, but the furnishings of the church were purged, the subsidiary altars dismantled, and a variety of images offensive to protestant taste obliterated or removed. The work was not undertaken with any notable zeal. The paintings on the backs of the stalls survived the storm, and the glass in the chancel windows was apparently saved for less sensitive times by being boarded over and whitewashed.[34] The roodloft and its organ also remained in place.

What was done in the church under the fellows' supervision was surpassed in the library in their despite. The royal commissioners who came to the university in 1549 were intent upon reformation, and at Merton in particular they found much to reform. The wanton destruction of the university library on that occasion was matched by the removal of a whole cartload of suspect books from the college, and although occasional volumes were concealed and saved by individuals the greater part of the collection was sacrificed. Globes, maps, and instruments, which had been accumulated in some numbers over

[32] See further J. M. Fletcher and C. A. Upton, 'Destruction, repair, and removal: An Oxford college chapel during the Reformation', *Oxoniensia*, xlviii (1983), 119–30, at 122–3. The lists of prayers probably derived from the common register referred to in an agreement with the rector of St Ebbe's in 1349: Reg. 1a, fo. 168, no. 311.
[33] But see further below, pp. 155–6.
[34] It took an order by 'the usurpers' in 1651 to obliterate the paintings behind the stalls, 'to the sorrow of curious men that were admirers of ancient painting': *LTAW* i. 309. See further the interesting remarks in Fletcher and Upton (above, n. 32), p. 123.

the previous two centuries, were probably also dispersed.[35] At the same time the commissioners were anxious to develop public teaching in the university, and they sought to mitigate the negative effects of their purges by exhorting the colleges to re-equip their libraries with more wholesome works.

Oxford was the scene of much excitement in Edward VI's reign, which though unsettling was less discordant than the scenes of public slaughter which disfigured his sister's. Despite the sudden disappearance of the houses of monks and friars between 1536 and 1538, which had a particularly marked effect on the faculty of theology, the general tone of the university was still conservative. Neither innovation nor direction from outside were welcome for their own sake, and though doctrinal divisions defined some new loyalties they did not entirely displace the old. There was also a spirit of accommodation which both the institution and many of its individual members found serviceable on occasion.

The principal conservative theologians, William Tresham and Richard Smith, were both Mertonians. Tresham was elected a fellow in 1516. He became registrar of the university in 1523, a member of Cardinal College, and then a canon of Christ Church when Henry VIII revived Wolsey's college in 1532. He was vice-chancellor of the university at the end of Mary's reign. Smith was a younger man than Tresham, whom he succeeded as registrar in 1532. He was elected to Merton in 1528, and subsequently became principal of St Alban Hall, prelector of theology at Magdalen, and then the first regius professor of divinity. Having accepted the royal supremacy in that office he at first followed the reformers. In 1547 he made a public retraction of his former conservative views at St Paul's Cross, but in 1548 on further examination he lost both his prebend at St Paul's and his chair.

Archbishop Cranmer sought to redress the condition of Oxford with an infusion of protestant refugees from the Continent. When Pietro Martire Vermigli, known in England as Peter Martyr, was brought to Oxford by the reformers, Tresham disputed with him in the Divinity School, and continued to resist doctrinal change so

---

[35] In 1512 the college lent a map of England to the dean of Wells to be copied, and there was some recrimination when it was damaged and no new map supplied in its place: *RACM 1483–1521*, pp. 431, 436, 442. The implication that the library had a useful map at that time is interesting. William Harrison, who was admitted in 1557 and died in 1564, bequeathed an astronomical instrument to the college, perhaps to make up recent losses.

vigorously that he was briefly imprisoned as an incorrigible conservative in 1551 and again in 1553. Vermigli had displaced Richard Smith as regius professor of divinity in 1548. Smith withdrew for a time from Oxford, first to St Andrews and then to Louvain, where he was appointed to a chair.

With Tresham and Smith out of the way the vocal opposition to reform was much reduced. Warden Raynolds was amongst those who conformed to the new regime, and in the aftermath of the commissioners' visitation Merton sold some £70 worth of plate to make good the losses in the library. The books which the college then bought marked not one departure but two. In the first place the library's notable holdings had been built up not by purchases but by gifts and legacies.[36] In the second, the new accessions were printed books, and there had been practically no print in the collection before 1550.

There was nothing exceptional in the practice of waiting upon donations, except that it had continued rather longer in Merton than elsewhere. There were many manuscripts for sale in the Middle Ages, and occasionally the college had bought some desirable work, but on the whole it had been comfortably stayed with gifts, and well able to spare the expense. Now it had to turn to the booksellers, and it chose to deal mainly with Herman Evans and Richard Garbrand in Oxford. Garbrand was a Fleming whose grandsons continued his business into the seventeenth century. His house became a meeting place for protestants under Mary, but his beliefs did not cloud his professional judgement. He was instrumental in saving some of the medieval texts ejected from Merton, which eventually found sanctuary in the Bodleian Library.[37]

Both New College and Magdalen had been buying printed books for several decades, and Magdalen's purchases in Oxford and London are documented in some detail. By contrast we know only that Merton sold the plate which the reformed liturgy was making superfluous and even illegal, and that most of the money realized was paid out to three Oxford booksellers shortly afterwards.[38] There was probably some explicit instruction from the commissioners, but their injunc-

---

[36] See above, pp. 80–8.

[37] One of them was John Mainsforth's collection, now MS Bodl. 52; see above, p. 123.

[38] The plate brought in £71. 8s. 7d., and payments totalling £68. 7s. 10d. were then made to Evans (£48. 9s. 11d.), Gore (£8. 19s. 7d.), and Garbrand (£10. 18s. 4d.): see [N. R. Ker], *Oxford College Libraries in 1556* (Oxford, 1956), p. 17.

tions to Merton were not entered in the college register, and have not survived. What we know of the books themselves comes, ironically, from lists which were prepared in Mary's reign to satisfy the demands of Cardinal Pole's legatine commissioners in 1556.[39] Pole shared with the Edwardian visitors a desire to see true doctrine allied to sound learning, and there was readier agreement on the means towards the second objective than towards the first.

In 1556 Merton had little more than 300 manuscripts in its library, which represented perhaps a quarter or less of the medieval college's holdings. Between 1549 and 1556 it acquired some 200 printed books, which on the evidence of the bursar's account came chiefly from Herman Evans. The new texts were almost entirely the product of recent scholarship, the work of Erasmus and his colleagues, which Fitzjames had regarded with such misgivings. They included critical editions of the works of twenty Greek and Latin fathers, amongst which the Greek text of the collected works of Epiphanius, bishop of Constantia, had been printed at Basle as recently as 1544. There were some modern editions of classical authors, both Latin and Greek, besides a number of scientific and medical works, but also some texts of medieval writers which had recently become available in print. Merton had owned exegetical works by Nicholas Gorran, OP, since the early fourteenth century, and a fine set of his commentaries was included in William Rede's bequest, but it now bought the first printed edition of the commentaries, which was published at Cologne in 1537, with illustrative woodcuts.

There was, naturally enough, no disposition to collect early printing for its own sake. The surviving texts in the library range only from 1516 to 1549. They do, however, include the great Polyglot Bible, in Hebrew, Syriac, Greek, and Latin, planned by Cardinal Francisco Ximenes, and printed at Alcalá de Henares by Arnaldo Guillen de Brocar. There was also a Vulgate from the house of Robert Étienne, of Paris, which had belonged to, and had presumably been given to the library by, Robert Huicke, a fellow since 1530, and a durable royal physician.[40] Those acquisitions, however, were later matched in number by the bequest made by James Leech, who was elected in 1557 and died in 1589, and in interest by the gift of books made by Robert

---

[39] See *Oxford College Libraries*, p. 15.

[40] Amongst Huicke's other accomplishments he was principal of St Alban Hall, censor and president of the Royal College of Physicians, and contracted a second marriage after being divorced by his first wife in 1547: *BRUO 1501–40*, p. 304.

Barnes, MD, in 1594. Barnes, who lived until 1604, was admitted a probationary fellow in 1537, and was the first higher lecturer on the Linacre foundation, in 1551.

When Mary succeeded her brother in 1553 and overturned the Edwardian reforms Warden Raynolds found himself able to return to the old order, with most of the fellows. The only member of the house deprived and expelled in 1553 was John Parkhurst, later bishop of Norwich, who had been John Jewel's tutor in the 1530s. There was no election in that year, but of the three fellows elected in 1554 one, Anthony Atkins, subsequently refused to take the oath of supremacy under Elizabeth I, and another, Gaspar Heywood, became a Jesuit. The third, however, John Wolley, became Elizabeth's Latin secretary, and had a long career as a diplomat and a member of parliament. Only fourteen fellows in all were admitted during Mary's reign, of whom six subsequently resigned or were removed by Elizabeth's commissioners. Any movement to the right was no more precipitate than the progress of reform in the previous reign.

It is perhaps significant that the warden's first care was to obtain a private act of Parliament effecting the formal incorporation of the college.[41] The restoration of services in the chapel seems to have been a less urgent affair, for it was not until 1556 that any obvious effort was made to re-establish the subsidiary altars, restore other fittings and furnishings that had been removed, or replace books, which seems to have been done piecemeal.[42]

Events at large had moved rather faster. By the time the Marian visitors descended on the university in 1556 Cranmer was dead, and his enemies triumphant. Richard Smith had been restored to his regius chair, and made a royal chaplain in 1554. He then pursued his opponents with some zest, joining with Tresham in debates against Cranmer, Latimer, and Ridley in 1554, preaching with unctuous relish before Ridley and Latimer's execution in 1556, and demonstrating in his subsequent testimony against Cranmer that he had not been corrupted by his old friendship with the archbishop, still less by Cranmer's forbearance towards him in adversity. The rule of Rome, however, was as short as Mary's reign. Deprived once again on Eliza-

---

[41] An Act for the Incorporation of the Warden and Scholars of Merton College in Oxford: 1 Mary, Session 2, Private Act c. 3.

[42] See Fletcher and Upton (above, n. 32), pp. 124–5. The work may simply have been slowed by a shortage of funds. The windfall from the sale of plate had been entirely devoted to restocking the library, and no fellows were admitted in 1555 or 1556.

beth's accession, Smith was placed in Archbishop Parker's keeping. Early in 1561 he escaped from a lenient restraint in Canterbury, and made his way to Louvain. From Louvain he moved to Douai, where he gathered his earthly reward, being first made dean of St.-Pierre and chaplain to Philip II, and then chancellor of the new Catholic university, an office which he held until his death in 1563.

Tresham was vice-chancellor in 1559 and a member of the deputation which conveyed the university's congratulations to Elizabeth on her succession, but he refused to take the oath of supremacy and was deprived of all his benefices except the rectory of Towcester. After a brief imprisonment he was allowed to live in retirement in Northamptonshire, his native county, where he died in 1569, and was buried at Bugbrooke, where he had once been rector.

Warden Raynolds had been vice-chancellor under Pole, and a chaplain to Philip and Mary from 1555. In 1558 he was nominated bishop of Hereford, but though he received the temporalities of the see ten days before Mary's death on 17 November he was never consecrated. The new government then deprived him of the wardenship and all his other benefices, and he was imprisoned in the Marshalsea, where he died on 26 November 1559. While he was in office he gave four books to the library, including a commentary on Aristotle's Physics printed at Venice in 1505, and a Greek text of Lucian printed at Florence in 1517. He was succeeded as warden by James Gervase, elected a fellow in 1548, who had since been a proctor, in 1555, and a student of law. Gervase held the post from 1559 to 1561, and then resigned, though he may have been moved to do so by Matthew Parker, now archbishop of Canterbury and visitor. The fellows then played into the archbishop's hands, upon some strange corporate impulse, by offering him five candidates for his consideration, an action which he was able to brush aside as unconstitutional. He thereupon appointed John Man, a Wykehamist, a fellow of New College, and one of his own chaplains.

Man presented himself at Merton on 30 March 1562, but secured admission only on 27 May after a lively resistance by some of the fellows and some unedifying scuffling at the gates. The leader of those who defied and affronted the warden was the sub-warden, William Hall, who had once made to throw an English psalter on the fire in hall when its contents were offered as a wholesome substitute for the traditional Christmas hymns. He was also reputed to have hidden service books and furnishings when the chapel was purged of monuments of superstition.[43] The opposition to the new warden plainly went beyond collegiate sensitivities, and had to be resolved by a visitatorial commission which after installing the warden expelled Hall, and went on to remove two other adherents of the old religion. Hall retired only as far as University College, where he died at the end of the year.

Man was sent to Merton to secure the Anglican settlement there and seems to have conducted himself with adequate dignity and wisdom. Both his scholarship and his protestantism were irreproachable, and he had turned to account his time abroad in Mary's reign by translating and publishing a selection of texts from the extensive writings of Wolfgang Müslin.[44] He was less successful as a diplomat, for when he was ambassador to the court of Spain in 1566–8 he spoke there so disobligingly of the pope that he was rusticated by Philip II. He had, however, largely succeeded in quietening the college, and his sufferings abroad were soothed by the deanery of Gloucester. Man died in London on 18 March 1569. He was followed by Thomas Bickley, a demy and fellow of Magdalen who had emerged as a vigorous protestant in Edward VI's reign, and returned from exile in France to become another of Parker's chaplains. Bickley seems to have been an undistinguished stalwart, dedicated to keeping good order in the church. At the time of his election he was archdeacon of Stafford and chancellor of Lichfield cathedral. He was admitted to Merton by proxy, without ructions of any kind, and ruled the house for sixteen years. He resigned in 1585 when he became bishop of Chichester, and on his death in 1596 he bequeathed to the college an endowment for an annual sermon which by the eighteenth century had degenerated into an unedifying sinecure as the Bickley lectureships.[45] On Bickley's resignation, however, the wardenship had fallen to Henry Savile, who since his election from Brasenose in 1565, at the age of sixteen, had emerged as a formidable scholar, courtier, and administrator. His colleagues included Thomas Bodley, a fellow since 1563. A new age of learning had begun.

---

[43] Henderson, p. 89.

[44] See below, p. 158 and n.

[45] Bickley himself had some reputation as a preacher, in an age when preaching was close to being a sacrament, but his only known published work is a set of visitation articles for his see which he had printed in London, in 1586. Merton's most celebrated preacher was Edmund Bunny, elected for his eloquence in 1565: *MMC*, p. 268

8

Merton in the Time of Bodley and Savile

In 1627 George Hakewell, rector of Exeter College, referring to Bodley and Savile asked 'What one college ever yeelded two such Heroical Spirits?'[1] Whatsoever the answer, there may be virtue in considering the history of Merton between *c.* 1563 when Bodley arrived as fellow, and Savile's death in 1622 in terms of the college's two most famous men. Bodley came to Merton from Magdalen when he was eighteen. He was born in Exeter in 1545, the son of John Bodley, a protestant merchant who fled abroad under Mary. John went first to Wesel, near Frankfurt, and moved on to Geneva. When he returned to England at the beginning of Elizabeth's reign he received a patent for publishing the Geneva Bible.[2] Thus his son was brought up in a world in which protestantism and printing went side by side. Indeed at Geneva Thomas had attended lectures by Calvin and Beza, and had there begun to acquire the learning for which he was afterwards famed. He learned Greek from Beroaldus,[3] and read Homer with Robert Constantine, the compiler of a Greek lexicon. When he was twelve he started Hebrew with the French protestant, Antoine Chevallier.[4] Greek and Hebrew were to remain two of his loves throughout his life. At Magdalen he was a commoner and a pupil of the redoubtable scholar and protestant, Lawrence Humphrey, subsequently president of that college.[5] His own expressed aims in buying books for the Bodleian showed him to be, in Dr Philip's words, 'precise and practical'.[6]

The wardens under whom Bodley served as fellow, John Man (1562–9) and Thomas Bickley (1569–86), were both noted protestants. Man

---

[1] Quoted in Garrod, *Study of Good Letters*, p. 118.

[2] In 1562 (*DNB*); Pollard, *Records*, no. xlviii, pp. 284–5 (8 Jan. 1561).

[3] Philip, *The Bodleian Library*, p. 3. Mattheus Beroaldus (Béroalde) was minister and professor of philosophy at Geneva (d. 1576).

[4] *Trecentale*, p. 4.

[5] Ibid., p. 5. Humphrey was a friend of Bodley's father.

[6] Philip, *The Bodleian Library*, p. 2.

was specifically appointed by Parker in 1562 after a disputed election.[7] Bickley, a former fellow of Magdalen, expelled by Bishop Gardiner in 1553, had studied abroad at Paris and Orleans during the hazardous Marian years. As the archbishop's chaplains both men had been exposed to the scholarly atmosphere of Parker's household and communicated something of it to the college.[8] Indeed Man had translated into English *Commonplaces of Christian Religion* gathered by Wolfgang Müslin, the Strasbourg reformer (1563).[9] It was entirely fitting that when John Jewell, a former postmaster and bishop of Salisbury, the intellectual defender of the Elizabethan Settlement, died in 1571 Bodley composed an epitaph for him in Hebrew.[10]

During his twenty-two years as fellow Bodley took his fair share of college offices, first as one of the three deans in 1567 (and again in subsequent years), twice as principal of the postmasters, three times as bursar, and once as Wyliot's bursar.[11] When many fellows fled the plague he stuck steadily to his post as bursar. As garden-master he cut down (with authority) twelve plum trees in the 'further orchard of the masters' and replanted them.[12] His standing in the university was shown by his election as junior proctor in 1569.[13] He started to lecture on Greek at Merton, and was appointed as the college's first lecturer in that language on 20 April 1565 with an allocation of 26s. 8d.[14] It is a testimony to his exercise of the office that when he laid it down it was made permanent. His interest in Hebrew led him to examine the college's medieval deeds, and was more prosaically reflected in the fact that he owned a Hebrew and Syriac Bible which he pledged in the Rede Chest in 1569.[15] That the college shared his tastes is shown

---

[7] *MMC*, p. 166; and above, pp. 155–6.

[8] For copies of the works of Calvin bought for the library in 1584 and of Peter Martyr in 1585 see Ker, 'Oxford Libraries', p. 500.

[9] *Commonplaces of Christian Religion gathered by W. Musculus for the use of suche as desire the Knowledge of Godly Truthe translated out of the Latin* ... (London, 1563). Man appended two further tracks by Müslin, on usury and oaths. The volume was dedicated to Parker, and was reprinted in 1578.

[10] C. Roth, 'Sir Thomas Bodley, Hebraist', *BLR* vii/5 (1966), 242–51; cf. *HUO* iii. 317.

[11] *RACM 1567–1603*, pp. 8, 13, 34, 37, 39, 43, 53.

[12] Ibid., p. 40.

[13] *Trecentale*, p. 6. He was also deputy public orator.

[14] *RACM 1521–67*, p. 251.

[15] John M. Fletcher and Christopher A. Upton, 'John Drusius of Flanders: Thomas Bodley and the development of Hebrew studies at Merton College, Oxford', in H. de Ridder-Symoens, *Academic Relations between the Low Countries and the British Isles* (Ghent, 1989), p. 124. For Bodley's translations of Merton College Records see MCR 1099 (Malden) of 30 Aug. 1574 and MCR 2423 (Ibstone), also C. Roth (n. 10 above).

by its welcoming into residence the Flemish Hebrew scholar, Drusius, like Bodley a pupil of Chevallier. He stayed from 1572 to 1576 during the period of Bodley's fellowship.[16]

Henry Savile came to Merton from Brasenose, his father's college, where he matriculated *c.* 1561[17] at a still earlier age – sixteen – than Bodley when he came to Magdalen. Born at Bradley in Yorkshire he belonged to the younger branch of the Saviles of Methley[18] and was thus closely related to the main Savile clan, whose estates in London gave Savile Row its name. As a young fellow he had not always found himself on the side of authority, siding with the dissidents in a quarrel between the fellows and Warden Man, when Bodley was dean. On that occasion the visitor, Archbishop Parker, had to intervene.[19] Nevertheless it appears that a friendship was springing up between Bodley and Savile by 1576. In that year Bodley was granted £6. 13s. 4d. and a licence to travel abroad to study.[20] He made his rooms available to Savile during his absence and inscribed to him a copy of a Hebrew book, evidently intending him to profit from its contents while he was away.[21] His example also showed Savile that the way to learning in the 1570s was to go to the Continent and visit the scholars and sources of Renaissance wisdom. We know that Bodley went to France, Italy, and Germany,[22] and that he extended his range of languages to French, Italian, and Spanish.[23]

By now Bodley had attracted attention at court and had become a gentleman usher to the queen. On his return one of his patrons, the Warden of the Cinque Ports, Sir Francis Cobham, put him up as MP for Hythe in the election to the parliament of 1584.[24] At the same time he was proposed for Portsmouth.[25] He was successful in both seats and chose to sit for Portsmouth, but it was not in the House of

---

[16] Fletcher and Upton, pp. 119–26.

[17] *Brasenose College Register, 1509–1909*, OHS lv (1910), i. 36–7.

[18] *DNB*.

[19] In 1566–7 (Garrod, *Study of Good Letters*, pp. 117–18).

[20] *RACM 1567–1603*, pp. 88–9.

[21] H. W. Garrod, 'Sir Thomas Bodley and Merton College', *BQR* vi (1931), 272. The book was *Elijah ben Asher the Levite: Sefer ha-Tischbi* (Isny, 1541). We owe the identification to the kindness of Dr Bendall. The inscription reads 'Henrico Savillo Thomas Bodlaius ad exteras nationes Oxonia proficiscens'.

[22] *Trecentale*, p. 7. He was in Paris in October 1579 (*CSP. Foreign, 1579–80*, p. 79).

[23] Philip, *The Bodleian Library*, p. 4.

[24] *DNB*.

[25] Philip, *The Bodleian Library*, p. 115 n. 20; J. E. Neale, *The Elizabethan House of Commons* (1949), p. 178, and cf. p. 219 and *DNB*.

Commons that he gained fame. His knowledge of languages led him in the direction of diplomacy, and he made his first mark in government service as a diplomat. That was on a mission to Denmark in 1585 which was subsequently extended to the courts of the German princes.[26] A year later he married a wealthy widow, Ann Ball, and broke his formal connections with Merton as he then had to resign his fellowship.[27] At the time he had been senior fellow for three years. His diplomatic career developed when he became the queen's representative at the Hague, which involved him in a series of tortuous negotiations. He eventually asked to be recalled.[28] The government was reluctant to agree, but at length he did succeed in 1596 in returning to England, and soon began to turn his mind to his most lasting project, the restoration of Duke Humfrey's Library and the foundation of the Bodleian. Bodley himself tells us that in that year both Burghley and Essex wanted him to be Secretary but he declined. It may be that Burghley turned against the idea when he knew that Essex was for it.[29] The idea of the secretaryship surfaced once again at the time of the Essex Rebellion since it was said that the earl, if he had been successful, would have asked Bodley to be Secretary of State.[30] It seems unlikely that Bodley would have been beguiled by the offer.

In the spring of 1598 Bodley visited the college and a dinner was given at which 57s. 4d. was spent on the meats and 11s. 6d. on the wines.[31] The occasion may have been of more consequence than the fare, for it was in that year that he decided to restore Duke Humfrey's library and found the Bodleian. It may be that the inspiration came from Savile, and Bodley certainly had before him the examples of two libraries which Savile had developed and restored between 1586 and 1598 at Merton and Eton,[32] and to each of which he had devoted his attention from the moment when he became head of the institution.

Neil Ker has chronicled the significant changes which began to occur in the College Library soon after Savile became warden. To quote his account:

[26] *Trecentale*, p. 7.

[27] *DNB*; *RACM 1567–1603*, p. 217.

[28] Philip, *The Bodleian Library*, pp. 4–5.

[29] Conyers Read, *Lord Burghley and Queen Elizabeth* (1960), p. 513.

[30] *CSP. Domestic, 1601–3*, p. 2. As late as 1602 the queen wished to send him back to the Netherlands (Philip, *The Bodleian Library*, p. 5).

[31] Garrod, *Study of Good Letters*, p. 117.

[32] Philip, *The Bodleian Library*, p. 2; for Savile, Merton, and Eton see below, pp. 162–3.

a set of library rules was issued on 1 August 1586, the lock of the library was renewed, and sixteen keys were issued to the fellows, who were henceforth required to bring their keys into the college hall on the first of August each year. The final event which made the warden and fellows decide to substitute stalls for lectern desks in part of their library was probably the news that a large bequest of books was coming to the college from Mr James Leech, fellow 1555–67. Leech's will, dated 8 August 1589, directed his executors to deliver an inventory of all his books in folio and quarto to the officers of the college. In the event the college received more than 200 books, many of them rare editions of high value.

The 'method of arranging books, in presses projecting from the walls, was applied to a chained library at Merton in the summer and autumn of 1589'.[33] It was a momentous change, and widely influential. The books were still arranged in divisions based on the medieval curriculum. 'Libri Artium' were in the west wing (Pl. 16). The south wing contained 'Libri theologiae' on its south side and 'Libri medicinae' and 'Libri jurisprudentiae' on the side looking into the quadrangle. Within each faculty, however, division was mainly by format to make economic use of the vertical space. The smallest volumes were kept in cupboards. The books on the shelves were chained. Locations were indicated by the abbreviated name of the faculty and a code of letters and numbers.[34]

Two more substantial gifts of books from former fellows came into the library in Savile's time. One was the collection of an Oxford physician, Robert Barnes (in 1594), the second that of a President of the Royal College of Physicians, Roger Giffard (in 1597).[35] After medicine it was the turn of law. A striking acquisition was that of the library of John Betts, a lawyer of Trinity Hall, Cambridge, a large and specialized collection which brought the college's holdings on law almost up to

[33] Ker, 'Oxford Libraries', pp. 507–8. Already in March 1572 the college had devised a method of raising a fund by decreeing that the admission fee payable by fellows at the beginning of their probationary year should be used to buy books for the library (ibid., p. 469).

[34] P. S. Morrish, 'Dr Higgs and Merton College Library', *Leeds Philosophical and Literary Society*, xxi/2 (1988), 29–30 (165–6). For a detailed description by John Newman cf. *HUO* iv. 146–7.

[35] Ker, 'Oxford Libraries', p. 508. In or about 1598 Savile was to claim in a letter to Archbishop Whitgift that he had enabled more than 500 marks to be spent on the library (P.3.25 (21)).

those of New College and All Souls'.[36] It seems likely that under Savile the library's holding of printed books increased from about 300, which it had been in 1556, to about 1,000 by 1595.[37]

While Bodley was still occupied in the Netherlands Savile was directing two of the fellows to make book purchases on the college's behalf on the Continent. His younger brother, Thomas Savile, was buying for the college in Italy in 1589[38] and at Frankfurt in 1591.[39] When Thomas Savile died in 1593 the responsibility was passed to another fellow, Henry Cuffe, when he too was in Italy. The titles of the books brought from abroad are entered into the college register. Neil Ker described them as 'largely classical, philosophical and scientific, and not as a rule theological; a good many books were in Greek and there was one Greek manuscript which cost £4'.[40]

At Eton the purchases of the first two years under Savile's provostship 'form in the main a collection of the Christian Fathers and of the classical Greek and Latin authors, printed for the most part in the second half of the sixteenth century, many by Henri Estienne. The works of the theologians of the Reformation follow these; subsequently scholastic theology is given its turn, and then the historical works of more recent times.'[41]

Fifty-two of the eighty-two works bought in 1596–7 have been identified by Robert Birley. The inscription in the Eton copy of the Savile Chrysostom says that Savile also presented many books on civil law, which shows an interest which can be matched at Merton by the purchase of John Betts's collection. Those two examples of libraries modernized at Merton and at Eton under Savile's supervision would have been well known to Bodley when he made his momentous resolution.

Early in 1599 the fellows of Merton, led by Savile, granted books to the value of £40 or £50 to be transferred to and chained up in Bodley's new library in order to further that 'pious and laudable institution'.[42]

---

[36] Ker, 'Oxford Libraries', p. 509.

[37] Alain Wijffels (ed.), *Late Sixteenth-Century Lists of Law Books at Merton College*, Libri Pertinentes (Cambridge, 1992). Doctor Wijffels checked the titles against two MS lists, one of which appears to be in Savile's hand.

[38] Ker, 'Oxford Libraries', pp. 508–9, cf. the important article by R. B. Todd, 'Henry and Thomas Savile in Italy', *Bibl. d'Humanisme et Renaissance*, lviii (1996), no. 2, 439–44, esp. 442–3.

[39] Ibid., p. 508.

[40] Ibid., p. 509.

[41] Birley, pp. 242–3.

[42] *RACM 1567–1603*, p. 333; Ker, 'Oxford Libraries', p. 509 and n. 6.

Their titles show that several of them came from the recently acquired Betts collection. Moreover Savile's personal interest in the work was steadily maintained. We read in Bodley's letters to his first librarian, Thomas James, of Savile's helping to choose books for the new library.[43] He helped again with the preface to the catalogue.[44] If uniquely in the early days he was allowed to borrow one or two books and manuscripts he also presented books from his own shelves. Above all he gave practical advice on the internal fittings of the new building. Bodley wrote of 'Sir Henry, whose affection to the stoaring and preserving of the Librarie, I knowe to be singular'.[45] Bodley employed the same Yorkshire masons, John Ackroyde and John Bentley, and the master carpenter, Thomas Holt, whom Savile had used for the construction of Fellows Quad in 1608–10 (Pl. 17). When the plan of Arts End was amended and Bodley learned that Savile approved of the change he wrote to James 'And above many others, Sir Henry Savile's [approval] is to me, as the iudgement of a mason'.[46] Bodley thought that Savile 'is like to becom, a very great benefactour to that place'. He did not quite become that, partly no doubt because of his intention to promote mathematical studies by founding two chairs, but he gave the library some Greek manuscripts in 1620, and after Bodley's death in 1613 continued to interest himself in the completion of the building. Lady Bullard has shown that it is likely that it was Savile who inspired the choice of the 'talking heads' in the frieze in the Upper Reading Room.[47]

John Chamberlain reckoned that Bodley had given about £7,000 to the library he had created.[48] To the college he left 200 marks with which to buy a chest from which loans could be made to the fellows, a most valuable assistance to a fellow faced with the problem of furnishing his rooms in the new quadrangle. A chest was promptly bought in 1614 for £13. 6s. 8d. and the rest of the money was put into it. When other college officers took up their posts at the beginning of

---

[43] *Letters of Thomas Bodley to Thomas James*, ed. G. W. Wheeler (Oxford, 1926), no. 24, p. 33.

[44] Ibid., no. 130, p. 137; no. 133, p. 140.

[45] Ibid., no. 174, p. 181.

[46] Ibid., no. 206, p. 210.

[47] Ibid., no. 183, p. 188; Wood, *History and Antiquities*, ii, pt.2, p. 937. He gave £20 in 1612 and £100 in 1616 (ibid., p. 791); M. R. A. Bullard, 'Talking Heads: The Bodleian Frieze, its inspiration, sources, designer and significance'. *BLR* xix/6 (April, 1994), 461–500.

[48] *John Dudley Carleton to John Chamberlain, 1603–1624: Jacobean Letters*, ed. Maurice Lee Jr (New Brunswick, NJ, 1972).

August each year keepers of the chest were appointed to check its accounts.[49] The executors of Bodley's will were Sir John Bennett and Master William Hakewill; Savile and Sir Ralph Winwood were the overseers.[50] Bodley had left the munificent provision of £666. 13s. 6d. for his funeral expenses and the cost of setting up a monument. The funeral was carried out with full ceremonial, and the occasion was marked by the publication of a profusion of verses in Latin, Greek, and Hebrew by the leading scholars of the day. The funerary address in college was made by a fellow of Merton, John Hales.[51] The monument by Nicholas Stone was in the event not as simple as Bodley in his will had requested it to be (Pl. 15). A preliminary drawing survives and has been examined in detail by Dr John Blair,[52] as the monument itself has been by John Woodward.[53]

Between 1570 and 1575 Savile lectured in the university on Ptolemy's *Almagest*.[54] In doing so he not only lectured on the texts themselves but took the occasion to discuss the views of such Continental scholars as Blanchin, Copernicus, Regiomontanus, Peurbach, Erasmus Reinhold, Tartaglia, Werner, and Faber. These were no lectures stuck in the past. It has been possible to demonstrate that because of the happy survival of seven notebooks, three of which concern Savile's lectures given for the MA course. Copernicus is referred to as 'Mathematicorum Modernorum Princeps'.[55] During the five years when he

[49] *Trecentale*, pp. 70–1. He named Savile his 'ever assured and special frinde' in his will and left him 'a standing salt of Sylver dowble guylt with my armes engraven in it to the value of Twentie pounds' (ibid., p. 75). The chest which he wished to be bought by the college to be put 'to the self same use as 'Read's' chest was instituted in that Coll.'. Rede's was a loan chest. Keepers of Bodley's chest were appointed from 1616 (Reg. 1.3, p. 257). The original chest, which has a very complicated lock, is a show-piece in the Upper Library.

[50] *Trecentale*, pp. 68, 75. By a codicil he added Archbishop Abbot, Lord Ellesmere, and Sir Edward Coke to the number of its overseers (ibid., pp. 82–3). The exalted nature of the circles in which Bodley moved is reflected in his having among the overseers of the will an archbishop, a lord chancellor, and a chief justice of the common pleas.

[51] Ibid., pp. 105–44. Mr Richard Corbet, deputy public orator, gave one university sermon in the Divinity School (ibid., pp. 87–103), Sir Isaac Wake, fellow of Merton, another. A full account is given in *Iusta Funebria Ptolomei Oxoniensis Thomae Bodleii Equitis aurati celebrata, Mensis Martii 29, 1613* (Oxford 1613). Twenty-two tributes by members of Merton in Latin, four in Greek, two in Hebrew and Italian, one in English were published in *Bodleiomnema* (Oxford, 1613), cf. *MMC*, p. 72.

[52] J. Blair, 'Nicholas Stone's Design for the Bodley Monument', *Burlington Magazine* (Jan. 1976), 23–4.

[53] J. Woodward, 'The Monument to Sir Thomas Bodley in Merton College Chapel', *BLR* v/2 (Oct. 1954), 69–73.

[54] Feingold, p. 47.

[55] Ibid.

lectured Savile covered such topics as mechanics, optics, the history of Greek mathematics, and trigonometry. The lectures seem to have been comparable with the best which were being given on the Continent, and their author must naturally have wished for an opportunity to discuss the problems raised with the leading experts of the day. Bodley had shown him the way and the college gave him his chance in 1578. On 3 April he had licence to travel for three years 'in Galliam et partes transmarinas' for the purpose of study, with the same allowance as Bodley had – £6. 13s. 4d.[56]

Savile went in the company of Robert Sidney, younger brother of Philip Sidney, Henry Neville, and George Carew.[57] On 25 March 1579 Philip wrote to Robert at Strasbourg 'I here you are fallen into consort and Fellowshyp wyth Sir Harry Nevellys son and Ayer, and one Mr Savell. I here of syngular Vertues of them both.' And again on 18 October 1580 he wrote[58] 'I have written to Mr Savile, I wish you kept still together, he is an excellent man ... Mr Savile will with ease help to set down such a table of remembrance to yourself, and for your sake I perceive he will do much, and if ever I be able I will deserve it of him ... Now (dear brother) take delight likewise in the mathematicals, Mr Savile is excellent in them.'[59]

Henry Neville was the son of Sir Henry Neville of Billingbear, Berkshire, and the first of three generations of his family to matriculate at Merton, which he did in 1577.[60] He was drawn dangerously deeply into the circle of Robert Devereux, second earl of Essex, and it will be necessary in due course to examine the links between a group of Mertonians including the warden and two of the fellows, Arthur Atye and Henry Cuffe, with the earl.

For the moment, it is enough to note that the continental journey of Savile, Neville, and Carew to France, Germany, Bohemia, Austria,

---

[56] *RACM 1567–1603*, p. 107, cf. Todd (above, n. 38), 440–2.

[57] Robert, younger brother of Sir Philip Sidney, became Governor of Flushing and corresponded with Bodley. He was an early subscriber to the Bodleian (Philip, *The Bodleian Library*, p. 8). George, Lord Carew, was a member of the first Society of Antiquaries, made an important historical collection in Ireland, and attempted a translation of Creton's poem on the deposition of Richard II (M. McKisack, *Medieval History in the Tudor Age* (Oxford, 1971), pp. 59–60).

[58] Feingold, p. 125 n. 8.

[59] *Correspondence of Philip Sidney and Hubert Languet*, ed. S. Pears (1845), pp. 199–201.

[60] Foster, *Alumni Oxonienses, 1500–1714*, iii. 1057; two of his sons, William and Edward, were fellows (*MMC*, pp. 280, 284); see also Blair Worden, 'Ben Jonson among the historians', in *Culture and Politics in Early Stuart England*, ed. Kevin Sharpe and Peter Lake (1994), p. 87.

and Italy was determined by their wish to visit and exchange views with certain great European scholars. Since Savile was acting as unofficial tutor to Neville and Carew it was doubtless he who decided that they should visit the Hungarian humanist Andre Dudith in Breslau, the German astronomer Joannes Praetorius at Altdorf, Thadeus Hajek, another Hungarian humanist, at Prague, and Johannes Sambuc at Vienna, before crossing the Alps into Italy to visit Wolfgang Zünderlin at Venice and Giovanni Vincenzo Pinelli at Padua.[61] In Germany they met a similar party at Nuremberg which included the diarist Sir Arthur Throckmorton.[62] The two groups travelled together for a while but then quarrelled and went their separate ways. They met again when they reached Padua. Sidney, Savile, and Neville made a good impression when they met Dudith, who wrote to Hajek, naming Savile as 'praestantissimi iuvenis'. Hajek printed the letter in the preface to his *Apodixis physica et mathematica de cometis* (Görlitz, 1578). It is clear that they had been discussing astronomy.

A commonplace book which Savile kept in Italy reveals some of his work in Venice and Padua.[63] It consists of lists of kings in ancient history and more specifically, cosmographical descriptions of different countries made up from mainly Venetian manuscript sources and books. The manuscripts were copies of the *relazioni* of Venetian ambassadors which were circulating and especially those from the envoys at the Porte. Savile writes mainly in Italian but from time to time slips into a phrase in Greek or French to remind himself and his reader of his accomplishments.

He also may have moved towards editing the works of Chrysostom, to judge from a letter dated 20 April 1580 from Alvise Lullini.[64] He was asked to seek for a map and certain 'undiscoverable books' in Patmos. An inventory of what might be found in Patmos could be obtained from one of Lullini's agents who lived in Candia, in Crete. Savile was already employing a professional searcher for records in order to accumulate Greek materials. He had been granted a fourth year of

---

[61] Feingold, pp. 128, 132. For five letters of Praetorius written during the tour and five after it see ibid., p. 127 n. 18. A Pinelli MS of Euclid has notes by Savile, cf. Todd (above, n. 38), 441–2.

[62] A. L. Rowse, *Ralegh and the Throckmortons* (1962), p. 84.

[63] Highfield, 'An autograph commonplace book', pp. 73–83.

[64] *CSP. Foreign, 1581–2*, p. 633. Dr A. Wright tells us that this may well be Alvise Lollius, bishop of Belluno, who with a Venetian-Greek background was well placed to advise on patristic subjects: 'Bellarmine, Baronius and Federico Borromeo' in *Bellarmino e la Controriforma*, ed. R. de Maio *et al.* (Sora, 1990), pp. 323–70, esp. p. 330 no. 20.

absence, but it was time to head for home. He seems to have done so by a roundabout route, for he returned first to Breslau in March.[65] He probably then met the astronomer Paul Wittich, who was teaching mathematics there between 1582 and 1584; but by the beginning of 1583 he was back in Merton.[66]

Henry's younger brother Thomas worked closely with him. He was a Merton undergraduate like Neville, and graduated in 1580 when he was at once elected to a fellowship.[67] He shared his elder brother's wide interests and collaborated with William Camden in the making of his *Britannia*.[68] Among his other friends were Richard Hakluyt the geographer, Alberico Gentili the civilian, the Hungarian Parmenius, and the Huguenot Jean Hotman. Parmenius stayed with Savile in 1583.[69] Then in 1588 Thomas Savile set off in his brother's steps with the college's permission; Henry wrote to Hugo Blotius on 12 March 1588 commending his brother to him and conveying the greetings of Sidney and Neville.[70] Naturally Thomas called on Dudith in Breslau and was present there during Dudith's last days, which he described in a letter to another of Henry's friends, Joannes Praetorius.[71] Thomas spent much time copying manuscripts and continued to do so when he eventually reached Italy. He was employed by the college to buy books there and later in Frankfurt. While he was in Italy he exchanged letters with Tycho Brahe with whom Henry had also been in touch.[72] He then returned to Oxford. He was elected proctor and had an important role to play on the occasion of the queen's visit,[73] but his promising career was cut short by his death in 1593.

The court of Queen Elizabeth began to affect Oxford and Merton in a variety of ways once Robert Dudley, earl of Leicester, became chancellor of the university in 1564. Some of its attentions were favourable, but some proved damaging. Leicester tried early to persuade the queen to visit Oxford, but she had already been to Cambridge under Burghley's aegis when in 1566 she agreed to come. The

[65] Feingold, p. 128.

[66] By January 1583 (ibid., p. 129).

[67] *MMC*, p. 273; *Register of the University of Oxford*, ed. A. Clark, OHS xii (1888), ii, pt. iii. 88–9.

[68] Feingold, p. 131.

[69] Ibid., and Birley, p. 244.

[70] Feingold, p. 131; for Thomas's letters to Blotius cf. Todd (above, n. 38), 443.

[71] Ibid., p. 132.

[72] Ibid.

[73] N. Robinson, in *Elizabethan Oxford*, p. 252.

warden of Merton, John Man, was then abroad as the queen's ambassador to Philip II of Spain, and with him was Arthur Atye, a fellow who was to become Leicester's secretary. Man's absence may account for the fact that the Spanish ambassador, Gómez de Silva, was accommodated in the Warden's Lodgings during the visit.[74] Despite the absence of the head of the house Merton was represented in several of the disputations mounted for the occasion. On 3 September a disputation in natural and moral philosophy was held at St Mary's before the earl as chancellor. The themes in moral philosophy were whether 'a prince should be made known by succession rather than by election' and that 'it would be better to be ruled by the best laws than by the best king'.[75] One of the four repliers was Mr James Leech, the senior proctor and a fellow of Merton since 1557. He argued with such force, saying that he was prepared to defend his principles through life and death, that it is recorded that he drew applause from the queen.[76] Another fellow to take part in a disputation before Elizabeth was Mr John Wolley (fellow from 1554). He must also have made a good impression, for he succeeded Roger Ascham as the queen's Latin secretary and eventually became a member of the privy council.[77] Elizabeth came to trust him so completely that she appointed him one of the commissioners for the trial of Mary, Queen of Scots. On 5 September there was another debate, this time involving members of the medical faculty. Again a Merton fellow took part – Robert Huicke, a former graduate of Cambridge. He had been a fellow of Merton since 1530 and was a natural choice since he was one of the royal physicians and a former President of the Royal College of Physicians.[78] He argued on the theme 'Whether human life can be defended by man's medical skill',[79] and quoted Galen 'De perfectione naturae et imperfectione'.

Savile's qualities had already become apparent to the chancellor by 1575, for in the following year Leicester asked for his reappointment as junior proctor. After a struggle the chancellor's choice prevailed,[80] but in 1578 the danger of the interest of the court was dramatically

---

[74] N. Robinson, in *Elizabethan Oxford*, pp. 200–1.

[75] 'An princeps declarandus esset successione potior quam electione' and 'An praestaret regi ab optima lege quam ab optimo rege': ibid., p. 182.

[76] Ibid., pp. xxii, 182. Mr Wolley, fellow of Merton, replied.

[77] Ibid., p. 175 n. 22.

[78] Ibid., p. 175 n. 14 and pp. 185–6.

[79] 'An vita humana arte medica prorogari possit'.

[80] *DNB* and McConica, *HUO* iii. 425–6.

demonstrated by the fate of Malden manor, one of the most valuable of the college estates. In Mary's reign the indebted twelfth earl of Arundel had bought the palace of Nonsuch from the crown, and was a next door neighbour to Malden manor. Elizabeth had been entertained there by the earl and wanted to show her appreciation. On 17 January 1579, without first seeking the college's views, she granted the earl the lease of Malden for 5,000 years at an annual rent of £40.[81] Only on 1 September following did she enter into a personally autographed indenture with the warden and fellows who then granted the queen the 5,000-year lease of the manor,[82] so sure was she that Warden Bickley and the fellows were impotent to resist the outrageous arrangement. Merton had to wait until the eighteenth century before it succeeded in breaking the lease.[83] The part which the earl's secretary, Arthur Atye, had played in the transaction is uncertain, but it was recorded that he was 'ingratus' to his college.[84]

Some time after Ascham died in 1576, and probably after he had returned from his travels abroad in 1582, Savile became a tutor in Greek to the queen.[85] He also became an accomplished courtier. Aubrey, writing long afterwards, records that 'the queen favoured him much'. Besides being 'a learned gentleman as most was of his time', he was 'an extraordinary handsome and beautiful man; no lady had a finer complexion'.[86] Thus when Warden Bickley was promoted to the bishopric of Chichester in 1585 Elizabeth, according to Wood, another seventeenth-century commentator, 'taking a liking to his parts and person' exercised herself in securing Savile's election to the wardenship of Merton. The sub-warden and the electors, the seven senior fellows, had the task of choosing three names to send to the visitor for him to take the final decision. The electors received a

---

[81] MCR 3351. For Elizabeth's visit to Nonsuch in 1559 see J. Dent, *The Quest for Nonsuch* (1962), pp. 158–9. For the queen's extortion of leases of 50 and 99 years of cathedral lands see C. Hill, *Economic Problems of the Church* (1956), p. 18, and of Oxford colleges, L. Pearsall Smith, *Life and Letters of Sir Henry Wootton* (1907), i. 32 and n. 4.

[82] The lease to the queen was dated 1 September 1579 and has her autograph (MCR 3351), cf. Ross, *Malden*, p. 68.

[83] In 1707 (Ross, *Malden*, p. 91).

[84] Savile Catalogue (Reg.4.18), p. 40; cf. *Register of the University of Oxford*, OHS xii, ii, pt. iii. 47, and Ross, *Malden*, p. 68. For a letter of Atye to Pérez from Islington, 27 March 1595, see Ungerer, *Spaniard in Elizabethan England*, ii. 255–6 and n. (letter 500). He was the translator of Pérez's *Relaciones* and a member of the Barbary Company promoted by Leicester. His eldest son was at Merton in 1601.

[85] Wood, *Athenae Oxonienses*, ii. 311, and *DNB*.

[86] Aubrey, *Brief Lives*, ii. 214.

joint letter on Savile's behalf from William Burghley and Sir Francis Walsingham.[87] The two ministers stated that the queen wished the fellows to choose their warden by election, but they trusted that when they did so they would 'seeke to concur also with Her Majesty's inclination'. Naturally the fellows took the hint; as did the visitor, Archbishop Whitgift, when he received notice of the three names chosen with that of Savile at the head.[88]

Leicester died in 1588, and when he did so Arthur Atye switched over to the patronage of Leicester's stepson and aspirant political heir, Robert Devereux, earl of Essex. Essex was present for the second visit which the monarch paid to Oxford in 1592. She had been staying at Woodstock when on 22 September she approached the city from the north and stopped at Wolvercote by Godstow Bridge, where, notwithstanding the 'foulness of the weather', Henry's younger brother, Thomas Savile, as senior proctor, made a short speech of welcome[89] from his knees. He yielded up to the queen the privileges and liberties of the universities, to receive them back immediately. He and the junior proctor attended the queen throughout the visit. On proceeding into Oxford she was greeted at Carfax by another Merton fellow, Henry Cuffe, the reader in Greek.[90]

On 23 September, after two philosophical questions had been argued before the queen and a respondent and repliers had said their pieces, the warden determined, that is, summed up the discussion, and brought proceedings to a formal end.[91] The two themes chosen were whether 'the study of warfare and philosophy can flourish in the same state' and whether 'judicial astrology should be extirpated in a well-ordered state'.[92] Two elegant Latin texts have survived in which Savile dealt with each question,[93] after which the warden added a speech of thanks. On the 24th in a debate among members of the medical faculty a former fellow, Richard Radcliffe, principal of St

---

[87] *RACM 1567–1603*, pp. 188–9 (28 February 1586). In 1545 at the time of the election of Warden Raynolds the three names had been chosen by the seven 'provectiores et discretiores' (*RACM 1483–1521*, p. 336).

[88] *RACM 1567–1603*, pp. 189–90 (7 March), pp. 194–6 (18 March).

[89] *Elizabethan Oxford*, p. 250.

[90] Ibid., p. 251.

[91] Ibid., pp. 253–4.

[92] 'Rei Militaris et Philosophiae studia in Republica una vigere'; 'Astrologiam Judiciariam e Civitate bene morata esse exterminandam'.

[93] *Elizabethan Oxford*, pp. 263–71. In 1619 Savile debarred his professor of astronomy from 'professing the doctrine of nativities and all judicial astrology without exception': Tyacke, 'Science and Religion', p. 74.

Alban Hall, argued from his own rotundity that the proposition 'that the body is changed more by air than by food and drink' must be negatived.[94] The great night of the visit for Merton was 25 September when the queen, the chancellor, and the lords in council all dined with the warden in Merton Hall. The sixty diners sat down at one table, which must have run down the axis of the hall. After dinner Henry Cuffe was the respondent and four other fellows, Thomas French, Richard Trafford, Henry Wilkinson, and Francis Mason, were the repliers or opponents.[95] The senior proctor, also a Mertonian, Thomas Savile determined on the theme 'whether civil disorders are useful to a state'. In doing so he commended Sir William Cecil (Lord Burghley), the Lord Treasurer, the Lord Chamberlain, and the Lord High Admiral, and the earl of Essex for his service in the Low Countries, Portugal, and France. Among those present was the French ambassador who with others in due course retired to Mr Colmer's rooms.[96] Merton's contribution towards the expenses of the 1592 visit was £400, which put the college sixth in wealth, on a par with St John's, whereas Christ Church at £2,000 and Magdalen at £1,200 were reckoned five and three times better off.[97]

After the visit the shadow of Robert Devereux, second earl of Essex began to fall over the college. His circle, centred on Essex House in the Strand, was a wide one, and we must not assume that all Mertonian contacts with the earl were as close as those of Henry Cuffe, one of his several secretaries. That of Bodley, for instance, seems to have been more distant, though when he was the queen's resident in the Netherlands, he sent information about events like the fall of Groningen to the earl of Essex before he sent them to Burghley. The slight made Burghley angry and he rebuked Bodley for his lapse.[98] However, the earl did not forget Bodley, for when Essex's rebellion broke out, as has been noted, Bodley was one of those considered for the secretaryship to replace Sir Robert Cecil.[99]

The warden was certainly a friend of Essex. Francis Bacon in his

---

[94] *Elizabethan Oxford*, pp. xxvii, 258; *Register of the University of Oxford*, ii, pt. iii, ed. A. Clark, p. 11.

[95] *RACM 1567–1603*, p. 288.

[96] Loc. cit.; cf. *Elizabethan Oxford*, p. 256.

[97] *RACM 1567–1603*, p. 287.

[98] R. B. Wernham, *After the Armada: Elizabethan England and the Struggle for Western Europe 1588–1595* (1984), p. 540.

[99] Joel Hurstfield, *Freedom, Corruption and Government in Elizabethan England* (1973), p. 127.

Apophthegms records that it was in answer to an enquiry of the earl touching poets that Savile replied 'He thought them the best of writers, next to those that write prose'.[100] Moreover in Bacon's 'Apologie' Essex demonstrates his love of knowledge by calling to witness his friendship with that 'most learned and trulie honest Mr Savile'. A letter of Antonio Pérez to Thomas Smith in 1594 shows that Savile was then staying at the earl's country seat of Barn Elms, and suggests that Pérez and the earl and Savile were about to pay a visit together to Oxford.[101] On 4 August 1597 the earl was allowed to hold a moiety of the college's valuable livings of Embleton and Ponteland.[102] When the rebellion began in 1599 the warden was for a time in custody and had his rooms in Eton searched, but it seems that no incriminating evidence was found;[103] and quite soon Savile was given charge of the earl's son, Robert, who was then a boy at Eton. Savile welcomed the future parliamentarian general as an undergraduate at Merton, and found accommodation for him in the Warden's Lodgings.[104] Thus the link between the college and the house of Devereux survived the strain of the earl's rebellion and disgrace.

Savile's old travelling companion and the queen's ambassador in France, Henry Neville was much closer to the fire, for he was judged to have been privy to the earl's plans even though he did not join in the *émeute* itself. He was imprisoned in the Tower and fined £5,000 for misprision of treason.[105] He was lucky not to be treated more harshly. Years later in 1612 another conspirator, the earl of Southampton, who also escaped, made a special visit to London in order to support Neville's candidature for a secretaryship to James I.[106]

Fully embroiled was Henry Cuffe, the former professor of Greek, and author of *The Differences of the Ages of Man's Life* and *A true Relation of the Action at Cadiz*, which he wrote as part of a propaganda

---

[100] Garrod, *Study of Good Letters*, pp. 102–3; David Womersley, 'Sir Henry Savile's translation of Tacitus and the political interpretation of Elizabethan texts', *Rev. Eng. Stud.* xli (1991), 313–42, at p. 316 and n.

[101] Letter 209 in Ungerer, *Spaniard in Elizabethan England*, i. 324–5; and see now Paul E. J. Hammer, 'The Use of Scholarship: The Secretariat of Robert Devereux, Second Earl of Essex, *c.* 1585–1601', *EHR* cix (Feb. 1994), 45, 49, 51.

[102] *RACM 1567–1603*, p. 329.

[103] Cf. *Cal S.P. Domestic* of 24. 2. 1601 in *DNB*.

[104] *DNB*. Admission on 23 January 1603 (*RACM 1567–1603*, p. 352).

[105] J. Spedding, ed. *The Letters and Life of Francis Bacon*, (1861–77) ii. 207, 343–50, and *DNB*; A. L. Rowse, 'The tragic career of Henry Cuffe', in *Court and Country*, pp. 211–41. Cuffe left Savile £100 in his will and £250 to Merton College for a commemoration on Lammas Day.

[106] *DNB* (Henry Neville).

campaign on Essex's behalf. For him there was no mercy and he was hanged for treason at Tyburn, a distinction which he shares with only one former fellow, on 13 March 1601.[107]

From 1585 to 1596 Savile endeavoured to run his interests at Merton and the court together. In 1587 he turned to Thomas Master, as sub-warden, as a trustworthy vicegerent whom he regarded with favour for his reliability in college business and on progress.[108] Nevertheless the warden could hardly attend to his business at court without neglecting his responsibilities in Oxford. Some of the fellows reacted with increasing impatience to the warden's long absences and reliance on deputies. When Savile sought at court to add the provostship of Eton to his Merton office their criticism found expression in a memorandum of complaint addressed to the visitor. Savile was successful in his attempt to become provost of Eton, an appointment in the queen's hand.[109] It was a real plum, but it did not prove an easy fruit to gather, for the statutes of Eton required that the provost should be in orders, and if he was not a dispensation was needed. At the same time Savile had a rival among the fellows in Henry Cuffe. But the warden outflanked him[110] and may finally have gained his point by making the queen anxious to free herself from his importunate attentions.

Savile's success at Eton moved his critics to attack him on two fronts. From 1591 to 1596 Thomas Master had been the sub-warden and the warden's choice as vicegerent.[111] When in 1597 Master obtained a benefice which might be judged richer (*uberius*) than was compatible with the holding of a fellowship a group of fellows appealed to the visitor, Archbishop Whitgift. They sought to persuade him to rule that the benefice was 'uberius' and so force the resignation of the warden's complaisant deputy. They wrote to Whitgift on 1 July 1598,[112] but unfortunately for them the visitor ruled in Master's favour. Their riposte was to refuse to elect the warden's choice for sub-warden when

---

[107] *DNB*. Rowse, loc. cit.; Hammer (above, n. 101), pp. 32–51.

[108] *RACM 1567–1603*, p. 230.

[109] He lobbied Essex first. When that did not answer he turned to Robert Cecil (Rowse, *Court and Country*, pp. 217–18).

[110] It seems that the queen at first offered him the Latin secretaryship and the deanery of Carlisle *in commendam* (cf. Maxwell-Lyte, *History of Eton College*, p. 179 and n. 1).

[111] *RACM 1567–1603*, pp. 279, 284, 305, 313, 320; *Register of the University of Oxford* (1888) ii, pt. iii. 70.

[112] P.3.25 (6). The benefice was said by the sub-warden and seniors to be worth more than £50.

the election of college officers came up on 1 August. Savile had written to say that he could not come because of sickness and asked the fellows to elect the proctor, Mr Trafford. They declined to do so and instead elected a senior fellow, Jasper Colmer.[113] Savile was furious. He protested against the election on the grounds that he had not been present to concur in the choice made and remitted the matter to the visitor. At this juncture the queen intervened in a letter from Sir John Stanhope to Whitgift.[114] She asked for an 'exemplary punishment' of the rebellious fellows. Whitgift needless to say supported Savile. He declared the election of Colmer to be 'disordered proceedings' and 'utterlie voide'. Colmer was deprived of his fellowship and three other senior fellows suspended. Master was reappointed sub-warden.[115] There is a revealing account in Chamberlain's letter to Sir Dudley Carleton: 'The Warden of Merton Colledge hath got a great victorie of his fellowes and raunsommed and punished divers of them and amongst the rest expelled Master Colmer who of griefe or curst hart died within five days after.'[116]

What lay behind the attack on Master? It is time to return to the memorandum of complaint. It was declared that Savile's government 'hath been negligent and unprofitable by his personall absence from the colledge for the most parte of the yeares he hath been warden ther'. It was alleged that he had failed to hold courts baron on the manors or to go on progress for five or six years together. He was said to have been 'detracting to call in money given by testament of a benefactor (deceased some ten yeres past or more) for speedie purchase of landes for th' encrease of commons; and after the receipt of the same money yet differring the said purchase'.[117]

He was also said to have made available favourable leases of college properties to some of his friends at rates unfavourable to the college. That looks like a reference to the grant made on 4 August 1597 to the

---

[113] Garrod, *Study of Good Letters*, p. 106.

[114] P.3.25 (11); Garrod, *Study of Good Letters*, pp. 106–7.

[115] Garrod, *Study of Good Letters*, pp. 107–8 (quoting Archbishop Whitgift's register). The suspended fellows were Robert Brizenden and Benjamin Bentham. Brizenden was a notable preacher, to judge from the remarkable petition from the mayor and corporation of the City of Oxford asking for his restoration to his fellowship as the 'publicke and onlie preacher to our citizens'.

[116] Quoted in Garrod, op. cit., p. 108.

[117] P.3.25 (5). The reference is to the will of Mr James Leech who had left the college 200 books and £200 with which to buy lands in Cheshire. He died in 1589. The difficulties experienced in Cheshire were partly the result of the failure of his brother to pay across the cash legacy.

earl of Essex.[118] Savile was alleged to have devised 'a whole manor of the college landes to a frend in trust for his owne use, in farre more ample terms than otherwise ordinarie, neither paying any fine for it nor levying the whole rent to the colledge (according to lawe) upon the lease reserved' and 'of receiving secret bribes or fines for the leases and turning the same to private use, to the common hinderance of the societie'.

Savile was criticized for having allowed the appointment of a probationer fellow but for having subsequently rejected him 'whom he once liked, without reason alledged and proved for the alteration of his judgment'. He was accused of advancing a protégé, designated a 'serving man', to a college copyhold and thence to a fellowship of Merton and an ushership of Eton;[119] he then secured him a fellowship there 'to which he had now disappeared, continuing the same man withal still fellowe at Merton College'. His appointment of a junior Linacre lecturer was criticized on the grounds that the man chosen did not live in college and had failed to give a lecture in the course of three years.[120] Finally he was criticized for 'suffering his brother[121] to change the college plate in great losse without the consent and noe good account made by the same'.

Returning to the fear that the critical fellows had of losing ground to Eton, 'some of the inconvenience of one man's being master of more houses than one at once and together' was stated at length. The linking of Merton and Eton was thought especially dangerous to the former since Henry VI's foundation ordinances required the provost of Eton to be 'continually restant there' which Merton's statutes did not for the warden. The complainants suggested that the five senior fellows[122] 'chosen before the present warden's comyng to the government' might be summoned to be examined on oath on these and other points. If the memorandum reached Whitgift, as it probably

---

[118] *RACM 1567–1603*, p. 329 (half the rectories of Ponteland and Embleton).
[119] This was perhaps Richard Wright, fellow 1595, who became a fellow and head master of Eton.
[120] P.3.25 (5); cf. the evidence summarized by R. G. Lewis in 'The Linacre lectureships subsequent to their foundation', in F. Maddison *et al.* (eds.), *Linacre Studies: Essays on the Life and Work of Thomas Linacre c.1460–1524* (Oxford, 1977), p. 238.
[121] The reference is to Thomas Savile in 1594 (*RACM 1567–1603*, p. 302).
[122] The senior fellows with their dates of election were Colmer and Fisher (1577), Brizenden and Bentham (1580). Thomas Savile was presumably not a complainant.

did,[123] it seems that he did nothing about it, no doubt in the light of the attempt to oust Master. That some criticism of the warden's absence and pluralism came to the chancellor of the university, Sir Thomas Sackville, Lord Buckhurst, is made clear in a letter which Savile wrote later to Whitgift,[124] defending himself against the pressure which Buckhurst evidently brought to bear on him to persuade him to resign Merton. In his letter to Whitgift he asked why he should be picked on. He argued that several of his predecessors as warden had often been absent, especially when serving their sovereign. Here he had a strong point. Richard FitzJames had thus been absent as royal counsellor (and almoner) to Henry VII, and Warden Chambers as physician to Henry VIII. Dr Phillips had been absent as vicar of Croydon, Dr Raynolds as dean of Exeter or when waiting on Queen Mary. Dr Man had even spent three years as Elizabeth's envoy at the Spanish court. Savile alleged that Dr Bickley, his predecessor, had not spent more than a month or so at Merton each year, and admitted that he himself was never there for more than two months at a time when he was warden and the earl of Leicester and Sir Christopher Hatton were running the queen's government (i.e. between 1587 and 1588).[125] As to other pluralists he quoted Dr Bill, provost of Eton, dean of Westminster, master of Trinity College, Cambridge, and royal almoner. He claimed that he himself was at Merton 'six or seven tymes a yeare and stay as longe as I have any business of the college to discharge'.

He then went on to the attack and to argue that his absence had had many beneficial results for the college. It had saved on allowances (wood, coal, utensils, and fruits) to the tune of £100 per annum. He had defended lawsuits affecting the college in the courts in London at his own expense. Financially he claimed that one year before his appointment the college 'had not one peny in treasure, but was endebted to the bursars'. By contrast since he took over he had been able to spend more than 1,000 marks in building 'one way and

---

[123] If Mr Fairhurst, the bookseller, is right these papers were among those seized from Archbishop Laud at the time of his downfall. Thence they passed to the Lambeth Selden/Hale Collection. The college bought them from Mr Fairhurst.

[124] P.3.25 (21).

[125] Hatton was chancellor, 29 April 1587–22 November 1591. Leicester died on 4 September 1588.

other',[126] and the college 'mayntayneth at this day very neare twyse as many felowes as usually it hath done in our memory and yet hath above a thousand pound in stocks'. It seems clear that he saw himself as a courtier as much as a head-of-house, but a head who paid regular though occasional visits to Oxford. If one was to lobby for the provostship of Eton permanent attendance at court was essential until the matter was settled. His task as tutor in Greek to the queen after 1582 may also have held him at Greenwich, Richmond, Windsor, Westminster, or wherever Elizabeth might be. The formal obligation to reside at Eton, once that plum had been picked, and the decision to print the Chrysostom at Eton in the reign of James I, must have drawn him more and more away from Oxford and towards Eton and the court. Nevertheless he did go on progress in 1606, achieved the construction of Fellows' Quad in 1608–10, brought Casaubon to Oxford in 1613, and turned his attention to the needs of the Bodleian after Bodley's death in that year. He suffered increasingly from illness (in 1611 and again in 1617). Only at the very end of his life does he seem to have become more or less fixed at Eton or at court.

In the closing years of Elizabeth's reign the warden enlarged his reputation for learning among his contemporaries when in 1591 he published *The Ende of Nero and the Beginning of Galba, Fower books of the Histories of Cornelius Tacitus. The life of Agricola*. He brought out a second edition in 1598, and three more before he died in 1622. To his translation he added an essay on the Roman art of war and sought to fill the gap left between the end of the *Annals* where they are cut short in AD 66 and 1 January 69 when the *Histories* begin, that is 'from the end of Nero to the beginning of Galba'. His restoration of the missing events is based on Suetonius' *Lives of Nero and Galba*, Plutarch's *Life of Galba*, and sections of Dio Cassius, but it also includes Savile's own interpretation of these events. Dr Womersley[127] has subjected his arguments to analysis and detects the strong influence of Machiavelli and a sympathy for the author of the rebellion against Nero, Julian Vindex. Jonson complimented Savile in verse on his

---

[126] P.3.25 (21). In 1589 he had had the north range of Front Quad rebuilt from the Front Gate to the Warden's Lodgings. For Fellows' Quad (Pl. 17) cf. *HUO* iv. 148–50. The projecting windows at each end of the south façade are at second-floor level (as was the warden's gallery, lit by the eastern one). After 1576 Merton, like other colleges, began to benefit from the effects of the Corn Rent Act as applied to its leases (cf. *HUO* iii. 534–7).

[127] David Womersley (above, n. 100). For the importance of Tacitus at the court of James I, cf. also J. H. M. Salmon, 'Seneca and Tacitus in Jacobean England' in *The Mental World of the Jacobean Court*, ed. Linda Levy Peck (Cambridge, 1991), 169–88.

translation and particularly on his filling in of the missing piece in Tacitus's story. He also suggested that the prefatory note to the reader signed A.B. was written by the earl of Essex, though that is a speculation.[128] The work is dedicated to the queen and Savile avers that one of his purposes was to persuade Elizabeth herself to publish on Tacitus. More recent authors than Jonson, including H. W. Garrod, have criticized Savile for the dullness of his translation. That may be partly because Savile himself is critical of Tacitus for his 'heresy of style'. He regarded his author as an historian of 'counsailes and causes', and believed that the subject would also interest the queen.[129] Another modern scholar, F. P. Wilson, is kinder than Garrod to the translation; he gives it as his opinion that some of the version retains 'a solemn music' which does honour to the original.[130] One reaction to the publication was a response to the appendix, *A view of certain military matters, or commentaries concerning Roman warfare*, which drew its author into an exchange of views with the great Burghley. Burghley was wrestling with the difficult problem of how to finance the new scheme for the militia which he was in process of launching. He evidently thought that he might learn directly from the experience of Roman history and so consulted the expert. Savile's learned reply in his *Report on the wages paid to the ancient Roman Soldiers* (1595) demonstrates his knowledge of Imperial Rome and also his recognition of the differences between the Roman and English situations.[131]

May McKisack showed that Savile also had it in mind to enter the field of medieval English history by writing an account of the English monasteries.[132] That he never did, but he did contribute to the editing of medieval chronicles, an interest which he shared with his friend William Camden. In 1596 he published *Rerum Anglicarum Scriptores post Bedam praecipui vetustissimis codicibus manuscriptis nunc primum in lucem editi*. It was his unhappiest publication from a modern point

---

[128] Womersley, op. cit., pp. 314–15 and n. 9, 316 n. 18. It is certainly true that a member of the Essex circle, Sir John Hayward, the translator of Sallust (1608), was to be indebted to Savile's Tacitus, cf. E. B. Benjamin, 'Sir John Hayward and Tacitus', *Rev. Eng. Stud.*, n.s. viii (1957), 29–32, 275–6.

[129] Garrod, *Study of Good Letters*, p. 112, Ungerer, *Spaniard in Elizabethan England*, ii. 372.

[130] F. P. Wilson, *Elizabethan and Jacobean* (Oxford, 1945, 1960), p. 39.

[131] For Savile's reply see 'Mr Henry Saville's Report of the Wages paid to the ancient Roman Soldiers for their Vittayling and Apparell, in a letter to Lord Burleigh, 1595', *Sommers Tracts*, 4th collection (1751), ii. 385–7.

[132] M. McKisack, *Medieval History in the Tudor Age*, p. 64 and n. 1.

of view. That is not because it was not a pioneering venture, as the title suggests, nor yet because the editor did not know a good text when he saw one, but because, after the practice of the sixteenth century, he mixed one text with another. The book contains editions of the *Gesta regum*, the *Historia Novella*, and *Gesta pontificum* of William of Malmesbury, the *Historia Anglorum* of Henry of Huntingdon, the *Chronica* of Roger of Howden, *Chronicles* of Aethelwaerd, and *Histories* of Ingulph of Croyland. The fact that the only known text of the chronicle of Aethelwaerd was destroyed in the Cottonian fire of 1731 has meant that Savile's text is particularly valuable as it seems to have been based on the lost chronicle.[133] But elsewhere, to quote McKisack, the editor 'followed his normal policy of omitting, abridging and "improving at will".' She gives an example of such an unhistorical improvement.[134] Stubbs who edited the *Gesta regum* for the Rolls Series describes Savile's edition in notably restrained terms as 'an eclectic or learned and critical recension of his own making based on a collection of good manuscripts but with only an indistinct recognition of their relation and bearing on one another'.[135] At the same time when Stubbs came to edit Roger of Howden's *Chronica* in the same series he was anxious that his criticisms of the weaknesses of the text should not detract from Savile's achievement. 'His edition is in all material respects so good and its usefulness for the last two hundred and seventy years has been so great, that I feel that no such criticism as this will be interpreted as directed to the depreciation of it.'[136] Hamilton in editing the *Gesta pontificum* of William of Malmesbury is less indulgent. The edition is 'full of errors, amounting at times to downright unintelligibility'.[137] Professor Douglas considers that the transcription of the chronicle of Pseudo-Ingulph is 'sometimes so inaccurate as to make it doubtful whether Savile himself ever revised his own proofs'.[138] A point which Savile himself made in his preface is of considerable importance for our grasp of the man. 'Though some have undertaken

---

[133] Ibid., p. 65.

[134] Ibid.

[135] *Willelmi Malmesbiriensis monachi de gestis regum Anglorum libri quinque: Historiae Novellae libri tres*, ed. W. Stubbs, RS i (1887), p. xciv.

[136] *Chronica Magistri Rogeri de Hovedene*, ed. W. Stubbs, RS ii (1869), p. xviii. The striking difference between the standard reached in the editing of the medieval chronicles and that achieved in the works of Chrysostom may be explained by the fact that those of the patristic father were approached with special piety and care.

[137] *Willelmi Malmesbiriensis monachi de gestis pontificum Anglorum libri quinque*, ed. N. E. S. A. Hamilton, RS lii (1870), p. x.

[138] David C. Douglas, *English Scholars* (1939), p. 210.

portions of our history,' he wrote, 'no one hitherto appears to have attempted to write the whole with that fidelity and dignity which the magnitude of the work demanded ... I have sought a remedy to this evil attempting to bring to light the most ancient of our authors if not the most eloquent certainly the most faithful recorders of facts to the end that others possessing both leisure and genius for the task might have their authors ready to their hand from which to derive their materials.'[139] In other words, here is the man of vision who looks forward to a complete history of 'Britons, Saxons and Normans', something better than the production of that 'ignorant foreigner' Polydore Vergil, and who sees as an essential preliminary the publication of the crucial source material. Certainly the defects decried by modern editors seem to have been invisible to contemporary users of the 1596 text, which was reprinted with the editor's additions and corrections at Frankfurt in 1601.

Savile's interest in British antiquities, evidenced in his edition of those chronicles, was shared with his brother Thomas and with their friend, William Camden. The friendship with Camden seems to have been established as early as the 1570s, and continued all his life. Camden on occasion sought to borrow for Savile manuscripts of Chrysostom and Euclid from the library of Lord Burghley through the intervention of Sir Robert Cotton. At the very end of his life Savile invited Camden to come and live with him in his house at Eton.[140]

Henry's brother Sir John was to become one of the founder members of the Society of Antiquaries.[141] His brother Thomas worked in close collaboration with Camden over the preparation of the compilation of the *Britannia*. It is not surprising therefore to find the warden leading the college to open and repair the damaged tomb of the founder at Rochester Cathedral in 1598–9.[142] A chalice and a ring were removed, a new alabaster effigy constructed, and a careful new inscription devised. The task of supervising the work was entrusted to a former fellow, William Wilson, who had resigned his fellowship on obtaining a 'uberius' benefice in the gift of the earl of Pembroke.[143]

---

[139] David C. Douglas, *English Scholars*, pp. 207–8.

[140] *DNB* (Camden); and see below, n. 153.

[141] *DNB* (Sir John Savile).

[142] For the inscription and restoration see *RACM 1567–1603*, p. 337, and cf. p. 332. The restoration was still being paid for on 13 July 1605 when £5 was spent (Reg. 1.3, p. 215). For an account of the opening of the tomb in the 19th cent. see E.1.22 (31 July 1849) and cf. F.3.46 (24 July 1849) (letter of E. Hawkins, provost of Oriel and canon of Rochester).

[143] *RACM 1567–1603*, pp. 80–1, 83–4; cf. *Register of the University of Oxford*, ii, pt. iii. 63.

As we have seen, Savile had had recent occasion to remember the authority which he considered he had received from Walter de Merton, when he quashed the election of Mr Jasper Colmer as sub-warden and referred the disputed election of college officers to the decision of the visitor.

The change of dynasty brought knighthoods to both Bodley and Savile in 1604. No wonder that there was a portrait of James I in the Warden's Lodgings. At the royal visit to the university in the following year, however, Savile does not seem to have been in Oxford. The king was received at the Bodleian on 30 August by the Librarian, and Bodley took a great deal of pains over the preparations for his reception. The principal Mertonian present was the public orator, Sir Isaac Wake, who elaborated his account of the visit in a publication – *Rex Platonicus*.[144] The king was ravished by the Bodleian. He offered to present to it manuscripts from the royal library and, though that seems to have been a promise which he did not keep, he did present to it a copy of his own Latin *Works* published in 1619.[145]

Savile meanwhile was about to become involved in that great scholarly enterprise which followed the meeting of the Hampton Court Conference in 1604 – the Authorized Version of the Bible.[146] It demonstrated that he was at his best as a scholar working in collaboration with a scholarly team, and on Greek texts rather than Latin.

He was by no means the initiator of the undertaking: that was President Raynolds of Corpus Christi College, Oxford. But relations with Raynolds were close. Was the president not the nephew of Warden Raynolds of Merton? Had he not been entered on the books of Merton before being elected to a scholarship at Corpus? At all events, when the six groups of translators had been drawn up, with two at Westminster, two at Cambridge, and two at Oxford, Savile and Raynolds each found themselves in one of the two Oxford groups. Raynolds and his colleagues attended especially to the prophets. They were the Hebrew group, whilst Savile in the 'Fifth company', a Greek group, worked on the Acts of the Apostles, the Gospels, and the Revelation of St John the Divine. We know from Merton sources

---

[144] *MMC*, p. 277 (27 August 1605).

[145] Philip, *The Bodleian Library*, pp. 15, 31.

[146] F. L. Cross, *Dictionary of the Christian Church*, 2nd edn. (1974), s.u. Bible (English Versions) Authorised Version.

that the Greek group met in the Warden's Lodgings.[147] Savile's work brought him in contact with some outstanding scholars. Foremost among them was George Abbot, dean of Winchester and master of University College, the future archbishop of Canterbury and visitor of Merton.[148] The names in the Merton Register enable us to identify the others in the group. They were Dr Ravis, the dean of Christ Church, Dr Giles Thompson, dean of Windsor, Dr Harmer, warden of St Mary's, Winchester, Dr John Aglionby, principal of St Edmund Hall (and not as in some lists Richard Edes, dean of Worcester), Dr Perrin or Pern, fellow of St John's, and Dr Hutton, canon of Christ Church.[149] Savile had a selection of books from the College Library carried up into his lodgings, including no doubt some of its dictionaries.[150] He later presented a handsome Hebrew–Latin dictionary to the library.[151] It should be remembered that the Authorized Version was rather a revision of earlier versions, such as that of William Tyndale, than a translation *ab initio*. The final revision was carried out by Dr Miles Smith and Thomas Bilson, bishop of Winchester. How much of the esteem which greeted this felicitous version was attributable to the individual groups of revisers is impossible to determine, but Savile had certainly been part of a very distinguished team.[152]

The other great co-operative venture with which the warden was associated was the *editio princeps* in Greek of the works of St John Chrysostom. Robert Birley calls it 'the one great work of Renaissance scholarship carried out in England'.[153] On that the Merton archives have less to say, because most of the work was done at Eton, where it was also printed and published. It was a very large-scale undertaking that Savile may have had in mind as early as 1582 when he was in

---

[147] Pollard, *Records*, pp. 52–3; Reg. 1.3, p. 214 (13 February 1605).

[148] Pollard, *Records*, p. 52.

[149] Reg. 1.3, p. 214. For Dr John Harmer, fellow of New College, reader in Greek (1585), proctor (1587), warden of Winchester for 17 years, see J. H. W. Binns, *Intellectual Culture in Elizabethan and Jacobean England* (Leeds, 1990), pp. 223–4, and Wood, *History and Antiquities*, ii, pt. 2, 853; for Dr John Aglionby, fellow of Queen's (1590), principal of St Edmund Hall, cf. J. N. D. Kelly, *St Edmund Hall: Nearly Seven Hundred Years* (Oxford, 1989), pp. 34–5; Dr John Perrin was a fellow of St John's (1597), canon of Christ Church and Regius professor of Greek (1597–1615) (Costin, *History of St John's*, p. 25). For Hutton see Pollard, *Records*, p. 53.

[150] Reg. 1.3, p. 214 (13 February 1605), Garrod, *Study of Good Letters*, p. 114.

[151] See the inscription in *Thesaurus Linguae Sanctae sive Lexicon Hebraicum* (Lyons, 1575). He also presented D. Cimchi's Hebrew Lexicon (Coxe, i. 130, Oriental MS.5).

[152] Cf. Pollard, *Records*, pp. 338–9, for the principles of the translation.

[153] Birley, p. 245.

Venice, and spoke of Greek resources to be searched for in Patmos.[154] The edition of individual items prepared by Erasmus (Basle, 1526, 1529) cried out for the whole work to be edited and for the complete replacement of the Latin editions. Before 1600 Savile had corresponded about it with his friends in the English diplomatic mission in Paris: Ralph Winwood, who had succeeded Savile's protégé Henry Neville[155] as ambassador, and Dudley Carleton, another diplomat, kinsman of George Carleton, later bishop of Chichester, and soon to be Lady Savile's son-in-law. Dudley Carleton collated manuscripts in Paris for him and, when he married Savile's step-daughter in 1607, took up his residence in the warden's house at Eton during the first year of his married life: 'plodding with my father Savile among his Greek letters'. Meanwhile the warden was borrowing a Greek manuscript of Chrysostom from the Bodleian in 1602[156] and trying to borrow a manuscript on Genesis from Lord Burghley with the help of William Camden and Sir Robert Cotton. A systematic search was pursued in foreign libraries both by correspondence and by sending out emissaries and copyists. The Royal and Imperial libraries were approached in Paris and Vienna, but also libraries in Augsburg, Munich, and Vienna, and in the Greek world in Mount Athos, Constantinople, and on the island of Chalce.[157] The emissaries included James Dalrymple of Ayr and Samuel Slade, fellow of Merton. Slade travelled extensively in Greece and died visiting Zante in 1613.[158] At the Vatican Savile used the copyist John Sanctamauras.[159] At Eton he was helped by Dudley Carleton, already noticed, by Boys, Hall, Richard Montague, another bishop of Chichester, and above all by another fellow of Merton, the 'ever memorable' John Hales, whose *Golden Remains* were to become a favourite book of the seventeenth century. Clarendon tells us that Hales 'had borne the greatest Part of the Labour of that excellent Edition and Impression of St Chrysostom's works, set out by Sir Henry

---

[154] Highfield, 'An autograph commonplace book ...', p. 80.

[155] *DNB* (Winwood, Ralph), and cf. S. Greenslade, 'The printer's copy for the Eton Chrysostom, 1610–1613' in *Studia Patristica*, vii (*Texte und Untersuchungen*, xcii: Berlin, 1966), 60–4.

[156] *Dudley Carleton to John Chamberlain* ... (above, n. 48), p. 107; *Original Letters of Eminent Literary Men*, Camden Soc., old ser., xxvi (1843), pp. 123–4.

[157] Ibid.

[158] Ibid., and *MMC*, pp. 274–5.

[159] Greenslade (above, n. 155), pp. 61–2.

Savile'.[160] Hales started life as a scholar of Corpus Christi, and was recruited by Savile as a fellow of Merton in 1588. He was a natural candidate for the college's Greek lectureship, once held by Bodley.[161] Savile secured a fellowship at Eton for him. Another fellow for whom the warden obtained an Eton fellowship (in 1604) was Thomas Allen, who lived at Eton for many years and was buried in the chapel there. Against one of Chrysostom's homilies in the printer's copy Savile has noted that it must be referred to Thomas Allen for his opinion.[162] At least five members of the Governing Body of Merton, Chamber, Slade, Allen, Wright, and Hales, were made fellows of Eton. Chamber was a fellow at the time of Savile's election as warden. He was a mathematician and astronomer and the founder of the Chamber's postmasterships. Richard Wright became first usher, then head master, and eventually fellow of Eton (1611). Slade and Hales helped the warden with his great undertaking. Chamber, Allen, and Hales lived and died at Eton.[163] One can guess that the fear which had surfaced at Merton when Savile became provost, that he might neglect his Oxford college, did not evaporate.

In his introduction to Chrysostom Savile presents a roll-call of European scholars who had helped him by correspondence or by opening their libraries to his emissaries. At their head he puts the name of Jacques Auguste de Thou, the French royal librarian. He calls him 'magnum lumen Galliae'.[164] Another librarian of a great library to be thanked is the lawyer Sebastian Tengnagel of the Imperial Library in Vienna.[165] A second protestant named is Isaac Casaubon. We know from the details of Casaubon's visit to Eton and Oxford that he did not relish being lionized by the warden, who took him in his carriage from Eton to Oxford and there introduced him to the scholars of the place. We know that Casaubon spent his twelve days in the Bodleian

---

[160] Clarendon, *Life*, p. 27, and cf. Aubrey, *Brief Lives*, i. 279; for Montague, see Wood, *Athenae Oxonienses*, 878–9; for Boys, Maxwell-Lyte, *History of Eton College*, pp. 191–3; for Hales, *HUO* iv. 581.

[161] Reg. 1.3, p. 225; *MMC*, pp. 277–8.

[162] Greenslade (above, n. 155), p. 64. For Allen see also Wood, *Athenae Oxonienses*, 603.

[163] *MMC*, pp. 278, 269, 275. Other possible helpers were Mr Andrew Downes, professor of Greek at Cambridge, and Chrysanthus, bishop of Lacedaemonia in Greece to whom payments were made at Eton (Maxwell-Lyte, *History of Eton College*, p. 193).

[164] Ioannes Chrysostom, *Opera* (Eton, 1612), i. p. v.

[165] Ibid. Other libraries tapped were those of Paris, Munich, Augsburg, Venice, and Constantinople (Aubineau, i, p. xvi).

pursuing his own interests.[166] Nevertheless he wrote some of the prefaces and notes for the Chrysostom. The mention of two Jesuits in Savile's list, Andreas Schott and Fronton du Duc, demonstrates that Savile had no narrow-minded approach to his editorial problems. For him the world of scholarship was still one. He drew on the advice of Gabriel Severus, the Greek archbishop of Philadelphia, an expert who had settled at Venice.[167] The remaining four names in his introduction, Marcus Velsus II of Augsburg, Georg Michael Lingelheim, I. Gruter, and David Hoeschel,[168] were all part of that network of Renaissance scholars on the continent who call to mind that similar group of mathematical scholars whom Savile had met at Nuremberg, Altdorf, Prague, and Vienna, when he went on the tour of 1578–82. They emphasize the wide vision of the man and his realization that the task on which he had embarked needed the co-operation of many of the leading European scholars who interested themselves in editions of works of the Fathers. The great edition was finally published in 1610–12 at Eton in eight volumes.[169] Merton helped the work forward by making a grant of £50 towards the publication of the first two volumes, to be paid back out of future sales.[170] The Greek type was presented to the university and the twenty-two dossiers of 15,800 pages of materials given to the Bodleian in 1620.[171] The editor of *Codices Chrysostomi Graeci*, Michel Aubineau, has observed, 'En se penchant sur ces pages marquées de l'écriture du Provost d'Eton, ils [les éditeurs modernes] admireront, comme nous l'avons fait, l'ampleur de son érudition, le sérieux de son sens critique'.[172]

The edition suffered from being pillaged by Morelli, for that published in Paris, 1609–33. Although copies were ceremonially presented

---

[166] Pattison, *Casaubon*, pp. 397–418. Casaubon recorded that it was his 'custom to kick all men who are generally considered learned, and to treat them as asses on two legs' (*Epistolae* (ed. 1709), p. 461, Maxwell-Lyte, *History of Eton College*, p. 182). However, he helped Savile with Chrysostom, visited the warden several times, and sent his son to Eton (Pattison, *Casaubon*, pp. 389, 397, 419, 436).

[167] Greenslade (above, n. 155), pp. 62–3. Another helper in Venice was Maximus Magounnios, Greek bishop of Kithira (A. D. Wright, 'Bellarmine, Baronius and Federico Borromeo' (*Centro di Studi Sorani V Patriarca* (1990), p. 330).

[168] Hoeschel had produced editions of individual texts (Augsburg, 1587, 1599, and 1602) (Aubineau i, pp. xv–xvi).

[169] 1,000 copies were printed. They sold at £9 the set; subsequently the price was reduced to £8, and some of the sets given to Eton were sold at £4 and £3 (*DNB*).

[170] Reg. 1.3, p. 201, 5 December 1602.

[171] Greenslade (above, n. 155), p. 60; H. Carter, *History of the Oxford University Press: i, to 1780* (1975), p. 25.

[172] Aubineau, i, p. xvii.

to the Prince Palatine, the United Provinces, and the Signory of Venice (for which the editor received handsome gifts in return) it seems that Savile was left with many copies on his hands if John Chamberlain is to be believed.[173] It is unlikely that Merton was paid back for its loan out of the profits of sales. Yet by contrast with his editions of Latin texts the edition of Chrysostom has retained its scholarly repute down the ages; and it may be that Hales succeeded in keeping the great enterprise on straight and narrow lines. Savile seems to have been in the mood for editing Greek texts, for in 1613 he brought out an edition of Xenophon's *Cyropaedia*, a natural choice for a provost of Eton and warden of Merton where the education of youth was a regular preoccupation.

Mention of Abbot leads naturally to another publication of the warden's declining years. For he tells us in the title of the book that it was at Abbot's instruction[174] that he prepared an edition of the *magnum opus* of a former archbishop of Canterbury, fellow of Merton and mathematician, Thomas Bradwardine. That was *De Causa Dei contra Pelagium et de virtute causarum ad suos Mertonenses libri tres*, published in 1618.[175] The defence of orthodoxy and Augustinianism against the Pelagians, who were the Ockhamists of the early fourteenth century, had a special interest for Abbot, since he was engaged in a defence of Calvinism at the time against the rising tide of opinion which was leading to Arminianism.[176] Bradwardine insisted 'on the necessity of grace' and the 'irresistible' efficacy of the Divine Will, and Abbot would have found a sympathetic echo in the scholastic's view of determinism. Yet, whereas Abbot was an out-and-out Calvinist it seems that Savile was not.[177] However, neither was he an Arminian, and the link with the visitor was maintained by his successor as warden, Nathaniel Brent, a civil lawyer, who became the archbishop's vicar-general.

After wrestling with Greek texts Savile turned to mathematics. More

---

[173] Garrod, *Study of Good Letters*, p. 113; Chamberlain, *Letters*, pp. 97–8; and cf. Maxwell-Lyte, *History of Eton College*, p. 186, and for the *Cyropaedia*, ibid., p. 187.

[174] *Libri tres iussu Reverendissimi Georgii Abbot Cantuariensis archiepiscopi* (title page).

[175] If Wood is correct it was based on six manuscripts (Wood, *Athenae Oxonienses*, ii. 314). One of these – Merton MS K.1.6 (Coxe 71) – Savile could consult in Merton Library.

[176] N. Cranfield and K. Fincham (eds.), 'John Howson's Answers to Archbishop Abbot's Accusations at his "Trial" before James I at Greenwich, 10 June 1615', *Camden Miscellany* xxix (1987), 4th ser., iv. 319–41; N. Tyacke, *Anti-Calvinists* (Oxford, 1987), pp. 56–7.

[177] Wood, *Historia et Antiquitates*, i. 304, 'vir a supervacaneis hisce Catharorum inventis alienissimus'.

than half a century later Dr Wallis, Savilian professor of geometry from 1649, is quoted by Aubrey[178] as saying that 'he look't on him to be as able a mathematician as any of his time'. Besides the half-bust of Savile himself, four figures adorn the monument erected in Merton Chapel after his death (Pl. 18). In the background, partly hidden behind pillars, are St John Chrysostom on his right and Tacitus on his left, but immediately on his right hand is the figure of Ptolemy. He stands for astronomy and the lectures which Savile had given on the *Almagest*. On his left is Euclid, personifying geometry, the last subject on which he lectured when he inaugurated the geometry chair.[179] Astronomy and geometry, the two subjects for which the Savilian chairs were founded in 1619, echo two subjects in the medieval arts course, but more recently they were subjects in which chairs had been established at Gresham College in London in 1597.[180] Moreover Savile observed in the preamble to his statutes that geometry had recently been totally unknown and abandoned at Oxford.

His interest in astronomy had been evidenced in the speech which he gave before the queen in 1592, when he advised that it should be cut off from judicial astrology.[181] In the same speech he argued a compatibility between the use of mathematics in warfare and philosophy – his own version of the debate about the need for both arms and letters in the education of a gentleman. He wished the choice of candidates for his chairs to be as wide as possible: they should be open to mathematicians 'from any part of Christendom'.[182] Savile naturally took a keen interest in the candidates. We are dependent on Seth Ward, Savilian professor of astronomy from 1649, as reported by Aubrey, for an account of the lively way in which the warden interviewed Edmund Gunter for the chair of geometry. Gunter was rejected with scorn because of his practical demonstration with math-

---

[178] Aubrey, *Brief Lives*, ii. 214.
[179] In his lectures on Euclid he especially commended study of the fifth book which deals with incommensurables and the theory of proportion (Garrod, *Study of Good Letters*, pp. 114–15, cf. Feingold, p. 128).
[180] Feingold, p. 5.
[181] *Elizabethan Oxford*, pp. 266–8.
[182] *DNB*. The three set books for the professor of geometry were Euclid's *Elements*, the *Conics* of Apollonius, and all Archimedes. He had also to give classes in surveying and arithmetic. For astronomy the set text was Ptolemy's *Almagest* (Tyacke, 'Science and Religion', p. 78).

ematical instruments.[183] Hill criticizes Savile for rejecting Gunter,[184] but he does not point out that Savile chose instead Briggs, the inventor of Briggsian logarithms, who was in every way an excellent candidate, even though the scorn with which Gunter was rejected was doubtless misplaced. Briggs came in from Cambridge via Gresham College. From Cambridge too came the first professor of astronomy, John Bainbridge, who was also, to judge from his papers, a first-rate choice.[185] Each new professor was endowed with a salary of £150 per annum and had a mathematical library made available to him, to which Savile gave some of his own books. A mathematical chest was also set up with an endowment of £100. Savile initiated the chair of geometry himself. His first lecture can be dated precisely to 9 a.m. in the Divinity School on Wednesday in Act Week, 12 July 1620. It was given before the vice-chancellor and all the doctors. He continued the course until the following Christmas, when he handed over to Briggs,[186] who began his lectures in Hilary Term 1621. Savile's own lectures were published along with others which he had given on Euclid in 1621. We must not exaggerate the importance of the establishment of the two chairs, but they were part of a rapidly changing scene. They reflected the new attitude to mathematics which was gradually invading the ancient university towards the end of the reign of James I.[187] Its effects cut right across the religious divide. Briggs was a Puritan, but several important mathematical figures of the 1630s were Arminians, and Laud himself was the patron of mathematics at St John's.[188] The Bodleian Library was already opening windows by its policy of acquisition, as when it bought by 1620 eight items of Kepler, Aaron Rathbone's *Surveyor*, and the translation by Edward Wright of Napier's *Logarithmes* (both published in 1616). Bainbridge's papers have enabled the 'new philosophy' to be identified in the 1630s. There are also links between Bainbridge and his successor, John Greaves,[189] and between Briggs and his successor, Peter Turner; both Greaves and

[183] Aubrey, *Brief Lives*, ii. 215; Feingold, p. 69.

[184] C. Hill, *Intellectual Origins of the English Revolution* (Oxford, 1965), p. 55; Aubrey, *Brief Lives*, ii. 215; cf. Feingold, p. 69, cf. *HUO* iv. 372–4.

[185] Feingold, pp. 143–7, cf. *HUO* iv. 288 n. 207, 380, 382–3, 486, 681.

[186] Wood, *History and Antiquities* ii (1796), p. 334; *Ultima Linea Savilii ... iusta academica*, (Oxford, 1622), pp. 22–3. Briggs 'also read Arithmetick thrice in a week in Merton College Refectory to the scholars thereof, being all the time of his abode in Oxford a commoner there', cf. *HUO* iv. 479–80, 485–6.

[187] Tyacke in 'Science and Religion', pp. 77–8.

[188] Feingold, p. 29; *HUO* iv. 581.

[189] Feingold, p. 70.

Turner were fellows of Merton.[190] The Civil War created a hiatus, but here were the foundations on which Ward and Wallis built during the Interregnum, when the group which formed first at Wadham and then in London initiated the Royal Society.

Of the two acquisitions of land by Merton during Savile's wardenship that at Bielby, Yorkshire, was closely associated with him. It came from a benefaction from John Chamber, fellow (1569), already noticed, who was himself a Yorkshireman and a friend. Indeed Chamber is said to have taught Savile some of his mathematics. Wood tells us that it was noted that Chamber was elected a fellow on merit, although coming from Yorkshire where the college held no land at the time of his election.[191] He was also a colleague of Savile in so far as he was a lecturer in astronomy in 1574[192] when Savile was lecturing on the *Almagest*. Moreover he shared Savile's pragmatic approach to Copernicus, and Feingold has found evidence to show that he approved of the 'Wittenburg interpretation', Melancthon, Peucer, and Erasmus Reinhold.[193] He also was present at Savile's election as warden in 1586, and shared with him the link with Eton, of which he became a fellow and where he died in 1604. His handsome legacy of £1,000 was to be put to buy lands in Yorkshire and to support two Eton postmasterships – the Chamber's postmasterships. They linked the two colleges over which Savile had presided until college awards were changed in the twentieth century. Warden Mure, an Etonian, was a Chamber's postmaster. Savile in all probability helped in the choice of Bielby. He also bought with college money originally given by Bishop Kempe the manor of Gamlingay Avenells, in 1599,[194] which was added to the lands which the college had owned in the village since the thirteenth century. The rents were to be set to help pay for the free robes which were due to the warden and fellows under the 1274 statutes, the cost of which was greatly increased by inflation in the sixteenth century. The last endowment for that purpose had been made by Bishop Kempe.[195]

---

[190] Feingold, pp. 69–70; Tyacke, 'Science and Religion', pp. 78–9, 89.

[191] Quoted in *MMC*, p. 269. For Chamber and his *Treatise against Judicial Astrology* (1601), see A. L. Rowse, *The Elizabethan Renaissance: The Life of the Society* (1971), pp. 236–9; *Register of the University of Oxford*, ii, pt. iii. 33.

[192] Cf. Wood, *Athenae Oxonienses*, 744–6.

[193] Feingold, p. 48.

[194] *RACM 1567–1603*, pp. 333–4. Shortly beforehand he had pointed out that owing to good husbandry the college had more than £1,000 in stock in hand (P.3.25 (21)).

[195] *RACM 1483–1521*, p. 522; and above, p. 130.

We should probably also attribute to Savile a radical change in keeping and recording the college accounts, which began when he assumed the warden's office in 1586. Henceforth the bursars' rolls were handsomely engrossed in books – the series known as 'Libri Rationarii Bursariorum'.

We do not know much about the way in which the fellows were elected under Bickley and Savile. The latter told Whitgift, when his rule was criticized in 1598, that in his time more fellows had been elected than hitherto because of the prosperity of the college's finances. Certainly a college which at times had as many as twenty-eight fellows was a powerful magnet. Moreover it is clear that Merton drew heavily on other colleges and halls for its new recruits. For instance under Savile there were about twice as many new fellows drawn from outside Merton as from within.[196] One feature of the new recruits was the high number from the halls – seventeen new fellows elected from them under Savile. St Mary Hall was especially prominent, with eight members.[197] Savile's old college, Brasenose, produced five new fellows.[198] Queen's came next with four.[199] Merton elected Bickley's nephew Richard Taylor.[200] Richard Fisher, to whose claim to kinship with the Founder Grindal testified, was nevertheless elected on merit and his claim to kinship rejected. Again pressure from Whitgift might not be enough to secure a fellowship, as it was not for Edmund Powell. We may assume that the method of election was by interview and oral examination, and that the warden took a keen interest in the process. We are told of Savile's 'hedge-beaters' who went out talent spotting, and Savile seems to have taken a leading role in the election of John Hales from Corpus Christi College in 1605.[201] Distinctly critical of the warden, however, was Robert Blake, the future admiral, who believed that Savile objected to his shortness of stature, 'it being the custom of Sir Henry Savile ... to pay much regard to the outward appearance of those who solicited preferment

---

[196] Out of 58 fellows elected under Savile 39 were from other colleges and only 19 from Merton (four unaccounted for).

[197] William Dainton, C. Dale, Edward Lee, James Marsh, Nicholas Marsh, John Morley, Peter Turner, and Leonard Yates.

[198] Thomas Allen, John Doughty, Peter Mason, Thomas Small, and perhaps William Fettiplace.

[199] Lawrence Hinton, John King, John Phillipson, and Henry Wilkinson.

[200] *RACM 1567–1603*, p. 255.

[201] *DNB*, Wood, *Athenae Oxonienses* (1817) iii. 410; Clarendon, *Life*, p. 27. In 1613 'He withdrew himself from all Pursuits of that Kind [i.e. preferment] into private Fellowship in the College of Eton, where his Friend Sir Henry Savile was Provost'.

in that society'.[202] How successful was the warden's seeking out of potential scholars? Notable reformers included Isaac Wake, elected in 1598[203] from Christ Church, public orator and ambassador to Switzerland, Venice, and France, and of two fellows elected in 1619 Edward Reynolds, a former postmaster, future dean of Christ Church, vice-chancellor, warden of Merton, and bishop of Norwich was outstanding. He was the composer of the 'General Thanksgiving' prayer.[204] John Earle, elected at the same time, became bishop of Salisbury and the author of the *Microcosmography* (1628).[205] Savile is normally supposed to have preferred the 'plodding scholar' to the wit and to have made an exception in the case of Earle who had both scholarship and wit. Theodore Gulston (1596) proved a notable medical scholar.[206] Griffin Higgs, later chaplain to the Winter Queen of Bohemia and dean of Lichfield, was a bibliophile of a high order, whose collection came to the college library.[207] Perhaps the best was the 'ever memorable' John Hales, already noticed as having helped Savile with the great edition of Chrysostom. Interestingly enough Briggs was never a fellow, but remained a professor and a commoner for reasons which are at present unknown.

Dr McConica has charted the stages by which after 1565 a matriculation register gradually came into being. On 14 December 1579 all students living in the town were ordered to move into colleges, and on 27 June 1580 convocation stated that all scholars must be brought into a college or hall.[208] The danger from recusants and the need to administer oaths were two of the reasons prompting the tighter

[202] For Wood's account of his choice of Doughty in 1619 see *Athenae Oxonienses* (1817), iii. 975–6.

[203] *MMC*, p. 277, *DNB*; he was MP for the university in 1623.

[204] *MMC*, p. 169. Wood says that he became a fellow 'by his skill in the Greek tongue', cf. *HUO* iv. 523, 597, 811–12, 823, 851.

[205] *MMC*, p. 282; Clarendon, *Life*, pp. 26–7. He was 'very notable for his Elegance in the Greek and Latin tongues'. He was author of the poem 'Hortus Mertonensis'.

[206] *MMC*, p. 276. He was editor of Aristotle, *De Rhetorica* (in Greek), and of works of Galen, the founder of the Gulstonian lectureship in anatomy, and a generous donor to the college library.

[207] *MMC*, p. 279, *Register of the University of Oxford*, ii, pt. iii. 296; W. C. Costin, *History of St John's*, pp. 59–60. Higgs endowed the librarianship with £10 p. a., and left £20 p. a. for a theological reader and £15 for the augmentation of the postmasters' commons. He left his 'musaeum', a notable collection of books, to the college library: Morrish, *Bibliotheca Higgsiana*.

[208] *HUO*, iii. 50–1. This was a reimposition of the rule that residence of a hall or college was a statutory requirement for all scholars, made as early as *c*. 1410 (A. B. Cobban, *The Medieval English Universities: Oxford and Cambridge to c. 1500* (Aldershot, 1988), p. 148).

arrangements. Whether the decrees of 1579 and 1580 provided the stimulus or not, a decision to extend the accommodation of the college and to bring the postmasters within the bounds was made during Savile's wardenship. The building of Fellows' Quad began in 1608 and was completed by September 1610 (Pl. 17). It was observed by John Chamberlain who, writing on 11 August 1612, noted after a visit 'the most pleasing thing I saw was the new quadrangle at Merton College, a graceful work, and that may stand for a sound foundation'.[209]

Merton matches only broadly the pattern established by Professor McConica for the social composition of the commoners and foundationers at Corpus Christi College, Christ Church, Broadgates Hall, Trinity, St John's, University College, Exeter, and Magdalen.[210] The matter is complicated by the fact that at Merton for the period in question the college evidence is largely made up by entries in the Register of the meetings of the Governing Body: the Postmasters' Register dates only from 1690. The register of matriculations is notoriously defective and recognizes neither 'portioniste' nor 'postmasters', the term which was coming in during the second half of the sixteenth century.[211] However, from the College Register it has been possible to identify nineteen of the matriculands as at some time holders of postmasterships and so as foundationers.[212] Two more, who are dubbed 'pauperi scholares' in the register of matriculations, may also perhaps be identified as postmasters.[213] Thus analysis of the undergraduate body has to be restricted to the combined figures for postmasters and commoners. They produce these results:

Baronis filius	Equitis filius	Armigeri filius	Generosi filius	Plebei filius	Clerici filius	Gentlemen & above
3 (1%)	13 (4%)	24 (8%)	38 (12.66%)	175 (58%)	19 (6.3%)	29 (9.66%)

The figures suggest that Merton was even less aristocratic than Magdalen, the least aristocratic of the colleges examined by Professor McConica. Nevertheless the movement towards admitting well-born commoners to the college can be seen developing, and had already

---

[209] Chamberlain, *Letters*, p. 98, *HUO* iv. 149–50.

[210] Stone, *The University in Society*, i. 158–71.

[211] *Register of the University of Oxford*, ii, pt. iii, pp. v, vi, 446–8.

[212] Thomas Whyte, John Dickin, George Jervis, Henry Lunde, George Potter, John Rociter, Humphrey Bother, Samuel Slade, Richard Tew, Robert Braye, John Farrer, George Daye, Thomas Durdent, Henry Pett, John Powell, Anthony Rowborrow, Henry Atwode, Nathaniel Brent, Edward Reynolds.

[213] *Register of the University of Oxford*, ii, pt. ii. 314 (William Barton and Lemuel Fouler).

begun under Bickley. Savile's well-heeled travelling companion, Henry Neville, matriculated at Merton on 20 December 1577.[214] Savile himself introduced members of his own family, such as his nephew, Sir Henry Savile, son of Sir John Savile, who matriculated aged 14 on 4 February 1594, and yet another Henry Savile, 'Long Harry', son of Thomas Savile of Banke (who matriculated on 11 October 1588).[215] The college register tells us of a grandee commoner, the son of Sir John Wolley, himself a Mertonian, but also a privy councillor and eventually a baron, who was admitted in 1595. The fellows then agreed that in order 'to retain and increase the good-will of the petitioner', at the suggestion of the warden, the privy councillor's son should take his commons at the table of the bachelor fellows.[216] After the débâcle of Essex's rebellion Savile found himself entrusted with the guardianship of the earl's heir who was then at Eton. Subsequently he entered Merton, and, as has been seen, Savile found quarters for him in a special room in the Warden's Lodgings.[217] Thus although there was no special building for well-born commoners at Merton, they might, when they arrived, receive special treatment. Brodrick drew attention to the resolution of 1607 that twelve 'pensioners' being the sons of knights and gentlemen 'of great name' should be admitted who should present the college with a silver cup at their admission.[218] But though the order was cancelled in 1616[219] the movement towards admitting gentlemen commoners was plain enough.

The undergraduate body was predominantly English. One Lumsden is labelled a Scot in the Matriculation Register; there was one Welshman, Maurice Vaughan from Merioneth, and one Channel Islander. Among the English an interesting feature is the extent of the warden's influence. It can be deduced from the fact that Warden Bickley, archdeacon of Stafford, who seems to have been a Staffordshire man himself, saw admitted no fewer than eighteen commoners from Staffordshire and Derbyshire, where the college had no land. They included two Bagots of Blithfield, two Curzons of Croxall, and the

---

[214] Son of Sir Henry Neville of Billingbear, Berks. (above, n. 60). For the movement in general see Stone, *The University in Society*, i. 24–8.

[215] Foster, *Alumni Oxonienses*, iv. 1319.

[216] *RACM 1567–1603*, p. 317.

[217] Above, p. 172 and n. 104.

[218] *MMC*, pp. 71–2.

[219] Ibid., p. 72. The cancellation was due to the adverse effects of their admission on discipline.

son of Bishop Bentham of Coventry and Lichfield.[220] The stream dried up as soon as Bickley resigned to become bishop of Chichester. In its place there was another from Yorkshire which was not there before: Yorkshire too was a county where the college had no land in 1586.[221] From that date onwards no fewer than twenty-four Yorkshiremen joined the college under Savile, including two other Henry Saviles, already noticed, and several of his Wilkinson cousins and kinsmen. Another feature worthy of mention is the tendency for Merton undergraduates once they had taken their BA to transfer to St Alban Hall where they would determine and incept after taking their MA.[222] Brodrick observes that Richard Radcliffe was the last principal of St Alban Hall to be directly appointed (1581) from among the fellows of Merton,[223] and it may be that once the chancellor appointed the principals, as he did from 1599, and the building of Fellows' Quad increased the accommodation at Merton, the attractions of such transfers lessened.

Among the postmasters of Savile's wardenship one of the most remarkable was Thomas Farnaby, who matriculated in 1590.[224] He was postmaster to Thomas French, a 'learned fellow' who had debated before Elizabeth in 1592 and became registrar of the university.[225] Farnaby pursued a more extraordinary career than his tutor. He came under Jesuit influence and attended a Jesuit college in Spain, but seems to have thought better of it, for he returned home to join the last expedition of Drake and Hawkins to the Canaries and Puerto Rico (August 1595). He subsequently fought in the Netherlands, but finding no fortune there, came back to Cornwall, where his grandfather

---

[220] Richard Asten, Anthony and Walter Bagot, Henry Bramall, Henry and William Curzon, William Dayrell, Hastings and Simon Grisly, John Heathcote, Robert Simons, John Tomkyns, John Walker, Henry Booth, Benjamin Bentham, Henry Whitgreve, Richard Tew, Arthur Pollard.

[221] William Lindley, Henry Clay, Henry Powell, John Wilkinson, Richard Deane, Henry Farrar, Richard Bates, Robert Claye, Samuel Wilkinson, Henry Savell (1594), James Maude, Robert Haulsworth, Henry Savell (1595), Matthew Wilson, Mark Graunte, Thomas Hopkinson, John Wilson, John Wilkinson, Henry Power, William Hodgson, John Heliwell, John Nelson, John Wilton, Samuel Basford.

[222] Richard Sherrar (or Sherwood) (1581), Arthur Pollard (1585), Thomas Durdent and Robert Braye (1588), Thomas Wilcocke (1590), Henry Savell (1592), Philip Evans (1593), Edward Deane (1594), Ralph Steare (1596), William Cladwell (1598), Edward Powell (1599), Gabriel Poultney (1600), Joseph Lee (1601), George Spurret (1602), Thomas Doe (1603), John Bonnett (1604), etc.

[223] *MMC*, p. 270.

[224] Foster, *Alumni Oxonienses*, ii. 485. For Farnaby, cf. *HUO* iv. 249 n. 105, 262.

[225] *MMC*, 273 (see above, p. 171 and n. 95).

had been mayor of Truro. Thence he migrated eastwards to Martock Grammar School in Somerset where he became a schoolmaster.[226] He had found his vocation, but soon moved to the capital where he set up a school in Goldsmith's Rents, Cripplegate.[227] In London editions of classical texts with commentaries began to pour from his pen – Juvenal and Persius' *Satires* in 1612, followed by Seneca's *Tragedies* (1613) and Martial's *Epigrams* (1615). He was then incorporated MA at Cambridge, but soon was back schoolmastering at Sevenoaks, Kent, whence the flow of classical texts continued. Lucan's *Pharsalia* (1618) was followed by Virgil (1634).[228] Meanwhile Farnaby acquired a minor canonry at St Paul's (1626), and opened a correspondence with Vossius (1630–42) which reveals him as a scholar of international standing.[229] His last publications were Ovid's *Metamorphoses* (1636) and Terence's *Comedies*, with Casaubon, published at Amsterdam in 1651. As a royalist, he was ruined by the Civil War and died in 1647; but in the course of his academic career he had outshone almost all other English teachers of the classics.[230] How much of his training he owed to his school, his college at Oxford, or his Jesuit training it is hard to say. He was certainly a nonpareil.

At a different level in the academic hierarchy were the brothers Davenport. They were pupils of Samuel Lane, elected fellow in 1602.[231] Their father was an alderman of Coventry who had many children. His two sons (matriculated at Merton in 1613) were batelers and took their commons with the chef,[232] until, if Wood is to be believed, Savile insisted that they must become full commoners or leave. Christopher did incorporate but then switched to Magdalen Hall, where he took his BA and where no doubt living was cheaper.[233] From there he is next found at Douai and had joined the Roman church. Unlike Farnaby he stayed with Rome and became a Franciscan friar as

---

[226] *DNB*, and cf. *LTAW* ii. 284.

[227] *DNB*.

[228] Binns, *Intellectual Culture*, p. 194.

[229] Vossius, *Epistolae* (London, 1690) in *DNB*.

[230] The leading classical scholar as well as the chief schoolmaster of his time (*DNB*).

[231] *MMC*, p. 277.

[232] Wood, *Athenae Oxonienses*, iii. 1221–2. The batteler 'bought his own food instead of eating it in the communal hall' (Stone, *The University in Society*, i. 11).

[233] Letters testimonial from Dublin 22 Nov. 1611; incorporated Oxford 23 May 1614 and allowed to count 15 months at Trinity College, Dublin (*Register of the University of Oxford*, ii, pt. i. 374, pt. iii. 327).

Franciscus a Sancta Clara.[234] Though he went on to take a doctorate at Salamanca, however, he had not finished with his native land, for he returned as chaplain to Queen Henrietta Maria and exercised an influence both on Richard Montague, bishop of Chichester, and Bishop Goodman of Gloucester. Indeed the seventh article of the impeachment of Archbishop Laud suggests that he also influenced him.[235] That he probably did not, and the archbishop stated that he had only met him four or five times. He nevertheless made an important contribution to the debate over Anglican and Roman Catholic orders in his *Paraphrastica expositio Articulorum Confessionis Anglicanae* (Lyons, 1634), which showed how closely they resembled one another and sufficiently alarmed Catholic opinion, let alone the Puritans, to get it placed on the *Index Purgatorius*.[236] An accomplished survivor, Sancta Clara was once again in England as the chaplain of Catherine of Braganza after the Restoration.

In striking contrast his brother John, who also moved from Merton to Magdalen Hall when Savile sought to change his status, went on to a chaplaincy at Hilton Hall, Durham.[237] He then found his way to London, first as a curate and lecturer at St Lawrence Jewry in 1619, and then as vicar of St Stephen's, Coleman Street, where he acquired a reputation as a Puritan preacher.[238] He helped to edit John Preston's sermons and became the friend of Nathaniel Ffiennes, Viscount Saye and Sele. He was one of those who sought to buy up lay impropriations in order to appoint to lectureships and thus incurred the hostility of Laud. A warrant for his arrest led him to resign his living in 1633 and face an uneasy spell in the Netherlands where Laud's long hand reached out to hamper him and where he fell out with his co-pastor at the English Church over the issue of infant baptism. He thus was ready to join Cotton's venture to New England in 1637. Laud did him the honour of stating that he was a 'most religious man who fled to

---

[234] *DNB*. For Sancta Clara see also M. Nédoncelle, *Trois aspects du problème anglo-catholique au xvii* siècle* (Paris, 1951). We owe this reference to the kindness of Dr A. D. Wright.

[235] *DNB*.

[236] Published separately and then as appendix to *Deus, Natura, Gratia* (Lyons, 1634); cf. Trevor-Roper, *Laud*, p. 309.

[237] Foster, *Alumni Oxonienses*, i. 376. Having continued at Magdalen Hall 'under severe and puritanical discipline for some time, he left without a degree'.

[238] *Letters of John Davenport*, ed. J. M. Calder (New Haven, 1937), in Trevor-Roper, *Laud*, p. 251; Valerie Pearl, *London and the Outbreak of the Puritan Revolution* (Oxford, 1961), p. 163.

New England for the sake of a good conscience'.[239] In 1638 he became with Theophilus Eaton one of the founders of New Haven and 'one of the Seven Pillars of the State'. He found himself invited to attend the Westminster Assembly but stayed in America. In 1654 he proposed a plan to establish a college in New Haven, but that was premature. In 1668 he was ordained minister of the First Church of Boston and died there two years later.[240] Davenport College in Yale University is named after him.

Savile would surely have been proud of Farnaby, and Bodley might well have had some sympathy for John Davenport. Christopher Davenport's career is there to remind us that when the authorities at Oxford insisted on the taking of oaths and the residence of graduates and undergraduates in settled halls and colleges they were taking precautions against a still powerful magnetic and effective counter-attraction on the Continent.

In the nineteenth century, when the sanctuary and chancel of the chapel were Gothicized by Blore and Butterfield, the two Renaissance monuments were removed from their honorific positions near the High Altar and banished to the ante-chapel. There Bodley and Savile were placed in the two blanked arches of the aisles which would have been built if the church had been extended to the west. In their new positions they easily hold their own and greet the visitor who enters by the north or south doors. Bodley's (by Nicholas Stone) is rightly the more severe.[241] Though the designer offers a joke in the fact that the pillars are made up of books, the prevailing impression is black and white – there is more than a touch of Geneva (Pl. 15). It is also, properly, closer to the Bodleian. The more southerly monument of Savile is truly magnificent.[242] The family arms behind the half-bust demonstrate pride in family proper to a swell. The picture of the two colleges he ruled, Merton on his right and Eton on his left, seem still to defy Chancellor Buckhurst's attempt to persuade him to resign Merton. The figures of St John Chrysostom, Ptolemy, Euclid, and Tacitus epitomize his scholarship and give the monument movement (Pl. 18). Away to Savile's right is the memorial of the first professor of

---

[239] *DNB*, Trevor-Roper, *Laud*, pp. 250–3. In Amsterdam Davenport was even less acceptable to John Paget, his presbyterian co-pastor at the English Church, than he had been in London.

[240] *DNB*.

[241] Bott, *Monuments*, pp. 86–7.

[242] Ibid., pp. 84–5.

astronomy, John Bainbridge, with a fine display of the mathematical instruments of his profession,[243] whilst to his left on the floor under the tower is a Puritanically simple slab for the first professor of geometry, inscribed with the two words 'Henricus Briggius'.[244]

Bodley and Savile were men of vision, and since Savile was the younger he had the opportunity to see further into the seventeenth century. He did not then like what he saw. On 16 February of the year Savile died – 1622 – Chamberlain observed that he had gone to Eton 'on Wednesday, in weak case but well resolved in mind, and willing to depart when it shall please God to call, the rather, he says, for that having lived in good times he doth fear or foresee worse'.[245]

[243] Bott, *Monuments*, pp. 82–3.
[244] Ibid., p. 54. Of the 68 tributes published in *Ultima Linea Savilii ... iusta academica* (Oxford, 1622) eight were by Mertonians, including those by the new warden (Brent), the sub-warden (Simonson), and both Savilian professors.
[245] Chamberlain, *Letters*, p. 263.

9

The Civil War and the Restoration
to 1700

THE worse things which Savile had foreseen came indeed under his successor. Nathaniel Brent was a postmaster and a fellow under Savile.[1] He came from Little Wolford, Warwickshire,[2] close to the college living of Great Wolford. In 1611 Bodley trusted him, with William Gent of Gloucester Hall, to supervise the building of Arts End at the Bodleian.[3] He resigned his fellowship to become a civil lawyer and to marry the daughter of Robert Abbot, bishop of Salisbury, about 1617,[4] and thus to join the family of the visitor, Archbishop Abbot. The archbishop sent him to Venice whence he smuggled out in parts the 'History of the Council of Trent' by Paolo Sarpi. On his return Brent translated Sarpi's seminal study and dedicated it to Abbot.[5] The archbishop once again advanced his career when he made Brent his vicar-general. It must have seemed to the electing seniors in 1622 that by including Brent's name among the three sent to the visitor, they were sure to please Abbot, and certainly Brent was his choice. The income of the warden of Merton was calculated at £200 per annum in 1612. That placed him fourth in order of income of heads of houses. Only Christ Church at £300 per annum and Magdalen and New College at £250 were superior.[6]

The new warden, drawing perhaps on his experience at the Bodleian, set to work to complete Savile's scheme for the college library.[7] Thus it is the arms of Abbot and Brent which grace the plasterwork at the east end of the south wing. The warden played a role when

---

[1] *MMC*, p. 167.

[2] *DNB*.

[3] Cf. *Letters of Sir Thomas Bodley to Thomas James*, ed. G. Wheeler (Oxford, 1926), nos. 190–2, 202, 204, 210–11, 214, 218, 221, 226.

[4] He became vicar-general and judge of the prerogative court.

[5] First edition printed by Robert Barker and John Bill, 1620.

[6] *MMC*, p. 96 n. 1.

[7] It included taking into the south wing the room at the east end (Henderson, p. 231). More work was to follow in 1641 (ibid., pp. 233–4).

parliament met in Oxford in 1625 because of the plague. The BAs and postmasters were sent out of Oxford while the MAs occupied Mob Quad.[8] Brent was knighted by Charles I in 1629 at Woodstock and subsequently entertained the king and queen to dinner in Merton.[9] At some time he installed the handsome staircase in his lodgings which led up to the warden's gallery. He added to the college's accommodation (1631) by constructing the staircase to the west of the porter's lodge – Front 1. It could just be fitted in beside the churchyard of St John the Baptist.

When Abbot died in 1633 the warden's career began to take a different turn. At first all seemed well and the new archbishop showed himself willing to help the college with the problem of Henry Jacob. Jacob had been elected in 1628, but after completing his year of probation seemed to have had difficulty in proceeding with the normal course of disputations. He was, however, a gifted linguist, and Laud as chancellor allowed the ancient post of grammar lecturer to be resuscitated so that he could be admitted to 'the study of philology' on condition that he lectured in the college hall on comparisons between Roman and Greek and Oriental antiquities.[10] He subsequently compiled a catalogue of Hebrew printed books and manuscripts in the Bodleian in 1639.[11]

When Charles I visited Oxford in 1636 Brent played a respectable if minor role. He entertained George Garrard, chaplain to the earl of Northumberland, William Seymour, 2nd earl of Hertford, and Robert Devereux, 3rd earl of Essex, who already knew the Warden's Lodgings.[12] On 30 August he presented Prince Charles and Prince Rupert for their MA degrees.[13] Laud continued Brent as vicar-general at first, though since he was one of Abbot's appointments he gave him a supervisor to keep an eye on him. He need have had no fears. Brent carried out the archbishop's wishes on his great three-year visitation

---

[8] Henderson, p. 108, *MMC*, p. 75 and n. 1.

[9] Henderson, p. 108, *DNB*.

[10] *MMC*, p. 286, Reg. 1.3, pp. 321–2. In 1638 he was explicitly allowed to choose the author on whom he lectured but was enjoined to post a bill in advance as an advertisement (Reg. 1.3, p. 335).

[11] E. Craster, 'Bibliotheca Rabbinica' in 'John Rouse, Bodley's Librarian', *BLR* v. 3 (1955), 135–6, cf. *HUO* iv. 266, 457, 478, 483.

[12] See above, p. 172. The earls of Hertford and Essex were made MA (Wood, *Fasti* in *Athenae Oxonienses*, ii, 490–1; A. J. Taylor, 'The Royal Visit to Oxford in 1636: a contemporary narrative', *Oxoniensia*, i (1936), 151–8).

[13] *DNB* (Brent).

of his province, it seems, 'au pied de la lettre'.[14] It was natural that during these years Brent had not much time to attend closely to college business. However, when complainants against the warden began to make themselves heard it seemed that they had more to complain of than merely a lax administration during his absences.

The complainants were led by Peter Turner, the Savilian professor of geometry, who had greatly helped the archbishop with the new codification of the University Statutes (1634-6). Brent had been, it seems, a great deal more careless with funds than had Savile during his absence in the 1590s, and certainly Laud was not another Whitgift. Brent was accused of having borrowed money from the college and of having left the debt unpaid for fourteen years. He had charged the college for a London house which he did not use.[15] His record for the recovery of the college's bad debts was poor: he had allowed debts to go unpaid, it was said, until they had become irrecoverable. No doubt some of that reflected his preoccupation with the archbishop's visitation. But in dissension between two fellows the warden's punishment of the offender had been so mild as to cause the offended party to appeal to the visitor.[16] At first sight none of that sounds decisively culpable. However, when the visitation of the college eventually came and five commissioners arrived on 29 March 1638 they found plenty of signs of neglect and worse. Postmasterships, it was said, had been awarded as a result of graft and bribery. College woods had been sold to kinsmen of the warden for less than half their value; the college had been overcharged for the supply of fuel for the warden's house. The warden had misrepresented the college accounts in order to conceal his mismanagement, and had taken the fellows into partnership of the profits which he had made.[17] To judge by the verdict of Gilbert Sheldon, warden of All Souls', one of the commissioners, it is hard to believe that Brent had been other than culpably negligent. 'If I were conscious of so much carelessness of the main affairs of this college, or of such practising upon the company, to the wasting of the common stock and my own advantage, I should

[14] Trevor-Roper, *Laud*, pp. 192-6.
[15] Ibid., pp. 355, 356, and cf. E. F. Percival (ed.), *The Foundation Statutes of Merton College, Oxford, AD 1270, with subsequent ordinances* (1847), p. 92 (ord. 19).
[16] Trevor-Roper, *Laud*, p. 355. This may be a reference to Mr Newman who had interrupted the Variations of Mr Nevill with contemptuous words and had been suspended from commons for a month (Reg. 1.3, p. 335).
[17] Trevor-Roper, *Laud*, p. 355.

not have the face to endure a visitation, but should lay the key under the door and be gone.'[18]

The five commissioners drew up a list of thirty-one injunctions on 15 October 1638.[19] Five more were added subsequently. They formed the basis of twenty-six ordinances which were eventually issued in 1640. The injunctions have the added interest that a list of fellows is attached which demonstrates that the commissioners were not simply intent on removing the warden. Mr Newman, for instance, was never to hold office again, though he might be a lecturer or a preacher. A new dean was to replace Mr French. He too was judged unsatisfactory though the registrar of the university. Other fellows like Mr Nevill senior, Mr Burton, and Mr Gibbs were put out of commons for varying lengths of time as punishments for delinquencies.[20] Notable among the general directives is the insistence that a sub-warden must be chosen yearly,[21] no doubt in order to defeat the temptation of an absentee warden to acquire a regularly complaisant sub-warden, as Savile had done in the days of Thomas Master. The Laudian insistence on Latin was underlined by the injunction that fellows and scholars were to speak it in college at all times except at college meetings.[22] Also the catechetical lecture, founded in 1635 by Richard Knightley and endowed with £10 per annum from rents at Badby, Northants., was to be given in Latin.[23] The tide was running against Latin, as the books in English entering the college libraries began to outnumber those in Latin, but Laud was determined to put up a brave fight in its defence. He also insisted on surplices and Divinity Disputations.[24] Absences and sales of woods were to be carefully controlled and recorded in registers.[25] Leases were to be strictly managed, to be of twenty-one years, and college was to benefit from half the profits.[26]

[18] Trevor-Roper, *Laud*, pp. 355–6.

[19] The commissioners were Dr Bayley, president of St John's, Richard Montague, the bishop of Oxford, Sir John Lambe, dean of arches, Dr Sheldon, warden of All Souls', and Dr Duck, chancellor of London (Reg. 1.3, p. 329). For the Injunctions see ibid., pp. 334–5.

[20] Ibid., p. 335. For Mr Nevill see also *A Complete Collection of State Trials in 6 volumes*, 2nd edn. (1730), i. 861.

[21] Injunction no. 3, ordinance no. 14 (Percival, *Statutes*, p. 90).

[22] Injunction no. 7, ordinance no. 17 (*Statutes*, p. 92).

[23] Injunction no. 13, ordinance no. 20 (*Statutes*, p. 92). It had been set up in 1635 (cf. MCR 3143).

[24] Injunctions nos. 1 and 2, ordinances nos. 3 and 4 (*Statutes*, pp. 82–3).

[25] Injunctions nos. 8 and 18, ordinances nos. 4 and 13 (*Statutes*, pp. 84–5, 90).

[26] Injunction no. 9, ordinance no. 8 (*Statutes*, pp. 86–7).

Strict regulations were set up to deal with multiple elections:[27] they must be of not more than five nor less than three candidates at a time and the total number of fellows was set at twenty-four. Chapel services were regulated to ensure that the Book of Common Prayer was properly followed[28] and that the parishioners of St John the Baptist and the members of St Alban Hall knew where they were to sit and when they could approach the communion table.[29] New rules were made to ensure that the accounts were regularly presented[30] and consideration given to the secure custody of college documents[31] and moneys.[32] Fellows' dress was to be modest; coloured boots, cut suits, and large bands were all to be avoided.[33] In a move presumably to raise the standing of the postmasters it was ordered that they should be chosen fellows before others *ceteris paribus*. It was reiterated that they should be selected by the warden, the principal of the postmasters, and three senior fellows according to the ordinance of *c.* 1383.[34]

The enquiry went on after the ordinances were made up, but Brent was not dismissed by Laud, and the ordeal of three-and-a-half years of investigation was reaching its end. The Long Parliament now cut short proceedings which the college register said 'threatened to rival the siege of Troy', and Brent became an opponent of the visitor. When war broke out he acted as judge marshall for Parliament and led a party in college who opposed the king in the Civil War. In 1641 he fled to London,[35] and in 1643–4 he appeared at the trial of Laud and took his revenge. Brent bore witness against the archbishop on a number of separate occasions, though not always very effectively, and Laud was able to remind the warden that he had had cause enough to have dismissed him but had forborne to do so. A royalist pamphleteer described the warden as being 'knuckle-deep in the archbishop's blood'.[36] Meanwhile in Oxford it was doubtless significant that when the war began and the parliamentary troops made a short stay in Oxford from 12 September 1642 their commander, Colonel Goodwin,

[27] Injunction no. 10, ordinance no. 9 (*Statutes*, p. 87).

[28] Injunction no. 16.

[29] Injunctions nos. 15 and 1, ordinance no. 1 (*Statutes*, p. 83).

[30] Injunction no. 20, ordinance no. 11 (*Statutes*, pp. 88–9).

[31] Injunction no. 19, ordinance no. 15 (*Statutes*, pp. 90–1).

[32] Injunction no. 21, ordinance no. 21 (*Statutes*, p. 93).

[33] Injunction no. 26, ordinance no. 16 (*Statutes*, p. 91).

[34] Injunction no. 29, ordinance no. 22 (*Statutes*, p. 93).

[35] *DNB*; and Birkenhead in 'The Assembly Man' (1810) *Harleian Miscellany*, v. 93.

[36] For Brent's accusations at the trial see *State Trials* (above, n. 20), i. 850–1, 861, 896. Pembroke is said to have promised him the vice-chancellorship (*HUO* iv. 692).

took up his quarters in Merton.[37] At the end of the next month those troops withdrew from Oxford and were replaced by royalists and by the king himself on 29 October.[38] By 1 January 1643 Merton along with other colleges was being asked to send in its plate to help to pay for the king's expenses. It sent in between 79 and 80 lbs for melting down in the mint in New Inn Hall Street: not a particularly large amount considering that Magdalen, All Souls', and Exeter each sent in over 200 lbs.[39] It was given as a loan, though in the event this was naturally one which was never repaid. The only items to escape were the communion plate from the reign of Queen Elizabeth, which was no doubt exempted, and a silver-gilt rose-water bowl of the reign of James I which seems to have been overlooked and left in a chest.[40] Dr Greaves was later accused of having disclosed that there was £400 in cash in the treasury. When he was dismissed by the parliamentary visitors after the siege of Oxford he was also accused of having consorted with courtiers and ingratiated himself with the confessors of Henrietta Maria.[41]

On 14 July 1643 the king brought the queen (Pl. 19) to Oxford and soon led her to take up quarters in Merton where the Warden's Lodgings, owing to their abandonment by Brent, lay conveniently empty. Anthony Wood records that the king took his consort to Merton from Christ Church through the back of Corpus. When she reached her destination she was greeted by a speech made for her entertainment and welcome.[42] The route was secured by opening a gate in the wall between Christ Church and Corpus which, since blocked, may still be seen. It is the origin of subsequent references to a secret passage which occur in later popular guide books. Once the queen reached Merton, if the weather was wet, it was open to her to take the route through the chapel and sacristy and over Rawlins's Arch in Patey's Quad into the Hall and so into the Warden's Lodgings. Wood tells us that a careful record was kept by Mr Gurgany, the chaplain, of the births, marriages, and deaths of members of the queen's retinue, but also that the register was later stolen from the window of his room – Mob 6.1.[43] Thus our information about her

---

[37] *LTAW* i. 60.
[38] Ibid., i. 67–8.
[39] Ibid., i. 94 and n. 4.
[40] Jones, *Catalogue of the Plate*, p. 26.
[41] See below n. 80, and *MMC*, p. 102.
[42] *LTAW* i. 103.
[43] Ibid., i. 130.

household is very fragmentary. She was certainly accompanied by her confessors, since, as has been seen, Dr Greaves was to be accused of feasting and dallying with them. Was one of them Franciscus de Sancta Clara? If so he would certainly have known his way round his old college. It seems that the countess of Northampton and Lady Cobham were in the queen's vicinity if not actually waiting on her.[44] One member of her retinue, Mr Ellis Roberts, died while she was at Merton, and his wife with him, since both were buried in the college chapel, he in the north transept and she in the south.[45] Two other members of the queen's retinue were also buried in the chapel: Mrs Mary Skevington in 1644 and in December 1643 Richard North, a stranger.[46] One of the two portraits of the queen now in the college seems to have come to the warden's house in the seventeenth century, though when is uncertain. A portrait of a royalist which was hidden under the floor of a fellow's set until it was found in the nineteenth century is that of Abraham Cowley,[47] a friend of William Harvey. Cowley was present in Oxford at St John's during the siege. The concealment of the portrait might seem to link it with the time when the royalists surrendered and it became prudent to conceal any royalist connections, but the picture is evidently a copy, and that is as far as one can go. The queen did not stay for the whole siege. Indeed before a full year was out she left for Exeter and Falmouth, on 17 April 1644, to take ship for France and to try to raise supplies for the king on the continent.[48] In the autumn of that year a devastating fire swept Oxford from George Street to the south side of Queen Street and consumed the college's property at Bull Hall,[49] thus weakening further the limited local resources on which the college could rely.

The queen's successor in the Warden's Lodgings was Merton's most famous warden, William Harvey. Having entered Caius College as long ago as 1593 and become a member of the Royal College of Physicians of London in 1607, Harvey had published the first edition of his great work, *De Motu Cordis*, in 1628. He had then gone steadily up the ladder of medical promotion. He was appointed physician to St Bartholomew's Hospital and then to the duke of Lennox, when the

[44] Reg. 1.3, pp. 360–2, and cf. n. 55; also the duchess of Richmond (*HUO* iv. 706).
[45] Bott, *Monuments*, pp. 49, 53.
[46] Ibid., p. 116.
[47] Poole, *Catalogue of Oxford Portraits*, ii. 51, cf. Henderson, p. 123 n.
[48] *DNB*.
[49] *DNB*; S. Porter, 'The Oxford Fire of 1644', *Oxoniensia*, xlix (1984), 289–300.

duke travelled on the continent. He filled the same office when he went abroad with Thomas Howard, earl of Arundel.[50] Charles made him royal physician in 1636. He was with the king in the field at Edgehill and followed him to Oxford when it became the royal capital.[51] He incorporated as Doctor of Medicine in 1642.[52]

Articles against Brent were promoted by the Savilian professor of astronomy, Dr Greaves, the sub-warden, on the grounds that he had taken the Covenant and abandoned his office.[53] As Laud's execution had left the see of Canterbury vacant the king stepped in on 24 January 1645 to urge the fellows to proceed to elect a new warden. He commended to them the name of William Harvey.[54] In answer to this royal injunction the seven electors failed to agree and one of them, Peter Turner, though a royalist, felt so strongly that the election was being improperly conducted that he resigned. Certainly the electors produced eight names for the king to choose from instead of the usual three for the archbishop. Moreover in naming Harvey those who did so had named a stranger, since Harvey had never been a fellow of Merton, and Turner argued that this had only happened once before in the previous three hundred years. He exaggerated, since both Wardens Man and Bickley had been outsiders. Among the eight names submitted five of the senior fellows including the sub-warden placed Harvey first. At the same time the heads of houses took it upon themselves to write to the king to urge him 'to appoint some fit and able man of that Society to be governor, who may revive the good and exemplary Orders of it'. Charles easily brushed aside this suggestion that he should choose a Mertonian and appointed Harvey.[55] On 9 April Harvey was admitted and addressed the fellows in the Hall. He said that some of his predecessors had sought the wardenship 'in order to enrich themselves, but he himself came truly with a far different mind, so that he might bring to the college greater wealth and benefit' and at the same time he exhorted the fellows to cultivate among themselves friendship and harmony.[56]

---

[50] *DNB* (Harvey).

[51] Ibid.

[52] Ibid.

[53] 7 Dec. (ibid.); *MMC*, p. 88.

[54] Reg. 1.3, pp. 355–6, *MMC*, p. 89.

[55] Reg. 1.3, p. 359 (9 April 1645) on the advice of the marquis of Hertford as chancellor (cf. *HUO* iv. 712).

[56] A. M. Cooke, 'William Harvey at Oxford', *Journal of the Royal College of Physicians of London*, ix/2 (1975), 185–6; J. Andrew, *Harveian Oration* (1891), pp. 6–7.

There are few documents from the period of his wardenship. College meetings, we are told, met regularly in the library since the warden's house and hall were unavailable.[57] An inventory of the goods in the warden's house was taken by Sir Charles Scarburgh and shows that the queen slept in the warden's dining-room, and that some of his belongings had been lent out to Penelope Lady Cobham, and to Mary, countess of Northampton.[58] During Harvey's reign the globes in the library (not the present set) were lent to the tutor of the young duke of York, the future James II, at Christ Church, for his edification.[59] We know that the warden regularly attended to the pursuit of unpaid rents in order to maintain the flow of the college's impaired revenues.[60] He checked the bursar's accounts, as can be seen from his signatures in the Libri Rationarii Bursariorum.[61] But we also know that he turned his mind to embryology. Sir Charles Scarburgh was interested in the same subject and Harvey secured his incorporation as a doctor of medicine by signing his letter testimonial.[62] The sub-warden of Merton, Dr Greaves, was also interested in the subject since he had written on the artificial hatching of birds' eggs which he had seen in Egypt,[63] but it was George Bathurst of Trinity 'who had a hen to hatch eggs in his chambers and would study the process of generation with Dr Harvey there'.[64] At Trinity too was Dr Nathaniel Highmore who testified to Harvey's dissections at Oxford and published his own book on the History of Generation in the same year (1651) as Harvey's *De Generatione Animalium* (Pl. 20).[65] When at Merton Harvey worked in the room 'at the end of the library',[66] which was presumably the present Beerbohm Room.

Towards the end of the war and during Harvey's wardenship there

---

[57] Reg. 1.3, pp. 364–5.

[58] Ibid., pp. 360–2. Some items were temporarily in the charge of Penelope Lady Cobham, widow of William Brooke, sometimes designated Lord Cobham, killed at the battle of Newbury, 20 September 1643, others in those of Mary, countess of Northampton, widow of Spencer Compton, earl of Northampton, killed at the battle of Hopton Heath, 18 March 1643.

[59] Ibid., p. 365.

[60] Ibid., p. 366. In 1645–6 (1 August to 1 August) the total of unpaid rents was £1,239. 5s. 3d.; ordinary receipts amounted to £158. 12s. 6d. (Reg. 3.2, pp. 81–2).

[61] Reg. 3.2, pp. 78ᵛ–79.

[62] *DNB* (Scarburgh); R. G. Frank, 'John Aubrey, F.R.S., John Lydall and Science at Commonwealth Oxford', *Notes and Records of the Royal Society* (1972–3), 195.

[63] Cooke, 'Harvey', p. 186.

[64] Ibid.

[65] *DNB* (Highmore); Cooke, 'Harvey', pp. 186–7.

[66] Ibid.

occurred an incident which has left its memory in a reputed haunting of Merton garden. In April 1645 Colonel Francis Windebank, the royalist commander of near two hundred men, surrendered Bletchingdon House and between two and three hundred muskets to Cromwell at the first summons, though the house was strong and well-manned and Cromwell had neither foot-soldiers nor a siege gun.[67] When he was allowed to march into Oxford Windebank found himself court-martialled for not having put up a better resistance, and was sentenced to be shot. By one account he was shot at Oxford castle,[68] but by another, picked up by Carlyle, it was 'with his back to the wall of Merton College'.[69] Tradition has attached the deed sometimes to the east terrace of Merton garden or to the path just outside and under the city wall. The last solution has found favour, since that would have him shot outside the jurisdiction of the city. Certainly the name of 'Dead Man's Walk' has survived there by oral tradition, and if the deed was done outside the city bounds, then the haunted walk should be the gravel path beneath the wall rather than the terrace above it.

When Oxford surrendered in June 1646 Harvey's wardenship came to an end. He received a passport under the articles of surrender[70] and returned to London in July. His *De Generatione Animalium* contained no less than seventy-two chapters devoted to the day-to-day development of the egg into a chicken,[71] and must have incorporated the work which he did under adverse conditions at Oxford. In his will he left 'my velvet gowne to my loving friend Dr Scarburgh' as well as 'all my little silver instruments of surgerie'.[72]

On Harvey's withdrawal Sir Nathaniel Brent returned to take up the wardenship[73] which he had left five years before and to enjoy a second reign. At once he found himself the principal head of a house to support the parliamentary regime. If Laud had learned to distrust Brent the Long Parliament had no hesitations. He was more or less

---

[67] *Letters and Speeches of Oliver Cromwell*, ed. T. Carlyle and Mrs S. G. Lomas, i (1904), pp. 193–4 and n. 1.

[68] *Diary of Sir W. Dugdale* (1827), p. 78, in C. E. Mallet, *History of the University of Oxford*, ii (1924), pp. 367–8 and n. 1.

[69] *Letters and Speeches*, i. 194 n. 1.

[70] Letter of F. J. Varley to K. J. Franklin, *William Harvey Englishman 1578–1657* (1961), p. 99.

[71] Cooke, *Harvey*, p. 186.

[72] *DNB* (Scarburgh); he had probably supported Harvey's candidature for the wardenship in 1645 (*HUO* iv. 712).

[73] *DNB* (Brent).

put in charge not only of Merton but of the University Commission which on 1 May 1647 was ordered to visit the university in 1648.[74] It operated until 1652. College support for the new regime was reflected in other ways. No fewer than three of the preachers appointed to give acceptable, that is to say presbyterian, sermons in Oxford were fellows of Merton,[75] Francis Cheynell, Edward Reynolds, and Edward Corbet, who were also all commissioners. When the visitatorial commission began work it made the Warden's Lodgings at Merton its headquarters and Brent its chairman.[76] Merton must have been very unpopular in royalist Oxford, but it made the most of its obloquy. The college provided the new vice-chancellor in Reynolds, the junior proctor in Ralph Button, and the public orator in Edward Corbet.[77] In order to strengthen the authority of the commission the chancellor, Philip Herbert, earl of Pembroke, arrived and stayed in Merton until April 1648.[78] Montague Burrows and Warden Brodrick described carefully the workings of the visitors, their expulsions and the appointment of those who were to replace the expelled or deprived.[79] The process was a slow one, made slower by the recalcitrance of many of those summoned to appear. Merton's own turn came on 12 May 1648. As the college had generally supported the Long Parliament the number of expulsions was limited, six fellows, at first all the postmasters and some others.[80] Brent and the other visitors seem to have been patient and at times lenient. Thus Brent through his friendship with the Wood family prevented Anthony Wood from losing his postmastership, and soon afterwards secured for him instead a rather more valuable bible clerkship which gave him rooms in Mob Quad to replace those which he had lost in the Front Quadrangle. He was kept on the college

---

[74] *LTAW* i. 142–3 and nn.

[75] *MMC*, pp. 94, 283, 285. Cheynell was to become president of St John's, and Reynolds dean of Christ Church. Corbet was public orator (but see n. 77) and married the daughter of Warden Brent. He refused a canonry of Chichester and died rector of Great Haseley. He had been chaplain to the earl of Essex (*HUO* iv. 210). For his presbyterianism cf. ibid. 589–90, 592–3, 596–9, 721–2.

[76] *LTAW* i. 141, *MMC*, p. 168.

[77] *MMC*, p. 97, though he soon resigned and gave place to another fellow of Merton, Ralph Button.

[78] Ibid.

[79] Visitors' Register, pp. 520–6 (Appendix E of *MMC*).

[80] Peter Turner, John Greaves, William Berkley, Francis Broad, John Lee, and William Owen.

books.[81] But by 1651 the warden's enthusiasm for his task was evidently ebbing. He made complaints in a petition against interference in the activities of the college and eventually on 27 November 1651 resigned.[82] Neither he nor Reynolds was prepared to take the Engagement, 'of Loyalty to the Commonwealth of England', so the vice-chancellor also resigned. Brent died the next year on 6 November in London aged 79.[83] The moderation of his rule in his second reign had gone some way to redeem the reputation which he had acquired in his first, though the college register states a little tamely that he was 'For many years the most vigilant and worthy Warden of Merton College'.

Under Jonathan Goddard (1651–60) and Edward Reynolds (1660–1) Merton had a breathing space after the heady days of the siege and the purge. Goddard, the son of a ship-builder, was at Magdalen Hall before he moved to take his medical degree at Cambridge.[84] As Cromwell's doctor he accompanied the army on its campaigns in Ireland (1649) and Scotland (1650–1) before returning to London, where he was available to the Long Parliament to replace Brent when the warden resigned.[85] Thus both Charles I and Cromwell saw their doctors wardens of Merton who continued the long-standing tradition of medical heads of the house. However Goddard, though not without distinction – he was one of the members of the first council of the Royal Society (after the Restoration) – was not in the same class as Harvey as a scientist. He was evidently an effective lecturer and had given lectures on anatomy for the Royal College of Physicians of London as a fellow after 1646 and again as Gulstonian lecturer in 1648,[86] but he had never been trained at Padua like Harvey or at Leiden. He became a professor of physic at Gresham College in 1655 and carried out many experiments in his laboratory there, but the published results do not suggest that he made many discoveries of importance, and 'Goddard's drops' which acquired fame as a powerful secret remedy against fainting turn out to have been little more than

[81] *LTAW* i. 144. His rooms in Front Quad were in the cockloft over his brother's set. Those in Mob Quad were Mob 2, ground floor right (J. R. L. Highfield, 'Some thoughts about Mob Quad in the eighteenth century', *Postmaster* (Oct. 1991), p. 55). See further below, p. 225.

[82] *MMC*, pp. 101–3.

[83] Ibid., p. 168, cf. *HUO* iv. 723.

[84] *DNB*. For Goddard's scholarship cf. *HUO* iv. 383, 586.

[85] Ibid.

[86] Ibid.

ammonia drops.[87] His heart seems to have been at Gresham College, and it is significant that he held his post there in plurality with the wardenship for five years.[88] However, he was evidently a man of moderation, and his wardenship coincided with a period of general recovery in the university at large. Merton was helped by the fact that at the Visitation of 1648 a higher proportion of its members submitted to parliament than at any other college – 37 out of a total of 52[89] – and only seven members of the fellowship were expelled. In their place the visitors appointed no more than six in that year, and another eleven in December 1649.[90] Thus Goddard, though an 'independent' while Brent was a presbyterian, took over a college which had been less distracted than most. Though the warden was often in London, he was MP for Oxford at the Nominated Parliament of 1653 and was appointed one of the visitors for the commission of 1654.[91] He was thus as well able as Brent to watch over the interest of the college under the Commonwealth and Protectorate.

During his rule a disaster occurred in the chapel on 17 October 1655 when part of the roof of the south transept fell to the floor, damaging many of the monumental stones.[92] The workmen who were brought in to mend the damage seem to have stolen some of the loose brasses in the course of their repairs, though Anthony Wood was careful to save some and to record their inscriptions.[93] The glass in the lower part of the east window had already been broken or removed at some time between 1646 and 1655.[94]

Soon after 1655 a new belfry was built (in January 1657) below the arches of the crossing and with timber which proved to be unsound. The five ancient bells were recast by Michael Darby into eight but rang with an unsatisfactory flatness so that some twenty-three years later they were recast.[95] Anthony Wood felt deeply about the error as he and his mother and brothers contributed £5 towards the cost of

---

[87] Ibid. The drops did at least work, and might well have been something worse.

[88] Ibid.

[89] Henderson, p. 131.

[90] The replacements in 1648 were Thomas Franks, Richard Franklyn, Joseph Harvey, Edward Wood, Edmund Dickenson, and Richard Trevor, and in 1649 (December) John Arnold, Robert Holly, Henry Hurst, Clinton Maund, Richard Parker, John Powell, Nathaniel Sterry, Charles Willoughby, Peter Nicholls, Robert Cripps, and Richard Pavier.

[91] *DNB*.

[92] *LTAW* i. 199, cf. *HUO* iv. 445, 597, 811–12, 814, 823, 857.

[93] Ibid.

[94] H. W. Garrod, *The Ancient Painted Glass in Merton College, Oxford* (Oxford, 1931), p. 28.

[95] *LTAW* i. 211–12, and see below, n. 140.

recasting. More happily under Goddard one of the college's royalist members, Griffin Higgs, the former dean of Lichfield, bequeathed a fine collection of books to the library[96] and also land to produce a stipend for a librarian. Coming from a fellow elected under Savile, his gift was to complete Savile's work of reformation in the library. Higgs left careful instructions to guide his librarian in his work. The first college librarian had been appointed early in 1658 in the person of Thomas Wilton, one of the chaplains.[97] Now that the job was salaried it took its place among the appointments annually made by the fellows on 1 August.

The transition of regime at the Restoration seemed at first to have been effected very peacefully. Dr Goddard retired to London, where he was able to continue as professor at Gresham's College and at the Royal College of Physicians of London. In the vacancy of the see of Canterbury, still unfilled since the execution of Laud, Charles II felt free to tell the fellows to elect his chaplain, Edward Reynolds, to replace Goddard.[98] Reynolds had protected himself by refusing to take the Engagement in 1651 and was a man who hoped to reconcile Anglicans and presbyterians. He was soon to be taken up fully with the negotiations of the Savoy Conference.[99] As a result of his moderation he was appointed to the see of Norwich in 1660, which after hesitation he accepted,[100] hoping that other presbyterians would follow his example. They did not do so. But with his removal to Norwich the wardenship was once more vacant, and this time the complexity of politics in the early years of Charles II's reign involved the college in a most unwelcome appointment.

The strongest internal candidate for the post was Sir Richard Browne, a former fellow, and principal clerk of His Majesty's Council, who for nineteen years had kept open the royalist embassy in Paris and its Anglican chapel.[101] Another aspirant for the position was Sir Thomas Clayton the younger, son of Sir Thomas Clayton the elder, of Pembroke College, and like his father regius professor of medicine.[102] He had been knighted in March and elected burgess for the

---

[96] Described in P. S. Morrish, *Bibliotheca Higgsiana*.

[97] P. S. Morrish, 'Dr Higgs and Merton College Library', *Leeds Philosophical and Literary Society, Lit. and Hist. sec.*, xxi/2, 179, and see below, Appendix C.

[98] *LTAW* i. 322 (royal letters of 7 July 1660, election of 18 July).

[99] *DNB* (Reynolds).

[100] *Handbook of British Chronology*, p. 263.

[101] *DNB* (Browne).

[102] Sinclair and Robb-Smith, pp. 11–12, cf. *HUO* iv. 518–19, 528, 543, 813, 866.

university in April 1660. He clearly had influence at court. On 9 September 1660 he wrote to Charles II to ask him to write to the sub-warden and fellows to suggest that when the election came on they would choose his name as one of the three to be sent to the visitor, the aged and ailing Archbishop Juxon.[103] Later in the same month we find a fellow of Queen's, Thomas Lamplugh, writing to his influential friend in London, Joseph Williamson, 'I guess Dick Lydall is the man for Merton College, but he has an antagonist, who will prove too strong for him. If you can help him with a letter of recommendation to the Fellows, this he desires, if it might be, and he would be thankful for it. But this to yourself.'[104] Lydall was a medical fellow of Merton. The college, as it turned out, though it was to choose his as one of the three names it sent forward, was all for Sir Richard Browne, or almost all. But Browne and Lydall were outmanœuvred by Clayton who had the support of only one of the seven seniors, Thomas Jones.[105] That was, ironically, enough to block both Browne and Lydall.

Wood tells us that one of the men behind Clayton's candidature was Thomas Barlow, provost of Queen's.[106] When the election followed on 5 March the sub-warden, Alexander Fisher, was asked to exclude Thomas Jones from the voting and to put another in his place.[107] Fisher not unreasonably refused to follow this suggestion. As a result Jones was able to nominate as his three Clayton, Sir Richard Browne, and Mr Priaulx, while the other six seniors chose as their three candidates Sir Richard Browne, Alexander Fisher, and Richard Lydall, all former or actual fellows.[108] This meant that there was a disputed election and the visitor was left to make his own choice as Parker had done in 1562. The situation was made doubly difficult by Sir Richard Browne's falling ill, so that he wrote to the archbishop on 9 March to tell him that he found his sickness very grievous to him.[109] In vain the sub-warden and twelve fellows wrote to the archbishop on behalf of Browne, for Juxon had received a letter from the king, asking him

---

[103] R. Beddard, *Restoration Oxford* (forthcoming publication OHS n.s. xxix), letter of 9 Sept. 1660.
[104] Ibid., letter of 22 Sept. 1660.
[105] Ibid., letter of 6 March 1661. Jones hoped to secure Clayton's support for his petition to replace Zouche as professor of civil law. He had been his deputy.
[106] *LTAW* i. 383.
[107] Beddard, *Restoration Oxford*, letter of 6 March 1661.
[108] Ibid.
[109] Ibid., letter of 9 March 1661.

to choose Clayton if one of the three names submitted was his, and if there was a dispute, to make the same choice.[110] Juxon at the end of his life, with the knowledge that Browne was sick, and under steady pressure from Clayton's brother-in-law, Sir Charles Coterel, master of the ceremonies, chose Sir Thomas Clayton. Nothing could have displeased the fellows more. Faced by the unwelcome decision they determined to try to prevent the warden from taking up his office. The story of how they twice shut the gates of the college against him and then stood siege for three weeks is well known and, set out in detail as it is by Wood, who was an eye-witness, does not need retelling here.[111] At all events when Clayton finally secured his entry nothing could have been more unpromising for the future relations between the warden and fellows than the manner of his entry.[112]

Anthony Wood makes the most of the stories which came out of the college during his wardenship. He explains how Clayton's main supporter at the time of his election, Dr Thomas Jones, was dropped as soon as the warden was safely in the saddle.[113] Thus set aside, Jones became crazed. When eventually he went to London to try to set up in Doctors' Commons he did not flourish and succumbed in the Great Plague of 1665.[114] Clayton meanwhile ran the college into debt with a lawsuit against the city over the college's rights in Holywell, a suit which Merton lost.[115] In the face of its debts the college postponed the fellowship election of 1667 until 1672.[116] Subsequently a major row broke out over the fellowship elections of August 1679. It seems that it had been agreed to elect six fellows. However, on 2 August when five had been elected the warden declined to support the possible sixth and dissolved the meeting with its business unfinished.[117] Subsequently he took his stand on the fact that he did not think that the college's finances would stand a sixth,[118] but that was evidently a

[110] Beddard, *Restoration Oxford.*

[111] *LTAW* i. 389–98.

[112] He resigned the regius chair of medicine in 1665 (Sinclair and Robb-Smith, p. 16). For his quarrels cf. *MMC*, pp. 110–19, 169–70.

[113] *LTAW* i. 395.

[114] Ibid.

[115] Ibid., ii. 107, 125.

[116] Ibid., i. 398 and n. 1. Unpaid revenues having stood at £191. 5s. 9d. in 1668–9 had risen alarmingly in 1669–70 to nearly £400 (Reg. 3.3, pp. 295, 311). In 1670–1 expenditure (£2039. 19s. 3¾d.) just matched receipts of £2,139. 2s. 1¾d. (ibid., p. 333). By 1673–4 receipts of over £2,000 (£2,011. 15s. 4¼d.) may be compared with £485. 8s. 6¼d. in 1660–1 (ibid., pp. 395, 150).

[117] Percival, *Statutes*, pp. 97–8.

[118] Ibid., p. 99.

device to cloak his personal opposition to the man in question. The sub-warden and seniors admonished the warden to complete the election. When he failed to do so, one of the seniors, William Bernard, took a petition on behalf of the sub-warden and six seniors to Lambeth. As he had failed to secure the warden's permission to absent himself, Clayton took the opportunity to suspend Bernard's fellowship and to send to the visitor a petition of his own which had the support of five fellows.[119] In London the law officers advising the archbishop took the view that the warden did not have a negative vote at a fellowship election against the wishes of the majority, but that he did have the right to expel or suspend a fellow without the consent of the seven senior fellows.[120] His treatment of one fellow who had supported the petition of Bernard was harsh and insensitive. Mr William Cardonnel had committed an indiscretion when accounting as bursar; for, when a gardener went to him at Clayton's suggestion to solicit payment for work done in the warden's garden, Cardonnel had said 'The warden be hanged'. For this Clayton exacted a public apology from Cardonnel on his knees. This preyed on his mind and he so much took the matter to heart that he hanged himself over his oak.[121] The warden reflected that he had one enemy the fewer, and Cardonnel was buried in unhallowed ground in the old chapel yard.

During Clayton's wardenship, characteristically perhaps, the one building which was added was the warden's summer house at the end of the warden's garden, where it commanded a view over the city wall and Christ Church Meadows. Wood naturally considered it a waste of money since the warden already had a fine view over the meadows from the great window at the southern end of his gallery.[122] In any case it did not last long, though it was still there in 1798, to judge by the *Oxford Almanack* of that year.[123]

One deed which can be adduced to Clayton's credit and which Wood overlooks is his gift of fourteen books and one manuscript to the library made in 1680. Though chiefly medical, they included works on law and theology. They suggest that the warden may have been

---

[119] Ibid., pp. 100–1.
[120] Ibid., pp. 107–10.
[121] On 23 Oct. 1681 (Reg. I. 3, p. 545) cf. *MMC*, pp. 118–19. Wood, *Athenae Oxonienses*, i, pp. xcii–xciii, id., *History and Antiquities*, Appendix, 212.
[122] *LTAW* i. 396.
[123] H. A. Petter, *The Oxford Almanacks* (Oxford, 1974), p. 81.

something of a bibliophile, for two of them have magnificent appliqué bindings which had been made for Julius Echter von Mespelbrunn, prince-bishop of Würzburg (1573–1617),[124] before the bishop's library was looted by the Swedes in the Thirty Years War and its contents dispersed. Even so, as the college register succinctly puts it, when he died he left in cash to the college £oo. os. od.[125] He had never forgiven the siege of 1661.

Improvements to the existing college buildings there were during his reign, but they were the result of gifts by fellows or former fellows. Thus in 1661, following an example set by Cambridge, Merton gave Oxford its first common room. Snugly placed over the kitchen, it served for nearly twenty years with its plastered walls painted[126] until it was wainscoted by the gift of Mr Peter Nicholls.[127]

One result of the Commonwealth and Interregnum had been the desolation of the interior of the chapel. We do not know precisely when the windows of the transepts and the bottom part of the great east window were broken,[128] but already in 1634–5 it had been decided to replace the medieval tiling of the floor with black and white marble.[129] Whether a start had been made before 1642 is unclear, but evidently during the Civil War and what followed the medieval screen and stalls were damaged.[130] In Ackermann's words 'During the usurpation they were treated with the despoiling contempt of that sacrilegious period, and rendered incapable of subsequent restoration'.[131] But who was to pay for their replacement? One of Savile's postmasters, Mr Alexander Fisher, came to the rescue. He had been elected fellow as long ago as 1619, but lost his fellowship after the Laudian visitation.

---

[124] See Appendix C (ii). For James of Vitriaco's *Sermones* (Antwerp, 1575) bound for the prince-bishop of Würzburg see *Fine Bindings, 1500–1700 from Oxford Libraries* (Bodleian Library, 1968), no. 116, p. 65. Clayton may have inherited them from his father, who had been a bibliophile (*HUO* iv. 517–18).

[125] Reg. 1.3, p. 600, Mallett, *History of the University of Oxford*, iii (1927), pp. 5–6.

[126] The painted walls were discovered when some of the wainscot was recently renewed.

[127] See below, pp. 217–18.

[128] Cf. above, p. 11 and n. 94. For the dates at which glass was broken cf. Garrod (above, n. 94), pp. 8–12. Some broken glass was for long preserved in the top of the north transept window until, at Garrod's suggestion, it was brought down and made up into a number of single lights for the two wings of the Old Library. Many of the eyelets from the spandrels of the tracery were also made into new library windows.

[129] Henderson, p. 212, *MMC*, pp. 108–9, 281; J. R. L. Highfield, 'Alexander Fisher, Sir Christopher Wren and Merton College Chapel', *Oxoniensia*, xxiv (1959), 71.

[130] Ibid., p. 73.

[131] Cf. Ackerman, *Oxford*, i. 11. Some of the medieval stalls could still be seen in the antechapel in 1815; see drawings by J. C. Buckler in Bott, *Short History of the Buildings*, p. 30.

He held many college offices: five times bursar, twice dean, once chaplain's chaplain, and once principal of the postmasters.[132] By 1653 he was senior fellow and in 1660 he had had to preside over the vexed election which brought Sir Thomas Clayton into the wardenship. Wood gives us a pen picture of the man:

> He left 1000 *li.* per annum to pave our chapple with marble and set up a skreen; 38 *li.* to the poor of Maidstone in Kent, where he was borne. A person fit to write a History especially Ecclesiastical, being very judicious that way; but timorous and love(d) to live in a whole skin; one that corrected and added to divers books which died with him and were scattered ... About half a yeare before he was taken suddenly with an apoplectical fit, but recovering, he set workmen on work to pave Mert. Coll. chapel with black and white marble at his owne charge.[133]

It remained to engage Sir Christopher Wren to design the stalls and screen in the same year that Fisher died (1671), probably by a decision of his executors.[134] Wren's servant, perhaps Edward Woodroffe, was paid for drawing 'the models of ye screen and seates'. The work cost £1,130. 19s. 2d. of which the five-arched screen and stalls cost £590. On or soon after 5 November 1673 the college feasted Wren at a reception which cost £4. 8s. 5d.[135] Subsequent generations did not appreciate what Fisher had done with his money. The Tractarians had the screen and stalls removed and replaced by Butterfield's work, but fortunately three of the arches survived, and were eventually replaced in 1959. The cartouche of the arms of Fisher recalls the benefactor in whose name Wren had been employed to do the work. Three years after Wren finished the stalls and screen another former postmaster from Savile's time, Dr Edward Reynolds, bishop of Norwich, bequeathed to the college 'a hundred pounds to be spent on adorning the chapel',[136] and in 1678 another gift came in from a senior fellow, Peter Nicholls, a great friend of Anthony Wood. He had been chaplain and vicar of St Peter's-in-the-East, and as senior fellow had enjoyed, like Fisher, the tithes of Burmington (1676–8). He gave a fine chalice, cover, and two patens of silver gilt for the altar, together a magnificent set,

[132] Highfield, 'Alexander Fisher', p. 70.
[133] Ibid.
[134] Ibid., p. 72.
[135] Ibid., p. 75, Reg. 3.3, p. 379.
[136] Reg. 1.3, p. 497. Fisher's money bought glass by Price for the east window (1702).

and £200 for panelling the Common Room and to buy books for the library.[137] On 21 June 1680 an agreement was made with the craftsman Arthur Frogley, to wainscot the Common Room and cover its painted walls.[138] The pheon of Nicholls appears in the carving of the mouldings. Thus thanks to Nicholls, who had frequently quarrelled with Clayton, and to Arthur Frogley, Merton acquired a fine decoration for what must be reckoned its most beautiful room.

The same year that Frogley set about his carving the college entered into another agreement with Christopher Hodson, the bell-caster of St Mary Cray, Kent, to recast the peal of bells, adding 25 cwt of good bell metal in the process.[139] Anthony Wood gives a vivid account of this operation. The recast peal of 1657 'did not at all please the curious and critical hearer'.[140] Moreover the belfry in which they were hung proved to be of bad timber and had to be rebuilt in 1675, when it was moved to the top of the tower arches, but in 1681 Hodson put right the mistakes of the bell-founder of 1657 and at last the bells rang 'to the content of the Societie'.[141]

Several notable Mertonians were contemporary with Clayton, but made their contributions beyond the confines of the college. Thus Sir Charles Scarburgh, William Harvey's friend from Cambridge and an adopted Mertonian, to whom Wren had been a demonstrator,[142] continued a distinguished medical career in London. He was Gulstonian lecturer and also lectured on the anatomy of the muscle for the Company of Barber Surgeons. He published a valuable guide to dissection – the *Syllabus Musculorum* – and became royal doctor to Charles II, James II, the Queens Mary II and Anne, and George, prince of Denmark.[143]

Another distinguished doctor was Daniel Whistler. He had benefited from a training at Leiden and had published *De morbo puerili* in 1645. In it he partly anticipated the contribution to the treatment of rickets made by Glisson in 1650. Whistler was twelve times censor and also registrar and president of the Royal College of Physicians of London (1684). Unfortunately he was a poor administrator and left the affairs

---

[137] Jones, *Catalogue of the Plate*, 1; *LTAW* ii. 401, 500.

[138] MCR, 2052 A and cf. *LTAW* ii. 500.

[139] MCR, 2052.

[140] *LTAW* i. 211–12, 219.

[141] Ibid., ii. 515.

[142] *DNB* (Wren); G. N. Clark and A. M. Cooke, *History of the Royal College of Physicians of London*, ii. 456, 526.

[143] *DNB* (Scarburgh).

of the college in disorder, though a recent attempt has been made to vindicate him.[144] An interesting Irish doctor was Charles Willoughby. He came to Merton from Trinity College, Dublin. He took his BA at Oxford and became a fellow in 1649. He also widened his medical experience by incorporating at Cambridge and then proceeding to take his MD at Padua.[145] While in Italy he made a notable collection of the flowers of Italy, the earliest to survive, a 'hortus siccus' known as Willoughby's Herbal, which he presented to the college library.[146] Meanwhile he had returned to Ireland where Charles II nominated him as a fellow of the Royal College of Physicians of Ireland. He was a founder member of the Philosophical Society of Dublin, to which he submitted papers. Some of his correspondence about Irish health statistics and other topics with William King, then bishop of Derry, survives. His observations on bills of mortality and the increase of population in Dublin were published by Sir William Wilde in 1857.[147]

Another Mertonian doctor, John Bateman, was doctor to Charles II and a candidate for the wardenship in 1693 and 1704. Like Whistler he became president of the Royal College of Physicians of London and, happily, proved a better administrator than Whistler. He founded a mathematical lectureship in geometry and algebra at Merton.[148]

The college produced an outstanding orientalist in Robert Huntington (1637–1701). He was a postmaster and had studied oriental languages when at Merton, and then obtained a chaplaincy with the Levant Company at its factory at Aleppo.[149] Elected in 1670 he went to Syria in the following year and took the chance to visit Palestine, Egypt, and Syria at large. He was thus able to amass a remarkable collection of oriental manuscripts. He resigned the chaplaincy in 1681 and returned to Merton, where the college allowed him to accumulate the profits of his fellowship.[150] He took his BD and DD in 1683 and

---

[144] A. M. Cooke, 'Daniel Whistler, PRCP', *Journal of Roy. Coll. Phys. London*, i/3 (April 1967), pp. 221–30, *MMC*, p. 288; Morrish, *Bibliotheca Higgsiana*, nos. 665–6, cf. *HUO* iv. 539, 550, 555.

[145] T. Percy Kirkpatrick, 'Charles Willoughby, MD', *Proc. Royal Irish Academy*, xxxvi, sec. C, p. 6.

[146] Herbarium Vivum, 1673.

[147] Kirkpatrick, 'Charles Willoughby, MD', pp. 15–23.

[148] *MMC*, p. 294, Clark and Cooke, *History of Roy. Coll. of Physicians of London*, ii. 489, 509, 532.

[149] *MMC*, p. 293, J. B. Pearson, *A Biographical Sketch of the Chaplains of the Levant Company . . . 1611–1706* (Cambridge, 1883), p. 57; P. E. Morrish, 'Dr Higgs and Merton College Library', p. 180, cf. *HUO* iv. 478, 491–2.

[150] For regular payments: see Reg. 3.3, pp. 339, 400, and 411.

accepted, though reluctantly, the provostship of Trinity College, Dublin, where he joined Willoughby in founding the Philosophical Society of Dublin.[151] He held the provostship until 1692 when he came home and was a candidate for the wardenship in 1693. He was appointed bishop of Raphoe in 1701, having turned down earlier the see of Lismore, but died soon afterwards. Of his great collection of oriental manuscripts about six hundred were bought for the Bodleian in 1693 for just over £1000 and thirty-five were presented by him to the same library;[152] he gave fourteen oriental manuscripts to Merton College Library in 1673,[153] and, perhaps stimulated by his example, William Fane, nephew of Frances Fane, 1st earl of Westmorland, gave four more to the library in 1675.[154]

Clayton was a courtier,[155] and once during his wardenship when the court came to Oxford the queen, Catherine of Braganza, stayed at Merton, when Charles II was housed in Christ Church. On Charles's first visit to Oxford after his coronation, that is in 1663, he had only stayed a few days[156] and there is no record that the queen then came to Merton, but when in September 1665 the court was seeking to avoid the plague, Queen Catherine stayed in the Warden's Lodgings for several months and brought her ladies with her. During the visit of the queen and the court Bishop Earle, a former fellow, died at University College and was buried in the chapel with full ceremony. Wood records that after the dean of Salisbury had read prayers the king's singers sang an anthem, a rare piece of evidence relating to the music in the chapel.[157] Robert Whitehall made a speech of commemoration. The chill of the chapel certainly impressed the court, for Anne Hyde, duchess of York, after she had set up a sermon there (on 10 December), had it moved to Christ Church on the following Sunday as Merton Chapel was too cold for her.[158] One of the queen's ladies, Barbara Villiers, Lady Castlemaine, gave birth to her son by the king in the college. He was George Palmer, later duke of Northumberland.[159] On

---

[151] *DNB*, and Kirkpatrick, 'Charles Willoughby, MD', p. 6.

[152] For Huntington's manuscripts at the Bodleian see Philip, *The Bodleian Library*, p. 60.

[153] *DNB*, and Coxe, *Catalogus*, pt. i *Codices Orientales*, pp. 130–2, cf. *HUO* iv. 491–2.

[154] Ibid., pp. 131–2.

[155] His friends included his brother-in-law, Sir Charles Coterel, master of ceremonies, see above, p. 220, cf. *HUO* iv. 518–19, 528, 543, 813, 866.

[156] 23–30 September 1661, cf. *LTAW* i. 492–9.

[157] *LTAW* ii. 66, cf. *HUO* iv. 675–6. For Merton 'music nights', see *HUO.* 630–1.

[158] *LTAW* ii. 67.

[159] A. J. Bott, *Baptisms and Marriages at Merton College* (Oxford, 1981), pp. 16–17.

the third occasion that Charles came to Oxford, for the Parliament of 1681, he once again brought the queen with him. Wood proudly records that she was presented with a copy of the cuts from his *History and Antiquities of the University of Oxford*, richly bound and gilt.[160] It seems that both king and queen stayed in Christ Church. The disappointment which the king experienced on finding parliament still bent on excluding his brother from the throne meant that his and the court's stay in Oxford was short.

By the 1680s the college had become attached to the Stuart cause and had no hesitation in expelling a probationer, Sir Strange Southby, who was a 'green-ribband' man and unwisely asserted that the old king died justly.[161] Thus the accession of James II was greeted with flares on the chapel tower and a bonfire in Fellows' Quadrangle round which the fellows knelt and drank healths in claret to the new king. Some of the college's members were enlisted to stand by the crown during Monmouth's rebellion.[162] The college even provided in John Massey an intruded dean of Christ Church.[163] Another fellow, Thomas Lane, fought for James II at the Battle of the Boyne. However, the college was not to be put to the test as was Magdalen in the months leading up to the Glorious Revolution, and by the time that Warden Clayton died in 1693 it had learned to live with the new regime. In the mean time it had welcomed Richard Steele, the future Whig pamphleteer, from Christ Church as a postmaster in 1691[164] and elected its first Whig warden, John Holland, in 1709.

[160] *LTAW* ii. 528.

[161] Ibid., ii. 511–12, cf. *HUO* iv. 611, 869, 898–9.

[162] *LTAW* iii. 129–30, 149, 151.

[163] *MMC*, p. 295, *LTAW* iii. 197–8, cf. *HUO* iv. 921–2, 929, 954, 614–15.

[164] Willard Connely, *Sir Richard Steele* (1934), pp. 41–5; *The Correspondence of Sir Richard Steele*, ed. Rae Blanchard (Oxford, 1941), p. 5 n. 3. The patron of his postmastership may have been William Sherwin, fellow, 1688 (*MMC*, p. 299), mentioned in surviving letters from Christ Church.

Anthony Wood, 1632–95

'When found, make a note of'
CAPTAIN CUTTLE

IN the second half of the seventeenth century the history of Merton College and, in a large measure, of the university itself, is dominated by a Mertonian who was neither a fellow nor an officer of the college, and one whom the university, in a moment of ignoble alarm, even deprived of his master's degree. Anthony Wood was born in the house known as Postmasters' Hall, in Merton Street, in 1632, and died in his rooms there in 1695. He was buried in the north transept of the church, a place to which he had some title as a parishioner, and it is perhaps a sign of grace on the part of the college that it did not seek to consign him to the common churchyard. He is commemorated in the transept by a small floor-slab, inscribed A.W., 1695, and by a mural tablet which displays his family's arms, and describes him succinctly as *Antiquarius*.[1] He was indeed an antiquary, and a notable example of his kind. The monument is as informative as any inscription of a normal length could be, and although there was much in Wood's life to which he took exception, he would probably have felt, may perhaps even feel, that in death he has not been unjustly treated.

To say that Anthony Wood lives in his works is something more than a commonplace. His *Athenae Oxonienses* and his histories of the city and university of Oxford broke entirely new ground.[2] His writings

---

[1] See Pl. 21, and Bott, *Monuments*, pp. 65, 93. Thomas Rowney, MP for the city of Oxford, paid for the tablet: *DNB*. *Antiquarius*, antiquary, is best understood as a student of the past: the early antiquaries laid the foundations of both history and archaeology as disciplines. It was incidentally Wood's intuitive concern with historical evidence that made him such a valuable commentator on change in his own time. See, e.g., his notes on, and appreciative use of, the flying coaches introduced in 1669 to ease the journey to London (*LTAW* ii. 153 and n.); and below, n. 13.

[2] *Historia et Antiquitates Universitatis Oxoniensis* (2 vols., Oxford, 1674); *Athenae Oxonienses: An Exact History of all the Writers and Bishops who have had their Education in Oxford from 1500 to 1690* (2 vols., London, 1691–2); *The History and Antiquities of the University of*

reveal, though they do not always acknowledge, that he had pre-decessors, notably Brian Twyne, and contemporaries whose work he used freely, but the imposing outcome was his own achievement, and everyone who has followed him has worked to the pattern which he set. It is not, however, simply Wood's industry and diligence in research and composition from which his extraordinary influence derives, and certainly not the published work which the university first patronized and then hastily disowned. He put his stamp upon his own century, and on the past which fascinated him, by his powers of close observation, and the pungency of his judgements, whether sound or unsound, and their utterance.[3] His lightest words are apt to remain in the mind, and even they are more abundant and better documented than those of his weightiest and most judicious con-temporaries. There is a vigour and a persistent fascination about them all, even when they are judged by the high standards of the English of Wood's day. It is a quality which he shares with his close contemporary John Aubrey, with whom he worked for some time in amity, and with whom he eventually and bitterly quarrelled, as he did with his family, his college, and most of his friends and colleagues.

Wood was born in Postmasters' Hall on 17 December 1632, about four o'clock in the morning, the fifth surviving son of Thomas Wood, BA, BCL, and the fourth of his second marriage, to Mary, daughter of Robert Petty, of Wyfold, Checkendon. Thomas had bought the lease of the house in 1608. The property comprised the portionists' hall of the medieval college, with a small annexe, or tenement, which now forms part of 6 Merton Street, built on behind it. It had been freed from college use when the Great Quadrangle was first ready to be occupied, after a fashion, and the postmasters were moved on to the main site to the rooms of their assigned fellows. The house was

Oxford, ed. J. Gutch (3 vols., Oxford, 1792–6); *Survey of the Antiquities of the City of Oxford*, ed. A. Clark (3 vols., OHS xv, xvii, xxxvii, 1889–99). The contents of the works are fully as imposing as their titles, and beyond them is the further mass of archival material edited by Andrew Clark in *The Life and Times of Anthony Wood* (OHS xix, xxi, xxvi, xxx, xl, 1890–1900; here abbreviated *LTAW*), and described by him at *LTAW*. i. 1–21. See also below, n. 14. For a recent commentary on the value of Wood's work, distinguishing some of his views in his earlier and his later years, see B. Worden in *HUO* iv. 771–2.

[3] 'Dr John Lloyd of Jesus Coll. took the place of vice-chancellor. A clowne, pedagogue, sot, not speak Latin': *LTAW* iii. 27. Dr Lloyd, himself a Mertonian, was in many others' eyes an estimable man, who became bishop of St David's in 1686: *DNB*. Wood's acrid phrases are entertaining enough at a distance, but those which became current did him much disservice.

then taken by John Lant, an MA of Christ Church, who sold the lease to Thomas Wood.

The Woods might reasonably be called a Mertonian family, not simply as parishioners of St John's, nor yet because Anthony and his elder brother Edward were members of the college. Thomas Wood's whole resource was to take leasehold properties and relet them. Postmasters' Hall became his wife's dower, and after her death the home of his son Robert and his wife Mary. Anthony Wood lived and died in the rooms behind it, and the mainstay of Anthony's income, as of his mother's in her lifetime, was the rent drawn from the Fleur de Luce Inn at Carfax,[4] which was one of Merton's chief city properties. The Woods were armigerous, but they had no landed estate, and no particular profession. In earlier times the farmers of the college properties had probably spent their substance in the country, and in later centuries there would be many other fields for carefully managed investments. In sevententh-century Oxford, Thomas Wood maintained a passable gentility by letting rooms and tenements and tennis courts, and his fifth son was thereby left free to browse on print and manuscripts at all hours, drink coffee, practise chamber music, and take notes.

Having learned to read at home from the psalter, Anthony Wood was sent to a small grammar school in Oxford at the age of eight, and then to New College school. There on the outbreak of war in 1642 he watched the young men of the university at muster, and the defences of the city being repaired. The king entered and garrisoned Oxford in October 1642, and the Woods' house was then commandeered for the Master of the Rolls, Sir John Colepeper, and his household. It was an unsettling time, and Anthony's father resolved to send him away from the town, but Thomas died early in 1643, and it was not until the next year that Anthony and his younger brother Christopher were finally settled at Lord Williams's school at Thame, which they attended together until 1646.[5] Wood's mother then wished to apprentice him to some trade, but in October 1647 Anthony was entered at Merton, and became postmaster to Edward Copley, later professor of moral philosophy. His brother Edward had already graduated from Trinity, and was elected a fellow of Merton in 1648.

---

[4] See above, p. 113.

[5] On Lord Williams's school see further *VCH Oxon.* i. 475–7. The master in Wood's time was William Burt, later warden of Winchester, who was married to Mary Wood's cousin, Elizabeth Petty: *LTAW* i. 108–9 and nn.

Although Wood much enjoyed the rituals and sociability of college life he was not a particularly apt student,[6] and did not complete his BA until 1652. In the mean time, having had his schooldays disrupted by war, he found his university life at peril from the strife which came with peace. When summoned before the parliamentary visitors in May 1648 he first returned a temporizing answer to their questions, but he then conformed, and kept his place, as did some other members of the college, his brother Edward amongst them, through the indulgence of Warden Brent. The intrusion of the politics of the Interregnum intensified rather than overlaid the tensions that were endemic in the university, and Brent, though a presbyterian, had no hesitation in circumventing the will of his fellow commissioners when he wished to protect the interests of his college.[7] He could not, however, prevent the ejection of some of the fellows, nor yet the intrusion of parliamentarian nominees in their places, but he did a particular service to Wood in 1650 by making him a Bible clerk. The supersession of chapel services made the clerkship largely a sinecure, whilst by the transfer Wood escaped a purge of the postmasters which followed soon afterwards.

During his undergraduate years Wood acquired some new tastes and a circle of friends. He learned to play the violin, for which he had some talent; he rode out on sight-seeing excursions. A friend took him home, to Bledlow in Buckinghamshire, and he particularly noticed, though he did not copy, old painted glass and epitaphs in the church there. In August 1652, shortly after his graduation, he fell sick with a recurrent fever, probably malarial, which came upon him after a day spent fishing at Wheatley, and was the first of the many illnesses which he suffered and documented to the last days of his life. He observed in 1650 the opening of the first coffee house in Oxford, but for the moment he left sociable coffee-drinking to those who delighted in novelty.[8]

Music was a continuing source of pleasure to Wood, but he found another in those years which framed his life's work. As a bachelor of

---

[6] He may not have benefited perfectly from the tuition of his brother Edward, 'pevish and . . . ever and anon angry': *LTAW* i. 162.

[7] See further above, pp. 208–10.

[8] Wood did not altogether approve of the results: 'The decay of study, and consequently of learning, are coffy houses, to which most scholars retire and spend much of the day in hearing and speaking of news, in speaking vily of their superiors': *LTAW* ii. 300. He nevertheless made a collection of the newsletters which helped to sell the coffee and fired the gossip: 'my coffey letters' (1687): *LTAW* iii. 215.

arts he gained access to 'the publik library', the Bodleian. He was allowed to use only the books in the Arts End until he had taken his master's degree, which he did in December 1655, though even then he was not formally admitted as a reader until 1658. In the mean time he fell to 'sedulous and close studying there', and was particularly moved by discovering William Burton's *Description of Leicestershire*, published in 1622, and a number of books on heraldry. Burton's work, which now seems only a modest achievement, has to be judged not against its many successors, but against the small number of antiquarian and topographical studies which were available at the time. To Wood it was a revelation, though there was another to come.

In April 1655 Edward Wood became junior proctor, but he died only a few weeks later, and was buried in the chancel of the church after lying in state in the hall. There were solemnities in hall, with gloves, wine, and biscuit in abundance for the distinguished mourners, and elegiac verses and escutcheons were displayed on the hearse. The family took pride and comfort in the college's and the university's formal display of grief, and Anthony was moved to edit and publish some of his brother's university sermons. The volume appeared in the following March, and was dedicated to Warden Goddard, to whom, at Gresham College, Wood sent a suitably bound copy.[9] He was now in print.

The decisive event in Wood's life as a student of the past was the appearance in 1656 of Sir William Dugdale's *Antiquities of Warwickshire*, which came to the Bodleian that summer. The first volume of Dugdale's comprehensive history of religious houses, *Monasticon Anglicanum*, which transformed the study of the English Middle Ages, had been published in the previous year. Now the *Antiquities* spoke directly and instantly to Wood. Dugdale had been a neighbour of Burton's in Warwickshire and admired the older man's work, but his own broke new ground in its wide scope and its learning. He was able to bring an exceptional knowledge of national and institutional records to bear upon the history of the local community, and he applied it with critical enthusiasm. The result was a striking folio, with maps, portraits, and other plates, many of them by Wenceslaus

---

[9] Γνωστὸν ιου Θεου καί νυωστὸν του Χριστου, *or that which may be known of God by the Book of Nature and the excellent Knowledge of Jesus Christ by the Book of Scripture. Delivered at St Mary's, Oxford, by Edward Wood.* Published since his death by his brother A. W., M. A. (Oxford, 1656). There was a second edition in 1674. On Warden Goddard and Gresham College, see above, pp. 210–11.

Hollar, a whole gallery of heraldry, and a notable apparatus of reference. It offered a model of systematic exposition to which Wood, whose 'tender affections and insatiable desire of knowledg were ravished and melted down by the reading', responded with his whole heart.

Wood had probably begun to identify and draw coats of arms under the stimulus of Burton's book, and in the autumn of 1656 he made systematic notes on the arms and inscriptions in Oxford churches and chapels. Spurred on by Dugdale's example, he pored over Leland's antiquarian notes, which he found in the Bodleian. He sketched the remains of Rewley Abbey, and made plans of Eynsham and Dorchester. He noted effigies, windows, and brasses; compiled pedigrees; visited the Baskervilles' house at Sunningwell and was pleased to find it isolated in 'a romancey place'. About the same time, though perhaps only coincidentally, he began to keep a journal each year in the blank spaces of his almanacs.[10] He also noted minutely what he spent from week to week, from £5 as a family contribution to the recasting of the Merton bells to 4*d*. 'for a physick drink', or 1*d*. at Pinnock's, 'when wee went to hear the nightingale sing'; and as he then preserved the accounts, he became an exceptionally well-documented man.

Although he ranged over the country around Oxford, on both what he called his frolics and his antiquarian excursions, Wood did not long see Oxfordshire, nor any other county, as a natural object of study. Unlike Burton and Dugdale, and despite his mother's affinity and acquaintance in the county, he was a townsman.[11] As an Oxonian, he was also, and by no means incidentally, a university man, with his natural habitat not only the study and the library, but also the favoured tavern, and, when common rooms came in, the common room. His eyes and ears missed little in the daily scene, and when his mind turned to consider the past, as it constantly did, it dwelt upon substantially the same community.

Though the medieval city and university loomed large in seventeenth-century Oxford, however, the very nature of Wood's interest in the Middle Ages is a reminder that his standpoint was modern. Despite his idiosyncratic sympathies there was nothing archaic about his tastes and principal interest, for his perception of the past and his scholarly work kept up to the most advanced thought of his day. His

---

[10] From 1657 onwards: *LTAW* i. 200.

[11] Mary Wood's mother, Penelope Taverner, was a daughter of Richard Taverner of Wood Eaton and Mary, daughter of Sir John Harcourt of Stanton Harcourt: *LTAW* i. 39–40.

view of history was necessarily self-taught, though as he absorbed it mostly from the archives he was spared many distortions. There were, indeed, few other aids to understanding. For his own part he deplored the destruction of antiquities that went on around him, and recognized the importance of recording what he found. He was generally on sure ground with archives, inscriptions, and, in large measure, heraldry. On the other hand he lacked the most elementary guide to medieval architecture, supposing that the remains of Eynsham abbey were, like the abbey itself, of pre-Conquest date, but he was not alone in that. The very term Gothick, for the dynamic phase of medieval architectural engineering, was only given currency in England much later in the century by Christopher Wren, whom Wood had distinguished as a coffee-house wit when he was a young fellow of All Souls' in the 1650s. It is interesting, for example, that although Wood noted and described the sedilia in the chancel of the abbey church at Dorchester, he plainly had no notion of their liturgical use.[12] At the same time his critical observations of change are generally valuable for their own sake, as when he remarked the contemporary taste for replacing stone-traceried windows with wooden-framed casements, an innovation which he characteristically, and not altogether unjustly, attributed to the influence of wives.[13]

His father's will gave Wood a modest independence, and early in 1660 he used his new means to build a fireplace and chimney on an upper floor of what is now 6 Merton Street, to make a study and bedroom there. He began his intensive study of Oxford by turning to the cartularies and other records of the religious houses, and so laid a better foundation for his history of the university than if he had started directly on that subject. However, in 1660 he gained access to the university archives, and began to shape his principal work.

For Wood's immediate purposes the most important contents of the archives were the antiquarian collections of Brian Twyne, a fellow and Greek lecturer of Corpus Christi College, who had been keeper

[12] See also above, p. 128 n. 41. The sedilia of Furness Abbey were a similar source of local bafflement in the late eighteenth cent.: 'I then visited the Seats, called by some people the Grand Chairs': *The History and Antiquities of Furness, being a Record of Journeys made in Furness, in the year 1777 with Descriptions of the Places visited*, ed. L. R. Ayre (Ulverston, 1887), p. 43.
[13] See e.g. his remarks on Warden Finch of All Souls', who removed an oriel and another stone-mullioned window on first coming in to his lodgings in 1687, and then in 1694 brought home a wife. 'More plucking down and altering windowes follow': *LTAW* iii. 208, 459. See also below, p. 235.

of the archives from 1634 to 1644. Twyne was one of the two principal draftsmen of Archbishop Laud's statutes for the university, and the author of a learned but purely fanciful history of the foundation of Oxford which was widely acclaimed outside Cambridge. Wood found that Twyne's work in the archives had largely anticipated his own, but Twyne had not brought it to a conclusion, and probably never contemplated publishing it in its entirety. He had assembled a mass of material, which ended shortly before his death in 1644 with a valuable account of the onset of the Civil War in Oxford and of the king's occupation of the town. Wood's use of those passages in particular fills out the memories of his own youth in a vivid way. His cheerful ransacking of Twyne's transcripts has been much reprobated. Andrew Clark observed from his first impression that 'there was no originality in [Wood's] work, for he merely put into shape Twyne's materials', but he added even then, before he was familiar with the whole collection, that Wood had manifestly returned to the records to verify Twyne's texts.[14] Wood's proceedings were in fact in the established tradition of early antiquarianism and, from an earlier age, of much medieval writing. He improved to the best of his capacity upon the accumulated material that he found, and he went beyond Twyne in committing it to print.

Wood's work in the university archives and the Bodleian brought him to the notice of Dr John Fell, dean of Christ Church from the autumn of 1660, and then bishop of Oxford from 1676 until his death in 1686. Fell was, like Wood, a former pupil of Lord Williams's school, though he had a studentship at Christ Church, upon the nomination of his father, the dean, at the age of eleven. He served in the king's army in the early years of the war, and was later a neighbour of the Woods in Merton Street, where he had celebrated Anglican services, in defiance of the authorities, during the Interregnum. He was a demon of energy.[15] He restored and reformed Christ Church, where Tom Tower and the north side of Tom Quad are to the outward eye his most commanding memorials; he imposed system and order upon the university at large. Amongst his other cares he galvanized the

---

[14] *DNB.* Clark edited Aubrey's *Brief Lives* as well as Wood's unpublished works, and was a perfect monument of editorial patience. He might well have given Wood more credit for his labours if he had written his notice for the *DNB* after rather than before he brought the *Life and Times* and the *City of Oxford* to the press.

[15] For a vigorous sketch of Fell's work in Christ Church, which could well have earned him, like Warden Sever at Merton, the title of a second founder, see E. G. W. Bill, *Education at Christ Church, Oxford, 1660–1800* (Oxford, 1988), pp. 20–36.

university press, transformed its typography, and promoted the publication of Greek texts and the study of Coptic.[16] He at once saw in
Wood's interests and dedication a unique opportunity to dignify the
university with a scholarly account of its past which would also be a
memorial to its current achievements.

Wood was flattered by Fell's patronage which, though Fell was
evidently a forbidding man, was accomplished with many acts of
kindness. A semi-official status made it easier for Wood to gain access
to archives, though every college was jealous of its privileges, and
there was often a lurking fear that too close an inquiry into the
evidences might reveal flaws in title.[17] It also took him to London, to
the Cottonian library at Westminster, and to consult the records in
the Tower, and there, to his great delight, to make the acquaintance
of Dugdale, whom he was later proud to assist in his work. At the
same time Fell was an autocrat, and a large part of his success depended
upon his remorseless attention to detail in pursuit of his imposing
schemes. He amended the text of Wood's history as a matter of course,
and he also decreed that it should be published in Latin rather than
English, and provided a translator, Richard Peers, of Christ Church,
of whom Wood naturally did not think highly.[18] The decision is
notable partly for the implication that Wood's Latin, though fully
equal to the business of research, was not elegant enough for Fell's
monumental purpose, and partly because the history was plainly
intended thereby to attract an international audience. Though Latin
held its own in academic exercises for a longer time, it would seem
eccentric within a century in England not to write scholarly works in
the vernacular, but that possibility would probably not have affected
Fell's judgement even if it had occurred to him.[19] In the mean time

[16] See e.g. P. Sutcliffe, *The Oxford University Press: An Informal History* (Oxford, 1978), pp.
xix–xxiii.

[17] Wood had quite ready access to the records of Magdalen, and of New College, and
was even allowed to borrow the first register of New College. At Queen's, he thought that
some material had been withheld from him, but he was well received at Exeter and
Lincoln: *LTAW* ii. 38, 44–5, 78–82. See, on the other hand, Dr Phineas Elwood's fear that
the *Historia* 'hath given advantages to the enimies of the universitie of Oxon to write
against it', an extremity of academic caution dismissed by Wood as 'Ridiculous': *LTAW*
iii. 277.

[18] See further *LTAW* ii. 199–200. It is difficult not to have some sympathy for Peers, 'a
sullen, dogged, clownish, and perverse fellow', ground between Fell as the upper and
Wood as the lower millstone. He seems, poor man, to have given Wood a manuscript
from Malmesbury abbey (Bodl. MS Wood D 8) as a placatory gesture.

[19] See also above, p. 202.

the work moved on, and the *Historia et Antiquitates* appeared in 1674.[20]

A second volume of the history was then to be devoted to *Fasti*, lists of office-holders in the university from the earliest times. It seems to have been Fell's idea to include them, but the work was highly congenial to Wood, and whilst he continued to collect materials for a comparable study of the city, he began to extend the *Fasti* into a biographical dictionary of Oxonian authors and prelates. It was at this point that he came to collaborate with John Aubrey, a kindred soul who willingly supplied material from his own abundant and disorderly files. At the same time Wood prepared an English version of the history, which remained in manuscript until it was published with scrupulous care by John Gutch in 1791–6. He also kept his diaries and accounts, frequented coffee-houses, read the journals, which were shaping a new political and intellectual community, and deplored the temper of the times. The second part of his work, now entitled *Athenae Oxonienses*, appeared in two volumes in 1691–2.

Catastrophe followed soon after. There were many acerbic reflections in the *Athenae*, and amongst them was a disobliging reference, provided by Aubrey, to the great Edward Hyde, sometime commoner of Magdalen Hall, and first earl of Clarendon. In the 1640s Clarendon had tried and failed to save Charles I from himself, and he was Charles II's principal councillor in exile. On his return to England in 1660 he became lord chancellor, but was driven into exile in 1667 when his overbearing manner finally grated upon the king as much as it did on his own political rivals. A man of sharp perceptions, he had something in common with Anthony Wood himself, though he was incomparably the greater stylist. His *History of the Great Rebellion* combines a resounding narrative with the most trenchant dissection of political humbug in the English language, but his wit and acumen and literary distinction could not save him from public obloquy, and he left England in a welter of denunciation. Now Clarendon's son, the second earl, who had been high steward of the university since 1676, decided that his father had been libelled by the university historiographer, and in November 1692 he took action against Wood in the vice-chancellor's court.

Wood (or Aubrey) had said that Clarendon was reputed to have taken bribes from office-seekers in 1660. He was certainly so reputed,

---

[20] '27 July [1674] Monday, my book published at Oxon. Full of base things put in by Dr Fell to please his partial humor and undo the author': *LTAW* ii. 290. Authors may suffer unparalleled torments of sensitivity, but can sometimes win the last word.

and it is very much more likely that he had accepted presents than that he had not. The facts are lost in the haze not of history but of politics. If Clarendon had stayed in England to be impeached in 1667 he would most probably have been convicted of those and many other offences. It is not clear that what was written in the *Fasti* would have been found defamatory if Clarendon had been alive, for he would then have been in exile or in prison, and it was and is not a common-law offence to libel the dead.

However, Wood did not argue that Lord Clarendon dead had no ground for action. He claimed instead that the offending words were not his own but the work of another hand, which was as close as he cared to go towards saying that they were Aubrey's. His defence was a characteristic tangle of pedantic exceptions and counter-accusations. Whether a more straightforward rebuttal would have served him better is questionable. The university was keenly conscious of its obligations to its patrons, and it not only ordered the offending pages burned outside the Sheldonian theatre, in July 1693, but expelled Wood from its outraged bosom.[21] The second earl, who had spent some time in the Tower for professing allegiance to William and Mary and to James II simultaneously, was reported to have considered having a medal struck to commemorate his victory. It was fitting that he should, for he never took part in a more glorious campaign, but he seems to have thought better of it, and it was subsequently said that he devoted the costs which he recovered against Wood to placing the figures on the gate of the Physic Garden.[22]

Wood dealt with the incident with some of the resolution which he showed in the face of death not long afterwards. Given though he was to captious recrimination over lesser trials, he dismissed the judgement and pursued his work as best he could.[23] He continued to observe and record the life of the university and city, and spoke sharply of Dr Lydall, the new warden of Merton.[24] He was called to

[21] See the account of the process in *LTAW* iv. 1–50. For Aubrey's side of the bitter estrangement between the friends which followed, see *Brief Lives and other Selected Writings by John Aubrey*, ed. A. Powell (London, 1949), pp. xvi–xx.

[22] See *LTAW* iii. 440, and iv. 50 and n. It should perhaps be said for Earl Henry that in 1685 he spoke against the notion of burning at the stake Dame Alice Lisle, the Edith Cavell of her day, and so disobliged his friend Judge Jeffreys, who greatly relished that side of his work.

[23] For his satirical recantation, see *LTAW* iv. 49–50.

[24] '[He is] a warden with a wife and 7 or 8 chidren, which being to be fed with the bread belonging to piety and learning is a great detriment to the college; what they eat and

Westminster to give evidence in the court of common pleas, as what would now be called an expert witness, in a cause between the chancellor of the university and the president and fellows of Magdalen College, over the appointment of the principal of Magdalen Hall.[25] His active friends in those last years included Arthur Charlett, the master of University College, who was caricatured in *The Spectator* as Abraham Froth, a busy correspondent, but who was an early and discerning patron of Humfrey Wanley, the palaeographer. Another was the young Thomas Tanner, later bishop of St Asaph, with whom Wood took antiquarian walks, and who presented him with a copy of his *Notitia Monastica* in 1695.

Much of Wood's sharpness can be attributed to his poor health. In addition to his other chronic ailments he suffered increasingly from deafness, which further drove him in upon himself.[26] Whilst he was undoubtedly the author of many of his own misfortunes, his apprehensions and some of his astringency must also be measured against the background of the times, and their high political tensions. He was a firm though moderate Anglican and a staunch royalist: in the language of the later part of the century, a Tory. Like many royalists he detested the Presbyterians as the fatuous architects of disaster in 1640–2. He did not forgive himself for having temporized under the Commonwealth, but he observed that many who persecuted Anglicans and prospered then, prospered equally well when the king returned and Anglicanism was in season again. Like other Tories he welcomed the restoration of the monarchy, but he could not find all the king's new friends congenial.

In his later years he watched the antics both of the Romanists and of their most vocal opponents with equal distaste. He could not approve of the attempts to exclude the duke of York from the succession, and yet feared the triumph of the Roman Church. Wood's increasing isolation at that time was aggravated by a widespread and specious delusion that he was a papist. His known distaste for Presbyterianism and what he categorized as fanaticism, his fondness for antiquities and for a past which lived on in the monuments of the medieval church, combined to give the impression to many who

---

drink [would] serve for exhibition of 7 or 8 poor scholars ... wholy bent for sneaking compliance, cares for no man, but for 1*d*. or 2*d*.': *LTAW* iii. 436. Dr Lydall was a physician, and a family man. See also above, p. 135 and n.
[25] *LTAW* iii. 456–8.
[26] See e.g. *LTAW* ii. 9, 163–4; and iii. 152–3 and nn.

did not share or understand his tastes that he favoured the cause of Rome. He was vehemently suspected of Romanism at the time of Titus Oates's grotesque impostures in 1678, when his rooms and papers were searched for treasonable correspondence. On that occasion he took the oaths of supremacy and allegiance before the vice-chancellor. Nothing could have been further from his mind than sedition, but for the most part he was too contemptuous of his enemies to say so. When James departed and William III and Mary came, Wood was much more concerned with the excesses of their professed supporters than with the deliverance which he acknowledged, yet his previous anxieties for the protestant cause had been as acute as anyone's else.[27]

Wood's health was clearly failing in the last two or three years of his life, but amid his many ailments it was probably some growth of his prostate gland which killed him. Convinced of the imminence of death by Arthur Charlett, who called to see him on 21 November 1695, he put his affairs in order with a calm resolve, burned some papers, though in the face of the multitudes that survive it is difficult to guess what they may have been, and committed the continuation of the *Athenae* to Thomas Tanner.[28] He made his will on 24 November, naming his nieces Anne and Frances Wood as his principal legatees and executors,[29] and died in the early hours of 29 November. He was buried in the evening of the same day, according to his own instructions: 'deeper than ordinary; under, and as close to the wall (just as you enter in at the north on the left hand) as the place will permit'.

Wood's eminent service to the history both of Oxford and of his own time was first the preservation of evidence, and then its publication. He had an intuitive understanding of the nature and value of documentary records, and his care for them extended to those of his own day as well as to those of the past in which he found most pleasure.[30] His personal papers are even now a rich mine of material,

[27] See e.g. *LTAW* iii. 286, 297, 308–9.

[28] Tanner observed in Wood's last days, 'Merton College people are mighty officious, sending him notes and paying him visits, either in hopes to suppress anything that he has writ (as they falsly imagine) to the scandal of their college, or else to prevail with him to give something to their library': *LTAW* iii. 501–2. Both the apprehensions and the hopes were natural enough, but nothing came of either.

[29] On Wood's estate, see further S. Gillam, 'Anthony Wood's trustees and their friends', *BLR* xv/3 (Oct. 1995), 187–210.

[30] See his recovery of the matriculation register for 1648–62, which was in danger of destruction in 1686, probably for political reasons: *LTAW* iii. 202–3. See also above, p. 222 n. 2.

ordered throughout by a lucid, acerbic mind. The *Historia* and the *Athenae* are great works, which were a service to those whose learning Wood digested and developed as well as to the reading world at large. His accomplishments outshine his sins both of commission and omission, whilst time has put most of, if not all his asperities into perspective. He did not admire Lady Clayton's face, but the appearance in the Warden's Lodgings of the pier glass in which she liked to contemplate her splendour is of at least as much historical interest as her long-forgotten features.[31] Nothing that any warden's wife did was likely to please Wood, but other innovations he could weigh upon their merits. Thus he came to terms with the coffee-house, but not with the idle habits of whistling, and walking hands-in-pockets, which the gentlemen of the court had communicated to the young men of his day, and so to their posterity. He found himself, at the last, an unwilling but perceptive chronicler of the rise of Whiggism and domesticity. Fortunately he not only recorded his multifarious expenditure and his daily irritations but also documented their occasions, and both the world of learning and its wider setting have ever since been the richer for it.

[31] They may not have been uncomely, though marriage to Sir Thomas Clayton cannot have done much for her inner radiance. In any event, it is arguably better to have won a place in the glass of history by being denounced by Anthony Wood than not to have been noticed at all.

II

Merton in the Eighteenth Century

The tradition of electing medical wardens continued into the eighteenth century, and the results were often disappointing to the college. Archbishop Tenison ensured that Richard Lydall (1693–1704) should become warden at his second attempt. But whereas in 1661 Lydall had been too young, in 1693 he was too old, and the fellows wanted Dr Conant.[1] Nor does Lydall seem to have been a distinguished head; indeed Wood said in his sweeping way that he was 'old and unserviceable, a man of no generous spirit, ignorant of learning, and so consequently no encourager thereof. He has been a packhorse in the practical and old Galenical way of physick, knows nothing else, buyes no books nor understands what learning is in the world ...'.[2] His successor, Dr Edmund Marten, also a doctor of medicine, was another archiepiscopal choice made against the wishes of the fellows. He was even less liked by Hearne than Lydall was by Wood. Hearne wrote that 'by a lazy, Epicurean life and utter Neglect of all Discipline [he] has very much prejudiced that noble and ancient Seminary'.[3] During his wardenship a 'Golden Election' of fellows was held in 1705 which may owe something to him.[4] He cannot be shown to have influenced another notable achievement of his time, the erection of the Fellows' Summer House and building up of the terrace which is the delight of

[1] The three candidates were Lydall, Conant, and Bateman.

[2] *LTAW* iii. 436. There is a portrait of him in the Old Warden's Lodgings (wrongly attributed to Sir Thomas Clayton in Mrs Poole's *Catalogue of Oxford Portraits*, ii. 52).

[3] T. Hearne, *Collections*, i. 231, cf. ii. 218 n., 'no better a governour than a scholar'. Archbishop Tenison chose him in preference to either J. Bateman or Dr Lane; for Holland's unfavourable view of Marten see *MMC*, p. 126. He left the college £200 for rebuilding the wall between the garden and Merton Street, but in the event the college only received £90, and left the wall largely as it was (Reg. 4.20, p. 37).

[4] Hearne, *Collections*, i. 115: 'They stile it ye Golden Election because they are all Excellent Scholars, especially three or four of them are said to be as good as any in Oxford of their standing'.

all Mertonians (Pl. 22). Then after the election of a Whig and a theologian in Warden Holland (1709–34), of whom more shortly, the last of the line of medical wardens, Robert Wyntle, was elected in 1734. He quickly ran head-on into collision with the fellows – a clash which led to an archiepiscopal visitation. Though Wyntle had been a Radcliffe Travelling Fellow he does not seem to have written anything memorable on medicine and his example seems to have ruled out any desire to appoint a medical warden thereafter.[5] At all events the last three wardens of the century were all Merton theologians, John Robinson (1750–9), Henry Barton (1759–90), and Scrope Berdmore (1790–1810). The domineering Wyntle's rule seems to have led to a reaction, so that *c.* 1760 a Magdalen observer could describe Merton as a college of twenty-four wardens and one fellow.[6] As the division between Whigs and Tories gradually died out after 1760 some harmony between the warden and fellows was restored. Robinson seems to have been an invalid for part of his wardenship. Barton, the son of an impecunious clergyman, was a humorous and easy-going warden.[7] Scrope Berdmore 'led a very quiet and gentlemanly life in his fine old College'; 'he was an estimable man' and 'undertook the office of Vice-Chancellor, but gave it up after a year's trial, preferring (it may be presumed) his wonted ease to public duties'.[8]

The best of the eighteenth-century wardens was Dr John Holland. His epitaph written in the college register describes him as

> a serious theologian who adhered closely to orthodoxy, a fluent and lively speaker. As far as his character and behaviour were concerned, he was endowed with a kindly and gentle nature which he improved

---

[5] Nias, *Dr John Radcliffe*, pp. 42–3.

[6] Ward, *Georgian Oxford*, p. 222.

[7] 'Dr Barton was a very singular character; he was an excellent scholar and had a great store of wit and humour, but his mode of living was strangely peculiar. In regard to all personal enjoyments and indulgence, his parsimony was excessive.' 'He had, it is said, an odd and ingenious way of coaxing a Barber to dress his wig for nothing.' 'He used to say it was not covetousness, but a habit of saving. When his Father (a Worcestershire clergyman) first brought him to College (such was his story) he put into his hands, with tears in his eyes, twenty pounds, begging of him to make it last as long as he could for that he had not anywhere, when he went home again, so large a sum at command, for the support of his mother and sisters and brother. And this he would say made so great an impression upon his mind, that he had ever since been in the habit of saving.' (E.2.41, i. 150–2.) There is a Vaslet crayon drawing of him in the Warden's Lodgings (Poole, *Catalogue of Oxford Portraits*, ii. 54 and pl. vii). Despite his parsimony he himself paid for repairs to the Founder's tomb (see below, p. 263 and n.).

[8] Cox, *Recollections*, pp. 168–9.

by application. He very rarely took offence, and if he did so, soon put the matter out of his mind and completely forgot it. Even those who were opposed to him he treated so kindly that you would have thought that he also loved them according to the rule of scripture. Nor did he let himself or his friends be troubled. He long administered Mertonian affairs peacefully and with the utmost leniency and frugality. He left the college £60 as a testimony of his affection for it.[9]

Though we may discount some of that as typical of the overwriting of the day, much still rings true. The two volumes of his personal registers which survive enable us to see the warden and former proctor conscientiously at work both as head of the house and as magistrate.[10] His comment on his predecessor's rule, that during his administration 'the major part of the society seem to have had greater regard for their own private interest than for the advancement of the college', suggests that he himself would by contrast strive for the second objective. Though Hearne denounced him as a Whig and a dullard, he was clever enough to outwit his opponents in 1716 and again in 1721 when the Merton Whigs split into two.[11]

To bring about the reforms made necessary by the easy-going habits of his predecessor proved distinctly difficult. The warden had to proceed by persuasion, and he was up against a faction several of whose members refused to be reconciled. The ringleader was John Marten, one of those elected at the Golden Election of 1705. He was a physician who, if Warden Wyntle is to be believed, went to George Street, London, later known as York Buildings, Charing Cross, to

---

[9] Reg. 1.4, p. 16. 'Theologus fuit gravis et fidei catholicae tenacissimus, Orator floridus, copiosus. Si indolem et mores spectes benignum et mite ingenium a natura inditus disciplinae excoluit. Offensiones rarissime accepit, acceptas cito deposuit, obliteravit. Et quos habuit sibi infestos adeo benigne tractavit ut ad scripturae normam illos etiam dilexisse crederes. Nec sibi nec suis molestus diu res Mertonenses pacatas summa cum lenitate et frugalitate administravit. Sexaginta libras collegio ut amoris pignus supremis tabulis legavit.' (I am grateful to Dr Nicholas Richardson for help with the translation in the text.) The money was to be put to buying an advowson. His is the only portrait of an eighteenth-cent. warden to be hung in the Hall (cf. Poole, *Catalogue of Oxford Portraits*, ii. 52).

[10] Reg. 4.21 and Reg. 4.22. See especially the way in which he secured the payment of Dr Tovey's debt as bursar (Reg. 4.22, p. 15), and his riding up to the north to visit Bielby (Yorks.) and Seaton Carew and Stillington (Co. Durham) in July 1723 (ibid., p. 3).

[11] Ward, *Georgian Oxford*, pp. 99–102; cf. Reg. 1.6, p. 68, when Marten, Abell, Byne, Watkinson, Sessions, Trowe, and Cox all left the room. For the 1716 election cf. the decree of Archbishop Wake of 1 August 1716 (*Statutes and Ordinances* (1853), pp. 61–3).

practise medicine,[12] but when his practice did not prosper returned to live at Headington with a woman to whom he was not married. He was one of the leaders of the 'Tory' faction[13] and, though he seems to have acquired considerable property, was not made to resign by the warden despite its incompatibility with his fellowship. He was later a thorn in the side of Holland's successor.

As soon as he was elected Warden Holland tried to revive the divinity disputations.[14] Though proud of its 'variations' or exercises based on themes from Aristotle,[15] the college had allowed its divinity disputations to lapse, and he had hard work in reviving them. The variations themselves needed support. If a fellow failed to vary, as did Henry Dunster, a budding lawyer, Holland fined him, but does not seem to have persuaded him subsequently to carry out the variations. When he proposed that there should be a fellowship election to make up numbers from the nineteen to which they had fallen, the fellows at first did not agree, but eventually here he got his way. It seems unlikely that he did so when he suggested that the gentlemen commoners should be subject to the same exercises and discipline as the other undergraduates.[16] Certainly they were all allotted tutors between 1716 and 1731, but what their tutors taught them is unclear. As the son of a leading citizen of Worcester Holland naturally became a canon of Worcester Cathedral and one of the founding trustees of Worcester College, Oxford.[17] Although Merton only had one direct link with the diocese of Worcester – its living of Great Wolford – Holland built up a considerable connection during his wardenship with the city and diocese of Worcester, from candidates for fellowships down to the lowliest poor boys seeking admission as servitors.[18]

[12] Reg. 1.6, p. 90.

[13] Ward, *Georgian Oxford*, p. 99. For the delay after election cf. *HUO* v. 238 n. 1.

[14] Reg. 4.21, p. 7 (17 Dec. 1709). He had been urged to do so by Archbishops Tenison and Wake (Reg. 1.6, p. 181). The practical observance of Divinity Disputations was insisted on by Archbishop Potter in 1738 (Injunction VII in *Statutes and Ordinances* (1853), p. 66).

[15] J. Pointer, *Oxoniensis Academia* (1749), pp. 18–19. They had not always been thus. For the earlier history of variations see *RACM 1483–1521*, pp. xxiii–xxiv.

[16] Reg. 4.21, p. 29 (1 Aug. 1711).

[17] He signed the Statutes of Worcester College, 12 June 1714 (Reg. 4.21, p. 52).

[18] The following fellows were from Worcester diocese: Philip Bearcroft (1717), John Cox (1717), James Stillingfleet (1721), Samuel Woolley (1721), John Cookesey (1727), Charles Lane (1731). The following servitors admitted by Warden Holland were from Worcestershire: E. Oldnall, F. Severs, C. Deacon, R. Butler, B. Lee, S. Nott, J. Hughes.

THE FELLOWS

The majority of the Merton fellows of the eighteenth century were home-grown. Of the 159 fellows eighty-five were Mertonians. The only other college to supply more than ten was Christ Church, whose numbers increased greatly towards the end of the century when its fame was ascendant.[19] Once Merton had become predominantly Whig, say by 1716, it attracted Whig refugees from 'Tory' colleges such as John Russell, from Brasenose.[20] In general, when the primate had himself become a government supporter, Merton, whose visitor he was, must have seemed an attractive berth for a cleric seeking to climb the ladder of promotion. The fellowship was never more aristocratic than in the second half of the century. There the influence of Christ Church was decisive. Five of the fellows were the sons of English earls and one of a Scottish earl.[21] All came from Christ Church. Three other fellows became baronets in their own right,[22] two more were sons of peers,[23] and one of a baronet.[24] Some of the fellows were the protégés of Whig aristocrats, as was James Stillingfleet of the earl of Dartmouth.[25] Others acquired tutorships or chaplaincies in aristocratic households,[26] as did Charles Bean as chaplain to the earl of Peterborough,[27] or Philip Bearcroft as chaplain to Lord Perceval.[28] Others became chaplains to bishops, as John Russell did to White Kennet, bishop of Peterborough.[29] Several were the kin of bishops. Edward Stillingfleet was the grandson of Bishop Stillingfleet. The bishop's great-grandson was James Stillingfleet. Both came to Merton from Wadham. George Willis (fellow 1768) was the grandson of Richard Willis, bishop of

---

[19] Cf *HUO* v. 624-5.

[20] Ward, *Georgian Oxford*, p. 99.

[21] The Hon. John Sherard (fellow, 1734), son of the earl of Harborough; the Hon. James Cornwallis (fellow 1763), son of the 3rd earl Cornwallis; the Hon. T. E. Capel (fellow, 1791), son of the earl of Essex; the Hon. A. G. Legge (fellow, 1794), son of the earl of Dartmouth; the Hon. William Herbert (fellow, 1799), son of the earl of Carnarvon; the Hon. G. Hamilton, son of the earl of Abercorn (fellow, 1744 from Christ Church and Exeter).

[22] John Doyly (fellow, 1727), John Parsons (fellow, 1738), George Burrard (fellow, 1791).

[23] John Cowper (fellow, 1717), Reginald Cocks (fellow, 1799).

[24] Richard Cust (fellow, 1751).

[25] Cf. J. S. Reynolds, *The Evangelicals at Oxford, 1735–1871* (1975), p. 183, and *HUO* v. 463. He was sub-warden and curate of Wolvercote, 1765.

[26] Catalogus Vetus, p. 82

[27] Foster, *Alumni Oxonienses*, i. 95.

[28] Ibid., i. 96.

[29] Ibid., iii. 1291.

Winchester.[30] Indeed of the 159 only two were written down in the University Matriculation Register as plebeians.[31] Some fellows became royal chaplains, as Philip Bearcroft did to George II, Henry Barton (as warden), the Hon. George Hamilton, Shute Barrington, and Erasmus Saunders to George III. Saunders was to serve as chaplain to four sovereigns, surviving into the reign of Queen Victoria.

Towards the end of the century Cox characterized the fellowship in the days of Warden Scrope Berdmore as 'becoming ... yearly more and more, not a provision and permanent residence for ecclesiastical students (as the Founder intended it), but a pleasant occasional resort, a kind of Club-house [as All Souls' had already become] for men of good family, with now and then a dash of military titles'.[32] The reference to the army may relate to the Hon. John Sherard, son of the earl of Harborough, who became lieutenant of the Yeomen of the Guard, or to the Hon. Edward Capel, son of the earl of Essex, who became a general in the army and was 'shot at, like a pigeon', at the siege of Cadiz in 1810.[33]

How were the fellows elected? We know from Warden Holland's registers that in his day there were competitive examinations which lasted three days, in 1712 and again in 1717.[34] Firstly it was decided which should be the authors selected for examination. Three Latin authors and three Greek were chosen, and also a topic for a Latin essay. The Latin authors selected in 1712 were Horace, Tacitus, and Juvenal; Homer, Xenophon, and Lucian were the Greek. The essay set was a quotation from Terence, 'a great and memorable deed is not achieved without danger'.[35] Thus the Merton candidates who were put to this test must have been taught these authors, as we know that comparable candidates at Christ Church were, by their tutors. How long this standard was maintained through the century is doubtful; we also know that other influences played at times a decisive role, such as whether a candidate was Whig or Tory at least until those divisions began to lose their relevance in the middle years of the century. By then, however, we have other evidence which shows what influences might be brought to bear on the fellows at an election

---

[30] Foster, *Alumni Oxonienses*, iv. 1355; ibid., p. 1576; Ward, *Georgian Oxford*, p. 101.

[31] Joseph Bullock (fellow, 1735) and Nathaniel Booth (fellow, 1763).

[32] Cox, *Recollections*, p. 168.

[33] G. C. Brodrick, *Memories and Impressions* (1900), p. 110.

[34] Reg. 4.21, pp. 39, 68. In 1712 there were twelve candidates, in 1717 ten.

[35] Ibid., p. 39; 'Non fit sine periculo facinus magnum et memorabile'.

for the parliamentary university seat or at an individual fellowship examination. There are three lists surviving from John Robinson's wardenship in which the influences are named for each individual fellow and in the fellowship elections for those which might affect the thirteen senior electing fellows.[36]

One influence affecting fellowship elections was undoubtedly kinship. Since the head of the house was free to marry and Warden Lydall had had seven or eight children,[37] it is not surprising to find that under his wardenship his son, John, was elected to a fellowship in 1700.[38] Warden Holland had no sons, but his nephew, Richard Meadowcourt, was elected, while he was warden,[39] and proved a very contentious Whig who sought to embroil the government and the university. He also hoped for promotion from a series of Whig patrons, Lord Cowper, Mr Craggs, and Baron Carteret, none of whom for different reasons gave him the high ecclesiastical promotion which he wanted, and when at last he became a canon and prebendary in his native Worcester cathedral, it was less than he had expected.[40]

The most striking dynasty of fellows was related to Charles Bean, the son of a Worcestershire clergyman who was himself elected to a fellowship from Magdalen Hall in 1700. Two of his sons, Charles Bean the younger (fellow from 1731) and Robert Bean (fellow from 1740), became members of the Governing Body and each of them was presented to a college living, Charles the younger to Lapworth in 1751 and Robert to the valuable vicarage of Malden, which he held from 1760 to 1792.[41] Appointments of father and son were quite common, where the father had begotten his son after resigning his fellowship and taking another career. Thus John Wall senior (fellow 1734), who had left Merton by 1740, lived to see his son, John Wall the younger, become a fellow in 1765.[42] To judge from Fanny Burney's description of him the son was nowhere near the equal of his father – 'the most queerly droll character, she had ever met, the most absurdly odd face and the most ridiculous of wigs'. He did, however, succeed in fol-

[36] Ward, *Georgian Oxford*, p. 284, quoting MSS BL Add. MS 39, 311, fos. 141; 34, 740, fos. 311–12; 37, 682, fo. 216.

[37] *LTAW* iii. 436.

[38] Catalogus Vetus, p. 50.

[39] 7 March 1716. Meadowcroft was dismissed from his fellowship because his prebend was found incompatible with his fellowship at the visitation of 1738; see below, n. 86.

[40] Ward, *Georgian Oxford*, p. 103.

[41] For Lapworth, see Hudson, *Memorials*, pp. 187–8; for Malden, Ross, *Malden*, p. 93.

[42] W. H. McMenemey, *History of Worcester Royal Infirmary*, pp. 108, 115.

lowing his father's profession as a physician, first at Worcester and then at Gloucester, where he oversaw the Poor Infirmary. A more fortunate pair of fellows who were father and son were Scrope Berdmore the elder and his son of the same name. The elder, the son of a clergyman at Nottingham, became a postmaster, fellow from 1731, principal of the postmasters, and a canon and prebendary of Southwell minster. His son (fellow from 1768) did even better for himself since, having been proctor in 1776, doctor of theology, and incumbent of a string of benefices, he was elected warden in 1790 and held the vice-chancellorship in 1797–8. Nares writes of him as of one who sought to reform the college in the years of his wardenship.[43] Two other pairs of fellows linked by kinship are worth mentioning, the Rudings and the Kilners; for Walter Ruding, a member of a well-known Whig family of Leicestershire,[44] after a medical training became a physician at Huntingdon and died senior fellow in 1789 when the author of the Catalogus Vetus described him as 'a man of manifold learning, most agreeable in his manners, and most notable for his singular modesty'. As one of the nine seniors nominating a postmaster he naturally nominated his nephew, Rogers Ruding, and Rogers became one of the most celebrated of the fellows engaged in the study of antiquity for his classic work, *Annals of the Coinage*.[45] It was antiquities also which preoccupied Joseph Kilner (fellow from 1741). One reason for his interest in the history of the college is suggested by the words of the inscription on his tomb at Cirencester, 'After a life of infirmity most graciously alleviated and wonderfully lengthened out to more than seventy-two years he died 3 June 1793': unable to lead a fuller life he took to scholarship. It is clear that as rector of Farleigh and of the sinecure moiety of Gamlingay and then vicar of Lapworth (1788–93) he was a steady non-resident on his benefices. He had to employ a curate at Lapworth to act on his behalf.[46] Samuel Kilner, his brother (fellow 1753–1815), was senior fellow when he died in college. As postmaster his patron had been Walter Ruding,[47]

---

[43] E.2.41., i. 154.

[44] From Westcotes Manor near Leicester.

[45] 'Vir multiplici eruditione moribus suavissimis et singulari modestia, spectatissimus' (Catalogus Vetus, p. 58) and see below, p. 257 and n. 113.

[46] Archbishop Tenison in 1710 specifically allowed Farleigh or Diddington to be held at the same time as a fellowship since neither was worth more than £50 (*Statutes and Ordinances*, pp. 59–60).

[47] Reg. 2.2 a, p. 161.

which is not surprising since he had 'a mother in Leicestershire'.[48] His elegant appearance is caught in Dighton's sketch of 1808, 'A view of Merton College'. The list of fellows linked by kinship could easily be continued with the Martens, the Ogles, and others, but enough has been said to demonstrate the close-knit relationship of many of the fellows and the important part played in establishing the web by the system of nominating the postmasters.

The Leicestershire links between the Rudings and the Kilners remind us that the college had been a Leicestershire landowner at Kibworth and Barkby since the days of Simon de Montfort. In 1788 it recruited a Leicestershire postmaster in Peter Vaughan. He was one of the sons of the notable Leicester doctor, James Vaughan, who furthered the foundation of Leicester Royal Infirmary.[49] Peter's brothers were all educated by their father and made successful careers. Peter became principal of the postmasters (1797), proctor (1805), and warden (1810–26). Although his wardenship cannot be said to have been distinguished his tenure of his office reflects the high point of the Leicestershire influence.

Another region where the college had livings and lands and which made itself felt in Oxford was Northumberland and County Durham. The fact that the two livings of Embleton and Ponteland were among the best-endowed probably had much to do with it.[50]

Another influence was political patronage, as is suggested by the valuable lists which Professor Ward has discussed. The purpose of one of the lists is made clear in its heading. 'The Warden, ye 13 electing members of Merton College together with the names of their patrons, their connections etc.'[51] The Warden and the thirteen fellows elected to the fellowships: the junior fellows who have no votes are specifi-

---

[48] BL Add. MS 37, 682, fo. 216.

[49] Reg. 2.2 a, p. 151. On some of Vaughan's family connections, see E. R. Frizelle and J. D. Martin, *The Leicester Royal Infirmary* (Leicester, 1971), pp. 44–51, and 74.

[50] We can identify the following fellows who came from Northumberland or Co. Durham, one of whom was the son of a warden: Robinson (fellow, 1721, vicar of Ponteland, 1753–61), Thomas Balliff (fellow, 1727), William Lambe (fellow, 1731), John Robinson (son of Thomas, fellow, 1738, warden, 1750–9), James Snowdon (fellow, 1740, vicar of Ponteland, 1762), Newton Ogle (fellow, 1748), Nathaniel Ellison (fellow, 1761), J. S. Ogle (fellow, 1788), Ralph Carr (fellow, 1789). Robinson, Bailiff, Snowdon, Ogle, and Ellison were all elected fellows from Lincoln College. Robinson, Bailiff, Snowdon, and Ellison had all enjoyed exhibitions at Lincoln, where links with the north-east had been enhanced by the long tenure of the see of Durham by Nathaniel, Lord Crewe, and by his foundation of the Crewe exhibitioners. We are grateful to Dr V. H. H. Green for information about the Crewe benefaction.

[51] BL Add. MS 37, 682, fos. 216–216ᵛ.

cally set aside at the bottom of the list. We learn that Dr Snowdon may be approached via the duke of Marlborough or the visitor. 'He comes very far north' (he was a Northumbrian). The duke of Marlborough is also named for two others, Mr Bell and Mr Blencowe, but he is specifically excluded in the reference to Mr Barclay, 'tho he was his patron'. Another local grandee, the earl of Macclesfield, is named for Mr Francis Rowden, who owed his postmastership to another gentleman in east Oxfordshire, Sir John Doyly of Chiselhampton. Rowden was presented in 1773 and 1774 to the college livings of Ibstone and Cuxham in the same area.[52] Bishops and local canons might naturally be named as influencing clerics, as were the bishop of Worcester and Canon Philip Barton of Christ Church for Henry Barton, the future warden; the bishop of Bath and Wells (Edward Willes, bishop 1743–73) might be turned to for Mr Wright, 'but not thro' his father'. Mr Stillingfleet, grandson of Bishop Stillingfleet, could be approached via the earl of Dartmouth, an old Whig connection. Mr Twynihoe, we are told, is 'a Dorset man' and so may be reached through Lord Shaftesbury. Poor Mr Kent 'may be gained by ye prospect of a good living. He is upon a poor curacy at Potterne.' His father came from Potterne, Wiltshire. Sometimes the information seems gratuitous. After telling us that Mr Bell has neither father nor mother, we are told that 'his sister keeps a boarding-school at Reading'. The junior fellow without a vote, who might succeed if a voting fellow died, was Mr Jennings. He might be approached through Lord Ligonier, to whom his brother, Captain Jennings, was an aide-de-camp. Altogether we are given a behind-the-scenes view of influences which could have been at work at fellowship elections in the late 1750s, for the document can be dated after 5 August 1755 and before the death of Warden Robinson in 1759. It remains a matter of great interest that at this date a fellowship election at Merton could still be of such concern to the government.

By the end of the century the nature of fellowship elections seems to have changed. The multiple elections of 1705, 1711, 1717, and 1723 had vanished as a result of the visitation of 1738. They had been inspired by the need to keep up the number of BA fellows for educational purposes until adequate replacements for them could be guaranteed. This had led to the deferment of elections of BA fellows to full MA status, to their annoyance. In 1752 the archbishop relented

---

[52] BL Add. MS 37, 740 (1750–3 August 1753).

a little and allowed three fellows to be elected together, but the old extreme position had been permanently abandoned.[53] By the end of the century we no longer hear of the selection of Latin and Greek texts set for viva-voce examination. Edward Nares was a candidate on three separate occasions, 1783, 1787 and finally, with success, 1788. Of the 1783 election he wrote: 'The elections always taking place on the 2nd of August. The candidates are nominated according to their standing in the university, and as they are nominated, elected or rejected. It so happens therefore often that the three vacancies were filled up before the junior candidates have an opportunity of being nominated, and this happened to myself twice' (i.e. in 1783 and again in 1787). Of the 1787 election he commented, 'I thought I had numerous friends among the electors, had I been high enough among the candidates.' Thus there was literally no chance of a junior being elected so long as anyone senior and electable was standing, and all semblance of serious competitive examination seems to have been dispensed with. Nares records that, when he was elected unanimously in 1788, it was 'under circumstances which would have served to set me aside, had there been any disposition so to do, for I kept my bed at the time and every form attending the election was obliged to be dispensed with'.[54]

Two Merton fellows who were elected in the eighteenth century subsequently held chairs, Gilbert Trowe of Abingdon and Thomas Hardcastle. Trowe was elected fellow at the 'Golden Election' of 1705. He attracted attention by writing a set of verses on the death in 1708 of George, prince of Denmark, the consort of Queen Anne. After 1714 he became a Hanover Tory and a doctor of medicine (1724), before being appointed Sherardian professor of botany and keeper of the Physic Garden. He kept his chair from 1724 to 1734 when he resigned; but he continued to reside in college, acting as deputy for the professor of medicine (Woodforde) for the next twenty years.[55]

Thomas Hardcastle (fellow, 1775) came from Queen's. He was a college tutor who worked in partnership with Nathaniel Booth, fellow, from 1784 to 1786 and with John Wall, fellow, from 1787 to 1795. He was appointed Rawlinson professor of Anglo-Saxon in 1800.[56] His

[53] *HUO* v. 235 and n.
[54] E.2.41, I.133 and cf. ibid. 49 (1783), 115–116 (1787). For the importance of seniority, see *HUO* v. 241–2.
[55] *HUO* v. 717.
[56] Ibid., p. 828 and n.

career is further evidence of the interest in Anglo-Saxon which developed during the eighteenth century.

Given the college's adherence to the Whig cause after 1709 it is not surprising that some of its members reached the episcopal bench. In England three fellows held important dioceses. John Gilbert, son of a fellow of Wadham, another Whig college, was elected a fellow of Merton from Trinity in 1717. He improved his prospects by marrying the sister of the Whig earl of Harborough. His daughter married into the Mount Edgcumbe family, and he seems to have exercised influence in the diocese of Exeter, of which he became dean in 1726. He reached the archbishopric of York in 1757, having travelled via the sees of Llandaff (1740) and Salisbury (1748). Several of his sermons were printed, but his soubriquet of 'leaden' suggests that he was anything but inspiring, whilst the record of a dispute in which he was involved at Salisbury demonstrates that he was all too ready to stand on his dignity.[57]

More interesting and influential was Shute Barrington, son of Viscount Barrington. He was a gentleman commoner of Merton, elected to a fellowship in 1755. He was also an active Whig politician, when a canon of Christ Church, though it may be to his credit that, sent down to Oxford by the duke of Newcastle to oppose the election of Henry Barton as warden in 1759, he was won over by Barton's claims and failed to carry out his instructions.[58] He won his way to the wealthy see of Durham through Llandaff and Salisbury, like Gilbert, in his ascent. His appointment at Salisbury seems to have owed much to George III and was opposed by the prime minister, Shelburne, who wanted the bishopric for a protégé.[59] The king was doubtless moved by the strong support which Barrington gave to the Protestant establishment. He set out his grounds for that support in print and entered into a controversy with John Lingard on the matter.[60] As bishop of Durham he interested himself in encouraging a system of parochial lending libraries and setting up the Barrington schools.[61] Yet although he became president of the society for promoting religious and Chris-

---

[57] *DNB*; Ward, *Georgian Oxford*, p. 164. He married Margaret Sherard, sister of Philip, earl of Harborough (whose son John became a fellow in 1734).

[58] *HUO* v. 147 n.

[59] J. Norris, *Shelburne and Reform* (1963), 251; cf. also Nichols, *Literary History*, v. 610–14.

[60] *Controversy between John Lingard and Shute Barrington* (1811).

[61] John C. Day, 'Parochial libraries in Northumberland', *Library History*, viii. 4 (1989), 100; Sir Thomas Bernard, *The Barrington Schools* (London, 1812). He contributed to the purchase of the Pinelli manuscripts by the Bodleian Library (*HUO* v. 745).

tian piety in the diocese of Durham neither he nor his clergy reached out in any effective way to the industrial population of his diocese.[62]

Another of the well-connected, the Hon. James Cornwallis, became bishop of Coventry and Lichfield in 1781. He had the unusual distinction of succeeding to the earldom of Cornwallis towards the end of his life as 14th earl Cornwallis and thus combined a temporal with a spiritual peerage in one person, making a fitting registrar of the Order of the Garter.[63] To Merton he gave its most beautiful and elegant set of four candlesticks.

John Hume, a former Merton commoner and graduate of Corpus, held the lesser sees of Bristol (1756–8) and Oxford (1758–68) before reaching the more ancient and better endowed see of Salisbury (1766–82). He was bishop of Oxford at the time of the expulsion of the 'methodists' from St Edmund Hall.[64]

To the church of Ireland Merton sent Robert Downes, successively bishop of Ferns (1744–52), Down (1752–3), and Raphoe (1753–63).

THE VISITOR AND THE VISITATION OF 1738

When John Holland died in May 1734 the fellows of Merton set Archbishop Wake a knotty problem. Of the three candidates whose names were sent to Lambeth two at least, the first and the third, must have seemed to Wake distinctly unattractive. The first, John Marten, sub-warden and senior fellow, and a doctor of medicine, had been a leader of the Tory interest in the largely Whig college.[65] The third, Richard Meadowcourt, was Holland's nephew, an able man, but one who had already shown himself to be tactless and ambitious. There remained the second, Robert Wyntle, who having been chosen one of Dr Radcliffe's first travelling fellows in 1715 had some claim to academic distinction.[66] For whatsoever reason Wake chose Wyntle. It was soon to prove a disastrous choice. Marten never reconciled

---

[62] W. B. Maynard, 'The response of the Church of England to economic and social change; the archdeaconry of Durham, 18 Oct. 1851', *JEH* 43/3 (1991), 437–62.

[63] *DNB*.

[64] *Handbook of British Chronology*, pp. 231, 264, and 272.

[65] Ward, *Georgian Oxford*, p. 99. His patron was Warden Marten, so he was probably a kinsman. He was a man of an imperious temper, to judge by his behaviour as librarian: see p. 265 and n.

[66] Nias, *Dr John Radcliffe*, pp. 42–3. A list exists of some 150 books in his library on 3 April 1716. Many were medical (P.3.26). See also above, p. 237.

himself to the preferment of his medical colleague from the Golden Election of 1705. Moreover Wyntle had shown himself to be a 'militant whig'. What was worse he was a reformer. How soon it emerged that the new warden was determined to continue Holland's attempts at reform is unclear. But once he had determined on asking the arch-bishop for a visitation on 13 May 1735[67] it was evident that he intended to raise a wide range of complaints against the sub-wardens of 1734 and 1735, against the bursars and individual fellows, and to prevent non-resident fellows from enjoying the full profits of fellowship for six weeks, as they had done from 1695 to the early years of Dr Holland's wardenship.[68] That the thirteenth-century statutes, as adjusted by successive archbishops and wardens, including both Laud and Savile, were creaking badly in the eighteenth century is hardly surprising, but to take on the task of looking at them afresh single-handed was brave of Wyntle, if not foolhardy. Moreover the warden was unlucky in his archbishop, since Wake was dying. Events had to wait on his death, the subsequent vacancy, and the election of Archbishop Potter. Gilbert Trowe, the sub-warden, told the warden 'in contumely' 'to take the labouring oar upon himself and to Lambeth'. He knew full well that for the moment nothing could be done in London.[69]

The first matter on which the warden, the sub-warden, and the bursars fell out was the question of the warden's allowances. Wyntle started to put the Warden's Lodgings to rights after what seems to have been a period of neglect. The ringleader of the hostile reaction to this process was his enemy Marten, then one of the bursars. He 'never hath nor will submit to Dr. Wyntle's being Warden of the College and therefore hath never paid him any appointments'.[70] The livery which under the statutes of 1264[71] covered the payment for a winter and a summer gown had had to be increased to meet the rising costs. Bishop Thomas Kempe had left money for the purpose with which the manors of Canes and Norton Mandeville in Essex had been bought in 1490.[72] Warden Savile followed in 1604 and 1622 by allotting the rent of the newly purchased farm of Gamlingay Avenells to the

[67] Reg. 1.6, p. 53; cf. Reg. 1.4, p. 37 (2 April 1737).

[68] Reg. 1.6, p. 161.

[69] Reg. 1.4, p. 38; Reg. 1.6, p. 99 (16 June); Dr Marten thought that the difference should be settled at a scrutiny and dissented from petitioning the visitor.

[70] Reg. 1.6, p. 54.

[71] *MM*, p. 15.

[72] *RACM 1483–1521*, pp. 140–1.

same purpose.[73] Bursar Marten during his term of office paid Wyntle no share of these liveries. He refused to pay bills sanctioned by the warden on the grounds that the college could not afford to increase the warden's allocation, and in denying him any additional payment for his liveries he positively reduced his allowances. The sub-warden, Gilbert Trowe, followed his bad example, but let the cat out of the bag. He instructed the bursars not to pay any of the warden's bills 'by way of punishment for endeavouring to reform the fellows'.[74] In December 1735 Charles Moseley, the third bursar, refused to pay one of the warden's bills.[75] Again the bursars for 1734/5, 1735/6 and 1736/7 all belonged to Marten's faction – besides Marten himself (one of the bursars in each of these years), Trowe (bursar twice), Moseley (bursar twice), and Woolley. The warden was brought to a standstill. Three of the junior fellows, Wall, Newey, and Williamson, called on the warden and, though they needed his permission before they could proceed to magistracy, and, it seems, though they had not performed the necessary bachelors' exercises, told him that they intended to proceed to their degrees 'in spite of his teeth'.[76] However Wyntle fought back gamely. John Potter, the bishop of Oxford, who must have well understood the situation and was himself a Whig, was translated from Oxford to Canterbury on 28 February 1737. By 13 June the fellows feared that the warden had called for a visitation. On 16 June Marten tried to delay matters by asserting that before recourse was had to the visitor, which would entail great expense, an attempt to settle the differences should be made at a scrutiny. The effort was vain. Too much damage had already been done, and visitation followed in 1738.

Marten made yet one more attempt to stave off retribution. On 1 June 1738 he applied for a writ of prohibition against Potter on the grounds that the archbishop of Canterbury was not the visitor of the college.[77] One cannot but admire Marten's cheek. He had noted that in the Foundation Statutes of 1264 the visitor named was the bishop of Winchester. But between 1274 and 1276 Walter de Merton had changed his mind and named or accepted the archbishop of Can-

---

[73] Reg. 1.6, pp. 24–5, and to encourage Divinity Disputations.

[74] Reg. 1.6, pp. 52–3.

[75] Ibid., p. 54; Reg. 1.4, p. 29. The warden wished to refer his complaints to the visitor. Moseley seems to have had an unhappy way with him. He was refused admission to the High Borlase Club of ultra Tories (*MMC*, p. 141) and as pro-proctor had his windows broken (July 1723) (Reg. 4.22, p. 2).

[76] Reg. 1.6, p. 177.

[77] Reg. 1.4, pp. 43–4; *MMC*, p. 147.

terbury. Potter's lawyers had little trouble in showing that successive archbishops had ever since fulfilled the office of visitor. The visitation went ahead and the archbishop's five commissioners proceeded. Already on 2 June 1738 Marten had been deprived of his fellowship on the grounds that he possessed estates which were of a value to make them incompatible with the tenure of a fellowship.[78]

In scrutinizing the extent to which the fellows were obeying the injunction making a fellowship incompatible with a 'richer benefice' (*uberius beneficium*), the visitor, the commissioners, and the warden were inviting trouble, for the Foundation Statutes did not define the value of a richer benefice. Archbishop Laud in 1640 had no hesitation in stating that anything more than eight marks per annum was inadmissible.[79] Archbishop Tenison muddied the waters in 1710 when he recognized that eight marks had become outdated, and set a lower limit of £50 per annum. He then named two of the college livings, Diddington and Farleigh, as being worth less than £50 per annum and thus compatible with the tenure of a fellowship. The fellows needed no such encouragement to seek to combine a fellowship with a compatible benefice. There was also a legal argument about what constituted a benefice. Marten argued that an estate in perpetuity was not a benefice.[80] Wyntle claimed that Marten had a freehold estate at Radford, Oxfordshire, of £80 per annum and the proceeds of the tithes of Burmington, to which he was entitled as senior fellow. They were not a benefice but worth £50 or £60 just the same. In addition he had freehold property from the church of Salisbury worth between £100 and £200 and more at Headington, Oxford, worth £30 per annum.[81] His was the most flagrant case, but there were others. Henry Dunster, a non-resident lawyer, whom we have already met when Holland fined him for his failure to carry out his variations,[82] was said to have an estate in Hertfordshire worth £700 per annum.[83] He had anticipated his fate by resigning his fellowship on 8 August 1737,[84] but for good

---

[78] Reg. 1.4, p. 42.

[79] *MM*, p. 15; *Statutes and Ordinances*, pp. 6, 53.

[80] *Statutes and Ordinances*, pp. 59–60, see above, pp. 243 and n. In 1754 the limit was raised to £50 (*HUO* v. 246). In the 19th cent. the disqualification was restricted to real property and freehold offices (E. Hobhouse, *Sermons and Addresses*, ed. W. Hobhouse (1905), p. xxxv).

[81] Reg. 1.6, p. 87.

[82] Reg. 4.22, p. 19 (17 Dec. 1728).

[83] Reg. 1.6, p. 87.

[84] Ibid., pp. 86–7.

measure he was deprived by the commissioners. Richard Streat, who held the sinecure moiety of Gamlingay, worth £80 per annum, had also resigned by the time Wyntle sent his name to the archbishop.[85] Then there was Richard Meadowcourt, Holland's nephew and one of the candidates at the election for the wardenship. He was a canon and prebendary of Worcester.[86] He may have hoped that by becoming warden he might have got away with holding the prebend, for it would have been compatible with being warden. Indeed his uncle as warden had held a prebend of Worcester. But he too fell under the axe of the commissioners and was deprived of his fellowship on the ground of incompatibility. Another fellow whom Wyntle accused of breaking Archbishop Laud's injunction was Samuel Woolley, vicar of St Peter's-in-the-East, who also had a living worth £80 per annum. In 1754 Archbishop Herring increased the limit to £80 per annum.

Wyntle met the argument that the college could not afford to put up his allowance in two ways. He noted that the fellows' stipends had been increased fifteen-fold since 1264 from fifty shillings to £38. 1s. 0d. per annum.[87] In the same period the warden's had only gone up four times. Again he drew attention to an extravagant practice which contravened the original statutes. An absent fellow on the necessary business of the college such as a riding bursar might be paid his fellowship quite legitimately.[88] However, we find that by 1714 it had become customary to pay some absent fellows £20 per annum in lieu of their allocation, liveries, and share of the fines.[89] This practice held for a fellow who, for instance, was serving as a chaplain in the household of a bishop, as Francis Astry was in the household of John Robinson, bishop of London. The same was allowable for John Tisser, for nine years chaplain to the English factory at Smyrna, and for Henry Stephens and John Nichol, who acted as chaplains to the English factory at Oporto.[90] Wyntle himself had enjoyed this benefit for the first two years when he was a Radcliffe Travelling Fellow. But more surprisingly the custom was extended to those who practised

---

[85] Reg. 1.6, p. 86.

[86] Ibid., pp. 86–7; *Statutes and Ordinances*, p. 68.

[87] For the fifty shillings allowance cf. *MM*, p. 15. For the 1274 Statutes and the warden's allowance, ibid., p. 25. Wyntle claimed that the wardenship though publicly thought to be worth £500 per annum was only worth £200 per annum (Reg. 1.6, p. 38). It had been estimated at £200 per annum in 1612 (*MMC*, p. 96 n. 1).

[88] For the comparable value of fellowships at other colleges see *HUO* v. 238–9.

[89] Reg. 4.21, p. 55.

[90] *MMC*, pp. 298–9; Reg. 4.21, pp. 17, 56.

medicine. Such were Martin Hartopp and Thomas Cox at Nottingham and John Wall at Worcester until he married.[91] Wyntle claimed that in this way the college was spending between £300 and £400 on payments to absent fellows clean contrary to the Founder's intentions.[92] Certainly absence meant that often little more than half the fellows resided.[93] On the other hand Marten as bursar had failed to pay Wyntle for the last year of his travelling fellowship although it had been agreed that he should be paid. One feels that there perhaps the warden was trying to have it both ways.

The commissioners certainly moved to control the absences of fellows. Henceforth they would require the express permission of the visitor if they were absent for more than six months.[94] The warden and five seniors could give permission for between four and six months. An absence register must be kept so that absences could be more carefully controlled, and this was done,[95] though the entries in it die out after 1757. Nor had the problem been solved for all time, as the future was to show.

A further very reasonable cause of complaint by the warden concerned the way in which both Marten when bursar, and Trowe as subwarden, acted or summoned meetings and took decisions without the warden being consulted. When their actions involved college servants they spread confusion, even if the episodes in themselves do not sound of major importance. Thus when a junior fellow, Mr Berdmore, was exceptionally presiding in Hall, he took the occasion to sconce the college groom, William Pain. When the next day the warden paid the groom's sconce, Mr Berdmore sconced him again for obeying the warden. When the warden again remitted the sconce the bursar sconced the groom and deprived him of seventeen weeks' wages and sustenance.[96] When Wyntle tried to maintain the rule that fellows who wished to enjoy their commons should do so at the common table and ordered that the commons of Mr Berdmore should be sent up into the Hall, Mr Berdmore had the order countermanded and had the commons sent down again[97] – exchanges very confusing

---

[91] A similar £20 was allowed in lieu of allocations, liveries, and share of fines for the year of grace, as in August 1714 to Mr Stephens (Reg. 4.21, p. 56).

[92] Reg. 1.6, pp. 40,44.

[93] *HUO* v. 239–40, 241 and n. 4.

[94] *Statutes and Ordinances*, pp. 64–5.

[95] Reg. 2.22.

[96] Reg. 1.6, p. 94, and see below, p. 275.

[97] Reg. 1.6, p. 82.

for the staff, to put it mildly. In another incident the servants again found themselves in the cross-fire. William Brown, the barber, who had been appointed by Warden Holland on the advice of Sir John Doyly, was expelled by the sub-warden, it seemed, without reason. On 31 December 1734 without the warden's knowledge the sub-warden held a scrutiny in the warden's absence and confirmed the expulsion of the barber: he held that the office had become obsolete and useless and instructed the bursars not to pay Brown in future.[98] Christopher Shute was accused of holding his fellowship while possessed of an estate worth £200–£300. Shute gave way and resigned.[99]

Other complaints against the fellows concerned the misuse of rooms in Fellows' Quad and the nuisance of their dogs in chapel. Wyntle stated that, when Fellows' Quad had been built, it had been the intention that the postmasters should occupy the ground-floor rooms under the rooms of the nine MA fellows, but that gradually these rooms had been usurped and turned into apartments or let to gentlemen commoners or to commoners. He asked that the post-masters should be allowed to occupy these rooms, if necessary in pairs and paying a rent of £40 per annum each.[100] As to the dogs, 'the [fellows'] dogs being frequently very troublesome in the chappel in the time of Divine Service', when the warden 'thought proper one morning after Prayers to order the sexton some way or other to get rid of the Dogs', Charles Bean, one of the junior masters, 'set up a whistle at the Warden's going out of chappel and whistled him to his Lodgings in the Presence of all the Young People that had been at Prayers that morning'. It seemed that one of the dogs belonged to him.[101] For their part the fellows complained of the warden whom 'scarce anything less than absolute power will satisfy'.

That Wyntle was in some measure to blame for the imbroglio is suggested by the fact that, although Archbishop Potter had appointed competent commissioners[102] to go over all the details of the settle-ment, his injunctions had no sooner been made than the warden disagreed with the fellows over their interpretation. At the election of 1738 the warden objected to three of the candidates because they

[98] Reg. 1.6, pp. 95–6, 98. and see below, p. 275.
[99] Reg. 1.6, p. 87.
[100] Ibid., p. 72.
[101] Ibid., p. 82.
[102] Reg. 1.4, p. 49. They included four heads of houses, Stephen Niblett, warden of All Souls' and vice-chancellor, John Mather, president of Corpus Christi College, Thomas Cockman, master of University College, and Dr Holmes, president of St John's College.

came from dioceses where in 1274 the college had no benefices or fees, but one of them, Theed Haywood, came from the diocese of Oxford where the college had both a living and land at Cuxham. The argument that the diocese of Oxford, as an Henrician foundation, had not existed at the time of the 1274 Statutes had already been dismissed by the visitor who for this purpose recognized that it was part of the diocese of Lincoln in the thirteenth century. Haywood was accordingly admitted and the warden's claim to the right of veto at a fellowship election was never made good.[103] By 1740 Potter had lost patience with the warden and fellows alike, and told Wyntle to seek to live in peace and concord with his society.[104]

The same Whig connection which after 1709 brought to its fellows royal chaplaincies, bishoprics, canonries and prebends, and, at a lower level, Whitehall preacherships,[105] also prevented it from providing heads of Tory colleges. Until 1760 or so its fellows would have been unacceptable at any college other, perhaps, than Wadham, Exeter, or Jesus, during the time that they were mainly Whig. It is also true that in the eighteenth century it was customary to elect heads from inside the colleges. At all events, apart from D'Blosiers Tovey who became principal of New Inn Hall in 1732,[106] the only other Merton fellow to become head of a house outside Merton was George Sandby, who was master of Magdalene College, Cambridge from 1760 to 1774. He was imposed there by the visitor, the countess of Portsmouth, to keep the post warm for her step-grandson, who in 1760 was a boy at Eton.[107] By contrast all six wardens of Merton were former fellows, even though Holland and Wyntle had begun life at other institutions, Magdalen Hall and Pembroke respectively.

---

[103] Cf. *HUO* v. 231 and n. Wyntle seems to have relied too closely on the original statutes. The restriction on drawing the fellows from the dioceses where the endowments were situated had been abolished by 1569 (*MMC*, p. 269).

[104] Reg. 1.4, p. 85 (31 Jan. 1740). He 'hopes you will in a peaceable way endeavour to settle everything with your society'.

[105] Edmund Gibson, bishop of London in 1723, had deliberately invented the Whitehall preacherships in order to extend his patronage (Ward, *Georgian Oxford*, pp. 131 ff.).

[106] Foster, *Alumni Oxonienses*, p. 1498. Tovey had been a Hanover Tory, which may explain his appointment as principal of New Inn Hall by a Tory chancellor.

[107] P. Cunich, D. Hoyle, E. Duffy, and R. Hyma, *A History of Magdalene College, Cambridge 1428–1988* (Cambridge, 1994), pp. 180–2.

DOCTORS OF MEDICINE, LAWYERS, THEOLOGIANS

As has already been noted the eighteenth century saw the end of the series of medical wardens.[108] Serious students of medicine no longer contented themselves with studying medicine at Oxford but went to Edinburgh or Leiden to pursue their studies. The foundation of the Radcliffe Travelling Fellowships[109] underlines the point, for Radcliffe, a highly successful doctor, saw the need for Oxford medical students to gain their knowledge somewhere other than at Oxford. Two of the Merton fellows enjoyed Radcliffe fellowships, Warden Robert Wyntle and David Hartley.[110] Though Wyntle took up his fellowship and travelled, he suffered himself from illness and is not known to have made a positive contribution to medicine, whilst David Hartley, though outstanding in many ways, did not settle to the medical career which tenure of the fellowship seemed to promise, but entered politics (Pl. 24).[111] The most notable doctor from among the fellows was undoubtedly John Wall senior, who is said to have gained his practical training at St Thomas's (Pl. 23). He attended the Oxford medical course and may have attended the lectures which were given in the laboratory of the Old Ashmolean. Wall became a member of the Royal Society and read a paper to it on the use of musk in cases of convulsions and another on Peruvian bark (quinine) in cases of smallpox (a pioneering study). His paper on distemper in cattle and man was also of practical value, and he went some way towards popularizing Malvern as a spa for taking the waters. He was one of the four original physicians of the Royal Infirmary in his native town of Worcester where he practised medicine. His principal fame, however, rests on the Royal Worcester Porcelain Works, which he founded. He used his experience of anatomical drawing to provide some of its early designs.[112] Though, apart from Wall, few Mertonians were active academic contributors to medical studies, that did not mean that the

---

[108] See above, p. 237.

[109] *HUO* v. 694–5.

[110] Nias, *Dr John Radcliffe*, pp. 42–3, 51–3.

[111] He entered Parliament as MP for Hull in 1774 and represented it till 1780 and again from 1782 to 1784 (*DNB*). There is a fine portrait of him by Romney, and a crayon drawing by Vaslet in the Warden's Lodgings (Poole, *Catalogue of Oxford Portraits*, ii. 55). The Vaslet drawing is reproduced by Nias in *Dr John Radcliffe*, facing p. 52. See Pl. 24.

[112] W. H. McMenemey, *History of Worcester Royal Infirmary* (1947), pp. 39–40, *DNB*. He was passionately interested in painting all his life and in 1765 presented to Merton an allegorical painting by his own hand entitled 'Paideia' which hung in the hall for many years (cf. D.I.47(ii)).

college did not produce practising doctors. Several of its former fellows and other members were active physicians, as was Edward Worth in Dublin,[113] John Wall junior at Gloucester and Worcester,[114] Walter Ruding at Huntingdon,[115] Martin Hartopp at Leicester,[116] and no fewer than three in Nottingham, Hartopp again, Thomas Cox,[117] and George Aldrich (a graduate).[118] It was from the fortune made by Aldrich that the most important academic benefit came, for he recognized the importance of chemistry in the training of doctors and founded the Aldrichian demonstratorship in Anatomy (1797).[119]

The Founder had hoped that most of the fellows would take their MA and then read for the higher degrees in theology, the BD and DD, but he left a loophole so that four or five might read law.[120] In the thirteenth century that meant Canon or Canon and Civil Law, but Canon Law disappeared at the Reformation. Civil Law continued as a more attractive degree for some than theology, since its holders were less exposed to accusations of theological error than were divines, and there was still some business in the church courts. It is interesting that the future bishop of Durham, Shute Barrington, took a DCL rather than a theological degree. In general, however, the law which the eighteenth-century fellows wanted to read was the Common Law. The foundation of the Vinerian chair in 1758 was an indication of the way things were going.[121] No fewer than fourteen fellows of Merton went to the Bar.[122] Two of them and one former commoner reached the Bench, Edward Willes, Sir Giles Rooke, and Sir Thomas Burnet. Willes was the most distinguished, for he not only became Solicitor-General (1766–8) (an appointment of Pitt's) but earned the com-

---

[113] Reg. 1.4, pp. 7–8.

[114] McMenemey, *History of Worcester Royal Infirmary*, p. 108.

[115] BL Add. MS 34, 740 (dated between 1750 and 3 Aug. 1753).

[116] Ibid.

[117] Hartopp was at Nottingham in 1723 (Ward, *Georgian Oxford*, p. 103); while retaining his fellowship and practising medicine there, he came up to vote at a fellowship election and brazenly claimed thirty guineas from the successful candidates for the cost of his travel from Nottingham and loss of earnings while he was away from his practice.

[118] For Cox, see BL Add. MS 34, 740.

[119] Sinclair and Robb-Smith, p. 41.

[120] *MM*, p. 21.

[121] *HUO* v. 489, Holdsworth, *History of English Law*, xii. 93–5.

[122] C. Moseley, H. Dunster, Hon. J. Sherard, T. Heywood, G. Rooke, E. Willes, J. St John, J. Milles, T. A. Davis, J. R. Hayes, W. Fendal, R. Carr, W. H. Hattley, Hon. C. Puller. Archbishop Potter had extended the number of fellows who might be excused from studying divinity to four or five. This was to cover law and medicine (*Statutes and Ordinances*, p. 64).

mendation of Holdsworth as a sound lawyer and a man of independence of mind.[123] Sir Giles Rooke combined his work as sergeant-at-law and Justice of the Common Pleas (1793–1808) with advising the college on legal affairs. His academic publications, *Scintilla Juris* (1792) and *Thoughts on the propriety of fixing the Easter Term* (1792) were no more than minor contributions even by the generous standards of the eighteenth century.[124] The former commoner, Sir Thomas Burnet, younger son of Bishop Burnet, had a mind of some distinction. He was a pamphleteer of no mean order in the early years of the century; 'an impudent brat', as Hearne has dubbed him, he nevertheless showed himself in *A Certain Information of a Certain Discourse* (2nd edn. 1712), *A Second Tale of a Tub* (1715), and *Mr Burnet's Defence or more reasons for an impeachment* ... (1715) a worthy opponent of Defoe in the pamphlet warfare between the Whigs and their critics.[125] His *Letters to Duckett*[126] show him to have been lively and very well informed. As Justice of the Common Pleas (1741) he enjoyed a reputation for uprightness and learning, but it must be admitted that Merton's benign influence played upon him for only a very short time.

The fellows who read for divinity degrees in the eighteenth century did not write much theology. Edward Welchman, whose work on the Thirty-Nine Articles was very popular,[127] was a rare exception. But many proceeded to the BD and nineteen went on to take the DD as well,[128] before filling college or other livings. Some resided and took their learning with them into the country. It is time to consider the college livings in the eighteenth century; their filling either with former fellows or with other members of the college lay at the heart of the university system.

---

[123] *History of English Law*, xii. 486.
[124] *DNB*; his portrait by Hoppner is in the Hall (Poole, *Catalogue of Oxford Portraits*, ii. 54).
[125] *DNB*.
[126] *Letters of Thomas Burnet to George Duckett, 1712–22*, ed. D. Nichol Smith (Oxford, 1914).
[127] *The XXXIX Articles of The Church of England, confirmed by Texts of Holy Scripture and Testimonies of the Primitive Fathers* (1744). There are five editions and a sixth in translation which was frequently reprinted. Welchman also wrote *A Defence of the Church of England* (1693), *The Husbandman's Manual* (1695), *Dr Clarke's Scripture Doctrine of the Trinity examined* (1714), etc.
[128] The BDs were W. Jennings, J. Norman, N. Booth, R. Ruding, P. Vaughan; and the DDs John Gilbert, F. Astry, J. Cowper, P. Bearcroft, T. Robinson, S. Berdmore the elder, J. Robinson, E. Saunders, J. Nichol, H. Barton, G. Sandby, J. Snowdon, F. White, H. Kent, R. Cust, T. Sainsbury, P. Gunning, S. Berdmore the younger, E. Nares.

COLLEGE LIVINGS

In the early part of the century the college sought to increase the number of its livings. In July 1714, for instance, it was proposed to set aside £60 per annum towards the purchase of advowsons.[129] The same point was made by Warden Holland when he left £60 to the college in his will to that end.[130] Similarly Henry Jackson in 1747 stated that when lands had been purchased whose rents were to provide the stipends of four scholars any residue should be spent on buying an advowson to a living worth £200 per annum.[131] At length in 1797 the college increased its number of fifteen livings by acquiring the advowson of Rushall, Wiltshire.[132] The value of many of the livings was much greater than that of a fellowship and all offered the chance of marriage. What a fellowship itself was worth is not easily determined. It seems to have brought in £38. 10s. 0d. in 1738.[133] We also know that in Warden Holland's time the value of a fellow's liveries, fines, and allocation was compounded at £20 per annum if he was given leave of absence, as Francis Astry was for the five years that he was chaplain to the bishop of London. The problem can also be approached from another direction. It is revealing that the eight fellows elected at the Golden Election of 1705 were unable to take up their fellowships until 1708 because of a lack of funds. It is also known from the evidence of 1738 that between 1716 and 1736 the available income of the college varied between £1761. 6s. 7d. in 1717 and £3013. 14s. 4½d. in 1729,[134] not taking into account half the fines. The warden claimed that his position was worth no more than £200, whilst his critics estimated it at £500.[135] If it was, say, £300 in 1717 that left no more than £1400 with which to pay for all other expenses including the stipends of perhaps twenty-four fellows. It is easy to see why permissible sinecure benefices like Farleigh or the moiety of Gamlingay, and college offices and the post of tutor were much sought

[129] Reg. 4.21, p. 53.

[130] Reg. 1.4, p. 16.

[131] Reg. 2.22, pp. 66–79.

[132] For the legislation of 1736 restricting the number of advowsons to half that of the fellowship see *HUO* v. 117. Merton had more livings than half the number of fellows. This may help to explain the long delay in acquiring Rushall. £20 was allowed to absent fellows in 1714, see above, p. 252 n. 89. £20 was also allowed as a composition for the year of grace after a fellowship had been resigned, see above, p. 253 n. 91.

[133] Reg. 1.6, p. 47.

[134] Ibid., p. 45.

[135] Ibid., p. 38.

after by the resident fellows. Those who had leave to serve as a chaplain to a factory overseas, as Henry Stephens did at Oporto in Portugal (*c.* 1707),[136] were benefiting the resident members of the society by drawing only £20.

In 1736 the college was anxious to point out that its livings were by no means monopolized by its members. At the time it was seeking to influence the debate which led to the Act of that year which restricted the number of advowsons which a college might hold. It then showed that in 45 presentations it had only presented its own fellows on nine occasions. Nevertheless if its more valuable livings are examined it will be seen that with one exception Embleton[137] and Ponteland[138] were held by Mertonians, if not necessarily by former fellows, throughout the century. The same was true of the rich living of Malden,[139] which had the additional advantage of being close to the capital, so that when Rogers Ruding, former fellow, was vicar he could keep in close touch with his fellow members of the Society of Antiquaries and friends in London. Less valuable livings such as Elham[140] in Kent, or Cuxham[141] in Oxfordshire can still show a respectable number of former fellows or graduates as vicars. Cuxham, though poor, might be combined with neighbouring Ibstone in plurality, as it was by both John Doyly and Francis Rowden. Since Doyly's family came from Chiselhampton that made especially good sense for him.

---

[136] He returned in 1707 after nine years as chaplain in Oporto to become proctor and to be presented to the college living of Malden in 1714.

[137] In this and subsequent notes, * denotes MA and/or fellow of Merton. V. Edwards,* 14 Jan. 1680–13 Jan. 1713; R. Parker,* 21 May 1713–28 (*VCH Northumberland*, ii. 71); Dr Tovey,* 2 May 1727–47; J. Parsons,* 4 Sept. 1747–56; W. Clifton (Balliol), 1756–90; G. Turner,* 1790–8; H. Hodges,* Merton MA, 1798–1811. In 1663 the impropriation had been judged worth £300 p. a., the stipend £60 p. a. (ibid., ii. 73), but by 1736, when Dr Tovey was non-resident and James Watson curate, its value was thought better than £200 (ibid.).

[138] (R. Whaley, 1692); R. Parker,* 14 July 1711–22 Dec. 1712; – Middleton, by 4 Aug. 1712; T. Dobbyns,* 1712; H. Byne,* 3 Jan. 1717–; J. Dix,* 23 Oct. 1717; (N. Ogle); T. Robinson,*, (before 1736)–61; J. Snowdon,* 1762–; T. Sainsbury,* 1779–87; J. Rawlins,* 1788–1811. The value of Ponteland was given in 1663 as the rectory £126, and the vicarage £90 (*VCH Northumberland*, xii. 420). Warden Holland said (presumably of the rectory) that it was worth £120 or £130 per annum (Reg. 4.21, pp. 27, 39). By 1736 the incumbent, Dr Robinson,* was non-resident. The living was in the hands of a curate, Edmund Lodge (ibid.).

[139] H. Stephens,* 1714–39; C. Moseley,* 1739–60; R. Bean,* 1760–92; Rogers Ruding,* 1792–(1820). Malden with Chessington was worth £120 per annum in 1657/8 (Ross, *Malden*, p. 86).

[140] Mr Hunt, 1707; Robert Harrison,* 22 Sept. 1707–; John Hill, 14 Nov. 1711–; P. Bearcroft,* 1731–; T. Thompson,* MA, 1773–; E. Fulham,* 1773–; W. Cornwallis,* 1778–.

[141] John Edwards,* 1693–1715; William Marten,* 1715–; John Doyly,* –1773; Francis Rowden,* 1774–1822.

The clearest record survives for the rectory of Lapworth, Warwickshire, where until 1736 Edward Welchman, a learned theologian and former fellow, was resident, and which from 1792 to 1806 was occupied by another former fellow, H. A. Pye. In between the living was held by three non-resident former fellows, William Darby (1739–57), Charles Bean the elder (1751–?66), and Joseph Kilner (1768–93). The Lapworth records show that the man who did the work was a curate, Owen Bonell.[142] As Archbishop Tenison had specifically declared Farleigh and Diddington so poor that they could be regarded as sinecures and combined with fellowships they naturally were, as by Joseph Kilner and Thomas Hardcastle, fellows and rectors of Farleigh.[143] The local Oxford livings of St Peter's-in-the-East, St Cross, Holywell, St John the Baptist, and Wolvercote were so close to the college that they could easily be held with a fellowship and no attempt was made to build them up in value, no doubt in order to observe the limits set by Archbishops Laud, Tenison, and Herring.[144] The provision of clergy continued to preoccupy the college during the century; and certainly many Mertonian clergy sought livings other than those of which the college had the presentation. How well qualified they were is another matter. In the years before 1738, as has been seen, efforts to restore the Divinity disputations met with limited success. Since neither Knightley's catechetical lecturer nor Bickley's lecturers seem to have been functioning, it may not have been easy for the would-be cleric to acquire the necessary learning and skills.

SCHOLARS

Setting aside learned theologians, doctors, and lawyers, the outstanding scholar among the fellows of the eighteenth century was undoubtedly Thomas Tyrwhitt (fellow, 1755–62: Pl. 25). He had come in from Queen's. His editions of Pindar and of Aristotle's Logic were important contributions to classical learning, and he was equally skilful with vernacular texts, as of Chaucer and Shakespeare, not to mention a Spanish *romancero*. His sharp eye detected the forgeries of Chatterton. Charles Burney called him 'one of the two bright stars of

[142] Hudson, *Memorials*, pp. 187–92.

[143] Mr Jones, –1707; Mr Abell,* 12 Nov. 1707–; Dr Tovey,* 1723–7; J. Kilner,* 1767–93; T. Hardcastle,* 1793–. For the succession of Mr Kilner's curates at Farleigh see Reg. 4.2.

[144] *Statutes and Ordinances*, p. 53.

classical scholarship'.[145] He was both FRS and FSA and was a close friend of Shute Barrington and the Reverend Clayton Cacherode of Christ Church, who used all to meet at Barrington's country house at Mongewell, Oxfordshire.[146] It must be admitted that his publications appeared after he had left college and become a student at the Middle Temple, deputy secretary at war (1756), and clerk to the House of Commons. Other careful students of classical texts were Thomas Robinson (fellow, 1721), who edited Hesiod,[147] and the Revd. James Beresford, who translated the *Aeneid* of Virgil,[148] though his best-known work in English was a strangely comic illustrated book called *The Miseries of Human Life* (1805),[149] which belies its title, whilst on vernacular poetry the restless Richard Meadowcourt towards the end of his life contributed to Miltonic studies.[150]

A strong interest in antiquarian studies is reflected in various ways. Joseph Abell (fellow, 1700) noted most of the inscriptions in the chapel and bought 'curious books and Antiquities' from the library of Warden Lydall. A reputed portrait of Duns Scotus was obtained by some agency. A similar picture by Edmund Ashfield (d. *c.* 1700) hangs in the Bodleian and another, probably the original, at Hampton Court. It seems to derive from an Italian *Commedia dell'arte* portrait. Since at least 1451–2 it had been mistakenly believed that Scotus was born in the college's parish of Embleton, Northumberland, and consequently had been a scholar at Merton. The assertion that he was a fellow is made in a late medieval hand against the word 'Douns' in the Catalogus Vetus under the fellows elected in Edward II's reign. Scotus

---

[145] *DNB*. For his edition of Aristotle's *Poetics* see *HUO* v. 529. 'T. was the only writer', wrote the Chaucerian scholar W. W. Skeat of the Chatterton affair, 'among those that handled the subject who had a critical knowledge of the language of the fourteenth and fifteenth centuries and who ... has on that account a real right to be heard.'

[146] His portrait was engraved by James Heath in 1792. For his friendship with Barrington and Cacherode see Nichols, *Literary History*, v. 61 5–6; cf. also Sandys, *History of Classical Scholarship*, ii. 419–20.

[147] *HUO* v. 527.

[148] *DNB*, and cf. Knox, *Reminiscences*, p. 120.

[149] He was vicar of the college living of Kibworth (Leics.), cf. J. Pycroft, *Oxford Memories: A retrospect after fifty years* (2 vols., 1886), i. 100–1.

[150] Ward, *Georgian Oxford*, p. 103. Milton also figured in a Mertonian benefaction: his head was to be depicted on one side of a silver medal for a prize poem to be established under the will of Sir John Parsons (fellow, 1738); Pope was to be shown on the other. The poem was to be of 200 lines on a divine or moral subject. £5 was to go to the winner; £5 was allowed for the publication of the poem, which was to be read in public in the Poetry School, cf. also n. 158. There seems to be no trace of this donation in the University Archives (information of S. Bailey).

continued to be claimed as a Mertonian into the eighteenth century. The Merton portrait, originally kept in the library, now hangs in the hall.[151]

Francis Astry and Joseph Kilner made catalogues of fellows, and Kilner collected four volumes of materials on the history of the college,[152] though he printed only one book, his *Account of Pythagoras School in Cambridge* (1790). He also made a fine collection of coins which is now in the Ashmolean,[153] whilst Rogers Ruding wrote his classic work on numismatics, the *Annals of the Coinage*, while he was vicar of Malden.[154] The interest shown by Warden Barton in securing the repairs to the Founder's tomb, and that of Warden Scrope Berdmore in presenting in 1796 the portrait of the Founder which he commissioned,[155] both show that the antiquarian interest was shared by the heads of the college. When the Hall was rebuilt by Wyatt in 1790–4 it was provided with armorial glass showing the arms of the warden (Barton) and fellows such as Richard Cust (fellow, 1751) and the Hon. John Sherard (fellow, 1734).

A pioneering work on the Jews in England was the *Anglo-Judaica* (1738) of D'Blosiers Tovey, which is still well regarded. Another of his works, *Winchester Converts or a full and true discovery of the real usefulness and design of a late treatise entitled a plain account of the nature and end of the Lord's supper in 3 dialogues* (Oxford, 1735),[156] was less happy and embroiled him in the Bangorian Controversy on the nature of the church and its relations with secular society.

Scholarship among the fellows was not confined to the Arts. One of the most interesting and studious of the fellows seems to have been Sir John Parsons. A former postmaster, he was a fellow from 1738

---

[151] On Abell, see *MMC*, p. 300. For Scotus, cf. Merton MS, G.3.4, fo. 260; Catalogus Vetus, fo. 5. The addition reads 'Hic doctor sutilis vulgariter nomen Duns et ordinis minorum'. See also Poole, *Catalogue of Oxford Portraits*, ii. 45.

[152] P.2.9; P.2.11; P.3.33–4; Q.1.1–7.

[153] J. D. A. Thompson, 'The Merton College Coin Collection', *Oxoniensia*, xvii–xviii (1952–3), 185–92.

[154] Author also of *A proposal for restoring the ancient constitution of the Mint, as far as it relates to the expense of coinage, and for the increasing of the difficulties of counter-feiting* (1798), and *Annals of the Coinage of Britain and its dependencies from the earliest period of authentick history to the end of the fiftieth year of George III* (1817), *Supplement* (1819).

[155] Poole, *Catalogue of Oxford Portraits*, ii. 45. It was based on a portrait in the Bodleian Library.

[156] For Tovey see S. Levy, 'Anglo-Jewish historiography', *Trans. Jew. Hist. Soc.*, England, vi (1911), 9, 'Tovey and the Bodleian Bowl'.

and had left to become vicar of Embleton in 1747.[157] In his will of 1745 he gave to Merton his microscopes, his hydrostatical balance, and ten guineas with which to buy a reflecting telescope. He left to the university £10 with which to buy the great edition of Caesar's *Commentaries* by Dr Clarke for the Bodleian Library, but also £60 for an orrery or planetarium, which was to be bought within five years of the receipt of the money or the offer would pass to Merton, and subsequently if not taken up by Merton to other colleges.[158]

The keen interest in science which this will reveals may be linked to the fact that one of the most popular lecturers in the university in the mid-eighteenth century was James Bradley, the Savilian professor of Astronomy, a future Astronomer Royal. Through his record of those attending his lectures (1739–60) we are able to see that about a third of all the matriculated members of the university attended them. Interestingly enough among the names of the Mertonians willing to pay three guineas for each of two courses is the name of the future bishop of Durham, Shute Barrington.[159] Another fellow who attended scientific lectures was Edward Nares (fellow, 1788). He records 'I voluntarily however entered my name, as an attendant upon every public lecture at Oxford, and applied myself with some diligence to the study of Chemistry, Mineralogy, Botany and Anatomy – being upon terms of intimacy with several of the lecturers ... I became a collector of Fossils, which were not to be obtained but at considerable cost.' In 1791 he passed the mineralogical specimens which he had collected to 'Dr Beddoes, then chemical lecturer'.[160]

---

[157] A postmaster on 30 June 1731, whose patron was Mr Cox, he was the son of Sir William Parsons, of St Andrew's, Holborn and matriculated at the age of fifteen (1731); BA, 1735, MA, 1739; he became vicar of Embleton, 1747–56, was presented to Wilford (Notts.) in 1756, and died vicar of Arnold (Notts.).

[158] E.2.3a (will of 30 Dec. 1745), proved 1760 (Borthwick Institute, York, probate rec. of York, Chancery Court 1760). He also had musical interests and left musical instruments and books to a Merton contemporary, the Rev. James Walker. Dr Simcock of the museum of the History of Science kindly informs us that there is no sign that the orrery was ever bought for the university.

[159] Bodley MS Bradley 3, p. 33. Barrington attended in 1754–5; 44 members were present between 1744 and 1760, including seven future fellows, Blencowe, Cust, Hartley, Lovell, Norman, Kilner, and Malmesbury. The course covered mechanics, optics, pneumatics, and a range of problems in natural philosophy. For Bradley see Alan Chapman, 'James Bradley, 1693–1762: an Oxford astronomer in eclipse', *Oxford Magazine* (Fourth Week, Trinity Term 1993), 17–19, and 'Pure Research and Practical Teaching; the astronomical career of James Bradley, 1693–1762', *Notes Rec. Royal Soc. Lond.* 47.2 (1993), 205–12.

[160] E.2.41, i. 141, 163.

THE LIBRARY

Funds for the library were not great, and depended on fees charged at admission or when members took their degrees. In 1754 we learn that BA fellows paid £3. 6s. 8d.; BAs and MAs paid 10s. per annum; gentlemen commoners £8 on admission and ordinary commoners 10s.[161] The administration of the library seems to have worked well in the 1690s, to judge by the careful entries in the Liber Benefactorum, but they end in the early eighteenth century, and when Marten became librarian in 1715 he proved negligent. It is true that he took out a subscription for William Williams, *Oxonia Depicta* in 1724,[162] a work which the library still has, but if Warden Wyntle is to be believed Marten was careless over his control of library keys. 'At Present many Persons have keys to the Library, the Door is often left open. It is an old Ruinous Place that lyes in neglect.'[163] Shortly before Dr Holland died Dr Marten 'would have some Logick books put out of the Library, which the Warden thought proper should remain therein; and upon this contest the Doctor ordered the Books to be throwed into the Quadrangle, from whence they were taken up and carried into the Warden's Gallery where they remain'. Wyntle accused Marten of having accumulated £100 worth of library funds which he did not spend on buying books but had lent to the junior fellows.[164] After the visitation proper accounting seems to have returned, to judge by subscriptions taken out by Dr Trowe as librarian and an account surviving for 1754–6. The college subscribed to Polybius, *History*, with a translation by Hampton (published 1757), to Demosthenes and Aeschines (in Greek and Latin), to Calasio's *Dictionary*, ed. W. Romaine (4 vols., 1747–9), and to Milton's *Paradise Lost* in Latin.[165] The library's income between 22 May 1754 and 8 February 1756 was £115. 14s. 9d., of which Trowe spent £31. 19s. 6d.[166] Twenty-one books were bought, including Johnson's *Dictionary*, nine volumes of *Viner's Abridgement*,

---

[161] Reg. 13.1, pp. 6–7. When Warden Holland was appointed in 1709 BA fellows were objecting to paying £3. 6s. 8d. (Reg. 4.21, p. 7). For an incipient undergraduate library see below, p. 274.

[162] 39 h.30, cf. D.3.19.

[163] Reg. 1.6, pp. 157–8. The fellows were supposed to bring their library keys to the college meeting in August to be surrendered, checked, and reissued (*RACM 1567–1603*, p. 216).

[164] Reg. 1.6, p. 158.

[165] D.3.19 (ed. W. Dobson), 2 vols. (Oxford, 1750–3).

[166] Reg. 13.1, pp. 6–7. Subscriptions were taken out for John Smith's *Memoirs of Wool*, 2 vols. (1747), to Miller for a map of Oxfordshire, and for J. Coneybeare, bishop of Bristol, *Sermons*, 2 vols. (1757).

five of the *Parliamentary History*, the *Acts of Parliament* of 28 George II, and vol. xlviii of the *Philosophical Transactions of the Royal Society*. Though the librarians did not keep up the Liber Benefactorum, benefactions continued, of which the most notable was a gift of 883 books from Henry Kent (fellow, 1745), a theologian.[167] His books reflect the wide interests of their owner, a parish priest and a Doctor of Divinity. Perhaps the most notable gift, however, was the copy of *The Tatler* (3 vols. in 4, 1710), made by a former postmaster, Sir Richard Steele.[168]

COLLEGE OFFICERS

The major college officers were usually appointed at the college meeting at the beginning of August by a committee consisting of the warden and five senior fellows, themselves chosen by the whole society from among the seniors. The meeting followed on the audit of the previous year's accounts and marked the start of the college year. It was the first of three annual meetings or scrutinies. The others were originally held eight days before Christmas and eight days before Easter. In the early sixteenth century it had still been customary to appoint the principal of the postmasters (or almoner) and the garden master and maltmen at the winter meeting, but by 1700 only the garden master remained to be chosen then. The major officers were the sub-warden, the three deans, three bursars, and the principal of the postmasters. The sub-warden had no special stipend in 1274 beyond his allocation of 50s. as a fellow, but he had a place at the warden's table, and was sometimes in a position to get his name put forward among the three names sent up to the visitor when the wardenship was vacant. When this manoeuvre was practised by sub-warden Marten on the death of Warden Holland it was detected by Archbishop Wake who chose one of the other two candidates.[169] The three deans, who

---

[167] His main interests covered English Literature (Chaucer), History of Ideas (Locke), Mathematics (Wallis's *Algebra*), Old Testament (Pocock, *On Joel*, Zouch, *On Hosea*), Spanish (Minscheu's *Dictionary*), theology (Hammond and Lightfoot).

[168] Reg. 1.3, p. 708. 'In eo tam amico foedere coeunt seria, jocosa, sensuum pondus, & sermonis nitor, ut tanti ingenii altrices haec aedes alumno suo merito exultent, quem universa Britannia jamdudum habuit in deliciis.'

[169] See above, p. 248. For the three college meetings or scrutinies see Archbishop Potter's decree in 1738 (*Statutes and Ordinances*, pp. 65–6). For the sub-warden's allocation and appointments in 1736 see Reg. 1.6, p. 46. They totalled £37. 2s. 1d. For the payment of college officers in general see *HUO* v. 249–55. For the election of garden masters at the winter scrutiny of 1711 see Reg. 4.21, p. 35 (Mr Wyntle) and Reg. 1.4, p. 37 (Mr Williamson, 31 Dec. 1736).

were in charge of the discipline and studies of the fellows, and the three bursars, each of whom was responsible for a third of the year's account, had each been granted by the Founder 3s. 4d. beyond the normal fellows' allocation. It had not always been easy to maintain the differential, notably for the deans; and it had sometimes been necessary to add to their stipend by other means. In 1568 the exhibition of the chapel's chaplain and of Wyliot's bursar had been equally divided between the three deans.[170] The bursars could be held responsible if they did not make up their account satisfactorily. One bursar who failed to do so, D'Blosiers Tovey, was held by Warden Holland to have committed an outrage and was pursued until he had made up his deficiency out of his pocket.[171] The considerable endowment of John Wyliot's exhibition, the foundation of the postmasterships, was enough in 1380 to allow the master, almoner, or principal 40s. per annum and the bachelor who assisted him with the supervision of the postmasters 13s. 4d. The office of principal was important not only for the stipend, but also for the patronage which it carried, as Dr Edward Nares, who held the post from 1792 to 1796, tells us in his autobiography.[172]

The endowments of the early sixteenth century provided three additional appointments, those of the senior and junior Linacre lectureships, at £12 and £8 respectively, and Hamsterley's gift. The last had endowed masses for Hamsterley's soul in 1515 and consisted of rents from lands at Hensington, Hampton Poyle, Kidlington, and Cricklade. In post-Reformation days his name was added to the commemoration prayers and the post became a sinecure. The late sixteenth century had added a catechist in 1589 at £3 per annum, Greek and Dialectic lecturers, and a senior and junior Bickley lecturer, endowed by Bishop Bickley who was warden from 1569 to 1585. He left £100 which went in 1627 to buy lands worth £4 per annum. Sir Richard Knightley in 1635 added lands worth £10 per annum, for a Catechetical lecturer, and it seems that the two Catechetical lectureships were amalgamated. Griffin Higgs in 1659 left provision for a stipend of £10 per annum to be paid to the librarian, and £20 for a Divinity lecturer which was available from 1672. The latest endowment was for a

---

[170] In 1276 they were allotted 4 marks, i.e. 3s. 4d. more than the 50s. allowance for the fellows (*Injunctions*, p. 121). Undergraduates on admission paid 10s. to the dean.

[171] Reg. 4.22, p. 16.

[172] See below, pp. 270–1.

mathematical lecturer in geometry and algebra, founded by Dr John
Bateman, a doctor, and fellow by 1709.

We know from the reference to the augmentation of the deans'
stipends in 1668 that an exhibition existed for paying the wage of the
chaplain who had the care of the vessels, ornaments, and expenses
of the chapel. Less certain was the pay of the grammar lecturer. His
was a post which went back to the foundation but which had fallen
into disuse and had to be revived in the early seventeenth century.
The three keepers of Rede's chest and the similar keepers of Bodley's
chest and the auditors were unpaid. The three deans and three bursars
seem to have taken it in turns to look after the chests, whilst the
warden, sub-warden, and five senior fellows were added for the audit,
and the auditors themselves could not also be bursars. There were
therefore many loaves and fishes for the committee of the college
meeting in the summer and the warden to distribute. How conscientiously the recipients attended to their duties is difficult to ascer-
tain. Holland commended warmly young Joseph Watkinson, fellow,
and appointed him first to the mathematical lectureship[173] and then
to the Greek lectureship also. The Linacre lecturers were accused by
Warden Wyntle,[174] who was free with his accusations, of neglecting
their duties. At that time they were fellows with medical degrees, such
as John Marten and Gilbert Trowe, but their duty laid down by
Linacre's executor of lecturing regularly on Galen and Hippocrates
had become outdated. Marten seems to have given no lectures, and
Trowe gave some but not as specified in the original foundation. One
may sympathize a little with Trowe and would much like to know
what he did lecture on, but Warden Wyntle had no hesitation in
criticizing him who 'hath of late read sometimes in the College Hall.
But in a manner different from what is prescribed by the Great
Linacre.'[175] Wyntle, himself a doctor, in 1738 had no doubt that the
lectures on Galen and Hippocrates should be continued. He had more
justification in complaining of the treatment of the post of Knightley's
catechetical lecturer by its incumbent. It had been held by Mr Woolley
for three years. He was non-resident, it was alleged, living on his cure

[173] Reg. 4.21, p. 5, and cf. pp. 33, 74.
[174] Reg. 1.6, p. 184. Since Marten lived at Headington he did not reside within the
university.
[175] Ibid. For the fate of the lectureships in the 19th cent. see M. Pelling, 'The refoundation
of the Linacre lectureships in the nineteenth century' in F. Maddison *et al.* (eds.), *Linacre
Studies: Essays on the Life and Work of Thomas Linacre, c. 1460–1524* (Oxford, 1977) pp. 265–
89.

in Worcestershire, and never read 'but once a peice of an old sermon after prayers in the chapple'. His successor, Mr Meadowcourt, had not even done so much. Again, if Wyntle is to be believed, a bishop examining a Merton BA candidate for ordination, and finding him wanting, had asked him whether there was any proper instruction in the college in Divinity, and on being told that there was not, had written to the warden to remonstrate over its lack.[176] Hamsterley's chaplaincy and the two Bickley lectureships, senior and junior, seem to have been treated simply as sinecures.

It fell to the warden to appoint to the two chaplaincies and to the office of tutor. The allocations to the chaplaincies, senior and junior at £6. 16s. 6d. and £19. 1s. 4d. respectively in 1736, were paid by the House,[177] but the tutors earned considerable sums by charging fees. Holland's admission lists show that the warden personally allotted the entrants to tutors, and could thereby augment the tutors' income. Between 1716 and 1731 he entrusted to ten of the fellows the responsibility of acting as tutor.[178] By the end of the century a tuition book for 1784–1800 tells us of the tutorial partnership which was entered into by a pair of tutors and of the profits which they made in exercising the tutorial office.[179] The entries relate to the partnership of Thomas Hardcastle and Nathaniel Booth, fellows, between 1784 and 1786, and to another partnership of Thomas Hardcastle and Robert Wall between 1787 and 1795. Since it seems that at that date a gentleman commoner paid £21 for four terms tuition in the year, a commoner eight guineas, a postmaster six guineas, a Jackson scholar and a bible clerk each four guineas, it can be seen that a tutor could add considerably to his income as a fellow. If there was time to teach undergraduates from other colleges, that might increase the earnings further accordingly. Thus the partnership which took over in 1795 from Hardcastle and Wall was run by Wall and the future warden, Peter Vaughan. In addition to Mertonians they took in three undergraduates from

---

[176] The Knightley lecturer should have lectured in Latin every Thursday in term for 3/4 of an hour. There was a rent of £10 to cover his fee (Reg. 2.2, pp. 283–6), cf. *Statutes and Ordinances*, p. 56. Higgs's Divinity lecture had been set up in 1672, but according to Warden Wyntle the stipend of £20 per annum had fallen to the 'senior divine' who 'receives their Stipend without any Intention to perform the Duty incumbent upon Him' (Reg. 1.6, p. 181).

[177] Reg. 1.6, p. 46. For the warden's examination of one of the chaplains for immorality and his dismissal in 1732 see *HUO* v. 350 and n. 4.

[178] Worcestershire Rec. Office doc.b.705, 353, 380/1, 2 in Hampden Collection.

[179] D.2.19, D.2.19 a.

Wadham, two from University College, and one each from Jesus and
Balliol.

The admission of undergraduates to Merton in the eighteenth century
took two different forms. First there were the postmasters. The system
by which the warden, the principal of the postmasters, and the nine
senior fellows nominated to the postmasterships was supplemented
by that for the two Chamber's postmasterships, which fell to the
provosts of Eton and King's College, Cambridge, respectively. Since
the last two awards were closed to Etonians there was a steady flow
of members of Eton into the college. Characteristic of their number
would be Richard Cust, nominated by the provost of King's,[180] whose
patron we know to have been his brother, Sir John Cust, a fellow of
King's. All those nominated had also to be examined. Holland's Register shows that this was regularly done, though in 1711 it seems to have
been quite a swift procedure. On 5 March 1711 Mr Barker, recommended by Mr Frank, fellow, was 'examined and admitted', as was
Mr Vaughan, son of the vicar of Little Tew, recommended by Mr
Parker, on the following day. On 16 March Mr Waterman of Southwark,
recommended by Dr King, was 'examined and admitted' and allotted
to Mr Martin as his tutor.[181] Or a servitor of the college might be
promoted to a postmastership, as Mr Prince was on 19 October 1730
on the advice of Dr Trowe.[182] In no instance do we hear of an applicant
failing the examination. The Postmasters' Register gives the names of
the patrons, who were the warden and nominating fellows. That the
appointments were considered as patronage is suggested by a passage
in the autobiography of Edward Nares, one of the principals of the
postmasters. The principal nominated to three of the scholarships.
Nares wrote:

> It is astonishing how civil the world is inclined to be to those who
> have anything to give away. The trifling patronage attached to the
> office I now held, together with my voice for fellowships of Merton,
> procured me the honour of numerous solicitations and attentions,

---

[180] Reg. 2.2 a, p. 161.
[181] Reg. 4.21, p. 13.
[182] Reg. 4.22, p. 22; see *HUO* v. 172, 230–1.

mediate or immediate, from Lords, and Dukes, Bishops and Archbishops, and even Princes of the Blood who had sons or nephews
or relations to serve.[183]

The Eton postmasters had their own room in Mob Quadrangle and
the postmasters as a group had their own table in Hall, to which
several of them presented silver.[184] Though some of them had once
lived in Fellows' Quad, in the eighteenth century they mostly lived
in Mob.

The postmasters were joined in the eighteenth century by four
other scholars of the foundation of Mr Henry Jackson. The foundation
dated from 1747 and the scholars were in post from 1755. They were
elected after examination and supported by the rents of lands at
Yarnton and Littlemore. The scholarships were restricted to boys born
in the city of Oxford and educated at Westminster or Eton, or failing
that, boys from Oxfordshire.[185] Below the postmasters and Jackson
scholars, but above the commoners came the Bible clerks, of whom
there were two at any one time. The most famous of their number
was Anthony Wood. His nearest eighteenth-century rival was Bob
Kirkham, the Merton member of John Wesley's Holy Club. In addition
between 1715 and 1731 the warden admitted on an average nine undergraduates of all types in a given year.[186] They arrived seriatim and were
examined as they arrived.

Thus the college was at this period admitting some eleven or twelve
undergraduates a year. Those who were not postmasters, Jackson
scholars, or Bible clerks fell into three categories. Firstly there were
the gentlemen commoners, usually one a year. Then there were the
ordinary commoners, of an age between fifteen and seventeen, about
six a year, and below them one or two servitors. In any given year
there would be therefore about thirty-eight in residence at any one
time. To them must be added about four graduates reading courses
after taking their BA. The total of graduates and undergraduates was
about forty-four. There would also be between nineteen and twenty-
four fellows, of whom perhaps something over half were in residence.
The fellows occupied Fellows' Quadrangle and some of the rooms in

---

[183] E.2.41, i. 159–60.

[184] Jones, *Catalogue of the Plate*, pp. 40, 42, 44–5, 47–50, 52–6.

[185] Reg. 2.2, pp. 69–70. If no suitably qualified candidate appeared preference was to be given to Phipps Weston, son of John Weston of Yarnton.

[186] Worcestershire Record Office doc.b 705, 353. For Kirkham and other clerks see below, n. 197.

Mob Quad as well. The remainder – chaplains, graduates, under-graduates, and servants – had to be fitted into Front and Mob Quad-rangles, though some servants occupied cocklofts in Fellows. The total number of residents may not have been much over sixty. It was a small society.

Among the undergraduates the gentlemen commoners came first in prestige. The most outspoken was certainly James Harris, later earl of Malmesbury. In words which recall those of Gibbon on Magdalen, or MacNeice in the twentieth century, he wrote long after he had left Merton:

> The two years of my life I look back to as most unprofitably spent were those I passed at Merton. The discipline of the University happened also at this particular moment to be so lax, that a Gentle-man Commoner was under no restraint and never called upon to attend either lectures, or chapel, or hall. My tutor, an excellent worthy man, according to the practice of all tutors at that moment gave himself no concern about his pupils. I never saw him but during a fortnight when I took into my head to be taught trig-onometry. The set of men with whom I lived were very pleasant, but very idle fellows. Our life was an imitation of High Life in London; luckily drinking was not the fashion, but what we did drink was claret, and we had our regular round of evening card parties to the great annoyance of our finances.[187]

It sounds as if Warden Holland's proposal that the gentlemen com-moners should be put under the same discipline as the other under-graduates, even if it had been imposed in his time, had by 1763 (when Harris matriculated) once again fallen into disuse. However, quite soon afterwards it can be shown that Richard Davis, fellow (from 1758) and tutor (from 1768), set out a sensible course for one of his gentleman commoners, Simeon Matveyevsky, a Russian. He was one of a group sent to Oxford by Catherine the Great. We know about the episode because the Russian failed to pay his tuition fees, and so Davis took him to law in the chancellor's court. The action was unsuccessful because Davis had forgotten to have Matveyevsky matriculated, so that he fell outside the jurisdiction of the court. That fact does suggest a careless approach by the college authorities, but the course itself, a

---

[187] *Diaries and Correspondence of the earl of Malmesbury*, ed. 3rd earl of Malmesbury (1845), p. xi. If Malmesbury paid the gentleman commoner's admission fee of £8. *os. od.* and the annual tuition fee of £21. *os. od.* he had every reason to complain.

kind of forerunner of the pass degree, consisted of moral philosophy, civil law, geometry, Greek and Latin in 1769, followed in 1769–70 by natural religion and philosophy.[188] It can also be observed that earlier in the century another gentleman commoner, Thomas Watson, son of the earl of Rockingham, took a different view from that of Harris. He showed his appreciation of the college by the presentation of two silver tankards 'in memory of the education he had received at Merton'.[189]

A small band of gentlemen commoners came from the West Indies and were generous donors of silver; Thomas Beckford came from Jamaica (1699), as did Thomas Bernard (1705) and the brothers Favell and Knight Peek (1721 and 1722); Robert Johnston was a Barbadian as was Thomas Stokes, who was an MD by diploma (1726). William Matthews was the son of Colonel Matthews, the governor of the Leeward islands; Sir John Williams, son of Sir John Williams, belonged to the Island of St Christopher (St Kitts) (1755).[190] Bernard and Beckford went on to the Inner and Middle Temple respectively. Dr Stokes presented the handsome grace cup which bears his name, and Sir John Williams a silver salver which is in daily use. Bernard gave a pair of silver salvers, and Beckford a monteith bowl.[191]

Out of the ordinary was John Skippe; he is said to have been a pupil of J. B. Jackson and Claude Joseph Vernet. He became a connoisseur of art and lived for many years in Italy. Between 1773 and 1781 he bought for his own collection Old Master drawings mainly of the Venetian and Italian schools which ended up in Herefordshire. They included drawings by Bellini, a Dürer, and a Rubens, and were catalogued by Christie's in 1958. Skippe did not forget his college and sent it in 1779 the Crucifixion of the school of Tintoretto which hangs at the back of the altar in chapel.[192]

Among the ordinary commoners it is possible to deduce that Merton's Whig affiliations may well have encouraged Bishop White Kennet to follow Bishop Burnet's example and send his son to Merton. The same is probably true of Ashley Cooper. The most interesting commoner, however, was perhaps Henry Jackson, son of the senior cook. His scholarships have already been noticed. He joined the choir

---

[188] R. L. Winstanley, 'No case for the Vice-Chancellor', *Oxford* (May, 1990), xlii/1, 82–5.

[189] Jones, *Catalogue of the Plate*, p. 2.

[190] Foster, *Alumni Oxonienses*, pp. 99 (Beckford), 115 (Bernard), 1427 (Stokes).

[191] Jones, *Catalogue of the Plate*, pp. 20, 28.

[192] *The Skippe Collection of Old Master Drawings (Christie Illustrated Catalogue)* (1958).

of Christ Church as a boy, and became junior chaplain of New College and eventually a minor canon of St Paul's. Born in a house opposite the north door of the chapel in Merton Street, he lived to accumulate enough money to buy what became Jackson's Farm, Yarnton, and land at Littlemore. There was enough money left after paying for four scholarships to buy the advowson of Rushall, Wilts.[193] Jackson's choral interests showed when he asked that at his funeral 'O Lord let me know mine end' should be sung, set to music by Green, the organist of St Paul's. Another undergraduate who remains anonymous showed unusual initiative. He presented two volumes of Rutherforth's lectures on Natural Philosophy. He left them to the undergraduates of Merton because there was no library for undergraduates who had had to rely on notes taken at lectures or on books which they bought for themselves. The donor said 'as a testimony of his gratitude to Merton College where he was educated these books are desired to be accepted by the undergraduates thereof. That they may more regularly circulate amongst them, the donor desires that they may be produced in Hall on every Monday before dinner to go round by seniority among the undergraduates who desire to have them.' In the second volume it states on the fly-leaf that a reader who returned the book late had to pay two pence to the porter, who had charge of the collection.

At the beginning of the century a servitor such as William Lancaster of Queen's could end up as head of his house, and at Merton at a lower-level Richard Parker could become vicar of the valuable living of Embleton (1713–28). Servitors were regularly admitted in the earlier part of the century: between 1717 and 1731 there were thirty-seven. Holland awarded Ironmongers' exhibitions to eleven and an Arnold exhibition to another,[194] but in the course of the century they gradually declined in numbers and eventually disappeared. As Dr Green has noted at Lincoln,[195] that was partly because their tasks were more and more carried out by college servants and partly because the wealthier undergraduates might bring their own servants with them.[196] Some servitors appear when they received book prizes from

[193] Reg. 2.2, p. 76,

[194] Reg. 4.21, p. 85; 4.22, p. 24. The eleven were B. Russel (1719), G. Deacon (1720), E. Oldnall (1717), H. Whishaw and T. Hurdis (1722), G. Wayte (1725), John Hancox (1726), Du Plessis (1727), Stinton (1728), N. Rose (1729), Thomas Wite (1731), and H. Wayte (1733), and the Arnold exhibitioner was White (1730).

[195] Green, *Commonwealth of Lincoln College*, p. 410.

[196] There were still two servitors in 1753, but they seem to disappear thereafter. Cf. Reg. 2.2 a, p. 20.

the principal of the postmasters. Thus on 7 April 1736 copies of Hammond's *Catechism* were given to Messrs Frewen, Walker, Downing, Bean, and Willes, postmasters, to Hale and Knight, (Bible) clerks, and to Turner and Astbury, servitors;[197] whilst copies of Hammond's *Whole Duty of Man* went to Hayley, postmaster, to Heath, Bible clerk, and to Pixel, Lynch, and Holland, servitors.[198]

THE STAFF

The staff in the eighteenth century did not yet receive wages, but there were signs that the medieval arrangement of maintaining them on the establishment was becoming outdated. On 20 July 1736 it was decided that not more than six servants should have accommodation in college,[199] and when Warden Wyntle and the fellows fell out one of the sub-warden's acts with which the warden disagreed, as has been seen, was the dismissal of the barber, William Brown, on the grounds that the office was out of date and useless.[200] The warden was similarly aggrieved because the groom, William Pain, had been sconced by a junior master in Hall, Mr Berdmore, who happened to be presiding when all the seniors were absent.[201] By the end of the century it was beginning to be felt that the servants' perquisites needed attention. Thus when in 1791 a scale was introduced for perquisites arising from the consumption of candles in the chapel, hall, and kitchen the servants to benefit were the porter, the senior cook, the manciple, the sexton, and the junior cook.[202] With the groom already mentioned here were six of the traditional nine servants, with the barber making a seventh. Unmentioned were the steward and the butler. We catch a glimpse of another member of the staff when the junior cook was reprimanded in 1736 for consuming an inordinate amount of the commons of the postmasters.[203] But equally if sub-warden Trowe could

---

[197] Reg. 2.2 a, p. 2.

[198] Ibid.

[199] Reg. 1.4, p. 33. This was the scrutiny at which in times past the principal of the postmasters, two maltmen, a garden master, and a grammar master were chosen. The number of the postmasters was fixed for the ensuing year, and the behaviour of the college servants was reviewed. The present Ceremony of the Keys is the last remnant of this custom. For the election of two garden masters see above, n. 169.

[200] Reg. 1.6, pp. 95–6. See above, p. 254.

[201] Ibid., p. 94. See above, p. 253.

[202] Reg. 1.4, p. 399, cf. *HUO* v. 255.

[203] Reg. 1.4, p. 37.

be peremptory with the barber, college could grant 20s. to Sarah Bedding, 'an ancient bedmaker who by sickness is reduced to low circumstances'.[204]

COLLEGE FINANCES

At the beginning of the century college finances were in a poor condition, judging by the fact that the eight fellows elected at the Golden Election of 1705 had to wait three-and-a-half years to take up their fellowships because of lack of money.[205] We know from the evidence collected in 1738 that, setting aside half the fines, the college's income varied between £1761. 6s. 7d. and £3013. 14s. 4½d. in the years between 1716 and 1736.[206] At that date it did not employ a regular banker. It bought South Sea stock in 1719, but does not seem to have bought very much; at least its income was not seriously affected after the bubble burst in 1721.[207] College was for a time advised by a banker who was a goldsmith called Hankey[208] and then by an attorney who was the brother of Twynihoe, one of the fellows. But eventually (in 1782) it realized the unsatisfactory nature of such expedients and opted for Child's Bank, following the examples of Magdalen and All Souls' in the 1720s.[209] The revenue from land was much affected by the current practice of beneficial leases. Such leases were for twenty-one years. If they were for land a fine was levied after seven years, if for houses after fourteen.[210] At the beginning of the century the fine was for one year's clear annual value. The difficulty was keeping up with the estimated value of the property. Bursars were naturally

---

[204] Reg. 1.5, p. 399. For the allocation for nine servants see Reg. 1.6, p. 46. In 1736 they cost £75. 1s. 6d.

[205] Each of the fellows thus delayed was to be compensated by £50 according to a decision of Archbishop Tenison in 1710 (*Statutes and Ordinances*, p. 60); cf. Reg. 1.3, p. 678 (21 May 1708); Henderson, p. 153.

[206] Reg. 4.22, p. 24; 'Snow to receive from the accountant of the South Sea Company 6% principal money on £850.0.0., as the annuity in the name of the Warden and Fellows of Merton College in the books of the South Sea Company'. For the finances 1716–36 cf. above, p. 259.

[207] See Reg. 1.6, p. 45.

[208] Reg. 4.22, p. 15.

[209] D. Adamson, 'Child's Bank and Oxford University in the eighteenth century', *Three Banks Review*, ccxxvi (1982), 45. The warden in 1738 claimed that the bursars were resorting to bankers in order to exclude him from the control of college business (Reg. 1.6, pp. 121–2).

[210] *HUO* v. 270.

uneasy about the arrangement, and we find the fine raised to one-and-a-quarter of the clear annual value by the middle of the century, and by its end to one-and-a-half.[211] When the fine was levied those who were present at the signing of the lease drew a share of it. The warden had two shares and the house received half the total fine. The signings took place in the Exchequer in Mob Quad. Evidently a fellow's stipend might be considerably affected by the number of occasions at which he was present and took his share. Throughout the century rents were producing more and more and beneficial leases proportionately less,[212] but those who benefited from the fines were naturally unwilling to abandon such leases.

College finances like those of many other colleges had greatly improved by the end of the century, and were well on the way to completing the change which occurred between the annual income of £2695. 7s. 8¼d. of 1736[213] and that of £7220 in 1853. In 1790–4 Merton even felt sufficiently self-confident to renew its dilapidated medieval hall. It diverted a bequest intended to establish an organ and set up a choir and commissioned James Wyatt to undertake the work.[214]

Three cartoons of Merton at the end of the eighteenth century hang in the Senior Common Room. The first, based on the Oxford Almanack of 1772, shows the entrance in Merton Street, the Chapel and Postmasters' Hall. The additions include an apple-woman following a fellow through the wicket, while another fellow supervises the rolling of barrels into the cellar of Postmasters' Hall. It is reproduced as the frontispiece of H. A. R. Gibb's *Rowlandson's Oxford* (1911), and has played its part in establishing popular perceptions of the eighteenth-century university. In a second, similarly based on an Oxford Almanack, that for 1788, a funeral procession of an undergraduate with its white pall and plumes crosses Front Quad on its way to the Chapel, followed by the master and bachelor Fellows two by two.[215] A third is of Magpie Lane with Merton chapel tower and the north transept at its end. It is highly probable that the artist drew his pictures in London, since he shows a fly being driven at a spanking

---

[211] Ibid. p. 277.
[212] Cf. Ibid., pp. 280–1.
[213] Reg. 1.6, p. 45 (with the value of half the fines omitted). For a comparison between the value of money rents, 'rents', and corn rents in a number of colleges as between 1739–40 and 1800 in constant 1740 pounds sterling see *HUO* v. 275.
[214] Bott, *Short History of the Buildings*, pp. 10–11.
[215] J. R. L. Highfield, 'Merton College Chapel', *Postmaster*, iii/4 (Dec. 1945), fig. 3.

pace into the kitchen yard of Oriel and on another occasion identified the west front of All Souls' as Magdalen College, Oxford.

By 1800 the trauma of 1738 had long been overcome and the college had recovered its poise. Its fellows in the second half of the eighteenth century could justly have borne Hearne's description of the fellows of All Souls' in the first – 'well born, well dressed, moderately learned'. 'Well born' they became more certainly as the influence of Christ Church was more strongly felt. 'Well dressed' they appear in portraits, as in the charming series of twelve crayon drawings made by Lewis Vaslet in 1779 and 1789 which now hang in the Warden's Lodgings. Even David Hartley, who was not famous for his dress, looks moderately smart. Still smarter is the man in the portrait of an MA seen against the city wall and the corner of Fellows' Quad painted by Knapton, which is now in the National Gallery at Washington. Yet as the fellows had become better born they had also become a narrower élite than they had been in Holland's day. The four best products were all middle-class or professional, Tyrwhitt and Rogers Ruding the sons of clergymen, and Hartley the son of a doctor, whilst John Wall's father was a citizen of Worcester. By any standard Tyrwhitt was more than moderately learned and so was Ruding, to judge by his published work. Hartley had had the advantage of training both in medicine and the law. Wall might be termed an amateur, given the existing medical course at Oxford, but he was a reflective physician, and also a versatile painter and entrepreneur who fathered the Royal Worcester Porcelain factory. Tyrwhitt and Ruding, the classical commentator and the numismatist, rose to the top of their chosen fields of study. The most spectacular of the four was Hartley, who came into Merton from Corpus. Leaving aside the tamer careers of physician and barrister he went into politics, with invention as his hobby. His speeches in the House though precise and practical in their criticism were judged boring, but his steady opposition to the American War proved sensible and in the end convincing, so that, partly through his friendship with Benjamin Franklin, when the fiasco had run its course he was the chosen envoy to draw up the Treaty of Paris which finished the war. He took with him a Mertonian secretary, George Hammond, a Yorkshireman, who became (in 1791) the first British minister to the United States.

12

Merton in the Nineteenth Century

It is a remarkable feature of the Governing Body of Merton College in the nineteenth century that its members were all sons of the clergy, of peers, or of fathers who called themselves gentlemen. The evidence comes from the matriculation register of the university. We must not lean too heavily on the terms 'armiger' or 'gentleman' which occur there, for they certainly do not mean that all these men were landed. The terms cover a multiplicity of backgrounds, but they do mean that those who used them wished to be thought of as gentry.

Only two colleges, other than Merton itself, supplied more than twenty members. They were Christ Church and Balliol. Of the Christ Church men all but three were elected before 1850.[1] Their diminishing number thereafter reflects the lesser role of Christ Church in the second half of the century. By contrast the numbers of Balliol men increased steadily as the century progressed, and by its end Balliol had won a clear pre-eminence over all other colleges. There were nineteen Balliol elections alone between 1850 and 1900.[2] The third of the reforming colleges, Oriel, produced eleven fellows of Merton.[3] No other college reached double figures, but all were represented except Magdalen. Moreover a clear change can be discerned in the extent to which Merton recruited from its own ranks. Among them it naturally drew most heavily on its postmasters. All but six of the twenty-nine Mertonians were postmasters before they were fellows, but there was a marked falling away after 1850, and only four were elected in the

[1] I. R. Williams (1866), E. R. Lankester (1891), and S. R. Gardiner (1892).
[2] W. H. Karslake (1851), C. S. Currer (Roundell) (1851), J. C. Patteson (1851), E. C. Cure (1851), Hon. G. C. Brodrick (1855), J. R. King (1859), E. Caird (1864), T. L. Papillon (1865), W. Wallace (1867), A. Lang (1868), J. W. Russell (1873), J. J. Massingham (1877), W. Scott (1879), W. Ashburner (1887), J. Burnet (1889), C. R. Beazley (1889), H. Joachim (1890), F. H. B. Dale (1893), E. Barker (1898).
[3] T. R. Barker (1802), Hon. L. P. Pleydell Bouverie (1802), M. R. Grey (1818), B. H. Bridges (1823), G. Tierney (1823), E. Denison (1826), G. Trevelyan (1826), Sir E. W. Head (1830), B. E. Bridges (1838), W. P. Dickins (1847), T. H. G. Wyndham (1867).

second half of the century.[4] The same tendency appears amongst Merton exhibitioners and commoners. Only one – Macdonald, an exhibitioner – gained his fellowship after 1850.[5] Thus in the second half of the nineteenth century Merton became a college whose Governing Body was largely recruited from other colleges and especially from Balliol. How had that come about?

Election in the early eighteenth century involved examination in Latin and Greek texts and had been in the hands of the thirteen senior fellows. In the early nineteenth century, we learn of the writing of a piece of Latin prose,[6] a test which was often set to candidates for ordination. We have no information until 1865 as to how mathematics was examined after the Honours School had appeared in 1800. In general a change seems to have set in after the first University Reform Act of 1854. Manning in later life could still complain of the wire-pulling to which he had to resort when securing a fellowship in 1832;[7] and James Hope-Scott, applying in 1837 for a close fellowship for those born in Buckinghamshire, records more precisely the names of all those who had exercised themselves on his behalf in order to secure his election.[8] They included a former Prime Minister, Lord Sidmouth, Lady Clarendon, and others of the well-connected. Of Goulburn's election in 1839, Berdmore Compton, a former fellow, wrote, 'the Fellowships were not then given by examination, but it was no longer the family borough, which it had been. It was a recognised principle of election that university distinction went very far to recommend a candidate.'[9] By the time of the election of the future Warden, Brodrick, in 1855 a real change could be observed. 'When I was a candidate for a fellowship', he wrote, 'and stress was laid by some of his colleagues on the duty of electing the man who might be placed first by the examiners Mr Griffith [a senior fellow] announced that he had come up from Bath to vote for my father's son and would certainly do so, whatever might be the result of the examination.'[10] Mr Griffith was a legacy from the eighteenth century, and Brodrick identifies in him

---

[4] The six were R. Hawker (1803), G. Rooke (1806), G. Rooke (1821), H. R. Farrer (1843), C. W. St J. Mildmay (1845), H. W. Sargent (1848). The four were G. N. Freeling (1852), M. Creighton (1866), R. J. Wilson (1867), and F. C. Crump (1896).

[5] In 1873.

[6] Manning's Latin Prose is E.1.23.

[7] Knox, *Reminiscences*, p. 84.

[8] Ornsby, *Memoirs*, i. 53–4.

[9] Berdmore Compton, *Edward Mayricke Goulburn* (1899), p. 28.

[10] G. C. Brodrick, *Memories and Impressions* (1900), pp. 110–11.

and his like the attitude which was passing. 'All these relics of that system were men of the old school, courteous, gentleman-like, and (in their own way) loyal to their College, which they regarded not exactly as a place of education, but rather as a pleasant resort in which sons of the landed gentry might profitably spend three years before entering into possession of their estates or launching forth into professions, and which fellows might use as a country house in vacations.'

WARDEN MARSHAM

The warden under whom that transformation occurred was Robert Bullock Marsham, one of the fellows elected from Christ Church. The report of the commissioners shows that his stipend was £1,050.[11] The son of the Hon. Jacob Marsham, canon of Windsor and brother of the earl of Romney, he was undoubtedly well-connected, and became even more so when he married Janet, widow of Sir John Carmichael-Anstruther. It seems likely that the link helped to persuade members of several Scottish low-country families to try for fellowships at Merton, as did James Robert Hope-Scott, son of Sir Archibald Hope, and James Bruce, second son of the 7th earl of Elgin, two of the three 'Jems',[12] and both former members of Christ Church. However, Bullock Marsham brought more to Merton than his good family. He was a skilled barrister of Lincoln's Inn and used his legal expertise when it came to guiding the college through the maze of the University Reform Commission of 1852, though sometimes in a notably conservative manner. He was sanguine enough to stand against Gladstone for one of the two Oxford University seats in the General Election of 1852. *The Times* devoted to him a leader headed 'Bos dixit', and, as a defeated candidate, he sanguinely advised Mr Gladstone to follow the lead given in the House by the senior MP for the university, Sir Robert Inglis.[13] Brodrick left a tempered pen picture of Bullock Marsham: 'My predecessor was a kindly and courteous old gentleman, more familiar with country life than with Academical studies, but not without scholar-like tastes, loyally attached to his College and justly

---

[11] *Oxford University Commission Report* (1852), p. 195. He was thus paid seven times as much as a fellow.

[12] Ornsby, *Memoirs*, i. 56.

[13] Brodrick, *Memories and Impressions*, p. 342.

popular with the junior members of it.'[14] Creighton was rather sharper, describing him in 1867 as 'a survival of a former state of things, in temper and tastes an old-fashioned country gentleman, whose main ambition for the College was that it should be filled with young men of good county families'.[15] His popularity with undergraduates may have had something to do with his enthusiastic patronage of cricket. When E. A. Knox joined Merton the following year he could describe Bullock Marsham as 'the only lay head of a house':

> For almost fifty years already he had been Warden of the College, had taken part in the great Hampden controversy debate in Convocation as the defender of Hampden ... was father of cricketers who had played in the University XI, and though now over the age of seventy and very blind used to ride his cob almost daily in and around Oxford. He was a fine old gentleman of the old school, courteous and genial, venerated by the undergraduates, but more lightly regarded by the fellows of the College ... If his appeals to the slothful to pass 'Smalls' for the honour of their county were rather antiquated, he made it clear that he would uphold the tutors in the exercise of authority. He never allowed his popularity to become a backstairs influence. A regular attendant and communicant, while health allowed, in College Chapel, he did what he could by way of example and high character to maintain the honour of the College.[16]

His tastes in architecture led him to employ an outstanding architect, Charles Cockerell, to build him a country residence at Caversfield House, near Bicester. They also led him, under the injunction of the University Commission, to provide more accommodation for undergraduates and at one point to agree to pulling down part of Mob Quadrangle including the Old Library, to be replaced by a quadrangle designed by Mr Butterfield. Fortunately, that startling decision was reversed at the end of the Long Vacation of 1861 as a result of a counter-movement led by Brodrick and Currer, fellows, and supported by public protest led by the Oxford Architectural and Historical Society.[17]

---

[14] Brodrick, *Memories and Impressions*, pp. 339–40.
[15] Creighton, *Life and Letters*, i (1904), p. 50.
[16] Knox, *Reminiscences*, pp. 83–4.
[17] Reg. 1.5, pp. 406–8, cf. Paul Thompson, *William Butterfield* (1971), p. 47.

I Interior of the Hall
(13th – 19th cent.)

II Warden FitzJames, bishop of
Rochester, in the robe of a Doctor of
Divinity, Commentary of St Jerome
on Isaiah (MS Coxe 25, fo. 1^r)

III Duns Scotus, *Quodlibets* (MS Coxe 65, fo. 119ʳ, c. 1455,
John Reynbold of Hesse, scribe)

IV Interior of the rooms of J. Hungerford Pollen (fellow; d. 1902),
by Josephine Butler

v T. S. Eliot OM (hon.
   fellow; d. 1965), by
   Sir Jacob Epstein

VI One of two vases given by
    HIM Emperor Akihito of Japan in
    March 1984 on the occasion of his
    visit to his son, HIH Prince
    Naruhito, now Crown Prince of
    Japan and hon. fellow

VII The garden and lime avenue in summer (1980)

VIII The Holywell Buildings (1995)

TRACTARIANISM

Topographically close to the centre of Tractarian Oxford at Oriel, it is not surprising that Merton found itself affected by Tractarianism and that four of its fellows turned Roman Catholic. That did not happen in a hurry. At Merton itself there was little sign of life in the chapel in the last years of Warden Vaughan (1810–26), to judge by the observation of William Sewell, who came up as a postmaster in 1823. 'When I went to Oxford ... we were required to attend a Chapel once in the term when the Holy Communion was administered, and we all attended as a form. But not one word of religious instruction did I receive during the whole time of my residence at Merton.'[18] Spirituality was there to be found, but it was hidden under a bushel. Next door to the east was St Alban Hall where in 1825 Newman was vice-principal to Whateley as principal, two men of widely different but deeply held views. Again, Manning was a full fellow in 1832–3 before he left in order to marry and take a living, his conversion to Catholicism came later.[19]

James Hope-Scott, fellow in 1832, was another matter (Pl. 26). He had it in mind to write a history of the colleges and in preparation for such a book examined carefully the foundation statutes as a guide to the intentions of the founder. As a lawyer he was especially interested in whether the fellows of the colleges were obeying the statutes by which they were governed. At one point he paid a visit to the tomb of Walter de Merton in Rochester cathedral and kept vigil there as he sought divine guidance.[20] One of the inspirations with which he returned was the idea that he should persuade all those of his colleagues who had not taken orders to proceed to do so and that, if still BAs, they should also take their MA. Thereafter they should begin to read for the degree of Bachelor of Theology.[21] Remarkably he persuaded some of them to do so. Another aim was to restore the chapel to its medieval Gothic state. With the advice at first of Edward

---

[18] Lionel James, *A Forgotten Genius: Sewell of St Columba's and Radley* (1945), p. 22. Sewell was in residence from 1823 to 1827.

[19] 6 April 1851, together with Hope-Scott (*DNB*).

[20] 29 July 1838 (Ornsby, *Memoirs*, i. 153).

[21] Ibid., i. 136–8, for his draft of the committee report on the statutes, charters, and muniments of the college. The resulting draft resolutions were passed with amendments at the meeting of the Governing Body in April 1839 (p. 139). Five fellows reading Law were exempted from the resolution (Reg. 1.5, pp. 158–61) requiring them to study theology. Fellows subsequently elected were to proceed to their MA after three years.

Blore the College decided to remove its Wren screen and stalls because they represented pagan architecture. When Blore resigned it fell to Butterfield to replace them with Gothic stalls and to effect a complete restoration of the interior.[22] The scheme included tapestries behind the stalls, a low wall at the west end of the chancel, and the fitting of encaustic tiles into the floor. The plan for the roof entailed the raising of the eastern ceiling of the chapel to clear the top of the east window, which was a great aesthetic improvement. John Hungerford Pollen (fellow, 1842–52) directed the painting of the roof, much of which he did himself reclining like some Victorian Michelangelo.[23] He later became a Roman Catholic and Newman's professor of fine art at the Catholic University of Dublin, before finishing his career as director of the Victoria and Albert Museum.

When Butterfield had completed his work the chapel became some-thing of a show-piece and famous for the beauty of its services. Its new fittings attracted the attention of Gerald Manley Hopkins.[24] A High Church tradition was sustained by Edward Denison and Walter Kerr Hamilton who successively became bishop of Salisbury. William Adams, fellow and author of *The Allegory* and *The Shadow of the Cross*, was to become a 'dear friend' of James Hope-Scott,[25] and Berdmore Compton, fellow, was appointed vicar of Butterfield's best-known church in London, All Saints, Margaret Street.[26]

It was in a High Church spirit and while still an Anglican that Hope-Scott with Sir John Gladstone in 1842–7 founded the Scottish public school of Trinity College, Glenalmond.[27] Like William Sewell, the other Mertonian to found a public school, Hope-Scott was reacting

---

[22] For the chapel, see J. R. L. Highfield, 'Alexander Fisher, Sir Christopher Wren and Merton College Chapel', *Oxoniensia*, xxiv (1959), p. 78. Blore was paid off in 1844 (Reg. 1.5, p. 205). Butterfield was invited, 25 November 1848 (ibid., pp. 249–50). For the encaustic tiles see Paul Thompson, *William Butterfield*, p. 234. For the roof Butterfield drew on the example of Trumpington (ibid., pp. 88, 188).

[23] For its painting cf. Thompson, *Butterfield*, p. 234, also *Who Was Who, 1897–1915*, p. 568. He was the author of *Ancient and Modern Furniture and Woodwork* (1875), *Ancient and Modern Gold and Silversmiths' Work* (1879), *Trajan's Column* (1874), *Narrative of 5 years at St Saviour's Leeds* (Oxford, 1851), etc. A watercolour of his rooms in Merton *c.* 1852 was made by Josephine Butler (P.2.25) and see Pl. IV.

[24] The *Journals and Papers of G. M. Hopkins*, ed. H. House and G. Storey (Oxford, 1959), i. 59, 330.

[25] Ornsby, *Memoirs*. ii. 42.

[26] 1873–86. For the continuation of a High Church tradition at Merton cf. M. Everitt, 'Merton Chapel in the nineteenth century', *Oxoniensia*, xlii (1977), 247–55.

[27] The proposal was initiated in 1840 when Hope-Scott discussed it with W. E. Gladstone (Ornsby, *Memoirs*, i. 212–21).

against the unsatisfactory state into which the great schools, Eton and Winchester, had fallen in the early nineteenth century. His intention was to establish an ecclesiastical school which should solve the problem of how 'young men of different ranks and fortunes shall have the benefit of a common education without allowing the growth of habits which will be injurious to one or other class – and particularly how the clergy shall receive a strict clerical education in contact with and yet without being secularised by the laity. Up to the age of twelve or thirteen all boys should be educated together. But thereafter those designed for Holy Orders should be separated from the rest. The latter boys should continue only till the age of fifteen or sixteen, unless it were as gentlemen-commoners with separate rooms allowed them, and at such a rate of payment as would secure the number from becoming very large.'[28]

Such was the dream of an idealistic old Etonian. A different solution was devised by a former Wykehamist and postmaster, William Sewell. The problem as Sewell saw it was how 'to make boys Christian gentlemen and scholars not by any artificial hothouse system of superintendence or excitement or asceticism, but by the tone and atmosphere in which they lived.'[29] The tone was to be that of the Christian family. Sewell began by founding with three others, all Irish gentlemen, a school at St Columba's, Stackallan, Co. Meath (in April 1843), later moved to Rathfarnam. But in 1847 he also established an English foundation at Radley, near Oxford. Both Trinity College, Glenalmond, and Radley represented the best part of the ideals of the older public schools, now as inspired also by the Tractarian Movement. Sewell believed that boys should be surrounded by the beauty of holiness, which was made evident in the splendid objects with which he adorned the chapel at Radley.

As has been seen, one of the strangest manifestations of Tractarianism at Merton was the decision of the Governing Body to eject the Wren screen and stalls from the chapel. It was proposed that, rather than fall into secular hands, the stalls should be burned.[30] Fortunately, Sewell was able to persuade the fellows that some of the

---

[28] Ibid., i. 216–17.

[29] James (above, n. 18), p. 139.

[30] Highfield (above, n. 22), p. 77; cf. Reg. 1.5, p. 213, resolution of 27 May 1847, which shows that they were originally intended for Radley chapel. Three of the arches after being temporarily housed in the College library have been returned to the chapel. Some of the woodwork is in Cuxham church, a college living.

stalls could safely be given to Radley since the school was under the eye of the bishop of Oxford. In that way some of them were saved and adorn Radley library to this day.

The revival of Christian zeal in a new age was also demonstrated by two fellows who went abroad as missionaries, Edmund Hobhouse to initiate the bishopric of Nelson, New Zealand, and J. C. Patteson to a martyr's death as bishop of Melanesia in 1871.[31] Yet after the High Church enthusiasms of the mid-century there was something of a lull in institutional religious life at Merton. It followed upon the death of H. W. Sargent, fellow and chaplain, in 1867.[32] An undergraduate who came up two years later commented unfavourably on the standard of the services in chapel.[33] At the same time the Governing Body had recruited a number of liberal-minded fellows on whom the High Church tradition sat very lightly.

THE FELLOWSHIP

The Reform Commission in its Act of 1854 had set a division of half and half between lay and clerical, but already by 1865 G. C. Brodrick had moved that this clause should be rescinded[34] and that the number of clerical fellowships should be no more than a third. His grounds were that candidates for the lay fellowships were of so much higher a standard that to restrict them to a half was to hold back the educational advance of the college. Neither the visitor, when appealed to, nor the Privy Council was prepared to shift from the division set by the ordinance under the Act.[35] Nevertheless by 1870 fourteen of the twenty-three fellows – more than half – were non-clerical. The distinction did not survive the Act of 1877, and it had not prevented the college from electing two outstanding clerical candidates, in

[31] 16 September (*DNB*). Patteson helped the college over the acceptance of the proposed University scheme for reform (1852–3). For his career see R. Symonds, *Oxford and Empire: The Last Lost Cause* (1986), pp. 221–2. Other missionaries were W. M. Richardson, a former postmaster and vicar of Ponteland, 1887–95, bishop of Zanzibar, 1895–1902, and H. Newton, DD (Merton 1889–93), bishop of Papua.

[32] *Merton Sundays*, a selection of his sermons, and *The Merton Tune-Book* (Oxford, 1863); cf. F. L. Cross, *Darwell Stone* (1943), pp. 11–12.

[33] Maude, *Memories*, p. 72.

[34] Reg. 1.5, p. 442. For the division into halves see c. 6 of *Ordinances concerning Merton College in pursuance of 17 and 18 Victoria c. 81* (1863), p. 6. For the resolution of 1846, Reg. 1.5, p. 225.

[35] Ibid., pp. 449–55.

Mandell Creighton (Pl. 27) and E. A. Knox (Pl. 29), who both subsequently became leading bishops. Indeed Creighton, a former postmaster, was also a major historian of the papacy, the first Dixie
professor of ecclesiastical history at Cambridge, and might well have
become archbishop of Canterbury had he not died prematurely as
bishop of London in 1901. As a Low-Churchman Knox was the very
opposite of a Tractarian, but he was also fearless and hard-working.
As a suffragan of the bishop of Worcester he ruled the diocese of
Birmingham and then another great urban diocese as bishop of Manchester.[36] Nevertheless, the writing was on the wall for the clerical
fellowships. It is true that the services in chapel, undistinguished
since Sargent's death, began to pick up with the return to Merton of
G. N. Freeling, who had been examining chaplain to Bishop Hamilton
of Salisbury. The college produced a clerical headmaster in C. T.
Cruttwell, headmaster of Bradfield (1877–88) and of Malvern (1880–
5),[37] but not another leading bishop. H. J. White (elected 1897) was
theology tutor (1898–1906), then professor of exegesis at King's College,
London, and eventually dean of Christ Church (1920–35),[38] but the
college was plainly becoming more secular.

How far did the clerical fellows go out into the college livings and
take their learning with them? The magnet which the livings offered
of the possibility of marriage, denied to the Oxford fellows until
1871, was coupled with the greater emphasis put on residence in the
parishes. The answer to the question is rather more certain than it was
in the eighteenth century, though college life still had its attractions.
Salary as a fellow amounted to £150 per annum in 1853–4 (£200 in
1877) plus free board and lodging. That might be combined with a
local benefice worth not more than £300[39] and with college offices

---

[36] Knox, *Reminiscences*, pp. 217–87. The bishop of Birmingham was still a suffragan of
the bishop of Worcester.

[37] J. Foster, *Oxford Men and their Colleges* (1893), p. 98.

[38] *Mert. Coll. Reg.*, p. 4.

[39] *Oxford University Commission Report* (1852), p. 195; *Ordinances concerning Merton College
in pursuance of 17 and 18 Victoria c. 81*, p. 7; the limit on an incompatible benefice was
raised to £500 in 1877 (*Statutes in pursuance of the Oxford and Cambridge Act, 1877*, p. 9). For
the estimated value of a fellowship in 1833 (£200) see Ornsby, *Memoirs*, i. 54. His father
brought it up to £300 and reckoned it 'poor bread' (ibid., p. 55). By 1871 all fellows were
paid £300 p.a. This could be increased by holding college offices. Creighton as senior
tutor was able to add £332. 1s. 0d., as principal of postmasters £50, and as senior dean £37
per annum, making a total of £719. 1s. 0d.: A. J. Engel, *From Clergyman to Don*, Oxford,
1983), p. 124 n. 58. Though Merton was in the van in allowing four of its fellows to marry,
the married don had appeared at Cambridge in 1860 (C. N. L. Brooke, *A History of Gonville
and Caius College* (Cambridge, 1985), p. 224 and nn. 4 and 5).

which, as Creighton showed in 1874, might bring the total to over £700.

In the two Northumberland livings six fellows in succession became vicars of Embleton between 1778 and 1895 (Henry Hodges, James Boulter, George Grimes, George Rooke, Mandell Creighton, and M. F. Osborn); similarly, four were vicars of Ponteland between 1783 and 1878 (John Rawlins, John Bartlam, John Lightfoot, and Kenrick Prescot). Not all were resident. Grimes, Rooke, and Creighton certainly were at Embleton – a valuable living worth £840 per annum in Creighton's day. Rawlins, Bartlam, and Lightfoot were non-resident at Ponteland. The visiting archdeacon in 1826 made a sharp distinction between James Boulter and George Grimes as vicars of Embleton, where later Creighton's work became a by-word. Louise Creighton left an unforgettable account of the conscientious way in which her husband carried out his duties at Embleton, while at the same time finding the time which he particularly sought for writing and scholarship.[40]

That there was a great deal to do in some of the livings comes out most clearly in the story of the Rev. W. C. Chetwynd Stapylton's resuscitation of the ancient living of Malden, Surrey (1850–94).[41] Another good account of parochial endeavour is that given by E. A. Knox of his time at Kibworth, Leicestershire.[42] Kibworth along with Cuxham (Oxon.), Diddington (Hunts.), Elham (Kent), Farleigh (Surrey), Gamlingay (Cambs.), and Lapworth (Warwicks.)[43] were all occupied on one or more occasions by former fellows as incumbents. That the chance of marriage, an uninterrupted opportunity to work, and material attractions were often matched by a sense of duty is

---

[40] Creighton, *Life and Letters*, i. 143–78, Engel, *From Clergyman to Don*, pp. 124–7.

[41] Ross, *Malden*, pp. 108–40.

[42] Knox, *Reminiscences*, pp. 119–33.

[43] *Kibworth* (Leics.): James Beresford, died 23. 9. 1840 (Reg. 1.5, p. 175); William Ricketts; S. E. Bathurst, resigned 8. 1844 (ibid., p. 207); M. F. F. Osborn, 7. 2. 1851 (ibid., p. 281)–84; E. A. Knox, 1885–91.

Cuxham (Oxon.): Francis Rowden, 1828–52; J. D. Piggott (former Bible clerk), 27. 1. 1853 (ibid., p. 303).

Diddington (Hunts.): Henry Williams, 1820–34.

Elham (Kent): Walter Woodhouse, 1846.

Farleigh (Surrey): J. C. Compton, d. 20. 4. 1835 (ibid., p. 126).

Gamlingay (Cambs., moiety): J. C. Compton, 1828–35 (20 April); H. A. S. Pye, DD, 1835–25. 3. 1839 (ibid., p. 157); G. Tyndall, 23. 7. 1839 (ibid., p. 163); d. reported 23. 2. 1848 (ibid., p. 240).

Lapworth (Warwicks.): H. A. S. Pye, d. 25. 3. 1839 (ibid., p. 157); G. Tyndall, 1839–48; C. W. St J. Mildmay, 21. 6. 1848 (ibid., p. 245)–64; J. R. T. Eaton, 1864–78.

Wolford (Warwicks.): E. H. B. Estcourt, 1830–43 (ibid., p. 201 (resigned)).

suggested by the few examples where there are reliable accounts by which to judge them, as with Creighton at Embleton, Knox at Kibworth, and Stapylton at Malden.

Meanwhile in those less valuable livings in the Oxford area, which could be combined with a fellowship by a bachelor, the records of St Peter's-in-the-East, St Cross, Holywell, St Peter's, Wolvercote, and St John the Baptist also suggest a general conscientiousness in the clerical fellows. St Peter's-in-the-East had no fewer than seven Merton fellows as vicars, of whom Edward Denison, Walter Kerr Hamilton, and Edmund Hobhouse, all future bishops, were outstanding. Hobhouse, vicar for fifteen years, sought to change the tradition by which the Oxford parishes passed rapidly through the hands of junior fellows who only held them until some more valuable living became vacant. He was also from 1848 vicar of St John the Baptist, and the college assigned £30 per annum for his stipend there.[44] If a fellow was unavailable, a chaplain or a Bible clerk might be presented. The chapel of St Cross, Holywell, was turned into a perpetual curacy and filled effectively by six of the fellows,[45] of whom Goulburn, a future dean of Norwich, was famous for his preaching, and G. N. Freeling for his work as a parish priest. Similarly at Wolvercote,[46] where seven fellows administered, the curacy was turned into a vicarage and help was given with the building of the church.

Only close at hand, in the north transept of the chapel where the parish of St John the Baptist worshipped, was there any discordancy. It arose from the difference in status between the parochial north

[44] *St Peter's-in-the-East* (from 1817 onwards incumbents license assistant curates): H. W. Buckley, 1821; Edward Denison (fellow, 1826–32), curate 6 Nov. 1834; Walter Kerr Hamilton, vicar 1837–41, resigned 1841 (*VCH Oxon.* iv. 400); William Adams, vicar 17 Dec. 1841 (Reg. 1.5, p. 186); Edmund Hobhouse, 1843–58 (*VCH Oxon.* iv. 400); Edward Capel Cure, 20 Oct. 1858 (Reg. 1.5, p. 382); John Richard King, 1 Oct. 1867 (ibid., p. 457, offer 20 June)–1907 (*VCH Oxon.* iv. 400).

[45] *St Cross*, Holywell (perpetual curacy): Peter Vaughan, 1799–1811 (*VCH Oxon.* iv. 377); C. St J. Mildmay, 1803; assistant curate Jos. Bardgett, 1807–29; R. E. Bridges, 1839–43 (30 Dec. 1839 (Reg. 1.5, p. 167), resigned 9. 2. 1843); S. E. Bathurst, nominated 1843, 1843–4; E. M. Goulburn, 1844–9; 2. 2. 1850 offer to Mr Pollen (ibid., p. 268) and to Mr Constantine Prichard; H. B. Walton, 10 June 1851–7 (ibid., p. 287, nomination); G. N. Freeling, 1871–92.

[46] *Wolvercote*: G. D. Grimes, 1826; George Rooke, 1828. Endowed perpetual curacy: Edward Denison, 1829; George Trevelyan, resigned April 1834; William Ricketts, 1834–7. Vicarage: Stephen Edwardes, vicar 1853–64, 1866–71; R. J. Wilson, 1875–9; F. W. Langton, 1889–95.

St John the Baptist (curacy until 1891 when united with St Peter's-in-the-East): Edmund Hobhouse nominated 23 Oct. 1847, 3 Nov. 1847 (Reg. 1.5, p. 238); H. W. Sargent, 29. 6. 1854 (ibid., p. 329), d. 18. 7. 1867 (ibid., p. 457); J. R. King, to be instituted before 18. 7. 1868 (ibid., p. 462); E. A. Knox, 1874–80 (*VCH Oxon.* iv. 384).

transept and the collegiate remainder of the church, of which the archbishop of Canterbury was the visitor. The bishop of Oxford, Samuel Wilberforce, ever a busy man, claimed the right of visitation. The fact that the college had allowed the parish to conduct some of its services in the main part of the chapel between 1850 and 1859 doubtless encouraged the bishop to press his claim. The fellows were also suspicious of their colleague, the vicar of St John the Baptist, since he had introduced a surpliced choir and when he added an organ was suspected of seeking to introduce more practices thought of then as High Church and milestones on the road to Rome. The college nevertheless emerged unscathed from the episcopal millstones.

College responsibility in its livings, where they had been appropriated, included the obligation to maintain their chancels, which were repaired regularly as at Wolvercote (Oxon.),[47] Elham (Kent),[48] and Diddington (Hunts.).[49] Naturally, too, the parsonage houses where fellows or former fellows might live were repaired and rebuilt, as at Wolvercote for William Ricketts in 1836,[50] at Farleigh in 1846,[51] or Wolford, or provided with new vicarages as at St Peter's-in-the-East, Oxford, and St Cross, which was built to a design by C. Buckeridge in 1864.[52]

A new interest appears with the movement initiated by the foundation of the National Society for promoting the education of the poor in the principles of the Established Church (1811), designed to rival a Nonconformist body set up in 1803 and entitled the British and Foreign School Society in 1814.[53] In 1839 Merton granted £25 to one of its fellows, W. K. Hamilton, the vicar of St Peter's-in-the-East, towards building a school house in his parish.[54] Parliamentary legislation was passed in 1841[55] and an increasing amount of government money was available to share between the societies, for building schools. The college then frequently tried to secure matching funds

[47] Reg. 1.5, p. 385 (1859).
[48] Ibid., p. 376 (1857).
[49] Ibid. (1857).
[50] Ibid., p. 133 (1836).
[51] Ibid., p. 226 (1846).
[52] *VCH Oxon.* iv. 376. The vicarage of St Peter's-in-the-East was let to tenants in the 16th and 17th cents., a workhouse in the 18th, and sold in 1804 (ibid., p. 398).
[53] E. L. Woodward, *The Age of Reform, 1815–1870* (1946), p. 458.
[54] Reg. 1.5, p. 166.
[55] 4 and 5 Victoria, c. 38.

to build schools in the parishes where it either held the living or was a substantial landowner.

However, the national movement had its focus in the towns, whilst the college's interests were chiefly in country villages. Since half the cost of the building of a school had often to be met by voluntary contributions it sometimes took a long time to raise the necessary funds. At Gamlingay (Cambs.), for instance, an initial grant of £20 towards the building of a school and £10 towards the salary of a schoolmaster of a school for boys and girls in 1847,[56] together with other contributions, proved inadequate. In the following year the college increased its contribution towards the building by £10.[57] Similarly at Ibstone (Bucks.), where the college had initially granted £50 towards the building of a school in 1847,[58] two years later we find it granting 2 roods and 29 perches for the site of the school to be administered by the trustees of the Goring Charity,[59] and in 1853 a further £50[60] to make good the deficit on the cost of the building which had already been erected.

Where the incumbent was a former fellow the initiative often came from him, as it did from Francis Rowden at Cuxham in 1848. College agreed to make £50 available to build a school;[61] two of its cottages near the church were set aside,[62] though subsequently the site was used for a National School instead;[63] a subscription for £5 per annum was raised in 1853 to £20.[64] At St Peter's-in-the-East, where another fellow, Edmund Hobhouse, was vicar and pursuing Hamilton's initiative, a piece of ground was provided for a site in Rose Lane[65] and later extended. At St Cross, Holywell, where Hobhouse was also the incumbent, the college gave a site close to the church, on part of what had been Holywell Common (1850). The vicar, in the first instance, himself advanced the cost of the building. The architect (as for the vicarage) was C. Buckeridge. An infant school was added a year later and a public subscription raised to clear the debt and provide £35 per annum for maintenance. The sums granted by the college to schools were often quite small, and doubtless it more or less had to join in a public subscription if it was a major landowner in the parish concerned. To build a school might cost anything from £650, the cost of

[56] Reg. 1.5, p. 228.
[57] Ibid., p. 253.
[58] Ibid., p. 228.
[59] Ibid., p. 264.
[60] Ibid., p. 315.

[61] Ibid., p. 241.
[62] Ibid., p. 256.
[63] Ibid., p. 258.
[64] Ibid., p. 305.
[65] Ibid., p. 203.

a school at Wolford in 1873,[66] to £1,200, the price for one at Ponteland in 1872.[67] Once the movement had gathered pace the college found itself making a large number of grants either towards building or maintenance or, as at Radstone, to paying £350 for a cottage in which the schoolmistress might live.[68] Thus it benefited schools at Ponteland and Embleton (Northumberland),[69] Bielby (Yorks.),[70] Barkby[71] and Kibworth (Leics.),[72] Wolford (Warwicks.),[73] Princes Risborough (Bucks.), Malden and Chessington (Surrey), Finmere, Eynsham, Littlemore, Wolvercote, and Cuxham (Oxon.), Newington and Elham (Kent), and several others.[74] Whether it liked it or not, it had been drawn into a national movement for educating the children of the poor up to the age of eleven, and some of its fellows and incumbents were certainly keen to take part. Nationally many of the schools built were on a scale too small to survive the reforms of the twentieth century, unlike the churches, ironically, which have often proved too big for dwindling congregations. One school of that kind, Holywell, has survived as part of St Cross College which has carefully preserved it. Thirty years and more before the great Education Act of 1870, the effects of which on her school were so tellingly described by the author of *Lark Rise to Candleford*, the parish schools to which the college subscribed made a notable contribution to the lives of the children who attended them.

LAWYERS AND MPS

In the early nineteenth century as in the late eighteenth a significant number of fellows wished to study law. The founder's tentative provision for legal studies was exploited particularly by those who aimed at a career at the bar. No fewer than twenty-nine fellows turned to

[66] Reg. 1.5, p. 522. The school was paid for by Lord Redesdale.
[67] Ibid., p. 509.
[68] Reg. 1.5 a, p. 284 (Radstone).
[69] Reg. 1.5, p. 331.
[70] Ibid., p. 344.
[71] Reg. 1.5 a, pp. 85, 202.
[72] Reg. 1.5, p. 486.
[73] Ibid., p. 522.
[74] Ibid., p. 386 (Princes Risborough, Lacy Green), p. 199 (Cheddington), p. 332 (Finmere), p. 219 (Eynsham), p. 512 (Littlemore), p. 348 (Wolvercote, where the school benefited from a legacy of £100 left to it by an incumbent, the Rev. L. E. Judge, a former chaplain of Merton (ibid., p. 412)), p. 486 (Newington), above nn. 61–3 (Cuxham, Elham).

the law after holding their fellowship for only a few years. The phenomenon was weaker after 1850, and two-thirds of the Merton fellows who turned barrister did so before the middle of the century. Lincoln's Inn was their favourite, perhaps because Warden Marsham was a Lincoln's Inn man, also because of its specialized chancery interests.

The most outstanding of these men was James Robert Hope-Scott, who quickly won renown as a parliamentary barrister. He was exceptionally fluent and persuasive even on behalf of unpromising causes and amassed a considerable fortune. He appeared in a series of cases involving railways which flooded in as the railway network spread. He also appeared in a famous case concerning the Mersey docks. Another Merton barrister fellow with a successful career was James Stuart-Wortley (fellow, 1832–46), MP for Halifax (1835–7) and for Bute (1842–59), who became a law officer of the Crown, first as Judge-Advocate-General in 1846 and then as Solicitor-General in Palmerston's government (1856–7). The most striking legal luminary of the later Governing Body was undoubtedly F. E. Smith, Lord Birkenhead, elected as fellow in 1896 from Wadham. He became the college's first lecturer in law in the following year. The appointment followed logically from the separation of the School of Law and Modern History in 1872. The committee headed by the warden recognized that Smith would not stay very long because of the lure of politics, but it judged that in the time that he taught he would be a notable stimulus to undergraduates reading law. He was not the only Merton lawyer to become Lord Chancellor. A Merton commoner, H. S. Giffard (later earl of Halsbury) was to reach that most senior office as a Tory Lord Chancellor (1885–6; 1886–1905), and at the age of 88 was the fiercest of the die-hard defenders of the powers of the House of Lords in the great constitutional struggle with the Commons in 1911. His more positive achievement was to preside over the compilation of *Halsbury's Laws of England* (1905–16) which has held its place throughout the twentieth century as the only modern encyclopaedic treatment of English law.[75]

A legal career was often combined with politics, but there were no more than five Merton MPs in the nineteenth century from the Governing Body. Brodrick, before he was warden, tried to secure

---

[75] Cf. R. E. V. Heuston, *Lives of the Lord Chancellors, 1885–1940* (Oxford, 1964), p. 35. Professor Beatson has kindly helped with the appraisal of Halsbury's contribution.

election three times, twice at Woodstock, as a Liberal. Two of the successful MPs were Stuart-Wortley, already mentioned, and Charles Savile Currer, who changed his name to Roundell. Stuart-Wortley was a Peelite Conservative, but Roundell represented Grantham (1880–5) and Skipton (1892–5) as a Liberal. A more spectacular figure, the apostle of Tory democracy, was a former commoner, Lord Randolph Churchill. He took a second class in Law and Modern History under Creighton's tuition. He sat for the pocket borough of Woodstock in 1874 and 1880, having stood on the first occasion against the future Warden Brodrick. He moved his seat to Paddington South in 1885 and was appointed Secretary of State for India in the short-lived Salisbury government of that year. In 1886, he was made Chancellor of the Exchequer, a position he resigned dramatically after only five months, never to hold office again.

A shift in the schools from which the fellows came ran parallel with the switch from a Christ Church-dominated to a Balliol-dominated entry. As long as the provosts of Eton and of King's College, Cambridge, regularly nominated a postmaster each (up to the University Reform Act of 1854) there was a steady small flow of Etonian post-masters, and five of them subsequently became fellows.[76] They were joined by fourteen other Etonian fellows who came in by examination, seven from Christ Church,[77] four from Balliol,[78] and two from Oriel,[79] all before 1855. Schools other than Eton appeared only rarely. There were, it is true, five Rugbeians before 1852,[80] four Old Westminsters by 1851,[81] and a Wykehamist in 1847.[82] After the University Reform Act that changed quite dramatically. Other public schools were now represented: Harrow (3),[83] Christ's Hospital (1),[84]

---

[76] T. Davies (1806), J. Lightfoot (1807), H. F. Whish (1812), G. Hamilton Seymour (1821), W. C. Stapylton (1847).

[77] R. B. Marsham (1811), R. Pollen (1811), A. Herbert (1814), C. Pigou (1821), G. Tyndall (1823), J. Hope-Scott (1833), J. Bruce (1835).

[78] E. Hobhouse (1841), E. M. Goulburn (1841), J. Hungerford Pollen (1842), the Hon. G. C. Brodrick (1855).

[79] G. Tierney (1823), E. Denison (1826).

[80] M. R. Grey (1818), B. Compton (1841), C. A. St J. Mildmay (1845), H. W. Sargent (1848), E. Capel Cure (1852).

[81] J. J. Randolph (1840), H. R. Farrer (1843), M. F. F. Osborn (1847), W. H. Karslake (1851).

[82] W. P. Dickins (1847).

[83] E. H. B. Estcourt (1826), C. S. Currer/Roundell (1851), H. H. Joachim (1890).

[84] W. Scott (1879).

Radley (1),[85] Uppingham (1),[86] Marlborough (3),[87] and Shrewsbury (1).[88] All those fellows came in from other colleges. The big London schools also began to put in an appearance, as St Paul's,[89] Blackheath School,[90] University College School,[91] and Merchant Taylors'.[92] Similarly, provincial grammar school pupils came in from Bristol Grammar School,[93] Manchester Grammar School,[94] Heversham School,[95] Macclesfield Grammar School,[96] and Birkenhead School.[97] The north was also represented by Durham School[98] and York.[99] Setting aside the Scottish schools from which the graduates of Scottish universities came, other schools represented on the Governing Body included Kingswood, the Methodist day and boarding school near Bath,[100] Magdalen College School,[101] Coventry School,[102] Queen Elizabeth School, Guernsey,[103] and Westward Ho.[104] The comparison with the first half of the century is striking. Through the opening of the fellowships, membership of the Governing Body had come to represent a wide range of pupils of English and Scottish schools, though as yet Welsh schools hardly appear and Irish not at all.

NATURAL SCIENCES

Another change in the middle of the century was a new emphasis put upon the natural sciences. The foundation of a School of Natural

---

[85] T. H. Wright (1874).
[86] J. H. Skrine (1877).
[87] T. L. Papillon (1865), F. H. Bradley (1870), L. T. Hobhouse (1887).
[88] J. C. Miles (1899).
[89] E. A. Knox (1868), C. R. Beazley (1889), E. R. Lankester (1891), F. H. B. Dale (1893).
[90] W. C. Sidgwick (1857).
[91] W. Ashburner (1887), B. W. Henderson (1894).
[92] C. T. Cruttwell (1870).
[93] T. Bowman (1877).
[94] E. Barker (1897).
[95] A. L. Selby (1886).
[96] K. Prescot (1853).
[97] F. E. Smith (1894).
[98] J. R. King (1859), M. Creighton (1866).
[99] A. W. Reinold (1866).
[100] J. W. Russell (1876), A. L. Dixon (1891), A. E. Taylor (1891).
[101] M. Hutton (1879).
[102] A. S. Peake (1890).
[103] J. R. T. Eaton (1847).
[104] E. A. Minchin (1892).

Sciences in 1849–50[105] was accompanied by the movement led by Henry Acland, which brought about the setting up of the University Museum. The first idea in 1850 was to establish the museum on land belonging to Merton immediately to the east of the city wall by Rose Lane.[106] Wisely a more extensive site was chosen – four acres of Merton land to the east of Parks Road and opposite the future site of Keble.[107] As a result, the whole of the science area was later built on land bought by the university from Merton. The college was equally involved in the appointments of two of the professors of science which followed the opening of the museum in 1860.[108]

The new Linacre chair of physiology came to Merton because in the sixteenth century Bishop Tunstall, Linacre's executor, had selected Merton for the seat of the lecturers on the works of the Greek medical authors, Galen and Hippocrates.[109] It was then the only Oxford college to have had a physician as its head. Once the Commissioners had become aware of the existence of lectureships the neglect into which they had fallen in the eighteenth century was made good. The revival of the Linacre link provided the college with its most important continuous modern scientific tradition. Warden Brodrick has recorded how he, as a young fellow, was involved in sounding out the great T. H. Huxley to persuade him to take up one of the new chairs.[110] Huxley was hesitant about coming to Oxford, but the new chair of physiology, created by the suppression of four Merton fellowships, went to one of his disciples, George Rolleston.

Rolleston had practical experience as a doctor of St Bartholomew's Hospital in London, in Smyrna during the Crimean War, and at the Great Ormond Street Hospital for Sick Children.[111] He was an excellent lecturer on anatomy and physiology though the content of his lectures was sometimes judged to be diffuse. He took advantage of the fact that Acland had organized the anatomy collection at Christ Church on Hunterian principles. He himself worked on comparative crania and encouraged studies on embryology and heredity. His pupils included two of his successors as Linacre professor, H. N. Moseley and

[105] C. E.Mallett, *History of the University of Oxford* (1927), iii. 297.
[106] T. Braun, 'The Garden from 1720', *Postmaster* (1986), p. 13, and cf. Reg. 1.5, pp. 270–1, 279, 305.
[107] *VCH Oxon*. iii. 57.
[108] Cf. Mallett, *History of the University of Oxford*, iii. 366; Sinclair and Robb-Smith, p. 60.
[109] See above p. 149.
[110] G. C. Brodrick, *Memories and Impressions* (1900), pp. 257–8.
[111] Sinclair and Robb-Smith, pp. 59–62.

E. Ray Lankester. The suppression of the fellowships took time, and meanwhile the chair changed its title. Rolleston had become professor of human and comparative anatomy by 1860. His official link with the college began in 1872.[112]

In the mean time another future professor of science, Robert Bellamy Clifton, had joined the Governing Body. He was attached in 1865 to Wadham, which had agreed to help pay for a chair in experimental philosophy,[113] and he laid out the Clarendon Laboratory in 1868. The following year he transferred to Merton, and although he gained his chair at Wadham in 1877 he remained a fellow of Merton until he retired in 1915. He had been, it seems, a successful professor of natural philosophy at Owen's College, Manchester, but his tenure of his Oxford chair was disappointing. It is true that he concentrated on the important matter of training teachers of science in schools, but in the words of one of his demonstrators he was 'very perturbed at the growing restlessness which the desire to research was introducing into physics'.[114] He personally did not intend to let research deflect him, and during his long reign it appears that only one serious piece of work can be identified in the Clarendon Laboratory, and that had been initiated in London. Lord Cherwell was probably not far off the mark when he said that Clifton held up the development of physics at Oxford for forty years. Science also suffered at Oxford in general in the last decades of the century from the way in which the 1877 Act tied its financing to an expected growth of income from the colleges. When college revenues fell during the agricultural depression of the 1880s, the funding of science fell with them.[115]

Meanwhile, the college reacted to the establishment of the school of natural sciences by appointing its first tutor in the subject, T. H. G. Wyndham of Oriel. He was elected to a fellowship in 1867 and then made lecturer and tutor in natural sciences in 1872, when he was spending up to £50 on apparatus.[116] He was also lecturer in mathematics, but was, it seems, a chemist, to judge from his appointment as Aldrichian demonstrator in 1873. When he died three years later he

---

[112] Ibid., p. 60. The 3rd, 5th, 7th and 9th fellowships had first to become vacant (*Ordinances concerning Merton College in pursuance of 17 & 18 Victoria c. 81* (1863), c. 22, pp. 10–11).

[113] *Ordinances in pursuance of 17 & 18 Victoria* (Wadham College).

[114] Letter of 16 September 1968 from O. F. Brown to T. C. Keeley, Fellow of Wadham, kindly lent by Professor Bleaney.

[115] J. Howarth, 'Science Education in late-Victorian Oxford: a curious case of failure', *EHR* cii (1987), 334–71.

[116] Reg. 1.5, p. 513.

was replaced as lecturer in natural sciences and as a demonstrator in the chemistry laboratory by W. H. Pike, who became professor at University College, Toronto, and then, in 1880, by a pupil of Faraday, a Balliol MA called John Watts. Watts held his lecturership until 1914 and forged the link through his pupil, B. Lambert, with the twentieth-century succession of Merton chemists. An ordinance of 1863 required that examinations for fellowships be held in the different subjects of the schools, and ensured that natural science regularly had its turn. Among the fellows thus elected in physics, A. W. Reinold from Brasenose became Dr Lee's reader in physics, A. S. Macdonald Millard lecturer in physics at Trinity, and A. L. Selby professor of physics at Cardiff. It was the Linacre professors especially who maintained the continuity of Merton science. The most notable was Professor Lankester, already mentioned. He was a large and quarrelsome figure, ready to assert himself in and out of college. He had already held the chairs of zoology and comparative anatomy at University College, London, and that of natural history at Edinburgh, and received the Gold Medal of the Royal Society before his election to the Linacre chair in 1891.[117] He held the chair for eight years before resigning in 1898 to become director of the Natural History Museum in London. He was an important figure with E. B. Poulton in developing Darwin's theory of evolution. In 1900, he entered into a lively debate with Warden Brodrick over the financing of science at Oxford.[118] Lankester argued that half the Oxford fellowships ought to be given to scientists. It was ironic that the warden, who had strongly advocated making two-thirds of the Merton fellowships available to laymen, should find himself opposing the proposition that half the fellowships should be for scientists. Since by the most favourable view no more than 32 of Oxford's 297 fellowships were held by scientists, it must be admitted that, though he stated his case too sharply, Lankester certainly had a strong point.[119] There is a good caricature of him by Max in the Beerbohm Room. Another zoologist, elected to a fellowship in 1893, was E. A. Minchin, demonstrator in comparative anatomy, who went on to become Jodrell professor of zoology in University College, London.

---

[117] *Who Was Who, 1929–1948*, p. 779.
[118] Cf. A. J. Engel, *From Clergyman to Don* (Oxford, 1983), pp. 227–9.
[119] Ibid., p. 228.

THE ENGLISH CHAIRS

In 1874 it seemed likely that the college would join in the movement towards establishing college laboratories. A committee which included both Rolleston and Clifton was set up to consider the question of building a laboratory for the study of chemical geology and lithology. The estimated cost was £4,000, and maintenance was set at £400 per annum,[120] but no positive steps were taken. Instead the college wrote to the vice-chancellor about the establishment of chairs in the light of the discussions of the second University Reform Commission. It proposed that it should support chairs in physics, classical archaeology, and English. The chair in physics went to Wadham, as had been earlier intended; classical archaeology eventually went to Lincoln, though Merton made a financial contribution. It was thus the chair in English with which Merton became preoccupied. It was to be worth up to £900 per annum and paid for by the suppression of four fellowships. While it took time for them to become available a hot debate began over the nature of the chair.

At first it was to be a chair of Anglo-Saxon, but subsequently, at the request of the college, literature was added to the professor's obligations. There were several exchanges between the Hebdomadal Council and the college before it was advertised as a chair of English language and literature in 1885 and filled by the distinguished philologist, A. S. Napier, who held a similarly described chair at Göttingen.[121] He brought to Oxford and to Anglo-Saxon learning in England the high standard of German philological studies. But Napier, once established, argued that the literary side should be defined in terms of early literature, that is, down to Chaucer. When it was proposed that the Rawlinson chair of Anglo-Saxon should be merged with a chair of English language only, and that the sum thus saved above the professor's salary of £900 should be set towards paying for a professor of literature, the proposition proved unacceptable to those who wished to keep the tradition of the Anglo-Saxon chair apart from the Merton chair. Nevertheless a view emerged that there should be

---

[120] Reg. 1.5, p. 528.

[121] *Who Was Who, 1916–1928*, p. 768, and N. Ker, 'A. S. Napier, 1853–1916', quoted in Engel, *From Clergyman to Don*, p. 240 n. 139. Cf. college request of 29 Nov. 1880 (Reg. 1.5 a, p. 59), *Statutes in pursuance of the Oxford & Cambridge Act, 1877* (1882), p. 11, c. 11 (salary of £700 plus emoluments of fellowship). The latter were formed out of the 2nd, 4th, and another fellowship to fall vacant (ibid., p. 26). For Churton Collins's efforts to turn it into a chair of literature, see Engel, *From Clergyman to Don*, pp. 239–44.

two chairs of English literature, one with the emphasis on language and the other on literature, yet to be established. Those two concepts were to prove valuable to the college in the twentieth century.

In 1897 when he joined the college as a young fellow, Ernest Barker especially appreciated its philosophers, but in addition to the representatives of classics, mathematics, natural science and English already referred to, he picked out modern history and law for special mention.[122] In modern history the outstanding man was Samuel Rawson Gardiner, the historian of the Puritan Revolution.[123] He was a dedicated research fellow, whose *History of England from the accession of James I* (1863–82) became a classic and held the field for many years. In law the notable figure was F. E. Smith. Here was a brilliant talker and a future Lord Chancellor, a star indeed.

PHILOSOPHY

Though the Merton fellowship proved a good recruiting-ground for professors of classics overseas (Walter Scott went to Sydney in 1884, and Maurice Hutton as professor of Greek to University College, Toronto, by way of Sheffield, in 1886), it was above all in philosophy that the Governing Body stood out in the second half of the nineteenth century. The stimulus came from Scotland via Balliol. Already in 1864 Edward Caird had brought his learning and experience from Glasgow University to the Greats tutorship and had numbered Creighton among his pupils. At Balliol he came under the influence of T. H. Green, who was a fellow-member of the Old Mortality Club. Caird was 'eager to direct students to use sources of thought opened by German philosophy and theology'. This gave a fresh excitement to the study of philosophy and led Caird, while at Glasgow (to which he had returned as professor of moral philosophy in 1866), to publish *A Critical Account of the Philosophy of Kant with an Historical Introduction* (1877, 2nd vol. 1889) and a monograph on Hegel (1883). Meanwhile his place as Greats tutor at Merton was taken by another Scot, William Wallace (born 1873), who arrived from St Andrews via Balliol. He

---

[122] E. Barker, *Age and Youth: Memories of Three Universities and Father of the Man* (Oxford, 1953), p. 34; *Mert. Coll. Reg. 1900–64*, p. 2.
[123] The School of Law and Modern History had split into two in 1872.

remained as tutor for thirty years. As Caird himself observed, 'as a teacher of philosophy to men reading for the Honours School of Literae Humaniores, he has had few rivals in the history of the University.'[124] That view may be set against that of one of his early pupils, John Maude, a classical postmaster (1869–73), who while describing Wallace as 'that really remarkable metaphysician' also wrote, 'an accurate thinker but a very poor lecturer'.[125] His achievement as tutor was the more notable as he was elected Whyte's professor of moral philosophy in 1882,[126] and at that time election to a chair did not mean that its holder had to resign his tutorship. It is even more remarkable that from 1871 he held the important college office of librarian, and, while holding it, carried through the Herculean task of publishing a catalogue of its printed holdings.[127] Small wonder that his publications came slowly, though come they did. When he published the *Logic of Hegel* in 1873, translating the text from Hegel's *Encyclopaedia of Philosophical Science*, its introduction was judged 'one of the earliest and most luminous expositions of the Hegelian point of view in English'. Other works of Hegel to be translated were the *Prolegomena* (1880) and his *Philosophy of Mind* (1890). After having made a pilgrimage to Koenigsberg Wallace published on Kant in 1882.

Wallace continued to extend his studies of German philosophers with a life of Schopenhauer, but when he was chosen to give the prestigious Gifford lectures he took as his topic the general relations between natural religion and moral philosophy. He gave his lectures in two series but did not live to complete their preparation for publication as he was killed in a bicycle accident in 1892. It was left to his friend Caird to edit them. Meanwhile a different philosophical tradition, though one similarly cast in an idealist mould, was being developed by F. H. Bradley, who had been elected to a fellowship in 1870. Bradley had read Greats at University College.[128] He was an admirer of Mill rather than of Kant, but despite their different approaches it seems that Wallace advocated his election. Bradley

---

[124] W. Wallace, *Lectures and Essays on Natural Theology and Ethics*, ed. E. Caird (Oxford, 1898), p. xvii.

[125] Maude, *Memories*, p. 67. His view may not be representative.

[126] Cf. Engel, *From Clergyman to Don*, pp. 251–2.

[127] *A Catalogue of the Printed Books in Merton College Library* (Oxford, 1880). On his election to his chair he was relieved by the college of pass work in the Final Schools (Reg. 1.5 a, pp. 89, 112).

[128] G. R. G. Mure, 'Francis Herbert Bradley', *Études philosophiques*, no. 1 (Jan./March 1960), p. 76.

suffered throughout his time as fellow from a kidney disease and as he grew older became increasingly deaf, which moved him to avoid teaching and college offices. His concentration on research work also helps to explain its intensity and his tendency to become something of a recluse. A very different side to Bradley emerges, however, in the record of his friendship with the romantic novelist, Elinor Glyn, whom he first met at the Hôtel Beau Rivage in St Raphael in 1910. Cheiron, the Professor in Glyn's novel *Halcyone* (1912), is a portrait of Bradley.[129] Though he was renowned for his courtesy he was greatly feared by his philosophical colleague, Harold Joachim, a future Wykeham professor of logic. Joachim was appointed as tutor to replace Wallace. By the end of the century Bradley had made four major contributions to philosophical studies in *Presuppositions of Critical History* (1874), *Ethical Studies* (1876), *Principles of Logic* (1883), and above all *Appearance and Reality* (1893). By then the philosophical element of the fellowship had been further strengthened by the elections of John Burnet who came in from Edinburgh and Balliol (in 1892) and of A. E. Taylor from New College. Taylor turned to Plato rather than to the Germans for the focus of his idealist studies and later pursued a very successful career as a teacher at McGill and St Andrews.

Sir Ernest Barker, elected in the year of Wallace's death, has given an evocative recollection of the Merton Senior Common Room at the end of the century:

> The essence of the character of Merton, as I knew or rather felt it, was determined for me by the company of Fellows to whose society I was admitted. To be admitted to that society was to enjoy the franchise of a fine tradition of scholarship. The tradition was primarily a tradition of the study of philosophy. Among the philosophical Fellows of my time the foremost was F. H. Bradley, whose swift and incisive mind would have terrified me if it had not been joined with a polished courtesy and a great generosity to a young colleague; there were also A. E. Taylor and Harold Joachim, both of them masters and afterwards professors of their subject, and John Burnet, once a fellow but then a professor in Scotland, would occasionally stay in the college and add his massive judgement to the stock of our common discourse. I say 'our discourse', but I was

---

[129] Anthony Glyn, *Elinor Glyn* (1955), pp. 195, 201–2, 205. This note is owed to the kindness of Mr P. J. Waller.

no more than a spell-bound listener; and I said to myself, in the words of a poem in the Greek Anthology, 'I know that I am mortal and the creature of a day ... but I sit at Jove's own table, and take my fill of the ambrosia that nourishes the gods.'[130]

THE VISITOR

Until the first University Reform Act (to which he had been opposed) the visitor had important powers in Merton College. The most influential lay in his right at the time of the election of a new warden to choose one of the three names presented to him by the electing fellows for confirmation. Under the Act of 1854 the fellows were for the first time given the power to send to him one name only for confirmation. But the visitor retained the right to refuse the nomination and then to revert to the old procedure.[131] His rights were, however, reduced under the Act of 1877. He lost his right to refuse the fellows' nomination, though when the voting was even he retained the right to give the casting vote.[132] He was also specifically enjoined to interpret the statutes, if asked to do so; he remained the supreme judicial authority to whom appeals might be sent in the case of grievance, or if it seemed that the statutes were being broken.[133] What did that mean in practice?

In 1864, Archbishop Longley visited the college for its sexcentenary. Remembering perhaps the experience of his predecessors, Archbishops Wake and Potter, Longley took the opportunity to observe that he rejoiced that his authority had not hitherto been invoked for disciplinary purposes.[134] He spoke too soon. If John Maude is to be believed, he appealed to the visitor in about 1870 against the decision of Mandell Creighton, as principal of the postmasters, that all members should keep four morning chapels during the week. Maude held that he was only obliged to keep chapel on Sundays, which he did. He reported that Archbishop Tait agreed with his interpretation, but Creighton hit back by introducing roll-calls instead.[135] Another

[130] Barker, *Age and Youth*, p. 34.
[131] *Ordinances in pursuance of 17 & 18 Victoria* c. 1, p. 4.
[132] *Statutes in pursuance of the Oxford and Cambridge Act, 1877*, p. 5.
[133] Ibid., pp. 6–7, 23–4.
[134] Reg. 1.5, p. 427.
[135] Maude, *Memories*, p. 73.

appeal reached the archbishop in 1880. Again it was against the authority of the principal of the postmasters, by now E. A. Knox. It was claimed that Knox was handing out punishments disproportionately severe in relation to the misdemeanours involved. The archbishop waited until there had been an exchange between the warden and tutors and the undergraduates and then withdrew from the dispute.[136] More significant is the way in which the college itself applied to the visitor for interpretation of the statutes. Already in 1866 and again in 1869 he had resisted an attempt by a group of fellows headed by Brodrick to alter the balance between lay and clerical fellows, established by the Act of 1854 at half and half, to two thirds lay and one third clerical.[137] In 1889 he gave judgement upon the incompatibility of holding a fellowship together with the wardenship of Keble.[138] He also adjudicated over the pension rights of a married fellow who became a professor.[139] There was a colourful correspondence between the visitor, the warden, and Professor Lankester when the latter appealed against what he claimed were the extravagant Common Room charges at Merton and the bursar's habit of deducting fees in advance from salaries.[140] Even so that was tame stuff in comparison with the days of the medieval archbishops or those of other centuries before his own.

TUITION AND DISCIPLINE

The most notable feature of the Merton undergraduates in the nineteenth century was the paucity of their numbers. In the years before the first University Reform Act they seem often to have mustered not many more than the twenty-three or twenty-four members of the Governing Body itself. By 1851, for example, there were thirty-five of whom only eight were on the foundation with twenty-seven ordinary commoners. If the foundationers had been at full strength there should have been fourteen postmasters, four Jackson scholars, and two Bible clerks,[141] but their numbers had evidently not been kept up.

---

[136] Reg. 1.5 a, pp. 53–6, 60.

[137] Reg. 1.5, pp. 442, 474–5.

[138] Reg. 1.5 a, pp. 171 (27. 4. 1889). He was also consulted over fellows' rights as electors (ibid., p. 227).

[139] Ibid., pp. 306–9.

[140] Ibid., pp. 233, 238–53.

[141] Cf. *Oxford University Commission Report* (1852) (evidence), pp. 319–20.

here were no gentlemen commoners as there still were at some other olleges, such as Christ Church.[142] Warden Marsham discontinued ie custom of admitting them, on the grounds that he judged their dmission 'hurtful to discipline'. He also changed the system by which the postmasters were examined and nominated in 1834, when iose arrangements were put in the hands of the warden, the principal f the postmasters, and the three senior fellows in residence.[143] Accordigly the Postmasters' Register in which the names of the postmasters nd their patrons had been carefully recorded since 1700 came to an nd. The last entry is for 1831. The examination under the new regime oes not seem to have been terrifying, to judge by the experience of Chetwynd Stapylton. He tells us that 'being fond of aquatics at Eton, nd a great winner of boat races in 1843 I had a great desire to see the oat races at Oxford'. He was informed that there was an examination or a scholarship in the very week of the boat races and that 'I might et leave to sit for the scholarship in the daytime'. In the evening he ould watch the races. His tutor at Eton asked why he had not let him now some months before in order to be prepared. He replied that he vas well up to the sixth form and 'should very much like to try for he scholarship', and leave was given. Stapylton adds modestly that ie had not the least expectancy of success, and was 'not a little urprised when I was successful'.[144] In consequence of the Act of 1854 he postmasterships were thrown open, including the two Chamber's Eton postmasterships, if an Etonian candidate of sufficient merit did iot present himself.

Not surprisingly the college was required by the Commissioners to ncrease its undergraduate numbers. In order to do so it began to extend its accommodation. The Butterfield building, now called Grove, of 1862–3 was the result. It added a beetling presence, and twenty sets of rooms. The Reverend John Wilkinson, MA of Merton College, in his evidence to the Commissioners in 1851 commented on the fact that 'Between the Heads and Fellows of the same society (not necessarily Merton) there is a distance, between Fellows and Undergraduates an impossible gulf'.[145] At Merton, it seems, that gulf had not much diminished by 1869, to judge from John Maude's

---

[142] Ibid.

[143] Reg. 1.5, p. 110.

[144] Ross, *Malden*, p. 127. For the old regime see the examination of Hartley Coleridge, postmaster, in *Letters of Hartley Coleridge*, ed. G. E. and E. L. Griggs (Oxford, 1936), p. 11.

[145] *Oxford University Commission Report* (1852) (evidence), p. 70.

observation that the only don with whom undergraduates came into personal contact was Creighton, his tutor and the principal of the postmasters.[146] Despite their small numbers, dons and undergraduates lived in different worlds. By Maude's day the number of junior members was between 50 and 60. He has left us a vivid picture of what it was like to be an Eton postmaster reading classics. He belonged to a rather idle set, mostly Etonians, who were more interested in hunting or playing cricket than in study. Reading men there were such as Mandell Creighton and George Saintsbury, both postmaster in their day, who attained academic distinction, but as Maude recalled then, reading men were rather lonely figures. E. A. Knox, coming a a don from Corpus, took it that it was his business as tutor and principal of the postmasters to turn an idle college into a reading one He flattered himself that he had done so by the time he left.

Though the Honours Schools and examinations began in 1800 Merton was slow in encouraging its undergraduates to take advantage of the innovation. It seems that William Sewell, postmaster, who matriculated in 1822, was the first Merton man to take first-class honours in the Final School of Literae Humaniores (Greats), which he did at Easter 1827.[147] Thereafter Mertonians appear regularly in the honours lists. When they obtained first classes they were granted book prizes in money.[148]

The regime in the college as it was in 1851 is described by J. H. T Eaton, one of its tutors, in his evidence to the first Reform Commission.[149] There were two tutors who were expected to give college lectures on the whole of the syllabus except for mathematics, which was covered by a lecturer. That entailed thirty-five weekly lectures in college on ten Greek and four Latin set books, besides lectures on the Greek New Testament, logic, and Bishop Butler, a modern author with whom the Greek philosophers might be compared. Since there were five mathematical undergraduates among the total of thirty-five, each tutor presumably looked after fifteen of the pupils who were not reading mathematics. The great majority of them would have been

[146] Maude, *Memories*, p. 67.

[147] See *University Calendar* (1828), p. 140. Hartley Coleridge, postmaster, had taken a 2nd in Lit. Hum. in 1818 (H. W. Hartman, *Hartley Coleridge* (Oxford, 1931), p. 70). In 1836 W. Adams, postmaster, took a double first in Lit. Hum. and in Maths and Physics.

[148] As were the following firsts in Maths., W. Lucas (1843), B. Compton (1848), S. Edwardes (1848), T. Fowler (1852), and in Lit. Hum., F. St J. Thackeray (1855).

[149] *Oxford University Commission Report* (1852) (evidence), pp. 319–20. In 1884 there were four lecture-rooms in Fellows' Quad (Reg. 1.5 a, p. 109).

reading for pass degrees. Not until 1928 was the senior tutor able in his report to congratulate the college on the fact that the majority of its undergraduates were reading for honours. The five men reading mathematics in 1851 covered in addition to arithmetic, algebra, Euclid, and mechanics. The focus of the reading was narrow even if the coverage in Greek literature was wide. Sir Edmund Head, a former fellow and tutor, in his evidence to the Commission commented on the absence in the university of a professor of Latin and the need to strengthen instruction in Latin literature.[150]

The same observer also noted the deficiency of teaching in the Natural Sciences. While admitting that his ignorance of them was such that he hardly dared venture to give a decisive opinion, he did state that the professorial system was the only one available for any good end, and asserted that 'the physical sciences have been most unjustly depreciated and discouraged at Oxford'.[151] A Merton Bible clerk and Jackson scholar (1844–8), called J. G. Wood, might well have agreed with him. The son of an Oxford surgeon, Wood had an interest in science which led him to become an assistant to Dr Acland when Acland became Dr Lee's reader in anatomy in 1845. Unable to read natural science, which only came in as a School in 1849, Wood made science his hobby. 'His rooms [at the top of the Tower Staircase over the entrance] were full of cages, and nets, and boxes of all kinds. At the time he was studying the development of the tiger-moth from the egg to the perfect insect, and had between five and six hundred of the "woolly bear" caterpillars simultaneously feeding in an enormous breeding-cage ... Other pets he had, too, at the same time, snakes again, which had a way of escaping from their cage and lying up in all sorts of nooks and corners, to the great dismay of the "bedmaker" and the scout, bats, and various other creatures.' He became a clergyman, whilst maintaining his hobby and becoming an immensely popular lecturer on natural history, and the author of a *Natural History*, besides a wide variety of other popular scientific writings.[152]

John Maude noted that in his day (1869–73) nearly half the college was made up of Etonians, like himself. Knox states that the personality of Warden Marsham had once 'attracted Public School men and especially Etonians, of whom the great Lord Randolph Churchill was

---

[150] *Oxford University Commission Report* (1852) (evidence), p. 161.
[151] Ibid.
[152] Theodore Wood, *The Reverend J. G. Wood* (1899), pp. 12–13; Sinclair and Robb-Smith, p. 52.

a type. They were, as a rule, not very industrious, not very frugal, but they were a dominant body in the College, and the postmasters did not easily hold their own ... For those who could afford it, and did not covet more than a Pass Degree, Merton was a College with distinct social *cachet*.'[153] Maude adds, 'A large group were hunting men who did not add much to the social pleasures of the College. They mostly lived in the more expensive sort of lodgings such as "Hippy's" in St Aldates, and we saw but little of them ... The others who were interested in cricket, football, and athletics were composed of a large group of Etonian men, some very pleasant Marlburians, and a still smaller, but most acceptable number of Bradfield old boys.'[154] Some at least of the postmasters contrived to read, and were at least sustained by their allowances. For commoners the cost must have been a limiting factor, even if, as Maude records, 'Magdalen alone gave equal advantages to its undergraduates.' The evidence submitted to the Reform Commission suggested that the cost of four years at Merton in 1851 might be £600, or £150 per annum.[155] In 1869 Maude calculated his income at £146 per annum, including a leaving exhibition from Eton, to which his father added at first £60 per annum and later £80. Thus his four-year course would have cost him £584 if he had not been a postmaster.[156]

By 1875 Knox says there was 'a sadly depleted list of entrants to the College and among them not a single Public School man'.[157] He thought that the advent of married tutorships had not helped matters. He seems here to be making a criticism of Creighton and Wallace, though chiefly of the Governing Body for permitting tutors to marry without providing residences for them near the college, and then leaving the undergraduates to look after themselves from 2 p.m. in the afternoon until 9 a.m. the next morning. Merton was one of the first colleges to allow married fellowships and had initiated four for college officers in 1871. Two were taken by Creighton and Wallace, both tutors. Creighton had to live in a small house in St Giles'.[158] As sub-warden in 1881 Knox master-minded the annexation of St Alban Hall (Pl. 29). That provided accommodation for some eighteen under-

---

[153] Knox, *Reminiscences*, pp. 92–3.
[154] Maude, *Memories*, p. 70.
[155] *Oxford University Commission Report* (1852) (evidence), p. 320.
[156] Maude, *Memories*, pp. 66–7.
[157] Knox, *Reminiscences*, p. 91.
[158] Creighton, *Life and Letters*, i. 127–8.

graduates, and in the former principal's house a residence for a married
tutor in the middle of the college.[159] The next step was to negotiate
with the city to acquire Grove House in Kybald Street as another
tutor's house and a site at the east end of Merton Street in exchange
for college property in Queen Street.[160] By 1899 the exchange included
the site of 19–22 Merton Street, also owned by the city.[161]

Between 1881 and 1882 there were in residence at any one time
about twenty-three postmasters, three exhibitioners, and eighty-five
commoners, or one hundred and eleven undergraduates in all.[162] No
one school predominated as Eton had once done, but schools where
there was a former fellow as headmaster, such as Malvern (C. T.
Cruttwell), were well represented: there were six Malvernians in 1881–
2. Marlborough, already noted by Maude in 1869, provided four in
1886–7 to Eton's five. The eighteen additional men from St Alban
Hall in 1881 who came in at the annexation included[163] two from
Manchester Grammar School. They made a good academic addition:
no fewer than four Albanians gained Merton awards and one, W.
Allison Phillips, a history exhibitioner, went on to become professor
of history at Trinity College, Dublin, and a scholar of distinction. The
principal's house became (1882) the house of a married don, G. R.
Scott (tutor from 1878), who taught Classical Moderations to Max
Beerbohm (1890–3). Brodrick's admissions register shows that the
range of schools from which entrants came was widening. College
resolved in 1868 that no questions about religious belief be asked
of candidates for admission,[164] and undergraduates who were not
members of the Church of England were, on their parents' decision,
excused from all attendance at chapel. From 1872 when L. E. Gould
arrived from the Oratory a small trickle of Roman Catholic entrants
defied the papal rescript of 1867 which forbade Catholics to enter non-
Catholic universities. Though the ban was not rescinded until 1895,
long before that boys from the Oratory, Beaumont, and Stonyhurst
began to appear. The fact that one of the Albanians came from

---

[159] Knox's claim to have initiated the move is not borne out by the entry in Reg. 1.5, p. 349 of 31. 5. 1855.

[160] Reg. 1.5 a, p. 275 (11. 3. 1895).

[161] Ibid., p. 316.

[162] Figures are from Warden Brodrick's admissions register.

[163] The figure eighteen is suggested by the number of members of the Hall who were incorporated as undergraduates in 1881 in Brodrick's Admissions Register. For the disciplinary advantages of annexation cf. Knox, *Reminiscences*, p. 97.

[164] Reg. 1.5, p. 464.

Kingswood, as did a Merton exhibitioner in 1890, a fellow (Dixon) i: the year later, and a postmaster in 1892, suggests that Methodists wer also admitted in Brodrick's time; and the names of Reggie Turner, A Birnbaum, and Leonard Messel show that Jews were represented as well

Two Australians and a South African made their appearance befor the end of the century, one each from King's School, Paramatta, Nev South Wales, Brisbane Grammar School, and Diocesan College, Cap· Town. Fellows and undergraduates had long since sought careers ir India, as did Sir John Boileau. He returned from India as a 'Nabob' t(buy up Ketteringham Hall in Norfolk and become its squire.[165] Othe Mertonians were the Hon. Christopher Puller, fellow 1795–1804, wh(became Chief Justice of Bengal (1823–4), and J. B. Norton, postmaster 1833–7, Judge Advocate General, Madras.[166] With the return to Englanc of another former postmaster and Puisne Judge of the High Court ir Calcutta, William Markby, as reader in Indian law, the college made proper arrangements for those who passed into the ICS and had tc spend a probationer year at a British university.[167] Markby became the tutor to all such men in Oxford.[168] The college also sold the site of the Indian Institute to the university at the request of Professor Monie! Williams[169] and contributed towards the cost. Two of its members, one a postmaster and the other a fellow, passed successfully into the service after taking firsts in Greats. One (Grimwood) became politica! agent at Manipur and was stabbed to death while trying to settle a dispute in 1891;[170] the other, Crump, a former fellow, also bore witness to the hazards of an Indian career when he died of fever at Hyderabad (Deccan) in 1900.[171] Merton's first West African seems to have been J. R. Maxwell, son of a chaplain at the Cape Coast; he matriculated at Merton in 1876 and, after taking a BCL, ended his career as Chief Justice of the Gambia. Its first Indian was Prince Moorut Ullea Moorut-Meerza who came up in 1897.[172]

---

[165] Foster, *Alumni Oxonienses, 1715–1886, A–D*, p. 128. For Sir John Boileau, see O. Chadwick, *Victorian Miniature* (1960).

[166] Cf. J. B. Norton, *Memories of Merton* (Madras, 1865); *In India at Christmas* (1883).

[167] R. Symonds, *Oxford and Empire: The Last Lost Cause* (1986), pp. 115, 188–9.

[168] Markby was offered the use of the hall and a lecture-room for his lectures (Reg. 1.5 a, p. 31). College agreed to grant £12 p.a. to each of its students attending the course (ibid., p. 104).

[169] Reg. 1.5 a, p. 68, Symonds, *Oxford and Empire*, pp. 109–10.

[170] Bott, *Monuments*, p. 76.

[171] Ibid., p. 92.

[172] Symonds, *Oxford and Empire*, pp. 270–1. Maxwell has left a warm tribute to the tutors and students. For Moorut-Meerza cf. Reg. 6.26, p. 111.

A new feature of the undergraduate body after 1854 was the arrival of the natural scientists. Once the University museum had been opened in 1860 interest in the natural sciences slowly grew. Mertonian scientists did well, to judge by their examination results. Out of seventeen reading the school between 1871 and 1885 ten were placed in the first class.[173] Two Merton natural scientists of the nineteenth century proved to be men of distinction. E. S. Goodrich (commoner, 1890–95), who acted as assistant to Professor Lankester and took a first class in natural science (morphology), became one of Lankester's successors as Linacre professor, and Frederick Soddy,[174] who received his training in the Balliol/Trinity laboratory in 1899, went on to work with Rutherford at McGill. He became Oxford's first Nobel Prize winner for his work on isotopes. In the first year of the new century Bertram Lambert was elected to an exhibition. He was awarded the OBE for his crucial work on the development of the gas mask in the First World War, and in 1920 he became the college's first tutor in chemistry.

When Brodrick (Pl. 29) became warden there were several signs that the relationship between the fellows and the undergraduates had begun to change. A stronger corporate spirit had already developed under Warden Marsham through sporting activities. The Merton 1st eight appeared on the river in 1838, and from 1845 Merton was represented in the University cricket XI. Warden Marsham especially had acted as a patron of cricket. A cricket field was laid out in 1865, which was levelled again in 1890 when tennis-courts were added on its edges.[175]

In college there were some helpful relaxations of rules. The library had been open to junior members for one hour a week since 1827.[176] Since it was neither heated nor lit (according to the regulations of 1483) what was really needed was a reading-room. At one stage the sacristy was considered for this purpose. A site was found in 1871 in what is now the Beerbohm Room.[177] To match that development the

---

[173] Eastgate, Macguire, Macdonald, Jones, Thornely, Judson, Quine, Richards, T. J. Richards, and D. Edward Chapman (matriculated 1860) who for 25 years was a successful natural science tutor at Magdalen (1882–1906).

[174] *Who Was Who 1951–1960*, p. 1022.

[175] For sport at Merton generally see Mallett, *History of the University of Oxford*, iii. 419, and Henderson, pp. 272–7. Group photographs of the 1st Eight (rowing) exist in the Archives from 1861 and for the 1st XI (cricket and soccer) from 1894.

[176] Henderson, p. 240.

[177] Reg. 1.5, p. 495.

Old Library was opened for not less than two hours a day on three weekdays, though still not on Sundays, from 1883.[178] The garden was also opened to undergraduates in 1881, at first only between the hours of 2 and 4 in winter and between 2 and 7 in summer.[179] It was closed on Sundays, smoking was not allowed, and it was closed when a fellow wanted to give a private party. The next year a set of rooms in Fellows' Quad was let to an undergraduate (Fellows 3, 2 pairs left), and furnished with 'plain and useful' furniture at the college's expense.[180] A notable decision was made in 1881 to consider the establishment of an 'undergraduates'' common room. The room was opened three years later.[181] Its popularity can be judged by the fact that it was found necessary to extend it in 1890, so that it occupied the south-west corner of Mob Quad.[182] A Debating Society and a Church Society were founded.[183] Finally, there was even music-making, and in mixed company. There had been a college concert in 1862, and in 1871 the choir of St Peter's-in-the-East was allowed to give a concert in the hall.[184] Ten years later, coinciding with the change of warden, a college Musical Society was formed and gave a concert in the hall, followed by regular meetings on Tuesday evenings after dinner.[185] By 1894 there was a Biological Club. All those developments should doubtless be seen against the background of a head-on collision which occurred between E. A. Knox, the principal of the postmasters, and the undergraduates. There had been a clash in 1880, when five miscreants who had played a practical joke by removing an associate's bedclothes were reported by the porter and sent down without much ceremony by Knox. Against what they took to be a disproportionate punishment

---

[178] Reg. 1.5 a, p. 101.

[179] Ibid., p. 72.

[180] Ibid., pp. 83, 85, 114, and cf. Reg. 1.5, p. 521. The furniture was to be rented to the undergraduates. A watercolour (1861) of undergraduate rooms belonging to E. Arkwright (commoner, 1858–64) exists, and photographs of those of George Chapman (commoner, 1867–73) and his friends (cf. D. 1.96 and Chapman's album (1868–73)). See also Pl. 28.

[181] Henderson, p. 278, Reg. 1.5 a, pp. 72, 117. It was lit by gas (ibid., p. 139).

[182] Reg. 1.5 a, p. 191.

[183] Minutes of the Debating Society (incomplete) survive from 21. Feb. 1881, and of the Church Society from 21. May. 1884.

[184] Reg. 1.5, p. 504.

[185] Reg. 1.5 a, p. 46. A programme of 2 Dec. 1887 survives (Q.2.36). Of the choir of 42 the Hon. Edith Brodrick and the Hon. Mrs Fremantle were to be found among the seven women altos, and the chaplain, Canon Freeling, among the thirteen basses. Miss Brodrick played as a piano solo Rubinstein's *Valse Allemagne*. In 1897 it was decided that ladies present must have had their names sent in beforehand and approved by the warden and Mr Scott.

and unsatisfactory procedure a large proportion of the undergraduate body appealed to Archbishop Tait as visitor.[186] The upshot was that the officer's authority was upheld, but in the third year of Brodrick's wardenship there was a petition to the warden in general terms against the way in which the principal of postmasters was exercising his authority.[187] His 'book of discipline' survives[188] and there is no doubt that he ruled strictly. To be caught climbing in was to be sent down till the end of term once six weeks had been kept. The petition was carefully considered by the warden and tutors. The warden could naturally do nothing against general complaints but ask for specific accusations to be made, which he did. None, it seems, materialized, but the greater consideration given to undergraduate needs implies an effort to achieve a better relationship. Knox himself comments on the contribution made by Mr Freeling, the chaplain, towards the same end.

We hear of an undergraduate charter which is said to have hung in the Junior Common Room for many years and to have taken the form of the warden's reply to specific complaints. It is said that when the principal, known familiarly as 'Hard Knox',[189] accepted the living of Kibworth in 1884 and appeared for the last time in chapel, the hymn 'Now thank we all our God' was sung with particular enthusiasm by the undergraduates present.

Knox thought that he had succeeded in turning Merton into a reading college. Careers such as those of Edmund Backhouse, postmaster, and Max Beerbohm (Pl. 31), commoner, suggest that he had not wholly succeeded. Both took honours, though neither got further than Classical Moderations. Backhouse secured a prize for good work in collections – an indication of his undoubted ability; and the full extent of his bizarre career as collector and forger of oriental documents remained unknown until exposed by Hugh Trevor-Roper in 1976.[190] By contrast, we have a vignette of Max and his friends relaxing in his rooms in Mob Quad from the pen of Eric Parker. 'While Reggie

---

[186] Reg. I.5 a, pp. 53–6 and p. 60. The petition was signed by 52 persons including 13 postmasters and two MAs (cf. also the visitor's correspondence of 11. Oct. 1880 and 26. Nov. 1880 (ibid., pp. 53, 60)).

[187] Cf. ibid., p. 112 (3. June 1884), and Knox, *Reminiscences*, p. 101.

[188] P.2.12. If men were caught climbing in, as soon as they had completed 6 weeks residence they were sent down for the rest of the term. Those who were convicted of profane language in Hall had their names withdrawn 'at their parents' request'.

[189] Knox, op. cit., pp. 98, 101; but see also W. Peck, *Home for the Holidays* (1945).

[190] H. R. Trevor-Roper, *A Hidden Life: The Enigma of Sir Edmund Backhouse* (1976).

Turner stares in a mirror and cries out "God! How ugly I am!" a game of roulette is being played."[191] Backhouse's unpaid bills at Rowell's, the jewellers, speak for themselves. Both men, brought up at Winchester and Charterhouse respectively, were being drawn by magnets other than classical learning.

At the same time the sense of a small but closer-knit family party to which both Creighton and Maude had borne witness was sustained by sport, especially rowing and cricket, by college 'wines' or 'smokers', and by clubs like the Myrmidons and the Septem contra Somnium.[192] The Myrmidons was established in 1865 for a limited number of twelve members. It held termly dinners in rooms over Adamson's, the tailors in High Street. There too was the club room adorned with photographs of past members on its walls. It began as a club of 'young bloods' and included Randolph Churchill in 1870, but by the 1890s a literary element had crept in, represented by Max Beerbohm and Reggie Turner. The club easily survived into the twentieth century (Pl. 32).

WARDEN BRODRICK

The warden had his own contribution to make to the milder air of harmony which began to be apparent in the 1880s and 1890s.

I had only an undergraduate's eye-view of Brodrick. *We* all loved him none the less because we laughed at his peculiarities ... His gifts were more social than academic: he entertained us to long and excellent dinners and the company of men eminent in what Oxford calls the outside world. I remember one evening suddenly receiving an invitation with barely time to dress for dinner. I was the last to arrive, and the Warden conducted me round his guests – one of whom was a Viceroy of India – saying 'This is Mr Fyfe, who has kindly consented to fill a gap at my dinner table'. In his mouth that rather ambiguous remark had, I am sure, no sting in its tail ... Verbose he was, but we did not think him pompous. Nor did we think him snobbish when he asked an embarrassed freshman from a village school for news of his cousin, the Duchess ... Was he not

---

[191] J. R. L. Highfield, 'Max at Merton', *Postmaster*, ii/4 (1960), 14.
[192] M. Beerbohm, *More* (1899), pp. 45–53; *Letters of Reggie Turner*, ed. R. Hart-Davis (1964), p. 27 n. 6, p. 29 n. 1.

twin brother to a peer? But he was also a very kindly old gentleman and his gentle kindness should not be forgotten.[193]

THE STAFF

Much more information becomes available in the nineteenth century about that essential element of the college – its staff. During the century the college sought to change from a system where servants were paid partly in kind. It was decided on 28 October 1841 that servants should be paid fixed wages,[194] but that was easier said than done. All through the subsequent years there are references to perquisites of one kind and another and to the need for their abolition. Thus in 1852 the porter was to be paid £60 per annum, plus gate fees and one third of the remains of high table dinner.[195] In 1868 we are told that his salary is to be £100 and once again the remains of High Table dinner, but that gate fees are now to go to the college.[196] The most highly paid servants for the first half of the century seem to have been the manciple,[197] the butler,[198] and the chef,[199] each receiving £200 per annum. Those levels were not sustained. In 1872 it was decided to abolish the offices of manciple and butler,[200] but the butler survived and came back at a salary of £180.[201] A highly responsible position was that of steward. He handled most of the business of the estates and presided at manor courts. He was the successor of the several stewards of medieval times. For much of the century this was Mr Caswall, who kept the muniments in exemplary order. We do not know his salary. The chef dropped to £130 when Goldsmith was appointed in 1872,[202] no doubt a sum appropriate to a young man coming in. The second cook and under-butler were paid £75 each in

[193] W. H. Fyfe, 'The Honourable George Charles Brodrick, Warden of Merton, 1881–1903' (sic), *Oxford Magazine* (1958), p. 432, repr. *Postmaster* ii/3 (1959), pp. 8–9.

[194] Reg. 1.5, p. 185.

[195] Ibid., p. 296 (Cullam). Where salaries are concerned it is worth noting that £1 in 1835 was very roughly worth £50 in 1991.

[196] Ibid., p. 463.

[197] Ibid., p. 193 (1842).

[198] Ibid., p. 405.

[199] Ibid., p. 193.

[200] Ibid., p. 509.

[201] Expressly in lieu of perquisites.

[202] Ibid., p. 512. It was increased to £140 in 1874 and £160 in 1892 (Reg. 1.5 a, p. 230), but Goldsmith eventually moved to Buckingham Palace.

315

1851,[203] the gardener £30 in 1843. The sexton had £55,[204] the messenger £50,[205] and the under-porter £30.[206] Valentine, a male bed-maker working in Fellows' Quad, had £80, but he had to find one male assistant at 5s. a week and two female assistants to work with him.[207] The clerk in the bursary was paid £25 in 1873, but by 1884 we learn that Chamberlain (Pl. 30), the bursar's clerk, was on a salary of £150 per annum.[208] The baker was paid 15s. per week.[209] The chef in addition to his wages of £150 had 10 per cent of the profits from the sale of dripping out of the kitchen and an allowance in place of beer money.[210] At the bottom of the pile the boy in the kitchen had 5s. per week and his board.[211] That may not sound much, but board was all important, and might be three times as valuable as the cash.

Housing was not provided until the building of the Manor Road houses for the upper servants and the Manor Place houses for the lower servants in the 1890s, except that Postmasters' Hall was let to the butler, James Kirkpatrick, in 1836 for £35 per annum,[212] and the cottage and nursery in Rose Lane were let to the gardener for £30.[213] In 1872 the college ran a scheme whereby a deduction from wages was made to provide a pension of £30 per annum for a servant retiring at 60.[214] Separate college-granted pensions existed for servants with long service, as for Betteris, a cook, in 1872 who was given a pension of £100 per annum and another cook one of £40.[215] James Patey, a retired butler, who, with his son Charles, ran a grocer's shop in 'an upper

[203] Reg. 1.5, pp. 193, 291.

[204] Ibid., p. 285 (1851); £40 in 1866 (ibid., p. 447).

[205] Put up from £45 in 1866 (ibid.).

[206] ibid., p. 285 (1851).

[207] Ibid., p. 342.

[208] Reg. 1.5 a, p. 109. For Chamberlain and some others, see C. Platt, *The Most Obliging Man in Europe* (1986), p. 22.

[209] Reg. 1.5, p. 193 (1842).

[210] Ibid., p. 291 (1852).

[211] Reg. 1.5 a, p. 230.

[212] Ibid., p. 133 (1836). It was occupied by a retired butler in 1921 (J. R. L. Highfield, 'The Pateys and their Quad', *Postmaster*, iv/2 (1970), 13). For the Manor Road houses see Reg. 1.5 a, p. 208. They were not to cost more than £7500, but in fact cost rather more. Those in Manor Place followed (cf. ibid., pp. 210, 265).

[213] In 1843.

[214] Reg. 1.5, p. 509.

[215] Ibid. The other cook was Mr Read; Betteris had become manciple in 1862 at the wage of £200 for long and meritorious service (ibid., p. 413).

room of the tiny quad in which the muniment room had place' was given a pension of £75 per annum in 1873.[216]

An entry concerning J. H. Hone, the head bed-maker in Mob Quad, reminds us that scouts often combined their work in college with other occupations, for in 1883 Hone was given a month's notice unless he agreed to give up his public house before the end of June. The contact between college and its servants was close and personal. Servants could be dismissed comparatively easily, as was Penrose, the gardener, although he was given warning of what was in store for him.[217] It seems to have been normal to give a month's notice or more, unless 'purloining' was involved. There was also a personal contact in areas which have now been taken over by the state. Thus when Boon, a labourer, was injured while taking down an old building near the college brew-house on the site of Grove buildings it was recognized that he had a mother who depended on him for support. She was paid £5 in weekly instalments by the porter.[218] When a man was injured during Scott's restoration of the hall in 1872 the college contributed to a subscription got up for him.[219]

Over one servant the college seems to have been unable to exercise control. He was John Bruce, the groom, who seems to have been a hard drinker and a generally bad influence. He also had some kind of semi-independent position, for in 1882 the Warden was reduced to decreeing that any servant found speaking to him was to be dismissed instantly and soon afterwards we hear that the office of groom had been abolished.[220]

COLLEGE HISTORY

In 1872–4 the Wyatt hall was rebuilt by G. G. Scott. The estimated cost was £3,690, and the design a restoration of the medieval hall as depicted by Loggan in 1675. Scott certainly succeeded in providing a magnificent roof (Pl. I).[221] College was fortunate to have avoided

---

[216] Reg. 1.5, p. 521, Maude, *Memories*, p. 68; cf. also 'The Pateys and their Quad' (above, n. 212), pp. 12–13; for a photograph of Charles Patey see Platt (above, n. 208) p. 22.

[217] Reg. 1.5, p. 174, entry for 9 June 1841. The porter was dismissed in 1876 with six months' notice.

[218] Reg. 1.5, p. 167.

[219] Ibid., p. 512.

[220] For caricatures of Bruce see Platt, op. cit., pp. 76, 79, and 92.

[221] Bott, *Short History of the Buildings*, pp. 11–13.

another proposal, in 1866, to build an arcaded cloister in the Gothic style in Fellows' Quad, at the expense of Mr Calvert,[222] which, though it would have given shelter on rainy days, would certainly have impaired the architecture of the seventeenth century.

An interest in the history of the college was maintained in the eighteenth century by the Reverend Joseph Kilner, fellow, through his antiquarian collections and the compilation of that strange book, *The School of Pythagoras* (1790). In 1796 Warden Scrope Berdmore presented the fanciful portrait of the Founder which still gazes out over the hall,[223] but it was really only in the nineteenth century that any serious investigations were pursued. As early as 1832 it was decided to alter the Muniment Room in order to make it fit for the records which were then being moved upstairs from the library in Mob Quad.[224] The fact that Hope-Scott was examining the college muniments for a projected history of colleges no doubt added to the awareness that both records and manuscripts needed better care. In 1837 the librarian was instructed to do what he should think necessary to restore the manuscripts.[225] Many volumes in the muniment room were rebound in 1839[226] and the cupboards there were altered for storing them.[227] An imaginative note is struck by a resolution of E. T. Bigge, the librarian, who installed in the east window of the south wing of the library the panels of sixteenth-century German glass which tell the story of the Passion. He also gave the college a portrait of Bishop Jewell. We are told by his colleague, Edmund Hobhouse, that it had been Bigge's intention in 1843 to introduce 'a series of commemorative windows in our Library for the purpose of recording the greater names that have reflected glory upon the House of Merton by their literary renown'. The idea had not been taken up after Bigge's death until lately (1858) 'when I got two erected in memory of the Founder of the Library, Bishop Rede, and the (almost) re-founder Warden Savile'. Hobhouse was anxious to press the scheme forward before leaving for a bishopric in New Zealand and wrote round to colleagues assuring them that the cost of one slit window was only £5. Time ran out on him, but did not prevent him from paying himself

---

[222] A drawing of the cloister hangs in the Estates Bursary.
[223] Poole, *Catalogue of Oxford Portraits*, ii. 44, and see above, p. 263.
[224] Reg. 1.5, p. 94.
[225] Ibid., p. 146.
[226] Ibid., p. 165.
[227] Ibid., p. 192.

to fill the south window of the vestibule. It displays the kneeling figure of the Founder, the college seal for letters testimonial, and seven heraldic shields.[228] He also completed his *Sketch of the Life of Walter de Merton* (1859), an admirable piece of scholarship which laid the foundations for all future work on the subject.

A high point of interest was reached with the sexcentenary of the college's foundation in 1864. A proposal was made that the hall should be adorned with portraits of present worthies, to be paid for by subscription. The persons proposed were Warden Marsham, Sir Edmund Head, the earl of Elgin, and Bishop Denison. At first the committee only raised enough to pay for the first two, though subsequently they were joined by Bishop Denison.[229] Meanwhile, the appeal to antiquity was answered when one fellow, Stephen Edwardes, presented a copy of a portrait of Sir Thomas Bodley,[230] and another, William Esson, a copy of one of Sir Henry Savile.[231] They are not among the best portraits in the college's collection. Then in 1876, when Warden Marsham had held his office for fifty years there was occasion for more commemoration. This time it took the form of filling five of the six windows of the hall with armorial glass celebrating the fame of past and present members. Of the twenty shields displayed five were of medieval fellows, two belonged to the sixteenth century, and three to the seventeenth; no fewer than nine to the self-confident nineteenth.[232] The shields of 'those two heroical figures', Bodley and Savile, were there and, interestingly enough, Manning, even though former fellows who had become Roman Catholics did not receive invitations to the sexcentenary dinner.

The movement to revive interest in the college's history was keenly pursued by Marsham's successor, Warden Brodrick. His most notable

---

[228] Q.2.4 (iv). The single windows commemorating Thomas Bradwardine and John Wyliot on the south side of the south wing also belong to the series. For Hobhouse's window in the vestibule, cf. Reg. 1.5, p. 381 (Committee to consider design).

[229] Ibid., p. 429, and cf. Poole, *Catalogue of Oxford Portraits*, ii. 57–60. Q.3.4 (b): one old member (B. Wagner) wrote of the proposal 'to which I object that none of our celebrities will ever live in force of the figure they cut in Merton Hall and we shall only be doing our best to immortalise the degradation of the art of portrait painting in this century'. He objected in particular to not being told by the committee organizing the subscription 'what artists they would propose to employ'.

[230] In 1865: Reg. 1.5, p. 431, Poole, *Catalogue of Oxford Portraits*, ii. 48.

[231] Reg. 1.5, p. 462, Poole, op. cit., ii. 49 (1868). In 1892 the road north of Manchester College was named by Merton Savile Road (Reg. 1.5 a, p. 231).

[232] D.2.4, D.2.4 a. A sixth window was filled in 1891 with glass showing the arms of Sir Richard Steele, Bishop Shute Barrington, J. Hope-Scott, and Warden Brodrick (Reg. 1.5 a, p. 218).

achievement was his *Memorials of Merton College* (1885), raised on the shoulders of previous annalists, such as Astry and Wood, but including judicious chapters of his own. He himself paid for half the cost of calendaring the medieval muniments. The work was carried out with exemplary skill by W. H. Stevenson.[233] Brodrick also paid for a valuable index in three volumes to the contents of the College Register.[234] He followed the passion for armorial bearings by arranging for those of former members and friends of the college to be painted on shields behind the High Table and down either side of the hall (Pl. I). He also added to the historical portrait gallery by presenting a seventeenth-century picture of Wyclif, a portrait of Warden Bickley, a crayon drawing by Richmond of Rolleston, the first Linacre professor, and engravings of Admiral Blake,[235] Dean Goulburn, and Bishop Hamilton. Meanwhile the muniments were inspected by H. T. Riley for a report for the Historical Manuscripts Commission,[236] and the northern records were inspected and utilized by Edward Bateson for the *County History of Northumberland*.

FINANCE AND LAND SALES

The two reform commissions naturally led the colleges in a variety of ways to examine their financial situation. Merton was no exception. The First Commission required the college every ten years to lay an account of its annual revenue before the visitor.[237] It estimated the income of the college at £7,220 and its expenditure at £8,410. The difference was met from an accumulation fund and was explained by delays in payments of fines due from the landed estates. The estates were reckoned by the Second Commission (1872–7) to amount in 1871 to 12,000 acres, which was less than half those of Christ Church, but enough to make Merton stand fifth among the colleges owning land.[238]

---

[233] Reg. 1.5, p. 527 (Mr Riley of Historical Manuscripts Commission requests permission to consult college archives), Reg. 1.5 a, pp. 152, 164. The cost of Stevenson's Calendar to the college was to be not more than £150. The warden paid half the cost.

[234] Reg. 1.5 a, p. 172.

[235] Poole, *Catalogue of Oxford Portraits*, ii. 44 (Wyclif), 60 (Rolleston), Reg. 1.5 a, p. 109 (Bickley), p. 172 (Blake).

[236] *Royal Commission on Historical Manuscripts 6th Report* (1877), pp. 545a–549a, and see above, n. 233.

[237] *Ordinances in pursuance of . . . 17 & 18 Victoria c. 81*, no. 26, p. 12.

[238] *Oxford University Commission Report*, Appendix (evidence), pp. 318–19; Mallett, *History of the University of Oxford*, iii. 334.

.t that date, too, the revenues were estimated at £19,000 (apart from
.uition fees), a sum which again brought Merton to fifth place among
the colleges. In 1874, the bursar put the total revenue at £16,380 per
.nnum.[239] One of the aims of the Second Commission was to enable
the university to draw on the resources of the colleges for its own
.urposes. Colleges were instructed to carry out an annual audit and
.o pay a contribution to the University Chest. As a result by 1886
.Merton was paying £2,293 to the university,[240] including payments
.owards the chair of English Language and Literature and to the
.3odleian Library. By that date too it had taken power to raise a
.uilding fund of £40,000.[241]

As sub-warden towards the end of Warden Bullock Marsham's long
.vardenship E. A. Knox nursed two significant ambitions. First, he
.ngineered an important exchange of land with Magdalen whereby
.Magdalen took over from Merton Holywell Ford, a property on the
.Cherwell at the back of the Deer Park, which Merton had owned since
.266 when it was part of Holywell Manor, and in exchange Merton
.icquired a block of properties at the south-west end of Logic Lane
.ormerly in the possession of the hospital of St John the Baptist. Here
.itood a small house opposite St Alban Hall. As a dividend Knox lived
.there when he was first married[242] and so was able to continue as a
.college officer. Secondly, he completed in the first years of Brodrick's
.vardenship the long-drawn-out process of the annexation of St Alban
.Hall. Although the primary aim of this development seems to have
.been disciplinary,[243] it also provided the college with accommodation
.for eighteen or more undergraduates[244] and in the principal's house
.another provision for a married tutor. The whole site cried out for
.redevelopment. At first the attention of the college was turned to the
.site opposite St Alban Hall. The architect T. G. Jackson, fresh from his
.triumphant work on the Examination Schools, was given the task of

---

[239] Reg. 1.5, p. 528, made up from £15,000 of corporate revenue and £1,380 from Trust
Funds.

[240] *Abstract of Accounts of the University of Oxford, 1883–86*, in Mallett, op. cit., iii. 349 n. 3.

[241] Mallett, op. cit., iii. 349, Statutes xiii, 2 under *Ordinances in pursuance of . . . Act of 1877*
(1882), p. 25.

[242] Knox, *Reminiscences*, pp. 98–9. The position of the property is marked by a crossing,
of the kind which crossing-sweepers kept clear, in the cobblestone surface of the street.
There is another crossing at the college gate.

[243] Ibid.

[244] That is the number of Albanians incorporated at Merton at the time of the annexation
(see above, p. 309).

designing a new building.[245] His plan was on a grand scale: a block of four stories with two wings, a forecourt, and two towers. But the project was deflected by the successful annexation of St Alban Hall and the death of Warden Marsham. Thus the future of the Warden's Lodgings and of St Alban Hall was brought under scrutiny. In face of the cost of rebuilding, funds were accumulated in different ways. Parts of the Holywell estate were sold or leased, and other sales pursued elsewhere. The cost of additional buildings had been set in 1879 at £50,000.

As early as 1832 a site had been sold to Wadham to the north of that college.[246] Then under the 1854 Act Merton was able to sell land for the university's scientific needs. That meant in the first phase the site of the museum and subsequently that of the science area. The college sold land on four occasions (1855, 1856, 1859, and 1865); 76 acres in all were sold for £24,857.[247] Merton also granted 99-year leases for domestic houses (1865–85) on the south side of what became South Parks Road. Land for the University Parks was made available to the university in what had been the northern fields of Holywell Manor Farm, where 22 acres were sold for £9,000.[248] In the last two decades of the century, a steady flow of sales followed from the Holywell estate, for new academic buildings or college playing fields. A site was made available to the Congregationalists to build Mansfield College in 1889 on the west of what became Mansfield Road.[249] It was followed by similar sales to the Unitarians to build Manchester College to the south of Mansfield.[250] To the Church of England the college gave the site for the vicarage of St Peter's-in-the-East at 4 South Parks Road and another to the south of St Cross Church for the vicarage and school of St Cross, Holywell. Opposite the church a group of Catholic laymen in 1896 bought a site for a projected Catholic college.[251] However, although Cardinal Manning, who had always opposed such a course,

---

[245] Howard Colvin, *Unbuilt Oxford* (New Haven and London, 1983), no. 153 (facing p. 148).

[246] 3.444 acres for £1,600. It included the site occupied by Rhodes House (Reg. 1.5, p. 129).

[247] 4 acres in 1854 (Reg. 1.5, p. 325), 22 acres in 1856 for £9,300, 50 acres on 29. Oct. 1857 for £16,000 (ibid., p. 376).

[248] Cf. Reg. 1.5, p. 325. Offer to sell remainder of interest in the Parks for £9,000.

[249] For £6,000.

[250] 1859 (£5,000); 1891 (£360); 1912 (£12,500).

[251] For the vicarage of St Peter's-in-the-East and the vicarage and school of St Cross, Holywell, see above, pp. 290, 291 and nn. 44, 65. The site for the Catholic college cost £12,500.

died in 1893, the Catholic college was never built, and the site was later sold to the university.

Merton laid out its own playing fields between Mansfield Road and St Cross Road in 1865,[252] and sold land for playing fields to Balliol[253] – the Master's Field – and to New College in 1891.[254] Balliol constructed a series of tutors' houses along the edges of its field. At the west end of Holywell Street a site was sold to the university for the Indian Institute at the corner of Holywell and Catte Street (1893–4),[255] and several houses on the south side of the street were sold to New College, which was able to build the Scott Building (1872) and its extension by Champneys (1885, 1896), together with a lodge which gave it an alternative entry to that in New College Lane. Altogether, by 1900 Merton had raised over £120,000.[256] In the 1890s it built ten houses for its upper servants in Manor Road and ten for its lower servants in Manor Place, which created the equivalent of a village community. They were designed in the bursary, and Warden Brodrick is said to

---

[252] Powers taken to acquire not more than 6 acres, 26. Oct. 1865 (Reg. 1.5, p. 437); ground opened 17. June 1867 (Q.3.4 (b)).

[253] 1859, £4,000; 1891, £10,000; 1894 £5,397; 6 acres in all, cf. E. Abbott and L. Campbell, *The Life and Letters of Benjamin Jowett*, ii (1897), p. 345.

[254] 1891, 10,750 acres for £15,000.

[255] 1893 (£3,600); 1894 (£42,162).

[256] Wadham (1835) £1,600 (Reg. 1.5, p. 129).

The University (1856–65) £24, 857
     (1893–94) £7,962

Balliol (1887–1896) £19,397

10 Dec. 1889 Conroy and Bickmore, Holywell Leaze and cottages – power to negotiate, (Reg. 1.5 a, p. 183)

18 March 1890 Sir John Conroy, 1 acre, 2 rods, 21 perches £4,000 (Reg. 1.5 a, pp. 185, 188)

1893 S. Davidson, Sir John Conroy and Dr Mee, 2 acres, 9 perches (ibid., p. 259) £8,000

Cricket Field 1¾ acres at £2,000 per acre.

New College (1858–91)

Nos. 40–9, 63–9, 70–1, 93–5 Holywell (Reg. 1.5, p. 509, Reg. 1.5 a, p. 31)

3 Feb. 1870 Merton ready to sell reversions of nos. 75–83, 86–92 Holywell (Reg. 1.5, p. 479)

27 May 1890 10¾ acres in Holywell for £15,080 of 2½% stock (Reg. 1.5 a, p. 188).

Mansfield College

22 Jan. 1886–9 £3,000 (Reg. 1.5 a, p. 130, cf. p. 145).

Manchester College

1889, 1891 £8,000 (ibid., pp. 159, 210).

Catholic Laymen

1896 3¾ acres £13,500 (ibid., p. 285).

Hertford College

1899 Nos. 45–50 Holywell not less than £6,500 (ibid., p. 318).

have observed that they did not need bathrooms when he did not have the benefit of that amenity in the Warden's Lodgings.

The sales of land on the Holywell estate were not the only way in which the college strengthened its liquid financial position and prepared itself to build.[257] Land was sold to railway companies whose lines crossed the college estates, as they did at Radstone, in Northamptonshire.[258] The first sale of a building lease at Motspur Farm, Surrey, to Mr Charles Blake[259] indicated that another portion of the 'Vetus Fundacio' with which the Founder had endowed the college was about to yield great dividends. There were still other opportunities to extend its academic commitments, though that was for the future. What can be said without reserve is that as the century ended Merton had evidently overcome the set-back caused by the agricultural depression. Because it owned non-agricultural property as well as farms, and although many rents had had to be reduced between 1883 and 1903, it had raised its income by 17 or 18 per cent.[260] It stood poised to proceed with much large-scale building, on or near the college, made possible by the acquisitions of 1878–81.

[257] For instance by the sale of lands at Basingstoke. Under the Statutes of 1270 a fellow falling into incurable sickness could have food and clothing for life at St John's Hospital, Basingstoke. See above, pp. 14, 19, 21. The last fellow known to have taken advantage of that privilege was Walter Staunton, *c.* 1381–1401–2. The site of the hospital and the local lands which sustained it were sold to the tenant, Mr Henry Portsmouth, in 1887. In the same year the hospital buildings were demolished (Reg. 1.5 a, p. 145, license to sell for £1,350; Baigent and Millard, *Basingstoke*, p. 640).

[258] Radstone, sale of land to the Manchester, Sheffield, and Lincolnshire railway of 25 acres, 2 rods, 28 perches. £3,000 in Oct. 1894 (Reg. 1.5 a, p. 272).

Other sales included:

West Tilbury estate, Essex £6,625 (ibid., p. 87)

The Rose and Crown, Watford £12,500 in 1887 (ibid., pp. 151–2).

[259] Reg. 1.5, p. 422.

[260] See A. J. Engel, *From Clergyman to Don* (Oxford, 1983), p. 204.

13

The Twentieth Century

When Warden Brodrick died in 1903 the fellows elected Thomas Bowman as his successor. Bowman's academic qualities were impeccable: he was a mathematician who was also proficient in classical scholarship. Yet the choice proved to be a mistake. Though his tenure of college offices had shown him to be an efficient administrator and a firm disciplinarian, Bowman soon turned into something of a recluse. He failed to provide either the leadership or the hospitality expected of the head of a house. When he did assert himself, the results could be unfortunate. For his new lodging Bowman asked that the sun should strike into the main rooms of the *piano nobile* over the top of the college roofs opposite. The resulting elevation gave the lodgings a jacked-up look. Champneys, the architect, had an impossible task. The result was a 'monstrum ... informe',[1] quite out of scale with the other houses in the street.

The new warden's subsequent reluctance to spend money had unexpected results. Whilst his close care of the college finances was generally helpful, his natural parsimony meant that throughout the thirty-three years of his wardenship the college only three times commissioned a work of art. It acquired a portrait of the philosopher, F. H. Bradley, after his death;[2] it contributed to a stained glass window in the library in memory of Professor Raleigh, and commissioned Eric Gill to design a monument and inscription to the memory of A. C. Irvine after the fatal Everest expedition of 1924.[3] In the words of one

---

[1] Sir William Hamilton Fyfe, in 'Thomas Bowman 1853–1945', *Postmaster*, ii/3 (1959), 19.

[2] Reg. 1.5 b, p. 204, agreement to pay 200 guineas to Mr Eves and 12 guineas for the frame, 16 Feb. 1929.

[3] Bott, *Short History of the Buildings*, p. 41. It takes the form of a sculptured flame set on a triangular column and bears the inscription 'ANDREW COMYN IRVINE, 1900–1924. Perished near the summit of Mount Everest – June, 1924'.

of the tutors who served under him the warden remained 'a figure not a man'.[4]

HAMILTON FYFE, H. JOACHIM, AND H. W. GARROD

Three other members of the Governing Body in the years before the First World War, however, emerge vividly from the pen of one of Bowman's successors as warden, Geoffrey Mure (Pls. 32, 38). Mure came up to Merton as an undergraduate in 1912, in Trinity Term which was not unusual in those days. The three fellows portrayed were his two tutors in Classical Moderations, Hamilton Fyfe and H. W. Garrod and the Greats tutor in philosophy, Harold Joachim. Here is his description of them when he arrived from Eton:[5]

> My first year at Merton was paradisal. In the *amplior aether* of Oxford after a public school I expanded rapidly. I counted my blessings with gratitude: to have one's own rooms and one's own scout who could serve one there with breakfast, luncheon and, if one didn't want to dine in Hall, cold supper; to have no engagement in the course of the day which one could not at a pinch cancel; to form much easier and franker friendships than one had at school; to deal no longer with schoolmasters, who, however benevolent, symbolised in the first instance discipline, but with dons, who took a much more intelligent, humorous, and on the whole affectionate interest in the young they taught, aiming to stimulate rather than drill, to advise rather than admonish, and if some incident demanded discipline, to impose it as unpedantically as possible. My first tutor was *William Hamilton Fyfe*, subsequently Headmaster of Christ's Hospital and then Vice-Chancellor of Aberdeen University, a delightfully amusing and friendly man of the world and the best ever 'Principal of the Postmasters', as in Merton the don responsible for discipline was called, but a not more than competent scholar. I was soon transferred to *H. W. Garrod*, who became my life-long friend. Garrod was a brilliant classic whose primary passions were

---

[4] W. Hamilton Fyfe, 'Thomas Bowman', p. 19.

[5] G. R. G. Mure, 'Impact of a War' (typescript), pp. 4–9. See also n. 25. Hamilton Fyfe's quality as a mentor also emerges from the correspondence of Walter Harrison, who anxiously canvassed his own response to the War in 1914–15. See R. Harrison, 'In the Shadow of War', *Oxford Magazine*, 135 (4th week MT, 1996), 4–13; and MCR Stack, W. B. Harrison correspondence, 13 Oct. 1914–19 June 1915.

poetry and the company of young men, whom he equally loved and teased with an outrageously impish tongue. It was an exciting and strenuous year, and in spite of the shortness of the time, I managed to achieve the desired first class in Honour Moderations with quite a fair margin. I should have liked to sit for the Hertford scholarship in Latin – at which, to my regret, I was rather better than at Greek – but I had no time for that...

By the 4th of August 1914 I had spent four terms reading 'Greats', the second part of *Literae Humaniores*, which covers ancient history and both ancient and modern philosophy. From the first this broad curriculum daunted me. Fascinating subjects, but even allowing for the fact that good marks on either history or philosophy would produce a first class if one's marks in the other half of the field were respectable, how could one in two short years gain sufficient mastery of either to persuade the examiners into giving one a first? Of course quite a few candidates did it every year, but I could not conceive how I could be one of them in 1915. I leaned to philosophy rather than history, because I already felt a dim need for it. When I was prepared for Confirmation at school my orthodox Anglican faith began to dwindle. I had no adolescent period of strong religious emotion, and I found over two hours of Chapel every Sunday something of a bore. The Commination Service was annually inflicted on us, and I remember my delight when Cyril Alington, then Master in College, told us to take any book we liked into Chapel and ignore what he regarded as a barbarous ritual. I read Stevenson's *Wreckers* with an exhilarating sense of authorised naughtiness. Nevertheless, if my orthodoxy had faded, my faith in the broad values of western civilisation (however vaguely I could have defined them) had not, and I wanted to see them somehow justified as rational. I cannot say that at Eton I regarded myth and miracle on the one hand and materialism on the other as opposite absurdities, but that was where I was getting to when I began to read Greats.

My philosophy tutor was *Harold Joachim*, a nephew of the famous violinist, whom he worshipped and whose daughter he had married. He had had thoughts of becoming a professional violinist himself, and he would sometimes illustrate the notion of an ideally perfect experience transcending the distinction of reason and emotion by the analogy of his uncle playing a masterpiece which he at once understood and felt. It suggested the music of the spheres in a dialectical counterpoint. But he would then remind me of the medieval thinker (I forget which) who prayed nightly to be delivered from the Devil and from metaphors. He was a constant student of Aristotle and Spinoza, to whose texts he supplied the most profound scholarship and the sharpest criticism. So thorough was he that, as he grew old and feared to lose his grip, he would either not read a new philosophical work or else read it three times. On the whole he was an Hegelian idealist, though he was usually loath to discuss Hegel. When he read Hegel, he said, some passages seemed to him brilliantly clear, others hopelessly dark. When he read the same page again the alternation continued, but unhappily the dark and the clear passages were not the same. He was an ally but also a critic of F. H. Bradley,[6] still the dominant figure of Oxford philosophy but almost a recluse in his Merton rooms owing to his deafness and his poor health. Joachim praised him especially for stubbornly working out his own view of things. Though Joachim believed that the only road to philosophy lay through the intense and detailed study of the great masters, he believed also that such effort was pointless if it did not teach one to think for oneself.

It might seem that I had met the ideally suitable tutor for me. I think I had, but my brief sketch of him owes almost everything to what I learned of him later; it is not the image of him that I had formed in 1914. Certainly I sensed a more powerful intellect than any I had met before, but for a long time I got little from the discussion of my weekly essay but a most humbling conviction of my own futility. That is of course a common enough experience among beginners in philosophy; Oxford philosophy tutors are by a sound tradition relentless in trying to make their pupils think and see little place for mercy in their destructive criticism. What I found quite shattering was Joachim's habit of taking a sentence or two from one's essay and assuming with a more than Socratic courtesy that one must have meant something definite when one wrote them. It soon became evident that one had not. He would suggest this or that possible meaning as seriously as if he were trying to interpret an obscure sentence in Aristotle. One quickly collapsed under this technique, and he would say, 'Perhaps you were a little confused', and pass on to explain how it might have been better

---

[6] Cf. G. R. G. Mure, 'Francis Herbert Bradley', *Postmaster*, ii/3 (1959), pp. 10–15, and for a fuller treatment, *Études philosophiques* (1960), pp. 75–89.

put. After four terms I was still frankly in a muddle, and the prospect of final schools filled me with apprehension. Examinations were not a subject one could discuss with Joachim. They seemed to him, however necessary, to be a great evil for both the victim and the executioner. Many years later, when I had succeeded him as philosophical tutor at Merton, he asked me whether I did not think that the reward for examining in Greats should be an ample pension for life. I should in fairness add here that after the effort of Honour Moderations I had worked less strenuously and allowed rowing and other social activities to take up a good deal of my time.

THE FIRST WORLD WAR AND AFTER

The First World War cost Merton College, like many other households, very dear. With a smaller college than during the Second and a shorter time span there were more than twice as many Mertonians killed – 109 in total.[7] They included a German Rhodes Scholar, C. F. L. von Wurmb,[8] and a German commoner, T. H. F. Erbe,[9] killed fighting for Germany. Geoffrey Vickers won a VC, and there were many French, Belgian, and Italian awards. The future warden, Geoffrey Mure, set down his reactions to the calamity in the largely unpublished autobiography quoted above. As an MC and with an eye-witness experience on the Somme and Passchendaele he gives a gruesome account of the battle front. Yet none of the dons was killed. The chaplain, Richard Brook, became chaplain to the forces (1916–18). Valuable war work was done in the civil service by Garrod at the Ministry of Munitions and by the law tutor, John Miles (Pl. 36).[10] But none was more valuable than that of the demonstrator and chemistry lecturer and future tutor, Bertram Lambert, RE, who by devising the carbon-filter for a gas mask saved many lives in the front line.[11] At Oxford life was sustained on an ever-narrowing base. St Albans Quad was taken over to accommodate nurses who served in the 3rd Southern General Hospital, established in the Examination Schools. In 1918 the Royal

---

[7] Bott, *Short History of the Buildings*, p. 15. To the 107 should be added the two Germans.

[8] *Mert. Coll. Reg., 1900–1964*, p. 92.

[9] Ibid., p. 34.

[10] Ibid., pp. 5, 23, cf. Reg. 1.5 b, p. 11. Miles acted as legal adviser to the Ministry of Munitions and assistant to the Director of Public Prosecutions. He was knighted for his services in 1919.

[11] *Mert. Coll. Reg., 1900–1964*, p. 20, and cf. C. S. G. Phillips, 'Bertram Lambert', in *Postmaster*, iii/2 (1963), 14–15.

Air Force took over Grove Buildings. Belgian refugees were accommodated at 59 Holywell. Overseas students were able to continue their studies. One was T. S. Eliot, up during the first year of the war (Pl. V). He had recently been at Paris where he felt lonely, and Oxford pleased him little more than the French capital,[12] though like Geoffrey Mure, he bore witness to the excellence of the philosophy teaching of Harold Joachim.[13]

Eliot came to Merton because of the fame in philosophy of F. H. Bradley, but Bradley was not a teaching fellow. Eliot experienced a certain numbness at Oxford.[14] This was no doubt partly due to the absence of women, which after life in Paris must have been particularly striking: no Gertrude Stein at Oxford. It is true that he met his first wife as a visitor to Oxford, but at the end of his first year he did not apply to renew his scholarship and escaped to London. By contrast may be observed the rewarding life led by an Indian Government Scholar, Kuruvila Zacharaiah, who has left a vivid testimony to his years in Merton (1912–15) in the form of a series of weekly letters which he sent home to his parents in Calicut.[15] He gives an appreciative account of his three years reading modern history under the college lecturer, Arthur Johnson, a fellow of All Souls'. He responded well to the spell-binding lectures of Ernest Barker, a former fellow. He also gives a detailed description of how an Indian student survived the Long Vacation when he could not afford to go home.

Before Garrod disappeared into the Ministry of Munitions Zacharaiah came to know him, and took a different view of his personality from that of Geoffrey Mure. 'I remember my early prejudices against him,' he wrote; 'I used to regard him as a shallow cynic, clever but blind to the lasting loveliness of life, a poetaster, a bear; as a matter of fact he seems to be a rather shy but exceedingly amiable man, whose ways are lonely and who walks them with a soul above or below the generous intoxication of enthusiasms.'[16]

After 1918 Warden Bowman became more and more of a recluse. He appeared in hall perhaps no more than twice a year. It might have been supposed that the absence of leadership would have a serious effect on the college. In some senses inevitably it did, but it also

---

[12] Cf. Peter Ackroyd, *T. S. Eliot* (1984), p. 43.
[13] *Letters of T. S. Eliot*, ed. Valerie Eliot (1988), p. 84.
[14] Ackroyd, *T. S. Eliot*, p. 59, and cf. *HUO* viii. 45.
[15] Kuruvila Zacharaiah, 'Oxford Letters 1912–1915' (typescript).
[16] Ibid., p. 574.

drove the tutors together into a friendly oligarchy. One element of continuity was provided when Garrod returned from war service, to take up for a few more years his tutorship in Classical Moderations. A third view of his elusive character is given by one of his last pupils, George Mallaby (1920–3):[17]

When I was up [in 1920] H. W. Garrod was still the Mods don and as such he was my tutor, and when he died some forty years later he was still my tutor – the only critic left whose good opinion I was resolute to obtain. Garrod was, I now think, a less renowned figure than his extraordinary talents deserved. Upon a deep foundation of classical learning he had erected an attractive superstructure of clever, if somewhat brittle, pavilions of ingenuity. He was alert and inventive, determined to find something new, to shake the elaborate fastnesses of what, in modern jargon, would be called the Establishment. He devoted perhaps more of his talents to this learned iconoclasm than would have seemed right to a maturer judgment. He was very clever and in Oxford this really means something. He was cleverer, it was generally thought, than the Balliol dons who [had] taught him. He knew this, but in a sense he was humble about it; he believed that others were much cleverer than he ... As a Renaissance scholar he was in the first rank, as a classical scholar, where the competition was closer, he could have been if he had had a mind to. For sheer cleverness – of any problem, the immediate grasp of understanding and his grasshopper leap to an ingenious solution – he was in his time unsurpassed ... During my years at Merton hardly a day passed without my spending some time in his company and the brilliance of his mind and of his conversation made a deep impression upon me. I was at once eager to develop my own critical judgment, to look at things as he did and to find phrases, not unworthy of his wit, in which to air my opinions. Many of us came under his spell and we caught not only his attitudes but his accents also. He spoke in a high quavering singsong, his voice often fading away into little more than a whisper, and in conversation on mundane topics he often confused – perhaps, on purpose – words and names. 'Do you like your tea hot or cold?' he would quaver out ...

I think I learnt from Garrod that, if you want to be learned and clever, there is no need to be prosy and bookish about it ...

[17] George Mallaby, *From My Level* (1965), p. 211.

From Garrod I did not learn scholarship – which indeed I never acquired – but I got a love of learning and a love of style. But above all, this man, separated from me by whole continents of academic skill and intellectual power, was my friend, generous, asking nothing in return, liking my company, it seemed shyly affectionate, a limp handshake and some scarcely audible words of welcome or farewell, knowing so much more of the practical world in which I lived than most dons, ready with well-informed opinions, again like Johnson, on matters which one would suppose he had never considered, courtly in his manners to women, gentle, kind and tender-hearted, with such a strong moral sense – for all his anti-clerical views – that I took pains not to deserve his reproof. In my life – my family apart – his influence has been the most powerful and the best.

A poet himself, Garrod always encouraged the college's poets and was endlessly patient in hearing their versions. Sensitively he suggested changes. A deep admirer of Matthew Arnold, it must be held against him that he never learned to appreciate Eliot. His own early poetry seems mawkish and lush. Yet as a translator he was hard to beat, and not simply in Latin and Greek. Rayner Heppenstall of the BBC used regularly to turn to him for a good translation from the French; as it might be of Ronsard. He could be equally efficient in English prose. When at the end of the First World War a suitable inscription was needed for the War Memorial in chapel he insisted that it should be in English not Latin. Naturally he was asked to compose it. This is what he wrote:

> Remember before God the men who died for freedom and justice. Their names, that they may be seen by all who enter the College, are inscribed under the Archway of the Great Quadrangle. Have them in honour here where for more than six hundred years it has been the custom daily to commemorate benefactors.[18]

Not all undergraduates were as lucky as Mallaby. Cecil Roth who came up in 1919 commented on the supercilious ex-officer environment. Moreover the arrival of the few scholars who had not been at public school might produce some bad moments. The largest group among the 120 or so undergraduates belonged to the lesser public

---

[18] Bott, *Monuments*, p. 66.

schools. Ieuan Thomas, a history exhibitioner of 1923, was not one of them. He came from Llanelly County Secondary School. He recruited A. J. P. Taylor of Oriel into the Communist Party. Taylor has testified to the fact that Merton was a difficult college in which to be a Communist.[19] He records that while he was at Oriel —

> All I suffered was a stream of drunken men calling each evening to convert me from Communism. When this became intolerable, I had to keep away from my rooms until late at night. Ieuan Thomas, a real Communist at Merton ... had a rougher time. He had his books burnt twice and his wardrobe four times in a single term. As he remarked to me 'People talk of a persecution complex. It is very easy to have a persecution complex if you are a Communist at Merton.' In the end persecution became too much for him and he went down. Years later I reminded a don at Merton of this story and was told that Thomas only got what he deserved.

Even if the story were true the western liberal tradition might have survived without help from the college rowdies.

There were now many fewer undergraduates from the greater public schools than from the lesser. There were no more than a handful from Eton, such as Billy Clonmore (1921–5) who moved in the circle of Evelyn Waugh,[20] and Robert Byron (1923–5),[21] the aesthete and traveller whose rooms were then famous for his collection of Victoriana. The college in the years just after the war remained a small community. The numbers of freshmen between 1919 and 1939 averaged 39. The entry was usually made up each year of four postmasters, three exhibitioners, four Rhodes Scholars, and just under thirty other commoners. Among the undergraduates a few bold spirits from the public schools showed a spirit of adventure reminiscent of the Victorian age to which Byron harked back aesthetically. Thus three Mertonians played an important role in the Spitzbergen expeditions of 1921 and 1923 and in the Everest expedition of 1924. Their leader was George Binney,[22] who in the Second World War achieved great success organizing and leading blockade running operations to Sweden through

---

[19] A. J. P. Taylor, *A Personal History* (1983), pp. 68–9. Taylor was mistaken in so far as I. Thomas did in fact take his degree. He and a friend from another college took an oath before the Vice-Chancellor to sever all links with the Communist party.
[20] *Mert. Coll. Reg., 1900–1964*, p. 148.
[21] Ibid., p. 150.
[22] Ibid., pp. 124–5.

the Skagerrak. Binney ran the Spitzbergen expedition of 1921 and was the leader of the 1923 expedition to the same island. He was joined by Geoffrey Milling and Sandy Irvine. The college gave Irvine permission to take two terms off from his course in engineering in order to take part in the Everest expedition in which he died. The monument to Irvine at the back of Grove building with an inscription carved by Eric Gill symbolizes the spirit of those young men, who came from Eton, Radley, and Shrewsbury respectively.

The changing composition of the college was commented on loftily by the poet Louis MacNeice, who came up as a postmaster in classics in 1926 (Pl. 34). Merton, he wrote, was 'a small college which contained comparatively few public school boys' (he must have meant from the greater public schools) 'and still fewer "intellectuals" ... The person I liked best was my scout.'[23] MacNeice dubbed the grammar-school boys 'monsters'. Early in his career he sat between two such monsters in hall and did not enjoy the experience. They were discussing Noel Coward and Bernard Shaw, topics which he considered beneath him. On the whole, however, he thought even less well of the dons:[24]

> As for the dons, they might just as well have been at Cambridge; I should hardly have missed them. Few of them were interested in teaching. They lived in a parlour up a winding stair and caught little facts like flies in webs of generalisation. For recreation they read detective stories. The cigar smoke of the Senior Common Rooms hid them from each other and from the world. Some of them had never been adult, their second childhood having come too early. Some of them had never been male, walked around in their gowns like blowsy widows or wizened spinsters. They had charm without warmth and knowledge without understanding. In appearance they were nearly as grotesque as the menials.
>
> There were exceptions of course, maybe the exceptions were a majority, but for me at least it was the grotesques who typified Oxford. When I think of Oxford dons I see a Walpurgisnacht, a zoo – scraggy baldheads in gown and hood looking like maribou storks, giant turtles reaching for a glass of port with infinitely weary flippers, and chimpanzees, codfish, washing blown out on a line.

---

[23] Louis MacNeice, *The Strings are False* (1965), p. 104. For a brief vignette of MacNeice at Merton see O. D. Holt, Autobiographical Letter (Stack 123 e. 9), p. 3, and for his biography, Jon Stallworthy, *Louis MacNeice* (1995).

[24] MacNeice, *The Strings are False*, p. 105.

Timid with pimples or boisterous with triple chins. Their wit and themselves had been kept too long; the squibs were damp, the cigars were dust, the champagne was flat. The word 'don' was uttered by most of my friends in a tone of superior pity. 'You're the sort of person (who) would become a don' was a serious insult. Becoming a don meant ossification.

Yet some of the dons, we had to admit, were very good indeed of their kind, masters of Socratic dialectic.[25] It was an excellent weapon though they never went out into the world with it. You have to have left Oxford and seen the mess that is everywhere caused by wishful thinking before you can be properly grateful to those dry old inheritors of reason who seemed to have no wishes at all but at least could think.

MacNeice evidently never entered the charmed circle of H. W. Garrod; and indeed had he done so his views on poetry would surely have clashed with those of a man whose tutelary deities were the Lake poets and Matthew Arnold.

Interestingly enough a very different view of the social composition of the undergraduate body was taken by Angus Wilson, who arrived only six years later than MacNeice. He himself came from Westminster, and he had a private income of £300 a year. It enabled him to eat out when he found the contrast between the food which his father had trained him to appreciate and that served in hall too extreme.[26]

The food, by the standards my father had given me from the Café Royal and the Trocadero, was vile, worse than that served at my brother's prep school, which was the nadir of my father's scale of feeding. After the first three weeks, I ate out in restaurants. At Merton, I was probably financially better off than most of the undergraduates, and could make my own standards. I count this as one of the most important of the many advantages Merton gave to me.

At first I didn't feel it so, however. All my Westminster friends were at other colleges. There was a very small rich set at Merton,

---

[25] One of the dons who was a master of socratic dialect was MacNeice's Greats philosophy tutor, G. R. G. Mure, an Hegelian scholar. It was probably his interest in Mure's writings on Hegel that brought Theodor Adorno to Merton as an Advanced Student in Philosophy and Music (1934–7).

[26] Angus Wilson, 'My Oxford', *Encounter* (Apr. 1977), pp. 28–32, and see also Margaret Drabble, *Angus Wilson: A Biography* (1995), ch. 6. Wilson sought a Hinchcliffe scholarship at Christ Church which he failed to secure and so came to Merton as a commoner.

and in my first weeks it made a great deal of drunken noise on many nights. As, with my father's assistance, I had chosen some excellent rooms over the Junior Common Room, I noticed this noise particularly. It seemed the blood-curdling prelude to heaven knows what roastings and defenestrations. I was very 'pansy' in manner and I was very conscious of it. The other new people who seemed out of it all were different. They came from various parts of the North and Midlands of England. A few of them were to become my close friends. But in those first weeks, I could as easily have confessed my loneliness and alarms to them as a warthog can communicate his fears of a lion to a herd of zebras...

The glory of Merton was that by the natural course of events, simply through casual encounters, and many more still through shared tutorials, I found myself among a group of people whose backgrounds were in varying kinds what I had been brought up to call 'working-class' and who came from various parts of the Midlands and North. I was so class-bound that I was not very class-conscious. Thus it came about that I knew these very agreeable and interesting men merely as my fellow history students, and only gradually realised that their backgrounds and assumptions were so entirely different from my own. It was the very best way that it could have come about and I am deeply grateful to Merton for it.

Robert Levens has recorded how a small group of tutors led by Idris Deane Jones, 'the moving spirit of twentieth-century Merton', set about lifting the college's academic standing and extending the number of its awards.[27] Apart from Levens himself, the group consisted of Geoffrey Mure and Robin Harrison, the Greats tutors, Edmund Blunden in English, Harold Newboult in mathematics, and Bertram Lambert in chemistry. By 1931 the senior tutor was able to report 'that we have this year been practically an Honours college and – which is far more important – that two-thirds of our actually classed entrants for Final Honour Schools, did not drop below the second class.' The tutors had to persuade the college regularly to elect its entitlement of six postmasters a year (usually three in classics, one each in modern history, mathematics, and natural science) and maintain the statutory number of not less than twenty-four. Then they had to persuade the university that, since the academic results were doing more than justice to the number of awards, that number should be increased.

[27] *Postmaster*, iv/2 (1968), 11–13.

Their success brought an additional number of postmasterships; in 1938 there were thirty-seven postmasters in residence. That in turn meant that an ambitious grammar-school boy who wished to max-imize his chances might well put Merton as his first choice in its group of colleges. Classics and arts generally continued to take the lion's share. In 1935–6 there were four or five postmasterships in classics as against one or two in mathematics and the same number in natural science. In 1938 eleven postmasters were elected and six exhibitioners. Next year the number was twelve and seven. Each time there were six postmasterships in classics. That policy combined with excellent teaching brought tangible results. Maidment's Hertford and Craven prizes (in 1929–30)[28] were followed by Walsh's Greek prose prize (1934)[29] and K. R. Brooks's Craven and Greek verse prizes (1935–6).[30] In 1938 R. M. Maudling (later Chancellor of the Exchequer)[31] and A. W. Peterson took firsts in Greats. In Robert Levens's own course, Classical Moderations, there were seven first classes in the same year, a record for any college. Meanwhile, there was a parallel development in graduate studies when three annual senior scholarships were founded under an endowment by an old member – Sir Hildebrand Harmsworth. It brought to the college a succession of intelligent graduates from all colleges. In that way a window was opened on to the world of graduate research at a time when there were few opportunities at that level in the university as a whole. The first Harmsworth senior scholars joined the college in 1931.[32] Twenty-five years later, because of the national and religious restrictions which the donor had set on the Harmsworth Scholarships, the college decided in 1956 to amplify the scheme by offering Domus senior scholarships without such restrictions and paid for out of the general revenues, but otherwise on the same terms and of the same standing.

By 1933 the warden was 78, increasingly deaf, and less and less able to transact business efficiently. An attempt was made in 1920 to secure unanimity among the fellows to persuade him to resign. It had not succeeded, and having been elected under the 1881 statutes the warden held his position for life. By June 1935 the tutors had lost patience and

---

[28] *Mert. Coll. Reg., 1900–1964*, p. 202.

[29] Ibid., p. 239.

[30] Ibid., p. 243.

[31] *Postmaster*, v/6 (1979), 10–11; vi/1 (1980), 13–14.

[32] *Mert. Coll. Reg., 1900–1964*, pp. 222–3, Merton College and Merton Society Annual Report for year 1931. The first Harmsworth Senior Scholars were E. S. Budden, F. E. Figgures, and H. F. Moseley.

started discussions to persuade the warden to resign. It was suggested that, if necessary, they should be ready to appeal to the visitor. The matter was handled by the sub-warden R. Campbell Thompson and, after the end of the academic year 1934–5, by Gavin de Beer, the Linacre professor. A halfway house was reached when the warden agreed to resign before September 1936, though he stated that the disability caused by his deafness was much exaggerated.[33] He stood out for a pension of £750 a year under the statutes of 1881; and he reminded the fellows that under those statutes 2/5 of the pension of a retiring warden was paid for out of the stipend of his successor. Since he was of the opinion that the college was well able to pay for the whole of the pension itself, he said that he had prepared a statute by which the necessary change might be effected. The fellows replied, forcing the issue. They asked him to resign as from the end of 1935. He was also asked to put the government of the college into the hands of the sub-warden. After a visit from Sir John Miles, the law tutor, that was the arrangement agreed. The fellows could now concentrate on the election of Bowman's successor, and Miles was their choice (Pl. 36). On his election a joyful old member presented the college with a silver cup. The warmth of the wording of the inscription conveys the sense of relief at Bowman's retirement.[34] It was just as well that he did not remain to die in office like his predecessors, Bullock Marsham and Brodrick, for he lived for another ten years at Bromley.

Early in Miles's wardenship the need to increase the number of scientific fellows was recognized by the election of G. M. Dobson, FRS, the reader in meteorology, whilst the college's medical tradition was strengthened by the election of A. G. Gibson, the Nuffield reader in morbid anatomy.[35] But the balance of the fellowship in the pre-war years remained firmly on the arts side. A notable feature of twentieth-century Merton has been its strength in poets and writers of English prose, though its greatest poet, T. S. Eliot, was attracted to Merton by its reputation in philosophy, just as earlier the prize fellow, Ernest Barker, had been in 1897.[36]

[33] Q.2.8 (letter of 7 July 1935). For the attempt made in 1920 see the correspondence in Q.2.9.

[34] Jones, *Catalogue of the Plate*, p. 15, 'Mertonensibus suis | Die quo officium Custodis auspicatus est Ioannes Carolus Miles | Hoc poculum dedit | Gratulabundus | Albertus Bernardus Burney commensalis'.

[35] *Mert. Coll. Reg., 1900–1964*, p. 280.

[36] Sir Ernest Barker, 'Memories of Merton', *Postmaster*, i/2 (1953), 6.

The fact that first one chair and then a second in English were attached to the college might be supposed to have had something to do with that literary effervescence. Some such effect seems to have worked upon J. R. R. Tolkien, who came to the college in 1945 when elected to the chair of English language and literature, but Tolkien's most famous works, his fairy story *The Hobbit* and his chef d'œuvre *The Lord of the Rings*, were written so to speak in his spare time over many years (Pl. 42). Neither Robert Byron nor Angus Wilson came to Merton because of the magnet of English literature. Both read modern history and were pupils of Idris Deane Jones. Nevertheless the brilliant lectures of Professor Walter Raleigh had raised an interest in English; and the excellent results in the Schools of undergraduates reading the subject[37] helped to persuade the college to elect a tutor in English in 1931 in the person of the poet, Edmund Blunden (Pl. 35). Since Blunden was well known and Merton drama began to flourish with the foundation of the 'Floats' in 1930,[38] those two developments helped to give a strong literary flavour to the decade before the opening of the Second World War. Blunden was himself responsible for the election of another poet, Keith Douglas, a man of outstanding calibre. Before that Louis MacNeice, an able postmaster in classics, was a notable figure who was subsequently influential at the BBC. Another classicist, Hugh Carleton Greene, became the Corporation's Director-General in 1960, and radio, television, acting, and drama criticism have all proved magnets to Mertonians. Outstanding in administration of the arts have been Sir Jeremy Isaacs (1951), and in their practice P. J. Kavanagh (1951).

In the traditional world of politics and the Civil Service two Merton Greats men, Reginald Maudling (Merton, 1935–8), Chancellor of the Exchequer, 1962–4, Home Secretary, 1970–2, and Burke Trend (Merton, 1932–6), Secretary to successive Cabinets (1963–73), and later, as Lord Trend, rector of Lincoln College, were clearly graduates of high calibre.

---

[37] A. B. Taylor (1920), J. N. Bryson (1922), H. V. H. Elwin (1924). Elwin went on to take a first in theology and to become an outstanding anthropologist of Central and North East India.

[38] The founding members were G. Playfair and K. Willing-Denton. For an account of the first production, 'A New Way to pay Old Debts' by Philip Massinger, see O. Holt, 'A biographical letter' (Stack 123 c. 9). For Blunden's encouragement of Keith Douglas cf. *HUO* viii. 417.

THE SECOND WORLD WAR AND AFTER

During the Second World War forty-six Mertonians were killed, fewer than half the number lost in the first. There were three VCs – Brigadier Lorne Campbell of the Argyll and Sutherland Highlanders, Captain John Randle of the Royal Norfolk Regiment (posthumously), and Group Captain Leonard Cheshire of the RAF (Pl. 37). Outstanding bravery on many occasions, not least as a prisoner escaping from Colditz camp, was shown by Lt.-Col. Airey Neave of the Royal Artillery, a future Under-Secretary of State for Air and victim of the IRA. Cheshire's war experience moved him after the war to found with his wife, Sue Ryder, the Cheshire Homes for the incurably sick. Again several members of the Governing Body served in the armed services or the Civil Service. Geoffrey Mure joined the General Staff at the War Office and SHAEF,[39] and was a war-time broadcaster to Italy. E. W. B. Gill[40] shared the interrogation of German prisoners of war with Hugh Trevor-Roper in military intelligence.[41] E. T. Williams served General Montgomery at the Headquarters of the 8th Army in Africa and Italy and subsequently was BGS(I) of 21st Army Group in Europe.[42] On the home front there was little work more important than that which Robin Harrison did at the Ministry of Food. He presided over the development of the Ration Book, and the introduction of the 'points' scheme, practically a new currency. From 1941 to 1945 he was private secretary to Lord Woolton.[43]

Meanwhile in Oxford some of the college's buildings were requisitioned, part of Grove I by the Ministry of Transport, and the rest of Grove, St Albans, Front, Fellows 1, 2, and 3, by the Ministry of Works with the single exception of H. W. Garrod's rooms.[44] They remained an oasis from which letters were sent out to members in the Forces and where a warm welcome was always ready for those on leave returning to the college.[45] Some Merton men were housed in Uni-

---

[39] *Mert. Coll. Reg., 1900–1964*, p. 87.

[40] Ibid., p. 69. He was a major in the Royal Corps of Signals and served in MI 8 and SHAEF.

[41] Ibid., p. 280.

[42] Ibid., p. 230. Other fellows who served in the Armed Forces were N. H. Gibbs (1st King's Dragoon Guards and the War Cabinet Office) and K. J. Maidment.

[43] Ibid., pp. 127–8, *HUO* viii. 386. F. H. Lawson, tutor in law since 1930, served at the Ministry of Supply.

[44] I. Deane Jones, *Merton College, 1939–1945* (Oxford, 1947), p. 5.

[45] Ibid., pp. 21–2.

versity College because of the requisitioning in Merton. A friendly arrangement of shared facilities was worked out between the two colleges. The wine-cellar under the hall became an air-raid shelter. Blunden and Gill acted as Air Raid Precaution officers, assisted by three college servants as air-raid wardens. A hideous shelter and a static water tank were erected in Front Quad. A large part of the ancient painted glass from the chapel, the college's medieval manuscripts, and some archives were stored under the New Bodleian. From 1942 to 1945 Naval, Army, and Air Force cadets were housed in college, and an organization for the repair of crashed aircraft was established there. The RAF officers stationed at Abingdon airport were adopted as a service unit by the College and from time to time appeared in common room. Those and other contrivances made Oxford a legitimate target, and the city was extremely lucky not to have been bombed from the air. By 1946 the long nightmare was over and in Trinity Term in that year there were 90 ex-service men in residence among a total of 130 to pick up the broken threads.[46] By October of the next year the total number had risen to 237 and by 1948 to 255, the highest it was to reach for some years.

It was time to turn to increasing the number of fellows, and especially of tutors to deal with the growing number of undergraduates; and also to recall the Founder's injunction that the number of fellows should increase as the revenues expanded. What was the basis on which the college could think of expansion in answer to the state of its revenues?

In 1918 the revenues had stood at £30,000 per annum. By 1923 they had risen to £47,802. 16s. 5d. and by 1927 to £51,876. 19s. od.[47] Warden Bowman had certainly been very careful with the finances, but more was required than that. From 1922 the college began to benefit from the expansion of London and a series of sales of its lands at Malden. By 1953 it had sold some 347 acres of leasehold and freehold land for £167,097.[48] With the deduction of costs and the addition of the sale of copyholds this meant that the college gained by £149,844. The rents before the sales had amounted to £846 per annum. By 1955 they had been increased to £7,500 per annum. The Ministry of Agriculture insisted that some of the proceeds should be invested at 4% so that

---

[46] Ibid., p. 25.
[47] *University of Oxford: Abstract of Accounts* (Oxford, 1924), p. 73; ibid. (1928), p. 95.
[48] F.3.42, p. 2.

the capital could accumulate and act as a defence against inflation over a period of years.

At the beginning of the Second World War Warden Miles had been in favour of selling much of the land and investing the proceeds in War Bonds as a patriotic gesture. He was successfully and fortunately opposed by Bertie Lambert as a member of the Finance Committee. Lambert took a more hard-headed if no less patriotic stand. The college undoubtedly profited from his advice and in 1944 began to invest in new land in Lincolnshire. Since 1917 its lands had been administered by a professional land agent, D. T. Thring, who from that year was known as estates bursar. It was part of the policy of his successor, the Hon. Wilfred Holland-Hibbert, to consolidate the existing estates. The more widely scattered and less remunerative holdings were sold off. Farms were bought at Marshchapel, Tetney, North Cotes, Rothwell, and Haugh, all in Lincolnshire, and first-class tenants were engaged for them. By contrast lands at Bielby, Yorkshire, and Ibstone, Buckinghamshire, were sold, along with scattered war-damaged properties in London. There the college was thought unable to undertake the necessary capital development. The historic site of the Dunnings in Cambridge was sold to St John's College, Cambridge, which was in a good position to develop the site for its own purposes. Another collegiate site was found in Oxford in Holywell Meadows. Seven acres there were sold to the university in 1959 for the future St Catherine's. Part of the purchase price was then given to St Catherine's to endow a tutorship in mathematics. At the same time another site was sold to the university for the new graduate college of St Cross where the former vicarage had stood in St Cross Road.

With the election of Warden Mure in 1947 the investments were reviewed. For twenty-five years the college had followed the advice of Sir William Goodenough of Barclays Bank that a third of its capital should be held in government stocks, a third in house property, and a third in land. Now a new College statute allowed investment in equities,[49] and it was decided to follow a general policy of balancing holdings in government stocks with holdings in land and house-property, whilst sums received in settlement of claims for loss of development rights were invested in equities. Reinvestment in land should only be considered if there were exceptional agricultural pros-

[49] Statute X (subsequently XI), Reg. 1.5 d, pp. 236–7 (30 July 1951), and cf. 1.5 e, pp. 412–13 (12 March 1956). For the move initiated by Queen's in 1945 to enable colleges to invest in equities see *HUO* viii. 670–1.

pects. In 1955 it was agreed that equities could be American or Canadian.[50] In the following year new income amounting to £13,000 had accrued, and it was decided to put £4,300 into an Investment Reserve Fund and to spend the remainder on a new physics tutor, a senior research fellow, and a junior research fellow.

After 1945 the pressure of applicants for admission at Oxford and at Merton greatly increased. The Education Act of 1944 was followed by the decision of the government in the Act of 1962 to offer a grant through his or her local education authority to any student who secured a university place.[51] So long as the system of scholarships and exhibitions provided almost the sole method by which a poor student could open the door to Oxford, so long had commoner-places attracted those who were not so much scholars as entrants who could pay their way. For many of them there had for long been the less taxing and more general courses leading to the pass degree, though their access had been controlled through separate commoner entrance examinations and the need to pass Responsions.[52] The entrance examinations were usually presided over by the head of the house. He often took the opportunity to achieve a balance in his college between the 'reading men' and those whose ambitions were less academic. At Merton the entrance examinations were held twice a year. They greatly favoured arts men, since the six papers set were in Latin prose, Latin and French unseens, a general paper, a special subject paper, as it might be in history, and mathematics.[53] Whilst all candidates offered the first five papers, that in mathematics was not obligatory and was only taken by those few who hoped to read mathematics or natural science. For many years it had also been possible to gain entrance by sitting the scholarship examinations, which were in classics or modern history or in mathematics or natural science. The government decision of 1962 gradually put paid both to the separate entrance examinations and to the pass degree. Local authorities would only subvent those who were reading for Honours. The whole admissions procedure became academically competitive and from 1962 was administered centrally by the Oxford Colleges Admissions Office.[54]

---

[50] Reg. 1.5 e, pp. 401–3 (5 December 1955).

[51] *Report of the Commission of Enquiry* (Oxford, 1966), the Franks Report, i. 65, no. 126, and i. 89, no. 187; *HUO* viii. 672.

[52] The first of three examinations which candidates for the BA degrees are required to pass.

[53] Cf. Reg. 6.31, pp. 183 (1921), 347 (1929), 399 (1931).

[54] *Report of Commission of Enquiry*, i. 77, no. 155.

That change came about at Merton towards the end of Mure's wardenship, and as a result it seemed that scholarships and exhibitions would become redundant. One or two tutors wished to abolish them and save the money for other purposes, but the college preferred to turn college awards into prizes for good work during the BA and BSc courses.[55] Thus the ancient order of postmasters which had lasted since about 1383 continued, though on a different basis.

The Robbins Report of 1963 emphasized the need to expand the number of undergraduates, and to meet that need more tutors were appointed. Between 1951 and 1986, setting aside lectureships, the tutorial body trebled, from eight to twenty-four.[56] The general policy was to strengthen existing subjects. Thus on the arts side there were two philosophy tutors instead of one, and they were joined by tutors in economics and politics to complete the trilogy of Modern Greats.[57] From 1951 there were three tutors in modern history instead of two. Modern languages, which Warden Mure believed any gentleman could get up for himself, was given two tutorships by combining the chaplaincy with Russian teaching and by appointing a full tutor in French. A tutor in music was added in 1970.

The core subject of mathematics went up from one to two tutors in 1966 and in 1974[58] to three, though it fell back to two in 1993. Most striking was the growth in science, where tutors had long been heavily outnumbered by colleagues in the arts. If medicine is counted with the natural sciences their number was increased when the lecturer in physiology became a tutor in 1951. Then tutors in organic and in due course physical chemistry were added to the tutorship in inorganic chemistry. The tutor in organic chemistry, a junior research fellow at the time of his appointment, R. O. C. Norman, from Balliol, later became the pioneering professor at York and rector of Exeter College.[59]

---

[55] Reg. 1.5 e, pp. 703–5 (19 March 1962), and Reg. Richards, pp. 146–7 (26 April 1984).

[56] The eight were in Classical Moderations, philosophy, modern history 1 and 2, chemistry, mathematics, ancient history, and English; the additional sixteen were in physiology, modern history 3 (1951), physics, economics (1956), chemistry 2 (1956), mathematics 2, Russian (1961), (engineering 1965–9 only), physics 2 (1966), philosophy 2, French (1967), music (1970), mathematics 3 (1971), physics 3 (1981), chemistry 3 (1983), zoology (1984), politics (1986).

[57] Mr Black, tutor in economics, from 1 April 1957 (Reg. 1.5 e, p. 461). Mr Markwell, tutor in politics, on 24 April 1986 (Reg. Roberts, p. 185).

[58] One of the mathematical postmasters of 1973, A. J. Wiles, went on to publish a proof of Fermat's Last Theorem.

[59] *Mert. Coll. Reg., 1891–1989*, p. 262. For Dennis Parsons's tutorship see Reg. 1.5 d, p. 225 (19 June 1961). His pupils included Sir Alec Jeffreys, pioneer of DNA fingerprinting.

The subject which showed the sharpest increase was physics. Before the war it was run by the domestic bursar, E. W. B. Gill, who was then a research physicist. The first full tutor was appointed from 1 January 1957.[60] Ten years later physics had three tutors. It only remained to add a tutor in zoology,[61] a development long hoped for by the Linacre professor.

RESEARCH AND TEACHING

In research progress was notable if not as easily achieved. In 1955, thanks to the initiative of the Linacre professor, Sir Alister Hardy, the college was able to elect Dr Nikolaas Tinbergen, later a Nobel prize winner, in animal behaviour.[62] In 1956 it was decided to add one senior and one junior research fellow. That led to the election of Professor Michael Polanyi as senior research fellow in 1958, and of Dr David Dick as an extra junior research fellow in the same year. The college's freedom to elect to a fellowship someone who was doing important research but not holding a university appointment was demonstrated when in 1969 it elected a former junior research fellow, Dr C. J. H. Watson, a scientific officer at the Culham centre of research in physics.[63]

In order to encourage existing tutors to maintain their research interests a system of sabbatical leave was initiated, together with a scheme by which fellows could qualify for grants for research. By 1970 the college was appointing on average three junior research fellows a year and sometimes, when there was an unusually strong field, four. At a time when it was becoming more and more difficult to acquire resident dons the new injection of young junior research fellows who were for the most part unmarried was especially valuable for the sense of the college as a coherent body. Sometimes one of them acted as an assistant disciplinary officer.

With the election of Warden Harrison (1963: Pl. 41) the college moved closer to the administrative life of the university. The warden

---

[60] Reg. 1.5 e, pp. 416–17 (19 April 1956), 419, 451 (10 December 1956).

[61] Dr Paul Harvey in 1984 (*Mert. Coll. Reg., 1891–1989*, p. 537). A method of keeping in touch with the schools emerged in April 1960. The colleges agreed to elect three schoolmaster students every year, one in each of the three terms (Reg. 1.5 e, p. 654).

[62] *Mert. Coll. Reg., 1891–1989*, p. 188.

[63] Ibid., p. 357.

himself had chaired the committee on entitlement which created 'Harrison fellowships' for non-dons, professors, and lecturers without fellowships, and made the first substantial move to confront that intractable university problem. Though its permanent solution was yet to be reached the first step was a great help to the university. Financially the proctorship of Dr Philip Watson (1955–6) also brought the college closer to the university, especially as he subsequently served for two periods on the university chest (1957–63 and 1977–89). As for the vice-chancellorship, Bullock Marsham, Brodrick, Miles, and Mure, either on grounds of health or age, had all declined to accept it when their turn came. Warden Harrison died before it could be offered to him, but his successor, Sir Rex Richards, held that office in 1977–81, and was thus the first Mertonian vice-chancellor since Scrope Berdmore in 1797–8. Then under the new procedure for election introduced by the Franks Commission, whereby the vice-chancellor did not need to be a head of house, the Linacre professor, Sir Richard Southwood, became vice-chancellor in 1989–93. Thus Merton filled that high university office twice in less than twenty years. Another link with the central administration of the university was established in 1961 when Brian Campbell, a deputy registrar and an old member, was made a fellow. The bond was reinforced in 1986 with the election to a fellowship of the secretary to the university chest, I. G. Thompson.

If Warden Harrison had wrestled with one university problem of first importance another soon fell to Warden Roberts. The Franks Report had drawn attention to the need to improve the standing and procedures of the university where its graduates were concerned. The Roberts Committee of 1987 devoted itself to those considerations and the excellence of its conclusions easily persuaded the university to implement them without delay.

As a result of the Harrison Report the college decided in 1962 to seek out four Harrison fellows. The first, David Witt, a lecturer in engineering, was elected in that year. John Boardman, reader in classical archaeology, and Stuart Sutherland, lecturer in experimental psychology, came one year later, to be followed by Alan Robson, lecturer in French philology and old French literature (1965).[64] A later Harrison appointment was that of Dr Edward Olleson, lecturer in music.

Merton also made two important appointments of non-tutorial

---

[64] *Mert. Coll. Reg., 1891–1989*, p. 357; for the Harrison Report (1962) see *HUO* viii. 724 n. 12.

fellows in medicine, a subject to which it was traditionally attached. The first, in 1965, was of John Badenoch, consultant physician to the Oxford hospitals and university lecturer in medicine. Two years later it elected as a Harrison fellow the university lecturer in pathology, Dr Michael Dunnill.[65] He was the director of clinical studies and helped to introduce a new curriculum at both final honours school and clinical levels. Historical research was represented by Martin Gilbert, a former junior research fellow, who in 1969 became the official biographer of Sir Winston Churchill.[66] The college's willingness to expand the fellowship meant that by 1973 it had more than doubled over the previous twenty years.

The popularity of law as an undergraduate subject was reflected by the fact that when John Barton was appointed as reader in Roman law a second law fellow was appointed in Jack Beatson (1973).[67] The wisdom of that choice was underlined when Beatson was made a Law Commissioner for five years in 1989, and then left to take up the Rouse Ball chair of law at Cambridge in 1994. Merton employed a succession of excellent weekenders including Gavin Lightman, QC, an outstanding teacher. Finally thanks to the generosity of a London law firm – Travers, Smith, Braithwaite – a third law fellowship was established in conjunction with a university lectureship in corporate law.[68]

'New Blood' appointments, made in order to ensure the entry of young teachers at a time when few new appointments were available, enabled the college to secure the services as tutor in organic chemistry of Dr Laurence Harwood who came in from Manchester in 1983. Meanwhile a committee on academic policy had been set up in 1978 so that whenever a vacant tutorship occurred the whole field of possibilities might be surveyed.

Another sign of change in Warden Mure's time was the appearance of a Middle Common Room, in which Merton followed the example of Lincoln.[69] It was first sited, in 1962, in the breakfast room of the Senior Common Room, but in 1971 was moved to the hall of the thirteenth-century warden's house, which had been prepared in the corner of Front Quad.[70] Each graduate was attached to a member of

[65] *Mert. Coll. Reg., 1891–1989*, p. 377, *HUO* viii. 343.
[66] *Mert. Coll. Reg., 1891–1989*, pp. 326–7.
[67] Ibid., p. 435.
[68] Ibid., p. 583 (Fidelis Oditah).
[69] Reg. 1.5 e, p. 681, and cf. p. 702. For the Middle Common Room in Bylaw 78 see Reg. 1.5 g, pp. 305–6 (16 January 1974). For the MCR at Lincoln in 1958 see *HUO* viii. 211.
[70] Bott, *Short History of the Buildings*, pp. 14–15.

the Governing Body as mentor, that is to say a college supervisor. The balance between undergraduates and graduate students was slowly changing in favour of the latter.[71] In 1985 the college stated that its aim was that the number of postgraduates should be about half of the number of undergraduates. By 1992 there were 145 graduates to 239 undergraduates. The cancellation by the government of favourable rates for overseas graduates in 1979 was opposed by the college as by the university. It was feared that it would damage Oxford's reputation as a centre of international scholarship, and that the numbers of overseas graduates would fall. Though opposition proved vain, the numbers did not drop, but their distribution among countries changed. Where the Chinese extended family was involved, as in Hong Kong, Singapore, and Malaya, there was certainly no decrease. Nor was there in those from the United States, though for a different reason: it might well cost more to take a postgraduate course there than in the United Kingdom. The anxiety of the university and colleges at large to sustain or expand their graduate numbers brought about a situation in which it was tempting to lower standards in order to admit self-financed students. There were, however, always those who kept a zealous watch.

The college's septencentenary in 1964 was blessed by the fact that every single planned event took place under perfect conditions between 29 May and 29 September. The sequence opened with the arrival of the visitor, the archbishop of Canterbury, Dr Michael Ramsey, who entertained his hosts after dinner in the hall with a survey of the corporate life and its value down the centuries. Next morning he celebrated Holy Communion in the chapel and was probably the first visitor to have taken a service there since Archbishop Peckham in the thirteenth century. A concert on the last day of May and the first of June was performed by the Bach Festival Chamber Orchestra, conducted by Laszlo Heltay, a pupil of Zoltan Kodály. After Handel's 'The King shall reign', Yehudi Menuhin played the Bach E Major violin concerto. Mozart's Coronation Mass followed and the concert concluded with the playing of a setting of O'Shaughnessy's poem *The Musicmakers*, specially written for the occasion by Kodály. From 15 to 20 June an exhibition of manuscripts, documents, and

---

[71] In 1960 there were 247 in residence (Senior Tutor's Report 1959–60); 32 were reading postgraduate courses. In 1962 the number in the last category rose to 50 (Senior Tutor's Report 1961–2). Between 1929 and 1939 the number of graduates in any given year had only once exceeded 20, see Appendix D.

books from Merton Library was mounted in the Divinity School by permission of the curators of the Bodleian Library. Floats put on a performance of Sir Richard Steele's play *The Funeral*. A ball and an evening reception followed. The reception was especially memorable. The kitchen succeeded in serving a buffet supper to over 1100 guests in the garden. The company of Mertonians and their wives subsequently lined the terrace to watch a forty-five-minute display of fireworks given by Messrs Brocks in Christ Church Meadow. The guests included Captain Balfour, who had come up in 1899, and Sir David Ross, an honorary fellow, who was a prize fellow in 1900. The occasion of the anniversary was taken to create five new honorary fellows: Professor Edmund Blunden, Sir Alister Hardy, Kenneth Sisam, Sir Burke Trend, and E. T. Williams, warden of Rhodes House. A lasting memorial of the year was provided by sponsoring three publications. The librarian edited the Founder's executors' accounts and the thirteenth-century rolls and charters from the muniment room, in *The Early Rolls of Merton College, Oxford*, published by the Oxford Historical Society. A former postmaster, Alan Bott, compiled a masterly account of the *Monuments in Merton College Chapel* and published the register of burials from the parish of St John the Baptist, and, finally, R. G. C. Levens edited the *Merton College Register 1900–1964*, a biographical survey of the members of the college and their activities in the twentieth century. The interest in college archives was subsequently followed up by J. M. Fletcher in his editions of the minutes of the governing body in two volumes, to continue the work of H. E. Salter for the years 1483–1521 and to take the record on through 1521–67 and 1567–1603.

The election of Professor Rex Richards as warden in 1969 brought Oxford its first chemist as head of house and Merton its first scientific warden since the physician Robert Wyntle in 1734 (Pl. 43). The appointment epitomized the strengthening of science in the college in the twentieth century. The governing body had long been inured to gas chromatography by Courtenay Phillips, and by the series of Linacre professors to the problems of zoology. Now magnetic-spin resonance and the enzyme group joined the college's interests and vocabulary. During the warden's four years as vice-chancellor John Roberts (who had already served as acting-warden when Sir Rex Richards's assumption of office was delayed) and Courtenay Phillips served as acting warden for two years apiece.

Another development was the admission of women in 1979. A first and very tentative sign came under Warden Mure when it was agreed to hold an annual dinner for the wives of fellows in December 1955 as a token of the part they played in supporting the college.[72] Five years later it was decided to hold six ladies' guest nights a term.[73] When New College in 1964 raised the possibility of admitting women students Merton instinctively moved more slowly. Though Anne Wallace-Hadrill became the first woman lecturer four years later in 1966[74] the university was told that 'within the next few years the college was not likely to seek to open to both sexes the admission of fellows, graduate students or undergraduates'. The first step would have to be in any case the cancellation of Statute I of the 1925 Statutes, which declared that Merton was a college for men only. To overturn that rule a two-thirds majority was needed. The JCR was less hesitant and passed a motion on 18 May 1977 favouring the change and that was reported to their seniors.[75] Though a majority of the governing body took the same view, a first attempt to overturn the crucial statute in April 1977 did not succeed, because the vote in favour was too small a majority. A second attempt succeeded on 8 February 1978,[76] and the first women graduate and undergraduate members were admitted in the following year. In anticipation of their arrival Dr Anne Grocock, the anatomy lecturer, was made adviser to women junior members. A little over ten years later Alison Durrant, writing in the alternative prospectus, could conclude that the college 'had adapted well to the advent of women'. The first woman fellow was an honorary appointment, Dr Julia de Lacy Mann, former principal of St Hilda's, a niece of Warden Bowman and as the founder of the Bowman Fund a valuable benefactor. Dinah Birch, a junior research fellow in English, became in 1980 the first woman member of the Governing Body. One of the early women undergraduates, Eleanor Grey, became president of the University Student Union. The balance between the sexes began slowly to change as the news percolated through the schools. Naturally enough the alteration came about much more slowly on the Governing Body. In 1995, even with Dr Jessica Rawson as warden

---

[72] Reg. 1.5 d, p. 380 (21 June 1955).
[73] Reg. 1.5 e, p. 595 (21 April 1960). From 19 June 1972 they could dine on any night when guests were permitted (Reg. 1.5 g, p. 206).
[74] Reg. 1.5 f, p. 133 (14 March 1966).
[75] JCR motion of 18 May 1977.
[76] Reg. 1.5 g, p. 616.

(Pl. 47) and seven fellows, women numbered only eight out of fifty-seven members.

The warden and tutors' meetings between the wars had frequently been concerned with levying fines arising from minor breaches of discipline, mostly noisy parties, occasional drunkenness, and returning to college after hours. All that turned on the fact that the college remained *in loco parentis* so long as the age of majority was fixed at 21. Once the age was lowered to 18, as it was in 1969,[77] a different mood naturally took over. Exeats, gate-bills, and fines for late entry had already disappeared; now undergraduates were allowed late-gate keys and could let themselves in or out of the college whenever they wished through a gate beyond St Alban's. The pre-war skills of climbing in became redundant.

THE STAFF

In 1900 the leading members of staff were the butler and the chef. The butler, for many years Charles Patey, was paid £500 per annum. The head chef had two chefs under him, a kitchen porter, two kitchen servants, and a boy, who at 6s. a week was the lowest-paid member of staff. Their numbers reflected the amount of preparation which had to be done by hand. The estates or senior bursar was a fellow and had a senior bursar's clerk and a second clerk, for several decades A. H. Rowley and his son. They were both masters of a neat hand and loyal members of the community. A steward of the manors supervised work on the farms. The lower bursars like the senior needed a senior and a junior clerk to handle the pen-and-ink work of the battels and college administration. The lodge was manned by the porter (at £110 per annum in 1904) and an under-porter. The groom had finally disappeared by 1900, but the sexton remained. There was a messenger (for over fifty years Christopher Wren by name) to carry the letters on the inter-collegiate mail. A servant in the stores had an under-storeman assistant. The scouts were known as staircase servants. Each quad had a senior staircase servant with a second-in-command. For Fellows' Quad there were also two bedmakers, because there was much more work in their large quadrangle.

Altogether before the rebuilding of St Alban's there seem to have

---

[77] S. i of Family Law Reform Act 1969, c. 46.

been eleven staircase servants to cover the three quadrangles and Grove Building. Though the hours were early and late the job was not considered full-time because the afternoons were free. Even so there were some limits to double jobs, and in 1907 a staircase servant was not allowed to combine his work with running a public-house. The female servants were confined to the kitchen and to bedmaking. A buttery boy and a coffee boy, apart from the boy in the kitchen, had the most menial positions (at 10*s.* a week) – they had prospects, however, whereas the boot-cleaner filled a post which would not last. A silverman and a gardener (at £80 per annum in 1908) completed a staff of just under forty, not counting the staff of the Warden's Lodgings.

In 1901 there were eighteen fellows resident in Oxford and 121 undergraduates, who were sustained by a staff of just under forty. By 1993 the administrative and domestic staff numbered eighty-three, though sixteen of them were part-time. Their college numbered sixty-five fellows (including 'emeritus' and one or two visiting fellows) and 388 graduate and undergraduate members. Thus the numbers dealt with had more than trebled, whilst the staff had no more than doubled. This is no doubt partly explained by the introduction of mechanization, electrification, and refrigeration. Mechanization was at its most intense and effective in the garden and the kitchen. One or two types of employee have vanished, like the boot-cleaner. Others have made their appearance, such as the accommodation manager, the college nurse, the bar manager and bar assistant, three maintenance men, two or three 'development' staff, and three academic secretaries. Most staircases are now cleaned by contract cleaners. But there are still twelve full-time scouts, even if they do not play as important a role as their staircase-servant forebears. The amount of business now transacted by the lodge has led to an increase to five porters. The kitchen staff who have to deal with two halls a night in term (one with cafeteria service) have also nearly doubled from seven to thirteen. They also have to cater for a large number of conferences, which were unheard of in 1900, but which now fill every vacation. The abiding impression is of admiration for a staff which manages to cope cheerfully and efficiently with the burdens which are put upon it.

The very special place which a member of staff can take in the life of the community was shown when the head porter, Peter Harrison, was made an honorary member of the JCR in 1990 and subsequently, when he died in office, by the full turn-out of senior and junior members alike at his moving memorial service in the chapel.

BUILDINGS

The death of Warden Brodrick enabled a rearrangement of the accommodation he had occupied in college and the transfer of his successor across Merton Street. Here lay the valuable site acquired by exchange with Magdalen. The task of designing the new warden's house (1908) according to the most difficult preconditions was given to Basil Champneys.[78] At the same time (1905–10) he also replaced all the old buildings of St Alban Hall, bar its gateway on to the street, with a neo-Jacobean quadrangle.[79] His scheme, though ruthless, had the scenic virtue of leaving the quadrangle open on the south to the garden. On the east side of Front Quad he built a staircase which replaced part of the medieval Warden's Lodgings, including regrettably the window of Sever's chapel. In memory of Warden Brodrick a new reading-room was constructed on the ground floor of the south wing of Mob Quad and into it were fitted some of the arches and woodwork of the Wren screen to a design made by the librarian, Professor Goodrich. Meanwhile at the east end of Merton Street E. P. Warren was employed to build three tutors' houses on land obtained from the city.[80] They were constructed on a generous scale and assumed that married fellows would have servants living in. Nothing further was done until after the First World War. Indeed it was to take fifty years to pay off the debt incurred in completing that ambitious programme.[81]

Ironically in 1929 the college sought not a new building but to rearrange an old one. So great had been the revulsion against the scale and aspect of Grove Building – 'Butterfield's packing case' – that the college was moved to employ T. Harold Hughes of Glasgow to take off the top storey, to maintain the number of rooms by tacking on two wings to the west, and to encase the whole in Bath stone

---

[78] Cf. Bott, *Short History of the Buildings*, pp. 9, 40. The first idea (1881) had been to build it east of St Alban Hall (Reg. 1.5 a, p. 67).

[79] Bott, *Short History of the Buildings*, p. 40. The fellows stipulated 'College does not approve of cupolas, cone-like ornaments, and spiral string-courses' for St Alban Hall (1904) (Reg. 1.5 a, p. 374).

[80] Reg. 1.5 a, p. 338 (31 October 1901).

[81] It was paid off in 1957.

(*Frontispiece*).[82] A. B. Burney, an old member, had in October 1928 contributed £10,000 towards the renewal. The result was commended by Max Beerbohm in 'A Sight that Gladdened me', though viewed from the east the façade is undeniably weak.[83]

By 1938 the college was rich enough to contemplate an additional building, and the Harmsworth benefaction called for some special rooms for the Harmsworth scholars. Rose Lane buildings were accordingly commissioned and built to the design of Sir Hubert Worthington in 1939–40.[84] Twenty-four sets of rooms and a porter's lodge together with two tutors' houses were provided, and a common room for the Harmsworth scholars. Bladon and Clipsham stone was used and the whole construction cost just under £40,000.[85] In the event the work was only finished during the first year of the war. The buildings would have been welcome at any time, but they proved difficult to love. Their heavy appearance was epitomized by Warden Mure's description of their entrance on Rose Lane as Agamemnon's tomb. Ironically when he became warden in 1947 he was glad to occupy one of the tutors' houses, the common room, and an accommodation block rather than move into the Champneys lodgings in a servantless era.

The saga of the warden's accommodation was not yet ended. Though the Champneys building had become hopelessly impractical, it was unsatisfactory to leave the warden in Rose Lane. An attempt to deal with the problem was made when first Harold Hughes and then Raymond Erith made a design for a building in Bath stone to occupy the site of 19 Merton Street and the summer house.[86] The proposal did not win support. A second attempt was then made more cheaply and using brick. It followed a design by Emil Godfrey and incorporated a flat for a member of staff. That was the house which was finally built in 1963[87] in Merton Street at a cost of £34,100. It was occupied for the first time by Warden Harrison. By the end of 1994 four wardens had

[82] Reg. 1.5 b, p. 205 (16 February 1929), pp. 209–10 (25 May 1929), cf. Bott, *Short History of the Buildings*, p. 41.

[83] 'A Sight that Gladdened me' (*Oxford*, i/2 (1934) 27–8. The work was less well received by H. S. Goodhart-Rendel, in *Vitruvian Nights* (1932). Mr Burney also gave the Bible Box in the Library and became the first president of the Merton Society (1931).

[84] (I. Deane Jones) *Merton College, 1939–45* (Oxford, 1947), p. 27.

[85] Ibid. Benfield and Loxley's estimate had been for £33,762 (13 March 1938). The loans raised for paying for the buildings had been paid off by 1962–3.

[86] Hughes's plan for 19 Merton Street was costed at £15,000, Erith's plan at £22,000 (Reg. 1.5 e, pp. 186–7), 17 May 1950.

[87] Ibid., pp. 639–40 (8 February 1961); p. 668 (19 June 1961); estimate of £32,940 (7 November 1962), p. 737.

occupied it, twice as many as had lived in the 1908 Warden's Lodgings. A plan had already been made in 1956 to build two tutors' houses in Savile Road, though in the event only one was put up. It was intended for the senior tutor,[88] but it was subsequently sold to Wadham to enable that college to expand eastwards from its own site. It was then demolished after the shortest recorded life of any of the college buildings.

In the older buildings the remaining three arches of the Wren screen were moved back from the library into the chapel though not into their original position. Elsewhere it was modernization that was most urgently needed, especially in the seventeenth-century kitchen. That was accomplished through the design of J. M. Surman in 1959–60 at a cost of £26,000.[89] It released a valuable space over the kitchen which was then used to make the Savile Room. As early as 1953 the college had commissioned from Mr R. Fielding Dodd a twenty-year plan for bringing all the old buildings up into good order. Five years later it appointed a new architect in Stephen Dykes Bower. He designed an extension of the undergraduate reading-rooms on the ground floor of Mob Quad before his duties were taken over by Robert Potter.[90] Meanwhile the Fielding Dodd plan proved an expensive undertaking and had to be spread out over more than forty rather than the original twenty years. In the early years the college was spending £4,000 to £5,000 per annum, but by 1993 the figure had risen to more than £136,000. In the closing years of the century repairs to the south side of the chapel remain to be completed. When the question arose as to whether to contribute to Lord Bridges' appeal for the restoration of the whole of the university's buildings Merton was one of the three colleges to stand out on the grounds that it would instead pay for its own necessary and expensive repairs.[91]

In 1963 in honour of the septencentenary old members were asked to contribute towards improving the existing undergraduate and graduate accommodation. A small accommodation block was accord-

---

[88] It cost £8,870. Cf. Reg. 1.5 e, pp. 413–14 (12 March 1956), 423 (19 June 1956), 476 (25 June 1957).

[89] Ibid., p. 573 (7 December 1959) and cf. p. 532 (Potter's scheme rejected, 16 March 1959). For the Wren screen see ibid., p. 530 (11 February 1959).

[90] Cf. Reg. 1.5 e, p. 506 (24 April 1958); termination of Dykes Bower's appointment, R. J. Potter to advise on alteration to the kitchen; appointed 23 April 1959 (ibid., p. 536).

[91] Reg. 1.5 e, p. 462 (18 March 1957) and cf. p. 484 (3 August 1957). In 1977 the estimated cost of repairing the chapel tower was £300,000 plus VAT (Reg. Richards, p. 584). In the event it cost £473,615.50 (ibid., p. 1209).

ingly fitted in between the Rose Lane buildings and the new warden's house at a cost of £53,000.[92] The architect was the same as for the new Warden's Lodgings – Emil Godfrey. Since then it has been principally undergraduate and graduate needs which claimed attention. A new cricket pavilion was built when the college had to change the position of its sports field. Designed by R. Sudell,[93] it seeks to fit in with its distinguished neighbour, the St Catherine's College buildings by Arne Jacobsen. In 1986 a working party on building possibilities was set up. One result was that the Rose Lane buildings were extended and improved in 1988–9 when an extra floor was added by Lee and Ross. It provided 28 new units of accommodation and was estimated to cost £1,360,850.[94] It also relieved the baldness of the original design by a bold but successful development of the roof line. The general need for more graduate accommodation was answered by taking over some of the college houses in Holywell. The special need of married quarters for graduates was met unexpectedly in 1974 when the estates bursar was able to buy from Techomes a site on the Iffley Road which already had the foundations for eight flats. An anonymous gift in Swiss francs enabled the setting up of a Higher Studies Fund with £40,000, whilst £25,559 provided about 40 per cent of the cost of the Iffley Road flats.[95]

However, as the numbers of junior members rose to meet the opportunities provided by the new tutorships and in accordance with the decisions of a size and shape committee (23 May 1984), the need for accommodation grew just as fast. It was underlined by the increasing difficulties experienced in finding lodgings in the town. The possibility of erecting a large new building was first broached in 1985.[96] A site was identified in the gardens of the Holywell houses where they reach Jowett Walk. Architects submitted plans which by 1992 had won approval. Foundations were dug in 1993. Remarkably the large sum required for this major expansion was successfully raised by the autumn of 1994. The buildings were designed by Architects Copartnership and provided 101 additional units of accommodation.[97] It was the most ambitious scheme to which the college had committed itself

---

[92] Reg. 1.5 e, p. 755 (18 March 1963) and cf. Reg. 1.5 f, p. 59, tender of £53,814 (7 October 1964).

[93] Estates Bursary file no. 10. Much of the work was carried out by M. G. D. Dixey.

[94] Reg. Roberts, p. 422 (22 June 1987 (estimated)).

[95] Cf. Reg. 1.5 g, p. 371 (12 February 1975). The total cost was to be £80,000.

[96] Reg. Roberts, p. 48 (13 February 1985). 'It is not impossible that we might at some time erect a new building, but no plans have been formulated in detail.'

[97] *Merton College: The Holywell Project*, p. 4.

since the building of Fellows' Quad constructed by Savile in the seventeenth century (Pl. VIII).

THE COMPUTER ROOM AND THE ARRIVAL
OF COMPUTERS

It was very properly under a warden who was a scientist that the revolution in computing first affected Merton. Microcomputers were introduced into the domestic bursary and tutorial office in 1983,[98] but computers appeared at large in the college only two years later. In 1985 IBM personal computers and Microsoft word-processors were made available to fellows who wished to use them. In the spring of the next year a computer room was set up in what had been part of the kitchen of the Old Warden's Lodgings, and inevitably became known as the computer kitchen. It housed twelve computers and two printers, and very soon it was a popular port of call for graduates struggling with their theses. In the autumn college appointed a fellow as computer officer (James Binney), who was given a graduate assistant.[99] In order to maintain a link with the mathematical past the assistant was known as the Henry Briggs scholar. Computerization of parts of the college offices was put into the hands of Philip Watson and James Binney,[100] and a whole college accounting system was installed. A little screen appeared in the lodge so that members of college could put their requirements for meals straight on to the accounts.

THE LIBRARY

In 1924 F. H. Bradley left the college a legacy of £2,000 and his philosophical books.[101] As a result the old Eton postmasters' room on the ground floor of Mob Quad was fitted up as the Bradley philosophical library. Further expansion and additions to the collections

---

[98] Reg. Richards, p. 1339; cf. Reg. Roberts, pp. 67, 82, 250.

[99] Reg. Roberts, pp. 271–2.

[100] Ibid., p. 273.

[101] Reg. Bibl. Coll. Mert. I (1901–67), p. 169 (2 January 1925) and for completion ibid., p. 193 (7 November 1928). In 1939 Miss Bull, his niece, added a collection of Bradley MSS. (Reg. 1.5 c, pp. 123–4).

came after the Second World War, when the warden's library was added and subsequently incorporated into the main collection.[102] Then under H. W. Garrod's direction a major programme of repair was begun for the books and their bindings in the old library. £600 was spent in 1950–1 and for each of the following two years.[103] The assistant librarian, Muriel Deane Jones, ran a workshop over the Senior Common Room, with two assistants. Under J. M. Wallace-Hadrill the whole of the upper library was fumigated, and new lighting and heating were installed. More room was obtained in Mob Quad by taking in a corridor and a room at the east end of the south wing; the whole was given new furnishings to the design of Dykes Bower (1958).[104] When in 1947 Warden Mure chose not to live in the Warden's Lodgings the building became known as the Old Warden's Lodgings and was leased to the university for two years and used for a variety of purposes. They included a home for the Chinese Faculty Library and a flat for the visiting Eastman professors. When the lease ran out, however, the lodgings were taken back for college use. The drawing-room was turned first into a lecture-room and then into a new science library, the old offices became a security book-stack (1971), and the law library, which had hitherto been kept in a room in Front Quad, became the Sir John Miles law library.[105] It houses a valuable collection of law books which Warden Miles left to the college. The library was thus in a good position to incorporate three special collections and two individual gifts which were soon to be presented to it.

The first collection, given by Lady Beerbohm in 1956,[106] consisted of drawings, books, and furniture formerly belonging to Sir Max Beerbohm. With the collaboration of Lady Beerhohm's sister and heir, Mrs Eva Reichmann, and on the advice of Sir John and Lady Rothenstein it was fitted up in Mob V.1 and made available to the general public in 1961. Further *Beerbohmiana* given by Mrs Schiff, Lord David Cecil, Mr and Mrs Jepson, and Mr Stephen Greene, greatly added to its value. Thanks to the generosity of Mr Judson

[102] Reg. I.5 d, p. 50 (2 August 1947). It was placed in the Sacristy, 6 December 1954 (ibid., p. 354).

[103] Ibid., pp. 205–6; Reg. Bibl. Coll. Mert. I, p. 272.

[104] Cf. Reg. 1.5 e, p. 464 (18 March 1957); Reg. Bibl. Coll. Mert. I, pp. 311–16.

[105] Reg. Bibl. Coll. Mert. I, p. 303 (Science and Law Libraries opened 22 October 1957, cf. Reg. 1.5 f, p. 291 (9 December 1968)).

[106] Reg. 1.5 e, p. 435 (10 December 1956), and cf. p. 623 (5 October 1960). The room was opened on 1 April 1961 (Reg. Bibl. Coll. Mert. I, p. 360).

of New York it was possible in 1960 to buy as an individual item an autograph commonplace-book of Sir Henry Savile.[107] Meanwhile a special series of gifts had begun to flow from Sir Basil Blackwell. By the time that it had finished on the donor's death eighteen Greek and Latin incunabula and *editiones principes* and the 1502 edition of Dante's *Terze Rime* had been added, most of them from the Aldine Press of which Blackwell was a great admirer. The most outstanding item was the Aldine edition of Aristotle (1495–8). As a former classical postmaster the donor hoped at a late date to offset the neglect of those works by the Mertonians of the end of the fifteenth and beginning of the sixteenth centuries – a truly imaginative provision (Pl. 14).

In 1976 Henrietta Dyson, sister of the English tutor, Hugo Dyson, left money to establish a Dyson memorial fund in her brother's memory.[108] As a result many valuable books have been bought, including a first edition of William Harvey's *De Generatione Animalium* (1651: Pl. 20). Then in 1986 a former postmaster (and later honorary fellow), Frank Brenchley, made a bequest to the college under his will of over 500 first editions of the printed works of T. S. Eliot, together with critical and biographical material which he deposited in the library.[109] The collection has the unusual distinction of a catalogue which the donor has made himself, and which he continues to keep up to date as he adds to the collection. He subsequently crowned his gifts with a bust of Eliot by Epstein which is housed in the Upper Library (Pl. V).

Important contributions to cataloguing were made by P. S. Morrish, formerly assistant librarian, who in 1990 published the catalogue of the library's most important seventeenth-century collection, that of the founder of the librarianship, Griffin Higgs, dean of Lichfield.[110] A list of Merton incunables was included by Dennis E. Rhodes in his *Catalogue of Incunabula in all the Libraries of Oxford outside the Bodleian* (1982). In 1987 6,000 titles of eighteenth-century books published in Great Britain were catalogued under a scheme initiated by UCLA[111] and in 1992 the bibliographer Alain Wijffels made an edition of the

[107] Reg. Bibl. Coll. Mert. I, pp. 339, 345, 352.
[108] Reg. 1.5 h, p. 477 (21 June 1976), £13,878.13 + £664.72 = £14,542.85.
[109] Reg. Roberts, pp. 257, 304.
[110] *Bibliotheca Higgsiana:* see also above, p. 212; and below, Appendix C.
[111] Reg. Bibl. Coll. Mert. II (1966–94), pp. 389–90.

sixteenth-century lists of law books and a catalogue of the books themselves.[112]

MUSIC

The college initiated an organ scholarship in 1907, overhauled the organ in 1923,[113] and nurtured a notable composer in Lennox Berkeley.[114] There was no dedicated place for practice or rehearsal until 1955 when in Michaelmas Term the Fellows' summer house on the garden terrace was turned into a Music Room (Pl. 22). Even so music only began to flourish at Merton by happy chance, when the college welcomed a pupil of Zoltan Kodály, Laszlo Heltay, during the Hungarian Revolt of 1956. He remained to found the Kodály choir (1958) which was for a time based on the college. As a conductor of an unaccompanied choir and an inspiration for amateurs Heltay was hard to beat. In 1964 an attempt to commission a piece of music from Benjamin Britten failed, but Kodály wrote a setting of O'Shaughnessy's *Musicmakers* and visited the college himself to conduct a performance of his *Te Deum*.[115] At the same time in answer to a request by the warden for a new organ, two were presented. That at the west end was given by Angus Acworth.[116] It was built by Walker, and has a case designed by Robert Potter. The other is a charming eighteenth-century instrument[117] set in the chancel. It was given by C. Balthazar and is used to accompany the choir.

THE CHAPEL

The first four chaplains of the twentieth century were, like most of their predecessors, also divinity lecturers and tutors in theology. H. J. White (1895–1905) left to become dean of Christ Church, Richard

---

[112] Alain Wijffels, *Late Sixteenth-Century Lists of Law Books at Merton College* (Cambridge, 1992).

[113] Reg. 1.5 a, pp. 413, 418 (Mr Norman Cocker elected); Reg. 6.31, p. 221 (10 December 1923), value £80, the overhaul of the organ cost £1, 812 7s. 3d.

[114] *Mert. Coll. Reg., 1900–1964*, p. 149 (1922–61).

[115] Reg. 1.5 e, p. 745 (17 January 1963). The Kodály MS is D.i.44.

[116] Reg. 1.5 f, p. 31 (16 March 1964); cf. ibid., p. 179 (18 January 1967). The programme of the opening recital, 11 May 1968, is E.1.50.

[117] Bott, *Short History of the Buildings*, p. 34.

Brook (1905–19) to become bishop of St Edmundsbury and Ipswich, and F. W. Green to join Norwich cathedral as a canon, whilst C. S. C. Williams (1932–62) was a distinguished New Testament and Armenian scholar. After 1962 the chaplaincy was joined to a tutorship in modern languages, and the present holder of the office, Mark Everitt, is also tutor in Russian.

Though the church society came to an end in 1975 the chapel has continued to serve a devoted minority. The regular communion services are especially popular. The most notable since the war was that presided over by the visitor, Archbishop Ramsey, at the time of the septencentenary. Roman Catholic members have used the chapel for Mass since 23 January 1967 when Fr Michael Hollings celebrated the first Mass since the Reformation and revived pre-Reformation practice. Organ scholars since 1976, like D. A. Warwick, have normally also conducted the enthusiastic mixed choir launched by Laszlo Heltay.

DRAMA

It happens that one of the early stage appearances of Mrs Patrick Campbell took place in Merton garden in 1889.[118] There was, however, no second house, and though many Mertonians belonged to OUDS from its beginning, drama at Merton itself in modern times only began when the College dramatic society – 'Floats' – was founded in 1930.[119] Its founding members were Giles Playfair, son of Sir Nigel Playfair, the West-End producer, and Kent Willing-Denton. The first play put on in December 1930 was *A New Way to Pay Old Debts* by Philip Massinger, himself a former member of St Alban Hall. Garrod wrote a special preface for the piece. The play was produced in hall by Sir Nigel Playfair, with Giles Playfair as Sir Giles Overreach, and Hermione Gingold as Maria. Four lively watercolours of the *dramatis personae* were drawn by Plowman.[120] Shaw's *Doctor's Dilemma* followed

---

[118] M. Peters, *Mrs Pat: The life of Mrs Patrick Campbell* (1984), p. 45. She played the part of Rosalind in 'As You Like It' with Ben Greet's Woodland Players, who went on to play 'A Midsummer Night's Dream' in the Hall. We owe this reference to the kindness of Dr Michael Dunnill.

[119] Reg. 1.5 b, p. 231 (30 May 1930).

[120] They hang in Mr Markwell's room (1997). For O. Holt's personal recollection of Miss Gingold and Sir Nigel Playfair on this occasion see Stack 123 e. 9.

in 1933. The most stalwart patrons of the Floats were Robert Levens and later Neville Coghill, who acted as producer for *All's Well that ends Well* and *Two Noble Kinsmen*.

Apart from the commissioned portrait of F. H. Bradley the portraits acquired under Wardens Bowman and Miles (1903–36; 1936–47) were gifts by individual donors or by subscriptions. In 1909 an enamelled portrait of Bishop Creighton by Professor Herkomer,[121] which is remarkable rather than beautiful, was presented by Sir John Schröder (Pl. 27). By other gifts or subscriptions the college obtained portraits of one former postmaster (Sir Richard Steele), two former fellows (Sir Walter Raleigh[122] and W. W. How[123]), and five honorary fellows (P. S. Allen,[124] the earl of Birkenhead,[125] Sir George Hill, Sir John Miles,[126] and Sir Max Beerbohm[127]). But undoubtedly its finest acquisition was William Nicholson's portrait of Professor George Saintsbury, another honorary fellow, bequeathed by the sitter himself.[128]

The college's first post-war commission was a portrait of its then probably most celebrated member of the common room, H. W. Garrod, from Rodrigo Moynihan.[129] This was followed by a sculpture of Warden Mure by the Yugoslav sculptor, Oscar Nemon. The warden (Pl. 38) chose his own sculptor since he considered that the art of portrait painting was in decay, an opinion which he did not keep entirely to himself. The sculpture, first placed in the hall, is now in the Mure Room, the old Rose Lane common room, where Geoffrey and his wife, Molly, regularly entertained undergraduates. Warden Harrison is also commemorated by a sculpture – the gift of a talented

---

[121] Poole, *Catalogue of Oxford Portraits*, ii. 61.

[122] The portrait said to be of Sir Richard Steele by Dahl was presented by Professor Nichol Smith, that of Raleigh by F. Dodd. Both now hang in the Senior Common Room.

[123] By Hugh Rivière, presented by A. B. Burney (Annual Report of Merton College and the Merton Society for 1931). It is on the staircase leading up to the Breakfast Room.

[124] By Herbert Olivier, given by Mrs Allen.

[125] Birkenhead's portrait, by Hugh Rivière, was given by A. B. Burney in 1933. It and the portrait of Sir George Hill (also by Rivière) are now in the Hall.

[126] By Hugh Rivière, over the entrance to the Sir John Miles Law Library.

[127] By William Rothenstein, in the lobby to the Senior Common Room.

[128] In the Upper Bursary.

[129] H. W. Garrod, *List of the Writings of H. W. Garrod* (1947), frontispiece.

schoolmaster student, G. W. Shield (Pl. 41).[130] Harrison's successor, Sir Rex Richards, is himself a connoisseur of modern painting and, taking a more sanguine view of it than Warden Mure, chose Brian Organ to paint his portrait, which now hangs in the hall (Pl. 43). It shows him as vice-chancellor. The college also decided to record the two acting-wardens of 1977–83 and its senior fellow. J. M. Roberts sat to David Tindall[131] for a portrait in acrylic, whilst C. S. G. Phillips was drawn by Harry Crooks,[132] and the senior fellow, R. G. C. Levens, by E. X. Kapp. The election of the Linacre professor, Sir Richard Southwood, as vice-chancellor in 1989 occasioned another vice-cancellarial portrait, by Mark Wickham (Pl. 44).[133] Merton for the first time had an artist in residence when in 1974 David Blackburn held a visiting research fellowship. He presented the college with a series of drawings entitled 'The Creation', which for a time hung in the Savile Room and then in the Zoology laboratory, and a set of six landscapes now in the Savile Room. A gift by an old member[134] enabled the purchase of a painting by Patrick Heron and another by Epstein which also hang in the Savile Room. Jeff Stultiens painted Roger Highfield, a fellow and tutor of forty years' standing, in the library of which he was for long librarian. Philip Watson, for many years mathematics tutor as well as finance bursar, was drawn by Bob Tulloch.

SPORT

Merton's outstanding achievement was on the river. Between 1921 and 1923 the college had supplied three members of the Oxford crew. That rate could not be maintained, but in 1950 the first Eight, regularly coached by Warden Mure, reached fourth place in the first division and went head of the river in 1951 (Pl. 39a).[135] A Head-of-the-River bowl was subscribed to, designed by a young silversmith, Eric Clements. It was a sign of the times that two members of the crew were graduates working for doctorates.

As the pressure to extend the Science Area to the south of South

---

[130] In the Savile Room.
[131] A second portrait by T. Schierenberg is in the Hall (Pl. 45).
[132] In the Upper Bursary, and see the Picture Register for a second drawing of Dr Phillips.
[133] In the Savile Room.
[134] Mr C. L. Burwell (Merton, 1932–5).
[135] Senior Tutor's Report for the year 1950–1.

Parks Road increased remorselessly it seemed prudent to find a new playing field. The site chosen was in that part of the Holywell Meadows which lay to the east of St Catherine's. The ground had to be carefully drained as it had been made-up flood meadow and it took some time to give general satisfaction. Yet by 1989 the 'pavilion complex' was 'said to be the best in the university', and there was 'quite a high rate of success among its [Merton's] teams'. Meanwhile the old playing fields between Mansfield and St Cross Roads were sold to the university. The northern strip was partly used for building and the wish expressed that the remainder would be kept as an open space.[136] Mansfield College joins with Merton in many of its sporting activities and enjoys all the facilities of the Merton playing fields.

A FINE AND PRIVATE PLACE?

Merton generally stood apart from the student unrest which led to the occupation of the Clarendon Building in 1970, and Merton undergraduates even sought to convince the Franks Commission that there were undergraduates who were contented with their lot.[137] Yet there were some discordant sounds within the walls. The traditional aspects of college life were not universally appreciated. The university students' alternative prospectus of 1982, dedicated to a rolling programme of reforms, described the college as 'placid, if not dead'.[138] One disgusted member in the same year said, 'the college is smug and insular. It should be more involved with the university and the outside world.'[139] Moreover the mingling of minds from all parts of the country, so much approved of by Angus Wilson, had not been an enduring success, to judge by some particular comments. 'Formal hall, Merton chapel, Drama Societies and rowing are seen by [us] solid northerners as obnoxious institutions. I have only been to formal hall once and avoid it studiously whenever it is at all possible, even to the extent of missing meals.'[140] Again 'I find formal hall ludicrous, antiquated, and symbolising all that is worst in the public school

---

[136] As was laid down in the Holford Report.
[137] *HUO* viii. 705 and n. 78.
[138] *Postmaster* (1982), p. 8.
[139] Ibid.
[140] Ibid., p. 9.

ethos.'[141] The fact that formal hall, chapel, and rowing, like party-going, are all voluntary no doubt has saved them for those who appreciate them, whether from north or south, but there were evident rifts in the family. Even the new-found academic excellence did not seem to be universally welcomed. Merton 'is not academically exciting nor does it have a vibrant social life. But the undergraduates on the whole work hard. And although the place seems so mediocre that it should produce only upper seconds, it's not so.'[142] Others were more plangent: 'Merton is beginning to fill up with faceless subject-orientated subclones who rarely see the light of day apart from through a library window . . .'[143] Another writer stated darkly, 'Merton is a rich college in resources and material wealth, but it is poor in the only way that counts – few Mertonians have any spirit.'[144] However, by 1989 Alison Durrant in the alternative prospectus could write, 'Academically Merton is strong and work is taken seriously, by the tutors at least. Despite this no one is placed under pressure, and life is not all work, there are ample opportunities to be involved in sports and societies.' 'Merton is small, very friendly and provides a "secure base" for your years in Oxford. People are easy-going and relaxed, no social set dominates and everyone should be able to find their own niche.' How typical those observations were and of what, is hard to determine. The critical comments suggest that the larger college of nearly 400 was in the early 80s experiencing growing-pains among some of its undergraduates, though they might also have been made at other times. In 1992, writing on Merton in *Oxford Today*, J. P. Walker chose to turn to the poet Marvell for his title 'A fine and private place'.[145] He commented on the family feeling but noted that with it comes 'a certain insularity'. The family feeling may have communicated itself more slowly to the college's foreign students, or to its growing number of graduates.

A graduate writing in 1961 made the point in a different way:[146]

No college, I think, is quite so removed from the world – so concentrated on itself – as Merton. Even Balliol men, though they like to think of the universe as compounded of aspiration to Balliolity,

---

[141] Ibid.
[142] Ibid., p. 8.
[143] Ibid., p. 9.
[144] Ibid.
[145] *Oxford Today*, 4/2 (Hilary, 1992), p. 41.
[146] *Postmaster*, ii/5 (1961), 34.

and degeneration from it, are immediately surrounded by things quite anti-Balliol – Trinity, for instance, and the Broad. We are not so rudely awakened into the recognition of non-Mertonian facts; all about us are walls, and the sweet influence of our name – Merton Street – Merton Grove – Merton Field.

There are echoes there of Cardinal Manning who said of his year, 'It was a quiet time, and Merton is the most perfect resting-place in the natural order'.

By the early 1960s, however, the whole university had become much more concerned with academic success. In 1962 A. L. P. Norrington, president of Trinity, invented a table by which to measure the examination results of the different colleges. In 1994 Merton found itself top of this table for the third year running and for the eighth time since 1964.[147] It might well be thought that in doing so it had reached the height of its academic ambition. Though the table was frequently criticized on technical grounds, nevertheless to secure the first position so regularly was taken as a distinction by all those who judged a college by the record of its undergraduates' academic performance. How had that been achieved and at what cost?

In the eighteenth century the college had been known for its isolation, chiefly because it was for long a Whig college in a Tory university.[148] Its warden was never chosen as vice-chancellor between 1652 and 1797. Its size and its topographical position on the southern periphery of the university served to increase a sense of remoteness. However, in the next century, as a result of the Reform Acts and the opening of its fellowships to competition, its governing body had by 1900 acquired for the college an enviable reputation for intelligence and scholarship, especially in the field of philosophy.[149] Then the long rule of Bowman, who turned into a recluse in the twentieth century (1903–36), more or less cut it off once more from the centre of university business until the two vice-chancellorships of Sir Rex Richards (1977–81) and Sir Richard Southwood (1989–93). None of that would have been so obvious to its undergraduates.

Meanwhile relations between dons and undergraduates had undergone a sea-change since the end of the Second World War. In the

---

[147] *Daily Telegraph*, 12. Aug. 1993, p. 12.
[148] See above, p. 255.
[149] See above, pp. 300–3.

1950s, when the college was sometimes thought of as 'top of the second division', the fellows and the undergraduates were in closer touch than they later became. Merton was a family. Warden Mure, Richard Walsh, and Leslie Beck, all three philosophers, frequently attended the meetings of the Bodley Club, an undergraduate literary society which was a focus of the intellectual life of the college. The warden himself coached the college eight and tirelessly encouraged its rowing. When rugby football matches were played fellows were often to be seen on the touch line. Warden Harrison (1963–9) ruled the college with a 'combination of integrity, innocence and toughness' and with his wife entertained every member at least once a year. Nevertheless the spirit of co-operation began to ebb away. The development seems to have reflected changes of attitude amongst both the fellows and the undergraduates. In the 60s many junior members, responding to a wider mood, began to resent the paternalism which was itself undermined when the age of majority was shifted back from 21 to 18. The college had no longer any business to act as a parent. Many undergraduates preferred to seek their outside interests in the university clubs, and the college clubs began to falter. The Church Society and the '1066 and All That Society' came to an end.[150] Meetings of the Bodley Club became fitful. Yet in the following generation those clubs were sadly missed. Have such trends been stayed since then?

Any attempt to assess the state of the college in 1995 must answer that question at three different levels. In the first place no one Oxford college in the twentieth century exercises the influence which Balliol did in the nineteenth. That is principally because all undergraduate colleges have for some years been pursuing similar objectives. Moreover where science is concerned the intellectual stimulus is necessarily provided by the university departments. In the days of the enzyme group under Warden Richards, he and Dr George Radda were operating on the frontiers of knowledge and there were many spin-offs at the college level, but the key experiments and debates took place in the science laboratories. The arrival of Professor May from Australia as a Royal Society professorial fellow in 1988 has given a great stimulus to graduates investigating infectious diseases. On the arts side, on the other hand, college life played a more important part, as with the

---

[150] The '1066 and All That Society' came to an end in 1966, the Church Society, outlasting History, in 1975.

research pupils of Professor John Carey, a leading critic in English Literature, who largely worked from his room in the Old Warden's Lodgings. The same was true of the influence of the philosophy tutor, John Lucas, whose interest in the border country between philosophy and other disciplines has brought him international repute and many visits from foreign scholars. In mathematics the skill of a former mathematics undergraduate in propounding a possible solution to Fermat's last theorem as a graduate inevitably drew him away from the college and across the Atlantic.

It is easy to enumerate the names of distinguished visiting research fellows and Sir Henry Savile fellows but hard to estimate their importance as influences on the governing body. Perhaps the visits of Professor Quine with his lectures on physics and philosophy and of Professor Frank Kermode as Clarendon lecturer may be allowed to stand out as highlights which helped to illuminate the fellowship as well as the university. The visit of Dr Karageorghis, the director of antiquities in Cyprus, was important for different reasons, not least because it led him to secure the establishment with the generous aid of Mr Leventis, a Cypriot businessman, of a graduate research scholarship attached to Merton to be held alternately by a Cypriot or Greek and an English graduate. It reflected the fact that Dr Karageorghis recognized that Oxford was the most favourable centre in which to train up staff who might later man the museums of Cyprus. Interest in the problems of eastern Europe was reflected in the election of Professor Fabry of the Charles University at Prague as a visiting research fellow (1968), the first of several, and by the contribution made by John Lucas to the circle of philosophers at Prague which played a key role in challenging the communist government of Czechoslovakia.

Another compliment was paid to Merton's system of senior scholarships when a Greenslade senior scholarship was added to enable a Swiss graduate to study at Oxford. The graduate section of the college was also distinguished when Crown Prince Naruhito of Japan, a graduate of Gakushuin university, came to Merton in 1983 to work for two years (Pl. VI) on a study which resulted in a book, *The Thames as Highway* (1989). The Middle Common Room has developed the habit of providing a forum in which two of its members offer papers to their colleagues and to members of the Senior Common Room. Productive discussions have taken place on subjects as widely different as galaxies and the current state of the fight against Aids. The talks have attracted an audience from fellows and graduates of every discipline. The Middle Common room is certainly alive.

The undergraduate body appears from the reports of societies in *Postmaster* to have much of that spirit which keeps its teams enjoying themselves, and often does much better than the small numbers of the college and of men for the major teams might lead one to expect (Pl. 39b). It is generally accepted that the shift of the university towards graduate studies puts undergraduates under some stress, and even under threat. Oxford has been strikingly successful in the past as a centre for the teaching of undergraduates, and Merton as one of its high academic performers can be proud of its academic record. In later years its graduates have risen in the public service, such as Sir Michael Palliser and Lord Wright, both heads of the Diplomatic Service, or Sir Michael Quinlan, first at the Ministry of Defence and then at Ditchley Park, Professor Richard Cobb or Professor Conrad Russell as academics, or Oliver Ford Davies on the stage, or Howard Davies, Deputy Governor of the Bank of England. The college has contributed to the development of Oxford and its colleges in a setting far removed from the university, the kingdom, and the world which Walter de Merton knew. Whether the present or some other combination of undergraduate and graduate studies will best serve his intentions in the Third Millennium, only time will tell.

STET FORTVNA DOMVS

Appendix A

(i) Wardens of Merton College, 1264–1994

[*Spelling as in Emden, *Biographical Register*]

1264–86	Peter Abingdon, de Abindon*
1286–95	Richard Worplesdon, de Werplesdon*
1295–9	John de la More
1299–1328	John Wanting, de Waneting*
1328–51	Robert Tring, de Tring*
1351–75	William Durrant, de Duraunt*
1375–87	John Bloxham
1387–98	John Wendover
1398–1416	Edmund Beckingham, Bekyngham*
1416–17	Thomas Rodbourne, Rodebourne*
1417–21	Robert Gilbert
1421–37	Henry Abingdon
1438–55	Elias Holcote
1456–71	Henry Sever
1471–83	John Gygour
1483–1507	Richard Fitzjames, FitzJames*
1507–8	Thomas Harper
1509–21	Richard Rawlins, Rawlyns*
1521–4	Roland Philipps
1525–44	John Chambers
1544–5	Henry Tyndall
1545–59	Thomas Raynolds
1559–62	James Gervase
1562–9	John Man
1569–85	Thomas Bickley
1585–1621	Henry Savile
1621–45	Nathaniel Brent
1645–6	William Harvey
1646–51	Nathaniel Brent

1651–60	Jonathan Goddard
1660–1	Edward Reynolds
1661–93	Thomas Clayton
1693–1704	Richard Lydall
1704–9	Edward Marten
1709–34	John Holland
1734–50	Robert Wyntle
1750–9	John Robinson
1759–90	Henry Barton
1790–1810	Scrope Berdmore
1810–26	Peter Vaughan
1826–80	Robert Bullock Marsham
1881–1903	George Charles Brodrick
1904–36	Thomas Bowman
1936–47	John Charles Miles
1947–63	Geoffrey Reginald Gilchrist Mure
1963–9	Alick Robin Walsham Harrison
1969–84	Rex Edward Richards
1984–94	John Morris Roberts
1994–	Jessica Mary Rawson

(ii) Principals of St Alban Hall

[* = fellow of Merton]

(1437)–1438	Roger Martyn*
1439–	Robert Assh
(1444)–(1446)	John Gygour*
(1450–1)	William Sheriff*
(1452–3)	William Rumsey*
1468–72	Thomas Danett*
1477–81	Richard Fitzjames*
1481–	Thomas Linley*
1501–3	Hugh Saunders*
(Sept. 1503)	John Foster*
(Apr. 1507)– Oct. 1507	John Beverston*
1507–(Sept. 1508)	William Bysse*
1509–10	Richard Walker*
1510–14	John Poxwell*
(1514 Oct.–)	John Hooper
(1526–7)	Simon Balle*

1527–30	Walter Buckler*
1530–2	Robert Taylor*
1532–4	William Pedyll*
1534–5	Robert Huicke*, deposed
1536–9	Richard Smythe*
1539–43	Humphrey Burneforde*
1543–7	John Estwycke*
1547–67	William Marshall*, expelled
1569–81	Arthur Atye*
1581–99	Richard Radcliffe*
1599–1603	Robert Master, resigned, fellow of All Souls', d. 1625
1603–14	Henry Master, resigned
1614–20	Anthony Morgen, resigned
1620–4	Richard Parker, resigned
1624–5	Edward Chaloner, fellow of All Souls'
1625–61	Richard Zouche, regius professor of civil law
1661–4	Giles Sweit
1664–73	Thomas Lamplugh, fellow of Queen's, later bishop of Exeter
1673–8	Narcissus Marsh, fellow of Exeter, later archbishop of Armagh
1679–1723	Thomas Bouchier, fellow of All Souls', regius professor of civil law
1723–36	James Bouchier, fellow of All Souls', regius professor of civil law
1736–59	Robert Leybourne, fellow of Brasenose
1759–97	Francis Randolph, fellow of Corpus Christi
1797–1823	Thomas Winstanley, Laudian professor of arabic
1823–5	Peter Elmsley, Camden professor of ancient history
1825–31	Richard Whateley, professor of political economy, later archbishop of Dublin
1831–61	Edward Cardwell, Brasenose, professor of ancient history
1861–81	W. C. Salter, former fellow of Balliol

Appendix B

(i) Presidents of Merton College Junior Common Room, 1922–95 (where known)

1922–3	A. R. W. Harrison
1924	P. B. Broadbent
1924–5	L. M. Campbell
1925–6	H. S. Kent
1926–7 or 1927–8	J. W. G. Hume
1928–9	E. T. Benson (?)
1929–30	G. L. Clutton
1930–1	J. T. Race
1931–2	R. B. Peacock
1932–3	H. S. Russell
1933–4	J. C. W. Buxton
1934–5	
1935–6	K. A. Merritt
1936–7	G. D. Leyland
1937–8	J. R. Bradshaw (absent in Mich.)
1938–9	J. R. Rossiter
1939–40	F. Brenchley (Mich.), A. G. Barson (Hil.), D. Greenlaw (Tr.)
1940–1	R. W. Pennock
1941–2	N. T. Iaco
1942–3	A. B. Garton-Sprenger
1943–4	Christopher Taylor
1944–5	D. A. Rees
1945–6	R. H. Hindmarsh
1947–8	J. T. Eva
1948–9	J. W. Mann
1949–50	W. A. B. Brown
1950–1	D. H. James
1951–2	R. F. M. Harley

1952–3	W. K. K. White
1953–4	P. R. H. Wright
1954–5	R. M. Medill
1955–6	E. S. A. Ions
1956–7	E. B. Mullins
1957–8	J. C. Mitchell
1958–9	L. R. Jebb
1959–60	R. O. Miles
1960–1	P. J. Parsons
1961–2	R. E. Abbott
1962–3	G. D. Q. Harrison
1963–4	S. N. Woodward
1964–5	T. J. Archer
1965–6	M. A. Hall
1966–7	J. A. H. Braime
1967–8	D. J. Barker
1968–9	W. R. Richards
1969–70	D. R. Holmes
1970–1	A. Hobson
1971	(Acting) J. D. C. Rosamond and B. Witherden
1972	G. Ellis
1972–3	W. J. Bailhache
1973–4	J. D. Heaton
1974–5	R. R. Lewis
1975–6	G. F. Maskell
1976–7	I. R. Taylor
1977–8	N. Craggs
1978–9	A. C. Jenkins
1980–1	M. Crickett
1981–2	D. Renton
1982–3	C. Smithers
1983–4	V. Knox (née Mitchell)
1984–5	J. W. Collings
1985–6	A. M. Phillips
1986–7	J. Layish
1987–8	H. J. Haywood (née Brindley)
1988–9	P. M. A. Wilson
1989–90	N. M. Davies
1990–1	D. A. Eames
1991–2	N. S. M. M. Abbas
1992–3	A. Webb
1993–4	S. Bolt
1994–5	J. V. I. Cooke

(ii) Presidents of Merton College Middle Common Room (for the academical year until 1985, then for the Calendar Year)

1962–3	H. G. Shue
1963–4	K. D. Elworthy
1964–5	G. Copland
1965–6	D. Summer
1966–7	J. Prichard
1967–8	A. D. B. Malcolm
Mich. 1968	E. G. Ranallo
1969–70	L. Woodward
1970–1	I. Rattray
1971–2	A. Sked
1972–3	J. D. C. Rosamond
1973–4	R. T. Walker
1974–5	W. Barton
1975–6	P. R. Lutzeier
1976–7	G. S. Bacal
1977–8	R. D. Hill
1978–9	J. M. Land
1979–80	A. P. Bridges
1980–1	T. J. Sutton
1981–2	J. L. Pethica
1982–3	N. W. S. Cranfield (Mich. and Hil.), J. E. Butcher (Tr.)
1983–4	J. E. Butcher
1984–5	C. J. Oetjen
1985–6	M. J. Kilroy
1986 (calendar year)	C. J. L. Murray
1987	M. J. Kempshall
1988	M. Newton
1989	J. Morrow
1990	B. Hogan-Howe, vice-president
1991	M. Somerville
1992	I. Haynes
1993	A. S. O. Mutambara
1994	M. T. E. Hughes
1995	L. Tsouyopoulos

Appendix C

(i) The Duties of the Merton Librarian, as defined by the founder of the office, Dr Griffin Higgs, in or before 1659

The Librarian shall be a fellow of the College, and a Master of Arts, in whatever Faculty, of not less than four years' standing. He shall be elected by the Warden and five senior Fellows at the same time and in the same manner as the other officers of the College. He shall be paid an annual stipend of £10 which shall be disbursed in three equal portions by the three bursars. He shall enjoy his office as long as he remains a Fellow of the College, unless (which God forbid!) he by neglect of his duties merit deprivation. This penalty, should it become necessary, shall be inflicted by the Warden and five Senior Fellows after three warnings.

It shall be his duty to arrange and classify the books according to the different subjects of study, to be responsible for the binding, chaining, and dusting of them, and for rescuing them from all harm. He shall draw up full alphabetical catalogues and subject catalogues. The manuscripts he shall bring forth out of their dust and darkness. Where necessary he shall prefix to them a contents page, so that printed lists of them may be made, when it seems in the interest of literature to do so; and in order that, not moth and worm, but bright intelligences, may be fostered by them. He shall from time to time advise the Warden and Fellows what books in each subject of study are likely to be most useful to the Library that these may be purchased out of the fees of probationer Fellows and other moneys. Day and night he shall use his best endeavours that the whole estate of the Library be kept unimpaired.

It shall also be his business to write to distinguished persons in Church and State, particularly to those who were educated in this training-ground of youth, adjuring them earnestly when they make their wills, to leave to the Library something of bibliographical interest. He shall provide, at the College expense, a sumptuous parchment Register, in which he shall make honourable record of the names of benefactors, and of books given by them or purchased by them for the Library. But above all, he shall make it his business to search with the utmost diligence into the Archives of the College and into the public records, making notes of anything that he may there find worthy of record about our most pious Founder, Walter de Merton, or about Scotus, Ockham, Bradwardine, Swineshead, Bodley, Savile, or others of earlier or later times who have been Wardens or Fellows. With the approval of the Warden and the Fellows, he shall place these notes among the MSS of the Library, in order that either himself or some succeeding librarian, furnished thus with the means of illustrating history, may publish and hand down to a late posterity lives of these great men which shall justly express the gratitude owed to them.

Compared with the original remaining in the hands of Mr Griffin Higgs, this 22nd of January, 1663; attested by Griffin Tudder.

Translated from E. 2. 3 and cf. Reg. 1.3, fo. 418 by H. W. Garrod. The text is also printed with the Latin original (from Reg. 1.3, fos. 486–8) in P. S. Morrish, 'Dr Higgs and Merton College Library', *Leeds Philosophical and Literary Society*, xxi/2 (1988), Appendix I a & b, pp. 198–9.

(ii) Works donated by Warden Clayton to the Library

Clemens Araneus: *Sacri Sermones* (Brescia, 1586)
Henningus Arnisaeus: *De subiectione et exemtione clericorum etc.* (Frankfurt, 1612)
Alexander Benedictus: *Omnium a vertice ad calcem morborum signa, causae, indicationes ... et remediorum* (Basle, 1539)
Georg Braun and Franz Hogenberg: *Civitates orbis terrarum* (Cologne, 1612)
Joannes Eusebius: *Historiae naturae maxime peregrinae* (Antwerp, 1635)
Melchior Junius: *Politicae quaestiones centum ac tredecim* (Strasburg, 1611)
Justinian: *Institutiones iuris* (Lyons, 1553)
Libri de re rustica (Venice, 1514)
Fortunius Licetus: *Athos perfossus sive rudens eruditus in Criomixi quaestiones de alimento dialogus prior* (Padua, 1636)
Jan Antonides van der Linden: *De scriptis medicis* (Amsterdam, 1637)
Ludovicus Mercatus: *De communi et peculiari praesidiorum artis medicae indicatione* (Cologne, 1588)
Joannes Eusebius Nierembergius: *Historia naturae* (Antwerp, 1635)
Joannes Royardus: *Homiliae* (Cologne, 1550)
Joannes Sambucas: *Icones veterum aliquot ac recentium medicorum philosophorumque* (Antwerp, 1574)
Jacobus de Vitriaco: *Sermones* (Antwerp, 1575)

Appendix D

Numbers of Undergraduates and Graduates, 1929–1994

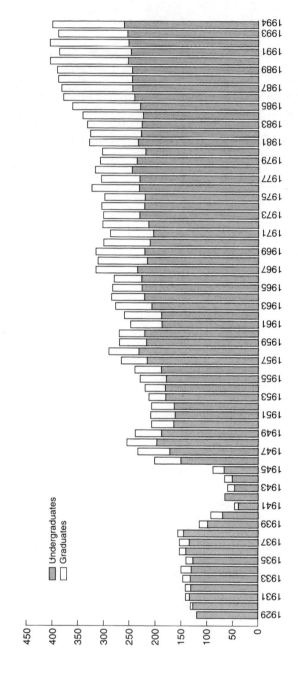

Bibliography

Printed works are published in London unless otherwise described

Unprinted Primary Sources: Merton College Records

MANUSCRIPTS (COXE AND POWICKE NOS. IN BRACKETS)

A.1.3 (52, P. 1180)

A.3.6 (32, P. 1190)

B.1.7 (249, P. 561)

B.3.3 (25, P. 1179)

B.3.4 (26, P. 1182)

C.1.12 (197, P. 567)

C.2.1 (I) (250 (I), P. 374)

C.2.13 (262, P. 603)

E.1.3 (267, P. 507)

F.1.1. (23, P. 1181)

F.1.2 (89, P. 1187)

G.2.1 (56, P. 134)

G.3.4 (64, P. 984)

H.1.10 (200, P. 705)

H.2.1 (118, P. 602)

H.3.3 (301, P. 513)

H.3.5 (231, P. 369)

H.3.9 (309, P. 101, 360)

K.1.6 (296, P. 126)

K.2.6 (71, P. 523)

L.1.2 (130, P. 1193)

L.1.3 (131, P. 983)

L.2.5 (111, P. 970)

L.2.7 (114, P. 319)

L.2.8 (115, P. 7)

L.3.2 (121, P. 978)

L.3.3 (116, P. 8)

N.1.6 (212, P. 852)

N.3.6 (223, P. 388)

N.3.7 (224, P. 363)

N.3.9 (226, P. 377)

O.1.12 (280, P. 207)

O.2.1 (285, P. 389)

O.2.5 (289, P. 515)

MSS NOW LOST

P. 664, 665

CARTULARY

Liber Ruber (Inventory of muniments with abstracts of deeds, *c.* 1288 (G. R. C. Davis, *Medieval Cartularies of Great Britain* (1958), p. 85)

Bibliography

CHARTERS AND ROLLS

MCR 1, 27, 122, 188–9, 195, 250–1, 1230, 1613, 1629
MR 2335, 2980, 3028, 3084, 3087, 3088, 3144, 3153, 3616, 4010–11, 4013, 4015–6, 4116, 4118

CATALOGUES OF FELLOWS

4.16 Catalogus Vetus (contains fellows' names and elections, first compiled *c.* 1412. Earlier names are taken from the bursars' rolls for the 13th and 14th cents. Some marginal comments. Complete to present)

4.18 Savile Catalogue (fellows' names 1585–1957, a copy of 4.16 written *c.* 1565–7 and kept up to 1 April 1957)

OTHER MATERIALS IN THE SACRISTY

D.1.44 Kodály MS., Setting for 'The Musicmakers' by O'Shaughnessy (1964)

D.1.47 (i) Correspondence about the picture 'Paideia' by John Wall
    (ii) Four photographs of 'Paideia'

D.1.96 Photograph of watercolour at the Ashmolean of Arkwright's rooms (1861)

D.2.19 Tuition Book, 1760–1804

D.2.19 (a) Notes on Tuition Book, 1784–1800

D.3.19 Proposals for publishing various books by subscription; receipts for subscriptions by Dr G. Trowe, librarian

E.1.22 Opening of the Founder's tomb, 31. 07. 1849

E.1.23 Latin prose written by Henry Manning when a candidate for a fellowship (1832)

E.1.50 Programme for the opening of the new organ, 11. 05. 1968

E.2.3 (a) Will of John Parsons, 30. 12. 1745

E.2.41 Autobiography of Dr E. Nares, fellow, i (*c.* 1770–1802)

E.2.42 (continuation of E.2.41) ii (1802–27)

F.3.42 Particulars of sale of part of Malden Manor, Surrey, 1922–53

F.3.46 Letter of Provost Hawkins of Oriel to Warden Marsham on the opening of the Founder's tomb at Rochester cathedral, 24. 07. 1849

P.2.9 Copy of Statutes given by F. Astry, fellow, to J. K[ilner], fellow

P.2.11 Statutes (14th cent. and later copies with notes by Kilner)

P.2.12 E. A. Knox's Book of Discipline (1865–81)

P.2.25 Watercolour by Josephine Butler of the rooms of Hungerford Pollen, fellow and senior proctor, *c.* 1852

P.3.25 (5), (6), (8–9) and (21) 5 letters on the quarrel between Warden Savile and the fellows

P.3.26 Books belonging to Robert Wyntle, fellow (later warden) in 03. 04. 1716

P.3.33 Kilner MSS
P.3.34 Kilner MSS
Q.1.1–6 Kilner MSS on college history
Q.1.7 Astry's Catalogue
Q.2.4 Notes on 19th-cent. windows in the library
Q.2.8 Correspondence between fellows and Warden Bowman over his resignation (1935–6)
Q.2.9 Correspondence between fellows over possible resignation of Warden Bowman
Q.2.36 Concert programme, 02. 12. 1887
Q.3.4 Cuttings and letters about the proposal to pull down the library in 1861 and replace it by buildings by Butterfield
Q.3.4 (b) Proposal to commission four paintings of past members for the hall (1864); opening of the cricket ground, 17. 06. 1867

Minutes of the Governing Body (1567–1994)

Reg. 1.3 (1567–1731)
Reg. 1.4 (1731–1822)
Reg. 1.5 (1822–77)
Reg. 1.5 a (1877–1914)
Reg. 1.5 b (1915–36)
Reg. 1.5 c (1935–47)
Reg. 1.5 d (1947–63) (i)
Reg. 1.5 e (1947–63) (ii)

Reg. 1.5 f (1963–9)
Reg. 1.5 g (1969–77) (i)
Reg. 1.5 h (1969–77) (ii)

A4 Format
Reg. Richards (05. 10. 1977–16. 10. 1984)
Reg. Roberts (10. 10. 1984–30. 09. 1994)

OTHER REGISTERS AND MATERIALS

Reg. 1.6 Warden Wyntle's Register
Reg. 2.2 Register of Trusts (accounts of 17 college trusts, 14th to 19th cent.)
Reg. 2.2 a, Postmasters' Register, 1695–1830
Reg. 2.22, Register of leaves of absence, 1738–60
Reg. 3.1 Liber Rationarius Bursariorum, 1585–1633 (1st vol. of enregistered bursars' accounts, 1585–1822)
Reg. 3.2 ditto, 1633–52
Reg. 3.3 ditto, 1652–77
Reg. 4.2, Manor of Farleigh, Surrey; valuation of 1767 by William Chapman
Reg. 4.20, Warden Holland's Daybook, 20. 04. 1709–25. 10. 1722
Reg. 4.22, ditto, 11. 07. 1723–10. 10. 1733
Reg. 5.25, Caswall's Reports (1841–51)
Reg. 6.31, Warden Bowman's Book (1911–32)

Reg. 13.1 Library Purchases, 1663, 1754–6, 1790–1852
Reg. Bibliothecae Collegii Mertonensis I (Minutes of the library committee, 1901–67); ditto, II (1966–94)
Senior Tutor's reports for 1950–1 and 1959–60
Stack, W. B. Harrison correspondence, 13 10. 1914–19. 06. 1915
Stack 123 e.9, letter of O. D. Holt (1928–31), July 1993
Goodrich's album of photographs (held in the library)
Mure, G. R. G., 'Impact of a War' (typescript in the library)
Picture Register (held in the library)
Zacharaiah, Kuruvila, 'Oxford Letters, 1912–15' (typescript in the library)

MATERIALS IN OTHER LIBRARIES

BL Add. MS 39, 311 (connections and patronage of electing fellows (1750 X 1759))
BL Add. MS 34, 740 (ibid., 1751)
BL Add. MS 37, 682 (ibid., 1758)
Bodley MS Bradley 3 (record of attendances (1744–61) at lectures of Professor James Bradley)
Worcestershire and Herefordshire Rec. Office doc. B 705, 353; 380/1, 2 (Hampden Coll.) Admissions of undergraduates by Warden Holland (1716–31)

Printed Primary Sources and Repertories

Account of the Visit of ... the Prince Regent and ... the Emperor of Russia and the Kimg of Prussia to the University of Oxford in June 1814 (Oxford, 1815)
Annual Report of Merton College and the Merton Society for 1931 (Oxford)
Aubineau, M., *Codices Chrysostomi Graeci* (Paris, 1968)
Aubrey, John, *Brief Lives, chiefly of contemporaries set down by John Aubrey between the years 1669 and 1696*, ed. A. Clark, 2 vols. (Oxford, 1898)
Bott, Alan, *The Monuments in Merton College Chapel* (Oxford, 1964)
—— (ed.), *Baptisms and Marriages at Merton College* (Oxford, 1987)
Bibliothecae Bodleianae Catalogus, 7 vols. (Oxford, 1843–51)
Bibliotheca Higgsiana: A Catalogue of the Books of Griffin Higgs (1589–1659), ed. P. S. Morrish (Oxford Bibliographical Soc., 1990)
Biographical Register of the Members of the University of Oxford to 1500, ed. A. B. Emden, 3 vols. (Oxford, 1957–9)
Biographical Register of the Members of the University of Oxford, A.D. 1501–1540, ed. A. B. Emden (Oxford, 1974)
Bodleiomnema (Oxford, 1913)
Bodley, Sir Thomas, *The Life of Sir Thomas Bodley* (Oxford, 1947)

Bibliography

Bradwardine, Thomas, *De Causa Dei contra Pelagium et de virtute causarum ad suos Mertonenses libri tres* (1618)

Brasenose College Register 1509–1909, OHS lv, 2 vols. (1910)

Braun, G., and Hohenberg, F., *Praecipuae Civitates Orbis Terrarum*, 2 vols. in 1 (Cologne, 1572–1612)

Calendar of the Charter Rolls, 1221–1615, 6 vols. (1913–27)

Calendar of the Close Rolls, Edward I, 5 vols. (1900–08)

Calendar of Papal Registers (Letters), ed. W. H. Bliss and others, 14 vols. (1895–1955)

Calendar of Patent Rolls, Edward II, 5 vols. (1894–1904)

——*Edward III*, 16 vols. (1891–1916)

Canterbury College: Documents and History, ed. W. A. Pantin, OHS n.s. vi–viii (1947–50)

Cartulary of the Monastery of St Frideswide, ed. S. R. Wigram, OHS xxviii, xxxi (1894, 1896)

A Catalogue of the Library of the Monastery of Syon, Isleworth, ed. M. Bateson (Cambridge, 1898)

A Catalogue of the Printed Books in Merton College Library (Oxford, 1880)

Chamberlain, John, *Letters (1597–1626): A Selection*, ed. H. McC. Thompson (1963)

Chronicon Magistri Rogeri de Hovedene, ed. W. Stubbs, RS ii (1869)

Clarendon, Edward, earl of, *The Life of Edward, Lord Clarendon, written by himself* (Oxford, 1759)

Close Rolls, Henry III, 15 vols. (1902–75)

Colvin, H. M., *Dictionary of British Architects, 1600–1840*, 2nd edn. (1978)

A Complete Collection of State Trials in 6 volumes, 2nd edn. (1730)

Controversy between John Lingard and Shute Barrington (1811)

Conybeare, John, *Sermons* (1757)

Correspondence of Philip Sidney and Hubert Languet (1845)

Coxe, H. O., *Catalogus Codicum MSS qui in collegiis aulisque Oxoniensibus hodie adservantur*, 2 vols. (Oxford, 1852)

Cross, F. L., *The Oxford Dictionary of the Christian Church*, 2nd edn. (1974)

Deus, Natura, Gratia (Lyons, 1634)

Dialogus de Scaccario, ed. C. Johnson (1950)

Diary of Sir William Dugdale (1827)

Dictionary of National Biography

Dudley Carleton to John Chamberlain, 1603–1624, Jacobean Letters, ed. Maurice Lee Jnr. (New Brunswick, NJ, 1972)

The Early Rolls of Merton College, Oxford, ed. J. R. L. Highfield, OHS n.s. xviii (1964)

Emden, A. B.: see *Biographical Register*

Elizabethan Oxford, ed. C. Plummer, OHS viii (1886)

Family Law Reform Act 1969, c. 46

Fine Bindings, 1500–1700, from Oxford Libraries (Bodleian Library, Oxford, 1967)

Formularies which bear on the History of Oxford, c. 1204–1420, ed. H. E. Salter, W. A. Pantin, and H. G. Richardson, OHS n.s. iv–v (1942)

Foster, Joseph, *Alumni Oxonienses, 1500–1714*, 4 vols. (Oxford, 1891–2)

——*Alumni Oxonienses, 1715–1886*, 4 vols. (Oxford, 1888)

Garrod, H. W., *List of the writings of H. W. Garrod* (Oxford, 1947)

Handbook of British Chronology, 3rd edn. (1986)

Hearne, *Collections*: see *Thomas Hearne*

Historical Monuments: see *Inventory*

The History and Antiquities of Furness, being a Record of Journeys made in Furness in the year 1777 with descriptions of the Places visited, ed. L. R. Ayre (Ulverston, 1887)

Injunctions of Archbishop Kilwardby, 1276, ed. H. W. Garrod (Oxford, 1929)

An Inventory of the Historical Monuments in the City of Oxford, Royal Commission on Historical Monuments (England) (1939)

Iusta Funebria Ptolomei Oxoniensis Thomae Bodleii militis aurati celebrata Mensis Martii 29 1613 (Oxford, 1613)

Jones, E. A., *Catalogue of the Plate of Merton College, Oxford* (Oxford, 1938)

The Journals of Gerard Manley Hopkins, ed. H. House and G. Storey (Oxford, 1959)

Knighton's Chronicle, 1337–96, ed. G. H. Martin (Oxford, 1995)

Knox, E. A., *Reminiscences of an Octogenarian* (1934)

Letters of Eminent Literary Men, ed. Henry Ellis, Camden Soc., old ser. xxvi (1843)

Letters of John Davenport, ed. J. M. Calder (New Haven, 1937)

Letters and Speeches of Oliver Cromwell, ed. T. Carlyle and Mrs S. C. Lomas, i (1904)

Letters of Thomas Burnet to George Duckett, 1712–22, ed. D. Nichol Smith (Oxford, 1914)

Letters of T. S. Eliot, ed. Valerie Eliot, i (1988)

Life and Times of Anthony Wood, ed. A. Clark, OHS xix, xxi, xxii, xxix, xl (1891–1900)

Loggan, David, *Oxonia Illustrata* (Oxford, 1675)

Malmesbury, William of: see Willelmi Malmesbiriensis

Manorial Records of Cuxham, Oxfordshire, c., 1240–1359, ed. P. D. A. Harvey (1976)

Maude, John, *Memories of Eton and Oxford, the Mountains and the Sea* (priv. pr., 1936)

Medieval Archives of the University of Oxford, ed. H. E. Salter, OHS lxx, lxviii (1917–19)

Merton College: the Holywell Project (Oxford, 1994)

Merton College Register, 1900–64 (Oxford, 1964): 2nd edn., *1891–1989* (Oxford, 1990)

Merton College, Senior Tutor's Report (1959–60)

Merton Muniments, ed. H. W. Garrod and P. S. Allen, OHS lxxxvi (1928)

Merton Tune-Book (Oxford, 1863)

Minschew, J., *Dictionary Spanish–English and English–Spanish with Spanish Proverbs and Dialogues* (1599)

Morrish, P. S., see *Bibliotheca Higgsiana*

Munimenta Academica or Documents illustrative of Academical Life and Studies at Oxford, ed. H. Ansty, 2 vols., RS l (1868)

Nichols, John, *Illustrations of the Literary History of the Eighteenth Century,* 8 vols. (1817–58)

Ordinances concerning Merton College in pursuance of 17 & 18 Victoria c. 81 (Oxford, 1863)

Ornsby, Robert, *Memoirs of James Robert Hope-Scott,* 2nd edn. (1884)

Oxford Balliol Deeds, ed. H. E. Salter, OHS lxiv (1913)

Oxford City Documents, ed. J. E. Thorold Rogers, OHS xviii (1891)

Oxford Council Acts 1555–1701, ed. M. G. Hobson, OHS n.s. ii (1939)

Oxford University Commission Report (1852)

Percival, E. F. (ed.), *The Foundation Statutes of Merton College, Oxford AD 1270, with subsequent ordinances* (1847)

Petter, H. M., *The Oxford Almanacks* (Oxford, 1974)

Poole, Mrs R. Lane, *Catalogue of Oxford Portraits,* OHS lvii, lxxxi, lxxxii (1911–24)

Powicke, F. M., *Medieval Books of Merton College, Oxford* (Oxford, 1931)

Pycroft, J., *Oxford Memories: A Retrospect after Fifty Years,* 2 vols. (1886)

The Records of Merton Priory in the County of Surrey chiefly from early and unpublished sources, ed. A. Heales (1898)

Records of the English Bible, ed. A. W. Pollard (1911)

Records of the Honourable Society of Lincoln's Inn, Admissions 1420–1729 (1896)

Register of the University of Oxford, ed. Andrew Clark, ii pt. 2, OHS xi (1887); xii, ii pt. 3 (1888)

Registrum Annalium Collegii Mertonensis 1483–1521, ed. H. E. Salter, OHS n.s. lxxvi (1921); *1521–67,* ed. J. M. Fletcher, OHS n.s. xxiii (1974); *1567–1603,* ed. J. M. Fletcher, OHS n.s. xxiv (1976)

Registrum Cancellarii Oxon., ed. H. E. Salter, OHS xciii, xciv (1930–1)

Registrum Epistolarum Johannis Peckham, ed. C. T. Martin, RS lxxvii, 3 vols. (1882–3)

Registrum Matthaei Parker, ed. E. M. Thompson and W. H. Frere, Canterbury and York Soc. xxxv–xxxvi (1928)

Report of the Commission of Enquiry, 2 vols. (Oxford, 1966)

Rogers, E. Thorold, *A History of Agriculture and Prices in England … 1259–1793,* 6 vols. (Oxford, 1886–7)

Bibliography

Rotuli Parliamentorum, House of Lords, 6 vols. (1783–1832)

Salter, H. E. (ed.), *Survey of Oxford*, OHS n.s. xiv (1960), xx (1969)

Select English Works of Wyclif, ed. T. Arnold, 3 vols. (1869–71)

Skelton, J., *Oxonia Antiqua Illustrata* (Oxford, 1821)

The Skippe Collection of Old Master Drawings (Christies' Illustrated Catalogue) (1958)

Snappe's Formulary, ed. H. E. Salter, OHS lxxx (1934)

The Sophismata of Richard of Kilvington: Introduction, Translation and Commentary, ed. N. and B. E. Kretzmann (Cambridge, 1990)

Spedding, James, *The Letters and Life of Francis Bacon*, 7 vols. (1861–77)

State Trials: see *A Complete Collection of State Trials*

Statutes of the Colleges of Oxford: Merton College (Oxford, 1853)

Statutes in pursuance of the Oxford and Cambridge Act, 1877 (1882)

Thesaurus Linguae Sanctae sive Lexicon Hebraicum (Lyons, 1575)

Thomas Hearne, Remarks and Collections, ed. C. E. Doble and H. E. Salter, OHS 11 vols. (1880–1918)

Trecentale Bodleianum (Oxford, 1913)

Ungerer, G., *A Spaniard in Elizabethan England: The Correspondence of Antonio Pérez's Exile*, 2 vols. (1975–6)

University of Oxford, Abstract of Accounts (Oxford, 1924)

Venn, I. and J. A. (eds.), *Alumni Cantabrigienses*, 2 prints (to 1751; 1752–1900), 4 and 6 vols. (Cambridge, 1922–54)

Victoria County History (Hampshire), 5 vols. (1903–14)

—— *(Oxfordshire)*, 12 vols. (1939–)

—— *(Surrey)*, 4 vols. (1902–14)

Vitriaco, James of, *Sermones* (Antwerp, 1575)

Westminster Chronicle, 1381–94, ed. L. C. Hector and B. F. Harvey, Oxford Medieval Texts (Oxford, 1982)

Wheeler, G. W., *Letters of Thomas Bodley to Thomas James* (Oxford, 1926)

Wijffels, Alain, *Late Sixteenth-Century Lists of Law Books at Merton College*, Libri Pertinentes (Cambridge, 1992)

Willelmi Malmesbiriensis monachi de gestis pontificum Anglorum libri quinque, ed. N. E. S. A. Hamilton, RS lii (1870)

Willelmi Malmesbiriensis monachi de gestis regum Anglorum libri quinque: Historiae Novellae libri tres, ed. W. Stubbs, RS xc, 2 vols. (1887–9)

Wood, Anthony, *Athenae Oxonienses: An Exact History of all the Writers and Bishops who have had their Education in Oxford from 1500 to 1690*, 2 vols. (Oxford, 1691–2)

Wood, Antonius, *Historia et Antiquitates Universitatis Oxoniensis*, 2 vols. (Oxford, 1674)

—— *Athenae Oxonienses to which are added Fasti Oxonienses*, ed. P. Bliss, 3rd edn., 4 vols. (1813–20)

———History and Antiquities of the University of Oxford, ed. J. Gutch, 2 vols. (1786–90), Appendix (1790)

———Survey of the Antiquities of the City of Oxford, ed. A. Clark, OHS xv, xvii, xxxvii (1889–99)

Wyclif's Latin Works, Wyclif Society, 22 vols. (1883–1922)

Select Secondary Sources

Ackermann, R., History of the University of Oxford, i (1814)

Ackroyd, Peter, T. S. Eliot (1984)

Adamson, D., 'Child's Bank and Oxford University in the eighteenth century', Three Banks Review, ccxxvi (1982), 45–50

Anon., 'MCR', Postmaster, ii/5 (1961), 34–5

Anon. 'Pride and Prejudice', Postmaster (1982), 8–10

Andrew, J., Harveian Oration (1891)

Aston, M., 'Corpus Christi and corpus regni: Heresy and the Peasants' Revolt', Past and Present, cxliii (1994), 1–47

Aston, T. H., 'The external administration and resources of Merton College to c. 1348', in HUO i. 269–309

———'Oxford's medieval alumni', Past and Present, lxxiv (1977), 3–40

Baigent, F. J., and Millard, M. J. E., A History of the Ancient Town and Manor of Basingstoke (Basingstoke, 1889)

Barker, (Sir) Ernest, Age and Youth: Memories of Three Universities and Father of the Man (Oxford, 1953)

———'Memories of Merton', Postmaster, i/2 (1953), 6–8

Bateson, Edward, Dodds, M. H., and others, A History of Northumberland, 12 vols. (Newcastle upon Tyne, 1893–1920)

Beddard, Robert, 'Restoration Oxford and the Remaking of the Protestant Establishment', in HUO iv. 803–62

———'Tory Oxford', ibid. 863–905

———'James II and the Catholic Challenge', ibid. 907–54

———Restoration Oxford, OHS n.s. xxix (forthcoming)

Benedictus, Alexander, Omnium a vertice ad calcem morborum signa, causae, indicationes . . . et remediorum (Basle, 1539)

Benjamin, E. B., 'Sir John Hayward and Tacitus', Rev. Eng. Stud. n.s. viii, 29–32 (1957), 275–6

Bennett, A. 'Antony Bek's copy of Statuta Anglie', in England in the Fourteenth Century, ed. N. M. Ormrod (Woodbridge, 1986), 1–27

Bernard, Sir Thomas, The Barrington Schools (1812)

Bill, E. G. W., Education at Christ Church, Oxford, 1660–1800 (Oxford, 1988)

Binns, J. W., Intellectual Culture in Elizabethan and Jacobean England (Leeds, 1990)

Bibliography

B[irkenhead] J[ohn], 'The Assembly Man', in *Harleian Miscellany*, v (1745), 93–8

Birley, R., 'The history of Eton College Library', *London Bibliographical Society* (1956), 231–61

Blair, J., 'Nicholas Stone's design for the Bodley Monument', *Burlington Magazine* (Jan. 1976), 23–4

Bony, J., *The English Decorated Style: Gothic Architecture Transformed, 1250–1350* (Oxford, 1979)

Bott, A. J., *Merton College: A Short History of the Buildings* (Oxford, 1993)

——and Highfield, J. R. L., 'The Sculpture over the Gatehouse of Merton College, Oxford, 1464–5', *Oxoniensia*, xlvii (1993), 233–40

Braun, Thomas, 'The Garden from 1720', *Postmaster* (1985), 45–50

Brodrick, Hon. G. C., *Memories and Impressions* (1900)

——*Memorials of Merton College*, OHS iv (1885)

Brooke, C. N. L., *A History of Gonville and Caius College* (Cambridge, 1985)

Bullard, M. R. A., 'Talking Heads: The Bodleian Frieze, its inspiration, sources, designer and significance', *BLR* xix/6 (April, 1994), 461–500

Bursill-Hall, G. L. (ed.), *Collected Papers on the History of Grammar in the Later Middle Ages* (Amsterdam, 1980)

Buxton, John, and Williams, Penry (eds.), *New College, Oxford 1379–1979* (Oxford, 1979)

Cambridge History of Later Medieval Philosophy, ed. N. Kretzmann, A. Kenny, and J. Piborg (Cambridge, 1982)

Carter, H., *History of the Oxford University Press*, i (1975)

Catto, I. J., 'Citizens, scholars and masters', in *HUO* i. 151–92

——'Theology and Theologians, 1200–1320', in *HUO* i. 471–517

——(ed.), *The History of the University of Oxford*, i. *The Early Oxford Schools* (Oxford, 1984)

——and Evans, T. A. R. (eds.), *The History of the University of Oxford*, ii. *Late Medieval Oxford* (Oxford, 1992)

Chamber, John, *Treatise against Judicial Astrology* (1601)

Chapman, Alan, 'James Bradley, 1693–1762, an Oxford astronomer in eclipse', *Oxford Magazine* (Fourth Week, Trin. Term 1993), 17–19

——'Pure Research and Practical Teaching: the astronomical career of James Bradley, 1693–1762', *Notes, Rec., Royal Society London*, xlvii/2 (1993), 205–12

Cheney, C. R., *Hubert Walter* (Oxford, 1967)

Cholmeley, H. P., *John of Gaddesden and the Rosa Medicinae* (Oxford, 1912)

Clark, G. N., and Cooke, A. M., *History of the Royal College of Physicians of London*, 3 vols. (Oxford, 1964–72)

——*The Care of Books* (Cambridge, 1902)

Cobban, A. B., 'Colleges and halls 1380–1500', in *HUO* ii. 581–633

—— *The Medieval English Universities: Oxford and Cambridge to c. 1500* (Aldershot, 1988)

Colvin, H. M., *Unbuilt Oxford* (New Haven, 1983)

Compton, Berdmore, *Edward Meyrick Goulburn* (1899)

Cooke, A. M., 'Daniel Whistler, PRCP', *Journal of Royal Coll. Phys. London* i/3 (April 1967), 221–30

—— 'William Harvey at Oxford', ibid. ix/2 (1975), 181–8

Cornford, F. M., *Microcosmographia Academica*, 5th edn. (Cambridge, 1953)

Corpus Musicalis Mensurabilis, ed. A. Hughes and M. Bent, 46 (1969)

Costin, W. C., *The Early History of St John's College, Oxford, 1598–1869*, OHS n.s. xii (1958)

Cox, G. V., *Recollections of Oxford* (1868)

Cranfield, N., and Fincham, K. (eds.), 'John Howson's answers to Archbishop Abbott's accusations at his trial before James I at Greenwich, 10 June 1616', *Camden Misc.*, xxix (1987), 4th ser. vol. 34, 319–41

Craster, H. H. E., 'Bibliotheca Rabbinica', in 'John Rous, Bodley's Librarian', *BLR* v/3 (1955), 130–46

Creighton, L., *Life and Letters of Mandell Creighton, D.D.*, 2 vols. (1904–6)

Cunrich, P., Hoyle, D., Duffy, E., and Hyma, F. R., *History of Magdalene College, Cambridge 1428–1988* (Cambridge, 1994)

Dahmus, J. H., *The Prosecution of John Wyclif* (New Haven, 1952)

Day, C., 'Parochial Libraries in Northumberland', *Library History*, viii/4 (1989), 93–103

Denholm-Young, N., 'Richard de Bury, 1287–1345', *TRHS* 4th ser. xx (1937), 135–68

Dent, J., *The Quest for Nonsuch* (1962)

Dickinson, J. C., *The Origins of the Austin Canons and their Introduction into England* (1950)

Douglas, David, *English Scholars* (1939)

Drabble, Margaret, *Angus Wilson: A Biography* (1995)

Duff, E. Gordon, *Fifteenth Century English Printed Books*, Oxford Bibliographical Society (1917)

Durham, B., 'The Thames crossing at Oxford', *Oxoniensia*, xlix (1985), 57–100

Eames, Penelope, 'Medieval Furniture', *Furniture History*, xiii (1977)

Emden, A. B., *Donors of Books to St Augustine's Canterbury*, Oxford Bibliographical Society, Occasional Publications, iv (Oxford, 1968)

—— 'Northerners and Southerners in the organization of the University to 1509', in *Oxford Studies presented to Daniel Callus*, OHS n.s. xvi (1964), 1–30

Engel, A. J., *From Clergyman to Don* (Oxford, 1983)

Evans, R., 'Merton College's control of its tenants at Thorncroft, 1270–

1349', in *Medieval Society and the Manor Court*, ed. Z. Razi and R. Smith (Oxford, 1996), pp. 199–259

Evans, T. A. R., and Faith, R. J., 'The numbers, origins and careers of scholars', in *HUO* ii. 485–538

—— 'College estates and university finances', in *HUO* ii. 635–707

Fairbank, F. R., 'The last earl of Warenne and Surrey', *YAJ* xix (1907), 193–204

Fasnacht, R., *A History of the City of Oxford* (Oxford, 1954)

Feingold, Mordechai, *The Mathematical Apprenticeship: Science, Universities and Society in England 1560–1640* (Cambridge, 1984)

—— 'The Humanities', in *HUO* iv. 211–357

—— 'The Mathematical Sciences and the New Philosophies', ibid. 359–448

—— 'Oriental Studies', ibid. 449–503

Fletcher, J. M., 'Linacre's lands and Lectureships', in *Linacre Studies* (below), pp. 107–97

—— and Upton, C. A., 'The cost of undergraduate study at Oxford in the fifteenth century: The evidence of the Merton College Founder's kin', *History of Education*, xiv (1989), 1–20

—— 'Destruction, repair, and renewal: an Oxford college chapel during the Reformation', *Oxoniensia*, xlviii (1983), 119–30

—— 'The renewal and embellishment of the Merton College library roof, 1502–3', *Library History*, viii/4 (1989), 104–9

—— 'John Drusius of Flanders, Thomas Bodley and the Development of Hebrew Studies at Merton College, Oxford', in H. de Ridder-Symoens, *Academic Relations between the Low Countries and the British Isles* (Ghent, 1989)

Fowler, T., *Corpus Christi College* (1898)

Frank, R. G., 'John Aubrey, F.R.S., John Lydall and Science at Commonwealth Oxford', *Notes and Records of the Royal Society* (1972–3), 193–217

Franklin, Kenneth J., *William Harvey Englishman 1578–1657* (1961)

Frizelle, E. R. and Martin, J. D. *The Leicester Royal Infirmary, 1771–1971* (Leicester, 1971)

Fyfe, W. H., 'The Honourable George Charles Brodrick, Warden of Merton, 1881–1903', *Oxford Magazine* (1958), 432, repr. *Postmaster*, ii/3 (1959), 19–20

Ganz, Paul, *Holbein: The Paintings* (1956)

Garrod, H. W., 'The Library Regulations of a medieval college', *Trans. Bibl. Soc.*, n.s. viii/3 (1927), 312–35

—— 'Sir Thomas Bodley and Merton College', *BQR* vi (1931), 272–3

—— *Anthony Wood 1632–1932* (Oxford, 1932)

—— *The Ancient Painted Glass of Merton College, Oxford* (Oxford, 1937)

Bibliography

—— *The Study of Good Letters*, ed. J. Jones (Oxford, 1961)

Gee, E. A., 'Oxford Masons, 1370–1630', *Archaeological Journal*, cix (1952), 54–131

—— 'Oxford Carpenters, 1370–1530', *Oxoniensia*, xvii–xviii (1953), 112–87

Gillam, Stanley, 'Anthony Wood's trustees and their friends', *BLR* xv/3 (Oct. 1995), 187–210

Glyn, Anthony, *Elinor Glyn* (1955)

Goodman, A., *John of Gaunt: The Exercise of Princely Power in Fourteenth-Century Europe* (Harlow, 1992)

Green, Vivian, *The Commonwealth of Lincoln College Oxford, 1427–1977*, (Oxford, 1979)

Greenslade, S. L., 'The printer's copy for the Eton Chrysostom 1610–13', in *Studia Patristica*, vii (*Texte und Untersuchungen*, xcii: Berlin, 1966), 60–4

Gunther, R. T., *Science at Oxford*, ii, OHS lxxvii (1922)

Hackett, M. B., 'The university as a corporate body', in *HUO* i. 37–95

Hammer, Paul E. J., 'Essex and Europe: evidence from Confidential Instructions by the Earl of Essex, 1595–6', *EHR* ciii (1966), 357–81

Harbison, E. H., *The Christian Scholar in the Age of the Reformation* (New York, 1956)

Harrison, Brian (ed.), *The History of the University of Oxford*, viii. *The Twentieth Century* (Oxford, 1994)

Hartmann, H. W., *Hartley Coleridge* (Oxford, 1931)

Harvey, P. D. A., *A Medieval Oxfordshire Village: Cuxham, 1240–1400* (1965)

Hasted, E., *A History and Topographical Survey of the County of Kent*, 4 vols. (Canterbury, 1778–90)

Henderson, Bernard, *Merton College* (1900)

Heuston, R. H. V., *Lives of the Lord Chancellors, 1885–1940* (Oxford, 1964)

Highfield, J. R. L., 'Alexander Fisher, Sir Christopher Wren and Merton College Chapel', *Oxoniensia*, xxiv (1959), 70–82

—— 'Max at Merton', *Postmaster*, ii/4 (1960), 12–16

—— 'An autograph common-place book of Sir Henry Savile', *BLR* vii/2 (July 1963), 73–83

—— 'The Pateys and their Quad', *Postmaster*, iv/4 (1970), 12–13

—— 'Two accounts of the death of Dr Peter Vaughan, warden of Merton College, Oxford', *Oxoniensia*, xxxix (1974), 92–5.

—— 'Some thoughts about Mob Quad in the eighteenth century', ibid. (Oct. 1991), 52–9

Hill, Christopher, *Economic Problems of the Church* (1956)

—— *Intellectual Origins of the English Revolution* (Oxford, 1965)

Holdsworth, W. H., *History of English Law*, 17 vols. (1922–72)

Howarth, J., 'Science Education in late-Victorian Oxford: a curious case of failure', *EHR* cii (1987), 334–71

Hudson, A., 'Wycliffism in Oxford, 1381–1411' and 'Wyclif and the English language', in Kenny, Anthony. (below), pp. 68–82, 85–103

—— *The Premature Reformation: Wycliffite Texts and Lollard History* (Oxford, 1988)

Hudson, Robert, *Memorials of a Warwickshire Parish* (1904)

Hurstfield, Joel, *Freedom, Corruption and Government in Elizabethan England* (1973)

James, Lionel, *A Forgotten Genius: Sewell of St Columba's and Radley* (1945)

Jones, I. Deane, 'Anthony Wood, the Oxford Antiquary', *Postmaster* (Oct. 1995), 24–31

—— *Merton College, 1939–45* (Oxford, 1947)

Jurkowsky, M., 'Heresy and factionalism at Merton College in the early fifteenth century', *JEH*, xlviii (1997)

Kelly, J. N. D., *St Edmund Hall. Nearly Seven Hundred Years* (Oxford, 1989)

Kenny, Anthony (ed.), *Wyclif and his Times* (Oxford, 1986)

Ker, N. R., 'Oxford College Libraries in the sixteenth century', *BLR* vi/3 (1969), 451–515

—— 'Oxford College Libraries before 1500', in *Books, Collectors and Libraries: Studies in the Medieval Heritage*, ed. Andrew G. Watson (1985), 301–20

—— 'The books of philosophy distributed at Merton College in 1372 and 1375', ibid., pp. 331–78.

Kibre, P., *The Nations in the Medieval Universities* (Cambridge, Mass., 1948)

Kilner, Joseph, *Account of Pythagoras's School* [n. p., 1790]

Kirkpatrick, T. Percy C., 'Charles Willoughby, M.D.' *Proc. Royal Irish Academy* (Dublin, 1923) xxxvi, sec. C, 5–23

Knowles, M. D., *The Religious Orders in England*, 3 vols. (Cambridge, 1948–59)

Lawrence, C. H., 'The University in State and Church' in *HUO* i. 97–150

Levens, R. G. C., 'Forty Years On', *Postmaster*, iv/2 (1968), 9–13

Levy, S., 'Anglo-Jewish Historiography', *Trans. Jew. Hist. Soc., England* vi (1911), 1–20

Lewis, R. G., 'The Linacre Lectureships subsequent to their foundation', in *Linacre Studies* (below), pp. 203–64

Licetus, *De Vita* (Geneva, 1607)

Life and Letters of Benjamin Jowett, ed. E. Abbot and L. Campbell, 2 vols. (1897)

Linacre Studies: Essays on the Life and Work of Thomas Linacre, c. 1460–1524, ed. F. Madison, M. Pelling, and C. Webster (Oxford, 1977)

Lovett, Roger, 'John Blacman: Biographer of Henry VI', in *The Writing of History in the Middle Ages: Essays presented to Richard Southern*, ed. R. H. C. Davis and J. M. Wallace-Hadrill (Oxford, 1981), 415–44

McConica, James (ed.), *The History of the University of Oxford*, iii. *The Collegiate University* (Oxford, 1986)

McFarlane, K. B., *John Wycliffe and the Beginnings of English Nonconformity* (1956)

McHardy, A. K., 'The dissemination of Wyclif's Ideas', *SCH Subsidia*, v (1987), 361–8

McMenemy, W. H., *History of Worcester Royal Infirmary* (1947)

MacNeice, Louis, *The Strings are False* (1965)

Maddicott, J. A. R., *Simon de Montfort* (Cambridge, 1994)

Maitland, F. W., *Township and Borough* (Cambridge, 1898)

Mallaby, (Sir) George, *From My Level* (1965)

Mallett, C. E., *History of the University of Oxford*, 3 vols. (1924–7)

Marples, B. J., 'The medieval crosses of Oxfordshire', *Oxoniensia*, xxxviii (1974), 299–311

Martin, G. H., 'Road travel in the Middle Ages: some journeys by the warden and fellows of Merton College, Oxford, 1315–1470', *Journal of Transport History*, iii (1976), 159–78

—— *The Early Court Rolls of the Borough of Ipswich* (Leicester, 1954)

—— 'The early history of the London saddlers' gild', *Bulletin of the John Rylands Library of the University of Manchester*, lxii (1992), 145–54

Maudling, Reginald, 'The Maudling Memoirs', *Postmaster*, v/6 (1979), 10–11

Maxwell-Lyte, H. C., *History of Eton College 1440–1840* (1889)

Maynard, W. H., 'The response of the Church of England to economic and social change: the archdeaconry of Durham, 18 Oct. 1851', *JEH* xliii/3 (1991), 437–62

Mayr-Harting, Henry, 'The foundation of Peterhouse, Cambridge (1284), and the rule of St Benedict', *EHR* ciii (1988), 318–38

Morrish, P. S., 'Dr Higgs and Merton College Library', *Leeds Philosophical and Literary Society*, Lit. and Hist. sec., xxi/2 (Leeds, 1988), 131–201

Munby, J., 'Zacharias's: a fourteenth-century Oxford new inn and the origins of the medieval urban inn', *Oxoniensia*, lvii (1993), 245–309

Mure, G. R. G., 'Francis Herbert Bradley', *Postmaster*, ii/3 (1959), 10–15

—— 'Francis Herbert Bradley', *Études Philosophiques*, no. 1 (Jan/March 1960), 75–89

—— 'Reggie Maudling', *Postmaster*, vi/1 (1980), 13–14

Neale, J. E., *The Elizabethan House of Commons* (1949)

Nédoncelle, M., *Trois aspects du problème anglo-catholique au xviie siècle* (Paris, 1951)

Newman, John, 'The Architectural Setting', in *HUO* iv. 135–77

Nias, J. B., *Dr John Radcliffe: A Sketch of his Life with an Account of his Fellows and Foundations* (Oxford, 1918)

Norris, J., *Shelburne and Reform* (1981)

North, J. D., 'Astronomy and Mathematics', in *HUO* ii. 103–74

Norton, J. B., *Memories of Merton* (Madras, 1865)

—— *In India at Christmas* (1883)

Orwin, C. S., and Williams, S., *A History of Wye Church and Wye College* (Ashford, 1913)

Parks, M. B., 'The provision of books', in *HUO* ii. 407–83

Pattison, M., *Isaac Casaubon, 1557–1614* (1875)

Pearl, Valerie, *London and the Outbreak of the Puritan Revolution* (Oxford, 1961)

Pearson, J. B., *A Biographical Sketch of the Chaplains of the Levant Company, 1611–1706* (Cambridge, 1883)

Pegues, F., 'The royal support of students in the thirteenth century', *Speculum*, xli (1956), 454–62

Peters, M., *Mrs Pat: The life of Mrs Patrick Campbell* (1954)

Philip, I., *The Bodleian Library in the Seventeenth and Eighteenth Centuries* (Oxford, 1983)

——, and Morgan, Paul, 'Libraries, Books, and Printing', in *HUO* iv. 659–85

Phillips, C. S. G., 'Bertram Lambert', *Postmaster*, iii/2 (1963), 14–15

Platt, Christopher, *The Most Obliging Man in Europe* (1985)

Platt, Colin, *The Monastic Grange in England: A Re-assessment* (1969)

Pointer, J., *Oxoniensis Academia* (1749)

Porter, S., 'The Oxford Fire of 1644', *Oxoniensia*, xlix (1984), 289–300

Postles, D., 'The acquisition and administration of spiritualities by Osney Abbey', *Oxoniensia*, li (1986), 69–77

—— 'Some differences between seignorial demesnes in medieval Oxfordshire', ibid., lviii (1994), 219–32

Raban, S., *Mortmain Legislation and the English Church, 1279–1500* (Cambridge, 1982)

Read, Conyers, *Lord Burghley and Queen Elizabeth* (1960)

Reynolds, J. S., *The Evangelicals at Oxford, 1735–1871* (1975)

Riewald, J. G., *Sir Max Beerbohm, Man and Artist* (1953)

Robson, J. A., *Wyclif and the Oxford Schools: The Relation of the 'Summa de ente' to Scholastic Debates at Oxford in the Later Fourteenth Century* (Cambridge, 1961)

Ross, K. N., *A History of Malden* (New Malden, 1947)

Roth, C., *The Jews of Medieval Oxford*, OHS n.s. ix (1951)

—— 'Sir Thomas Bodley, Hebraist', *BLR* vii/5 (1966), 242–51

Rowse, A. L., *Ralegh and the Throckmortons* (1962)

—— 'The tragic career of Henry Cuffe,' in *Court and Country: Studies in Tudor Social History* (Brighton, 1987), 211–41

Roy, I., and Reinhart, D., 'Oxford and the Civil Wars', in *HUO* iv. 687–731

Bibliography

Rubin, M., *Corpus Christi: The Eucharist in Late Medieval Culture* (Cambridge, 1991)

Salmon, J. H. M., 'Seneca and Tacitus in Jacobean England', in *The Mental World of the Jacobean Court*, ed. Linda Levy Peck (Cambridge, 1991), 169–88

Salter, H. E., 'An Oxford mural mansion', in *Historical Essays in Honour of James Tait*, ed. J. G. Edwards, V. H. Galbraith, and E. F. Jacob (Manchester, 1933)

Sandys, J. E., *History of Classical Scholarship*, 3 vols. (Cambridge, 1902–8)

Sharpe, Kevin, and Lake, Peter (eds.), *Culture and Politics in Early Stuart England* (1994)

Sheehan, M. W., 'The religious orders, 1220–1370', in *HUO* i. 193–221

Shrewsbury, J. F. D., *A History of Bubonic Plague in the British Isles* (Cambridge, 1971)

Sinclair, H. M., and Robb-Smith, A. H. M., *History of Anatomy at Oxford* (Oxford, 1958)

Smith, John, *Memoirs of Wool*, 2 vols. (1747)

Smith, L. Pearsall, *Life and Letters of Sir Henry Wootton*, 2 vols. (1907)

Southern, R. W., 'From schools to university', in *HUO* i. 1–36

Stone, L. (ed.), *The University in Society*, 2 vols. (Princeton, 1975)

Streeter, B. H., *The Chained Library: A Survey of Four Centuries in the Revolution of the English Library* (1931)

Sutherland, L. S., and Mitchell, L. G. (eds.), *The History of the University of Oxford*, v. *The Eighteenth Century* (Oxford, 1986)

Symonds, Richard, *Oxford and Empire: The Last Lost Cause* (1986)

Synans, E. A., 'Richard of Campsale: an English theologian of the fourteenth century', *MS* xiv (1952), 1–8

Taylor, A. J., 'The Royal Visit to Oxford in 1636: a contemporary narrative', *Oxoniensia*, i (1936), 151–9

Taylor, A. J. P., *A Personal History* (1983)

Thompson, A. H., 'The registers of John Gynewell, bishop of Lincoln, for the years 1347–50', *Archaeological Journal*, lxviii (1911), 301–60

—— 'The pestilences of the fourteenth century in the diocese of York', *Archaeological Journal*, lxxi (1914), 98–154

—— *The History of the Hospital and the New College of the Annunciation of St Mary in the Newarke, Leicester* (Leicester, 1937)

—— *The Abbey of St Mary of the Meadows, Leicester* (Leicester, 1949)

Thompson, Paul, *William Butterfield* (1971)

Todd, R. B., 'Henry and Thomas Savile in Italy', *Bibl. d'Humanisme et Renaissance*, lviii/2 (1996), 439–44

Trevor-Roper, H. R., *Archbishop Laud*, 2nd edn. (1962)

—— *A Hidden Life: The Enigma of Sir Edmund Backhouse* (1976)

Turner, H., 'The mural mansions of Oxford: attempted identifications', *Oxoniensia*, lv (1991), 73–9

Tyacke, N., 'Science and Religion at Oxford University before the Civil War', in *Puritans and Revolutionaries: Essays in Seventeenth-Century History presented to Christopher Hill*, ed. D. Pennington and G. Aylmer (Oxford, 1978)

—— 'Introduction', in *HUO* iv. 1–24

—— 'Religious Controversy', ibid. 569–619

—— (ed.), *The History of the University of Oxford*, iv. *The Seventeenth Century* (Oxford, 1997)

Walker, J. P., *Oxford Today*, iv/2 (Hilary 1992), 41

Wallace, W., *Lectures and Essays on Natural Theology and Ethics*, ed. E. Caird (Oxford, 1898)

Ward, W. R., *Georgian Oxford* (Oxford, 1958)

Weisheipl, J. A., 'Ockham and Some Mertonians', *MS* xxx (1968), 163–213

—— 'Repertorium Mertonense', *MS* xxxi (1969), 174–224

Wernham, R. B., *After the Armada: Elizabethan England and the Struggle for Western Europe 1588–1595* (1984)

Willis, R., and Clark, J. W., *The Architectural History of the University of Cambridge and of the Colleges of Cambridge and Eton*, 4 vols. (Cambridge, 1886)

Wilson, Angus, 'My Oxford', *Encounter* (April 1977), 27–33

Wilson, F. P., *Elizabethan and Jacobean* (Oxford, 1960)

Winstanley, R. E., 'No case for the Vice-Chancellor', *Oxford*, xlii/1 (May 1990), 82–5

Womersley, David, 'Sir Henry Savile's translation of Tacitus and the political interpretation of Elizabethan texts', *Rev. Eng. Stud.*, xli (1991), 313–42

Wood, Theodore, *The Reverend J. G. Wood* (1899)

Woodward, F. L., *The Age of Reform, 1815–1870* (1946)

Woodward, J., 'The Monument to Sir Thomas Bodley in Merton College', *BLR* v/2 (Oct. 1954), 69–73

Worden, Blair, 'Cromwellian Oxford', in *HUO* iv. 733–72

Workman, H. B., *John Wyclif: A Study of the English Medieval Church*, 2 vols. (Oxford, 1926)

Wright, A. D., 'Bellarmine, Baronius and Federico Borromeo', in *Bellarmino e la Controriforma*, ed. R. de Maio and others, Centro di Studi Sorani V Patriarca (Sora, 1990), 323–70

General Index

Index

Bull Hall, Oxford 25 and n, 27, 74, 205
Bullard, Margaret R. A., Lady Bullard 163
Bullock, Joseph* 241 n
Bunny, Edmund (1540–1618)* 156
Burdett, Thomas 133
Burghley, Lord, see Cecil, William
Burley, Walter (c.1274–c.1345)* 53 and n, 54–6, 59
Burmington (Warwicks.), tithes 217, 251
Burneforde, Humphrey (d. c.1555)* 372
Burnell, William (c.1268–1304) 80 n
Burnet, Gilbert (1643–1715), bishop of Salisbury 258, 273
Burnet, John (1863–1928) 279 n, 302
Burnet, Sir Thomas (1664–1753) 257–8
Burney (Birnbaum), Albert B. 310, 338 n, 354 and n, 362 n
Burney, Charles (1757–1817) 261
Burney, Frances, see Arblay
Burrard, George* 240 n
Burrows, Montagu (1819–1905) 209
Burt, Elizabeth (d. 1683) (wife of William) 224 n
Burt, William (d. 1679) 224 n
Burton, William* 202
Burton, William (1575–1645) 226–7
Burwell, Clayton Lee 363 n
Bury, Richard (1281–1345), bishop of Durham 56, 58, 60, 62
Butler, Joseph (1692–1752), bishop of Durham 306
Butler, Josephine Elizabeth (1828–1906) 380
Butler, R. 239 n
Butterfield William (1814–1900) 41, 197, 217, 282, 284 and n, 305, 381
Button, Ralph* 209 and n
Byne, Henry* 238 n, 260 n
Byrde, John*†, see Bird
Byron, Robert (1905–41) 333, 339
Bysse, William* 371

Cacherode, Clayton 262 and n
Cadiz (Cádiz), siege of (1810) 241
Caird, Edward* (1835–1908), master of Balliol College 279 n, 300–1

Caius College, Cambridge, see Gonville and Caius
Calais (Pas-de-Calais) 120
Calasio's Dictionary 265
Calcutta 310
Calicut (Kerala) 330
Calvert, Frederic* 318
Calvin, Jean (1509–64) 157–8 and n
Cambridge (Cambs.) 16 n, 17, 39 n, 103, 127, 167
University of 1, 7 n, 130, 168, 181, 188, 195, 210, 216, 218–19, 229, 287 and n, 334, 347
see also Dunnings manor; and individual colleges
Camden, William (1551–1623) 167, 178, 180, 183
Campbell, Brian Guy* 346
Campbell, Beatrice Stella (Mrs Patrick Campbell) (1865–1940) 361 and n
Campbell, Brigadier Lorne Maclaine, VC 340
Campsale, Richard (d. c.1350)* 59–60
Candia (Crete) 166
Canes, manor of, see North Weald Basset
Canon Law 16, 21, 50, 63, 86, 257
Canterbury (Kent), religious houses:
Christchurch cathedral priory 102
St Augustine's abbey 59 and n, 67 and n, 102 n
Canterbury, archbishop of 20, 57, 206, 212, 287, 290
see also Abbot, George; Arundel, Thomas; Bourchier; Bradwardine; Chichele; Courtenay; Cranmer; Grindal; Herring; Islip; Juxon; Kemp; Kilwardby; Laud; Longley; Parker, Matthew; Peckham; Pole; Potter, John; Ramsey; Reynolds, Walter; Sheldon; Sudbury; Tait; Tenison; Wake, William; Walter, Hubert; Warham; Whitgift
Canterbury, province of 120
Canterbury College, Oxford 101–2
Cape Coast (Ghana) 310
Capel, Thomas Edward (d. 1855)* 240 n, 241
Capetown Diocesan College 310
Carden and Godfrey, architects 354

402

The Index

Index

Wolvercote (Oxon.) 170, 290, 292 and n
St Peter's church 34, 261, 289
women, admission of 349–50
Womersley, Dr David 177 and n
Wood, Anne (b. 1669) 234
Wood, Anthony (1632–95) 26 n, 70 n, 72 n, 118 n, 128 n, 135 n, 169, 186 n, 189, 191 n, 195, 204, 209–10, 214–15, 217–18, 220, 222–35, 271, 320
Athenae Oxonienses (1691–2) 222, 231, 234–5
Historia et Antiquitates (1764) 231, 235
History and Antiquities of the University of Oxford (1791–6) 221
Wood, Christopher (d. 1684) 224
Wood, Edward (d. 1655)* 38 n, 211 n, 224, 225 and n, 226
Wood, Frances (b. 1672) 234
Wood, John (d. 1475)*, archdeacon of Middlesex 84 n
Wood, John George (1827–89) 307
Wood, Robert (d. 1686) 72 n, 224 and n
Wood, Thomas (d. 1643) 223–4
Wood, William, *see* Boys*, William
Woodforde, William (d. 1758) 246
Woodhall, Hugh 66
Woodhouse, Walter 288 n
Woodroffe, Edward (c.1621–75) 217
Woodstock (Oxon.) 170, 200, 294
Woodville, queen Elizabeth, *see* Elizabeth
Woodward, John 164
Woolley, Samuel* 239 n, 250, 252, 268
Woolton, earl of, *see* Marquis, Frederick James
Worcester 253, 257
  bishop of 60, 245, 287; *see also* Latimer; Stillingfleet, Edward
  cathedral 242; priory 60
  city 239, 243
  diocese of 60, 97, 120, 239
  Royal Infirmary 256
  see of 120
Works, Ministry of 340
World War:
  First 329–30, 332
  Second 340–1, 342, 358, 366

Worplesdon, Richard (d. 1295)*(W) 66, 70 and n, 75 and n, 84 n, 370
Worth, Edward 257
Worthington, Sir Hubert (1886–1963) 354
Wortley, James Archibald Stuart (d. 1881)* 293–4
Wotton, William, organ builder (1488) 137
Wren, Christopher, messenger 351
Wren, Sir Christopher (1632–1723) 217–18, 228
Wright, Dr Anthony David 166 n, 196 n
Wright, Edward (c.1558–1615) 188
Wright, Nicholas (d. 1499)*, provost of Wye College 126 n, 136 and n
Wright, Richard* 175 n, 184
Wright, —* 245
Wright*, Patrick Richard Henry, Lord Wright, GCMG 369
Wright, Thomas Howard 295 n
Wriothesley, Henry (1573–1624), earl of Southampton 172
Wrocław 166–7
Wryght, Nicholas*†, *see* Wright, Nicholas
Wurmb, Carl Friedrich Lothar von (1893–1918) 329
Würzburg, prince-bishop of 216 and n
Wyatt, James (1746–1813) 263, 277
Wychwood (Oxon.) 30 and n
Wyclif, John (d. 1384)* 54, 89 n, 93, 99–108, 110, 117 and n, 119 and n, 123, 320
Wyclif, William 100
Wycliffe (Yorks.) 100
Wye (Kent) 129
  College of St Gregory and St Martin 129, 136; *see also* Wright, Nicholas
Wyfold, Checkendon (Oxon.) 223
Wykeham, William of (1324–1404), bishop of Winchester 17, 91–2, 111 and n, 114, 121, 126
Wylie beguylie 145 n
Wyliot, John* 93, 97, 112 and n, 113–14, 137, 319 n
  bursar 267
Wyliot foundation 267
Wylyot, John*†, *see* Wyliot

435

Index